1981
SEASON

THE COMPLETE HANDBOOK OF BASEBALL

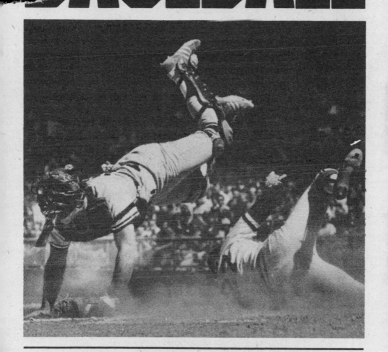

EDITED BY ZANDER HOLLANDER

A SIGNET BOOK

NEW AMERICAN LIBRARY

TIMES MIRROR

Wirz, Vince Nauss, Bob Fishel, Phyllis Merhige, Blake
Katy Feeney and the publicity directors of the 26 major league teams.

Zander Hollander

PHOTO CREDITS: Cover–Rich Pilling. Back Cover–Mitchell B. Reibel. Inside photos: George Gojkovich, Nancy Hogue, Rich Pilling, Mitchell B. Reibel, UPI, Wide World, Montreal Canadiens, Jockey International and Sports Photo Source.

SIGNET, SIGNET CLASSICS, MENTOR, PLUME, MERIDIAN AND NAL BOOKS
are published by The New American Library Inc. 1633 Broadway
New York, New York 10019

First Printing, March, 1981

1 2 3 4 5 6 7 8 9

PRINTED IN THE UNITED STATES OF AMERICA

CONTENTS

Editor's Note: The material herein includes trades and rosters up to final printing deadline.

JIM PALMER: Master of Mound, Mike & Modeling

By PETER PASCARELLI

You'd expect the turning heads and pointing fingers in more logical settings. You'd expect the undisguised attention to be riveted upon the tall man in the designer jeans if it were beer-drinking sports fans doing the gawking.

But this was a fashionable little restaurant in Kansas City's chic Country Club Plaza area and these weren't baseball aficionados gushing over the sight of Jim Palmer, winner of 242 Baltimore Orioles games, striding through the lunchtime crowd.

These were young secretaries on their noon break, middle-aged housewives nibbling on their quiche and taking a respite from overworking their credit cards, even a scattered grandmother. And they reacted to the sight of Palmer as if he were a matinee idol.

They probably had some vague knowledge of Palmer's baseball career, some distant scrap of awareness that he had a certain prowess in throwing a baseball. But the majority of these women and the ones that have flocked to Palmer's scheduled appearances in department stores all over the country couldn't tell you what number he wears or for what team he plays.

But without hesitation, these women could tell you what Jim Palmer looks like in his underwear.

It is all the offshoot of an aggressive advertising campaign conducted by Jockey International that has used Palmer and his good looks and lean body as the model of a line of fashion men's underwear. The response to the ads has surpassed Jockey's wildest dreams. Letters have poured into the company, asking that

Peter Pascarelli covers Jim Palmer at home and abroad for the Baltimore News-American.

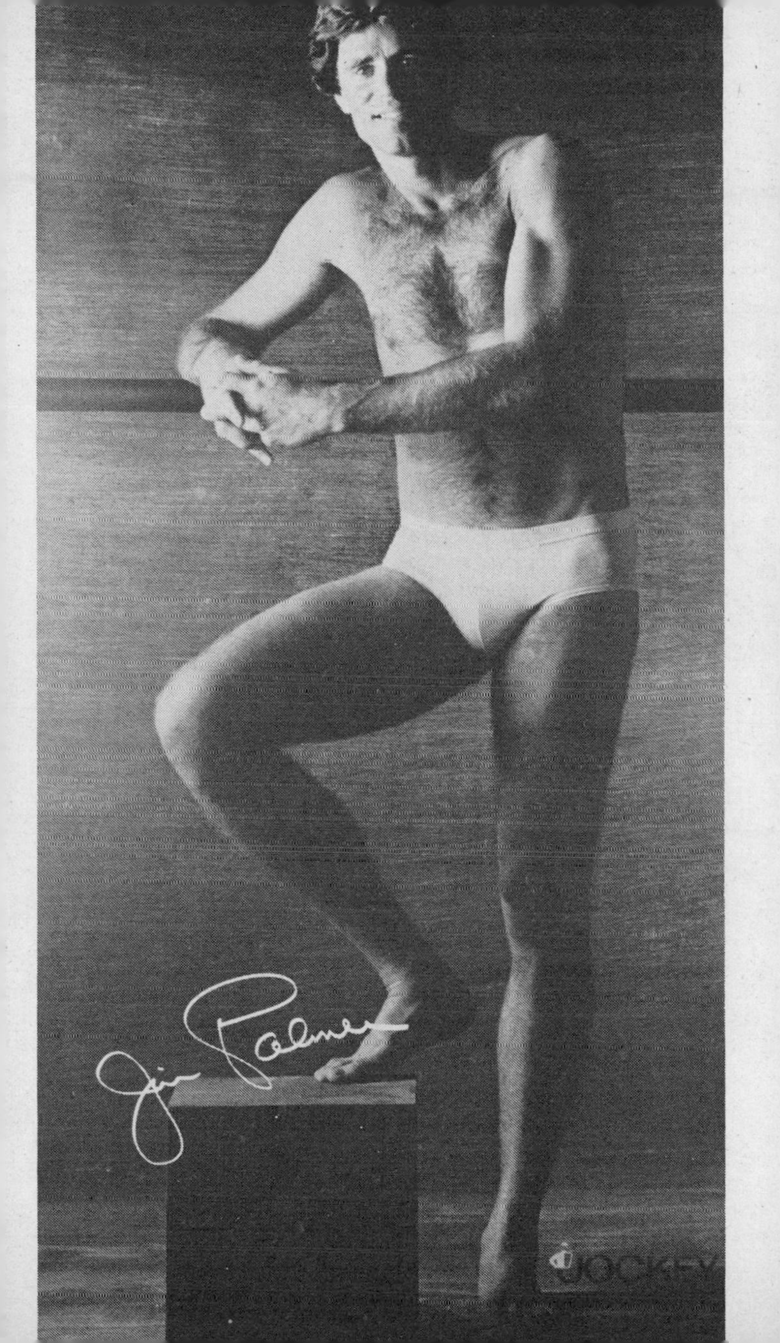

Jim Palmer
JOCKEY

the bare-chested Palmer pose become a poster, à la Farrah Fawcett or Cheryl Tiegs.

For example, there was the following letter from an office of 17 women that was sent to Jockey. Such correspondence has become common.

May 1, 1980

Jockey International, Inc.
Kenosha, Wisconsin 53140

Gentlemen:

I have been elected from an office of seventeen women, to write to you concerning your Micro 3 Briefs advertisement with Jim Palmer as the model.

I purchased an issue of People Magazine *and got as far as page 7 at which time I spotted your advertisement mentioned in the above paragraph. It was three days before I could get past page 7! I brought your ad to work and it was unanimously agreed that posters should be made. Do you realize the market you are missing?*

As executive secretaries of a major firm, we have learned the value of a marketable item so thought we ought to bring it to your attention. As women, we are just plain selfish! For whatever reason you may choose to look at the above suggestion, we do hope you consider it.

Sincerely,

Sweet Seventeen

And there are letters from female baseball fans who have suddenly made Jim Palmer their new favorite—like the woman who sent Palmer this letter:

March 11, 1980

Mr. Jim Palmer
Miami Stadium
2301 N.W. 10th Avenue
Miami, FL 33127

Dear Mr. Palmer:

I have been a Los Angeles Dodger fan most of my life and like Tom Lasorda, I thought my blood was Dodger blue. But I just picked up an April issue of Playboy *magazine and saw your picture. That is enough to make any girl switch teams and leagues, and that is just what I have done.*

I am not a groupie, nor am I a fickle female. I am a 32-year-old secretary who thinks you look as good with your clothes on as you do off. I also think you are a super pitcher, even better than my idol, Sandy Koufax.

Since it may be some time before I get to Baltimore to see you perform in person, I would sure like to have a picture of you. The girls in our office have almost mutilated the one from Playboy.

If Bo Derek is a perfect 10, then you have got to be at least 20.

A Baltimore Fan Forever

P.S. Have a wonderful spring training, and thanks for motivating a secretary with spring fever.

What makes this most American of cheesecake phenomenons something more than a jock being photographed in briefs is that the commercials haven't been Palmer's only mass exposure. He won universally rave reviews for his articulate and smooth performance as an ABC analyst during the American League playoffs last fall, handling the potentially ticklish role of being a foil for Oakland manager Billy Martin with aplomb and good humor.

Thus in the space of a year has Palmer come to the threshold of that definable line that separates sports idols from mass-media entities. And like O.J. Simpson parlayed running through airports, B movies and touchdowns, like Joe Namath combined panty hose, popcorn poppers and show biz, so may Palmer be the latest athlete to be crossing the great divide between the lockerroom and tinsel.

The irony of it all is that without the blast of publicity generated by the underwear ads, Palmer would have likely gone on about his distinguished baseball career and occasional forays into broadcasting in relative anonymity. As Palmer's teammate Mike Flanagan, the 1979 Cy Young Award winner, pointed out with his wry wit, "It's pretty weird that Cakes (the Orioles' nickname for Palmer) has won 240 games, but it took a picture of him standing in his underwear to get nationally known."

Throughout the whole year of attention that the Jockey commercials have generated, Palmer has remained calm in the eye of the hurricane his scantily-clad body has produced. The whole thing amuses him rather than turns his head.

"It might be one thing if I was single (Palmer and his wife Susan live with their two daughters in a bucolic northern suburb of Baltimore) but my family is pretty cool about the whole thing," said Palmer. "I guess all the attention is flattering. My daughters have heard people say that their dad is good-looking and all this is much the same thing.

"It's how people interpret the ads. It wasn't my idea to establish myself as a sex symbol or anything like that. All I had in mind was modeling underwear. No one knew how well it would be received, but I had worked with Jockey before, so I knew that everything would be done in good taste and it has."

Palmer acknowledges that he gets his share of letters from women, who describe in some detail what pleasures may be in store if the two were to meet. But he adds, "It really doesn't happen that much and I don't think a lot of the women who are buying the posters really know who I am or what I do for a living."

However, Palmer's recognition level was enhanced by his network TV stint during the playoffs. And it is an area that Palmer is very serious about pursuing. Throughout the three-game series swept by the Kansas City Royals, Palmer worked hard, not opting for a role as a mere ornament to the telecasts. He was at the stadium several hours early, compiling notes from players and coaches and reporters, trying to avoid being interviewed himself while preferring to be the interviewer, instead.

Having done similar work during the 1978 playoffs, Palmer was much more polished and confident last fall.

"One thing that Howard (Cosell, who was not on the same ABC team with Palmer) always told me was that it is important to develop a story line as the game proceeded," said Palmer. "And with Al Michaels doing the play-by-play and Billy there to provide an insight to the various managerial decisions in a game, I felt that I should try to bridge them.

"At least that is what I tried to do, along with trying to offer some idea of how a pitcher might go about getting the various hitters out. One thing I've learned after doing these games is that it often isn't necessary to overexplain. The action can often explain itself. And I also learned that I am in the booth as a reporter, not just a ballplayer. Which made me almost root that the Series would have gone longer than three games because I was really enjoying myself."

From all accounts, ABC was just as pleased with Palmer. Palmer and his Cleveland-based agent Ed Keating have been negotiating a long-term agreement with the network that might have Palmer doing commentating work outside of baseball, in addition to future postseason appearances.

Palmer needs only 58 victories to join the 300-win club.

Similarly, Keating added that there has been a marked increase in the possibilities opening up to Palmer.

"People sometimes get the incorrect impression that companies are lining up for athletes to endorse their products," said Keating. "But over the year, there has been a lot of interest in Jim, several possibilities that we are investigating."

One of the most likely deals is a line of men's toiletries to which Palmer would lend his name and promotion expertise that has been gained through his underwear exposure.

The paradox of all this is that it comes at a time when Palmer's baseball future has never been more cloudy. Unlike past years, when doubts about Palmer dealt with his oft-volatile contract skirmishes with the Orioles or his frequent spats with Birds' manager Earl Weaver, the current uncertainity surrounds his ability to continue being a big major-league winner.

At a time when Palmer is secure with a contract extension negotiated during last season that ties him to the Orioles through 1983 and when he and Weaver have mellowed into a Odd Couple sort of co-existence, he worries about his physical condition. Palmer is 35 and after winning 20 games eight out of nine years beginning in 1970, he has spent '79 and '80 plagued by assorted arm, shoulder, elbow and back miseries.

And though he still managed to win 17 games in the Orioles' 100-victory 1980 season, Palmer was hardly satisfied with the shaky way he had to gain many of those wins.

"It all stemmed from a knot in my back that developed during spring training," said Palmer. "I probably should have just stopped pitching and got the problem treated properly. But Scotty McGregor started the year with a sore elbow and Dennis Martinez started the season on the disabled list with a bad shoulder and I figured that I could at least go out there.

"But because of the back, I had to alter my delivery to compensate. And because of that, I just couldn't throw like I should and ended up creating a tight shoulder. It became difficult to get loose warming up and I couldn't get my arm properly extended to get anything extra on my fastball.

"And it just about came to the point where I couldn't keep going out there. I finished the season but I really wasn't helping the club with the way I was throwing. I didn't have anything.

"When the season ended, I vowed to myself that I wouldn't ever go through a season like this one again. I had always kept myself in good physical condition all the time but I had never done much throwing. And I never needed conditioning like I realize I now need. So my winter is going to be spent on finding a good program for my back and shoulder and sticking with it. I will be working harder this winter than I have ever worked before."

Palmer has investigated various rehabilitation methods, including a trip to Philadelphia to discuss with Phillies' pitcher Steve Carlton a strengthening program designed by the Phils' strength coach and martial-arts expert Gus Hoefling. Palmer has also consulted with various sports medicine experts around the country.

"I want to give myself every possible option because I'd hate to think I overlooked anything if I can't pitch again like I know I can," said Palmer.

"Sure, I know I'm 35 but I've kept myself in good shape all my life. And I am confident I can again be a consistent winner. I know that if I can't get over this back problem, it won't be from lack of work."

Certainly, the Orioles believe Palmer can again be the stopper he used to be. Weaver constantly says that Palmer's new contract means that Palmer can win his 300th in a Baltimore uniform. The club's general manager Hank Peters and owner Edward Bennett Williams obviously wouldn't have signed him to the new contract extension (reportedly worth in the neighborhood of $700,000 a year) if they didn't feel that Palmer could still be a big winner.

And Palmer's teammates, especially the pitchers, still look up to him. "He just has so much knowledge about pitching and the game that it is impossible not to have some rub off," said Flanagan. Adds Orioles' pitching coach Ray Miller, "The thing about Cakes that I have always admired is that he never cuts corners on his work. He shows the younger guys by example when he is the first one out there to do the spring-training drills or is out there doing his daily running without complaining.

"And Jim is quick to help out teammates, no matter if they're rookies or established players. Every guy on our pitching staff sees him working hard, sees how many games he's won and realizes that's the best way to do it."

Palmer's elder-statesman status even has Weaver talking in glowing terms. "Hell, see all these gray hairs," said Weaver. "Palmer is responsible for a lot of them. But the guy is a pro and all the stuff with him has sort of calmed down. I try to speak to him and he tries not to irritate me.

"But the guy saved our pitching staff by his going out there this year when everyone knew he wasn't physically right. And with a few breaks, he still could have won his 20, which tells you something about him."

Barring a physical setback, Palmer will likely pitch at least three more years. But his future obviously lies somewhere beyond baseball, in broadcasting, in modeling, perhaps in show business. He was nearly the person to help host the show "That's Incredible," which has gotten such high ratings. In the end, Fran Tarkenton got the spot for which Palmer auditioned. And reportedly, the reason was that Palmer was too good-looking and therefore would have detracted from the show's big star, John Davidson.

But good looks haven't hurt Palmer's modeling career. And as he enters the homestretch on his race toward 300 victories, he has become just as famous for his underwear and his commentating.

President Reagan As a Sportscaster

By STAN ISAACS

That was quite a collection of names at the Chicago Cubs training camp in Catalina Island off Los Angeles in 1937: Charlie Grimm, manager; Rip Collins, 1b; Billy Herman, 2b; Billy Jurges, ss; Stan Hack, 3b; Gabby Hartnett, c; Augie Galan, lf; Joe Marty, cf; Frank Demaree, rf; and pitchers Bill Lee, Larry French, Tex Carleton, Charley Root, Roy Parmelee, Clay Bryant, Curt Davis and Clyde Shoun.

Yet the most significant name at that training camp may have been that of Ronald Reagan. He was there as a radio announcer for station WHO in Des Moines. A staff announcer who did re-creations off a Western Union ticker of Cubs games, he had persuaded his bosses that a trip to Catalina and close association with the Cubs would prove invaluable to his regular-season broadcasts.

Reagan parlayed that trip to the Coast into an acting career. In Los Angeles, he looked up some friends who introduced him to an agent which led to a screen test at 26 which led to a seven-year contract with Warner at $200 a week.

Reagan wrote fondly of his sports announcing career in his 1965 autobiography *Where's the Rest of Me?* (his famous line in the movie *King's Row*). He tells about being hired at his first job at WOC in Davenport, Iowa, by being able to do an impromptu broadcast of a football game when he applied for work. He had been a football player, a right guard, at Eureka College in Illinois and when asked to do a game on the spot, recalled the events in Eureka's epic victory over Western State in 1931.

He wrote: "I battled them back and forth, exchanged kicks, and kept watching the clock to make it come out long enough to

---

Stan Isaacs is TV sports columnist for Newsday. *This article has been excerpted from* Newsday.

Ronald Reagan announces at WHO (Des Moines) in the mid-30s.

pass for a quarter. When 15 minutes had gone by, I figured it was safe to maneuver us Red Devils down to our own 35 and go for the old college try finish . . . Now 20 minutes had gone by . . . I wound it up and even threw in that familiar line, 'We return you now to our main studio.' "

He broadcasted Iowa U. football games at WOC, then went on to the bigger WHO, where he did re-creations of White Sox and Cubs games for Des Moines' listeners. Many stations were doing the games at the time, some of them live from the park, Reagan recalled, so it was important to keep right on top of the action off the telegraphic relay. He said his commentary would go something like this:

" 'The pitcher [whatever his name] has the sign, he's coming out of the windup, here's the pitch,' and at that moment Curly [the telegrapher] would slip me the blank. It might contain the information S2C, and without a pause I would translate this into 'It's a called strike breaking over the inside corner, making it two strikes on the batter.' If the Cubs were in the field, I would continue while I waited for the next dot and dash, saying, 'Hartnett

Sal Bando made the candidate No. 1 before the election.

returns the ball to Lon Warneke, Warneke is dusting his hands in the resin, steps back up on the mound, is getting the sign again from Hartnett, here's the windup and the pitch.' "

Once, the telegraphic wire went dead when Reagan had a pitch on its way to batter Augie Galan in the ninth inning of a scoreless tie. "I was convinced that a ball game tied up in the ninth inning was no time to tell my audience we had lost contact with the game and they would have to listen to recorded music. I knew of only one thing that wouldn't get me in the score column and betray me–a foul ball. So I had Augie foul this pitch down the left field foul line . . . He fouled for six minutes and 45 seconds until I lost count. I began to be frightened that maybe I was establishing a new world record for a fellow staying at bat hitting fouls, and this could betray me . . ."

Finally, the wire resumed with the word that Galan popped out on the first pitch. Reagan wrote, "Not in my game he didn't –he popped out after practically making a career of foul balls."

Jim Zabel, the current sports announcer at WHO, who is 58, recalls listening to Reagan when he was growing up in Davenport. "Reagan was one of the best sports announcers I ever heard. He had all the elements, being concise, accurate, quick and glib. He was in a class with the greats, Bill Stern and Ted

Reagan played the movie role of Grover Cleveland Alexander in "The Winning Team." He's with Mrs. Alexander.

Husing, and he told me on one of his visits back here that he would have stayed in sportscasting if he hadn't gotten that Hollywood break—and I'm sure he would have gone on to the networks."

Zabel has interviewed Reagan on many of his trips back to Iowa. "He still recalls small details from those games he broadcast—the temperature, the names of the players. He once told me those years as a broadcaster here were the happiest years of his life. He was doing what he liked to do, everybody liked him and there was a minimum of controversy."

Will George Brett Or Anyone Else Reach the Magic .400?

By HAL BOCK

Call it The Chase—a pulsating day-by-day struggle staged over the final two months of the season, a battle George Brett fought not against other hitters, but with himself. The other hitters had been left behind long ago, lost in Brett's afterburners as he soared toward .400, that magical, mystical batting average achieved by so very few major-league players.

With six weeks left in the 1980 season, there was little question that George Brett would win the batting championship. What people wondered—Brett included—was whether this marvelously-talented hitter could make it to .400, a plateau which had not been dented since 1941.

Brett's flirtation with .400 captivated the country. And it's fair to say it fascinated him as well. He started the season in a funk and on May 21, the day before the strike deadline set by the Major League Players Association, he was batting a very un-Brettian .247. When the settlement was reached, Brett's bat came alive. But then he damaged ligaments in his right ankle June 10 and spent a month on the disabled list.

"I was probably swinging the bat the best I'd ever swung it in my life before I got injured," Brett said. "But then, when I got out of the hospital and I was able to take batting practice, I was swinging bad. I had missed 26 games. You just don't come back without losing something."

Brett's injury forced him to miss the All-Star Game, although he had been named the American League's starting third baseman for the fifth straight year. After the midseason break, Brett returned to the Kansas City lineup and went on a batting tear.

"I tried to block out of my mind that I'd missed a month of the

Hal Bock swings a big bat as baseball columnist for the Associated Press.

It's conquerable, like Mount Everest, but few ever achieve it.

season," he said. "I just kept telling myself, 'I'm hot. I'm swinging the bat good.' Everytime I'd walk up to the batter's box I just kept telling myself, 'Hey, you're the best! You're hot, you're hot.' I know I'm not the best hitter in baseball, but if you keep telling yourself you are, you're going to believe it."

Not the best? You'd have trouble convincing those who tried to get Brett out during the second half of the season. In one August game, with runners on first and second and the score tied in the ninth inning, Earl Weaver, manager of the Baltimore Orioles, ordered Brett walked to load the bases. After reliever Tim Stoddard then walked Amos Otis to force in the Royals' winning run, Weaver wasn't prone to second-guessing himself.

"I would be a dumb so-and-so coming in here saying I'm not going to let Brett beat me and then let him beat me," said the scrappy Orioles' skipper. Of course, George had already singled and tripled in the game, extending a hitting streak to 25 consecutive games.

Brett was batting .388 after that game and a week later, on Aug. 17, he pushed his average past .400 for the first time, going 4-for-4 against Toronto. The Kansas City crowd gave him a standing ovation when his final hit of the night–a double–pushed him past the magic mark. Standing on second base, Brett acknowledged the roar of the crowd with a tip of his hat. Inside, he was churning. "I got goose bumps standing there," he said. "It was a tremendous feeling, something that will live with me, something I don't think I will ever forget."

There were 44 games left in the season at that point, a lot of baseball, a long stretch over which to maintain .400. The combination of that factor and the absence of a pennant race–the Royals were light years ahead of the rest of the American League West when Brett reached .400–convinced some baseball people that he could not crack the barrier.

Stan Musial, whose .376 in 1948 is the closest any National Leaguer has come to .400 in half a century, thought a race would have helped Brett.

"If the lead was a lot smaller, if George felt the pressure to deliver because the team's success was at stake, it would be easier on him," Musial said. "Now, all he's got to concentrate on is .400."

In the midst of his run at .400, Brett reeled off a 30-game hitting streak. Musial thought that batting streaks are easier to maintain than a season-long .400 average.

"He can think about one game at a time, about keeping that streak going," Musial said. "But for .400, the thing is, he doesn't just need one hit a game. He needs a couple every day."

EIGHT PREREQUISITES FOR REACHING .400

- Concentration and dedication of Ted Williams
- Speed and daring of Jackie Robinson
- Quick wrists of Henry Aaron
- Contact abilities of Rod Carew
- Sustained good health
- Ability to overcome rigors of 162-game schedule
- Must be slump-proof
- Must be pressure-proof

Specifically two hits in every five at-bats, or four in every ten. It is a monumental task, one accomplished by only eight players since 1900. Musial thinks it can be done again and that Brett has the tools to do it.

"He's in good position to do it," Stan the Man said. "Around September, he's got to be at .400 or above, though. I was up to .390 in September, 1948, then I fell off a little. He's got to avoid going into any kind of a slump. Once you drop below .400, it's hard to build up to it again."

Brett knew that. There was one stretch when he cracked eight straight hits and pushed his average from .394 to .407. "It doesn't matter if you drop under (.400)," he said. "All you've got to do is have one good day and you're back over. I've had 'em for a week at a time. I feel if I get hot for one solid week and just hit the ball like I've done in the past and accumulate a lot of hits, it should give me enough padding so I won't have to worry about it. That would be fantastic . . . I think I've been up to .407 now three times. I'd like to get back to .407 and then have a good four-hit game or a five-hit game and that would give me the leeway that I really need."

But it never happened. On Sept. 6, with his average at .399, Brett went 0-for-3 against Cleveland and injured his right hand swinging at an outside pitch. At first the injury was considered minor but it nagged him and kept him out of the lineup for some 10 days. At the time, he was still short of the 502 official plate appearances needed to qualify for the batting crown and that quickly became a source of as much speculation as whether or not he really could hit .400.

When Brett returned, his average slipped below .390 and time began running out on him. Still, he thinks he could have reached the magic .400 figure if he had not lost that oh-so-important hitter's ally, patience.

"A lot of pressure was put on me to hit .400," he said. "But in the end, it wasn't the pressure I got from the media that got to me. It was the pressure I put on myself. At first, I didn't think I could do it. Then everybody started talking about it and all of a sudden, talking about it so much, I found out I wanted it.

"I knew every time I didn't get a hit, it was hurting my chances. So I started getting impatient, swinging at bad balls. I put the nail in my own coffin."

When the Royals reached the playoffs against the New York Yankees and then the World Series against the Philadelphia Phillies, his teammates may have felt the pressure, but Brett was cool and calm.

"I've had my pressure," Brett said of The Chase. "For a month-and-a-half, I had my pressure. Nothing can match that. Maybe if it's the fifth game of the playoffs with the winning run at second and two out and I'm up, it might come close.

"The toughest part of the .400 pressure was our last road trip to Seattle and Minnesota the next-to-the-last week of the season. That was by far the worst because I was running out of time, the other teams were throwing a lot of lefthanders at me and I got impatient. I started to swing at bad pitches. If we hadn't clinched the division so early, the other teams might have been a little more fair to me. But their pitchers just seemed to care about giving George Brett an 0-for-4."

So he finished with .390, 24 home runs and 118 runs batted in, not terribly shabby figures. But the questions persist: Could he have hit .400 if he had been healthy all year?—he did miss a total of 45 games because of injuries—and can anyone hit .400 in this day and age?

"I hope I get another shot at it," said Brett. "Maybe I will. But the one thing I had going for me this year was those three hot months. I went from .240 to .404 and that would be awfully hard to do again."

To hit .400, a number of factors have to go a hitter's way. For one, he must avoid any serious slumps like the one Brett had to recover from after the first six weeks of the season. Harry "The Hat" Walker, a hitting encyclopedia who batted .363 in 1947, has an idea about that.

"You have to take it a week at a time," he said. "That's what I

The wide-ranging Brett owns a show horse.

did in '47. I'd take a week and figure that if I was going to bat, say 30 times, I knew I needed about 12 hits during that time. I treated each week separately. I'd battle that one. Then, when it was over, I'd put it out of my mind and go on to the next one.

"Each week would be like a new season to me," Walker continued. "Doing it that way kept me enthusiastic. I wouldn't let down if I had a bad day, or even a bad week."

Brett finished with 175 hits in 449 at-bats. To bat .400 with that number of swings, a man would need 180 hits, only five more than Brett managed. That's the difference of less than one hit per month over the course of a six-month season.

Brett's shot at .400 is enhanced by Royals Stadium. The artificial surface certainly adds hits and points to any batter's average.

"He's playing in a hitter's ball park, there's no question about that," said Pete Rose of the Phillies, who got his first look at Royals Stadium during the World Series. "But anytime you hit .390 . . . well that's some accomplishment. I don't believe any hitter in the National League can hit that high. We've got too many good, young pitchers. After all (Bill Buckner's) .324 won it this year. Last year it was (Keith Hernandez') .344."

Brett has his favorite teams to swing against.

"I always hit well against the Yankees, the Orioles, the Angels, Texas and the Red Sox," he said. "I always feel very comfortable in those ball parks and I always like hitting in Kansas City because of the artificial surface."

Brett was asked to describe his hitting style.

"I'm an average hitter," he said.

Average?

"Not average routine," he explained. "I hit for average."

And how!

Yet, for all his success, Brett does have a weakness. Despite all his injuries, despite his impatience at the end, Brett still would have hit .400 last year if he had been able to handle the Oakland A's pitching staff. Against the A's in 1980, baseball's best hitter batted a feeble .233, managing only 10 hits in 43 swings.

Manager Billy Martin chortled over the success his pitchers enjoyed with Brett in 1980.

"It was more than just luck," said George Steinbrenner's favorite ex-employee. "We did everything to him. We never pitched him the same way twice. We pitched him in different patterns. If you pitch to him the same way and stay that way, he'll hurt you."

Martin said the A's did not pitch around Brett. "It's better location and selection of pitches," the A's manager said. "When you're dealing with a super, super player, you've got to keep changing and changing.

"We're not going to let him sit on one thing because he's that good and that strong that he'll adjust quickly. He's like a hitting coach doing the hitting."

When Martin managed the Yankees, the club's book on Brett said to jam him and force him to hit the ball away. "We found out that he takes you downtown when you pitch him in and he hits line drives to left field when you pitch him away," said Martin. "You come back inside and he's waiting for you again. He was thinking the same way as the pitchers."

And that's another reason why baseball people feel Brett is a legitimate threat to .400. He is a smart hitter, much like Rod Carew, who flirted with .400 in 1977 and finished with .388. Pitching and hitting is a cat-and-mouse game and batters who can't be fooled wind up with big averages.

When Carew made his run at .400, Ted Williams, the last man to hit that much, was asked about the accomplishment by *Sports Illustrated*.

"For sure, you don't fluke into a .400 season," Williams said.

"A lot of guys have lucked into .300, but there are no flash-in-the-pan .400s. Hitting a baseball—I've always said it—is the single most difficult thing to do in sport, and a .400 season is a magnificent achievement. You have to have the talent, the opportunity and the circumstances to make it happen."

Williams liked Carew's chances for .400 because, like Brett, Rod is a contact hitter who sprays the ball.

"He's the classic straightway hitter," Williams said of Carew. "Historically, the highest average hitters were straightaway hitters. Good form, good plate coverage, good style, a quick bat."

The description fits Brett every bit as well as it does Carew.

In Williams' magic season of 1941, his average soared as high as .436 in June. By season's end, his bat was dragging a bit and he was losing about a point per day. On the last day of the season, his average was at .3996—rounded off to .400. Red Sox manager Joe Cronin offered Williams the last day off, a tactic that would have safeguarded .400. Williams chose to play and went out that final day by getting six hits in eight swings in a doubleheader. He finished at .406 and no one has been over .400 since. But Williams has always insisted that someone would.

"As time went by, I began to think, at least privately, that maybe people were right, that .400 was too tough, especially because I wasn't seeing the devotion I thought was necessary to make a .400 hitter. Today ballplayers have a thousand distractions and too much time on their hands, and the money comes in a lot easier. In my case, nothing else mattered but the hitting. I lived to hit. I was willing to practice until the blisters bled. And then I practiced some more. A trip to the plate was an adventure—and a time to store up information too."

If you were putting together the prototype .400 hitter, he would need the concentration and dedication of a Ted Williams, the speed and daring of a Jackie Robinson, the quick wrists of a Hank Aaron, the contact abilities of a Rod Carew. He has to stay healthy, be able to overcome the rigors of the modern 162-game schedule and its endless night games and coast-to-coast road trips which sometimes deposit his body in California while his stomach is still in Texas. He must be slump-proof, a consistent day-in, day-out hitter who will never go into a long, extended dry spell. He must be pressure-proof, able to ignore the swarms of media that his bid will attract, especially in its final weeks.

Is there such a guy around? Quite possibly.

He can be found in Kansas City, wearing No. 5, and playing third base. Five more hits last year and George Brett would have answered the question then and there. Don't bet against him getting those five—and a few more—some year soon.

An Astrologic Preview WORLD SERIES 1981-1991

By JOE GERGEN

Sea of Tranquility, Nov. 1, 1991—Workmen were spraying the final coat of green paint on the left-field wall and installing the last row of bleacher seats up above the bullpen in right-center-field when Bill Lee walked to the mound. His three-piece suit was slightly rumpled and his running shoes were coated with moon dust from his jog through the countryside outside this first boom town in space. Lee had neither a ball nor a glove but that didn't stop him from going through the motions which, deep down, he still identified with Fenway Park.

Lee had not pitched in nine years, since the 1982 World Series in Montreal at which former commissioner Bowie Kuhn lost three fingers and two toes to frostbite and surrendered the job on the advice of his physician. But it all came back to the lefthander as he stood on the mound of the first old ballpark built in his lifetime. The replica of Fenway, identical to the original, even to the Jimmy Fund sign atop the one-deck grandstand in right, was almost finished. Lee had made good on a promise.

"A Return to Old-Fashioned Values" was Lee's campaign theme. He had run for commissioner on the Regressive Party ticket, stressing baseball should be moved out of the massive, concrete stadiums with artificial turf and placed in odd, mis-shapen parks with grass where so many people had discovered the joys of the game. Since no one on earth was willing to be identified with anything so antiquated, Lee had turned to the

---

Joe Gergen, farflung correspondent for Long Island's Newsday, *already has his press credentials for such 1991 classics as Super Bowl XXV on Mars, the NBA championship on Lovetron and the World Series on the Sea of Tranquility.*

Commissioner Bill Lee ponders under his astral beanie.

moon. After all, during his playing days, he had been called Spaceman.

Two days from now, in the man-made environment of a city under glass, the first Out of This World Series will get underway. It will feature neither designated hitters, designated runners, designated shortstops or orange baseballs, which afflicted baseball during the decade of the 1980s. Lee, acting under a mandate from fans in the third general election since Kuhn's resignation, rolled back the "refinements" which had been incorporated into the game during the reign of Kuhn and his successors, George Steinbrenner and Charlie Finley.

"I profess oldtime baseball," Lee said in the great debate among himself, Jimmy Carter and John Anderson on election eve, "the way it used to be played, with more of what we say are humanist values off the field. The establishment likes serfdom. They are wrong. I identify with the people in the bleachers."

It was thought by many that Lee's strongest appeal to voters, especially the older variety, was a film clip featuring Fenway Park, leveled for a multi-level parking garage in 1983 by the penniless owners of the Boston Red Sox (Carl Yastrzemski stayed on as attendant in what was left field), Chicago's Wrigley Field, which gave way to a drive-in theatre following the 1986 season, and such fondly remembered palaces as Brooklyn's Ebbets Field and St. Louis' Sportsman's Park. The clip was accompanied by the Sinatra recording of "There Used to Be a Ballpark Right Here." Apparently, many wept all the way to the polls.

Lee has promised to rebuild all the famous parks of yesteryear with the old technology available here and in other earth settlements, technology no longer available on the mother planet. This area is particularly rich in rafters from which oldtime fans frequently hung. The foundation for Wrigley Field already has been set and the park is expected to open in time for the 1992 season, provided the outfield vines arrive on time.

The commissioner, who once went to mainland China in search of the real Big Red Machine during his playing days, also has smoothed relations between major teams from North America and foreign powers. The series starting Tuesday will mark China's first appearance in the fall classic. Ironically, they will be represented by graduates of the great Taiwan Little League system, wearing the uniforms of the Shanghai Shippers. They will be opposed by the Toronto Blue Jays. And Lee, whose taste ran to Warren Zevon a decade ago, promised to lead the men on the moon in a chorus of "Take Me Out to the Ball Game" before the first game.

Judging by the interest exhibited here, Lee appears to have hit upon an idea whose time has come again. The series, to be played in the daytime, offers a respite from the high-powered productions of the '80s which turned many people from the game. To wit:

1981

KANSAS CITY—The Royals reversed the outcome of the 1980 season by beating the depleted Philadelphia Phillies, 6-4, in the seventh game. Dan Quisenberry, appearing in his 58th consecutive game, dating back to early August, saved the victory by striking out Mike Schmidt with the bases loaded in the ninth. The strikeout pitch was Quisenberry's first overhand curve of his career and broke the reliever's arm.

The Phillies were on the verge of winning the Series in five games when several of the 6,312 police dogs encircling Veterans

Royals' Dan Quisenberry wins seventh game in '81 Series.

Stadium got loose in the ninth inning. They mauled pitcher Steve Carlton and five Phillie regulars, who missed the remainder of the Series, and the Royals rallied to win that game in 10 innings. Philadelphia hopes were dealt another blow when manager Dallas Green, fed up with whining on the flight to Kansas City, personally sent five more players to the hospital. The Phillie Phanatic was forced to play first base in the final two games. The winning hit in the seventh game was a three-run homer by Ken Brett in the eighth inning. Ken was batting for his brother George, baseball's first .500 hitter, who was suffering from diarrhea.

Philadelphia	**002**	**011**	**000**	**—**	**4**	**10**	**2**
Kansas City	**101**	**100**	**03x**	**—**	**6**	**8**	**0**

Ruthven, Reed (6), Lyle (8) and Boone; Gura, Leonard (5), Quisenberry (6) and Wathan. WP-Quisenberry. LP-Reed. HRS-Rose, Wilson, K. Brett.

1982

MONTREAL—The strife-plagued series ended on a bitter-cold note in Olympic Stadium as the Montreal Expos overcame the Oakland A's, 5-4, in 12 innings. Guy Lafleur, a late-season acquisition, skated across home plate after a marvelous deke around catcher Darrell Porter, who had the misfortune of playing in spikes on the ice which formed on the artificial surface. The Expos' use of blades on their shoes prompted a furious first-inning argument which Oakland's Billy Martin resolved by punching Montreal's Dick Williams in the nose. Martin thus became the first manager to be banished from baseball during the course of a World Series.

The ruling was made by commissioner Bowie Kuhn, who was dressed in Bermuda shorts, t-shirt and sandals, apparently to convince a national television audience that it was not cold. Temperature at the start of the night game was 25 degrees and reportedly it had dipped below 20 before Lafleur tagged up and scored on Larry Robinson's slapshot to medium centerfield. It was discovered after the game that Kuhn could not move from

Guy Lafleur ices the Expos' World Series triumph in '82.

his seat and he had to be borne by ambulance to the hospital, where his frostbite was treated.

Oakland .... **020 002 000 000 – 4 12 1**
Montreal......... **001 030 000 001 – 5 13 2**

Langford, Norris (5), Lyle (9) and Porter; Rogers, Lee (5), Sosa (9), Fryman (11) and Carter. WP-Fryman, LP-Lyle. HRS-Henderson, Parrish.

1983

NEW YORK–Although it had been billed as baseball's first Subway Series in 27 years, no one arrived by train at either Yankee Stadium or Shea Stadium. The subway, burdened by a shortage of funds and an excess of graffiti, had shut down in late September after desperately raising the fares to $3 for one way and $5.50 roundtrip during the summer. The inconvenience caused massive traffic jams in both Queens and Brooklyn, which were not alleviated until Thanksgiving Day.

George Steinbrenner, who had added the commissioner's duties to his position as owner of the Yankees, invited himself to throw out the first ball in Yankee Stadium. He accepted. The owners had been deadlocked through 25 ballots on a new commissioner when Steinbrenner, tired of such inefficiency, offered to buy the job. He spent so much time in his Rockefeller Center office firing off telegrams and firing personnel that he lost interest in third-base coaches and the Yankees, who enjoyed a peaceful and successful season. The series was a one-sided affair settled in the fifth game by Reggie Jackson's towering home run off Tom Seaver, the cornerstone of the old Mets' staff which included Nolan Ryan, Jerry Koosman and Tug McGraw.

New York (A)..... **000 001 420 – 7 9 0**
New York (N)..... **100 100 10x – 3 6 1**

John, Gossage (7) and Cerone; Seaver, Allen (7), McGraw (8) and Stearns. WP-John. LP-Seaver. HRS-Swoboda, Jackson, Winfield.

1984

ATLANTA–Ted Turner played Big Brother in the Brave New World Series of 1984. Turner, whose exuberance was such that he once appointed himself manager during his first years as owner of the Braves, threw the most lavish party in the history of the classic. It started in Atlanta the night before the first game and somehow wound up at Newport, site of Turner's 1977 America's Cup triumph, two weeks later. Turner and those who went for the ride didn't miss much in the way of action.

The Braves, who became the first team to represent three cities in the Series (Boston, Milwaukee and Atlanta), hammered the Denver Indians in the first three games, lost two one-run contests on Joe Charboneau homers which reportedly traveled 650 feet in the mile-high air, and then breezed to a 7-0 victory in the sixth game. Phil Niekro, the 45-year-old knuckleball pitcher, allowed the Indians three scratch singles.

Denver	**000 000 000 —**	**0**	**3**	**1**
Atlanta	**301 001 20x —**	**7**	**8**	**1**

Waits, Garland (1), Morton (7), Lyle (8) and Alexander; Niekro and Nolan. WP-Niekro. LP-Waits. HRS-Murphy 2, Chambliss.

1985

SAN DIEGO—There were those who assumed it was just another of Ray Kroc's ill-advised brainstorms. This, after all, was the man who offered Oscar Gamble millions to play the outfield and who decided Jerry Coleman was better suited to managing than announcing. So when Kroc announced that the Chicken was taking over operation of the Padres' franchise, many scoffed. Sure, the Chicken was the most popular sports figure in San Diego but his fortune had been made on looks.

Well, the Chicken surprised them all in 1985. Dressing the Padres in uniforms identical to his own, he fashioned a remarkable flock. Communication was the key, his players said, as they fluttered to the National League pennant and then swept the Baltimore Orioles in four straight. The team's entertainment value made the Padres a bigger draw than Disneyland, although humorless opponents bridled at being "shown up." Rollie Fingers, who had changed his name to Fingers Lookin' Good although he retained his handlebar mustache, saved three of the four games for the Padres.

Baltimore	**000 110 000 —**	**2**	**6**	**0**
San Diego	**000 003 010 —**	**4**	**8**	**0**

Stone, Martinez (6), Stoddard (8) and Dempsey; Chicken Littell, Fingers Lookin' Good (7) and Chicken Cacciatore. WP-Chicken Littell. LP-Stone. HRS-Chicken Stanley.

1986

CHICAGO—The most bizarre Series in history ended in mid-play during the sixth game when the temporary lighting system installed in Wrigley Field by the American Broadcasting Com-

Mark (still the Bird) Fidrych figures in 1986 Series.

pany shorted at the instant Steve Kemp drove a bases-loaded pitch toward Dave Kingman with the Chicago Cubs and the Detroit Tigers locked in a scoreless tie in the sixth inning. Neither the ball nor Kingman was found, the argument on the field precipitated a riot in the stands and Detroit was awarded a 9-0 forfeit victory.

As a result of the chaotic finish, it was decided Wrigley Field no longer was suitable for major-league baseball unless permanent light towers were erected. The Wrigley family refused and three weeks after the end of the season the brick ballyard was demolished. Steinbrenner resigned under fire and Charlie Finley scored a landslide victory in the first general election of a commissioner by pointing out that if they had been using the orange baseballs he long ago prescribed, Kemp's drive could have been located.

***Detroit**	**000 00**	**9**	**5**	**0**
Chicago	**000 00**	**0**	**3**	**0**

Fidrych and Parrish; Reuschel and Foote. HRS-Kemp?
*Forfeit

1987

NEW ORLEANS—Artificiality was the theme of this Series. All seven games between the Houston Astros and the New Orleans Mariners were played indoors on AstroTurf and Mardi Grass. In addition to the designated hitter, the teams were permitted to use the designated runner. Commissioner Finley entered the arenas on his personal mule as the organists played "Donkey Serenade" and then everyone sat back to applaud with the moving hands on the scoreboard.

Both the Astros and the Mariners, who had been transferred at the start of the season from another domed stadium in Seattle, averaged slightly more than two runs per game during the season. The combination of their strong pitching and the lack of air currents in the Astrodome and the Superdome, however, curtailed more powerful opponents. Each game of the Series was decided by a score of 2-1. The winning run in the seventh game was scored by Terry Puhl, who walked on three pitches (another Finley innovation), stole second, advanced to third on a ground ball and came home on a squeeze bunt by Craig Reynolds.

New Orleans	**000 100 000**	**1**	**5**	**1**
Houston	**100 000 10x**	**2**	**6**	**0**

Honeycutt and Hirt; Niekro, Sambito (8) and Ashby. WP-Niekro. LP-Honeycutt. HRS-None.

1988

HAVANA–Gleefully, the citizens of this old city rummaged around in their attics for signs and banners which hadn't seen the light of day in more than two decades. They produced them at Fidel Castro Stadium before the first game of the Series which would make baseball the international pastime. "Cuba si, Yanquis no," some signs said. "Yanquis go home" said others.

Ironically, the New York Yankees qualified to meet the Havana Cigars in the first Series not held exclusively on the North American continent. The Yankees had been the most popular U.S. team among Cubans before the revolution and now they would be the first American team to visit Havana in the realigned structure of Organized Baseball. Havana had won the Caribbean division which included teams from Venezuela, Mexico, the Dominican Republic, Panama and Puerto Rico.

Castro, the manager of the Cuban team and a former prospect before he turned to guerilla activities, pitched the first game but

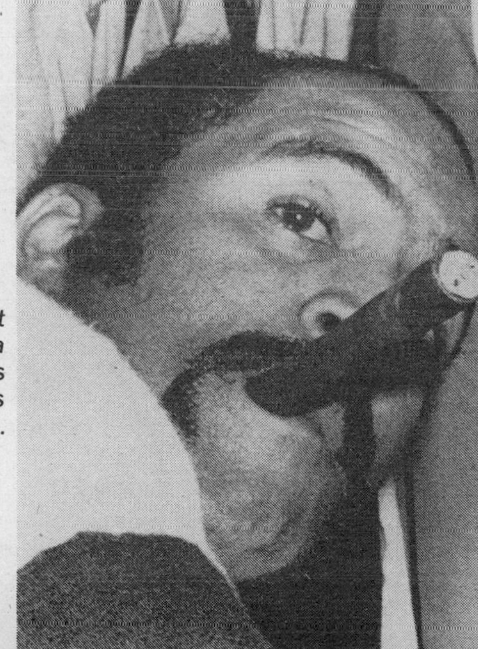

Luis Tiant lights up Havana as he four-hits the N.Y. Yanquis in 1988 Series.

was shelled. He played the rest of the Series at first base, relegating Tony Perez to the role of designated hitter. The star who emerged was a native of Havana who, according to some reports, was 50. Luis Tiant, pitching with a cigar in his mouth, baffled his former teammates in the second and concluding sixth game.

New York (A)	**000 001 100**	**—**	**2 8 0**
Havana	**000 022 00x**	**—**	**4 7 0**

Righetti, Lyle (6) and Cerone; Tiant and Azcue. WP-Tiant. LP-Righetti. HRS-Perez, Oliva.

Oh pinch-hits in Tokyo.

Charlie Finley's ode to cricket.

1989

TOKYO—The year the Series went worldwide also qualified as the year of the Giants. From the shores of San Francisco Bay to

Tokyo Bay, the Giants dominated baseball. The San Francisco Giants, descendants of the New York Giants, met the Tokyo Yomiuri Giants, patterned after the New York Giants right down to their uniforms.

An earthquake had left Candlestick Park unusable and the San Francisco team agreed to play all Series games in Tokyo. Only five games were required for the Japanese Giants to defeat their American counterparts. Of particular note was the appearance of Sadaharu Oh as a pinch-hitter in the final game. Although the legendary Japanese home run king had retired to the manager's office, he had continued to take batting practice. Baseball officials implored him to play in order to add a sense of occasion to this first significant meeting of East and West on a baseball field. He did so in the sixth inning, lifting his leg and lining a single off Vida Blue to start a four-run rally.

San Francisco.....	**030**	**000**	**110**	**—**	**5**	**10**	**2**
Tokyo...........	**001**	**204**	**00x**	**—**	**7**	**11**	**1**

Blue, Green (6), Black (8) and White; Murakami, Datsun (7) and Toyota. WP-Murakami. LP-Blue. HRS-Clark.

1990

LONDON—The English agreed that what those men in the strange britches were doing wasn't cricket. But nonetheless a crowd of curiosity seekers had convened on Lord's, the shrine of bowlers the world over, in northwest London for a look at this game called baseball. In a sense, baseball was returning to its roots.

This was the last year of Finley's stewardship, and he was determined to go out in style. He had decided to convert the world to baseball, or at least his vision of it, and had scheduled the World Series for London. As a concession to British tradition, there was a tea break every three innings. Which meant that the fifth and final game, which lasted 13 innings, set a Series time endurance record of six hours, three minutes. Jim Rice's long home run was the margin of victory for the California Angels over the Singapore Slings.

California........	**000**	**200**	**001**	**000**	**01**	**—**	**4**	**15**	**2**
Singapore........	**000**	**110**	**100**	**000**	**00**	**—**	**3**	**12**	**2**

Perry, Clear (7), Lyle (12) and Downing; Chan, Kipling (9) and Raffles. WP-Lyle. LP-Kipling. HRS-Fish, Rice.

MIKE SCHMIDT'S PHILADELPHIA EXPLOSION

By GARY SMITH

Mike Schmidt climbed aboard the flat-bed truck at 18th and Market Sts. It was time for the victory parade Philadelphia had been planning for 97 years and he wasn't so sure he was going to like it.

Yeah, yeah, he figured. Half a million people, half-drunk and half-crazy. Same ones who throw beer cans, throwing confetti. Same ones who booed me, wanting to climb on my bandwagon, not to mention my flat-bed truck.

Four miles of humanity later, Mike Schmidt's mind had changed. The truck pulled into JFK Stadium, where 90,000 more were waiting to embrace the Phillies. Schmidt felt his throat and his eyes begin to do things he hadn't asked them to do. The man they call Captain Cool was starting to cry.

"I got chills and I actually started crying," said the World Series MVP. "I was moved by the whole concept. It was shocking. You could make a movie about it. Never will you see more unity over one isolated thing in the world.

"I started out the day with mixed feelings. You always question the sincerity of the Philadelphia fans when there's so much of a love/hate relationship. You can hit three home runs to win the first game of a doubleheader and they'll go crazy and then strike out twice in the second game and they'll boo you all the way to the dugout. But the further we got into the parade, the

---

Gary Smith covered the Philadelphia sports scene, including Mike Schmidt, for the Philadelphia Daily News *and now is a staff writer for* Inside Sports.

And now Schmidt looks for an encore.

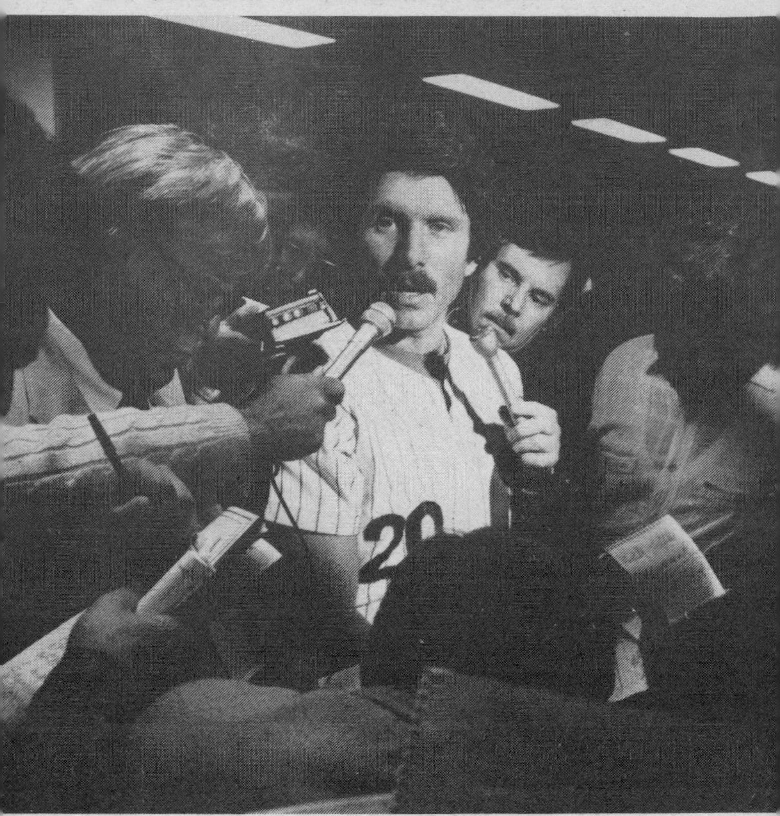

When you're MVP, the media world engulfs you.

look of sincerity on faces, and the warmth, the things they were yelling . . . I can't even describe it."

Captain Cool is dead, an image ransacked by two months Mike Schmidt will never forget. September and October of 1980 took turns lifting him to the clouds and rubbing his face in the dust. He was thrilled by four game-winning hits in the last week of the season, humbled by an 0-for-5 and two critical strikeouts in the playoff clincher in Houston, overwhelmed by a world championship, reduced to tears by the victory parade, jubilant over receiving the World Series MVP award and then mortified the same day when reporters told him a teammate said he didn't deserve it.

Those who always complained that he was too cool were

struck silent. In the autumn of 1980 Mike Schmidt got his emotions dirty, if not his pants.

The biggest piece of satisfaction that Schmidt got from these two months was not the watch for being Series MVP or the trophy for being the league MVP. It was the glow inside from knowing that he had finally reached up and grabbed a fuzzy edge of the potential that had always been waiting there over his head, waiting since the day he was born.

"The last two-three weeks of the season, and then the playoffs and the Series, surviving it the way we did and I did, really gave me a sense of fulfillment of the purpose in my life," said the third baseman. "The purpose of my life is to use the tools and abilities and coordination God gave me at birth. The most gratifying thing is I have an opportunity to communicate that feeling, the idea of fulfillment of purpose, to youths wherever I go."

He will have plenty of opportunities. Wherever Schmidt goes now, people freeze and stare. Before October, his was never a face that started traffic jams. He was a .255 career hitter with some fancy home-run numbers and one national TV commercial for 7-Up, but that's as far as it went.

Now there is no town in America where he can seek asylum. He says the change struck home a week and a half after the Series, when he was sauntering over a golf course in South Carolina. Every time he walked down the fairway, construction workers building houses on an adjacent lot would go on a five-minute wildcat strike. Hammers stopped and there was silence until Schmidt was just a speck in the distance.

"They'd stop hammering and start staring every time I went by," Schmidt recalled. "It gives you an idea of the impact of a World Series when people stop working for five minutes when you walk by. It's awesome, really. Everywhere I go, from South Carolina to New York to Philadelphia, I'm recognized now."

Everyone wants a piece of Schmidt since the Series, and he has had a hard time divvying himself up. There are two daughters, a wife, a book coming out this spring, appearances, TV shows, interviews and commercials all vying for time.

"My life has been ridiculous," he sighed. "It's a rat race I can't stop."

He brought it all on himself, of course. He had one of those, *See here, world, I can do it* seasons, the kind when an athlete stands up and, flexing his muscles, shrugs off all his critics at once. He hit .286 and led the league in four categories–home runs (48), RBI (121), slugging percentage (.624) and total bases (324). But that, awesome as it was, would not have been enough had Schmidt not saved some of his gunpowder for postseason.

This was the label he had to kick harder than any other, the label of the big man with the tiny stats whenever the pressure was on. Terrifying on a June day with no one on base, but clog them in September and watch him strand them like orphans.

He had a .182 average in three playoffs and once was quoted by a Philadelphia columnist as admitting he had choked. But in 1980 he tore the tag clean off his collar.

He carried the Phillies down the stretch, hit two massive homers in back-to-back games on the season's final weekend in Montreal, had a game-winning hit in the playoffs and then in the Series had seven RBI, two game-winning hits and a single that ignited a ninth-inning rally in the pivotal fifth game.

"I got through the pressure-filled games," said Schmidt. "Every ballplayer wants to be known as a guy that plays under pressure. There are only three or four hitters in baseball that are talked of in terms of being clutch hitters. I doubt if that will be said about me now . . . all it takes is one strikeout in Houston on national TV in the playoffs to get the old label.

"But this year I hit as well with men on base as any player in the league. I may be improving in that more than any player. I'm not trying to carry the burden of the team on my back as I did in the past. I was able to keep my sanity more than ever before. I didn't go into a coma, feeling like I had to hit three home runs to make up for an 0-for-10. I cut down on the 0-fors, so I was always doing just a little something. There were less 0-fors . . . and less agonizing.

"I felt learning to hit under pressure was the one item I wanted in my repertoire, in my baseball life. I knew when I retired they were going to say, 'He could hit a baseball as far as anybody, he was a great third baseman, but he could have been a better clutch hitter.'

"Just because I did it this year doesn't automatically make me a career clutch hitter. But there's going to be other pressure-filled at-bats, and to be able to look back on how I did it this year, to know I've had success under pressure, makes it easier the next time it comes up. You have to have it happen to you to know what it's like."

This time he stopped trying to haul a franchise by himself, stopped pressing to be the .350 hitter he was not meant to be. He had added 12 pounds by weightlifting over the offseason and he moved farther away from the plate. He let the muscles in his arms and wrists work and let the ones inside his skull rest. Less agonizing about yesterday, more mashing today.

It was the one mountain Schmidt had to climb with his bare hands, the one he couldn't leap over and laugh at with his sheer athletic grace. Everything else in life had come easily, had come as a birthright, except for the ability to produce with consistency all season, in the heat of October as well as the cool of June.

He was born to an upper-middle class family in Dayton, Ohio, with a park, a pool and a car all waiting within 50 feet of his house. Schoolwork was no sweat and sports he picked up like a kid picks pennies up off a parking lot. He played baseball, basketball and football in high school and one college, Marietta, offered him a scholarship in all three. Everyone talked about what a great future he had.

"People were always talking about my potential," he said. "The media started picking it up and started telling the world, 'Hey, this guy should maybe be the best ever.' I knew I had it. There was no way you could ever tell me that the guy on the mound or the guys hitting in front of me or behind me had any more ability. It was just a matter of me putting together a couple of monster years to prove it."

His rookie year with the Phils was a monster of another kind. He hit .196 but the whispers and grumbles had not yet started. It wasn't until he became the first Phillie to sign a fat multi-year contract, it wasn't until the potential and the dollar signs linked arms and paraded down the third-base line, that Philadelphia turned on Schmidt. He was fair game; big money and big potential commanded big results.

He hit .251 with 21 home runs in 1978 and they scalded him every time his curly hair popped out of the dugout. His wife, Donna, even stopped coming to games. But in 1979 he doubled his home-run production to 45 and the fans found a new whipping boy, Greg Luzinski. By the World Series of '80, he was routinely getting standing ovations and, along with Tug McGraw, had emerged as one of the city's favorite players. Mike Schmidt was finally loved.

"I'm no dummy," he says. "I know it can change right back. I just hope this town would appreciate a team if it didn't win. Maybe the fans will learn. Maybe there'll be a change of heart. As for myself, anytime you think you have the game conquered, the game will turn around and punch you right in the nose."

Part of Schmidt's new peace of mind may stem from his conversion to religion. He is not one of the new generation of athletic God Squadders that clubs you over the head with it, the kind that turn people off immediately. Instead, he accomplishes far more for the cause by quietly and naturally stitching it into the conversation. He says he plays the game to glorify God and believes the Phillies finally found a way to win because it was God's will.

"I thought those last three weeks, when we played so many crucial games, where it came right down to 'Win it and you're in the World Series' or 'Hit a line drive right at somebody and the other team goes to the Series,' it's got to be God's will," he said. "It's just that this was supposed to be the Phillies' year. It wasn't supposed to be before this. We had the same heart, the same character we have now, or supposedly have been labeled with now."

Imagewise, Schmidt did as much for the Phils with his mouth as he did with his bat and glove during the playoffs and Series. The national media grumbled daily about the way the Phillies hid in the trainer's room and players' lounge after games, but they knew they could always find Schmidt, 0-for-5 or 3-for-4, in front of his locker, ready with intelligent and courteous answers.

He has had his collisions with the press, however. He was angered when a Philadelphia newspaper sent a reporter to ask his neighbors in Media, Pa., about the Schmidts, and horrified when his name was smeared across the front page in a midseason story that claimed the state was investigating amphetamine use on the Phillies. The story was later denied.

His latest jolt came on the day he appeared in New York to accept his Series MVP award. He expected it to be a day of smiles and handshakes, but suddenly reporters were asking him how he felt about Bake McBride saying he didn't deserve the honor—or the regular-season MVP, for that matter.

"It really ruined the most thrilling day of my life," said Schmidt. "I haven't made any judgments of Bake McBride as a person. I was disappointed in Bake, but I held back my true feelings. They're still held back.

"It truthfully re-established my bitterness toward the Philadelphia press. It was vintage Philadelphia journalism, bringing that up at a time when everything in town was positive. Here I'm being asked if I really deserve the award, *while* I'm getting the award.

"It couldn't have happened at a more powerful time. You talk about bleeping on my parade. But regardless of what anyone says, let's just leave it at this: statistics don't lie. Let people think what they want."

He knows his life will never be simple in Philadelphia, not with four newspapers squabbling for stories and a lockerroom stocked with snipers in red baseball hats.

"We'll never be one big happy family in Philadelphia," he said. "There's too many newspapers, too many radio stations, too many players, too many opinions."

Teammates may rip, fans may boo, the media may criticize,

but at age 31, Mike Schmidt seems to have mustered the strength of mind to keep his eyes focused dead-ahead, walk through it all and produce. If he ever doubts, if he ever wavers, he has a good watch and a trophy as proof that 1980 was the year he conquered all that . . . and conquered himself.

As a young Phillie.

"I'll look at this (watch) and think, that was the 1980 World Series, and the greatest thrill in my life was becoming a world champion," said Schmidt. "And the other award, when I look at that, I'll think about what went into it—162 games, a lot of sleepless nights, a lot of knockdown pitches, a lot of tough road trips, grinding it out for 162 games.

"1980," said Mike Schmidt, with reverence, "what an unbelievable year it's been in my life."

THE ULTIMATE EYE TEST FOR HITTERS

By PHYLLIS and ZANDER HOLLANDER

As Dr. Donald S. Teig sees it, the day may not be far off when big league teams carry eye coaches on their rosters. They would work eye-in-hand with the hitting coaches in a coordinated effort to improve a player's eye.

"I'm not going to teach anyone how to hit the curve ball," assures Dr. Teig, a Ridgefield, Conn., optometrist, "but you've got to agree that with all the emphasis on physical fitness, you still have to see the ball before you can hit it."

The innovative, sports-oriented Dr. Teig has developed tests and devices for dealing with an athlete's visual problems that go beyond the standard eye-chart exam. His eye-opening study of more than 275 major league players, including pitchers, brought enthusiastic cooperation from the players, and some intriguing results.

Dr. Teig and associates–under the sponsorship of Bausch & Lomb's Council on Sports Vision–did their tests on the Los Angeles Dodgers, Chicago White Sox, Houston Astros, Atlanta Braves, Kansas City Royals, Toronto Blue Jays and Seattle Mariners.

"We discovered that more than 50 percent of the players had cross-dominant vision (righthanded with a dominant left eye, or lefthanded with right-eye dominance. This is in contrast to the 20 percent normal population we estimate to be cross-dominant. The other 80 percent are unilateral dominant–when the eye dominance agrees with the hand preference."

What does all this mean to the hitter?

"To be cross-dominant is to clearly have an advantage in pick-

Phyllis and Zander Hollander each have cross-dominant vision and are still reaching for .300.

Dr. Teig's 10 Ballplayers Tested With the Best Eyes for Hitting

1. Steve Garvey
2. Willie Mays Aikens
3. George Brett
4. Chet Lemon
5. Bob Molinaro
6. Rico Carty
7. Dale Murphy
8. Gary Mathews
9. Bruce Bochte
10. Tom Paciorek

ing up the flight of the ball, since the batter can sight it from the proper angle with the stronger eye. Players with 'normal' (same side) dominance are at a disadvantage," says Dr. Teig, "and must compensate since the dominant eye is at an angle with the oncoming pitch. These players are advised to open up their batting stance to compensate for the dominant eye being behind them."

The Teig tests, for all but Seattle, were conducted in spring

Dr. Teig readies Tom Paciorek for depth perception test.

training 1980, and Dr. Teig sees some significance in the fact that the American League champion Royals had 70 percent cross-dominant players and the Astros, National League West winner, were next highest with 61 percent, followed by the Braves (55) and Dodgers (51), with the weaker-hitting Blue Jays, White Sox and Mariners in the 40s.

It's commonly thought that 20-20 vision translates into a good hitter. But Dr. Teig notes: "Actually over 75 percent of the players tested had 20-20 (some even better with 20-17), yet a large group of those were not good hitters, so obviously having good vision is not enough. Visual concentration is another important factor."

Dr. Teig and his peers tested this concentration by giving an eye reaction time test with a tachistascope, which flashes visual images at speeds of 1/100 of a second.

"We made slides of the various stages of 10 different pitches. We hooked the tachistascope on to a simple Carousel projector and flashed the slides for each pitch on the screen. We showed the batter the slides from the beginning of the pitch and asked him what kind of a pitch it was going to be and then whether it would be a strike or a ball. One man, interestingly a catcher, Larry Cox of the Mariners, called the pitch on the first slide every time. And he's not a great hitter. But being a catcher, he was attuned to the delivery. For the most part, the better hitters identified the pitch along its course sooner than the poorer hitters."

Among those who did especially well in the eye concentration test were Bob Welch and Steve Garvey of the Dodgers; Willie Mays Aikens and Dan Quisenberry of the Royals; Joe Morgan, J.R. Richard, Enos Cabell, Dennis Walling and Joe Niekro of the Astros; Jeff Burroughs and Dale Murphy of the Braves; Britt Burns of the White Sox, and the now retired Rico Carty of the Blue Jays.

And there were two others–Hall of Famers Hank Aaron and Hank Greenberg–who happened to be around when Dr. Teig did his tests. They had better-than-average results. And consider that Greenberg is around 70 years old.

The Teig testers also examined players for depth perception. Those who tested highest were Darrell Porter (with glasses), Dennis Leonard, Frank White, Ken Kravec, Kevin Bell, Ross Baumgarten, Nolan Ryan, Alan Ashby, Dale Murphy, Phil Niekro, Ron Cey, Bob Welch, Steve Garvey and Bill Russell.

Dr. Teig discovered, with amazement, that many of the players he tested had never had a complete eye exam. There were a few who needed vision correction for near-sightedness and the like. He prescribed corrective lenses. And, studying the 1980 sea-

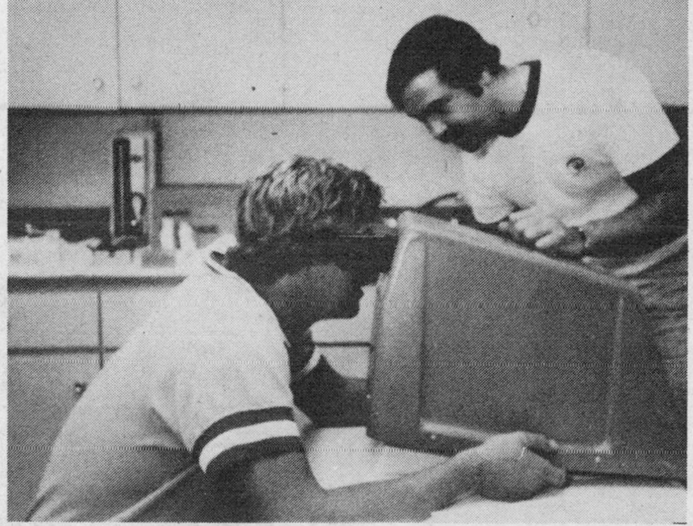

K.C.'s Pete LaCock undergoes night vision exam.

son's averages, he notes, "Their averages improved."

Dr. Teig's prescriptions for improving hitting performance go beyond corrective lenses and suggested open stances. For the player low in concentration, he recommends use of the flashing light approach: "A strobe light, going on and off as the batter practices. When you cause a visual disturbance, the batter has to tune in twice as hard if he wants to hit the ball. If he could do this for a half hour every day in the batting cage, he'd improve."

Can the Little Leaguer benefit from any of this?

"There can be an application to the training of children. If a cross-dominant trait is picked up in examination, it can be helpful in showing the youngster how to bat, lefty or righty. When you're dealing with, say 16-year-olds or beyond, it's obvious you can't change which hand they bat with, but with a child just learning, it would be a simple matter to have him bat with the hand that would produce the best result right away (a left-eye dominant should be trained to bat righty, and visa versa). Such a youngster could become a switch-hitter.

"As a matter of fact, I have a nine-year-old, a lefty who normally bats right. He is right-eye dominant and when he picked up the bat with his right hand I suggested he try hitting with his left. He hates getting up lefthanded, but he does pretty well that way. So he's a switch-hitter."

Tug McGraw, $1,750,000 signee, savors the good life.

The New Millionaires V

When will it all end? That's what major league owners and a number of fans were asking after the latest round of free agents signed for astronomical sums.

The most supercalifragilistic, of course, was Dave Winfield's $15 million contract with the Yankees. Winfield, who played out his option with the Padres, will be paid approximately $1.4 million a year over the course of the 10-year pact, with provisions for a cost-of-living raise, as if he might need one.

The money explosion this time began auspiciously enough with an unlikely performer named Claudell Washington who seemed to set the tone, if not the standard, for fringe players to become members of The Millionaire Club. Washington, an outfielder who was *waived* out of the American League in mid-season last year, signed a five-year, $3.5 million agreement with Atlanta.

And so it was that utilityman Dave Roberts, a lifetime .240 hitter, signed with Houston for $1.1 million over five years; Jim Essian, a journeyman catcher, became a millionaire with the White Sox, and Mike Cubbage, who had toiled in obscurity in Minnesota, signed a million-dollar deal with the Mets.

PLAYER	TEAM	YEARS	TOTAL
Dave Winfield	Yankees	10	$15,000,000
Darrell Porter	St. Louis	5	3,500,000
Don Sutton	Houston	4	3,500,000
Claudell Washington	Atlanta	5	3,500,000
Ron LeFlore	White Sox	4	2,425,000
Tug McGraw	Philadelphia	4	1,750,000
John D'Acquisto	California	4	1,100,000
Dave Roberts	Houston	5	1,100,000
Mike Cubbage	Mets	3	1,000,000
Jim Essian	White Sox	4	1,000,000
Rusty Staub	Mets	3	1,000,000
Geoff Zahn	California	3	1,000,000

INSIDE THE NATIONAL LEAGUE

By NICK PETERS
Oakland Tribune

PREDICTED ORDER OF FINISH	*East*	*West*
	Montreal Expos	Los Angeles Dodgers
	Philadelphia Phillies	Houston Astros
	St. Louis Cardinals	San Francisco Giants
	Pittsburgh Pirates	Cincinnati Reds
	Chicago Cubs	Atlanta Braves
	New York Mets	San Diego Padres

Playoff winner: Los Angeles

EAST DIVISION	Owner		Morning Line Manager
1 EXPOS scarlet, white & royal blue Third time a charm.	Charles Bronfman	1980 W 90 L 72	3-2 Dick Williams
2 PHILLIES crimson & white Age takes its toll.	R.R.M. Carpenter	1980 W 91 L 71	3-2 Dallas Green
3 CARDINALS red & white New jockey cracks whip.	August A. Busch	1980 W 74 L 88	10-1 Whitey Herzog
4 PIRATES old gold, white & black No longer a great finisher.	John Galbreath	1980 W 83 L 79	12-1 Chuck Tanner
5 CUBS royal blue & white No chance, but more interesting.	William Wrigley	1980 W 64 L 98	80-1 Joe Amalfitano
6 METS orange, white & blue Same old horse.	Nelson Doubleday	1980 W 67 L 95	100-1 Joe Torre

Like the other derby, it's a two-horse race with youthfulness and the fact repeaters are rare giving **EXPOS** slight edge over **PHILLIES**. Improved **CARDINALS** have lots of get-up-and-go, but not in same class yet. **PIRATES** a big disappointment as fade begins earlier. **CUBS** have a different look, but it's not enough to beat anyone but the **METS**, who did nothing to improve chances by falling short in the Winfield Stakes.

HOLLYWOOD HANDICAP

105th Running. National League Race. Distance, 162 games, plus playoff. Purse (based on '80): $13,000 per winning player, division, up to $35,000 total per winning player, World Championship. A field of 12 entered in two divisions.

Track Record 116 wins–Chicago 1906

WEST DIVISION	Owner		Morning Line Manager
1 **DODGERS** royal blue & white Healthy and hungry.	Peter O'Malley	1980 W 92 L 71	3-2 Tommy Lasorda
2 **ASTROS** orange & white Clipped at the wire.	John McMullen	1980 W 93 L 70	3-2 Bill Virdon
3 **GIANTS** white, orange & black New look brings improvement.	Bob Lurie	1980 W 75 L 86	20-1 Frank Robinson
4 **REDS** red & white Slowing down with age.	Louis Nippert	1980 W 89 L 73	20-1 John McNamara
5 **BRAVES** royal blue & white Lots of power, little else.	Ted Turner	1980 W 81 L 80	30-1 Bobby Cox
6 **PADRES** brown, gold & white Frisky, but needs seasoning.	Ray A. Kroc	1980 W 73 L 89	100-1 Frank Howard

A two-horse race between patched-up **DODGERS** and **ASTROS** which may require a photo at the finish. A repeat of last year's exciting derby, only both horses aren't crippled this time. **GIANTS** far back, but a tranquil season gets most out of talent, enough to nip aging **REDS** for show money. **BRAVES** imposing in own stable, but fall behind on a fast track. **PADRES** plucky, but youthful nervousness costly at the starting gate.

CHICAGO CUBS

TEAM DIRECTORY: Chairman of Exec. Committee: William Wrigley; Pres.: William J. Hagenah, Jr.; Exec. VP: Bob Kennedy; VP-Dir. Park Operations: E.R. Saltwell; Dir. Player Development: C.V. Davis; Dir. Scouting: Vedie Himsl; Dir. Info.: Buck Peden; Mgr.: Joe Amalfitano. Home: Wrigley Field (37,-471). Field distances: 355, l.f. line; 400, c.f.; 353, r.f. line. Spring training: Mesa, Ariz.

SCOUTING REPORT

HITTING: Can't help but improve with the addition of Leon Durham and Ken Reitz and the possible return to form of Dave Kingman, but the building Cubs simply aren't in the same league with the big boys despite playing in a ballpark that is the envy of sluggers.

Even Reitz might be able to avoid his second-half slump in friendly Wrigley, perhaps even adding to his power totals. But the key newcomer, and the reason Bruce Sutter was swapped, is Durham, a youngster who batted .271 and exhibited flashes of power as a St. Louis rookie in 1980.

Another pleasant surprise last year was catcher Tim Blackwell, who stepped in when Barry Foote was injured and responded with a .272 average. Bill Buckner (.324) is the batting king and obviously the most dependable stick in the lineup. Ivan DeJesus is capable of improving on a .259 average and Joe Strain should brighten the offensive contribution from second base.

PITCHING: Only the Cardinals had a higher team ERA than the Cubs' 3.89 and you can't count on an improvement with Bruce Sutter gone. The staff is really shaky and relievers Dick Tidrow, Bill Caudill and Willie Hernandez figure to have a really busy summer.

The starters are stale and undependable, though Rick Reuschel, Lynn McGlothen, Dennis Lamp and Mike Krukow could win in double figures, as they did last year. Trouble is, there won't be a Sutter to bail them out, which means the foursome may not be able to improve on its dismal 43-56 output of 1980.

FIELDING: The Cubs made more errors (174) than any club in the N.L. and were last in fielding percentage (.974), so they can't help but improve with Reitz at third base. But that's where it stops, for the remainder of his teammates are merely adequate, or worse, and they'll likely be fielding a few more shots with Sutter gone.

Bill Buckner led the league with a .324 average.

OUTLOOK: Dismal, but at least the club tried to change its image with a few changes over the winter. The big question will be whether the new faces will be able to compensate for the loss of the incomparable Sutter, a man who finished 43 games, saved 28 and won five.

The club lost the key to its staff and made no significant additions to fill the gap. The pitching isn't so good and neither is the fielding, so it'll take a hitting miracle to lift the Cubs higher than fifth. That may be too much to expect of Durham, Reitz and Kingman, for Buckner is the only proven hitter. The team undoubtedly will try Joe Amalfitano's patience and could easily finish dead last if the Mets' youth movement pays off.

CHICAGO CUBS 1981 ROSTER

MANAGER Joe Amalfitano
Coaches—Gene Clines, Jack Hiatt, Peanuts Lowrey, Les Moss, Cookie Rojas

PITCHERS

No.	Name	1980 Club	W-L	IP	SO	ERA	B-T	Ht.	Wt.	Born
35	Capilla, Doug	Chicago (NL)	2-8	90	51	4.10	L-L	5-8	175	1/7/52 Honolulu, HI
36	Caudill, Bill	Chicago (NL)	4-6	128	112	2.18	R-R	6-1	175	7/13/56 Santa Monica, CA
50	Churchill, Norm	Quad City	2-3	36	29	2.25	L-L	6-4	205	4/16/58 Hempstead, NY
		Wichita	3-1	24	15	4.50				
		Midland	3-2	65	50	3.88				
38	Hernandez, Willie	Chicago (NL)	1-9	108	75	4.42	L-L	6-2	180	11/14/55 Puerto Rico
54	Howell, Jay	Indianapolis	5-11	98	73	5.05	R-R	6-3	200	11/26/55 Miami, FL
		Cincinnati	0-0	3	1	15.00				
39	Krukow, Mike	Chicago (NL)	10-15	205	130	4.39	R-R	6-4	195	1/21/52 Long Beach, CA
47	Lamp, Dennis	Chicago (NL)	10-14	203	83	5.19	R-R	6-3	190	9/23/52 Los Angeles, CA
31	Mack, Henry	Midland	5-11	142	115	6.27	R-R	6-2	185	11/10/58 Winchester, KY
34	Martz, Randy	Wichita	8-6	107	53	3.11	L-R	6-4	210	5/28/56 Harrisburg, PA
		Chicago (NL)	1-2	30	5	2.10				
40	McGlothen, Lynn	Chicago (NL)	12-14	182	119	4.80	L-R	6-2	195	3/27/50 Monroe, LA
55	Myrick, Bob	Tidewater	0-1	6	3	1.50	R-L	6-1	195	10/1/52 Hattiesburg, MS
		Wichita	6-2	73	45	2.59				
–	Nastu, Phil	Phoenix	4-8	93	39	5.42	L-L	6-2	185	3/8/55 Bridgeport, CT
		San Francisco	0-0	6	1	6.00				
44	Parker, Mark	Wichita	7-11	157	70	5.10	L-R	6-1	175	6/12/56 Huntington, IN
48	Reuschel, Rick	Chicago (NL)	11-13	257	140	3.40	R-R	6-3	230	5/16/49 Quincy, IL
37	Riley, George	Wichita	3-3	47	32	4.40	L-L	6-2	200	10/6/56 Philadelphia, PA
		Chicago (NL)	0-4	36	18	5.75				
43	Segelke, Herman	Midland	7-10	129	88	4.74	R-R	6-4	215	4/24/58 San Mateo, CA
46	Smith, Lee	Wichita	4-7	90	63	3.70	R-R	6-5	220	12/4/57 Jamestown, LA
		Chicago (NL)	2-0	22	17	2.86				
41	Tidrow, Dick	Chicago (NL)	6-5	116	97	2.79	R-R	6-4	213	5/14/47 San Francisco, CA
56	Viskas, Steve	Midland	4-2	55	36	4.42	R-R	6-2	185	11/5/59 San Diego, CA
		Wichita	3-5	78	30	4.85				

CATCHERS

No.	Name	1980 Club	H	HR	RBI	Pct.	B-T	Ht.	Wt.	Born
9	Blackwell, Tim	Chicago (NL)	87	5	30	.272	B-R	5-11	185	8/19/52 San Diego, CA
8	Foote, Barry	Chicago (NL)	48	6	28	.238	R-R	6-3	215	2/16/52 Smithfield, NC
16	Hayes, Bill	Wichita	84	8	48	.229	R-R	6-0	195	10/24/57 Cheverly, MD
		Chicago (NL)	2	0	0	.222				

INFIELDERS

No.	Name	1980 Club	H	HR	RBI	Pct.	B-T	Ht.	Wt.	Born
22	Buckner, Bill	Chicago (NL)	187	10	68	.324	L-L	6-1	185	12/14/49 Vallejo, CA
11	DeJesus, Ivan	Chicago (NL)	160	3	33	.259	R-R	5-11	175	1/9/53 Puerto Rico
15	Dillard, Steve	Chicago (NL)	55	4	27	.225	R-R	6-1	180	2/8/51 Memphis, TN
12	Macko, Steve	Wichita	80	9	42	.252	L-R	5-10	160	9/6/54 Burlington, IA
		Chicago (NL)	6	0	2	.300				
–	Reitz, Ken	St. Louis	141	8	58	.270	R-R	6-0	185	6/24/51 San Francisco, CA
29	Turgeon, Mike	Wichita	122	13	75	.249	B-R	6-2	180	3/9/56 New London, CT
–	Strain, Joe	San Francisco	54	0	16	.286	R-R	5-10	169	4/30/54 Denver, CO
18	Tyson, Mike	Chicago (NL)	81	3	23	.238	R-R	5-9	170	1/13/50 Rocky Mount, NC
–	Waller, Ty	Springfield	110	6	53	.262	R-R	6-0	180	3/14/57 Fresno, CA
		St. Louis	1	0	0	.083				

OUTFIELDERS

No.	Name	1980 Club	H	HR	RBI	Pct.	B-T	Ht.	Wt.	Born
–	Cruz, Hector	Cincinnati	16	1	5	.213	R-R	5-11	180	4/2/53 Puerto Rico
–	Durham, Leon	Springfield	33	5	23	.258	L-L	6-1	185	7/31/57 Cincinnati, OH
		St. Louis	82	8	42	.271				
24	Hall, Mel	Midland	34	1	14	.266	L-L	6-0	185	9/16/60 Lyons, NY
		Quad City	102	6	42	.294				
10	Kingman, Dave	Chicago (NL)	71	18	57	.278	R-R	6-6	210	12/21/48 Pendleton, OR
30	Lezcano, Carlos	Wichita	68	19	56	.232	R-R	6-2	185	9/30/55 Puerto Rico
		Chicago (NL)	18	3	12	.205				
19	Rosinski, Brian	Wichita	123	19	79	.315	L-R	6-2	205	10/12/56 Chicago, IL
25	Thompson, Scot	Chicago (NL)	48	2	13	.212	L-L	6-3	175	12/7/55 Grove City, PA
23	Tracy, Jim	Wichita	130	16	63	.320	L-R	6-3	193	12/31/55 Hamilton, OH
		Chicago (NL)	31	3	9	.254				

CUB PROFILES

BILL BUCKNER 31 6-1 185 — Bats L Throws L

Had one of best all-around seasons while winning first batting title . . . Hit .344 in June and had a 10-game streak in September, batting .488 . . . Avoided controversy after troubled '79 season in which he was verbally criticized by manager Herman Franks for allegedly being jealous of Kingman . . . Still reached career highs in all extra-base categories in '79 . . . Born Dec. 14, 1949, at Vallejo, Cal. . . . Solid hitter with five seasons above .300 in 10-year major league career . . . No telling what he might have accomplished without bad wheels . . . Turned down more than 60 grid scholarship offers to sign with Dodgers . . . Batted .356 last September . . . Difficult to strike out.

Year	Club	Pos.	G	AB	R	H	2B	3B	HR	RBI	SB	Avg.
1969	Los Angeles.....	PH	1	1	0	0	0	0	0	0	0	.000
1970	Los Angeles.....	OF-1B	28	68	6	13	3	1	0	4	0	.191
1971	Los Angeles.....	OF-1B	108	358	37	99	15	1	5	41	4	.277
1972	Los Angeles.....	OF-1B	105	383	47	122	14	3	5	37	10	.319
1973	Los Angeles.....	1B-OF	140	575	68	158	20	0	8	46	12	.275
1974	Los Angeles.....	OF-1B	145	580	83	182	30	3	7	58	31	.314
1975	Los Angeles.....	OF	92	288	30	70	11	2	6	31	8	.243
1976	Los Angeles.....	1B-OF	154	642	76	193	28	4	7	60	28	.301
1977	Chicago (NL)....	1B	122	426	40	121	27	0	11	60	7	.284
1978	Chicago (NL)....	1B	117	446	47	144	26	1	5	74	7	.323
1979	Chicago (NL)....	1B	149	591	72	168	34	7	14	66	9	.284
1980	Chicago (NL)....	1B	145	578	69	187	41	3	10	68	1	.324
	Totals..........		1306	4936	575	1457	249	25	78	545	117	.295

DAVE KINGMAN 32 6-6 210 — Bats R Throws R

Well-traveled slugger can't seem to dodge controversy . . . Was N.L. Player of Month in April with six homers, 16 RBI and .375 average, but it was downhill thereafter . . . Suffered a shoulder injury that was reaggravated when he played in All-Star Game . . . Kong missed more than 75 games because of injuries, reducing home run total from 48 to 18 in one year . . . Went homerless for 10 weeks during one stretch of season . . . Born Dec. 21, 1948, at Pendleton, Ore. . . . Troubles with press intensified when he became a weekly columnist for Chicago Tribune after refusing to grant interviews . . . Abandoned column during midseason . . . Seemed to alienate teammates as well as reporters because of aloof nature . . . Had two three-homer games in '79 . . . Former USC pitching and hitting standout.

Year	Club	Pos.	G	AB	R	H	2B	3B	HR	RBI	SB	Avg.
1971	San Francisco ...	1B-OF	41	115	17	32	10	2	6	24	5	.278
1972	San Francisco ...	3B-1B-OF	135	472	65	106	17	4	29	83	16	.225
1973	San Francisco ...	3B-1B-P	112	305	54	62	10	1	24	55	8	.203
1974	San Francisco ...	1B-3B-OF	121	350	41	78	18	2	18	55	8	.223
1975	New York (NL)..	OF-1B-3B	134	502	65	116	22	1	36	88	7	.231
1976	New York (NL)..	OF-1B	123	474	70	113	14	1	37	86	7	.238
1977	NY (NL)-SD.....	OF-1B	114	379	38	84	16	0	20	67	5	.222
1977	Calif-NY (AL)....	1B-DH-OF	18	60	9	13	4	0	6	11	0	.217
1978	Chicago (NL)....	OF-1B	119	395	65	105	17	4	28	79	3	.266
1979	Chicago (NL)....	OF	145	532	97	153	19	5	48	115	4	.288
1980	Chicago (NL)....	OF	81	255	31	71	8	0	18	57	2	.278
	Totals..........		1143	3839	552	933	155	20	270	720	65	.243

TIM BLACKWELL 28 5-11 185 Bats S Throws R

After faltering in trials with Red Sox, Phillies and Expos, made most of opportunity with Cubs when regular catcher Barry Foote was injured . . . Called "most improved player in the majors" by general manager Bob Kennedy . . . Will challenge for No. 1 job this spring because of impressive work . . . Batted .317 in August to lift average to .270s . . . Born Aug. 19, 1952, at San Diego . . . Best known for fielding prowess . . . Strong arm and provides leadership . . . Good-field, no-hit reputation until he batted .293 in Triple-A in '78 and earned promotion to Cubs . . . Attained career highs in virtually every statistical department last season.

Year	Club	Pos.	G	AB	R	H	2B	3B	HR	RBI	SB	Avg.
1974	Boston.........	C	44	122	9	30	1	1	0	8	1	.246
1975	Boston.........	C	59	132	15	26	3	2	0	6	0	.197
1976	Philadelphia.....	C	4	8	0	2	0	0	0	1	0	.250
1977	Phil.-Mtl.........	C	17	22	4	2	1	0	0	0	0	.091
1978	Chicago (NL)....	C	49	103	8	23	3	0	0	7	0	.223
1979	Chicago (NL)....	C	63	122	8	20	3	1	0	12	0	.164
1980	Chicago (NL)....	C	103	320	24	87	16	4	5	30	0	.272
	Totals..........		339	829	68	190	27	8	5	64	1	.229

IVAN DeJESUS 28 5-11 175 Bats R Throws R

A good, steady shortstop who is underrated in a league full of good ones . . . Stole a career-high 44 bases last season and hit in vicinity of lifetime average . . . Durable, has played in at least 155 games each of last four years . . . Came to Cubs in Buckner-Monday swap and impressed immediately with .266 average in first year as a regular, 1977 . . . Born Jan. 9, 1953, at Santurce, Puerto Rico . . . Topped N.L. with 104 runs in

'78 . . . His 41 steals that year were most by a Cub since Kiki Cuyler's 43 in 1929 . . . Had best year in '79, missing only two games and reaching career highs in average, hits, triples and RBI . . . Signed by Dodgers while still in high school.

Year	Club	Pos.	G	AB	R	H	2B	3B	HR	RBI	SB	Avg.
1974	Los Angeles.....	SS	3	3	1	1	0	0	0	0	0	.333
1975	Los Angeles.....	SS	63	87	10	16	2	1	0	2	1	.184
1976	Los Angeles.....	SS-3B	22	41	4	7	2	1	0	2	0	.171
1977	Chicago (NL)....	SS	155	624	91	166	31	7	3	40	24	.266
1978	Chicago (NL)....	SS	160	619	104	172	24	7	3	35	41	.278
1979	Chicago (NL)....	SS	160	636	92	180	26	10	5	52	24	.283
1980	Chicago (NL)....	SS	157	618	78	160	26	3	3	33	44	.259
	Totals..........		720	2628	380	702	111	29	14	164	134	.267

KEN REITZ 29 6-0 185 — Bats R Throws R

A notoriously great early-season hitter, he batted at .417 clip in April and .358 in May, but sank to his lifetime level by hitting .182 from June 3 to Aug. 17 . . . Never mind, for he's most valuable for his glove . . . Schmidt gets the Gold Gloves, but Reitz has the records . . . Set record with only nine errors at third base in '77 and lowered mark with only eight last year . . . Also topped N.L. with .980 fielding percentage that year, but didn't win Gold Glove . . . Born June 24, 1951, at San Francisco . . . Joined Giants in '76, but wanted to get back to St. Louis, so was swapped back to Cards after one year . . . Traded to Chicago when Cubs agreed to throw in $150,000 as compensation.

Year	Club	Pos.	G	AB	R	H	2B	3B	HR	RBI	SB	Avg.
1972	St. Louis.......	3B	21	78	5	28	4	0	0	10	0	.359
1973	St. Louis.......	SS-3B	147	426	40	100	20	2	6	42	0	.235
1974	St. Louis.......	3B-SS-2B	154	579	48	157	28	2	7	54	0	.271
1975	St. Louis.......	3B	161	592	43	159	25	1	5	63	1	.269
1976	San Francisco...	3B-SS	155	577	40	154	21	1	5	66	5	.267
1977	St. Louis.......	3B	157	587	58	153	36	1	17	79	2	.261
1978	St. Louis.......	3B	150	540	41	133	26	2	10	75	1	.246
1979	St. Louis.......	3B	159	605	42	162	41	2	8	73	1	.268
1980	St. Louis.......	3B	151	523	39	141	33	0	8	58	0	.270
	Totals..........		1255	4507	356	1187	234	11	66	520	10	.263

RICK REUSCHEL 31 6-3 230 **Bats R Throws R**

An accomplished eater and pitcher . . . Has been mainstay of Cubs' rotation since '72 . . . Had sub-par season until 5-0, 2.08 August brought figures to respectability . . . Was 7-0 in August of '79 . . . Has won in double figures every season in bigs, including 10-8 in half year as rookie in '72 . . . Earned promotion that year by going 9-2, 1.33 at Wichita . . . Born May 16, 1949, at Quincy, Ill. . . . Combined with brother Paul to blank Dodgers in 1975 . . . Was a 20-game winner and a N.L. All-Star in '77 . . . Was 10-0, 1.29 his final year at Western Illinois U. . . . Owns a farm in Wisconsin . . . As usual, was staff leader in most areas in 1980.

Year	Club	G	IP	W	L	Pct.	SO	BB	H	ERA
1972	Chicago (NL)............	21	129	10	8	.556	87	29	127	2.93
1973	Chicago (NL)............	36	237	14	15	.483	168	62	244	3.00
1974	Chicago (NL)............	41	241	13	12	.520	160	83	262	4.29
1975	Chicago (NL)............	38	234	11	17	.393	155	67	244	3.73
1976	Chicago (NL)............	38	260	14	12	.538	146	64	260	3.46
1977	Chicago (NL)............	39	252	20	10	.667	166	74	233	2.79
1978	Chicago (NL)............	35	243	14	15	.483	115	54	235	3.41
1979	Chicago (NL)............	36	239	18	12	.600	125	75	251	3.62
1980	Chicago (NL)............	38	257	11	13	.458	140	76	281	3.40
	Totals..................	422	2092	125	114	.523	1262	584	2137	3.42

DENNIS LAMP 28 6-3 190 **Bats R Throws R**

Earned reputation as tough-luck hurler in '78 by going 7-15 with a solid 3.29 ERA . . . In dozen of those losses, Cubs were either blanked or scored only once . . . A sinkerball pitcher who usually gets better as game progresses . . . Hasn't pitched to '78 form last two years, but has been more successful in won-lost percentage . . . Born Sept. 23, 1952, at Los Angeles . . . Pitched a one-hitter against San Diego in '78 . . . Posted flashy figures at all levels of minors before joining Cubs in '77 . . . Was 7-2, 1.93 at Bradenton in '72 and 11-4, 2.94 at Wichita (AAA) the first half of the '77 season as an American Assn. All-Star.

Year	Club	G	IP	W	L	Pct.	SO	BB	H	ERA
1977	Chicago (NL)............	11	30	0	2	.000	12	8	43	6.30
1978	Chicago (NL)............	37	224	7	15	.318	73	56	221	3.29
1979	Chicago (NL)............	38	220	11	10	.524	86	46	223	3.51
1980	Chicago (NL)............	41	203	10	13	.435	83	82	259	5.19
	Totals..................	127	677	28	40	.412	254	192	746	3.96

LYNN McGLOTHEN 31 6-2 195 **Bats L Throws R**

Battling back following injury-riddled 1977-78 campaigns . . . Still a hard thrower, but just hasn't achieved consistency . . . Hasn't enjoyed truly satisfying season since going 16-12 with 2.70 ERA for '74 Cardinals . . . Won 44 games in 1974-76 with St. Louis, but a disappointment with S.F. before he was virtually given to Cubs in June 1978 . . . Promptly went 5-3, 3.04 down the stretch for Chicago and followed with 13 wins in '79 . . . Born March 27, 1950, at Monroe, La. . . . A four-sport star as a prep, he attended Grambling before signing with Red Sox . . . Was 30-15 in low minors in 1969-70 and made it to Boston after going 9-2, 1.92 at Louisville in '72.

Year	Club	G	IP	W	L	Pct.	SO	BB	H	ERA
1972	Boston	22	145	8	7	.533	112	59	135	3.41
1973	Boston	6	23	1	2	.333	16	8	39	8.22
1974	St. Louis	31	237	16	12	.571	142	89	212	2.70
1975	St. Louis	35	239	15	13	.536	146	97	231	3.92
1976	St. Louis	33	205	13	15	.464	106	68	209	3.91
1977	San Francisco	21	80	2	9	.182	42	52	94	5.63
1978	San Fran.-Chic. (NL)	54	93	5	3	.625	69	43	92	3.29
1979	Chicago (NL)	42	212	13	14	.481	147	55	236	4.12
1980	Chicago (NL)	39	182	12	14	.462	119	64	211	4.80
	Totals	283	1416	85	89	.489	899	535	1459	3.93

TOP PROSPECTS

JIM TRACY 25 6-3 193 **Bats L Throws R**

Probably the club's first baseman of the future . . . Batted .355 at Midlands in '79 and came up with Cubs after batting .320 with 16 homers and 63 RBI at Wichita (AAA) last year . . . Looked good down the stretch, being used in the outfield . . . Cubs also liked pitcher Randy Martz, 8-6, 3.11 at Wichita.

MANAGER JOE AMALFITANO: He certainly has had a relatively long-time Cub connection—as player, coach and manager, and with interruptions along the way . . . But now he has a chance to start a season as manager—following the Cub's third-worst season in history, 64-98 . . . Joe took over from Preston Gomez last July 25 when the Cubs were 38-53 . . . As Joey Amalfitano he was a big league infielder for

10 years (starting in 1954) with the New York and San Francisco Giants, the Astros and the Cubs . . . After retiring as a Cub he was a coach with the team for five years, went off for stints with the Giants and San Diego before returning to Chicago in 1978 . . . He was born Jan. 23, 1934, at San Pedro, Cal.

GREATEST TEAM

Since the franchise has had little success—and no pennants—during the post-war period, it's safe to go way back to 1906 for the Cubs' finest hour. That team posted a remarkable 116-36 record, unsurpassed in major league history. The crosstown White Sox spoiled things by taking the Series, 4-2, but that record .763 percentage during the regular season is tough to overlook.

No team since 1900 has allowed fewer runs than the '06 Cubs, who posted a 1.76 ERA. Tinker-to-Evers-to-Chance was the club's celebrated double-play combination, but the main reason for the success story was the pitching staff.

Three Finger Brown was 26-6 with a league-leading 1.04 ERA, Jack Pfeister went 20-8 and Ed Reulbach was 19-4. The Cubs, who won the pennant by 20 games over the Giants, were led at the plate by newly acquired third baseman Harry Steinfeldt, who batted .327 and topped the N.L. with 83 RBI. Player-manager Frank Chance batted .319 and catcher Johnny Kling .312. With a year like that, no wonder the club suffered a letdown in the Series.

ALL-TIME CUB LEADERS

BATTING: Rogers Hornsby, .380, 1929
HRs: Hack Wilson, 56, 1930
RBIs: Hack Wilson, 190, 1930
STEALS: Frank Chance, 67, 1903
WINS: Mordecai Brown, 29, 1908
STRIKEOUTS: Ferguson Jenkins, 274, 1970

It's 51st anniversary of Hack Wilson's 56 HRs, 190 RBI.

MONTREAL EXPOS

TEAM DIRECTORY: Chairman of the Board: Charles Bronfman; Pres.-GM: John McHale; Asst. to Pres.: Danny Menendez; VP-Player Development and Scouting: Jim Fanning; VP-Marketing: Roger Landry; VP-Sec.-Treas.: Harry Renaud; Admin. Asst., Player Relations: Gene Kirby; Dirs. Pub. Rel.: Richard Griffin, Monique Giroux; Trav. Sec.: Peter Durso; Mgr.: Dick Williams. Home: Olympic Stadium (59,984). Field distances: 325, l.f. line; 375, l.c.; 404, c.f.; 375, r.c.; 325, r.f. line. Spring training: West Palm Beach, Fla.

SCOUTING REPORT

HITTING: The Expos suffered from Larry Parrish's slump (.307 to .254 in one year) and the absence of Ellis Valentine for 76 games, yet they still made enough things happen offensively to

Bill Gullickson struck out 18 Cubs in one game last year.

finish one game behind the Phillies. Even without Ron LeFlore's 97 steals, the club has an exciting attack with the likes of Gary Carter, Andre Dawson, Warren Cromartie, Willie Montanez and Parrish pounding the ball.

Carter, just beginning to blossom at 26, figures to improve with age, though his 29 homers and 101 RBI are not to be taken lightly. The Expos probably won't swipe 237 bases again with LeFlore gone, but Rodney Scott can fly (63 steals) and newcomer Tim Raines (77 SB at Denver) could pick up where LeFlore left off. Raines, possibly switched to the outfield, also batted a gaudy .354 in Triple-A. The club will make room for outfielder-first baseman Tim Wallach, who had 36 homers and 124 RBI at Denver.

PITCHING: Late-season sensation Bill Gullickson gave a much-needed boost to the starters in the wake of Bill Lee's demise and Scott Sanderson (16-11) developed into the standout the club anticipated. Steve Rogers (16-11) is still the ace and big things are expected of David Palmer and newcomer Richard Wortham.

The question mark, again, is the bullpen, one reason the club was trying to land a "name" reliever over the winter. There was nothing wrong with Woodie Fryman's performance in 1980, but he'll be 41 shortly after Opening Day and the club could use another able body to complement Fryman, Elias Sosa and Stan Bahnsen.

FIELDING: Tailed off last year, especially since the club was forced to break up the dynamite outfield of Dawson, Valentine and Cromartie. LeFlore alone made 14 errors, so the defense should tighten if Cromartie returns to the outfield and Montanez plays first. Carter has developed into a Gold Glove catcher and is easily the best in the league with John Bench de-emphasizing work at the position.

OUTLOOK: Excellent, if the young pitchers continue to improve and if the bullpen can be shored up. LeFlore didn't hit well in his one year in the N.L., so Raines or Wallach will give the club more punch, as will the full-season return of Valentine, who totaled 67 RBI in only 86 games, and Montanez.

Parrish was the surprise of '79 and the disappointment of '80, so a strong comeback by the former team MVP would also boost the club's stock. The young pitching starters also are impressive and a big year by either Gullickson or Palmer could be enough to push the club over the top. Since the hitting, pitching and fielding all figure to improve, why not a pennant for Dick Williams?

MONTREAL EXPOS 1981 ROSTER

MANAGER Dick Williams

Coaches—Felipe Alou, Galen Cisco, Pat Mullin, Vern Rapp, Norm Sherry, Ozzie Virgil, Steve Boros

PITCHERS

No.	Name	1980 Club	W-L	IP	SO	ERA	B-T	Ht.	Wt.	Born
22	Bahnsen, Stan	Montreal	7-6	91	48	3.07	R-R	6-3	198	12/15/44 Council Bluffs, IA
28	Dues, Hal	Denver	7-4	98	39	3.40	R-R	6-3	185	9/22/54 Dickinson, TX
		Montreal	0-1	12	2	6.75				
51	Engle, Rick	Denver	12-7	168	90	4.50	L-L	5-11	180	4/7/57 Corbin, KY
35	Fryman, Woodie	Montreal	7-4	80	59	2.25	R-L	6-2	215	4/12/40 Ewing, KY
34	Gullickson, Bill	Denver	6-2	66	64	191	R-R	6-3	198	2/20/59 Marshall, MN
		Montreal	10-5	141	120	3.00				
20	James, Bob	Denver	9-2	87	79	3.83	R-R	6-4	215	8/15/58 Glendale, CA
53	Lea, Charlie	Denver	0-0	12	9	1.50	R-R	6-4	194	12/25/56 France
		Memphis	9-0	75	54	0.84				
		Montreal	7-5	104	56	3.72				
37	Lee, Bill	Montreal	4-6	118	34	4.96	L-L	6-3	190	12/28/46 Burbank, CA
–	Mendon, Kevin	Memphis	7-2	95	59	2.75	R-R	6-4	175	8/7/56 Corona, CA
		Denver	7-1	74	40	4.26				
32	Norman, Fred	Montreal	4-4	98	58	4.13	B-L	5-8	172	8/20/42 San Antonio, TX
46	Palmer, David	Montreal	8-6	130	73	2.98	R-R	6-1	205	10/19/57 Glens Falls, NY
47	Ratzer, Steve	Denver	15-4	163	50	3.59	R-R	6-1	192	9/9/53 Paterson, NJ
		Montreal	0-0	4	0	11.25				
45	Rogers, Steve	Montreal	16-11	281	147	2.98	R-R	6-1	177	10/26/49 Jefferson City, MO
21	Sanderson, Scott	Montreal	16-11	211	125	3.11	R-R	6-5	195	7/22/56 Dearborn, MI
27	Sosa, Elias	Montreal	9-6	94	58	3.06	R-R	6-2	205	6/10/50 Dominican Republic
–	Wortham, Rich	Chicago (AL)	4-7	92	45	5.97	R-L	6-0	185	10/22/53 Odessa, TX

CATCHERS

No.	Name	1980 Club	H	HR	RBI	Pct.	B-T	Ht.	Wt.	Born
8	Carter, Gary	Montreal	145	29	101	.264	R-R	6-2	210	4/8/54 Culver City, CA
44	Ramos, Bobby	Denver	72	4	30	.295	R-R	5-11	208	11/5/55 Cuba
		Montreal	5	0	2	.156				
11	Tamargo, John	Montreal	14	1	13	.275	B-R	5-10	195	1/7/51 Tampa, FL
–	Wieghaus, Tom	Memphis	101	4	44	.272	R-R	6-0	195	2/1/57 Chicago Heights, IL

INFIELDERS

No.	Name	1980 Club	H	HR	RBI	Pct.	B-T	Ht.	Wt.	Born
49	Cromartie, Warren	Montreal	172	14	70	.288	L-L	6-0	190	9/23/53 Miami, FL
–	Hostetler, Dave	Denver	122	9	58	.269	R-R	6-4	215	3/27/56 Pasadena, CA
14	Hutton, Tommy	Montreal	12	0	5	.218	L-L	5-11	172	4/20/46 Los Angeles, CA
11	Macha, Ken	Montreal	31	1	8	.290	R-R	6-2	218	9/29/50 Wilkinsburg, PA
43	Manuel, Jerry	Denver	136	3	61	.277	R-R	6-0	155	12/23/53 Hahira, GA
		Montreal	0	0	0	.000				
54	Mills, Brad	Memphis	56	6	44	.295	L-R	6-0	195	1/19/57 Lemon Cove, CA
		Denver	58	2	27	.289				
		Montreal	18	0	8	.300				
–	Montanez, Willie	SD-Mont	136	6	64	.272	L-L	6-1	185	4/1/48 Puerto Rico
15	Parrish, Larry	Montreal	115	15	72	.254	R-R	6-3	205	11/10/53 Winter Haven, FL
30	Raines, Tim	Denver	152	6	64	.354	B-R	5-8	170	8/16/59 Sanford, FL
		Montreal	1	0	0	.050				
3	Scott, Rodney	Montreal	127	0	46	.224	B-R	6-0	160	10/16/53 Indianapolis, IN
–	Smith, Chris	Memphis	102	12	70	.304	B-R	6-0	185	7/18/57 Torrance, CA
		Denver	5	1	3	.200				
4	Speier, Chris	Montreal	103	1	32	.265	R-R	6-1	175	6/28/50 Alameda, CA

OUTFIELDERS

No.	Name	1980 Club	H	HR	RBI	Pct.	B-T	Ht.	Wt.	Born
33	Briggs, Dan	Denver	135	13	74	.316	L-L	6-0	180	11/18/52 Scotia, CA
10	Dawson, Andre	Montreal	178	17	87	.308	R-R	6-3	180	7/10/54 Miami, FL
–	Johnson, Tony	Memphis	153	8	89	.299	R-R	6-3	195	2/23/56 Memphis, TN
25	Office, Rowland	Montreal	78	6	30	.267	L-L	6-0	170	10/25/52 Sacramento, CA
24	Pate, Bob	Denver	86	8	65	.323	R-R	6-3	196	12/3/53 Los Angeles, CA
		Montreal	10	0	5	.256				
–	Rooney, Pat	Memphis	135	28	102	.280	R-R	6-1	190	11/28/57 Chicago, IL
17	Valentine, Ellis	Montreal	98	13	67	.315	R-R	6-4	205	7/30/54 Helena, AR
58	Wallach, Tim	Denver	144	36	124	.281	R-R	6-3	220	9/14/58 Tustin, CA
		Montreal	2	1	2	.182				
18	White, Jerry	Montreal	56	7	23	.262	B-R	5-11	172	8/23/52 Shirley, MA

EXPO PROFILES

GARY CARTER 27 6-2 210 Bats R Throws R

Slipped at the plate, but power figures as good as ever, including career-high 101 RBI last year . . . Vital to pennant push by batting .360 with seven homers and 22 RBI in September, earning N.L. Player of Month honors . . . Hit seven homers in a nine-game span in May-June . . . Batted .314 with seven homers, 17 RBI in May . . . Born April 8, 1954, at Culver City, Cal. . . . With Bench and Simmons past their prime, ranks as best all-around catcher in league . . . Rookie of Year in '75 . . . Set club record for homers with 31 in '77 . . . Late-season injury in '79 damaged Expos' pennant chances . . . Three-time N.L. All-Star . . . First Montreal player to hit three homers in a game . . . Avid baseball card collector.

Year	Club	Pos.	G	AB	R	H	2B	3B	HR	RBI	SB	Avg.
1974	Montreal	C-OF	9	27	5	11	0	1	1	6	2	.407
1975	Montreal	OF-C-3B	144	503	58	136	20	1	17	68	5	.270
1976	Montreal	C-OF	91	311	31	68	8	1	6	38	0	.219
1977	Montreal	C-OF	154	522	86	148	29	2	31	84	5	.284
1978	Montreal	C-1B	157	533	76	136	27	1	20	72	10	.255
1979	Montreal	C	140	505	74	143	26	5	22	75	3	.283
1980	Montreal	C	154	549	76	145	25	5	29	101	3	.264
	Totals..........		849	2950	406	787	135	16	126	444	28	.267

WARREN CROMARTIE 27 6-0 190 Bats L Throws L

Switched to first base when LeFlore joined club and had best season in major league career . . . Batted .353 in June . . . Posted career highs in average, homers and RBI . . . Played in at least 155 games fourth consecutive year . . . Totaled 40 assists as leftfielder in 1978-79, tops in majors for that span . . . Had extra-base hit in nine straight games in '79 . . . Also set club records that year with 659 at-bats, 46 doubles and a 19-game batting streak . . . Born Sept. 29, 1953, at Miami . . . Team batting leader in '78 . . . Sensational pro debut at Quebec City in '74, batting .336 and earning promotion to parent club . . . Up for good after batting .336 for Denver (AAA) in '76.

Year	Club	Pos.	G	AB	R	H	2B	3B	HR	RBI	SB	Avg.
1974	Montreal	OF	8	17	2	3	0	0	0	0	1	.176
1976	Montreal	OF	33	81	8	17	1	0	0	2	1	.210
1977	Montreal	OF	155	620	64	175	41	7	5	50	10	.282
1978	Montreal	OF-1B	159	607	77	180	32	6	10	56	8	.297
1979	Montreal	OF	158	659	84	181	46	5	8	46	8	.275
1980	Montreal	1B-OF	162	597	74	172	33	5	14	70	8	.288
	Totals..........		675	2581	309	728	153	23	37	224	36	.282

ELLIS VALENTINE 26 6-4 205 Bats R Throws R

Outstanding season despite missing more than 60 games with injuries . . . Batted .329 in May, but struck by pitch and fractured cheekbone May 30 . . . Out 40 days . . . Returned and had eight hits in first five games . . . Missed 22 more games with hip injury . . . Despite limited play, neared career high for RBI . . . Strong-armed rightfielder, won Gold Glove in '78 . . . Born July 30, 1954, at Helena, Ark. . . . A gifted, all-around talent who can throw, hit and run . . . Stole 14 straight bases in '77, when he also smacked two inside-the-park homers . . . Part of what is considered best outfield in N.L. . . . Joined Expos for good after batting .309 for Denver in '76.

Year	Club	Pos.	G	AB	R	H	2B	3B	HR	RBI	SB	Avg.
1975	Montreal	OF	12	33	2	12	4	0	1	3	0	.364
1976	Montreal	OF	94	305	36	85	15	2	7	39	14	.279
1977	Montreal	OF	127	508	63	149	28	2	25	76	13	.293
1978	Montreal	OF	151	570	75	165	35	2	25	76	13	.289
1979	Montreal	OF	146	548	73	151	29	3	21	82	11	.276
1980	Montreal	OF	86	311	40	98	22	2	13	67	5	.315
	Totals..........		616	2275	289	660	133	11	92	343	56	.290

LARRY PARRISH 27 6-3 205 Bats R Throws R

Club's most underrated player in '79, but slumped sharply from .307 to .254 when hindered by a wrist injury . . . On April 25 at Atlanta, hit three homers and totaled seven RBI in 11-inning loss . . . Sizzled down stretch in '79, batting .327 with 21 homers and 50 RBI in final 75 games . . . Set club records with 71 extra-base hits, 300 total bases and .551 slugging percentage while playing solid third base . . . Born Nov. 30, 1953, at Winter Haven, Fla. . . . Became only third Expos' player to bat .300 in '79 . . . Fourth in MVP voting in '79 and Expos' Player of Year . . . Only Montreal player with trio of three-homer games, connecting against St. Louis in '77 and Atlanta in '78.

Year	Club	Pos.	G	AB	R	H	2B	3B	HR	RBI	SB	Avg.
1974	Montreal	3B	25	69	9	14	5	0	0	4	0	.203
1975	Montreal	3B-2B-SS	145	532	50	146	32	5	10	65	4	.274
1976	Montreal	3B	154	543	65	126	28	5	11	61	2	.232
1977	Montreal	3B	123	402	50	99	19	2	11	46	2	.246
1978	Montreal	3B	144	520	68	144	39	4	15	70	2	.277
1979	Montreal	3B	153	544	83	167	39	2	30	82	5	.307
1980	Montreal	3B	126	452	55	115	27	3	15	72	2	.254
	Totals..........		870	3062	380	811	199	21	92	400	17	.265

ANDRE DAWSON 26 6-3 180 Bats R Throws R

Home run total dropped, but Andre enjoyed best all-around season in '80 . . . Second in N.L. with 17 game-winning RBI . . . Best average ever . . . Also had career-high stolen base total, obscured by LeFlore-Scott rampage . . . N.L. Rookie of Year in '77 with .282 average . . . Born July 10, 1954, at Miami . . . Needed very little minor league seasoning, batting .343 in 186 games to earn promotion . . . Entered '80 season as Expos' career stolen base leader with 85, a figure exceeded by LeFlore in one season . . . Hit two home runs in one inning at Atlanta in '78 . . . Batted .357 at Quebec City in '76 and shipped to Triple A, where he hit 14 homers in first month at Denver . . . Gold Glove winner.

Year	Club	Pos.	G	AB	R	H	2B	3B	HR	RBI	SB	Avg.
1976	Montreal	OF	24	85	9	20	4	1	0	7	1	.235
1977	Montreal	OF	139	525	64	148	26	9	19	65	21	.282
1978	Montreal	OF	157	609	84	154	24	8	25	72	28	.253
1979	Montreal	OF	155	639	90	176	24	12	25	92	35	.275
1980	Montreal	OF	151	577	96	178	41	7	17	87	34	.308
	Totals..........		602	2350	334	656	115	36	86	316	118	.279

RODNEY SCOTT 27 6-0 160 Bats S Throws R

With 63 steals, enabled Expos to set two-man record with LeFlore . . . Total of 160 smashed previous mark of 148 by Cards' Lou Brock and Bake McBride . . . A master at stealing third base, often doing it when catcher throws back to pitcher . . . Won second base job from Dave Cash in '79, but tailed off sharply at plate last year . . . Born Oct. 16, 1953, at Indianapolis . . . A clutch hitter and a snappy fielder . . . Can be valuable despite meager average . . . Stole 85 bases in Class A in '74 . . . Has played with five major league clubs and could be on the move again if pushed by promising prospect Tim Raines, also a speedburner.

Year	Club	Pos.	G	AB	R	H	2B	3B	HR	RBI	SB	Avg.
1975	Kansas City.....	2B-SS	48	15	13	1	0	0	0	0	4	.067
1976	Montreal	2B-SS	7	10	3	4	0	0	0	0	2	.400
1977	Oakland.........	2B-SS-3B-OF	133	364	56	95	4	4	0	20	33	.261
1978	Chicago (NL)....	3B-OF-2B-SS	78	227	41	64	5	1	0	15	27	.282
1979	Montreal	2B-SS	151	562	69	134	12	5	3	42	39	.238
1980	Montreal	2B-SS	154	567	84	127	13	13	0	46	63	.224
	Totals..........		571	1745	266	425	34	23	3	123	168	.244

STEVE ROGERS 31 6-1 177 Bats R Throws R

Still ace of the staff after so many tough-luck years . . . From May 16 to June 26, he was 7-1 with a 2.15 ERA . . . Didn't win for more than a month in mid-season . . . Rallied to post 4-1, 2.16 stats in September, including two of his four shutouts . . . A career of low ERAs and unspectacular records . . . Born Oct. 27, 1949, at Jefferson City, Mo. . . . Best pitcher in Montreal history, yet still under .500 . . . Lost 10 more than he won in '76 despite 3.21 ERA . . . In '78, won only 13 games despite never allowing more than three runs in first 21 starts . . . Critics questioned if he could perform under pressure, but he proved them wrong down the stretch last year . . . Attended Tulsa U. and was 31-5 as an All-America pitcher.

Year	Club	G	IP	W	L	Pct.	SO	BB	H	ERA
1973	Montreal	17	134	10	5	.667	64	49	93	1.54
1974	Montreal	38	254	15	22	.405	154	80	225	4.46
1975	Montreal	35	252	11	12	.478	137	88	248	3.29
1976	Montreal	33	230	7	17	.292	150	69	212	3.21
1977	Montreal	40	302	17	16	.515	206	81	272	3.10
1978	Montreal	30	219	13	10	.565	126	64	186	2.47
1979	Montreal	37	249	13	12	.520	143	78	232	3.00
1980	Montreal	37	281	16	11	.593	147	85	247	2.98
	Totals..................	267	1921	102	105	.493	1127	594	1745	3.11

SCOTT SANDERSON 24 6-5 195 Bats R Throws R

Joined Rogers to form solid one-two veteran punch in rotation . . . Blazing start: 4-1, 2.36 in May . . . Gave indication of what was to come with 2.51 ERA in brief '78 trial and was 9-8 with 3.43 ERA as rookie in '79 . . . Fired a one-hitter against Giants in '79 . . . Pitched only 28 games in minors and hardly spectacular, but won club Player-of Month honors for 4-0 mark in September 1978 . . . Born July 22, 1956, at Dearborn, Mich. . . . A standout at Vanderbilt U., where he majored in business finance and history . . . Earned rave notices as top Venezuelan League hurler in winter of '77, going 9-2, 1.41.

Year	Club	G	IP	W	L	Pct.	SO	BB	H	ERA
1978	Montreal	10	61	4	2	.667	50	21	52	2.51
1979	Montreal	34	168	9	8	.529	138	54	148	3.43
1980	Montreal	33	211	16	11	.593	125	56	206	3.11
	Totals	77	440	29	21	.580	313	131	406	3.15

WOODIE FRYMAN 40 6-2 215 **Bats R Throws L**

Blossomed as club's top reliever in '79 and was even better last year, improving saves from 10 to 17 . . . Was a starter until '79, getting new life with swap from Phillies to Tigers in '72 . . . Expos' Player of Year in '76, but swapped to Reds for Tony Perez that winter and was reluctant to go . . . Retired in middle of '77 season, went to Cubs in '78 and returned to Expos that June . . . Born April 12, 1940, in Ewing, Ky. . . . Named to All-Star team in '68 and '76 . . . A tobacco farmer in off-season . . . Four career one-hitters . . . Considering success out of bullpen, probably was wasted as a journeyman starter, 1966-78 . . . Pitched only 12 games in minors before making grade with Bucs in '66.

Year	Club	G	IP	W	L	Pct.	SO	BB	H	ERA
1966	Pittsburgh	36	182	12	9	.571	105	47	182	3.81
1967	Pittsburgh	28	113	3	8	.273	74	44	121	4.06
1968	Philadelphia	34	214	12	14	.462	151	64	198	2.78
1969	Philadelphia	36	228	12	15	.444	150	89	243	4.42
1970	Philadelphia	27	128	8	6	.571	97	43	122	4.08
1971	Philadelphia	37	149	10	7	.588	104	46	133	3.38
1972	Philadelphia	23	120	4	10	.286	69	39	131	4.35
1972	Detroit	16	114	10	3	.769	72	31	93	2.05
1973	Detroit	34	170	6	13	.316	119	64	200	5.35
1974	Detroit	27	142	6	9	.400	92	67	120	4.31
1975	Montreal	38	157	9	12	.429	118	68	141	3.32
1976	Montreal	34	216	13	13	.500	123	76	218	3.38
1977	Cincinnati	17	75	5	5	.500	57	45	83	5.40
1978	Chicago-Montreal	32	150	7	11	.389	81	74	157	4.20
1979	Montreal	44	58	3	6	.333	44	22	52	2.79
1980	Montreal	61	80	7	4	.636	59	30	61	2.25
	Totals	524	2296	127	145	.467	1515	849	2255	3.78

TOP PROSPECTS

BILL GULLICKSON 22 6-3 198 **Bats R Throws R**

Perhaps no longer a "prospect" because of swift rise last season, but too important to be ignored . . . Started season at Denver and went 6-2, 1.91 before promotion . . . Incredible three-game streak in September . . . Blanked Giants on three hits, struck out 18 Cubs and shut out Pirates on three-hitter . . . 4-1, 2.84 in August and 4-1, 1.64 in September . . . Born Feb. 20, 1959, at Marshall, Minn. . . . Two other fine prospects are slugger Tim Wallach, who hit 36 homers and had 124 RBI at Denver, and infielder Tim Raines, American Assn. bat king with .354 at Denver.

MANAGER DICK WILLIAMS: Just missed joining elite group of skippers who have won pennants in both leagues and who have done it with three different clubs . . . Carried Expos into final weekend of season tied with Phillies . . . Also second in '79 when 95 victories set club record . . . Manager of Year a third time in '79 . . . Has a gruff exterior to strangers . . . A no-nonsense manager who lays down law . . . Born May 7, 1929, at St. Louis . . . Twice played for Montreal as minor league player in Dodgers' chain . . . A journeyman outfielder, but a successful skipper . . . As rookie manager in '67, guided Red Sox to World Series . . . Won three straight division crowns and two World Series titles in 1971-73 with Oakland . . . Was to become Yankees' pilot in '74, but Charlie Finley wouldn't release him from contract . . . If he had, Billy Martin might never have made it back to New York . . . A's 101 wins were club's most in 40 years . . . Posted 1,000th victory in '80.

GREATEST TEAM

The addition of LeFlore and a solid bullpen made the '80 Expos better than the '79 version, so it rates as the best club in Montreal history. Manager Dick Williams' team posted 90 wins and wasn't eliminated from division title contention until the day before the conclusion of the regular season, falling victim to torrid Mike Schmidt and the Phillies.

The '80 Expos had everything: speed, power and pitching. The loss of Ellis Valentine for a large chunk of the season probably cost the club a few wins—and a possible pennant—but most Expos had banner seasons, including Dawson, Cromartie, Carter, Fryman, Rogers, Sanderson, rookie pitching sensation Gullickson and the blurring LeFlore and Scott on the basepaths.

ALL-TIME EXPO LEADERS

BATTING: Rusty Staub, .311, 1971
HRs: Gary Carter, 31, 1977
RBIs: Ken Singleton, 103, 1973
STEALS: Ron LeFlore, 97, 1980
WINS: Ross Grimsley, 20, 1978
STRIKEOUTS: Bill Stoneman, 251, 1971

Warren Cromartie batted solid .288 during 1980.

NEW YORK METS

TEAM DIRECTORY: Chairman of the Board: Nelson Doubleday; Pres.: Fred Wilpon; Exec. VP-GM: Frank Cashen; VP-Baseball Operations: Lou Gorman; Dir. Scouting: Joe McIlvaine; Dir. Pub. Rel.: Jay Horwitz; Mgr.: Joe Torre. Home: Shea Stadium (55,300). Field distances: 338, l.f. line; 371, l.c.; 410, c.f.; 371, r.c.; 338, r.f. line. Spring training: St. Petersburg, Fla.

SCOUTING REPORT

HITTING: Shows marked improvement with the progress made by rookies Wally Backman, Mookie Wilson and Hubie Brooks last year. Lee Mazzilli, Frank Taveras, Steve Henderson and Joel Youngblood also were solid at the plate and a healthy John Stearns will add more punch to the receiving corps.

There is a definite lack of power, a situation not aided by the departure of Claudell Washington. The club tried to remedy the situation with the signing of free agents Rusty Staub (.300) and Mike Cubbage (.246) and the acquisition of Bob Bailor (.236). The only blessing is that the club has sufficient speed to stretch out some of those singles, for game-winning homers are few and far between.

PITCHING: Once the key to pennants in 1969 and 1973, pitching no longer is the Mets' strong suit, a fact sometimes guised by capable young relievers like Neil Allen and Jeff Reardon and veteran Dyar Miller, who pitched well after coming from the Angels.

The starters are young and potentially outstanding, but Pat Zachry and Craig Swan can't seem to stay healthy. And one wonders whether ex-San Diegoan Randy Jones can return to his old form. The most impressive starter last year was Mark Bomback, the club's big winner at 10-8. This is a staff which has to develop in a hurry if the Mets have any hopes of climbing in the standings.

FIELDING: Another problem area, though second baseman Doug Flynn was the best in the league at his position last year, fielding .991 while making only six errors in 659 chances. Shortstop Taveras was inconsistent and Mazzilli was a better outfielder than a first baseman, so there are gaps all over.

OUTLOOK: Not good, though there is sufficient talent to keep the club ahead of the Cubs, thanks particularly to a significant bullpen edge now that Sutter is a Cardinal. The club's big problem is consistent starting pitching because there is enough punch in the lineup to provide some runs.

Things would have been a lot brighter for the club if it had won its battle with the Yankees for Dave Winfield, or if another slugger had been acquired. Trouble is, everyone was talking about Allen and the Mets seemingly weren't willing to part with him.

This is a key year for Joe Torre, for the new ownership is intent on producing a winner and is willing to spend some money to do it. But because of pitching and fielding problems, it would take a miracle to move the club into the first division.

Doug Flynn won Gold Glove at second for Mets.

NEW YORK METS 1981 ROSTER

MANAGER Joe Torre
Coaches—Bob Gibson, Deron Johnson, Joe Pignatano, Chuck Cottier, Rube Walker

PITCHERS

No.	Name	1980 Club	W-L	IP	SO	ERA	B-T	Ht.	Wt.	Born
13	Allen, Neil	New York (NL)	7-10	97	79	3.71	R-R	6-2	195	1/24/58 Kansas City KA
36	Bomback, Mark	New York (NL)	10-8	163	68	4.09	R-R	5-11	170	4/14/53 Portsmouth, VA
43	Berenguer, Juan	Tidewater	9-15	157	178	3.84	R-R	5-11	186	11/30/54 Panama
		New York (NL)	0-1	9	7	6.00				
33	Falcone, Pete	New York (NL)	7-10	157	109	4.53	L-L	6-2	185	10/1/53 Brooklyn, NY
48	Glynn, Ed	New York (NL)	3-3	52	32	4.15	R-L	6-2	180	6/3/53 Flushing, NY
32	Hausman, Tom	New York (NL)	6-5	122	53	3.98	R-R	6-5	200	3/31/53 Mobridge, SD
26	Holman, Scott	Tidewater	3-3	48	16	4.88	R-R	6-0	190	9/19/58 Santa Paula, CA
		New York (NL)	0-0	7	3	1.29				
35	Jones, Randy	San Diego	5-13	154	53	3.92	R-L	6-0	180	1/12/50 Fullerton, CA
–	Lynch, Ed	Tidewater	13-6	163	91	3.15	R-R	6-5	210	2/25/56 Brooklyn, NY
		New York (NL)	1-1	19	9	5.21				
49	Miller, Dyar	New York (NL)	1-2	42	28	1.93	R-R	6-1	202	5/29/46 Batesville, IN
		Tidewater	4-2	52	35	4.70				
47	Orosco, Jesse	Jackson	4-5	91	93	3.71	R-L	6-2	174	4/21/57 Santa Barbara, CA
44	Reardon, Jeff	New York (NL)	8-7	110	101	2.62	R-R	6-1	190	10/1/55 Pittsfield, MA
–	Roberts, Dave	Pittsburgh	0-1	2	1	4.50	L-L	6-3	192	9/11/44 Gallipolis, OH
		Seattle	2-3	80	47	4.39				
30	Scott, Mike	Tidewater	13-7	170	88	2.96	R-R	6-3	215	4/26/55 Santa Monica, CA
		New York (NL)	1-1	29	13	4.34				
27	Swan, Craig	New York (NL)	5-9	128	79	3.59	R-R	6-3	225	11/30/50 Van Nuys, CA
39	Thurberg, Tom	Jackson	7-2	92	84	2.82	R-R	6-1	190	10/16/57 Unavailable
46	Von Ohlen, Dave	Tidewater	5-4	86	44	3.21	L-L	6-2	200	10/25/58 Unavailable
40	Zachry, Pat	New York (NL)	6-10	165	88	3.00	R-R	6-5	175	4/24/52 Richmond, TX

CATCHERS

No.	Name	1980 Club	H	HR	RBI	Pct.	B-T	Ht.	Wt.	Born
15	Benton, Butch	Tidewater	63	5	34	.297	R-R	6-1	193	8/24/57 Tampa, FL
		New York (NL)	1	0	0	.048				
42	Hodges, Ron	New York (NL)	10	0	5	.238	L-R	6-1	185	6/22/49 Franklin County, VA
12	Stearns, John	New York (NL)	91	0	45	.285	R-R	6-0	185	8/21/51 Denver, CO
29	Trevino, Alex	New York (NL)	91	0	37	.256	R-R	5-10	165	8/26/57 Mexico

INFIELDERS

No.	Name	1980 Club	H	HR	RBI	Pct.	B-T	Ht.	Wt.	Born
3	Backman, Wally	Tidewater	117	1	51	.293	B-R	5-9	160	9/29/59 Hillsboro, OR
		New York (NL)	30	0	9	.323				
7	Brooks, Hubie	Tidewater	124	3	50	.297	R-R	6-0	178	9/24/56 Los Angeles, CA
		New York (NL)	25	1	10	.309				
–	Cubbage, Mike	Minnesota	70	8	42	.246	L-R	6-0	180	7/21/50 Charlottesville, VA
23	Flynn, Doug	New York (NL)	113	0	24	.255	R-R	5-11	165	4/18/51 Lexington, KY
17	Giles, Brian	Jackson	128	10	58	.286	R-R	6-1	165	4/27/60 Unavailable
22	Jorgensen, Mike	New York (NL)	82	7	43	.255	L-L	6-1	192	8/16/48 Passaic, NJ
21	Maddox, Elliott	New York (NL)	101	4	34	.246	R-R	5-11	185	12/21/48 East Orange, NJ
16	Mazzilli, Lee	New York (NL)	162	16	76	.280	B-R	6-1	180	3/25/55 New York, NY
11	Taveras, Frank	New York (NL)	157	0	25	.279	R-R	6-0	170	12/24/50 Dominican Republic

OUTFIELDERS

No.	Name	1980 Club	H	HR	RBI	Pct.	B-T	Ht.	Wt.	Born
–	Bailor, Bob	Toronto	82	1	16	.236	R-R	5-10	160	7/10/51 Connellsville, PA
28	Beltre, Sergio	Jackson	46	3	19	.311	R-R	6-2	175	10/22/58 Unavailable
5	Henderson, Steve	New York (NL)	149	8	58	.290	R-R	6-1	197	11/18/52 Houston, TX
25	Howard, Mike	Jackson	148	9	54	.292	B-R	6-2	185	4/2/58 Unavailable
10	Staub, Rusty	Texas	102	9	55	.300	L-R	6-2	205	4/1/44 New Orleans, LA
1	Wilson, Mookie	New York (NL)	26	0	4	.248	B-R	5-10	170	2/9/56 Bamberg, SC
		Tidewater	152	4	44	.295				
18	Youngblood, Joel	New York (NL)	142	8	69	.276	R-R	5-11	175	8/28/51 Houston, TX

MET PROFILES

STEVE HENDERSON 28 6-1 197 Bats R Throws R

Established himself as club batting leader while bouncing back from a serious ankle injury . . . Hit .306 in '79, but missed 64 games . . . Was Player of Week following 12-for-26 June streak . . . Got a chance to play with New York after trade from Reds as part of Tom Seaver swap . . . Paid off instantly with .297 average in '77, missing Rookie-of-Year honors by one vote . . . Born Nov. 18, 1952, at Houston . . . Set career major league high with 23 steals last year . . . A good fielder . . . A standout at Prairie View A&M before signing with Reds . . . Raised average every year in minors, capped by .326 at Indianapolis first half of '77 season . . . Though only playing 99 games as rookie, topped club in RBI and shared lead in homers.

Year	Club	Pos.	G	AB	R	H	2B	3B	HR	RBI	SB	Avg.
1977	New York (NL)..	OF	99	350	67	104	16	6	12	65	6	.297
1978	New York (NL)..	OF	157	587	83	156	30	9	10	65	13	.266
1979	New York (NL)..	OF	98	350	42	107	16	8	5	39	13	.306
1980	New York (NL)..	OF	143	513	75	149	17	8	8	58	23	.290
	Totals..........		497	1800	267	516	79	31	35	227	55	.287

JOEL YOUNGBLOOD 29 5-11 175 Bats R Throws R

Another solid season at the plate, though his power figures tailed off . . . Batted .329 in June . . . Can play several positions, but seems to be settling in at third base . . . Started '79 as third baseman, but shifted to outfield when Rich Hebner was acquired . . . Elliott Maddox won right field job, but was injured in early April and Joel took over . . . Responded with .275 average and 16 homers . . . Less power last year, but averaged a career-high .276 . . . Born Aug. 28, 1951, at Houston . . . Had 18 outfield assists in '79 and played second base with N.L. squad in post-season Japan tour, batting .316 . . . Came up with Reds, but swapped to Cardinals before joining Mets in trade for Mike Phillips . . . A steal.

Year	Club	Pos.	G	AB	R	H	2B	3B	HR	RBI	SB	Avg.
1976	Cincinnati	OF-3B-2B-C	55	57	8	11	1	1	0	1	1	.193
1977	St.L.-N.Y. (NL) ..	2B-OF-3B	95	209	17	51	13	1	0	12	1	.244
1978	New York (NL)..	OF-2B-3B-SS	113	266	40	67	12	8	7	30	4	.252
1979	New York (NL)..	OF-3B-2B	158	590	90	162	37	5	16	60	18	.275
1980	New York (NL)..	OF-2B-3B	146	514	58	142	26	2	8	69	14	.276
	Totals..........		587	1636	213	433	89	17	31	172	38	.265

JOHN STEARNS 29 6-0 185 Bats R Throws R

Considered one of game's top catchers, but was hindered by injury last year and emergence of Alex Trevino, Stearns balking over some use at first base . . . Batted .322 in May . . . Fractured finger in August and required surgery . . . Frequently mentioned in trade rumors . . . Born Aug. 21, 1951, at Denver . . . Set Modern N.L. record for catchers by stealing 25 bases in '78 . . . Batted .285 in 91 games last year, but went homerless after averaging 12 per year first three seasons as regular . . . Has also played left field and third base for Mets . . . A former football star at Colorado U., where he played four bowl games as a defensive back . . . NCAA home run champ in '73.

Year	Club	Pos.	G	AB	R	H	2B	3B	HR	RBI	SB	Avg.
1974	Philadelphia.....	C	1	2	0	1	0	0	0	0	0	.500
1975	New York (NL)..	C	59	169	25	32	5	1	3	10	4	.189
1976	New York (NL)..	C-3B	32	103	13	27	6	0	2	10	1	.262
1977	New York (NL)..	C-1B	139	431	52	108	25	1	12	55	9	.251
1978	New York (NL)..	C-3B	143	477	65	126	24	1	15	73	25	.264
1979	New York (NL)..	C-3B-1B-OF	155	538	58	131	29	2	9	66	15	.243
1980	New York (NL)..	C-1B-3B	91	319	42	91	25	1	0	45	7	.285
	Totals..........		619	2039	255	516	115	6	41	259	61	.253

DOUG FLYNN 30 5-11 165 Bats R Throws R

Considered by some the best defensive second baseman in the N.L. . . . A fractured wrist suffered against S.F. knocked him out of lineup in August . . . Became first player since Ernie Banks in '66 to hit three triples in a game, Aug. 5, against Montreal . . . Another acquisition in Seaver swap . . . Poor hitter in bigs, but started to make progress at plate last year . . . Runnerup in Gold Glove voting 1978-79 and won it in 1980 with .991 percentage . . . Born April 18, 1951, at Lexington, Ky. . . . Played basketball at U. of Kentucky . . . Nephew of coaching great Adolph Rupp . . . Joined Mets in summer of '77 and became shortstop when Bud Harrelson was injured.

Year	Club	Pos.	G	AB	R	H	2B	3B	HR	RBI	SB	Avg.
1975	Cincinnati	3B-2B-SS	89	127	17	34	7	0	1	20	3	.268
1976	Cincinnati	2B-3B-SS	93	219	20	62	5	2	1	20	2	.283
1977	Cin.-N.Y. (NL)...	SS-2B-3B	126	314	14	62	7	2	0	19	1	.197
1978	New York (NL)..	SS-2B	156	532	37	126	12	8	0	36	3	.237
1979	New York (NL)..	2B-SS	157	555	35	135	19	5	4	61	0	.243
1980	New York (NL)..	2B-SS	128	443	46	113	9	8	0	24	2	.255
	Totals..........		749	2190	169	532	59	25	6	180	11	.243

FRANK TAVERAS 30 6-0 170 Bats R Throws R

Enjoyed another solid season at the plate and on the basepaths . . . Was Player of Week in May while blasting 29 hits in 56 at bats over a two-week stretch . . . Batted .362 in May and .333 in August . . . Made three errors in first nine games with Pittsburgh in '79 and was swapped to New York for Tim Foli . . . Bucs won pennant, but Frank settled down and gave Mets better long-range shortstop . . . Played in 164 games in '79 and once went 38 games without an error . . . Born Dec. 24, 1950, at Villa Vasquez, Dominican Republic . . . Set Mets' record with 42 steals in '79 . . . Topped N.L. with 70 steals in 1977, setting Bucs' record since broken by Omar Moreno . . . Batted .300 in 1974 playoffs.

Year	Club	Pos.	G	AB	R	H	2B	3B	HR	RBI	SB	Avg.
1971	Pittsburgh......	PR	1	0	0	0	0	0	0	0	0	.000
1972	Pittsburgh......	SS	4	3	0	0	0	0	0	0	0	.000
1974	Pittsburgh......	SS	126	333	33	82	4	2	0	26	13	.246
1975	Pittsburgh......	SS	134	378	44	80	9	4	0	23	17	.212
1976	Pittsburgh......	SS	144	519	76	134	8	6	0	24	58	.258
1977	Pittsburgh......	SS	147	544	72	137	20	10	1	29	70	.252
1978	Pittsburgh......	SS	157	654	81	182	31	9	0	38	46	.278
1979	Pitt-NY (NL)....	SS	164	680	93	178	29	9	1	34	44	.262
1980	New York (NL)..	SS	141	562	65	157	27	0	0	25	32	.279
	Totals..........		1018	3673	464	950	128	40	2	199	280	.259

LEE MAZZILLI 26 6-1 180 Bats S Throws R

Exciting and inconsistent, yet rates as good bet for future stardom . . . Maz had no homers until his 165th at-bat and only two in first 70 games . . . Then he batted .325 with 11 homers and 25 RBI in July before hitting only one homer in August . . . A roller-coaster season, but final totals made him club leader in several offensive categories . . . Born March 25, 1955, in New York City, so is an obvious hometown favorite . . . Playing more first base than outfield because of weak arm . . . Spurred N.L. to '79 All-Star Game win at Seattle with pinch-homer in eighth for tie and bases-loaded walk in ninth for the victory . . . Stole seven bases for San Jose in seven-inning game in '75.

Year	Club	Pos.	G	AB	R	H	2B	3B	HR	RBI	SB	Avg.
1976	New York (NL)..	OF	24	77	9	15	2	0	2	7	5	.195
1977	New York (NL)..	OF	159	537	66	134	24	3	6	46	22	.250
1978	New York (NL)..	OF	148	542	78	148	28	5	16	61	20	.273
1979	New York (NL)..	OF-1B	158	597	78	181	34	4	15	79	34	.303
1980	New York (NL)..	1B-OF	152	578	82	162	31	4	16	76	41	.280
	Totals..........		641	2331	313	640	119	16	55	269	122	.275

NEIL ALLEN 23 6-2 195 **Bats R Throws R**

Shows signs of brilliant future in bullpen . . . Despite club's poor standing, battled Sutter for N.L. saves lead and finished with 22 . . . Had eight as a rookie in '79, becoming full-time reliever . . . Was 2-0, 1.59 in May . . . Allowed on run in 13 innings in August, posting 0.69 ERA . . . Switched to bullpen after losing four of first five starts in '79 . . . Born Jan. 24, 1958, at Kansas City, Kan. . . . On disabled list with rib injury in May 1979, but flourished upon recovery, posting 2.05 ERA in last 38 appearances . . . Had seven saves last two months . . . Signed football scholarship letter with Kansas State as QB, but went with Mets instead . . . Was 10-2, 2.79 at Lynchburg in second year of pro ball, 1977.

Year	Club	G	IP	W	L	Pct.	SO	BB	H	ERA
1979	New York (NL)...........	50	99	6	10	.375	65	47	100	3.55
1980	New York (NL)...........	59	97	7	10	.412	79	40	87	3.71
	Totals....................	109	196	13	20	.394	144	87	187	3.63

CRAIG SWAN 30 6-3 225 **Bats R Throws R**

Became highest-paid Met after signing lucrative contract in '80, but severe arm injury dampened season, limiting him to 21 games, 5-9 record . . . Had intestinal problem in '79, but not serious enough to detract from banner 14-win season . . . Won eight more games than any teammate that year . . . Career has been plagued by injury . . . Born Nov. 30, 1950, at Van Nuys, Cal. . . . Set school records for victories (47), strikeouts and innings at Arizona State, going 16-1 as senior All-American . . . Mets' top prospect in '72, but early development retarded by injuries and ailments . . . Up to stay after 13-7, 2.24 year at Tidewater (AAA) in '75.

Year	Club	G	IP	W	L	Pct.	SO	BB	H	ERA
1973	New York (NL)...........	3	8	0	1	.000	4	2	16	9.00
1974	New York (NL)...........	7	30	1	3	.250	10	21	28	4.50
1975	New York (NL)...........	6	31	1	3	.250	19	13	38	6.39
1976	New York (NL)...........	23	132	6	9	.400	89	44	129	3.55
1977	New York (NL)...........	26	147	9	10	.474	71	56	153	4.22
1978	New York (NL)...........	29	207	9	6	.600	125	58	164	2.43
1979	New York (NL)...........	35	251	14	13	.519	145	57	241	3.30
1980	New York (NL)...........	21	128	5	9	.357	79	30	117	3.59
	Totals....................	150	934	45	54	.455	542	281	886	3.52

PAT ZACHRY 28 6-5 175 **Bats R Throws R**

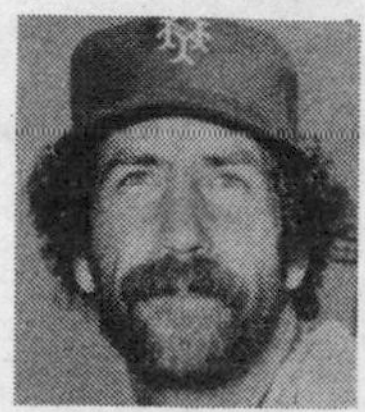

Enjoyed best season with the Mets . . . Better than record shows, for 6-10 mark disguised a solid 3.00 ERA . . . At best in July with 4-0 record, three shutouts and 1.40 ERA . . . Those were his only blankings and he was winless in August . . . Like Swan, also is injury-plagued . . . Elbow problem limited him to seven games in '79, but he was 5-1 . . . Was 5-0 before losing final start, June 8 . . . In first full year with Mets made N.L. All-Star squad and was 10-6 with 3.33 ERA when foot fracture knocked him out . . . Born April 24, 1952, at Richmond, Tex. . . . Signed by Reds in '70 and co-winner of Rookie-of-Year award in '76, going 14-7, 2.74 . . . Fine future if he stays healthy.

Year	Club	G	IP	W	L	Pct.	SO	BB	H	ERA
1976	Cincinnati	38	204	14	7	.667	143	83	170	2.74
1977	Cin.-N.Y. (NL)	31	195	10	13	.439	99	77	207	4.25
1978	New York (NL)	21	138	10	6	.625	78	60	120	3.33
1979	New York (NL)	7	43	5	1	.833	17	21	44	3.56
1980	New York (NL)	28	165	6	10	.375	88	58	145	3.00
	Totals	125	745	45	37	.549	425	299	686	3.35

RANDY JONES 31 6-0 180 **Bats R Throws L**

Injury-plagued veteran from San Diego has chance to return to Cy Young Award form of '76 with Mets . . . Was Player of Week for successive shutouts against Cubs and Pirates in May, but a damaged nerve led to more arm trouble and he dropped 12 of 13 decisions in mid-summer . . . Born Jan. 12, 1950, at Fullerton, Cal. . . . Seemed on road to recovery after logging 263 innings and 39 starts in '79 . . . A control artist who is known for working quickly, thereby keeping teammates alert . . . Was 42-26 in 1975-76, ranking among top lefthanders in baseball . . . Injuries have reduced him to journeyman status . . . Also in tough-luck category . . . Was a 13-14 loser in '78 despite 2.88 ERA.

Year	Club	G	IP	W	L	Pct.	SO	BB	H	ERA
1973	San Diego	20	140	7	6	.538	77	37	129	3.15
1974	San Diego	40	208	8	22	.267	124	78	217	4.46
1975	San Diego	37	285	20	12	.625	103	56	242	2.24
1976	San Diego	40	315	22	14	.611	93	50	274	2.74
1977	San Diego	27	147	6	12	.333	44	36	173	4.59
1978	San Diego	37	253	13	14	.481	71	64	253	2.88
1979	San Diego	39	263	11	12	.478	112	64	257	3.63
1980	San Diego	24	154	5	13	.278	53	29	165	3.92
	Totals	264	1765	92	105	.467	677	414	1710	3.30

RUSTY STAUB 37 6-2 205 **Bats L Throws R**

Returns for another round at his restaurant, "Rusty's," and another fling at Shea, where he was so popular . . . What a way to come back: a guaranteed three-year $1 million contract, active duty at first base and a shot at membership in the 300 Home Run Club (he has 279) . . . Born April 1, 1944, in New Orleans . . . Received a reported $100,000 for signing Astro contract in 1961 . . . Was "Le Grand Orange" in Montreal before first tour of duty with the Mets . . . Selected for N.L. All-Star team five straight years 1967-71, although he didn't play in '71 game . . . Batted .423 for the Mets in 1973 World Series . . . Although a DH in Detroit, he played 90 games at first for the Rangers and hit .300, which didn't hurt his free-agent appeal when he sat down to negotiate with the Doubleday gang in December.

Year	Club	Pos.	G	AB	R	H	2B	3B	HR	RBI	SB	Avg.
1963	Houston........	1B-OF	150	513	43	115	17	4	6	45	0	.224
1964	Houston........	1B-OF	89	292	26	63	10	2	8	35	1	.216
1965	Houston........	OF-1B	131	410	43	105	20	1	14	63	3	.256
1966	Houston........	OF-1B	153	554	60	155	28	3	13	81	2	.280
1967	Houston........	OF	149	546	71	182	44	1	10	74	0	.333
1968	Houston........	1B-OF	161	591	54	172	37	1	6	72	2	.291
1969	Montreal.......	OF	158	549	89	166	26	5	29	79	3	.302
1970	Montreal.......	OF	160	569	98	156	23	7	30	94	12	.274
1971	Montreal.......	OF	162	599	94	186	34	6	19	97	9	.311
1972	New York (NL)..	OF	66	239	32	70	11	0	9	38	0	.293
1973	New York (NL)..	OF	152	585	77	163	36	1	15	76	1	.279
1974	New York (NL)..	OF	151	561	65	145	22	2	19	78	2	.258
1975	New York (NL)..	OF	155	574	93	162	30	4	19	105	2	.282
1976	Detroit.........	OF	161	589	73	176	28	3	15	96	3	.299
1977	Detroit.........	DH	158	623	84	173	34	3	22	101	1	.278
1978	Detroit.........	DH	162	642	75	175	30	1	24	121	3	.273
1979	Detroit.........	DH	68	246	32	58	12	1	9	40	1	.236
1979	Montreal.......	1B-OF	38	86	9	23	3	0	3	14	0	.267
1980	Texas..........	1B-DH	109	340	42	102	23	2	9	55	1	.300
	Totals.........		2533	9108	1160	2547	468	47	279	1364	46	.280

TOP PROSPECTS

MOOKIE WILSON 25 5-10 170 **Bats R Throws R**

Fleet outfielder batted .295 at Tidewater (AAA) and looked good in late-season trial with Mets . . . Also at Tidewater in '79, stealing 49 bases and earning Rookie of Year honors . . . Born Feb. 9, 1956, at Bamberg, S.C. . . . Star for U. of South Carolina, led club to finals of College World Series . . . Second baseman Wally Backman also a standout . . . Batted .293 at Tidewater and continued hot pace with Mets down the stretch.

MANAGER JOE TORRE: Finally was acknowledged with a two-year contract after there had been some doubt as to whether he'd be back . . . Now he's a $100,000 manager starting his fourth full season . . . A product of Brooklyn, where he was born July 18, 1940, Joe was an outstanding player with the Milwaukee and Atlanta Braves, Cardinals and Mets . . . He retired with a .297 lifetime average soon after succeeding Joe Frazier May 31, 1977 . . . Played in eight All-Star Games, and at three positions–catcher, third and first . . . As a Brave, was runnerup in 1961 Rookie-of-Year voting (to Billy Williams of the Cubs) . . . Traded to St. Louis for Orlando Cepeda in 1969 and the following year shifted from catcher to third . . . In 1971 he won the N.L. batting title with .363 and wound up as MVP . . . As a schoolboy at Brooklyn's St. Francis Prep, he was the chubbiest on the team, but now he's a streamlined 200-pounder who is a fashion model for a men's clothier.

GREATEST TEAM

This one is easy. The Miracle Mets, a ragamuffin expansion club throughout most of the Sixties, not only captured their first pennant in 1969, they also clobbered the Orioles, 4-1, in the World Series after sweeping the Braves in the first N.L. championship series.

It was no fluke, for the pitching-rich New Yorkers posted a 100-62 record to win the N.L. East by eight games over the Cubs. Tom Seaver was 25-7, Jerry Koosman 17-9 and young reliever Tug McGraw 9-3. All three had ERAs below 2.30, helping the club post a 2.99 mark for the season. Cleon Jones paced the batters at .340.

New York showed it could hit in the historic playoffs, sweeping Atlanta, 9-5, 11-6, 7-4. Koosman was 2-0 in the Series, upstarts Al Weis and Ron Swoboda batting .455 and .400, respectively. Incredibly, manager Gil Hodges' champions were 73-89 and 24 games back in ninth place in 1968.

ALL-TIME MET LEADERS

BATTING: Cleon Jones, .340, 1969
HRs: Dave Kingman, 37, 1976
RBIs: Rusty Staub, 105, 1975
STEALS: Frank Taveras, 42, 1979
WINS: Tom Seaver, 25, 1969
STRIKEOUTS: Tom Seaver, 289, 1971

PHILADELPHIA PHILLIES

TEAM DIRECTORY: Chairman of the Board: R.R.M. (Bob) Carpenter, Jr.; Pres: R.R.M. (Ruly) Carpenter III; Exec. VP: William Y. Giles; VP-Dir. Player Personnel: Paul Owens; VP-Dir. Finances: George F.H. Harrison; Dir. Minor Leagues: Howie Bedell; Adm.-Scouting: Jack Pastore; Dir. Pub. Rel.: Larry Shenk; Trav. Sec.: Ed Ferenz; Mgr.: Dallas Green. Home: Veterans Stadium (56,581). Field distances: 330, l.f. line; 408, c.f.; 330, r.f. line. Spring training: Clearwater, Fla.

SCOUTING REPORT

HITTING: An outstanding attack, one which got a big boost last season from rookies Lonnie Smith and Keith Moreland. Only the Cardinals had a higher batting average than the Phillies' .270 and only St. Louis scored more runs. By placing Greg Luzinski on the block and apparently phasing him out of the lineup, the club loses some power, yet only the Dodgers belted more homers in 1980. Pete Rose and Garry Maddox tailed off at the plate, but big years by Mike Schmidt, Bake McBride and Smith more than compensated.

Schmidt, if necessary, can be a tremendous one-man offense, as evidenced by his potent hitting down the stretch last season. Always a streaky home-run hitter, Schmidt was much more consistent in 1980 and there's no reason to expect him to tail off at age 31. Rose may no longer be a .300 hitter, but he still stroked 185 hits and topped the league in doubles. Smith, at .339, showed he's ready to step in for Luzinski, giving the club additional speed.

PITCHING: It all starts with Steve Carlton and the Cy Young lefthander may be hard pressed to repeat his 24-9, 2.34 success at age 36. But the staff has Larry Christenson bouncing back from injury and impressive newcomers in Bob Walk and Marty Bystrom, a combined 16-7 last year, ready to pick up the slack.

Tug McGraw heads a stout bullpen corps, one which figures to be even stronger this season with the fulltime work of Sparky Lyle. The staff is deep and talented, Carlton and Dick Ruthven forming a solid one-two punch. Imagine the potential if Nino Espinosa and Randy Lerch (a combined 7-19 last year) bounce back to respectability.

FIELDING: The Phils slumped to fifth in the league after being tops the year before, which makes one wonder if there truly is a correlation between solid defense and winning a championship.

Manny Trillo excelled at second base in the World Series.

St. Louis and San Diego, for instance, fielded better than Philadelphia in 1980, but the Phils still got Gold Glove seasons from Schmidt and Garry Maddox, who is regarded as the best centerfielder in the circuit by his peers.

OUTLOOK: A lot better than it was last spring, when the aging Phillies were generally regarded as the third-best club in the division behind Pittsburgh and Montreal. The success of youngsters like Smith, Moreland, Bystrom and Walk gave the club a breath of fresh air, as did the direction of manager Dallas Green.

But the main men still were Schmidt and Carlton, whose accomplishments under pennant pressure made them the best players in the league. Add Rose and McGraw to the group for the intangible leadership they provided, though it didn't show up in the box scores until McGraw's impeccable performance down the stretch. The Phillies had to believe–and they did.

PHILADELPHIA PHILLIES 1981 ROSTER

MANAGER Dallas Green

Coaches—Billy DeMars, Bobby Wine, Herm Starrette, Lee Elia, Mike Ryan

PITCHERS

No.	Name	1980 Club	W-L	IP	SO	ERA	B-T	Ht.	Wt.	Born
40	Brusstar, Warren	Peninsula	1-1	14	8	4.61	R-R	6-3	200	2/2/52 Oakland, CA
		Philadelphia	2-2	39	21	3.69				
50	Bystrom, Marty	Okla. City	6-5	91	68	3.65	R-R	6-5	200	7/26/58 Miami, FL
		Philadelphia	5-0	36	21	1.50				
32	Carlton, Steve	Philadelphia	24-9	304	286	2.34	L-L	6-5	210	12/22/44 Chesterfield, MO
38	Christenson, Larry	Philadelphia	5-1	74	49	4.01	R-R	6-4	213	11/10/53 Everett, WA
43	Davis, Mark	Reading	19-6	193	185	2.47	L-L	6-3	180	10/19/60 Livermore, CA
		Philadelphia	0-0	7	5	2.57				
35	Espinosa, Nino	Spartanburg	1-1	17	11	2.65	R-R	6-1	186	8/15/53 Dominican Republic
		Philadelphia	3-5	76	13	3.79				
47	Lerch, Randy	Philadelphia	4-14	150	57	5.16	L-L	6-3	195	10/9/54 Sacramento, CA
39	Lyle, Sparky	Texas	3-2	81	43	4.69	L-L	6-1	195	7/22/44 Reynoldsville, PA
		Philadelphia	0-0	14	6	1.93				
45	McGraw, Tug	Philadelphia	5-4	92	75	1.47	R-L	6-0	184	8/30/44 Martinez, CA
34	Munninghoff, Scott	Philadelphia	0-0	6	2	4.50	R-R	6-0	180	12/5/58 Cincinnati, OH
		Oklahoma City	4-9	92	30	5.07				
48	Noles, Dickie	Philadelphia	1-4	81	57	3.89	R-R	6-2	178	11/19/56 Charlotte, NC
42	Reed, Ron	Philadelphia	7-5	91	54	4.05	R-R	6-6	225	11/2/42 LaPorte, IN
44	Ruthven, Dick	Philadelphia	17-10	223	86	3.55	R-R	6-3	190	3/27/51 Sacramento, CA
41	Walk, Bob	Oklahoma City	5-1	49	36	2.92	R-R	6-3	200	11/26/56 Van Nuys, CA
		Philadelphia	11-7	152	94	4.56				

CATCHERS

No.	Name	1980 Club	H	HR	RBI	Pct.	B-T	Ht.	Wt.	Born
8	Boone, Bob	Philadelphia	110	9	55	.229	R-R	6-2	202	11/19/47 San Diego, CA
17	McCormack, Don	Oklahoma City	109	14	64	.265	R-R	6-5	205	9/18/55 Omak, WA
		Philadelphia	1	0	0	1.000				
6	Moreland, Keith	Philadelphia	50	4	29	.314	R-R	6-0	200	5/2/54 Dallas, TX
24	Virgil, Ozzie	Reading	123	28	104	.270	R-R	6-1	195	12/7/56 Puerto Rico
		Philadelphia	1	0	0	.200				

INFIELDERS

No.	Name	1980 Club	H	HR	RBI	Pct.	B-T	Ht.	Wt.	Born
16	Aguayo, Luis	Oklahoma City	71	9	40	.244	R-R	5-9	173	3/13/59 Vega Baja, PR
		Philadelphia	13	1	8	.277				
15	Aviles, Ramon	Oklahoma City	–	–	–	–	R-R	5-9	155	1/22/52 Manati, PR
		Philadelphia	28	2	9	.277				
10	Bowa, Larry	Philadelphia	144	2	39	.267	B-R	5-10	155	12/6/45 Sacramento, CA
–	Franco, Julio	Peninsula	178	11	99	.321	R-R	5-11	155	8/23/58 Dominican Republic
22	Loviglio, Jay	Oklahoma City	138	6	39	.277	R-R	5-9	160	5/30/56 Freeport, NY
		Philadelphia	0	0	0	.000				
–	Matuszek, Len	Oklahoma City	78	7	35	.305	L-R	6-2	190	9/27/54 Toledo, OH
14	Rose, Pete	Philadelphia	185	1	64	.282	B-R	5-11	200	4/14/41 Cincinnati, OH
–	Sandberg, Ryne	Reading	152	11	79	.310	R-R	6-1	175	9/18/59 Spokane, WA
20	Schmidt, Mike	Philadelphia	157	48	121	.286	R-R	6-2	198	9/27/49 Dayton, OH
9	Trillo, Manny	Philadelphia	155	7	43	.292	R-R	6-1	164	12/25/50 Venezuela

OUTFIELDERS

No.	Name	1980 Club	H	HR	RBI	Pct.	B-T	Ht.	Wt.	Born
–	Culmer, Wil	Peninsula	184	18	93	.369	R-R	6-4	210	11/11/58 Bahamas
30	Dernier, Bob	Reading	160	10	57	.299	R-R	6-0	160	1/5/57 Kansas City, MO
		Philadelphia	4	0	1	.571				
23	Gross, Greg	Philadelphia	37	0	12	.240	L-L	5-11	175	8/1/52 York, PA
28	Isales, Orlando	Oklahoma City	88	8	51	.262	R-R	5-9	175	12/22/59 Puerto Rico
		Philadelphia	2	0	3	.400				
19	Luzinski, Greg	Philadelphia	84	19	56	.228	R-R	6-1	225	11/22/50 Chicago, IL
31	Maddox, Garry	Philadelphia	142	11	73	.259	R-R	6-3	175	9/1/49 Cincinnati, OH
21	McBride, Bake	Philadelphia	171	9	87	.309	L-R	6-2	190	2/3/49 Fulton, MO
–	Sanchez, Alejandro	Spartanburg	139	15	76	.284	R-R	6-0	175	2/26/59 Puerto Rico
27	Smith, Lonnie	Philadelphia	101	3	20	.339	R-R	5-9	170	12/22/59 Chicago, IL
25	Unser, Del	Philadelphia	29	0	10	.264	L-L	5-11	180	12/9/44 Decatur, IL
29	Vukovich, George	Philadelphia	13	0	8	.224	L-R	6-0	198	6/24/56 Arlington Hts., IL

PHILLIE PROFILES

MIKE SCHMIDT 31 6-2 198 Bats R Throws R

Not many players did it better than this N.L. and World Series MVP in 1980 . . . Belted a career-high 48 homers to lead majors and also captured RBI crown with 121 . . . Two-run single in Game 6 clinched club's first-ever Series victory . . . Connected for 12 homers and knocked in 29 runs while batting .305 in May and was voted N.L. Player of Month . . . Batted .472 in a 10-game August stretch and finished the month at .327 with eight homers and 22 RBI to fuel pennant push . . . While slamming his 260th homer, passed Del Ennis as club's all-time leader . . . Born Sept. 27, 1949, at Dayton, Ohio . . . Second-squad third baseman on team of decade . . . Four-time N.L. home run king . . . Consistent Gold Glove winner . . . A streaky slugger, once belted seven homers in five games in '79 . . . Majors' most prolific home run hitter last seven years . . . Hit four homers in game at Chicago in '76 . . . Nine homers last 17 games in 1980 . . . Broke Ed Mathews record for homers by a third baseman.

Year	Club	Pos.	G	AB	R	H	2B	3B	HR	RBI	SB	Avg.
1972	Philadelphia.....	3B-2B	13	34	2	7	0	0	1	3	0	.206
1973	Philadelphia.....	3B-2B-1B-SS	132	367	43	72	11	0	18	52	8	.196
1974	Philadelphia.....	3B	162	568	108	160	28	7	36	116	23	.282
1975	Philadelphia.....	3B-SS	158	562	93	140	34	3	38	95	29	.249
1976	Philadelphia.....	3B	160	584	112	153	31	4	38	107	14	.262
1977	Philadelphia.....	3B-SS-2B	154	544	114	149	27	11	38	101	15	.274
1978	Philadelphia.....	3B-SS	145	513	93	129	27	2	21	78	19	.251
1979	Philadelphia.....	3B-SS	160	541	109	137	25	4	45	114	9	.253
1980	Philadelphia.....	3B-SS	150	548	104	157	25	8	48	121	12	.286
	Totals..........		1234	4261	778	1104	208	39	283	787	129	.259

PETE ROSE 39 5-11 200 Bats S Throws R

Had string of five .300 seasons snapped, but still a standout with league-leading 42 doubles and made dramatic catch of foul pop for next-to-last out of Series clincher. Off to a slow start, batting .205 on May 5, before gradually lifted average . . . Outfielder on team of decade . . . In '79, set major league record with 10th 200-hit season . . . Charlie Hustle still as aggressive as ever, but feats obscured by Schmidt and Carlton . . . Born April 4, 1941, at Cincinnati . . . Rookie of Year in '63 . . . MVP in '73 and World Series MVP in '75 . . . Batted .378 in 19 playoff games for Reds . . . Three-time batting champ . . .

Climbed on career lists after playing in all 162 games last year . . . Ranks eighth in games, second in at-bats, ninth in runs, fourth in hits (3,557) first in singles, fourth in doubles and fifth in total bases in major league history . . . N.L.-record-tying 44-game batting streak in '78.

Year	Club	Pos.	G	AB	R	H	2B	3B	HR	RBI	SB	Avg.
1963	Cincinnati	2B-OF	157	623	101	170	25	9	6	41	13	.273
1964	Cincinnati	2B	136	516	64	139	13	2	4	34	4	.269
1965	Cincinnati	2B	162	670	117	209	35	11	11	81	8	.312
1966	Cincinnati	2B-3B	156	654	97	205	38	5	16	70	4	.313
1967	Cincinnati	OF-2B	148	585	86	176	32	8	12	76	11	.301
1968	Cincinnati	OF-2B-1B	149	626	94	210	42	6	10	49	3	.335
1969	Cincinnati	OF-2B	156	627	120	218	33	11	16	82	7	.348
1970	Cincinnati	OF	159	649	120	205	37	9	15	52	12	.316
1971	Cincinnati	OF	160	632	86	192	27	4	13	44	13	.304
1972	Cincinnati	OF	154	645	107	198	31	11	6	57	10	.307
1973	Cincinnati	OF	160	680	115	230	36	8	5	64	10	.338
1974	Cincinnati	OF	163	652	110	185	45	7	3	51	2	.284
1975	Cincinnati	3B-OF	162	662	112	210	47	4	7	74	0	.317
1976	Cincinnati	3B-OF	162	665	130	215	42	6	10	63	9	.323
1977	Cincinnati	3B	162	655	95	204	38	7	9	64	16	.311
1978	Cincinnati	3B-OF-1B	159	655	103	198	51	3	7	52	13	.302
1979	Philadelphia.....	1B-3B-2B	163	628	90	208	40	5	4	59	20	.331
1980	Philadelphia.....	1B	162	655	96	185	42	1	1	64	12	.282
	Totals..........		2830	11,479	1843	3557	654	117	155	1077	167	.310

GREG LUZINSKI 30 6-1 225 — Bats R Throws R

Had second straight injury-plagued season, but still made big contribution prior to World Series . . . Belted three-run homer in first at bat of season . . . Batted .312 with eight homers and 18 RBI in May . . . On May 19-21, hit four homers in six at-bats . . . Went on disabled list and had knee surgery in July . . . Returned and hit homer against Giants in first game back Aug. 24 . . . Born Nov. 22, 1950, at Chicago . . . Averaged 32 homers and 111.5 RBI in four years, 1975-78, before stricken by injuries . . . This will be a key year, for youngsters are waiting in wings and ready to take over . . . Only got into three World Series games and failed to hit in nine at-bats . . . Has played in four All-Star Games.

Year	Club	Pos.	G	AB	R	H	2B	3B	HR	RBI	SB	Avg.
1970	Philadelphia.....	1B	8	12	0	2	0	0	0	0	0	.167
1971	Philadelphia.....	1B	28	100	13	30	8	0	3	15	2	.300
1972	Philadelphia.....	OF-1B	150	563	66	158	33	5	18	68	0	.281
1973	Philadelphia.....	OF	161	610	76	174	26	4	29	97	3	.285
1974	Philadelphia.....	OF	85	302	29	82	14	1	7	48	3	.272
1975	Philadelphia.....	OF	161	596	85	179	35	3	34	120	3	.300
1976	Philadelphia.....	OF	149	533	74	162	28	1	21	95	1	.304
1977	Philadelphia.....	OF	149	544	99	171	35	3	39	130	3	.309
1978	Philadelphia.....	OF	155	540	85	143	32	2	35	101	8	.265
1979	Philadelphia.....	OF	137	452	47	114	23	1	18	81	3	.252
1980	Philadelphia.....	OF	106	368	44	84	19	1	19	56	3	.228
	Totals..........		1289	4620	618	1299	253	21	223	811	29	.281

MANNY TRILLO 30 6-1 164 Bats R Throws R

Had best year at the plate in '80, batting .292 after being above .300 much of the way, and earned MVP honors in playoffs . . . Joined Phillies in '79 and promptly won a Gold Glove . . . Was batting .303 in May that year when fractured forearm sidelined him 40 games . . . Has always been a quick starter, batting .388 in mid-May of '77 . . . Originally signed as a catcher by Phillies in '68 . . . Played as pro rookie under manager Dallas Green in Huron, Mich., that year . . . Was in A's system and swapped to Cubs for Billy Williams in '74 . . . Played at least 152 games four straight years with Cubs . . . Born Dec. 25, 1950, at Caritito, Venezuela . . . Solidified Phillies' infield.

Year	Club	Pos.	G	AB	R	H	2B	3B	HR	RBI	SB	Avg.
1973	Oakland........	2B	17	12	0	3	2	0	0	3	0	.250
1974	Oakland........	2B	21	33	3	5	0	0	0	2	0	.152
1975	Chicago (NL)....	2B-SS	154	545	55	135	12	2	7	70	1	.248
1976	Chicago (NL)....	2B-SS	158	582	42	139	24	3	4	59	17	.239
1977	Chicago (NL)....	2B	152	504	51	141	18	5	7	57	3	.280
1978	Chicago (NL)....	2B	152	552	53	144	17	5	4	55	0	.261
1979	Philadelphia.....	2B	118	431	40	112	22	1	6	42	4	.260
1980	Philadelphia.....	2B	141	531	68	155	25	9	7	43	8	.292
	Totals..........		913	3190	312	834	120	25	35	331	33	.261

GARRY MADDOX 31 6-3 175 Bats R Throws R

Signed lucrative six-year contract before '80 season and proceeded to have worst season in bigs since rookie year of '72 . . . Was benched part of time because reserves were producing . . . Still had solid totals in doubles and RBI and fielded well . . . Average on gradual descent since .330 campaign in '76, his best . . . Born Sept. 1, 1949, at Cincinnati . . . Won sixth straight Gold Glove in '80, only Phils' outfielder to win as many as one . . . Former Vietnam veteran who came up in Giants' system . . . Swapped to Phillies for Willie Montanez during '75 season . . . Dropped fly in '78 playoffs costly to club and embarrassing to star fielder.

Year	Club	Pos.	G	AB	R	H	2B	3B	HR	RBI	SB	Avg.
1972	San Francisco ...	OF	125	458	62	122	26	7	12	58	13	.266
1973	San Francisco ...	OF	144	587	81	187	30	10	11	76	24	.319
1974	San Francisco ...	OF	135	538	74	153	31	3	8	50	21	.284
1975	S.F.-Phil.	OF	116	426	54	116	26	8	5	50	25	.272
1976	Philadelphia.....	OF	146	531	75	175	37	6	6	68	29	.330
1977	Philadelphia.....	OF	139	571	85	167	27	10	14	74	22	.292
1978	Philadelphia.....	OF	155	598	62	172	34	3	11	68	33	.288
1979	Philadelphia.....	OF	148	548	70	154	28	6	13	61	26	.281
1980	Philadelphia.....	OF	143	549	59	142	31	3	11	73	25	.259
	Totals..........		1251	4806	622	1388	270	56	91	578	218	.289

BOB BOONE 33 6-2 202 **Bats R Throws R**

Troublesome post-operative left knee hampered his bat for most of the 1980 regular season after he posted his career-best average (.286) in 1979 . . . But in the Phils' stretch run and post-season play, Boone regained his stroke and wound up hitting .412 with four RBI in the World Series . . . Three-time All-Star, two-time winner of the Gold Glove, Boone remains one of the most respected defensive backstops in the game . . . Son of 12-year major league infielder Ray Boone, who also wore No. 8 . . . Father was originally a catcher converted to an infielder, while Bob was an infielder (at Stanford) and converted to catcher . . . Born Nov. 19, 1947, in San Diego . . . Fitness enthusiast who owns and operates racquetball and Nautilus fitness centers in New Jersey . . . An astute, no-nonsense guy.

Year	Club	Pos.	G	AB	R	H	2B	3B	HR	RBI	SB	Avg.
1972	Philadelphia.....	C	16	51	4	14	1	0	1	4	1	.275
1973	Philadelphia.....	C	145	521	42	136	20	2	10	61	3	.261
1974	Philadelphia.....	C	146	488	41	118	24	3	3	52	3	.242
1975	Philadelphia.....	C-3B	97	289	28	71	14	2	2	20	1	.246
1976	Philadelphia.....	C-1B	121	361	40	98	18	2	4	54	2	.271
1977	Philadelphia.....	C-3B	132	440	55	125	26	4	11	66	5	.284
1978	Philadelphia.....	C-1B-OF	132	435	48	123	18	4	12	62	2	.283
1979	Philadelphia.....	C-3B	119	398	38	114	21	3	9	58	1	.286
1980	Philadelphia.....	C-3B	141	480	34	110	23	1	9	55	3	.229
	Totals..........		1049	3463	330	909	165	21	61	432	21	.262

LONNIE SMITH 25 5-9 170 **Bats R Throws R**

Tabbed as club's best prospect last spring, he justified faith by batting .339 in part-time role . . . Filled in admirably when Luzinski was hurt . . . Despite limited duty, led club in stolen bases . . . Club's No. 1 selection in '74 draft . . . Outstanding minor league credentials . . . Batted .315 with league-leading 66 steals in '78 at Oklahoma City and .330 with league-leading 106 runs for same Triple-A club in '79 . . . Battled Dodgers' Steve Howe for Rookie-of-Year honors . . . Born Dec. 22, 1955, at Chicago . . . Batted .340 in August . . . Created tough decision for Dallas Green when Luzinski was ready to play . . . Seems ready to start somewhere.

Year	Club	Pos.	G	AB	R	H	2B	3B	HR	RBI	SB	Avg.
1978	Philadelphia.....	OF	17	4	6	0	0	0	0	0	4	.000
1979	Philadelphia.....	OF	17	30	4	5	2	0	0	3	2	.167
1980	Philadelphia.....	OF	100	298	69	101	14	4	3	20	33	.339
	Totals..........		134	332	79	106	16	4	3	23	39	.319

STEVE CARLTON 36 6-5 210 **Bats L Throws L**

A Cy Young Award shoo-in last year, winning for third time . . . His 24 wins second highest total of career (27 in '72), embellished by the two biggest victories—in the World Series . . . But still won't talk to reporters . . . Voted top lefthander on team of decade . . . N.L. Pitcher of Month in May for 6-1 record, 1.65 ERA and 70 strikeouts in 60 innings . . . Majors' strikeout leader with 286 . . . Born Dec. 22, 1944, at Miami . . . Passed Mickey Lolich as all-time strikeout leader among southpaws . . . Lefty was 4-1 with a 2.11 ERA in June, when eight-game win string was snapped by Mets . . . Posted 4-2 record, 2.21 ERA in August . . . Set N.L. record with sixth career one-hitter, April 26, against Cardinals . . . Shares nine-inning strikeout mark of 19 . . . Winningest pitcher last 10 years.

Year	Club	G	IP	W	L	Pct.	SO	BB	H	ERA
1965	St. Louis	15	25	0	0	.000	21	8	27	2.52
1966	St. Louis	9	52	3	3	.500	25	18	56	3.12
1967	St. Louis	30	193	14	9	.609	168	62	173	2.98
1968	St. Louis	34	232	13	11	.542	162	61	214	2.99
1969	St. Louis	31	236	17	11	.607	210	93	185	2.17
1970	St. Louis	34	254	10	19	.345	193	109	239	3.72
1971	St. Louis	37	273	20	9	.690	172	98	275	3.56
1972	Philadelphia	41	346	27	10	.730	310	87	257	1.98
1973	Philadelphia	40	293	13	20	.394	223	113	293	3.90
1974	Philadelphia	39	291	16	13	.552	240	136	249	3.22
1975	Philadelphia	37	225	15	14	.517	192	104	217	3.56
1976	Philadelphia	35	253	20	7	.741	195	72	224	3.13
1977	Philadelphia	36	283	23	10	.697	198	89	229	2.64
1978	Philadelphia	34	247	16	13	.552	161	63	228	2.84
1979	Philadelphia	35	251	18	11	.621	213	89	202	3.62
1980	Philadelphia	38	304	24	9	.727	286	90	243	2.34
	Totals	525	3788	249	169	.596	2969	1292	3311	3.02

BAKE McBRIDE 32 6-2 190 **Bats L Throws R**

Regained his '77 touch by batting above .300 last year . . . Got going with .330 May and kept it up . . . Underrated, yet ranked with Schmidt and Rose as club's top run producers with career-high game-winning RBI (14) and RBI (87) totals . . . Started slowly in '79, but batted .371 in September to finish at .280 . . . Rookie of Year in '74, batting .309 with Cardinals . . . Came to Phillies in '77 swap and batted .339 in 85 games as club's new leadoff batter . . . Born Feb. 3, 1949, at Fulton, Mo. . . . Because of 9.8 speed in 100, is one of toughest players to double on basepaths . . . Has degree in P.E. from Westminster (Mo.) College.

Year	Club	Pos.	G	AB	R	H	2B	3B	HR	RBI	SB	Avg.
1973	St. Louis	OF	40	63	8	19	3	0	0	5	0	.300
1974	St. Louis	OF	150	559	81	173	19	5	6	56	30	.309
1975	St. Louis	OF	116	413	70	124	10	9	5	36	26	.300
1976	St. Louis	OF	72	272	40	91	13	4	3	24	10	.335
1977	St. L.-Phil.	OF	128	402	76	127	25	6	15	61	36	.316
1978	Philadelphia.....	OF	122	472	68	127	20	4	10	49	28	.269
1979	Philadelphia.....	OF	151	582	82	163	16	12	12	60	25	.280
1980	Philadelphia.....	OF	137	554	68	171	33	10	9	87	13	.309
	Totals..........		916	3317	493	995	139	50	60	378	168	.300

DICK RUTHVEN 30 6-3 190 — Bats R Throws R

Made marvelous comeback in '80 following injury-riddled '79 in which he went 7-5 . . . Won career-high 17 games and formed solid one-two punch with Carlton . . . Did some of finest work in August, going 3-1, 2.61 . . . Originally signed by Phils in '73, jumping from college campus (Fresno State) to majors . . . Returned to minors for seasoning in '75 . . . Was swapped to White Sox and then to Atlanta before Phils reacquired him in middle of '78 . . . Born March 27, 1951, at Sacramento, Cal. . . . Was 13-5 after joining Phils in '78 and off to a 6-0 start in '79 when elbow problems struck . . . Beat Expos to break first-place tie Oct. 3.

Year	Club	G	IP	W	L	Pct.	SO	BB	H	ERA
1973	Philadelphia..............	25	128	6	9	.400	98	75	125	4.22
1974	Philadelphia..............	35	213	9	13	.409	153	116	182	4.01
1975	Philadelphia..............	11	41	2	2	.500	26	22	37	4.17
1976	Atlanta..................	36	240	14	17	.452	142	90	255	4.20
1977	Atlanta..................	25	151	7	13	.350	84	62	158	4.23
1978	Atlanta-Philadelphia	33	232	15	11	.577	120	56	214	3.38
1979	Philadelphia..............	20	122	7	5	.583	58	37	121	4.28
1980	Philadelphia..............	33	223	17	10	.630	86	74	241	3.55
	Totals....................	218	1350	77	80	.490	767	532	1333	3.93

LARRY BOWA 35 5-10 155 — Bats S Throws R

A key man in Phillies' rush to the top . . . Got clutch hits in Games 4 and 5 of playoffs vs. Astros and then followed with .375 average (9 for 24) in Series . . . Had steady season at plate with .267 average, two homers and 39 RBI . . . Stole 21 bases, too, for seventh straight season of 20-or-more SBs . . . Holds major league record for lifetime fielding percentage by a shortstop playing a minimum of 1,000 games . . . Won Gold Gloves in 1972 and 1978 . . . Born Dec. 6, 1945, in

Sacramento . . . Has lost some of his range afield, but what he gets to, he catches . . . At plate he goes up swinging; he drew only 24 walks last season.

Year	Club	Pos.	G	AB	R	H	2B	3B	HR	RBI	SB	Avg.
1970	Philadelphia.....	SS-2B	145	547	50	137	17	6	0	34	24	.250
1971	Philadelphia.....	SS	159	650	74	162	18	5	0	25	28	.249
1972	Philadelphia.....	SS	152	579	67	145	11	13	1	31	17	.250
1973	Philadelphia.....	SS	122	446	42	94	11	3	0	23	10	.211
1974	Philadelphia.....	SS	162	669	97	184	19	10	1	36	39	.275
1975	Philadelphia.....	SS	136	583	79	178	18	9	2	38	24	.305
1976	Philadelphia.....	SS	156	624	71	155	15	9	0	49	30	.248
1977	Philadelphia.....	SS	154	624	93	175	19	3	4	41	32	.280
1978	Philadelphia.....	SS	156	654	78	192	31	5	3	43	27	.294
1979	Philadelphia.....	SS	147	539	74	130	17	11	0	31	20	.241
1980	Philadelphia.....	SS	147	540	57	144	16	4	2	39	21	.267
	Totals..........		1636	6455	782	1696	192	68	13	390	272	.263

TUG McGRAW 36 6-0 184 Bats R Throws L

N.L. lifetime leader in saves (164), adding to total with 20 last season . . . Regained form as premier fireman, keeping ERA under 2.00 . . . Went on 21-day disabled list in June, but didn't allow a run in first seven appearances after coming off . . . One of game's grand characters, rose to prominence with Miracle Mets of '69 . . . Born Aug. 30, 1944, at Martinez, Cal., also birthplace of Joe DiMaggio . . . Set Mets' club record with 27 saves in '72 . . . A clubhouse wit who doesn't take himself seriously . . . Has game in perspective . . . Saved division-clincher at Montreal and added two more saves in playoffs and a win and two saves in the Series.

Year	Club	G	IP	W	L	Pct.	SO	BB	H	ERA
1965	New York (NL)...........	37	98	2	7	.222	57	48	88	3.31
1966	New York (NL)...........	15	62	2	9	.182	34	25	72	5.37
1967	New York (NL)...........	4	17	0	3	.000	18	13	13	7.94
1969	New York (NL)...........	42	100	9	3	.750	92	47	89	2.25
1970	New York (NL)...........	57	91	4	6	.400	81	49	77	3.26
1971	New York (NL)...........	51	111	11	4	.733	109	41	73	1.70
1972	New York (NL)...........	54	106	8	6	.571	92	40	71	1.70
1973	New York (NL)...........	60	119	5	6	.455	81	55	106	3.86
1974	New York (NL)...........	41	89	6	11	.353	54	32	96	4.15
1975	Philadelphia.............	56	103	9	6	.600	55	36	84	2.97
1976	Philadelphia.............	58	97	7	6	.538	76	42	81	2.51
1977	Philadelphia.............	45	79	7	3	.700	58	24	62	2.62
1978	Philadelphia.............	55	90	8	7	.533	63	23	82	3.20
1979	Philadelphia.............	65	84	4	3	.571	57	29	83	5.14
1980	Philadelphia.............	57	92	5	4	.556	75	23	62	1.47
	Totals...................	697	1338	87	84	.509	1002	527	1139	3.08

TOP PROSPECTS

KEITH MORELAND 26 6-0 200 Bats R Throws R
Perhaps the club's catcher of the future . . . Bob Boone's backup batted above .300 in bigs after posting .300 credentials in Triple A . . . Born May 2, 1954, at Dallas . . . Strong arm and rated good defensively . . . Stock improved considerably in one year . . . So did righthander Marty Bystrom, who was a mere 6-5, 3.65 at Oklahoma City before going 5-0 with a 1.50 ERA with Phillies in September.

MANAGER DALLAS GREEN: Guided club to 19-11 record after succeeding Danny Ozark in September 1979, but most experts figured Phils no better than third in '80 . . . Green fooled them by taking club to its first World Championship ever . . . Off to a 10 start, the Phils were emphatically chewed out when Bucs swept four games . . . Then they won seven of next eight . . . Born Aug. 4, 1934, at Newport, Del. . . . Pitched pro ball from 1955 to 1967, including parts of six years with Phillies . . . Began managing in '68 and won a pennant in '69 . . . Headed club's minor league development from 1972 until named manager . . . Proved his worth in first full year as big league skipper . . . Earned respect of the players but there were the disgruntled ones . . . Attended U. of Delaware . . . Best year in bigs was '63, 7-5 with a 3.23 ERA for Phils. . . . Also worked briefly for Senators and Mets.

GREATEST TEAM

Philadelphia hadn't won a pennant since 1950 and was teased in the mid-Seventies by division champs, but no club stirred the imagination like the '80 Phillies. Picked to finish third behind the Pirates and the Expos, the Phils surged behind rookie manager Dallas Green and won the division title on the final weekend, rallied to beat Houston in the playoffs and the Royals in six games to win their first World Series in the 77-year history of the event.

It ended, appropriately, in Philadelphia, with Tug McGraw on the mound after Cy Young Award winner Steve Carlton had kept the Royals at bay for seven innings. And it ended the way it did because the season's MVP Mike Schmidt put together eight hits (including a two-run single in the finale) and seven RBI for Series MVP honors.

It was more than McGraw and Carlton and Schmidt. The parade of Philadelphia factors in the Series ranged from Larry Bowa and Bob Boone to Del Unser and a hustler named Pete Rose, who in his exciting fashion snared a foul ball that popped out of Boone's glove in the ninth inning of the final game. It was something even Pete–like Philadelphia–had never done before.

ALL-TIME PHILLIE LEADERS

BATTING: Frank O'Doul, .398, 1929
HRs: Mike Schmidt, 48, 1980
RBIs: Chuck Klein, 170, 1930
STEALS: Sherry Magee, 55, 1906
WINS: Grover Alexander, 33, 1916
STRIKEOUTS: Steve Carlton, 310, 1972

PITTSBURGH PIRATES

TEAM DIRECTORY: Chairman: John Galbreath; Pres.: Daniel Galbreath; Exec. VP: Harding Peterson; Dir. Minor Leagues-Scouting: Murray Cook; VP Marketing/Dir. Pub. Rel.: Jack Schrom; Trav. Sec.: Charles Muse; Mgr.: Chuck Tanner. Home: Three Rivers Stadium (53,869). Field distances: 335, l.f. line; 375, l.c.; 400, c.f.; 375, r.c.; 335, r.f. line. Spring training: Bradenton, Fla.

SCOUTING REPORT

HITTING: What a difference a year makes for the 1979 World Series champs. Virtually everyone slumped last season—except standout reserves Lee Lacy and Mike Easler—and the sudden demise of Willie Stargell splintered the once-mighty Lumber Company.

There's still plenty of thunder, but only Dave Parker, the circuit's top active lifetime hitter, seems a cinch to have a solid year at the plate. Age is creeping up on most of the other regulars and many of those veterans didn't respond last September in the manner to which Chuck Tanner is accustomed.

Easler was phenomenal at .338 and punched a team-leading 21 homers as a part-time player, but it remains to be seen if the 1980 sensation can do it again. Ditto for Lacy, who slapped the ball at a .335 clip off the bench and isn't likely to play much more this year.

PITCHING: It should be better than last year's version if John Candelaria (11-14) and Don Robinson (7-10) live up to their potential, but age is definitely a factor with ace Jim Bibby (19-6 at age 35) and a veteran bullpen. Even Bibby had trouble winning during the second half.

The bullpen is the deepest in baseball, but how long will Kent Tekulve, Grant Jackson and Enrique Romo be able to perform at peak efficiency? Newcomers Bob Owchinko and Victor Cruz will add depth to the staff, with Owchinko and Rick Rhoden expected to compensate for the loss of disenchanted Bert Blyleven.

FIELDING: Also slipped, though Tim Foli had the highest fielding percentage (.981) among N.L. shortstops and outfielders Omar Moreno and Parker ranked with the best. The shift of Phil Garner to second to make room for Bill Madlock at third worked so well in the pennant drive of '79, but was less than suc-

Jim Bibby led the league in winning percentage (.760).

cessful last year. If Stargell's knees keep him inactive, either Madlock or Bill Robinson may get the job at first.

OUTLOOK: Not encouraging after a late-season fade and talk of dissension among the ranks. The Family simply isn't as together as it was two years ago and does not seem capable, on paper at least, of keeping up with the improving Expos and Phillies.

In fact, Pittsburgh may be heading the other way. If the youth movements underway in St. Louis, Chicago and New York suddenly bear fruit, it's conceivable the Bucs could suddenly find themselves in the second division instead of battling for a pennant.

There's just too much age and too many question marks to take this club as seriously anymore. Tanner still has the ability to get the most out of his entire roster, but the truth is that the Bucs don't have 25 better players than either the Expos or the Phillies, nor do they have the influx of young talent that those two other clubs possess.

PITTSBURGH PIRATES 1981 ROSTER

MANAGER Chuck Tanner
Coaches—Harvey Haddix, Joe Lonnett, Al Monchak, Bob Skinner

PITCHERS

No.	Name	1980 Club	W-L	IP	SO	ERA	B-T	Ht.	Wt.	Born
–	Barez, Angel	Salem	11-5	–	–	4.14	R-R	6-1	180	9/15/60 Puerto Rico
26	Bibby, Jim	Pittsburgh	19-6	238	144	3.33	R-R	6-5	250	10/29/44 Franklinton, NC
–	Britt, Douglas				Did not play		L-L	6-5	185	11/2/57 Orange, CA
45	Candelaria, John	Pittsburgh	11-14	233	97	4.02	L-L	6-7	232	11/6/53 New York, NY
–	Cruz, Victor	Cleveland	6-7	86	88	3.45	R-R	5-9	215	12/24/57 Dominican Republic
23	Jackson, Grant	Pittsburgh	8-4	71	31	2.92	B-L	6-0	204	9/28/42 Fostoria, OH
–	Lee, Mark	Haw-Portland	5-5	57	36	4.11	R-R	6-4	225	6/14/53 Inglewood, CA
		Pittsburgh	0-1	6	2	4.50				
–	Long, Robert	Portland	4-4	92	54	4.26	R-R	6-3	178	11/11/54 Jasper, TN
–	Mahler, Mickey	Portland	13-8	164	128	2.69	B-L	6-3	190	7/30/52 Montgomery, AL
		Pittsburgh	0-0	1	1	63.00				
–	Mohorcic, Dale	Salem	7-5	111	85	2.18	R-R	6-3	205	1/25/56 Cleveland, OH
–	Owchinko, Bob	Cleveland	2-9	114	66	5.29	L-L	6-2	195	1/1/55 Detroit, MI
–	Perez, Pascual	Portland	12-10	160	106	4.05	R-R	6-2	162	5/17/57 Dominican Republic
		Pittsburgh	0-1	12	7	3.75				
43	Robinson, Don	Pittsburgh	7-10	160	103	3.99	R-R	6-4	231	6/8/57 Ashland, KY
29	Rhoden, Rick	Portland	6-3	52	24	2.94	R-R	6-3	195	5/16/53 Boynton Beach, FL
		Pittsburgh	7-5	127	70	3.83				
15	Romo, Enrique	Pittsburgh	5-5	124	82	3.27	R-R	5-11	185	7/15/47 Mexico
57	Scurry, Rod	Pittsburgh	0-2	38	28	2.13	L-L	6-2	180	3/17/56 Sacramento, CA
44	Solomon, Eddie	Pittsburgh	7-3	100	35	2.70	R-R	6-3	190	2/9/51 Perry, GA
27	Tekulve, Kent	Pittsburgh	8-12	93	47	3.39	R-R	6-4	167	3/5/47 Cincinnati, OH
–	Vasquez, Rafael	Tacoma	8-10	139	55	5.37	R-R	6-0	160	6/28/58 Dominican Republic
–	Wiltbank, Ben	Buffalo	7-11	163	86	4.09	R-R	6-1	195	3/13/56 Lewes, DE

CATCHERS

No.	Name	1980 Club	H	HR	RBI	Pct.	B-T	Ht.	Wt.	Born
35	Alexander, Gary	Cleveland	40	5	31	.225	R-R	6-2	200	3/27/53 Los Angeles, CA
16	Nicosia, Steve	Pittsburgh	38	1	22	.216	R-R	5-10	185	8/6/55 Paterson, NJ
–	Ortiz, Adalberto	Buffalo	178	12	78	.346	R-R	5-11	174	10/24/59 Puerto Rico
		Portland	3	0	3	.111				
14	Ott, Ed	Pittsburgh	102	8	41	.260	L-R	5-10	190	7/11/51 Muncy, PA
–	Pena, Tony	Portland	148	9	77	.327	R-R	6-0	175	11/20/57 Dominican Republic
		Pittsburgh	9	0	1	.429				

INFIELDERS

No.	Name	1980 Club	H	HR	RBI	Pct.	B-T	Ht.	Wt.	Born
4	Berra, Dale	Pittsburgh	54	6	31	.220	R-R	6-0	190	12/13/56 Ridgewood, NJ
–	Bevacqua, Kurt	SD-Pittsburgh	26	0	16	.228	R-R	6-2	195	1/23/48 Miami, FL
10	Foli, Tim	Pittsburgh	131	3	38	.265	R-R	6-0	175	12/8/50 Culver City, CA
3	Garner, Phil	Pittsburgh	142	5	58	.259	R-R	5-10	177	4/30/49 Jefferson City, TN
49	Law, Vance	Portland	100	5	54	.295	R-R	6-2	185	10/1/56 Boise, ID
		Pittsburgh	17	0	3	.230				
5	Madlock, Bill	Pittsburgh	137	10	53	.277	R-R	5-11	180	1/12/51 Memphis, TN
8	Stargell, Willie	Pittsburgh	53	11	38	.262	L-L	6-3	225	3/6/41 Earlsboro, OK
–	Vargas, Hediberto	Buffalo	138	24	87	.271	R-R	6-4	205	2/23/59 Puerto Rico

OUTFIELDERS

No.	Name	1980 Club	H	HR	RBI	Pct.	B-T	Ht.	Wt.	Born
–	Boyland, Dorian	Portland	116	14	67	.281	L-L	6-4	204	1/6/55 Chicago, IL
24	Easler, Mike	Pittsburgh	133	21	74	.338	L-R	6-1	196	11/29/50 Cleveland, OH
27	Lacy, Lee	Pittsburgh	93	7	33	.335	R-R	6-1	175	4/10/48 Longview, TX
18	Moreno, Omar	Pittsburgh	168	2	36	.249	L-L	6-3	175	10/24/52 Panama
39	Parker, Dave	Pittsburgh	153	17	79	.295	L-R	6-5	220	6/9/51 Jackson, MS
28	Robinson, Bill	Pittsburgh	78	12	36	.287	R-R	6-3	197	6/26/43 McKeesport, PA
–	Rodriguez, Jose	Salem	132	13	75	.288	R-R	6-1	173	2/25/59 Dominican Republic

PIRATE PROFILES

DAVE PARKER 29 6-5 220 — Bats L Throws R

Plagued by injuries, slipped below customary high level in '80, but still batted respectable .295 . . . Named to second squad on team of decade . . . Menacing appearance at plate led to nickname, Cobra . . . Injuries to heel, elbow and knee made '80 frustrating, but biggest problem was abusive Pittsburgh fans, who threw objects and compelled Dave to ask for trade . . . Batted .354 in August to help keep defending champs in contention . . . Born June 9, 1951, at Cincinnati . . . Had three game-winning RBI in post-season play in '79 . . . Two-time batting champ in 1977-78 . . . MVP of 1979 All-Star Game for game-saving throw . . . A Gold Glove outfielder . . . MVP in '78 . . . In '80, failed to hit .300 for first time since '74 . . . A great talent because of all-around skills.

Year	Club	Pos.	G	AB	R	H	2B	3B	HR	RBI	SB	Avg.
1973	Pittsburgh......	OF	54	139	17	40	9	1	4	14	1	.288
1974	Pittsburgh......	OF-1B	73	220	27	62	10	3	4	29	3	.282
1975	Pittsburgh......	OF	148	558	75	172	35	10	25	101	8	.308
1976	Pittsburgh......	OF	138	537	82	168	28	10	13	90	19	.313
1977	Pittsburgh......	OF-2B	159	637	107	215	44	8	21	88	17	.338
1978	Pittsburgh......	OF	148	581	102	194	32	12	30	117	20	.334
1979	Pittsburgh......	OF	158	622	109	193	45	7	25	94	20	.310
1980	Pittsburgh......	OF	139	518	71	153	31	1	17	79	10	.295
	Totals..........		1017	3812	590	1197	234	52	139	612	98	.314

BILL MADLOCK 30 5-11 180 — Bats R Throws R

Mad Dog was just that last year when an incident with umpire Jerry Crawford led to a 15-day suspension and a $5,000 fine . . . The altercation affected his season, but couldn't keep him from batting a torrid .388 in August . . . Failed to reach .300 level a second straight season after six in a row, including successive batting titles with Cubs in 1975-76 . . . Unappreciated by Giants and swapped in June '79 after .261 start . . . Batted .328 with Bucs and hit .375 in World Series . . . Born Jan. 12, 1951, at Memphis . . . Bucs were 36-33 when Madlock was acquired in '79, soaring to 62-31 with him . . . As a Rangers' farmhand, tied PCL record with six hits in as many at-bats for Spokane in '73 . . . A controversial player because he spoke his mind—at least until he reached Pirates.

Year	Club	Pos.	G	AB	R	H	2B	3B	HR	RBI	SB	Avg.
1973	Texas	3B	21	77	16	27	5	3	1	5	3	.351
1974	Chicago (NL)	3B	128	453	65	142	21	5	9	54	11	.313
1975	Chicago (NL)	3B	130	514	77	182	29	7	7	64	9	.354
1976	Chicago (NL)	3B	142	514	68	174	36	1	15	84	15	.339
1977	San Francisco	2B-3B	140	533	70	161	28	1	12	46	13	.302
1978	San Francisco	2B-1B	122	447	76	138	26	3	15	44	16	.309
1979	SF-Pitts.	3B-2B-1B	154	560	85	167	26	5	14	85	32	.298
1980	Pittsburgh	3B-2B	137	494	62	137	22	4	10	53	16	.277
	Totals		974	3592	519	1128	193	29	83	435	115	.314

MIKE EASLER 30 6-1 196 — Bats L Throws R

A remarkable season as a part-timer last year, batted way above .300 all season and topped club in homers . . . Batted .382 with six homers and 16 RBI in June . . . Became first Buc to hit for the cycle since 1974 when he connected June 12 against Cincy . . . Had 10 homers in first 82 at-bats . . . Known as Hit Man among teammates . . . Born Nov. 29, 1950, at Cleveland . . . Long and distinguished minor league career until he stayed with Bucs in '79 . . . Won batting titles at Tulsa (.352) in '76 and at Columbus (.330) in '78 . . . Made the grade relatively late, but is here to stay and likely will be a regular this season . . . Previously saw service with Astros and Angels . . . Adequate outfielder . . . Batted .341 in September.

Year	Club	Pos.	G	AB	R	H	2B	3B	HR	RBI	SB	Avg.
1973	Houston	OF	6	7	1	0	0	0	0	0	0	.000
1974	Houston	PH	15	15	0	1	0	0	0	0	0	.067
1975	Houston	PH	5	5	0	0	0	0	0	0	0	.000
1976	California	DH	21	54	6	13	1	1	0	4	1	.241
1977	Pittsburgh	OF	10	18	3	8	2	0	1	5	0	.444
1979	Pittsburgh	OF	55	54	8	15	1	1	2	11	0	.278
1980	Pittsburgh	OF	132	393	66	133	27	3	21	74	5	.338
	Totals		244	546	84	170	31	5	24	94	6	.311

LEE LACY 32 6-1 175 — Bats R Throws R

Supersub on a team which always boasts of a strong bench . . . Unspectacular as a free-agent acquisition in '79, but zoomed to .335 in '80 . . . Good start set tone . . . Collected 25 hits in 59 trips, .424, in May . . . Batted .314 as Dodgers' part-timer in '75 . . . Went to Braves in swap for Dusty Baker in '76, But was reacquired by L.A. one year later . . . Originally a second-baseman, but has been used mostly as an outfielder by Bucs . . . Born April 10, 1948, at Longview, Tex. . . . Made jump from Double-A to bigs after batting .372 for El

Paso in '72 . . . Joined Dodgers that summer and hit safely in 12 of first 13 games.

Year	Club	Pos.	G	AB	R	H	2B	3B	HR	RBI	SB	Avg.
1972	Los Angeles.....	2B	60	243	34	63	7	3	0	12	5	.259
1973	Los Angeles.....	2B	57	135	14	28	2	0	0	8	2	.207
1974	Los Angeles.....	2B-3B	48	78	13	22	6	0	0	8	2	.282
1975	Los Angeles.....	SS-2B-OF	101	306	44	96	11	5	7	40	5	.314
1976	Atl.-L.A.	2B-OF-3B	103	338	42	91	11	3	3	34	3	.269
1977	Los Angeles.....	OF-2B-3B	75	169	28	45	7	0	6	21	4	.266
1978	Los Angeles.....	OF-2B-3B	103	245	29	64	16	4	13	40	7	.261
1979	Pittsburgh	OF-2B	84	182	17	45	9	3	5	15	6	.247
1980	Pittsburgh	OF-2B	109	278	45	93	20	4	7	33	18	.335
	Totals..........		740	1974	266	547	89	22	41	211	52	.277

PHIL GARNER 28 5-10 177 Bats R Throws R

Slumped after batting a career-high .293 in '79 and went back to previous .260 level . . . Still a vital member of squad because of fielding and clutch-hitting ability . . . A thinking player with managerial potential . . . Wanted badly by Chuck Tanner in '77, so Bucs relinquished some top young prospects to get him . . . Can play all infield positions, but shifted from third to second when club obtained Madlock . . . Born April 30, 1952, at Jefferson City, Tenn. . . . Became first N.L. player to hit grand-slam homers in successive games since 1901 when he did it in '78 . . . Batted .417 in '79 playoffs and tied seven-game record with .500 mark in Series . . . An All-America at U. of Tennessee.

Year	Club	Pos.	G	AB	R	H	2B	3B	HR	RBI	SB	Avg.
1973	Oakland........	3B	9	5	0	0	0	0	0	0	0	.000
1974	Oakland........	3B-SS-2B	30	28	4	5	1	0	0	1	1	.179
1975	Oakland........	2B-SS	160	488	46	120	21	5	6	54	4	.246
1976	Oakland........	2B	159	555	54	145	29	12	8	74	35	.261
1977	Pittsburgh	3B-2B-SS	153	585	99	152	35	10	17	77	32	.260
1978	Pittsburgh	2B-3B-SS	154	528	66	138	25	9	10	66	27	.261
1979	Pittsburgh	2B-3B-SS	150	549	76	161	32	8	11	59	17	.293
1980	Pittsburgh	2B-3B,SS	151	548	62	142	27	6	5	58	32	.259
	Totals..........		966	3286	407	863	170	50	57	389	148	.263

TIM FOLI 30 6-0 175 Bats R Throws R

Didn't match his outstanding .288 season which helped club to '79 championship, but still made solid contribution . . . Went on disabled list with shin injury, but returned to hit in 18 straight games in July . . . Was nation's No. 1 draft choice for Mets in '68 and was known for feisty demeanor while with Mets, Expos and Giants . . . Not a favorite with umpires at the time, but settled down after joining Bucs in '79 . . . Born Dec. 8, 1950, at Culver City, Cal. . . . Turned down

Notre Dame and USC scholarships in football following prep quarterback success . . . Traded from Mets for Frank Taveras at start of '79 season . . . Starred in post-season play, batting .333 with no strikeouts in 10 games.

Year	Club	Pos.	G	AB	R	H	2B	3B	HR	RBI	SB	Avg.
1970	New York (NL)..	3B-SS	5	11	0	4	0	0	0	1	0	.364
1971	New York (NL)..	2B-3B-SS-OF	97	288	32	65	12	2	0	24	5	.226
1972	Montreal.......	SS-2B	149	540	45	130	12	2	2	35	11	.241
1973	Montreal.......	SS-2B-OF	126	458	37	110	11	0	2	36	6	.240
1974	Montreal.......	SS-3B	121	441	41	112	10	3	0	39	8	.254
1975	Montreal.......	SS-2B	152	572	64	136	25	2	1	29	13	.238
1976	Montreal.......	SS-3B	149	546	41	144	36	1	6	54	6	.264
1977	Mtl.-S.F.........	SS-2B-3B-OF	117	425	32	94	22	4	4	30	2	.221
1978	New York (NL)..	SS	113	413	37	106	21	1	1	27	2	.257
1979	N.Y. (NL)-Pit....	SS	136	532	70	153	23	1	1	65	6	.288
1980	Pittsburgh......	SS	127	495	61	131	22	0	3	38	11	.265
	Totals..........		1292	4721	460	1185	194	16	20	378	70	.251

OMAR MORENO 28 6-3 175 — Bats L Throws L

Like most of his teammates, Omar slumped at the plate last year, but made most of opportunities by swiping 96 bases . . . Batted .303 in June . . . Set Bucs' standard with 71 steals in '78 and improved to 77 in '79 . . . Increased total last year while battling N.L. newcomer Ron LeFlore for title . . . Batted .333 in '79 World Series, but failed to steal . . . Born Oct. 24, 1952, at Puerto Armuelles, Panama . . . An excellent outfielder who has supplanted Garry Maddox as premier N.L. gloveman in center . . . Was only 16 when he broke into pro ball in '69, batting .290 at Bradenton . . . Stole only 59 bases in first four years until exploding for 77 in Class A in '73.

Year	Club	Pos.	G	AB	R	H	2B	3B	HR	RBI	SB	Avg.
1975	Pittsburgh......	OF	6	6	1	1	0	0	0	0	1	.167
1976	Pittsburgh......	OF	48	122	24	33	4	1	2	12	15	.270
1977	Pittsburgh......	OF	150	492	69	118	19	9	7	34	53	.240
1978	Pittsburgh......	OF	155	515	95	121	15	7	2	33	71	.235
1979	Pittsburgh......	OF	162	695	110	196	21	12	8	69	77	.282
1980	Pittsburgh......	OF	162	676	87	168	20	13	2	36	96	.249
	Totals..........		683	2506	386	637	79	42	21	184	313	.254

JIM BIBBY 36 6-5 250 — Bats R Throws R

Obviously improving with age, had best season in '80 with 19-6 record . . . Credits experience and support for making him a big winner with Pittsburgh . . . Was 4-0 in June and 4-0 in July, making All-Star team . . . Lost three straight trying for No. 16 . . . In '79, had 1.29 ERA in playoffs and 2.70 mark in Series, but didn't receive a decision in post-season play . . . Born Oct. 29, 1944, at Franklinton, N.C. . . . Hurled a no-hitter for Texas against Oakland in '73 . . . Topped N.L. with .750 percentage (12-4) in '79 . . . Was 8-2 down the stretch after joining rotation for good . . . Was a spot starter and long reliever for Bucs in 1978-79 until injuries to others gave him big break . . . Brother of NBA guard Henry Bibby.

Year	Club	G	IP	W	L	Pct.	SO	BB	H	ERA
1972	St. Louis	6	40	1	3	.250	28	19	29	3.38
1973	St. Louis	6	16	0	2	.000	12	17	19	9.56
1973	Texas	26	180	9	10	.474	155	106	121	3.25
1974	Texas	41	264	19	19	.500	149	113	255	4.74
1975	Tex.-Clev.	36	181	7	15	.318	93	78	172	3.88
1976	Cleveland	34	163	13	7	.650	84	56	162	3.20
1977	Cleveland	37	207	12	13	.480	141	73	197	3.57
1978	Pittsburgh	34	107	8	7	.533	72	39	100	3.53
1979	Pittsburgh	34	138	12	4	.750	103	47	110	2.80
1980	Pittsburgh	35	238	19	6	.760	144	88	210	3.33
	Totals	289	1534	100	86	.538	948	636	1375	3.68

GRANT JACKSON 38 6-0 204 Bats S Throws L

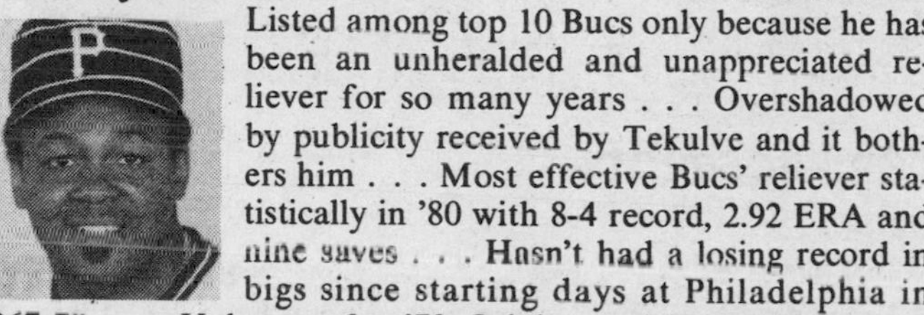

Listed among top 10 Bucs only because he has been an unheralded and unappreciated reliever for so many years . . . Overshadowed by publicity received by Tekulve and it bothers him . . . Most effective Bucs' reliever statistically in '80 with 8-4 record, 2.92 ERA and nine saves . . . Hasn't had a losing record in bigs since starting days at Philadelphia in 1967-70 . . . Unbeaten for '73 Orioles and '76 Yankees . . . ERA under 3.00 in six of last 10 years as reliever . . . Born Sept. 28, 1942, at Fostoria, Ohio . . . Pitched in six World Series games and is 1-0 with two runs allowed in 10 and two-thirds innings . . . Attended Bowling Green U.

Year	Club	G	IP	W	L	Pct.	SO	BB	H	ERA
1965	Philadelphia	6	14	1	1	.500	15	5	17	7.07
1966	Philadelphia	2	2	0	0	.000	0	3	2	4.50
1967	Philadelphia	43	84	2	3	.400	83	43	86	3.86
1968	Philadelphia	33	61	1	6	.143	49	20	59	2.95
1969	Philadelphia	38	253	14	18	.438	180	92	237	3.34
1970	Philadelphia	32	150	5	15	.250	104	61	170	5.28
1971	Baltimore	29	78	4	3	.571	51	20	72	3.12
1972	Baltimore	32	41	1	1	.500	34	9	33	2.63
1973	Baltimore	45	80	8	0	1.000	47	24	54	1.91
1974	Baltimore	49	67	6	4	.600	56	22	48	2.55
1975	Baltimore	41	48	4	3	.571	39	21	42	3.38
1976	Balt.-N.Y. (AL)	34	78	7	1	.875	39	25	57	2.54
1977	Pittsburgh	49	91	5	3	.625	41	39	81	3.86
1978	Pittsburgh	60	77	7	5	.583	45	32	89	3.27
1979	Pittsburgh	72	82	8	5	.615	39	35	67	2.96
1980	Pittsburgh	61	71	8	4	.667	31	20	71	2.92
	Totals	626	1277	81	72	.529	853	471	1185	3.40

KENT TEKULVE 34 6-4 167 **Bats R Throws R**

Leader of bullpen regarded as deepest in N.L. . . . Lost more games and had highest ERA last year, but still finished with 21 saves . . . Totaled 31 in both '78 and '79 . . . The lithe reliever has been consistently outstanding, ranking second only to Sutter for effectiveness . . . "I don't see how righthanders hit him," said Orioles' skipper Earl Weaver after Teke's three saves in '79 World Series . . . Born March 5, 1947, at Cincinnati . . . A late bloomer, didn't reach bigs to stay until age 28 . . . Made up for lost time . . . Had 10-1 record in '77 and league-leading 91 appearances in '78 and 94 in '79, a club record . . . Began pitching professionally at 22 . . . Graduated from Marietta (Ohio) College with education degree.

Year	Club	G	IP	W	L	Pct.	SO	BB	H	ERA
1974	Pittsburgh	8	9	1	1	.500	6	5	12	6.00
1975	Pittsburgh	34	56	1	2	.333	28	23	43	2.25
1976	Pittsburgh	64	103	5	3	.625	68	25	91	2.45
1977	Pittsburgh	72	103	10	1	.909	59	33	89	3.06
1978	Pittsburgh	91	135	8	7	.533	77	55	115	2.33
1979	Pittsburgh	94	134	10	8	.556	75	49	109	2.75
1980	Pittsburgh	78	93	8	12	.400	47	40	96	3.39
	Totals	441	633	43	34	.558	360	230	555	2.76

TOP PROSPECTS

VANCE LAW 24 6-2 185 **Bats R Throws R**

A lot of people in Bucs' organization hope he makes it because of tradition . . . Father Vern was star hurler for Pirates . . . Batted .310 in Triple A in '79 and .295 last year . . . Good shortstop prospect . . . Battling Dale Berra for chance to succeed Foli . . . Born Oct. 1, 1956, at Boise, Ida. . . . Reliever Rod Scurry also commands a long look after some sharp performances over second half last year.

MANAGER CHUCK TANNER: Is known for directing strong

finishes, but it didn't happen last year as Expos and Phillies left Bucs standing down the stretch . . . Loss of Willie Stargell, Madlock's slump and problems with pitchers Bert Blyleven and John Candelaria kept Bucs back . . . Was at his best in '79, guiding club to 98 wins, most since 1910, and a dramatic World Series triumph . . . Born July 4, 1929, at New

Castle, Pa. . . . Known as skipper who gets maximum out of bench—Easler and Lacy prime examples—thereby keeping players fresh at the finish . . . Placed second three straight years before grabbing gold ring in '79 . . . His '78 club just fell short with 37-12 record down to the wire . . . Took Phillies into final weekend after trailing by 11½ games on Aug. 12 . . . As a Braves' rookie in '55, Tanner homered on the first pitch he saw.

GREATEST TEAM

Going by the assumption that the modern ballplayers are more proficient than the turn-of-the-century variety, Pittsburgh's 1971 champions rate the edge over the 1909 club as the best Pirates ever. It's a tough decision, though, because the '09 group established a record which may never be broken. Manager Fred Clarke's club went 110-42 for a .724 percentage.

But the '71 Bucs were tough, too. They defeated the Cardinals by seven games to win the N.L. East with a 97-65 mark, took three out of four from the Giants in the playoffs and outlasted defending champion Baltimore to win the World Series, 4-3.

That was the year Willie Stargell won home run (48) and RBI (154) crowns, Roberto Clemente batted .341 one year before his death, Manny Sanguillen batted .319, Dock Ellis posted a 19-9 record and Dave Giusti saved 30 games. Bob Robertson whacked three homers in a playoff game, Clemente batted .414 in the Series and Steve Blass went 2-0 against the O's, including a four-hit, 2-1 clincher.

The '09 squad was powered by Honus Wagner's .339 average and Howie Camnitz' 25-6 record. Babe Adams was 3-0 in the Series as the Bucs edged Detroit and Ty Cobb, 4-3. The Pirates' team ERA that season was an astounding 2.07.

ALL-TIME PIRATE LEADERS

BATTING: Arky Vaughan, .385, 1935
HRs: Ralph Kiner, 54, 1949
RBIs: Paul Waner, 131, 1927
STEALS: Omar Moreno, 96, 1980
WINS: Jack Chesbro, 28, 1902
STRIKEOUTS: Bob Veale, 276, 1965

ST. LOUIS CARDINALS

TEAM DIRECTORY: Chairman of the Board-Pres.: August A. Busch, Jr.; GM-Mgr.: Whitey Herzog; Senior VP: Stan Musial; Dir. Player Personnel: Jim Bayens; VP Pub. Rel.: Jim Toomey; Trav. Sec.: Lee Thomas. Home: Busch Memorial Stadium (50,-100). Field distances: 330, l.f. line; 414, c.f.; 330, r.f. line. Spring training: St. Petersburg, Fla.

SCOUTING REPORT

HITTING: Wow! Nobody did it better than the Cardinals last year, but it didn't do them any good because the pitchers

Keith Hernandez narrowly missed his second batting title.

couldn't stop anyone. Still, the St. Louis batting order is imposing and there's plenty of young talent in the wings to make up for the loss of Ted Simmons and Kenny Reitz, who didn't do much hitting after May anyway.

The lineup remains tough from top to bottom and the addition of Sixto Lezcano and Darrell Porter may even hike the team batting average from the league-leading .275 of last year. Keith Hernandez (.321) and Garry Templeton (.319) were two-three in the batting race and George Hendrick (.302) cracked the Top 10.

Ken Oberkfell, the new third baseman, didn't qualify for the batting title, but batted .303 in 422 at-bats and new second baseman Tom Herr was a .312 hitter in Triple-A. The prospects for another hit-happy season are awesome, even if Bobby Bonds doesn't bounce back.

PITCHING: Here's the rub. The Cardinals' pitching was as putrid as the hitting was superb. St. Louis had a collective team earned-run average of 3.93, worst in the league, but there's been one significant improvement. Even if the starters don't get better, it's comforting for Whitey Herzog to know that Bruce Sutter is in the bullpen.

Sutter is simply baseball's best reliever and is assured of seeing plenty of work, because the starters are suspect. Bob Shirley will help, and so could a healthy John Fulgham and continued improvement from rookie Andy Rincon, who looked good down the stretch. Lary Sorensen, ex-Brewer, will take Pete Vuckovich's spot.

FIELDING: Almost as good as the hitting, for the Birds' .981 percentage was second best in the league. It's bound to slip a little with Reitz no longer at third, but Porter is tough behind the plate. Look for centerfielder Tony Scott, who made only one error in 330 chances last year, to keep busy. The DP combination is solid with Templeton and Herr.

OUTLOOK: Extremely encouraging since Herzog revamped things and accomplished his goal of landing Sutter. He simply couldn't afford to keep Rollie Fingers, too, so the bullpen isn't quite as strong as it was for a couple of days during the winter meetings.

If things break right and Sutter does what is expected, the Cardinals may even be able to challenge for a pennant. The offense and defense obviously are sound, so it all depends on the pitching. An additional standout on the mound could be all the club needs to make a strong bid this summer.

ST. LOUIS CARDINALS 1981 ROSTER

MANAGER Whitey Herzog
Coaches—Herb Kittle, Red Schoendienst, Hal Lanier, Chuck Hiller, Dave Ricketts

PITCHERS

No.	Name	1980 Club	W-L	IP	SO	ERA	B-T	Ht.	Wt.	Born
–	Edelen, Joe	Arkansas	13-5	161	100	2.63	R-R	6-0	165	9/16/55 Durant, OK
31	Forsch, Bob	St. Louis	11-10	215	87	3.77	R-R	6-4	200	1/13/50 Sacramento, CA
39	Frazier, George	Springfield	1-3	60	55	3.00	R-R	6-5	205	10/13/54 Oklahoma City, OK
		St. Louis	1-4	23	11	2.74				
41	Fulgham, John	St. Louis	4-6	85	48	3.39	R-R	6-2	195	6/9/56 St. Louis, MO
36	Kaat, Jim	New York (AL)	0-1	5	1	7.20	L-L	6-5	195	11/7/38 Zeeland, MI
		St. Louis	8-7	130	36	3.81				
–	LaPoint, Dave	Vancouver	7-4	93	64	2.81	L-L	6-3	205	7/29/59 Glens Falls, NY
		Milwaukee	1-0	15	5	6.00				
32	Littell, Mark	St. Louis	0-2	11	7	9.00	L-R	6-3	210	1/17/53 Cape Girardeau, MO
–	Little, Jeff	Springfield	3-4	62	46	4.50	R-L	6-6	220	12/25/54 Fremont, OH
		St. Louis	1-1	19	17	3.79				
–	Martin, John	Evans-Springfield	2-2	38	31	5.92	B-L	6-0	190	4/11/56 Wyandotte, MI
		Arkansas	1-1	27	19	1.67				
		St. Louis	2-3	42	23	4.29				
35	Martinez, Silvio	St. Louis	5-10	120	39	4.80	R-R	5-11	160	8/31/55 Dominican Republic
–	Rincon, Andy	Arkansas	10-7	172	138	3.40	R-R	6-3	195	3/5/59 Pico Rivera, CA
		St. Louis	3-1	31	22	2.61				
–	Sorensen, Lary	Milwaukee	12-10	196	54	3.67	R-R	6-2	200	10/4/55 Detroit, MI
–	Shirley, Bob	San Diego	11-12	137	67	3.55	R-L	5-11	185	6/25/54 Cushing, OK
–	Stuper, John	St. Petersburg	1-4	39	28	2.31	R-R	6-2	200	5/9/57 Butler, PA
		Arkansas	7-2	88	57	2.45				
–	Sutter, Bruce	Chicago (NL)	5-8	102	76	2.65	R-R	6-2	190	1/8/53 Lancaster, PA
42	Sykes, Bob	St. Louis	6-10	126	50	4.64	B-L	6-2	200	12/11/54 Neptune, NJ

CATCHERS

No.	Name	1980 Club	H	HR	RBI	Pct.	B-T	Ht.	Wt.	Born
–	Brummer, Glenn	Springfield	83	1	40	.257	R-R	6-0	185	11/23/54 Olney, IL
–	Porter, Darrell	Kansas City	104	7	51	.249	L-R	6-0	193	1/17/52 Joplin, MO
–	Tenace, Gene	San Diego	70	17	50	.222	R-R	6-0	190	10/10/46 Russelton, PA

INFIELDERS

No.	Name	1980 Club	H	HR	RBI	Pct.	B-T	Ht.	Wt.	Born
–	Calise, Mike	Arkansas	21	3	16	.362	R-R	6-2	190	3/16/57 Norwalk, CT
		Gastonia	24	3	16	.312				
–	DeSa, Joe	Springfield	124	9	74	.293	L-L	5-11	170	7/27/59 Honolulu, HI
37	Hernandez, Keith	St. Louis	191	16	99	.321	L-L	6-0	185	10/20/53 San Francisco, CA
28	Herr, Tom	Springfield	44	1	16	.312	B-R	6-0	175	4/4/56 Lancaster, PA
		St. Louis	55	0	15	.248				
24	Oberkfell, Ken	St. Louis	128	3	46	.303	L-R	6-1	185	5/4/56 Highland, IL
–	Ramsey, Mike	Springfield	18	0	6	.261	B-R	6-1	170	3/29/54 Roanoke, VA
		St. Louis	33	0	8	.262				
1	Templeton, Garry	St. Louis	161	4	43	.319	B-R	5-11	170	3/24/56 Lockey, TX

OUTFIELDERS

No.	Name	1980 Club	H	HR	RBI	Pct.	B-T	Ht.	Wt.	Born
27	Hendrick, George	St. Louis	173	25	109	.302	R-R	6-3	195	10/18/49 Los Angeles, CA
19	Iorg, Dane	St. Louis	76	3	36	.303	L-R	6-0	180	5/11/50 Eureka, CA
–	Landrum, Tito	Springfield	106	12	46	.303	R-R	5-11	175	10/25/54 Joplin, MO
		St. Louis	19	0	7	.247				
–	Lezcano, Sixto	Milwaukee	94	18	55	.229	R-R	5-10	175	11/28/53 Puerto Rico
–	Penniall, Dave	Arkansas	53	4	23	.294	R-R	5-10	175	9/26/54 Coronade, CA
		Springfield	49	13	39	.297				
–	Roof, Gene	Springfield	124	10	57	.258	B-R	6-2	180	1/13/58 Mayfield, KY
30	Scott, Tony	St. Louis	104	0	28	.251	B-R	6-0	175	9/18/51 Cincinnati, OH

CARDINAL PROFILES

GARRY TEMPLETON 25 5-11 170 Bats S Throws R

Regarded as best all-around shortstop in N.L., but has angered some people by snubbing All-Star Game because he hasn't been picked to start . . . Missed several games with finger and thumb injuries last year after becoming first major leaguer to reach 100 hits . . . Batted .336 in June . . . Came off disabled list and collected 12 hits in 23 trips to take N.L. batting lead . . . Was on DL twice, yet still went down to wire in batting race . . . Born March 24, 1956, at Lockey, Tex. . . . In '79, became first switch-hitter ever to collect 100 hits from each side . . . Led league in hits and triples in '79 . . . Batted .401 in Double-A in '75 . . . Set N.L. mark by leading league in triples three straight years.

Year	Club	Pos.	G	AB	R	H	2B	3B	HR	RBI	SB	Avg.
1976	St. Louis	SS	53	213	32	62	8	2	1	17	11	.291
1977	St. Louis	SS	153	621	94	200	19	18	8	79	28	.322
1978	St. Louis	SS	155	647	82	181	31	13	2	47	34	.280
1979	St. Louis	SS	154	672	105	211	32	19	9	62	26	.314
1980	St. Louis	SS	118	504	83	161	19	9	4	43	31	.319
	Totals..........		633	2657	396	815	109	61	24	248	130	.307

KEITH HERNANDEZ 27 6-0 185 Bats L Throws L

Tailed off slightly following co-MVP campaign of '79, but reached career high with 16 homers . . . Just missed in attempt to win two batting titles in a row . . . Off to fast start, batting .364 in May . . . Became a father for the second time (Melissa Sue) in June . . . Batted .333 in August with 21 RBI . . . Born Oct. 20, 1953, at San Francisco . . . Father Tony was an outfielder in the Cards' farm system in the Forties . . . Raised average from .255 in '78 to league-leading .344 in '79 . . . Became first first-baseman to win N.L. crown since Stan Musial in 1957 . . . Also topped N.L. with 48 doubles and 116 runs in '79.

Year	Club	Pos.	G	AB	R	H	2B	3B	HR	RBI	SB	Avg.
1974	St. Louis	1B	14	34	3	10	1	2	0	2	0	.294
1975	St. Louis	1B	64	188	20	47	8	2	3	20	0	.250
1976	St. Louis	1B	129	374	54	108	21	5	7	46	4	.289
1977	St. Louis	1B	161	560	90	163	41	4	15	91	7	.291
1978	St. Louis	1B	159	542	90	138	32	4	11	64	13	.255
1979	St. Louis	1B	161	610	116	210	48	11	11	105	11	.344
1980	St. Louis	1B	159	595	111	191	39	8	16	99	14	.321
	Totals..........		847	2903	484	867	190	36	63	427	49	.299

GENE TENACE 34 6-0 190 Bats R Throws R

Used a September spurt to make power figures respectable, but Padres' youth movement triggered trade to Cards . . . Second on Padres in home runs . . . Back problem contributed to low average and RBI figures . . . Born Oct. 10, 1946, at Russellton, Pa. . . . Never a great player, but rode 1972 World Series success to fame and fortune . . . Belted four homers and batted .348 against Reds to spur A's Series upset and it's been downhill ever since . . . Angered Padres' owner by not producing commensurate to his free-agent contract when he joined club in '77 . . . Twenty homers and .263 average in 1979 his best figures with club.

Year	Club	Pos.	G	AB	R	H	2B	3B	HR	RBI	SB	Avg.
1969	Oakland........	C	16	38	1	6	0	0	1	2	0	.158
1970	Oakland........	C	38	105	19	32	6	0	7	20	0	.305
1971	Oakland........	C-OF	65	179	26	49	7	0	7	25	2	.274
1972	Oakland........	C-OF-INF	82	227	22	51	5	3	5	32	0	.225
1973	Oakland........	1B-C-2B	160	510	83	132	18	2	24	84	2	.259
1974	Oakland........	1B-C	158	484	71	102	17	1	26	73	2	.211
1975	Oakland........	1B-C	158	498	83	127	17	0	29	87	7	.255
1976	Oakland........	1B-C	128	417	64	104	19	1	22	66	5	.249
1977	San Diego......	C-1B-3B	147	437	66	102	24	4	15	61	5	.233
1978	San Diego......	1B-C-3B	142	401	60	90	18	4	16	61	6	.224
1979	San Diego......	1B-C	151	463	61	122	16	4	20	67	2	.263
1980	San Diego......	1B-C	133	316	46	70	11	1	16	50	4	.222
	Totals..........		1378	4075	602	987	158	20	188	628	35	.242

GEORGE HENDRICK 31 6-3 195 Bats R Throws R

Member of the silent minority in baseball . . . Lets bat do the talking . . . An awesome start last year gave him 50 RBI by mid-June, but slower pace down the stretch enabled Mike Schmidt to win title . . . Belted six homers and had 24 RBI in June . . . Batted .333 in August . . . Born Oct. 18, 1949, at Los Angeles . . . Came out of shell, at least with teammates, and is one of most popular players on club . . . Found a home with Cards by batting .300 in '79, and repeated last year . . . Had five-hit game against Pittsburgh in '79 . . . Collected three homers for Indians against Detroit in '73 . . . Appeared in five World Series games with Oakland in '72 . . . Played in three All-Star Games, including '80.

Year	Club	Pos.	G	AB	R	H	2B	3B	HR	RBI	SB	Avg.
1971	Oakland........	OF	42	114	8	27	4	1	0	8	0	.237
1972	Oakland........	OF	58	121	10	22	1	1	4	15	3	.182
1973	Cleveland.......	OF	113	440	64	118	18	0	21	61	7	.268
1974	Cleveland.......	OF	139	495	65	138	23	1	19	67	6	.279
1975	Cleveland.......	OF	145	561	82	145	21	2	24	86	6	.258
1976	Cleveland.......	OF	149	551	72	146	20	3	25	81	4	.265
1977	San Diego......	OF	152	541	75	168	25	2	23	81	11	.311
1978	SD-St. Louis....	OF	138	493	64	137	31	1	20	75	2	.278
1979	St. Louis.......	OF	140	493	67	148	27	1	16	75	2	.300
1980	St. Louis.......	OF	150	572	73	173	33	2	25	109	6	.302
	Totals..........		1226	4381	580	1222	203	14	177	658	47	.279

BRUCE SUTTER 28 6-2 190 — Bats R Throws R

Slipped slightly from Cy Young Award form of '79, but was still outstanding . . . Registered 28 saves after equaling N.L. mark with 37 in '79 . . . "I'd trade in all my accomplishments for a shot at the playoffs and World Series," he insists . . . Had been mentioned prominently in trade talks before Cubs finally sent him to St. Louis . . . Born Jan. 8, 1953, at Lancaster, Pa. . . . Developed split-finger fastball out of necessity following 1973 arm surgery . . . Didn't allow Reds and Giants a run in '80 . . . Giants didn't score off him in '79 either, collecting one hit . . . The nonpareil reliever, remarkably consistent . . . Has replaced Fingers as best in business . . . Has hitters talking to themselves because of sharp drop split-finger fastball makes at plate.

Year	Club	G	IP	W	L	Pct.	SO	BB	H	ERA
1976	Chicago (NL)............	52	83	6	3	.667	73	26	63	2.71
1977	Chicago (NL)............	62	107	7	3	.700	129	23	69	1.35
1978	Chicago (NL)............	64	99	8	10	.444	106	34	82	3.18
1979	Chicago (NL)............	62	101	6	6	.500	110	32	67	2.23
1980	Chicago (NL)............	60	102	5	8	.385	76	34	90	2.65
	Totals..................	300	492	32	30	.516	494	149	371	2.40

TONY SCOTT 29 6-0 175 — Bats S Throws R

Another defensive specialist overlooked on the heavy-hitting Cards . . . Blossomed as centerfielder in '79 after switching positions with Hendrick . . . Also helped offensively with 10 triples and 37 stolen bases . . . Slumped last year, but still sharp afield . . . Considered Cards' best defensive centerfielder since Curt Flood . . . Born Sept. 18, 1951, at Cincinnati . . . Didn't make an error at Denver in '76, batting career-high .311 . . . Batted .291 with Cards in '77 until suffering knee injury that required surgery . . . Came up in Expos' farm system and was swapped to Cards following '76 season.

Year	Club	Pos.	G	AB	R	H	2B	3B	HR	RBI	SB	Avg.
1973	Montreal	OF	11	1	2	0	0	0	0	0	0	.000
1974	Montreal	OF	19	7	2	2	0	0	0	1	1	.286
1975	Montreal	OF	92	143	19	26	4	2	0	11	5	.182
1977	St. Louis	OF	95	292	38	85	16	3	3	41	13	.291
1978	St. Louis	OF	96	219	28	50	5	2	1	14	5	.228
1979	St. Louis	OF	153	587	69	152	22	10	6	68	37	.259
1980	St. Louis	OF	143	415	51	104	19	3	0	28	22	.251
	Totals..........		609	1664	209	419	66	20	10	163	83	.252

KEN OBERKFELL 24 6-1 185 — Bats L Throws R

Proved consistency by batting .303 last year following .301 rookie season . . . Good second baseman and leadoff hitter . . . Topped N.L. with .985 fielding percentage in '79 . . . Entered that season with a .119 lifetime average in bigs . . . Showed promise as a hitter by batting .351 in first year of pro ball in '75 . . . Born May 4, 1956, at Highland, Ill. . . . In first start at second base in April '79, banged four hits against Reds . . . Beat veteran Mike Tyson out of job . . . Once went zero for 32 while batting .120 for Cards in '78 . . . One of best bargains in baseball after signing as a free agent in '75.

Year	Club	Pos.	G	AB	R	H	2B	3B	HR	RBI	SB	Avg.
1977	St. Louis	2B	9	9	0	1	0	0	0	1	0	.111
1978	St. Louis	2B-3B	24	50	7	6	1	0	0	0	0	.120
1979	St. Louis	2B-3B-SS	135	369	53	111	19	5	1	35	4	.301
1980	St. Louis	2B-3B	116	422	58	128	27	6	3	46	4	.303
	Totals..........		284	850	118	246	47	11	4	82	8	.289

BOB SHIRLEY 26 5-11 185 — Bats R Throws L

Traded by Padres in 11-player deal last December . . . Started 25 games and relieved in 24 during '79 season, but did most work out of bullpen last year because of addition of free agents John Curtis and Rick Wise and development of youngsters . . . Valuable member of staff because of versatility . . . Born June 25, 1954, at Cushing, Okla. . . . Had a 1.47 ERA out of bullpen in '79 and posted solid 3.38 overall ERA despite 16 losses . . . Was Padres' biggest winner in '77 with 12 . . . Struck out 11 Reds in major league debut in '77 and beat them four times that season . . . Former star at U. of Oklahoma.

Year	Club	G	IP	W	L	Pct.	SO	BB	H	ERA
1977	San Diego	39	214	12	18	.400	146	100	215	3.70
1978	San Diego	50	166	8	11	.421	102	61	164	3.69
1979	San Diego	49	205	8	16	.333	117	59	196	3.38
1980	San Diego	59	137	11	12	.478	67	54	143	3.55
	Totals	197	722	39	57	.406	432	274	718	3.58

BOB FORSCH 31 6-4 200 Bats R Throws R

Had best record on staff, thanks to fast finish which included a 3-1 mark and a 2.77 ERA in August . . . Has been in a rut since banner '77 season in which he went 20-7 . . . Lost nine in a row in '78, but fired a no-hitter against the Phillies, April 17 . . . Became Cards' first 20-game winner since 1971 in '77 . . . Born Jan. 13, 1950, at Sacramento, Cal. . . . With Astros' Ken, only brother combo ever to pitch no-hitters . . . Won seven of last eight decisions in '79 . . . In first full season as major leaguer, fashioned 15-10 record and 2.86 ERA in '75 . . . Was an all-star third baseman as rookie pro in '63, but turned to pitching two years later.

Year	Club	G	IP	W	L	Pct.	SO	BB	H	ERA
1974	St. Louis	19	100	7	4	.636	39	34	84	2.97
1975	St. Louis	34	230	15	10	.600	108	70	213	2.86
1976	St. Louis	33	194	8	10	.444	76	71	209	3.94
1977	St. Louis	35	217	20	7	.741	95	69	210	3.48
1978	St. Louis	34	234	11	17	.393	114	97	205	3.69
1979	St. Louis	33	219	11	11	.500	92	52	215	3.82
1980	St. Louis	31	215	11	10	.524	87	33	225	3.77
	Totals	219	1409	83	69	.546	611	426	1361	3.54

DARRELL PORTER 29 6-0 193 Bats L Throws R

Signed as free agent after playing out option with Royals . . . Bounced back from a bout with alcoholism and drug abuse to become productive hitter again . . . Does not mind repeatedly telling the story of his struggle . . . When he returned after six weeks of therapy and immediately began swinging a hot bat, Jim Frey quipped, "Some people can come out of a snow bank and hit." . . . Born Jan. 17, 1952, in Joplin, Mo. . . . The first catcher ever to lead the league in walks while squatting behind the plate for 100 or more games . . . Did not enjoy an outstanding World Series . . . Was thrown out twice at home plate . . . Still, considered one of the top all-around catchers in the game.

Year	Club	Pos.	G	AB	R	H	2B	3B	HR	RBI	SB	Avg.
1971	Milwaukee......	C	22	70	4	15	2	0	2	9	2	.214
1972	Milwaukee......	C	18	56	2	7	1	0	1	2	0	.125
1973	Milwaukee......	C	117	350	50	89	19	2	16	67	5	.254
1974	Milwaukee......	C	131	432	59	104	15	4	12	56	8	.241
1975	Milwaukee......	C	130	409	66	95	12	5	18	60	2	.232
1976	Milwaukee......	C	119	389	43	81	14	1	5	32	2	.208
1977	Kansas City.....	C	130	425	61	117	21	3	16	60	1	.275
1978	Kansas City.....	C	150	520	77	138	27	6	18	78	0	.265
1979	Kansas City.....	C	157	533	101	155	23	10	20	112	3	.291
1980	Kansas City.....	C	118	418	51	104	14	2	7	51	1	.249
	Totals..........		1092	3602	514	905	148	33	115	527	24	.251

SIXTO LEZCANO 27 5-11 175 — Bats R Throws R

Owns one of the strongest arms in baseball . . . Nicknamed "The Sixto Kid." . . . Signed with Brewers as free agent in 1970 after outstanding amateur career in Puerto Rico . . . A good clutch hitter . . . Especially effective against lefthanded pitching . . . Born Nov. 28, 1953, in Arecibo, P.R. . . . Was one of the best rightfielders in A.L. . . . Was named Brewers' MVP in 1979 . . . Came to Cards in Ted Simmons deal . . . Won Gold Glove for his defense in '79 . . . First caught pro scout's eye when he was 12 years old.

Year	Club	Pos.	G	AB	R	H	2B	3B	HR	RBI	SB	Avg.
1974	Milwaukee......	OF	15	54	5	13	2	0	2	9	1	.241
1975	Milwaukee......	OF	134	429	55	106	19	3	11	43	5	.247
1976	Milwaukee......	OF	145	513	53	146	19	5	7	56	14	.285
1977	Milwaukee......	OF	109	400	50	109	21	4	21	49	6	.273
1978	Milwaukee......	OF	132	442	62	129	21	4	15	61	3	.292
1979	Milwaukee......	OF	138	473	84	152	29	3	28	101	4	.321
1980	Milwaukee......	OF	112	411	51	94	19	3	18	55	1	.229
	Totals..........		785	2722	360	749	130	22	102	374	34	.275

TOP PROSPECTS

ANDY RINCON 22 6-3 195 — Bats R Throws R

Made jump from Double-A, where he was 10-7, 3.41 with Arkansas, to sizzle down the stretch with big club . . . Posted 3-0 record with 1.08 ERA in September . . . Infielder Tom Herr batted .312 at Springfield (AAA) and hit ball at .338 clip in September for Cards . . . Club also high on outfielder Tito Landrum, who hit 12 homers and batted .303 at Springfield before reaching bigs.

MANAGER WHITEY HERZOG: Back in the dugout again by his own decree . . . Will be aided in GM duties by Joe McDonald, brought over from the Mets . . . Had the best record of any of the four managers who led the Cardinals last season (38-35), but relinquished manager's job to coach Red Schoendienst to give him time to map organization's overhaul . . . Born Dorrel Norman Elvert Herzog, Nov. 9, 1931 in New Athens, Ill. . . . Sincere, outspoken and well-liked . . . After taking Royals to playoffs three times only to lose to Yankees, he wondered aloud if KC might be better off with a new manager . . . Soon after, the club agreed with him . . . Spent eight years in majors as outfielder and first baseman with Washington, Kansas City, Baltimore and Detroit . . . As Mets' director of development (1967-72), he played key role in bringing along players who led team to '69 and '73 championships.

GREATEST TEAM

The Cardinals, led by Bob Gibson, were plenty good in 1967-68, but the club reached its acme in the late Twenties and early Thirties, dominating the National League. The best of the bunch was Gabby Street's 1931 squad, one which went 101-53 and defeated John McGraw's Giants by 13 games.

It was a grand season in which Chick Hafey batted .349 to nip teammate Jim Bottomley (.348) for the N.L. crown. Frankie Frisch batted .311 and Pepper Martin .300 for a team which collectively connected at a .286 rate.

Wild Bill Hallahan (19-9), Paul Derringer (18-8) and Burleigh Grimes (17-9) topped a balanced staff. Frisch was the MVP, but Martin came of age in the Series as the Cardinals jolted Connie Mack's A's, 4-3. Martin batted .500 with four doubles and a homer and Derringer went 2-0.

ALL-TIME CARDINAL LEADERS

BATTING: Rogers Hornsby, .424, 1924
HRs: Johnny Mize, 43, 1940
RBIs: Joe Medwick, 154, 1937
STEALS: Lou Brock, 118, 1974
WINS: Dizzy Dean, 30, 1934
STRIKEOUTS: Bob Gibson, 274, 1970

ATLANTA BRAVES

TEAM DIRECTORY: Chairman of the Board: Bill Bartholomay; Pres.: Ted Turner; VP-Dir. Player Personnel: John Mullen; Dir. Player Development: Hank Aaron; Trav. Sec.: Bill Acree; Dir. Pub. Rel.: Wayne Minshew; Mgr.: Bobby Cox. Home: Atlanta Stadium (52,870). Field distances: 330, l.f. line; 402, c.f.; 330, r.f. line. Spring training: West Palm Beach, Fla.

SCOUTING REPORT

HITTING: Surprisingly, the Braves are not a good hitting team. They have power and are in a ballpark suited for it, yet despite 144 homers–second to the Dodgers' 148 in the N.L.–the club batted a lowly .250, 11th in the league.

Nobody ranked among the league leaders, for Chris Chambliss' .282 topped the club, closely followed by Dale Murphy's .281 and Gary Matthews' .278. The most feared hitter, however, is Bob Horner, who is dynamite in a compact 6-1, 210-pound frame. Horner cut down his strikeouts, lifted his average to .268 and blasted 35 homers following an early-season spat with management.

Claudell Washington hit well in his introduction to the N.L. as a Met last year and could blossom with regular duty in a park which should make him a 20-homer hitter. Murphy, with 33 homers, is another outstanding power hitter. Both he and Horner could hike their RBI totals should the club do a better job with the top of the order.

PITCHING: The club lost Doyle Alexander and his 14 wins, so the rotation remains shaky. Newcomer John Montefusco, from San Francisco, could pick up some of the slack, but Phil Niekro may be slipping a bit at 42 and other starters have been inconsistent. Tommy Boggs, Rick Matula and Larry McWilliams, however, could be ready to blossom.

Rick Camp was outstanding in relief last year and the bullpen would get a big boost if Gene Garber and/or Al Hrabosky bounce back. This seems to be an absolute necessity, especially since the starters figure to need plenty of help during a steamy summer in Atlanta.

FIELDING: The Braves were shabby afield last season–only the Cubs were worse–and there isn't a Gold Glove candidate on this year's squad either. Many of the Braves seem to regard fielding as an inconvenience while itching to get to the plate, but

Dale Murphy, only 25, already has hit 79 career homers.

Glenn Hubbard is a scrapper at second, Murphy is improving as a centerfielder and Chambliss ranks with the best at first.

OUTLOOK: Manager Bobby Cox created a positive attitude down the stretch last season and hopes that it carries over, yet it remains to be seen if the winter dealings will have a significant effect. It's doubtful Montefusco will be as effective as Alexander, or that Washington will play up to his superstar contract.

There's no question the Braves can bash it. Horner, Murphy, Chambliss and Matthews form an imposing heart of a batting order. But the club will continue to languish in the second division until it finds a better way to field the ball and pitch it.

ATLANTA BRAVES 1981 ROSTER

MANAGER Bob Cox
Coaches—Tommie Aaron, Cloyd Boyer, Bobby Dews, John Sullivan

PITCHERS

No.	Name	1980 Club	W-L	IP	SO	ERA	B-T	Ht.	Wt.	Born
–	Bedrosian, Steve	Savannah	14-10	203	161	3.19	R-R	6-3	200	12/6/57 Methuen, MA
40	Boggs, Tom	Atlanta	12-9	192	84	3.42	R-R	6-2	200	10/25/55 Pougheepsie, NY
34	Bradford, Larry	Atlanta	3-4	55	32	2.45	R-L	6-1	205	12/21/51 Chicago, IL
–	Brizzolara, Tony	Richmond	10-15	206	128	3.17	R-R	6-5	210	1/14/57 Santa Monica, CA
37	Camp, Rick	Atlanta	6-4	108	33	1.92	R-R	6-1	198	6/10/53 Trion, GA
–	Cole, Tim	Savannah	10-13	154	108	4.68	L-L	6-0	189	5/1/59 Kingston, NY
26	Garber, Gene	Atlanta	5-5	82	51	3.84	R-R	5-10	175	11/13/47 Lancaster, PA
49	Hanna, Preston	Atlanta	4-2	79	35	3.19	R-R	6-1	185	9/10/54 Pensacola, FL
39	Hrabosky, Al	Atlanta	4-2	60	31	3.60	R-L	5-10	180	7/21/49 Oakland, CA
42	Mahler, Rick	Richmond	12-6	188	101	2.59	R-R	6-1	190	8/5/53 Austin, TX
		Atlanta	0-0	4	1	2.25				
29	Matula, Rick	Atlanta	11-13	177	62	4.58	R-R	6-0	190	11/22/53 Wharton, TX
27	McWilliams, Larry	Atlanta	9-14	164	77	4.94	L-L	6-5	175	2/10/54 Wichita, KS
–	Melson, Gary	Richmond	7-10	139	110	2.85	R-R	6-1	180	2/27/53 New Albany, IN
–	Montefusco, John	San Francisco	4-8	113	85	4.38	R-R	6-1	192	5/25/50 Keansburg, NJ
–	Morogiello, Dan	Richmond	11-12	196	71	4.04	L-L	6-1	200	3/26/55 Brooklyn, NY
35	Niekro, Phil	Atlanta	15-18	275	176	3.63	R-R	6-2	180	4/1/39 Blaine, OH
–	Pettaway, Felix	Durham	11-4	91	95	2.08	R-R	6-2	200	2/9/55 Mobile, AL

CATCHERS

No.	Name	1980 Club	H	HR	RBI	Pct.	B-T	Ht.	Wt.	Born
20	Benedict, Bruce	Richmond	3	0	0	.300	R-R	6-1	185	8/18/55 Birmingham, AL
		Atlanta	91	2	34	.253				
15	Nahorodny, Bill	Atlanta	38	5	18	.242	R-R	6-2	195	8/31/53 Hamtramck, MI
4	Pocoroba, Biff	Atlanta	22	2	8	.265	B-R	5-10	170	7/25/53 Los Angeles, CA
–	Sinatro, Matt	Savannah	125	11	50	.278	R-R	5-9	174	3/22/60 Hartford, CT

INFIELDERS

No.	Name	1980 Club	H	HR	RBI	Pct.	B-T	Ht.	Wt.	Born
10	Chambliss, Chris	Atlanta	170	18	72	.282	L-R	6-1	215	12/26/48 Dayton, OH
9	Gomez, Luis	Atlanta	53	0	24	.191	R-R	5-9	150	8/19/51 Mexico
5	Horner, Bob	Atlanta	124	35	89	.268	R-R	6-1	195	8/6/57 Junction City, TX
17	Hubbard, Glenn	Richmond	45	2	25	.315	R-R	5-8	160	9/25/57 Hann AFB, Germany
		Atlanta	107	9	43	.248				
28	Lum, Mike	Atlanta	17	0	5	.205	L-L	6-0	185	10/27/45 Honolulu, HI
–	Perry, Gerald	Durham	124	15	92	.249	L-R	5-11	172	10/30/60 Savannah, GA
47	Ramirez, Rafael	Atlanta	44	2	11	.267	R-R	6-0	170	2/18/59 Dominican Republic
		Richmond	79	5	38	.281				
–	Smith, Ken	Richmond	103	12	53	.246	L-R	6-1	195	2/12/58 Youngstown, OH

OUTFIELDERS

No.	Name	1980 Club	H	HR	RBI	Pct.	B-T	Ht.	Wt.	Born
30	Asselstine, Brian	Atlanta	62	3	25	.284	L-R	6-1	190	9/23/53 Santa Barbara, CA
–	Hall, Albert	Durham	139	4	41	.283	R-R	5-11	155	3/7/59 Birmingham, AL
19	Harper, Terry	Richmond	143	13	72	.279	R-R	6-1	195	8/19/55 Douglasville, GA
		Atlanta	10	0	3	.185				
–	Landis, Craig	Phoenix	134	7	49	.282	R-R	6-2	195	12/29/58 Richmond, CA
–	Linares, Rufino	Savannah	85	2	38	.425	R-R	6-0	170	2/20/55 Dominican Republic
		Richmond	77	3	41	.329				
36	Matthews, Gary	Atlanta	159	19	75	.278	R-R	6-3	180	7/5/50 San Fernando, CA
3	Murphy, Dale	Atlanta	160	33	89	.281	R-R	6-5	185	3/12/56 Portland, OR
1	Royster, Jerry	Atlanta	95	1	20	.242	R-R	6-0	165	10/18/52 Sacramento, CA
–	Washington, Claudell	Chicago (AL)	26	1	12	.289	L-L	6-0	190	8/31/54 Los Angeles, CA
		New York (NL)	78	10	42	.275				
–	Whisenton, Larry	Richmond	103	9	37	.252	L-L	6-1	190	7/3/56 St. Louis, MO

BRAVE PROFILES

GARY MATTHEWS 30 6-3 180 Bats R Throws R

Benched after 10 games while batting .162 with four errors, he still rebounded to have a strong season, though his production, overall, fell off . . . Batted .342 in May to get on right track . . . Has been a solid major leaguer ever since winning Rookie-of-Year distinction with Giants in '73, batting .300 . . . Came within a few thousand dollars of re-signing with S.F. in 1976 and Braves lured him with fat contract amid charges of tampering . . . Born July 5, 1950, at San Fernando, Cal. . . . Despite consistency over entire major league career, has generally been overshadowed by more illustrious teammates . . . Name mentioned in trade rumors following slow '80 start, Cubs being most prominently mentioned.

Year	Club	Pos.	G	AB	R	H	2B	3B	HR	RBI	SB	Avg.
1972	San Francisco ...	OF	20	62	11	18	1	1	4	14	0	.290
1973	San Francisco ...	OF	148	540	74	162	22	10	12	58	17	.300
1974	San Francisco ...	OF	154	561	87	161	27	6	16	82	11	.287
1975	San Francisco ...	OF	116	425	67	119	22	3	12	58	13	.280
1976	San Francisco ...	OF	156	587	79	164	28	4	20	84	12	.279
1977	Atlanta.........	OF	148	555	89	157	25	5	17	64	22	.283
1978	Atlanta.........	OF	129	474	75	134	20	5	18	62	8	.283
1979	Atlanta.........	OF	156	631	97	192	34	5	27	90	18	.304
1980	Atlanta.........	OF	155	571	79	159	17	3	19	75	11	.278
	Totals......		1182	4406	658	1266	196	42	145	587	112	.287

CLAUDELL WASHINGTON 26 6-0 190 Bats L Throws L

Became popular player with Mets following mid-season acquisition from White Sox . . . Signed incredible $3.5 million contract with Braves after playing out option . . . Ended one-for-17 slump by belting three homers at L.A. June 22 . . . Also hit three for Sox against Tigers in '79, joining Babe Ruth and Johnny Mize as only players to accomplish feat in both leagues . . . Born Aug. 31, 1954, at Los Angeles . . . Went to high school (Berkeley, Cal.) with Yankees' Ruppert Jones, but didn't play as a prep . . . Signed off sandlots by A's and batted .308 for Oakland in first full season, 1975 . . . Batted

.344 in August . . . In short time with Mets provided much-needed punch.

Year	Club	Pos.	G	AB	R	H	2B	3B	HR	RBI	SB	Avg.
1974	Oakland........	OF	73	221	16	63	10	5	0	19	6	.285
1975	Oakland........	OF	148	590	86	182	24	7	10	77	40	.308
1976	Oakland........	OF	134	490	65	126	20	6	5	53	37	.257
1977	Texas..........	OF	129	521	63	148	31	2	12	68	21	.284
1978	Texas-Chi (AL) ..	OF	98	356	34	90	16	5	6	33	5	.253
1979	Chicago (AL)....	OF	131	471	79	132	33	5	13	66	19	.280
1980	Chicago (AL)....	OF	32	90	15	26	4	2	1	12	4	.289
1980	New York (NL)...	OF	79	284	38	78	16	4	10	42	17	.275
	Totals..........		824	3023	396	845	154	36	57	370	149	.280

DALE MURPHY 25 6-4 185 — Bats R Throws R

Horner gets much of the attention, but Murphy is a rising star in his own right . . . Good in both halves of season . . . Batted .317 with seven homers, 21 RBI in June . . . Named to All-Star squad . . . Batted .312 with eight homers, 26 RBI in August . . . Versatility is evidenced by fact he can catch, play first and center field for the Braves, though he appears set in latter position . . . Born March 12, 1956, at Portland, Ore. . . . Off to great start in '79 with .348 average, 13 homers and 36 RBI when he tore cartilage in knee on May 23 . . . Belted three homers against Giants May 18 that year . . . Turned down Ohio State football scholarship to sign as Braves' No. 1 draft choice in '74 . . . Tied for team RBI lead.

Year	Club	Pos.	G	AB	R	H	2B	3B	HR	RBI	SB	Avg.
1976	Atlanta.........	C	19	65	3	17	6	0	0	9	0	.262
1977	Atlanta.........	C	18	76	5	24	8	1	2	14	0	.316
1978	Atlanta.........	C-1B	151	530	66	120	14	3	23	79	11	.226
1979	Atlanta.........	1B-C	104	384	53	106	7	2	21	57	6	.276
1980	Atlanta.........	1B-OF	156	569	98	160	27	2	33	89	9	.281
	Totals..........		448	1624	225	427	62	8	79	248	26	.263

CHRIS CHAMBLISS 32 6-1 215 — Bats L Throws R

Provided stability with banner maiden season in N.L. . . . Hit well from the start and enjoyed a .325 June . . . Only disappointment until the Braves' blazing stretch run was RBI total . . . Came to Atlanta after first going from Yankees to Toronto in winter of '79 . . . "A good hitter can hit anywhere," said Chris, disdaining adjustment problems after nine years in A.L. . . . Home run gave Yankees '76 playoff victory over Royals . . . Batted .524 in that series and .340 in 14 playoff games . . . Born Dec. 26, 1948, at Dayton . . . Was an All-America slugger at UCLA . . . Gold Glove winner with Yankees in '78 . . . Durable and consistent . . . Cousin of former NBA star JoJo White.

Year	Club	Pos.	G	AB	R	H	2B	3B	HR	RBI	SB	Avg.
1971	Cleveland.......	1B	111	415	49	114	20	4	9	48	2	.275
1972	Cleveland.......	1B	121	466	51	136	27	2	6	44	3	.292
1973	Cleveland.......	1B	155	572	70	156	30	2	11	53	4	.273
1974	Cleve.-N.Y.(AL) ..	1B	127	467	46	119	20	3	6	50	0	.255
1975	New York (AL) ..	1B	150	562	66	171	38	4	9	72	0	.304
1976	New York (AL) ..	1B	156	641	79	188	32	6	17	96	1	.293
1977	New York (AL) ..	1B	157	600	90	172	32	6	17	90	4	.287
1978	New York (AL) ..	1B	162	625	81	171	26	3	12	90	2	.274
1979	New York (AL) ..	1B	149	554	61	155	27	3	18	63	3	.280
1980	Atlanta.........	1B	158	602	83	170	37	2	18	72	7	.282
	Totals..........		1446	5504	676	1552	299	35	123	678	26	.282

BOB HORNER 23 6-1 195 — Bats R Throws R

An outrageous power hitter . . . Collected 25 of his homers after the All-Star break following problem-plagued start . . . Had only two hits in 34 trips, no homers and no RBI after 10 games, so owner Ted Turner banished him to Triple-A . . . Horner balked and lost $2,250 per day when he left club . . . Came back with a bang, belting 15 homers and slugging .930 from June 27 to July 22 . . . N.L. Player of Month for July, hitting .327 with 14 homers, 32 RBI . . . Born Aug. 1, 1957, at Junction City, Kan. . . . Greatest young slugger in game . . . Also missed 14 games with sprained back . . . Still finished second to Schmidt in homers . . . Rated best bet to break Roger Maris' one-season record, especially if he stays in Atlanta . . . Set NCAA mark with 58 career homers at Arizona State.

Year	Club	Pos.	G	AB	R	H	2B	3B	HR	RBI	SB	Avg.
1978	Atlanta.........	3B	89	323	50	86	17	1	23	63	0	.266
1979	Atlanta.........	3B-1B	121	487	66	153	15	1	33	98	0	.314
1980	Atlanta.........	3B	124	463	81	124	14	1	35	89	3	.268
	Totals..........		334	1273	197	363	46	3	91	250	3	.285

GLENN HUBBARD 23 5-9 160 — Bats R Throws R

Rewarded club with solid season at second base in first full year in bigs . . . Had identical .336 averages at Richmond in 1978-79 before earning promotion from Triple-A for good . . . An aggressive, hustling ballplayer who looms large in club's future plans . . . Has decent power for size . . . Born Sept. 25, 1957, at Hann AFB, Germany . . . Impressed club by batting .400 in seven games after recall from Richmond in September 1979 . . . As rookie in 1978, participated in triple play against Phillies . . . A 20th-round selection as a Utah prep in 1975 . . . Batted .385 in Class A ball in 1977 . . . Batted .315 at Richmond at start of '80 season.

Year	Club	Pos.	G	AB	R	H	2B	3B	HR	RBI	SB	Avg.
1978	Atlanta.........	2B	44	163	15	42	4	0	2	13	2	.258
1979	Atlanta.........	2B	97	325	34	75	12	0	3	29	0	.231
1980	Atlanta.........	2B	117	431	55	107	21	3	9	43	7	.248
	Totals..........		258	919	104	224	37	3	14	85	9	.244

JERRY ROYSTER 28 6-0 165 Bats R Throws R

Versatile infielder-outfielder a valuable member of club . . . Gives dimension of speed to team laden with power . . . Slipped back into utility role after enjoying finest season in majors as a regular in '79 . . . That year batted 601 times, hit .273 and tied Ralph Garr's club record with 35 steals . . . Born Oct. 18, 1952, at Sacramento, Cal. . . . Can play most positons on club—and has . . . Was highly-rated Dodgers' prospect when he joined Braves in Dusty Baker deal in '75 . . . Promoted to L.A. after .333 season in PCL in '75 . . . A three-sport prep whiz, he could have gone to UCLA on a basketball scholarship.

Year	Club	Pos.	G	AB	R	H	2B	3B	HR	RBI	SB	Avg.
1973	Los Angeles.....	3B-2B	10	19	1	4	0	0	0	2	1	.211
1974	Los Angeles.....	2B-3B-OF	6	0	2	0	0	0	0	0	0	.000
1975	Los Angeles.....	OF-2B-3B-SS	13	36	2	9	2	1	0	1	1	.250
1976	Atlanta.........	3B-SS	149	533	65	132	13	1	5	45	24	.248
1977	Atlanta.........	3B-SS-2B-OF	140	445	64	96	10	2	6	28	28	.216
1978	Atlanta.........	3B-SS-2B	140	529	67	137	17	8	2	35	27	.259
1979	Atlanta.........	3B-2B	154	601	103	164	25	6	3	51	35	.273
1980	Atlanta.........	3B-2B-SS	123	392	42	95	17	5	1	20	22	.242
	Totals..........		735	2555	346	637	84	23	17	182	138	.249

PHIL NIEKRO 42 6-1 180 Bats R Throws R

Off to slow start, but bounced back to respectability with 4-1 August . . . King of the knuckleballers seems like he can go on indefinitely after topping staff in most categories in '80 . . . Experienced a rarity in '79 by topping N.L. in wins and losses with 21-20 record . . . Forty-four starts that year were most in league since Grover Cleveland Alexander's 44 in 1917 . . . Born April 1, 1939, at Blaine, Ohio . . . Holds several all-time Braves' records, including most wins by a righthander (233) and lowest season ERA, league-leading 1.87 in '67 . . . Thrice a 20-game winner . . . A workhorse who cut down on innings last year because of development of other pitchers . . . A Gold Glove fielder . . . Active in charity work . . . A rock of stability for club since 1967.

Year	Club	G	IP	W	L	Pct.	SO	BB	H	ERA
1964	Milwaukee	10	15	0	0	.000	8	7	15	4.80
1965	Milwaukee	41	75	2	3	.400	40	26	73	2.88
1966	Atlanta	28	50	4	3	.571	17	23	48	4.14
1967	Atlanta	46	207	11	9	.550	129	55	164	1.87
1968	Atlanta	37	257	14	12	.538	140	45	228	2.50
1969	Atlanta	40	284	23	13	.639	193	57	235	2.57
1970	Atlanta	34	230	12	18	.400	168	68	222	4.27
1971	Atlanta	42	269	15	14	.517	173	70	248	2.98
1972	Atlanta	38	282	16	12	.571	164	53	254	3.06
1973	Atlanta	42	245	13	10	.565	131	89	214	3.31
1974	Atlanta	41	302	20	13	.606	195	88	249	2.38
1975	Atlanta	39	276	15	15	.500	144	72	285	3.20
1976	Atlanta	38	271	17	11	.607	173	101	249	3.29
1977	Atlanta	44	330	16	20	.444	262	164	315	4.04
1978	Atlanta	44	334	19	18	.514	248	102	295	2.88
1979	Atlanta	44	342	21	20	.512	208	113	311	3.39
1980	Atlanta	40	275	15	18	.455	176	85	256	3.63
	Totals	648	4044	233	209	.527	2578	1218	3661	3.14

TOMMY BOGGS 25 6-2 200 — Bats R Throws R

Blossomed in first full season with club, becoming mainstay in rotation . . . Earned promotion by going 20-11 in parts of two seasons with Richmond Triple-A club . . . A hard thrower, he was second draft pick in nation when Texas took him in 1974 . . . Was 1-10 in parts of two years with Rangers before becoming part of Willie Montanez deal in 1977 . . . Born Oct. 25, 1955, at Poughkeepsie, N.Y. . . . Was International League workhorse in '79, topping Triple-A league in starts, complete games, innings and strikeouts . . . Began last season with dubious 3-20 major league mark before impressively turning career around.

Year	Club	G	IP	W	L	Pct.	SO	BB	H	ERA
1976	Texas	13	90	1	7	.125	36	34	87	3.50
1977	Texas	6	27	0	3	.000	15	12	40	6.00
1978	Atlanta	16	59	2	8	.200	21	26	80	6.71
1979	Atlanta	3	13	0	2	.000	1	4	21	6.23
1980	Atlanta	32	192	12	9	.571	84	46	180	3.42
	Totals	70	381	15	29	.341	157	122	408	4.23

RICK CAMP 27 6-1 198 — Bats R Throws R

Success story of 1980 squad after coming to spring training as a non-roster player . . . Failures of Gene Garber and Al Hrabosky thrust Rick into role of top reliever and he responded with 22 saves . . . Allowed one run in 22 innings in August . . . Shoulder injury set him back early in career and was unspectacular at Richmond in '79, posting 3-2 record and 4.25 ERA in 22 games . . . Born June 10, 1953, at Trion, Ga. . . . Earned spot on roster with fine spring and became bullpen workhorse, appearing in 77 games . . . Best previous season was '77, when he went 6-3 in 54 games . . . Fast finish last year kept ERA under 2.00.

Year	Club	G	IP	W	L	Pct.	SO	BB	H	ERA
1976	Atlanta	5	11	0	1	.000	6	2	13	6.55
1977	Atlanta	54	79	6	3	.667	51	47	89	3.99
1978	Atlanta	42	74	2	4	.333	23	32	99	3.77
1980	Atlanta	77	108	6	4	.600	33	29	92	1.92
	Totals	178	272	14	12	.538	113	110	293	3.21

TOP PROSPECT

RICK MATULA 27 6-0 190 Bats R Throws R

The spring training sensation of 1979, Matula was 8-10 with a 4.16 ERA during regular season, but could not earn a spot on the roster last year . . . Brushed up skills at Richmond, where he was a solid 12-6 with a 2.89 ERA . . . Appears ready to stick for good this time . . . Born Nov. 22, 1953, at Wharton, Tex. . . . Has 3-0 career mark against Dodgers.

MANAGER BOBBY COX: Strong Manager-of-Year credentials after Braves overcame 0-8 start to finish with a torrid second half . . . Guided club to 11-1 record against defending World Series champion Pittsburgh . . . Job on line after successive last-place finishes in 1978-79 . . . Club posted most victories since 88 in '74 . . . Placed in tough position by owner interference early in the season, but is respected, and well-liked by players . . . Born May 21, 1941, at Tulsa, Okla. . . . Lackluster playing career came to a halt because of bad knees . . . Successful minor league player, but not as big leaguer . . . In second year as manager won pennant for West Haven (Eastern) in '72 and again guided champion with 1976 Syracuse club . . . Coached under Billy Martin at New York in '77 and was lured away by Braves after season . . . Never finished lower than fourth as a minor league manager . . . Father of five children . . . Promised a .500 season in spring and delivered.

Brief walkout didn't stop Bob Horner from hitting 35 HRs.

GREATEST TEAM

It would be fair to consider two different phases of this nomadic franchise: the Boston era and the Milwaukee-Atlanta years. The Miracle Braves of 1914 were the best of the Boston teams, while the modern Braves were best represented in 1957-58, winning back-to-back flags against such worthy competition as the Dodgers' Boys of Summer.

The 1914 club truly was miraculous. Manager George Stallings' club, a fifth-place finisher in '13, was mired in last place halfway through the season, July 18. The Braves won 34 of 44 to take first place in early September and kept rolling to down the stunned Giants by 10½ games.

Outfielder Joe Connolly was the batting leader at .306, shortstop Rabbit Maranville fielded brilliantly and Dick Rudolph (27-10) and Bill James (26-7) formed a potent one-two pitching punch. The capper was a 4-0 World Series sweep of the A's, who scored but six runs as Rudolph and James each went 2-0 and Hank Gowdy batted .545.

Of the moderns, the '57 club gets the nod because it edged the mighty Yankees, 4-3, in the Series behind Lew Burdette's three wins. Henry Aaron won home run (44) and RBI (132) titles, Red Schoendienst batted .310, Warren Spahn was 21-11 and Ed Mathews belted 32 homers and totaled 94 RBI. Aaron batted .322 during the season and .393 with three homers in the Series.

ALL-TIME BRAVE LEADERS

BATTING: Rogers Hornsby, .387, 1928
HRs: Eddie Mathews, 47, 1953
Hank Aaron, 47, 1971
RBIs: Eddie Mathews, 135, 1953
STEALS: Ralph Meyers, 57, 1913
WINS: Vic Willis, 27, 1902
Charles Pittinger, 27, 1902
Dick Rudolph, 27, 1914
STRIKEOUTS: Phil Niekro, 262, 1977

CINCINNATI REDS

TEAM DIRECTORY: Chairman of the Board: Louis Nippert; Pres.: Dick Wagner; Scouting Dir.: Joe Bowen; Dir. Minor Leagues: Mike Compton; Dir. Publ.: Jim Ferguson; Trav. Sec.: Doug Bureman; Mgr.: John McNamara. Home: Riverfront Stadium (52,392). Field distances: 330, l.f. line; 404, c.f.; 330, r.f. line. Spring training: Tampa, Fla.

SCOUTING REPORT

HITTING: The Big Red Machine wasn't its usual devastating self last season, but scored enough runs to keep the club within

Tom Seaver needs 55 wins to crack 300 barrier.

striking distance down to the wire. Dave Collins did his part with a .303 average and 79 steals and Ken Griffey bounced back to bat .294, but most of the Reds slumped. Mike Vail should add some punch.

Ray Knight plunged from .318 to .264, George Foster managed only 25 homers while enduring a long dry spell, Dave Concepcion slipped to .260 and mighty John Bench checked in at .250. Yes, the Reds are getting old and it's the dawning of a new era at Riverfront Stadium.

Trouble is, many of the newcomers are not in the same class as the players who terrorized the N.L. in the Seventies. Perhaps Knight's big season of '79 was merely a fluke. Second baseman Junior Kennedy waited a long time for his chance, but Ron Oester proved he was better. A lot of people are looking over their shoulders.

PITCHING: A perennial Cincy problem once again is a sore spot because of the question marks surrounding veterans Tom Seaver and Bill Bonham. Tom Terrific will have to prove that his injury-riddled 10-8 campaign merely was an aberration and Bonham will have to prove he can pitch, period.

That situation has placed additional pressure on youngsters, so it's to their credit that Frank Pastore, Mario Soto, Mike LaCoss, Charlie Liebrandt, Joe Price and Paul Moskau have done a decent job. Pastore, in particular, is a star on the rise following a 13-7 season. Tom Hume was sharp in relief, but the Reds need a strong comeback from Doug Bair to stabilize the bullpen.

FIELDING: The club's strong suit last year, perhaps explaining the high finish despite problems in other areas. Cincy topped the N.L. with a .983 percentage and had solid performances afield from first baseman Dan Driessen, second baseman Oester, third baseman Knight, shortstop Concepcion and catcher Bench.

OUTLOOK: The Reds are having aging problems, but unlike the Dodgers, they don't seem to have the quality depth to cope with it. Because of the questionable pitching and bench, it's inconceivable Cincy has the horses to overtake either the Astros or the Dodgers.

Rather, it seems more of a case of looking out for the Braves and Giants, who could replace the Reds in the first division. For it to be otherwise, the veteran Reds have to rebound and the youngsters must prove worthy of carrying on the tradition.

CINCINNATI REDS 1981 ROSTER

MANAGER John McNamara
Coaches—Harry Dunlop, Bill Fischer, Russ Nixon, Ron Plaza, Ted Kluszewski

PITCHERS

No.	Name	1980 Club	W-L	IP	SO	ERA	B T	Ht.	Wt.	Born
40	Bair, Doug	Cincinnati	3-6	85	62	4.24	R-R	6-0	185	8/22/49 Defiance, OH
38	Berenyi, Bruce	Indianapolis	5-8	123	121	4.32	R-R	6-3	215	8/21/54 Bryan, OH
		Cincinnati	2-2	28	19	7.71				
42	Bonham, Bill	Tampa	1-0	16	14	0.56	R-R	6-3	195	10/1/48 Glendale, CA
		Cincinnati	2-1	19	13	4.74				
54	Brito, Jose	Waterbury	12-6	172	175	3.14	R-R	6-2	160	10/28/59 Dominican Republic
53	Brown, Scott	Indianapolis	6-7	123	73	3.44	R-R	6-6	220	8/30/56 DeQuincy, LA
37	Combe, Geoff	Indianapolis	2-2	77	72	2.22	R-R	6-1	185	2/1/56 Melrose, MA
		Cincinnati	0-0	7	10	10.29				
47	Hume, Tom	Cincinnati	9-10	137	68	2.56	R-R	6-1	180	3/29/53 Cincinnati, OH
51	LaCoss, Mike	Cincinnati	10-12	169	59	4.63	R-R	6-4	190	5/30/56 Glendale, CA
48	Lahti, Jeff	Waterbury	7-8	91	78	2.77	R-R	6-0	180	10/8/56 Oregon City, OR
44	Leibrandt, Charlie	Cincinnati	10-9	174	62	4-24	R-L	6-4	200	10/4/56 Chicago, IL
31	Moskau, Paul	Cincinnati	9-7	153	94	4.00	R-R	6-2	205	12/20/53 St. Joseph, MO
35	Pastore, Frank	Cincinnati	13-7	185	110	3.26	R-R	6-3	205	8/21/57 Alhambra, CA
49	Price, Joe	Indianapolis	4-4	79	83	3.87	R-L	6-4	220	11/29/56 Inglewood, CA
		Cincinnati	7-3	111	44	3.57				
52	Scherrer, Bill	Waterbury	7-8	151	58	3.34	L-L	6-4	180	1/20/58 Tonawanda, NY
41	Seaver, Tom	Cincinnati	10-8	168	101	3.64	R-R	6-1	208	11/17/44 Fresno, CA
36	Soto, Mario	Cincinnati	10-8	190	182	3.08	R-R	6-0	185	7/12/56 Dominican Republic

CATCHERS

No.	Name	1980 Club	H	HR	RBI	Pct.	B-T	Ht.	Wt.	Born
5	Bench, Johnny	Cincinnati	90	24	68	.250	R-R	6-1	215	12/7/47 Oklahoma City, OK
62	Christmas, Steve	Waterbury	84	7	44	.242	L-R	6-0	215	12/9/57 Orlando, FL
9	O'Berry, Mike	Midland	42	1	23	.243	R-R	6-2	190	4/20/54 Birmingham, AL
		Wichita	6	0	6	.261				
		Chicago (NL)	10	0	5	.208				
17	Nolan, Joe	Atl-Cin	54	3	26	.307	L-R	6-0	190	5/12/51 St. Louis, MO
60	Van Gorder, Dave	Indianapolis	57	3	26	.225	R-R	6-2	205	3/27/57 Cleveland, OH

INFIELDERS

13	Concepcion, Dave	Cincinnati	162	5	77	.260	R-R	6-2	175	6/17/48 Venezuela
22	Driessen, Dan	Cincinnati	139	14	74	.265	L-R	5-11	190	7/29/51 Hilton Head, SC
55	Esasky, Nick	Waterbury	115	30	79	.271	R-R	6-3	190	2/24/60 Hialeah, FL
59	Foley, Tom	Waterbury	119	4	41	.249	L-R	6-1	160	10/9/59 Columbus, GA
26	Kennedy, Junior	Cincinnati	88	1	34	.261	R-R	6-0	185	8/9/50 Ft. Gibson, OK
25	Knight, Ray	Cincinnati	163	14	78	.264	R-R	6-2	185	12/28/52 Albany, GA
56	Lawless, Tom	Waterbury	137	2	29	.275	R-R	6-0	165	12/29/56 Erie, PA
16	Oester, Ron	Cincinnati	84	2	20	.277	B-R	6-2	185	5/5/56 Cincinnati, OH
61	Redus, Gary	Tampa	136	16	68	.301	R-R	6-1	180	11/1/56 Limestone, AL
12	Spilman, Harry	Cincinnati	27	4	19	.267	L-R	6-1	190	7/18/54 Albany, GA

OUTFIELDERS

29	Collins, Dave	Cincinnati	167	3	35	.303	B-L	5-10	175	10/20/52 Rapid City, SD
15	Foster, George	Cincinnati	144	25	93	.275	R-R	6-1	185	12/1/48 Tuscaloosa, AL
20	Geronimo, Cesar	Cincinnati	37	2	9	.255	L-L	6-2	175	3/11/48 Dominican Republic
30	Griffey, Ken	Cincinnati	160	13	85	.294	L-L	5-11	200	4/10/50 Donora, PA
21	Householder, Paul	Cincinnati	11	0	7	.244	B-R	6-0	180	9/4/58 Columbus, OH
		Indianapolis	137	9	50	.295				
28	Mejias, Sam	Cincinnati	30	1	10	.278	R-R	6-0	170	5/9/52 Dominican Republic
57	Milner, Eddie	Indianapolis	118	5	37	.252	L-L	5-11	170	5/21/55 Columbus, OH
		Cincinnati	0	0	0	.000				
–	Vail, Mike	Chicago (NL)	93	6	47	.298	R-R	6-0	185	11/10/51 San Francisco, CA
58	Walker, Duane	Indianapolis	87	6	30	.248	L-L	6-0	180	3/13/57 Pasadena, TX

RED PROFILES

DAVE COLLINS 28 5-10 175 Bats S Throws L

National League's first Player of Week, going 8 for 10 in three games against Braves after zero for five Opening Day . . . Stole 22 bases in a row before being caught June 29 at Houston . . . Doubled his previous career high in steals with 79, a Reds' record . . . Failed to make grade in A.L. and batted lowly .216 with Reds in '78 . . . Got big chance when Griffey and Foster were injured in '79 and flourished, batting .318 . . . Born Oct. 20, 1952, at Rapid City, S.D. . . . Batted .357 in '79 playoffs . . . Has 9.6 speed . . . Proved Angels and Mariners made a mistake by giving up too soon . . . A hyper, enthusiastic player who has talked with a hypnotist by telephone to calm down.

Year	Club	Pos.	G	AB	R	H	2B	3B	HR	RBI	SB	Avg.
1975	California.......	OF	93	319	41	85	13	4	3	29	24	.266
1976	California.......	OF	99	365	45	96	12	1	4	28	32	.263
1977	Seattle.........	OF	120	402	46	96	9	3	5	28	25	.239
1978	Cincinnati	OF	102	102	13	22	1	0	0	7	7	.216
1979	Cincinnati	OF-1B	122	396	59	126	16	4	3	35	16	.318
1980	Cincinnati	OF	144	551	94	167	20	4	3	35	79	.303
	Totals..........		680	2135	298	592	71	16	18	162	183	.277

KEN GRIFFEY 30 5-11 200 Bats L Throws L

Showed flashes of former brilliance after battling back from knee surgery . . . Should be even better this year . . . Was involved in trade talks, but finally signed with Cincy . . . Batted .365 in May and .324 in June . . . Was MVP of '80 All-Star Game after his homer started N.L. on way to victory . . . Had 27 doubles and .316 average in 95 games when felled by knee injury in '79 . . . Second on club in RBI, batting average and steals . . . Born April 19, 1950, at Donora, Pa. . . . Entered '80 with .310 average, fifth best in majors during Seventies . . . Was going to be used as leadoff batter upon Pete Rose's departure, but Collins' emergence and injury changed all that . . . A .313 hitter in nine playoff games . . . Outstanding minor league career topped by .342 at Tampa and .327 at Indianapolis.

Year	Club	Pos.	G	AB	R	H	2B	3B	HR	RBI	SB	Avg.
1974	Cincinnati	OF	88	227	24	57	9	5	2	19	9	.251
1975	Cincinnati	OF	132	463	95	141	15	9	4	46	16	.305
1976	Cincinnati	OF	148	562	111	189	28	9	6	74	34	.336
1977	Cincinnati	OF	154	585	117	186	35	8	12	57	17	.318
1978	Cincinnati	OF	158	614	90	177	33	8	10	63	23	.288
1979	Cincinnati	OF	95	380	62	120	27	4	8	32	12	.316
1980	Cincinnati	OF	146	544	89	160	28	10	13	85	23	.294
	Totals..........		946	3461	607	1063	180	54	58	390	138	.307

GEORGE FOSTER 32 6-1 185 — Bats R Throws R

An inconsistent year for one of the premier power hitters in the game . . . Hit only one homer in June . . . Solid August with six homers, 20 RBI and .320 average . . . Homers on steady decline since 52 in '77 . . . Though injured part of '79, collected 19 game-winning RBI to prove worth in clutch . . . Had only nine homers at All-Star break last year . . . Born Dec. 1, 1948, at Ralph, Ala. . . . Black bat is his trademark . . . A steal for Cincy when he was obtained from Giants for Frank Duffy and Vern Geishert in 1971 . . . Willie Mays predicted stardom and hated to see him go . . . Won three straight RBI titles in 1976-78, averaging 130 per year . . . Named MVP of major league tour to Japan after '79 season, using trip as a honeymoon.

Year	Club	Pos.	G	AB	R	H	2B	3B	HR	RBI	SB	Avg.
1969	San Francisco ...	OF	9	5	1	2	0	0	0	1	0	.400
1970	San Francisco ...	OF	9	19	2	6	1	1	1	4	0	.316
1971	S.F.-Cin.	OF	140	473	50	114	23	4	13	58	7	.241
1972	Cincinnati	OF	59	145	15	29	4	1	2	12	2	.200
1973	Cincinnati	OF	17	39	6	11	3	0	4	9	0	.282
1974	Cincinnati	OF	106	276	31	73	18	0	7	41	3	.264
1975	Cincinnati	OF-1B	134	463	71	139	24	4	23	78	2	.300
1976	Cincinnati	OF-1B	144	562	86	172	21	9	29	121	17	.306
1977	Cincinnati	OF	158	615	124	197	31	2	52	149	6	.320
1978	Cincinnati	OF	158	604	97	170	26	7	40	120	4	.281
1979	Cincinnati	OF	121	440	68	133	18	3	30	98	0	.302
1980	Cincinnati	OF	144	528	79	144	21	5	25	93	1	.273
	Totals..........		1199	4169	630	1190	190	36	226	784	42	.285

RAY KNIGHT 28 6-2 185 — Bats R Throws R

Tailed off sharply following .318 debut as Reds' regular in '79 . . . Though average dropped, other offensive figures remained solid . . . Broke zero-for-15 slump by cracking two homers, including a grand-slam, in the eighth inning against the Mets May 13 . . . Made fans forget Pete Rose by coming through in great style at third base in '79 . . .

Born Dec. 28, 1952, at Albany, Ga. . . . His .318 season amazed everyone because he never batted above .285 previously in pro ball . . . Named Reds' MVP of '79 . . . "There were times I thought I would never get a chance, that Pete Rose would play here forever," he said in '79 . . . Got chance and made the best of it.

Year	Club	Pos.	G	AB	R	H	2B	3B	HR	RBI	SB	Avg.
1974	Cincinnati	3B	14	11	1	2	1	0	0	2	0	.182
1977	Cincinnati	3B-2B-OF-SS	80	92	8	24	5	1	1	13	1	.261
1978	Cincinnati	3B-2B-OF-SS	83	65	7	13	3	0	1	4	0	.200
1979	Cincinnati	3B	150	551	64	175	37	4	10	79	4	.318
1980	Cincinnati	3B-2B	162	618	71	163	39	7	14	78	1	.264
	Totals..........		489	1337	151	377	85	12	26	176	6	.282

DAN DRIESSEN 29 5-11 190 Bats L Throws R

Unfairly pressured when fans expected another Tony Perez after latter went to Montreal in '77 . . . Batted .300 in '77 and averaged 16 homers last four years, but simply not as capable in clutch as Perez . . . A good player hurt by comparison to predecessor . . . Batted .345 last May . . . Born July 29, 1951, at Hilton Head, S.C. . . . Batted .342 after Labor Day in '79 to help club to division title . . . A solid, if not flashy, fielder at first base . . . Earned promotion to bigs by batting .409 in first 47 games of Triple-A ball at Indianapolis in '73 . . . Finished rookie season batting .301 for Cincy . . . Has .313 average in six World Series games, including first homer ever hit by a DH.

Year	Club	Pos.	G	AB	R	H	2B	3B	HR	RBI	SB	Avg.
1973	Cincinnati	3B-1B	102	366	49	110	15	2	4	47	8	.301
1974	Cincinnati	3B-1B-OF	150	470	63	132	23	6	7	56	10	.281
1975	Cincinnati	1B-OF	88	210	38	59	8	1	7	38	10	.281
1976	Cincinnati	1B-OF	98	219	32	54	11	1	7	44	14	.247
1977	Cincinnati	1B	151	536	75	161	31	4	17	91	31	.300
1978	Cincinnati	1B	153	524	68	131	23	3	16	70	28	.250
1979	Cincinnati	1B	150	515	72	129	24	3	18	75	11	.250
1980	Cincinnati	1B	154	524	81	139	36	1	14	74	19	.265
	Totals..........		1046	3364	478	915	171	21	90	495	131	.272

DAVE CONCEPCION 32 6-2 175 Bats R Throws R

A key year for the slender shortstop . . . Voted tops at his position for the Seventies, but slipped somewhat last season, .260 average being lowest since 1972 . . . Elbow injury contributed to problems at plate and basestealing also suffered . . . Won Gold Glove fifth time in six years in '79 and also enjoyed best offensive year in terms of homers and

RBI . . . Born June 17, 1948, at Aragua, Venezuela . . . Best run-producer among N.L. shortstops, often batting clean-up last year . . . Posted .351 average in 15 playoff games . . . A very consistent performer who blossomed with the Big Red Machine in '73, batting .287 . . . Has played in 20 World Series games.

Year	Club	Pos.	G	AB	R	H	2B	3B	HR	RBI	SB	Avg.
1970	Cincinnati	SS-2B	101	265	38	69	6	3	1	19	10	.260
1971	Cincinnati	SS-2B-3B-OF	130	327	24	67	4	4	1	20	9	.205
1972	Cincinnati	SS	119	378	40	79	13	2	2	29	13	.209
1973	Cincinnati	SS-OF	89	328	39	94	18	3	8	46	22	.287
1974	Cincinnati	SS-OF	160	594	70	167	25	1	14	82	41	.281
1975	Cincinnati	SS-3B	140	507	62	139	23	1	5	49	33	.274
1976	Cincinnati	SS	152	576	74	162	28	7	9	69	21	.281
1977	Cincinnati	SS	156	572	59	155	26	3	8	64	29	.271
1978	Cincinnati	SS	153	565	75	170	33	4	6	67	23	.301
1979	Cincinnati	SS	149	590	91	166	25	3	16	84	19	.281
1980	Cincinnati	SS	156	622	72	162	31	8	5	77	12	.260
	Totals..........		1505	5324	644	1430	232	39	75	606	232	.269

JOHNNY BENCH 33 6-1 215 — Bats R Throws R

The standard by which other catchers are compared . . . Voted tops on majors' team of the decade . . . Set record for career homers by a backstop when he belted No. 314 against Montreal July 15, breaking Yogi Berra's mark . . . Also tied Bill Dickey's career record by catching at least 100 games for a 13th year . . . Wants to lessen catching load in future, but management reluctant . . . Born Dec. 7, 1947, at Oklahoma City . . . Batted .359 in June . . . Socked three home runs at San Diego May 28, third time in career he'd done it . . . Hit two grand-slams last year despite fears that injury has reduced effectiveness as power hitter . . . His 1,013 RBI during Seventies were most by any major leaguer in that decade . . . Club's all-time home run and RBI leader . . . Two-time MVP and earned similar honor for '76 World Series . . . Five career Series homers.

Year	Club	Pos.	G	AB	R	H	2B	3B	HR	RBI	SB	Avg.
1967	Cincinnati	C	26	86	7	14	3	1	1	6	0	.163
1968	Cincinnati	C	154	564	67	155	40	2	15	82	1	.275
1969	Cincinnati	C	148	532	83	156	23	1	26	90	6	.293
1970	Cincinnati	C-OF-1B-3B	158	605	97	177	35	4	45	148	5	.293
1971	Cincinnati	C-1B-OF-3B	149	562	80	134	19	2	27	61	2	.238
1972	Cincinnati	C-OF-1B-3B	147	538	87	145	22	2	40	125	6	.270
1973	Cincinnati	C-OF-1B-3B	152	557	83	141	17	3	25	104	4	.253
1974	Cincinnati	C-3B-1B	160	621	108	174	38	2	33	129	5	.280
1975	Cincinnati	C-OF-1B	142	530	83	150	39	1	28	110	11	.283
1976	Cincinnati	C-OF-1B	135	465	62	109	24	1	16	74	13	.234
1977	Cincinnati	C-OF-1B-3B	142	494	67	136	34	2	31	109	2	.275
1978	Cincinnati	C-OF-1B	120	393	52	102	17	1	23	73	4	.260
1979	Cincinnati	C-1B	130	464	73	128	19	0	22	80	4	.276
1980	Cincinnati	C-1B	114	360	52	90	12	0	24	68	4	.250
	Totals..........		1877	6771	1001	1811	342	22	356	1259	67	.267

TOM SEAVER 36 6-1 208 — Bats R Throws R

Selected top righthander of the decade, but threw a big scare into Reds with retirement talk last season . . . Comment was made following loss at S.F. June 30, when injuries had reduced Tom Terrific to just another pitcher . . . Finished '79 season with a 14-1 record and again was strong down the stretch last year, 4-1 in September . . . Won 11 in a row in '79 . . . Born Nov. 17, 1944, at Fresno, Cal. . . . Four 20-win campaigns and three Cy Young Awards with Mets . . . Was 16-14 in first full season with Reds in '78 while victimized by non-support . . . Topped N.L. in strikeouts five times and just shy of 3,000 for career.

Year	Club	G	IP	W	L	Pct.	SO	BB	H	ERA
1967	New York (NL)	35	251	16	13	.552	170	78	224	2.76
1968	New York (NL)	36	278	16	12	.571	205	48	224	2.20
1969	New York (NL)	36	273	25	7	.781	208	82	202	2.21
1970	New York (NL)	37	291	18	12	.600	283	83	230	2.81
1971	New York (NL)	36	286	20	10	.667	289	61	210	1.76
1972	New York (NL)	35	262	21	12	.636	249	77	215	2.92
1973	New York (NL)	36	290	19	10	.655	251	64	219	2.07
1974	New York (NL)	32	236	11	11	.500	201	75	199	3.20
1975	New York (NL)	36	280	22	9	.710	243	88	217	2.38
1976	New York (NL)	35	271	14	11	.560	235	77	211	2.59
1977	New York (NL)-Cincinnati	33	261	21	6	.778	1&6	66	199	2.59
1978	Cincinnati	36	260	16	14	.533	226	89	218	2.87
1979	Cincinnati	32	215	16	6	.727	131	61	187	3.14
1980	Cincinnati	26	168	10	8	.556	101	59	140	3.64
	Totals	481	3622	245	141	.635	2988	1008	2895	2.60

FRANK PASTORE 23 6-2 205 — Bats R Throws R

Reds' pitching star of the future . . . Was 5-2 down the stretch in '79, including four-hitter over Atlanta to clinch the division crown . . . Bolted to 8-2 start last year before finger injury placed him on disabled list and marred solid season . . . Was 3-1 in May . . . Rated a can't-miss prospect . . . Made club in spring of '79, but was ineffective . . . Shipped to Indianapolis, he was 7-2, 2.78 in Triple-A and came back to stay . . . Born Aug. 21, 1957, at Alhambra, Cal. . . . Had 2.10 ERA down the stretch in '79 . . . In crucial series with Astros, Reds dropped first two games before Pastore posted 7-1 victory with first complete game in bigs.

Year	Club	G	IP	W	L	Pct.	SO	BB	H	ERA
1979	Cincinnati	30	95	6	7	.462	63	23	102	4.26
1980	Cincinnati	27	185	13	7	.650	110	42	161	3.26
	Totals	57	280	19	14	.576	173	65	263	3.60

TOM HUME 27 6-1 180 **Bats R Throws R**

Has become club's bullpen ace, replacing Doug Bair . . . Showed promise with 17 saves in '79 and finished with 25 last season . . . Registered seven saves and 1.44 ERA in July . . . Followed with 3-1 record, 1.44 ERA in August . . . Became exclusively a reliever after years of spot starting . . . Born March 29, 1953, at Cincinnati . . . Second behind J.R. Richard in '79 ERA race . . . Poor professional pitching record (55-71) until he found his niche in '79 . . . After All-Star Game in '79, posted 15 saves and 1.44 ERA to rise from obscurity to prominence . . . Had 2.02 ERA out of bullpen in '79 and again topped club in ERA last season.

Year	Club	G	IP	W	L	Pct.	SO	BB	H	ERA
1977	Cincinnati	14	43	3	3	.500	22	17	54	7.12
1978	Cincinnati	42	174	8	11	.421	90	50	198	4.14
1979	Cincinnati	57	163	10	9	.526	80	33	162	2.76
1980	Cincinnati	78	137	9	10	.474	68	38	121	2.56
	Totals	191	517	30	33	.476	260	138	535	3.53

TOP PROSPECTS

PAUL HOUSEHOLDER 22 6-0 180 **Bats S Throws R**

An outfielder who can hit and field, appears ready for big time after batting .295 with nine homers and 50 RBI at Indianapolis . . . Born Sept. 4, 1958, at Columbus, Ohio . . . Reliever Geoff Combe, 25, was 2-2 with a 2.22 ERA in 60 games for Triple-A club and also is highly touted . . . Neither impressed with parent club in September, however.

MANAGER JOHN McNAMARA: Came up short in an improved division and failed to repeat last year

after keeping club in contention until final week . . . Injuries to Seaver and Bill Bonham didn't help, nor did plate slumps by Foster and Concepcion . . . Did a tremendous job in '79 with a team supposedly in transition . . . Dodgers and Giants slumped that year and Reds outlasted Astros for N.L. West title,

Mac's first as a big league manager . . . Born June 4, 1932, at Sacramento, Cal. . . . He was 29 when 1961 Lewiston (Wash.) club won Northwest League pennant . . . Captured back-to-back flags for A's Birmingham and Mobile farm clubs in 1966-67 and joined new Oakland A's as coach in '68 . . . Succeeded Hank Bauer as skipper late in '69 and guided '70 A's to second place . . . Started managing at age 26 while still a minor league catcher . . . Considered firm and fair and especially effective with younger players . . . Reds' success the last two years would verify that belief.

GREATEST TEAM

It's easy to argue the merits of Bill McKechnie's repeat winners in 1939-40 and the worth of the Big Red Machine of the Seventies, so the best Cincy club obviously emerges from those two choices.

The '39 champs were swept by the Yankees in the Series, but the '40 club went 100-53, won the flag by 12 games and edged Detroit, 4-3, in the Series. Bucky Walters was 22-10 with a league-leading 2.48 ERA and Paul Derringer went 20-12. Both won two games in the Series, wiping out a 3-2 Tigers' edge. Catcher Ernie Lombardi was the batting leader at .319.

But the '75 Reds were even more impressive, setting a club record with 108 victories, sweeping the Pirates in the playoffs and shading the Red Sox in what many consider the most exciting World Series ever. What made the season even more amazing was that the Reds were 20-20 at one stage.

Joe Morgan batted .327, Pete Rose .317 and Ken Griffey .305. Johnny Bench had 28 homers and 110 RBI and George Foster added 23 homers as a blossoming star. Gary Nolan, Jack Billingham and Don Gullett each won 15 games and Clay Carroll was the bullpen star. A great team. Rose batted .370 in the Series and reliever Rawly Eastwick was 2-0.

ALL-TIME RED LEADERS

BATTING: Cy Seymour, .377, 1905
HRs: George Foster, 52, 1977
RBIs: George Foster, 149, 1977
STEALS: Bob Bescher, 80, 1911
WINS: Adolfo Luque, 27, 1923
Bucky Walters, 27, 1939
STRIKEOUTS: Jim Maloney, 265, 1963

HOUSTON ASTROS

TEAM DIRECTORY: Executive Committee: John J. McMullen, Jack Trotter, Herb Neyland; Pres.-GM: Al Rosen; Asst. to GM: Tony Siegle; Admin. Asst.-Trav. Sec.: Donald Davidson; Dir. Minor League Clubs: Bill Wood; Dir. Scouting: Lynwood Stallings; Dir. Publ.: Ed Wade; Mgr.: Bill Virdon. Home: Astrodome (45,000). Field distances: 340, l.f. line; 390, l.c.; 406, c.f.; 390, r.c.; 340, r.f. line. Spring training: Cocoa, Fla.

SCOUTING REPORT

HITTING: The Astros' lack of punch is the brunt of jokes, but guess who's laughing last? Besides, the club raised its home run output from 48 to a whopping 75 and collectively batted .261, sixth-best in the league, so Houston's lineup isn't exactly feeble at the dish.

Joe Morgan's spark down the stretch, including a total of 11 game-winning RBI, may be missed, as might Enos Cabell's con-

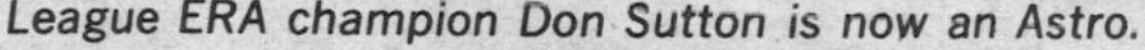

League ERA champion Don Sutton is now an Astro.

tribution, but with all that pitching, a lot of sock isn't needed. Still, outfielders Jose Cruz (.302), Cesar Cedeno (.309) and Terry Puhl (.282) can hit and rookie first baseman Danny Heep adds power.

PITCHING: Simply overwhelming. If the Astros stopped trading after the winter meetings, they would have had seven starters –Joe Niekro, Nolan Ryan, Don Sutton, Bob Knepper, Ken Forsch, Vern Ruhle and Joaquin Andujar–not counting J.R. Richard. Forsch, however, was reported to be headed for the Giants.

The problem will be finding a place for everyone, so a trade or two seems to be a necessity. Besides a solid rotation, the bullpen is excellent with Joe Sambito, Frank LaCorte and Dave Smith. If it remains intact, it is difficult to recall a pitching staff with more quality and depth.

Sutton and Knepper, of course, were acquired as insurance in the event Richard cannot make a comeback in 1981. Since the Astros won the 1980 team ERA title with a classy 3.10 and have obtained the individual ERA king in Sutton, how can they help but improve?

FIELDING: As with their hitting, the Astros' fielding also is in the middle of the pack, but it could improve with Art Howe at third base in place of Cabell. The outfield is swift and sure and the catching duties were handled nicely last season by Alan Ashby and Luis Pujols. Free agent Dave Roberts should be valuable at catcher and around the infield.

OUTLOOK: The team lacks power, but it is perfectly suited for the Astrodome, where its 55-26 home record was the best in the league. Speed is emphasized more than power, so new second baseman Rafael Landestoy could prove to be more exciting than Morgan.

The hitting doesn't figure to improve, but the fielding and pitching could. Forsch and Andujar had off-years and Ryan surely wasn't an overnight sensation in his return to the N.L. Look for an improvement from The Express and also from Knepper, who didn't get the maximum out of his ability the last two years as a Giant.

Manager Bill Virdon earned his post-season honors for a great job last year. The Astros could have collapsed without Richard, but they didn't panic and registered the franchise's first winner. It could be No. 2 coming up, but it'll take beating the Dodgers to do it in what shapes up as a two-team race.

HOUSTON ASTROS 1981 ROSTER

MANAGER Bill Virdon
Coaches—Deacon Jones, Don Leppert, Bob Lillis, Mel Wright

PITCHERS

No.	Name	1980 Club	W-L	IP	SO	ERA	B-T	Ht.	Wt.	Born
47	Andujar, Joaquin	Houston	3-8	122	75	3.91	B-R	5-11	180	12/21/52 Dominican Republic
43	Forsch, Ken	Houston	12-13	222	84	3.20	R-R	6-4	215	9/8/46 Sacramento, CA
54	Hessler, John	Columbus	8-7	144	110	4.56	R-R	6-3	200	6/3/57 Kansas City, MO
—	Knepper, Bob	San Francisco	9-16	215	103	4.10	L-L	6-2	200	5/25/54 Akron, OH
31	LaCorte, Frank	Houston	8-5	83	66	2.82	R-R	6-1	180	10/13/51 San Jose, CA
33	Leatherwood, Del	Columbus	7-4	102	59	2.82	R-R	6-1	185	3/30/55 Houston, TX
49	Leland, Stan	Columbus	7-12	192	94	3.84	R-R	6-4	190	5/17/59 Wabash, IN
36	Niekro, Joe	Houston	20-12	256	127	3.55	R-R	6-1	190	11/7/44 Martins Ferry, OH
46	Niemann, Randy	Tucson	4-1	52	26	4.85	L-L	6-4	200	11/15/55 Scotia, CA
		Houston	0-1	33	18	5.45				
26	Pladson, Gordie	Tucson	10-5	128	66	3.59	R-R	6-4	210	7/31/56 Canada
		Houston	0-4	41	13	4.39				
50	Richard, J. R.	Houston	10-4	114	119	1.89	R-R	6-8	220	3/7/50 Vienna, LA
42	Roberge, Bert	Tucson	5-3	49	47	4.78	R-R	6-4	190	10/3/54 Lewiston, ME
		Houston	2-0	24	9	6.00				
48	Ruhle, Vern	Houston	12-4	159	55	2.38	R-R	6-1	187	1/25/51 Coleman, MI
34	Ryan, Nolan	Houston	11-10	234	200	3.35	R-R	6-2	195	1/31/47 Refugio, TX
35	Sambito, Joe	Houston	8-4	90	75	2.20	L-L	6-1	190	6/28/52 Brooklyn, NY
45	Smith, Dave	Houston	7-5	103	85	1.92	R-R	6-1	195	1/21/55 San Francisco, CA
41	Sprowl, Bobby	Tucson	10-11	180	89	4.35	L-L	6-2	190	4/14/56 Sandusky, OH
		Houston	0-0	1	3	0.00				
—	Sutton, Don	Los Angeles	13-5	212	128	2.21	R-R	6-2	185	4/2/45 Clio, AL

CATCHERS

No.	Name	1980 Club	H	HR	RBI	Pct.	B-T	Ht.	Wt.	Born
14	Ashby, Alan	Houston	90	3	48	.256	B-R	6-2	190	7/8/51 Long Beach, CA
11	Knicely, Alan	Tucson	149	22	105	.318	R-R	6-½	194	5/19/55 Harrisonburg, VA
		Houston	0	0	0	.000				
6	Pujols, Luis	Houston	44	0	20	.199	R-R	6-1	195	11/18/55 Dominican Republic
—	Roberts, Dave	Texas	56	10	30	.238	R-R	6-3	205	2/17/51 Lebanon, OR

INFIELDERS

No.	Name	1980 Club	H	HR	RBI	Pct.	B-T	Ht.	Wt.	Born
16	Bergman, Dave	Houston	20	0	3	.256	L-L	6-2	185	6/6/53 Evanston, IL
23	Cabell, Enos	Houston	167	2	55	.276	R-R	6-1	185	10/8/49 Ft. Riley, KS
10	Fischlin, Mike	Tucson	117	3	49	.281	R-R	6-1	165	9/13/55 Sacramento, CA
		Houston	0	0	0	.000				
9	Gonzalez, Julio	Tucson	44	2	25	.295	R-R	5-11	165	12/25/53 Puerto Rico
		Houston	6	0	1	.115				
20	Heep, Danny	Tucson	129	17	69	.343	L-L	5-11	185	7/3/57 San Antonio, TX
		Houston	24	0	6	.276				
18	Howe, Art	Houston	91	10	46	.283	R-R	6-1	185	12/15/46 Pittsburgh, PA
17	Landestoy, Rafael	Houston	97	1	27	.247	B-R	5-9	163	5/28/53 Dominican Republic
8	Morgan, Joe	Houston	112	11	49	.243	L-R	5-7	160	9/19/43 Bonham, TX
1	Pena, Bert	Columbus	88	9	47	.243	R-R	5-11	165	7/11/59 Puerto Rico
12	Reynolds, Craig	Houston	86	3	28	.226	L-R	6-1	175	12/27/52 Houston, TX

OUTFIELDERS

No.	Name	1980 Club	H	HR	RBI	Pct.	B-T	Ht.	Wt.	Born
—	Bourjos, Chris	Phoenix	170	9	86	.295	R-R	6-0	185	10/16/55 Chicago, IL
		San Francisco	5	1	2	.227				
28	Cedeno, Cesar	Houston	154	10	73	.309	R-R	6-2	190	2/25/51 Dominican Republic
25	Cruz, Jose	Houston	185	11	91	.302	L-L	6-0	175	8/8/47 Puerto Rico
30	Leonard, Jeff	Houston	46	3	20	.213	R-R	6-4	200	9/22/55 Philadelphia, PA
22	Loucks, Scott	Columbus	124	10	45	.248	R-R	6-0	178	11/11/56 Anchorage, AK
		Houston	1	0	0	.333				
21	Puhl, Terry	Houston	151	13	55	.282	L-R	6-1	190	7/8/56 Canada
27	Rajsich, Gary	Tucson	143	21	99	.321	L-L	6-2	190	10/28/54 Youngstown, OH
29	Walling, Dennis	Houston	85	3	29	.299	L-R	6-1	185	4/17/54 Neptune, NJ
19	Wiedenbauer, Tom	Tucson	98	0	33	.255	R-R	6-1	175	11/5/58 Menomonie, WI
15	Woods, Gary	Tucson	162	8	86	.313	R-R	6-2	190	7/20/54 Santa Barbara, CA
		Houston	20	2	15	.377				

ASTRO PROFILES

CESAR CEDENO 30 6-2 190 — Bats R Throws R

Without much fanfare, Cesar had his best season at the plate since 1973, going over .300 for the first time in seven years . . . Went back to outfield and prospered after giving way to rookie Jeff Leonard and playing first base most of '79 . . . A strong Comeback-of-Year candidate after suffering through career-low .262 season in '79 . . . Born Feb. 25, 1951, at Santo Domingo, Dominican Republic . . . Topped club in extra-base hits . . . 1978 knee surgery limited him to 50 games and reduced his power potential . . . Still a gifted gloveman . . . Was hurt early in career by comparison to Willie Mays . . . Never reached level others expected of him, but has been a solid major leaguer . . . Batted .341 in September . . . Broke ankle in playoffs.

Year	Club	Pos.	G	AB	R	H	2B	3B	HR	RBI	SB	Avg.
1970	Houston........	OF	90	355	46	110	21	4	7	42	17	.310
1971	Houston........	OF-1B	161	611	85	161	40	6	10	81	20	.264
1972	Houston........	OF	139	559	103	179	39	8	22	82	55	.320
1973	Houston........	OF	139	525	86	168	35	2	25	70	56	.320
1974	Houston........	OF	160	610	95	164	29	5	26	102	57	.269
1975	Houston........	OF	131	500	93	144	31	3	13	63	50	.288
1976	Houston........	OF	150	575	89	171	26	5	18	83	58	.297
1977	Houston........	OF	141	530	92	148	36	8	14	71	61	.279
1978	Houston........	OF	50	192	31	54	8	2	7	23	23	.281
1979	Houston........	OF-1B	132	470	57	123	27	4	6	54	30	.262
1980	Houston........	1B-OF	137	499	71	154	32	8	10	73	48	.309
	Totals..........		1430	5426	848	1576	324	55	158	744	475	.290

JOSE CRUZ 33 6-0 175 — Bats L Throws L

Houston's most consistent hitter over the last five years . . . Batted .333 in May and .339 in August . . . Extremely popular player who commands cheers of "Crooz, Crooz, Crooz" when he strides to the plate in the Astrodome . . . The best clutch hitter in a lineup without much punch . . . Born Aug. 8, 1947, at Arroyo, Puerto Rico . . . Comes from a baseball-playing family, including brothers Hector and Tommy . . . Possibly the most underrated player in the N.L. considering his consistency and value to the Astros . . . Roberto Clemente Award winner in '79 . . . Batted above .300 in three of six seasons with Astros, also .299 in '77 when he was the club MVP . . . Once had eight RBI in a doubleheader against S.F. in '79.

Year	Club	Pos.	G	AB	R	H	2B	3B	HR	RBI	SB	Avg.
1970	St. Louis	OF	6	17	2	6	1	0	0	1	0	.353
1971	St. Louis	OF	83	292	46	80	13	2	9	27	6	.274
1972	St. Louis	OF	117	332	33	78	14	4	2	23	9	.235
1973	St. Louis	OF	132	406	51	92	22	5	10	57	10	.227
1974	St. Louis	OF-1B	107	161	24	42	4	3	5	20	4	.261
1975	Houston........	OF	120	315	44	81	15	2	0	49	6	.257
1976	Houston........	OF	133	439	49	133	21	5	4	61	28	.303
1977	Houston........	OF	157	579	87	173	31	10	17	87	44	.299
1978	Houston........	OF-1B	153	565	79	178	34	9	10	83	37	.315
1979	Houston........	OF	157	558	73	161	33	7	9	72	36	.289
1980	Houston........	OF	160	612	79	185	29	7	11	91	36	.302
	Totals..........		1325	4276	567	1209	217	54	86	571	216	.283

DAVE ROBERTS 30 6-3 205 Bats R Throws R

A millionaire ballplayer, even if his stats don't show it . . . Played out option in Texas and was selected by 12 clubs, one under maximum, in free-agent draft . . . Why? Versatility is the answer . . . Catcher-infielder Roberts will play anywhere, and the Astros are paying him $1.1 million over the next five years . . . Born Feb. 17, 1951, in Lebanon, Ore. . . . Was drafted by Padres out of University of Oregon June 7, 1972, and played in San Diego lineup that same day . . . Had best year in 1973, when he amassed 21 HR and 64 RBI with Padres.

Year	Club	Pos.	G	AB	R	H	2B	3B	HR	RBI	SB	Avg.
1972	San Diego	3B-2B-SS-C	100	418	38	102	17	0	5	33	7	.244
1973	San Diego	3B-2B	127	479	56	137	20	3	21	64	11	.286
1974	San Diego	3B-SS-OF	113	318	26	53	10	1	5	18	2	.167
1975	San Diego	3B-2B	33	113	7	32	2	0	2	12	3	.283
1977	San Diego	C-3B-2B-SS	82	186	15	41	14	1	1	23	2	.220
1978	San Diego	C-1B-OF	54	97	7	21	4	1	1	7	0	.216
1979	Texas..........	C-OF-INF	44	84	12	22	2	1	3	14	1	.262
1980	Texas..........	C-OF-INF	101	235	27	56	4	0	10	30	0	.238
	Totals..........		654	1930	188	464	73	7	48	201	26	.240

TERRY PUHL 24 6-1 190 Bats L Throws R

Another underrated player on a team full of them . . . Had four hits in Game 5 of N.L. playoffs . . . Collected seven hits in a double-header against Atlanta July 13 . . . Replaced Cedeno in center field in '79 and made no errors . . . Batted .301 when promoted to bigs at end of '77 season and torrid at start of '78 season with 18-game batting streak . . . Tailed off last year as lifetime average dipped below .290, but still a valuable member of club . . . Second to Cruz in game-winning

RBI . . . Born July 8, 1956, at Melville, Sask. . . . High school didn't field a baseball team and was rejected by Expos in tryout camp . . . Entered '80 season with 152 consecutive errorless games, a club record.

Year	Club	Pos.	G	AB	R	H	2B	3B	HR	RBI	SB	Avg.
1977	Houston........	OF	60	229	40	69	13	5	0	10	10	.301
1978	Houston........	OF	149	585	87	169	25	6	3	35	32	.289
1979	Houston........	OF	157	600	87	172	22	4	8	49	30	.287
1980	Houston........	OF	141	535	75	151	24	5	13	55	27	.282
	Totals..........		507	1949	289	561	84	20	24	149	99	.288

KEN FORSCH 34 6-4 215 — Bats R Throws R

Established a career high with 12 victories . . . Came out of bullpen to go 11-6 as starter in '79, including a no-hitter against Atlanta April 7 in the second game of the season . . . Joined brother Bob of the Cardinals as only brothers in major league history to notch no-hitters . . . Born Sept. 8, 1946, at Sacramento, Cal. . . . Was Astros' top reliever in 1976-77 . . . Despite quick start and N.L. Pitcher of Month honors in April '79, season was marred by shoulder problems which limited him to 24 starts . . . Pitched perfect inning in '76 All-Star Game . . . Starred in baseball at Oregon State U.

Year	Club	G	IP	W	L	Pct.	SO	BB	H	ERA
1970	Houston................	4	24	1	2	.333	13	5	28	5.63
1971	Houston................	33	188	8	8	.500	131	53	162	2.54
1972	Houston................	30	156	6	8	.429	113	62	163	3.92
1973	Houston................	46	201	9	12	.429	149	74	197	4.21
1974	Houston................	70	103	8	7	.533	48	37	98	2.80
1975	Houston................	34	109	4	8	.333	54	30	114	3.22
1976	Houston................	52	92	4	3	.571	49	26	76	2.15
1977	Houston................	42	86	5	8	.385	45	28	80	2.72
1978	Houston................	52	133	10	6	.625	71	37	136	2.71
1979	Houston................	26	178	11	6	.647	58	35	155	3.03
1980	Houston................	32	222	12	13	.480	84	41	230	3.20
	Totals..................	421	1492	78	81	.491	815	428	1439	3.18

JOE NIEKRO 36 6-1 190 — Bats R Throws R

It's said that knuckleball pitchers improve with age, and Joe has done nothing to disprove that theory . . . He didn't quite match a 21-win season of '79, but Phil's little brother topped the Astros in victories (20) and complete games . . . Won 20th in special playoff after Dodgers had won three straight for tie . . . Tied Phil for most victories in N.L. in '79, year he blossomed as a starter after years of shuffling between rotation and bullpen . . . Born Nov. 7, 1944, at Martins Ferry,

Ohio . . . Knuckler becomes more effective at Houston, where it provides a sharp contrast to blazers thrown by Richard and Ryan . . . Took off as a starter with 6-0 record and two shutouts in May 1979, earning N.L. Pitcher of Month award . . . Set club mark with nine wins in row . . . 6-1 down stretch last year.

Year	Club	G	IP	W	L	Pct.	SO	BB	H	ERA
1967	Chicago (NL)	35	170	10	7	.588	77	32	171	3.34
1968	Chicago (NL)	34	177	14	10	.583	65	59	204	4.32
1969	Chi. (NL)-S.D.	41	221	8	18	.308	62	51	237	3.71
1970	Detroit	38	213	12	13	.480	101	72	221	4.06
1971	Detroit	31	122	6	7	.462	43	49	136	4.50
1972	Detroit	18	47	3	2	.600	24	8	62	3.83
1973	Atlanta	20	24	2	4	.333	12	11	23	4.13
1974	Atlanta	27	43	3	2	.600	31	18	36	3.56
1975	Houston	40	88	6	4	.600	54	39	79	3.07
1976	Houston	36	118	4	8	.333	77	56	107	3.36
1977	Houston	44	181	13	8	.619	101	64	155	3.03
1978	Houston	35	203	14	14	.500	97	73	190	3.86
1979	Houston	38	264	21	11	.656	119	107	221	3.00
1980	Houston	37	256	20	12	.625	127	79	268	3.55
	Totals	475	2127	136	120	.531	990	718	2110	3.62

NOLAN RYAN 34 6-2 195 — Bats R Throws R

A disappointment immediately after signing four-year, $4-million contract as a free agent . . . Winless from June 19 through August 4 . . . But vital to Astros' pennant push down the stretch, posting 4-0 record and 2.45 ERA in August . . . Achieved 3,000th career strikeout against Reds, July 4 . . . Fourth on all-time strikeout list behind Walter Johnson, Bob Gibson and Gaylord Perry . . . Born Jan. 31, 1947, at Refugio, Tex. . . . Has four career no-hitters, tying Sandy Koufax for the most by a major leaguer . . . Has thrown seven one-hitters . . . Fastball has been clocked above 100 mph, but control problems have kept him from being much over .500 lifetime . . . Has registered 15 or more strikeouts 21 times, a record . . . Also has mark for five 300-strikeout seasons.

Year	Club	G	IP	W	L	Pct.	SO	BB	H	ERA
1966	New York (NL)	2	3	0	1	.000	6	3	5	15.00
1968	New York (NL)	21	134	6	9	.400	133	75	93	3.09
1969	New York (NL)	25	89	6	3	.667	92	53	60	3.54
1970	New York (NL)	27	132	7	11	.389	125	97	86	3.41
1971	New York (NL)	30	152	10	14	.417	137	116	125	3.97
1972	California	39	284	19	16	.543	329	157	166	2.28
1973	California	41	326	21	16	.568	383	162	238	2.87
1974	California	42	333	22	16	.578	367	202	221	2.89
1975	California	28	198	14	12	.538	186	132	152	3.45
1976	California	39	284	17	18	.486	327	183	193	3.36
1977	California	37	299	19	16	.543	341	204	198	2.77
1978	California	31	235	10	13	.435	260	148	183	3.71
1979	California	34	223	16	14	.533	223	114	169	3.59
1980	Houston	35	234	11	10	.524	200	98	205	3.35
	Totals	431	2926	178	169	.513	3109	1744	2094	3.18

JOE SAMBITO 28 6-1 190 — Bats L Throws L

The class of the Astros' stout bullpen with 17 saves and eight victories . . . Proved great '79 campaign was no fluke . . . Didn't allow an earned run in 27 consecutive appearances in '79, a streak covering 40 and two-thirds innings . . . Had a perfect 13-game streak in '78 . . . Born June 28, 1952, in Brooklyn . . . A football and baseball star at Adelphi U., he gained All-America honors as a pitcher in '73 . . . Outstanding minor league career (38-21) earned quick promotion to majors and he came up to stay in '76.

Year	Club	G	IP	W	L	Pct.	SO	BB	H	ERA
1976	Houston	20	53	3	2	.600	26	14	45	3.57
1977	Houston	54	89	5	5	.500	67	24	77	2.33
1978	Houston	62	88	4	9	.308	96	32	85	3.07
1979	Houston	63	91	8	7	.533	83	23	80	1.78
1980	Houston	64	90	8	4	.667	75	22	65	2.20
	Totals	263	411	28	27	.509	347	115	352	2.50

J.R. RICHARD 31 6-8 220 — Bats R Throws R

Baseball's tragedy of the 1980 season found the league's most imposing righthander stricken by a stroke . . . The blow left Richard's career in jeopardy, the Astros without their ace and teammates and newsmen embarrassed because they doubted the star pitcher's claim that something was wrong . . . Voted N.L. Player of Month for April after going 3-0 with a 1.80 ERA and 40 strikeouts in 30 innings . . . Hadn't allowed a homer in 135-plus innings until Dale Murphy and Chris Chambliss connected back-to-back at Atlanta, July 3 . . . Extended his record against L.A. to 13-0 since '76 with a two-hitter and a one-hitter . . . Coupled with 11-2 finish in '79, he was 21-6 in less than a year before being disabled . . . Too early to tell at presstime whether J.R. would even attempt a comeback in 1981 . . . Born March 7, 1950, at Vienna, La.

Year	Club	G	IP	W	L	Pct.	SO	BB	H	ERA
1971	Houston	4	21	2	1	.667	29	16	17	3.43
1972	Houston	4	6	1	0	1.000	8	8	10	13.50
1973	Houston	16	72	6	2	.750	75	38	54	4.00
1974	Houston	15	65	2	3	.400	42	36	58	4.15
1975	Houston	33	203	12	10	.545	176	138	178	4.34
1976	Houston	39	291	20	15	.571	214	151	221	2.75
1977	Houston	36	267	18	12	.600	214	104	212	2.97
1978	Houston	36	275	18	11	.621	303	141	192	3.11
1979	Houston	38	292	18	13	.581	313	98	220	2.71
1980	Houston	17	114	10	4	.714	119	40	65	1.89
	Totals	238	1606	107	71	.601	1493	770	1227	3.15

DON SUTTON 36 6-2 185 **Bats R Throws R**

Traded in his Dodger blue for a set of Astro double-knits when he signed a four-year, $3.5 million pact last December . . . Holds Dodger records for victories, strikeouts, innings and shutouts . . . Led N.L. in ERA (2.21) . . . Was unbeaten from May 27 to July 22, but won only three games in that span . . . Has won at least 11 games every year in majors, but a 20-game winner only once . . . Born May 2, 1945, at Clio, Ala. . . . Object of bidding war between Yankees and Astros, but desire to stay in N.L. and the far reaches of the Astrodome induced Don to sign in Houston . . . Wants broadcasting career after playing days are over.

Year	Club	G	IP	W	L	Pct.	SO	BB	H	ERA
1966	Los Angeles..............	37	226	12	12	.500	209	52	192	2.99
1967	Los Angeles..............	37	233	11	15	.423	169	57	223	3.94
1968	Los Angeles..............	35	208	11	15	.423	162	59	179	2.60
1969	Los Angeles..............	41	293	17	18	.486	217	91	269	3.47
1970	Los Angeles..............	38	260	15	13	.536	201	78	251	4.08
1971	Los Angeles..............	38	265	17	12	.586	194	55	231	2.55
1972	Los Angeles..............	33	273	19	9	.679	207	63	186	2.08
1973	Los Angeles..............	33	256	18	10	.643	200	56	196	2.43
1974	Los Angeles..............	40	276	19	9	.679	179	80	241	3.23
1975	Los Angeles..............	35	254	16	13	.552	175	62	202	2.87
1976	Los Angeles..............	35	268	21	10	.677	161	82	231	3.06
1977	Los Angeles..............	33	240	14	8	.636	150	69	207	3.19
1978	Los Angeles..............	34	238	15	11	.577	154	54	228	3.55
1979	Los Angeles..............	33	226	12	15	.444	146	61	201	3.82
1980	Los Angeles..............	32	212	13	5	.722	128	47	163	2.21
	Totals....................	534	3728	230	175	.568	2652	966	3200	3.07

TOP PROSPECTS

DANNY HEEP 23 5-11 185 **Bats L Throws L**

Hit well in brief trial last year after solving Triple-A pitching for .343 average, 17 homers and 69 RBI in 129 games at Tucson . . . Southern League co-MVP in '79 after batting .327 at Columbus, Ga. . . . Born July 3, 1957, at San Antonio . . . Astros also high on outfielder Gary Woods, who belted some big hits down the stretch last season after .315 year at Tucson.

MANAGER BILL VIRDON: Did an amazing job holding club together after potentially demoralizing loss of Richard . . . Proves that nice guys don't have to finish last . . . Named UPI Manager of Year in '79 for keeping punchless Astros in race most of the way . . . Did even better last year with a weaker team—minus Richard—and a stronger division . . . Born June 9, 1931, at Hazel Park, Mi. . . . Guided Astros to only division crown in their history after winning dogfight from Dodgers . . . Doesn't have the colorful personality of some skippers and his low-key demeanor is reflected in his club . . . Quiet and confident, Virdon has been a winner at every level . . . As rookie manager with Pirates in '72 he won a career-high 96 games and a division title . . . Finished second in first year as Yankees' pilot in '74, starting club back on road to recovery . . . Set Astros' victory high with 89 in '79, and then topped that with 93 last season . . . Played in majors 12 years as an outfielder, batting .319 with Cards and Bucs in 1956.

GREATEST TEAM

Like the expansion Expos, the teenage Astros also enjoyed their best success in '80, surviving a last-ditch scare from the Dodgers to win with 93 victories. Manager Bill Virdon gave the franchise its first winner despite the loss of ace righthander J.R. Richard at mid-season. The club was expected to collapse under the circumstances, but it didn't.

Again, there was little punch in a anemic lineup, but Cruz, Cedeno, Puhl, Cabell, Dennis Walling and Art Howe were superb in spraying basehits and late-season surges by rookie Gary Woods and Joe Morgan made it easier for a crack pitching staff to pick up the slack for Richard. Sambito, Niekro and Ruhle were especially effective and Ryan perked down the stretch. Loss of Cedeno hurt Astros in N.L. playoffs, which they dropped to Phillies after taking 2-1 lead.

ALL-TIME ASTRO LEADERS

BATTING: Rusty Staub, .333, 1967
HRs: Jimmy Wynn, 37, 1967
RBIs: Bob Watson, 110, 1977
STEALS: Cesar Cedeno, 61, 1977
WINS: Joe Niekro, 21, 1979
STRIKEOUTS: J.R. Richard, 313, 1979

LOS ANGELES DODGERS

TEAM DIRECTORY: Pres.: Peter O'Malley; VP-Player Personnel: Al Campanis; VP-Public Relations: Fred Claire; VP-Minor Leagues: Bill Schweppe; Dir. Publ.: Steve Brener; Trav. Sec.: Bill DeLury; Mgr.: Tom Lasorda. Home: Dodger Stadium (56,000). Field distances: 330, l.f. line; 370, l.c.; 395, c.f.; 370, r.c.; 330, r.f. line. Spring training: Vero Beach, Fla.

SCOUTING REPORT

HITTING: Plenty of sock left for a club which topped the league in home runs (148) despite the abasence of Reggie Smith for 70 games and Davey Lopes' power de-emphasis from 28 to 10 hom-

Dusty Baker slammed 29 homers for Dodgers in '80.

ers. The club has so much punch, in fact, it was able to throw a giant scare into the pitching-rich Astros and take them into a playoff last year.

Everyone insists the infield of Steve Garvey, Lopes, Ron Cey and Bill Russell is getting too old, but they don't seem ready for retirement. Garvey is one of the most disciplined and consistent hitters in the league, blending power and skill (26 homers, .304). Cey hammered 28 homers.

Dusty Baker, who chose the Dodgers over free agency, was right behind Garvey in consistency, belting a team-leading 29 homers and batting .294 while assuming more of a leadership role. Smith's comeback from an injury could mean the difference, for he batted .322 with 15 homers and 55 RBI before being sidelined. Pedro Guerrero, also a .322 hitter, is ready to step in as a regular.

PITCHING: The rotation can't possibly be any better without unappreciated Don Sutton, who merely topped the N.L. with a 2.21 ERA and posted 13 victories. Jerry Reuss, Burt Hooton and Bob Welch are solid, but Dave Goltz, Rick Sutcliffe or Doug Rau must bounce back to ease the loss of Sutton.

The bullpen is potentially outstanding, especially if Don Stanhouse and Terry Forster reach their previous form. If not, there's still N.L. Rookie of the Year Steve Howe, Bobby Castillo, Joe Beckwith and Fernando Valenzuela.

FIELDING: There were periods of sloppy play and nobody won a Gold Glove, but the Dodgers collectively fielded .981, good for third in the N.L., so somebody had to be doing something right. Garvey missed by one error of winning the fielding title, making six errors to Rose's five at first base. Lopes, Cey, Baker, Smith and Rudy Law also are solid.

OUTLOOK: As usual, the Dodgers have what it takes to go all the way. Time may be running out for some of the veterans, but youngsters like Law, Guerrero, Mike Scioscia and Mickey Hatcher are ready to make their move and the "oldtimers" may be seeing less playing time, with the exception of ironman Garvey and Baker.

The most critical area is starting pitching. Will losing Sutton, for instance, have the same effect that Tommy John's departure did in 1978? Management, of course, feels otherwise because of the steady flow of young talent. It is a team of character, as evidenced in 1980, and seems capable of being even better this summer, aided by an always-strong bench.

LOS ANGELES DODGERS 1981 ROSTER

MANAGER Tom Lasorda
Coaches—Monty Basgall, Mark Cresse, Manny Mota, Danny Ozark, Ron Perranoski

PITCHERS

No.	Name	1980 Club	W-L	IP	SO	ERA	B-T	Ht.	Wt.	Born
27	Beckwith, Joe	Albuquerque	2-1	14	12	2.57	L-R	6-3	185	1/28/55 Auburn, AL
		Los Angeles	3-3	60	40	1.95				
37	Castillo, Bob	Los Angeles	8-6	98	60	2.76	R-R	5-10	170	4/18/55 Los Angeles, CA
51	Forster, Terry	Los Angeles	0-0	12	2	3.00	L-L	6-3	210	1/14/52 Sioux Falls, SD
38	Goltz, Dave	Los Angeles	7-11	171	91	4.32	R-R	6-4	215	6/23/49 Pelican Rapids, MN
55	Holton, Brian	San Antonio	15-10	207	130	3.43	R-R	6-1	174	11/29/59 Buena Vista, PA
46	Hooton, Burt	Los Angeles	14-8	207	118	3.65	R-R	6-1	200	2/7/50 Greenville, TX
57	Howe, Steve	Los Angeles	7-9	85	39	2.65	L-L	6-1	180	3/10/58 Pontiac, MI
25	Power, Ted	Albuquerque	13-7	155	113	4.53	R-R	6-4	220	1/13/55 Tulsa, OK
31	Rau, Doug	San Antonio	0-1	15	7	5.40	L-L	6-2	175	12/15/48 Columbus, TX
41	Reuss, Jerry	Los Angeles	18-6	229	111	2.52	L-L	6-5	217	6/19/49 St. Louis, MO
26	Stanhouse, Don	Los Angeles	2-2	25	5	5.04	R-R	6-2	198	2/12/51 DuQuoin, IL
48	Stewart, Dave	Albuquerque	15-10	202	125	3.70	R-R	6-2	200	2/19/57 Oakland, CA
43	Sutcliffe, Rick	Los Angeles	3-9	110	59	5.56	L-R	6-6	200	6/21/56 Independence, MO
34	Valenzuela, Fernando	San Antonio	13-9	174	162	3.10	L-L	5-11	180	11/1/60 Mexico
		Los Angeles	2-0	18	16	0.00				
35	Welch, Bob	Los Angeles	14-9	214	141	3.28	R-R	6-3	190	11/3/56 Detroit, MI

CATCHERS

No.	Name	1980 Club	H	HR	RBI	Pct.	B-T	Ht.	Wt.	Born
13	Ferguson, Joe	Los Angeles	41	9	29	.238	R-R	6-2	215	9/19/46 San Francisco, CA
14	Scioscia, Mike	Albuquerque	53	3	33	.331	L-R	6-2	200	11/27/58 Upper Darby, PA
		Los Angeles	34	1	8	.254				
7	Yeager, Steve	Los Angeles	48	2	20	.211	R-R	6-0	200	11/24/48 Huntington, WV

INFIELDERS

No.	Name	1980 Club	H	HR	RBI	Pct.	B-T	Ht.	Wt.	Born
10	Cey, Ron	Los Angeles	140	28	77	.254	R-R	5-10	185	2/15/48 Tacoma, WA
36	Frias, Pepe	Texas	55	0	10	.242	R-R	5-10	165	7/14/48 Dominican Republic
		Los Angeles	2	0	0	.222				
6	Garvey, Steve	Los Angeles	200	26	106	.304	R-R	5-10	190	12/22/48 Tampa, FL
44	Hatcher, Mickey	Albuquerque	65	7	40	.359	R-R	6-2	195	3/15/55 Cleveland, OH
		Los Angeles	19	1	5	.226				
15	Lopes, Dave	Los Angeles	139	10	49	.251	R-R	5-10	170	5/3/46 E. Providence, RI
5	Marshall, Mike	San Antonio	151	16	82	.321	R-R	6-5	215	1/12/60 Libertyville, IL
45	Perconte, Jack	Albuquerque	143	2	46	.326	L-R	5-10	160	8/31/54 Joliet, IL
		Los Angeles	4	0	2	.235				
18	Russell, Bill	Los Angeles	123	3	34	.264	R-R	6-0	175	10/21/48 Pittsburg, KS
52	Sax, Steve	Vero Beach	149	2	58	.283	R-R	5-11	185	1/20/50 Sacramento, CA
1	Weiss, Gary	Albuquerque	123	6	51	.291	L-R	5-10	170	12/27/55 Brenham, TX
		Los Angeles	0	0	0	.000				

OUTFIELDERS

No.	Name	1980 Club	H	HR	RBI	Pct.	B-T	Ht.	Wt.	Born
12	Baker, Dusty	Los Angeles	170	29	97	.294	R-R	6-2	195	6/15/49 Riverside, CA
22	Bradley, Mark	San Antonio	117	12	76	.249	R-R	6-1	180	12/3/56 Elizabethtown, KY
28	Guerrero, Pedro	Los Angeles	59	7	31	.322	R-R	5-11	176	6/29/56 Dominican Republic
21	Johnstone, Jay	Los Angeles	77	2	20	.307	L-R	6-1	190	11/20/46 Manchester, CT
3	Law, Rudy	Los Angeles	101	1	23	.260	L-L	6-1	165	10/7/56 Waco, TX
47	Maldonado, Candy	Lodi	139	25	102	.305	R-R	6-0	185	9/5/60 Puerto Rico
17	Mitchell, Bob	Albuquerque	111	3	53	.320	L-L	5-10	170	4/7/55 Salt Lake City, UT
		Los Angeles	1	0	0	.333				
16	Monday, Rick	Los Angeles	52	10	25	.268	L-L	6-3	200	11/20/45 Batesville, AR
50	Roenicke, Ron	Albuquerque	80	7	47	.296	B-L	6-0	180	8/19/56 Covina, CA
8	Smith, Reggie	Los Angeles	100	15	55	.322	B-R	6-0	195	4/2/45 Shreveport, LA
30	Thomas, Derrel	Los Angeles	79	1	22	.266	B-R	6-0	160	1/14/51 Los Angeles, CA
9	Thomasson, Gary	Los Angeles	24	1	12	.216	L-L	6-1	180	7/29/51 San Diego, CA

DODGER PROFILES

STEVE GARVEY 32 5-10 190 Bats R Throws R

Had more trouble with his wife's comments than with baseball in 1980, once again displaying the consistency that has characterized his career . . . Batted above .300 for seventh time in eight years and extended consecutive games streak to 835 . . . Barely collected 200 hits to lead N.L. . . . Sixth time he has hit 200 mark . . . Second-squad first baseman on majors' team of the decade . . . Batted .398 in July with nine homers, 20 RBI . . . Brunt of jokes because of wife Cyndy's popping off in national mag . . . May have affected performance, for Steve was in 1-for-28 slump at end of August and also had a September dry spell before finishing fast . . . Had 100 RBI four straight seasons . . . Born Dec. 22, 1948, at Tampa . . . Former Michigan State athlete . . . Portrays a wholesome, nice-guy image which has caused problems with teammates . . . Only major leaguer to have a junior high named in his honor.

Year	Club	Pos.	G	AB	R	H	2B	3B	HR	RBI	SB	Avg.
1969	Los Angeles.....	3B	3	3	0	1	0	0	0	0	0	.333
1970	Los Angeles.....	3B-2B	34	93	8	25	5	0	1	6	1	.269
1971	Los Angeles.....	3B	81	225	27	51	12	1	7	26	1	.227
1972	Los Angeles.....	3B-1B	96	294	36	79	14	2	9	30	4	.269
1973	Los Angeles.....	1B-OF	114	349	37	106	17	3	8	50	0	.304
1974	Los Angeles.....	1B	156	642	95	200	32	3	21	111	5	.312
1975	Los Angeles.....	1B	160	659	85	210	38	6	18	95	11	.319
1976	Los Angeles.....	1B	162	631	85	200	37	4	13	80	19	.317
1977	Los Angeles.....	1B	162	646	91	192	25	3	33	115	9	.297
1978	Los Angeles.....	1B	162	639	89	202	36	9	21	113	10	.316
1979	Los Angeles.....	1B	162	648	92	204	32	1	28	110	3	.315
1980	Los Angeles.....	1B	163	658	77	200	27	1	26	106	6	.304
	Totals..........		1455	5487	722	1670	275	33	185	842	69	.304

DUSTY BAKER 31 6-2 195 Bats R Throws R

Hey, what does a guy have to do to get recognition? . . . Dusty has never been invited to the All-Star Game and his '80 snub infuriated some of his teammates, who consider him club MVP . . . Topped club in game-winning RBI and homers . . . Enjoyed a monster June with 10 homers, 26 RBI and .349 average for N.L. Player-of-Month honors . . . Hit five homers in four games during streak . . . Not a bad August either: .354, six homers, 21 RBI . . . Born June 15, 1949, at Riverside, Cal. . . . Underrated, but no longer underpaid following free agent option year . . . Enjoyed 16-game batting streak . . . Credits Jim Lefebvre's weight training program for development . . . Batted .399 in '77 World Series . . . Regarded as one of toughest clutch hitters in league.

Year	Club	Pos.	G	AB	R	H	2B	3B	HR	RBI	SB	Avg.
1968	Atlanta.........	OF	6	5	0	2	0	0	0	0	0	.400
1969	Atlanta.........	OF	3	7	0	0	0	0	0	0	0	.000
1970	Atlanta.........	OF	13	24	3	7	0	0	0	4	0	.292
1971	Atlanta.........	OF	29	62	2	14	2	0	0	4	0	.226
1972	Atlanta.........	OF	127	446	62	143	27	2	17	76	4	.321
1973	Atlanta.........	OF	159	604	101	174	29	4	21	99	24	.288
1974	Atlanta.........	OF	149	574	80	147	35	0	20	69	18	.256
1975	Atlanta.........	OF	142	494	63	129	18	2	19	72	12	.261
1976	Los Angeles.....	OF	112	384	36	93	13	0	4	39	2	.242
1977	Los Angeles.....	OF	153	533	86	155	26	1	30	86	2	.291
1978	Los Angeles.....	OF	149	522	62	137	24	1	11	66	12	.262
1979	Los Angeles.....	OF	151	554	86	152	29	1	23	88	11	.274
1980	Los Angeles.....	OF	153	579	80	170	26	4	29	97	12	.294
	Totals..........		1348	4788	661	1323	229	15	174	700	97	.276

REGGIE SMITH 36 6-0 195 Bats S Throws R

Shoulder problems marred what might have been slugging rightfielder's best season ever . . . Limited to 92 games, yet had 15 homers, 55 RBI and a career-high .322 average . . . Can't seem to evade controversy, like the other Reggie . . . Required 60 stitches after slashing his wrist slamming the door of the clubhouse cooler in anger over a disagreement with Derrel Thomas . . . Partial dislocation necessitated second shoulder surgery in three years in September . . . Born April 2, 1945, at Shreveport, La., but reared in L.A. . . . Led Dodgers to pennants in 1977-78 . . . Club weakened with him out of lineup in 1979-80 . . . Can he come back again?

Year	Club	Pos.	G	AB	R	H	2B	3B	HR	RBI	SB	Avg.
1966	Boston.........	OF	6	26	1	4	1	0	0	0	0	.154
1967	Boston.........	OF-2B	158	565	78	139	24	6	15	61	16	.246
1968	Boston.........	OF	155	558	78	148	37	5	15	69	22	.265
1969	Boston.........	OF	143	543	87	168	29	7	25	93	7	.309
1970	Boston.........	OF	147	580	109	176	32	7	22	74	10	.303
1971	Boston.........	OF	159	618	85	175	33	2	30	95	11	.283
1972	Boston.........	OF	131	467	75	126	25	4	21	74	15	.270
1973	Boston.........	OF-1B	115	423	79	128	23	2	21	69	3	.303
1974	St. Louis.......	OF-1B	143	517	79	160	26	9	23	100	4	.309
1975	St. Louis.......	OF-1B-3B	135	477	67	144	26	3	19	76	9	.302
1976	St. L-LA........	OF-1B-3B	112	395	55	100	15	5	18	49	3	.253
1977	Los Angeles.....	OF	148	488	104	150	27	4	32	87	7	.307
1978	Los Angeles.....	OF	128	447	82	132	27	2	29	93	12	.295
1979	Los Angeles.....	OF	68	234	41	64	13	1	10	32	6	.274
1980	Los Angeles.....	OF	92	311	47	100	13	0	15	55	5	.322
	Totals..........		1840	6649	1067	1914	351	57	295	1028	130	.288

DAVEY LOPES 34 5-10 170 **Bats R Throws R**

Tailed off in several offensive categories last season, but still is regarded as the club's leader . . . Most pronounced drop was in homers, from 28 to 10 . . . Named second-team second baseman on majors' team of decade . . . Had a 44-game errorless string snapped May 17 after enjoying a 48-game streak in 1978-79 . . . A popular player who was embarrassed at being named an All-Star Game starter when he felt undeserving . . . Born May 3, 1946, at East Providence, R.I. . . . Reduced his base stealing, but his career percentage above .800 is major league record . . . Stepped down as team captain in '79 . . . Seems to be the glue that holds the Dodgers together . . . Once a premier base thief, but age has taken its toll on legs.

Year	Club	Pos.	G	AB	R	H	2B	3B	HR	RBI	SB	Avg.
1972	Los Angeles.....	2B	11	42	6	9	4	0	0	1	4	.214
1973	Los Angeles.....	2B-OF-SS-3B	142	535	77	147	13	5	6	37	36	.275
1974	Los Angeles.....	2B	145	530	95	141	26	3	10	35	59	.266
1975	Los Angeles.....	2B-OF-SS	155	618	108	162	24	6	8	41	77	.262
1976	Los Angeles.....	2B-OF	117	427	72	103	17	7	4	20	63	.241
1977	Los Angeles.....	2B	134	502	85	142	19	5	11	53	47	.283
1978	Los Angeles.....	2B-OF	151	587	93	163	25	4	17	58	45	.278
1979	Los Angeles.....	2B	153	582	109	154	20	6	28	73	44	.265
1980	Los Angeles.....	2B	141	553	79	139	15	3	10	49	23	.251
	Totals..........		1149	4376	724	1160	163	39	94	367	398	.265

RON CEY 36 5-10 185 **Bats R Throws R**

Penguin struggled through early season, but bounced back strong in September to bring power figures up to normal level . . . All-time L.A. home run leader with 190 after belting 28, 16 of them after ASG . . . Home run downed Astros on final day to force playoff . . . Born Feb. 15, 1948, at Tacoma . . . Attended Washington State U. . . . Set Dodgers' fielding mark for third baseman with .977 percentage in '79, tying Ken Reitz' N.L. record with fewest errors, nine . . . Fielded solidly again last year . . . Set major league mark with 29 RBI in April 1977 . . . L.A. never had a reliable third baseman until Cey took over in '73 . . . Surprising power for his size . . . A Giant-killer in the finest Dodger tradition.

Year	Club	Pos.	G	AB	R	H	2B	3B	HR	RBI	SB	Avg.
1971	Los Angeles.....	PH	2	2	0	0	0	0	0	0	0	.000
1972	Los Angeles.....	3B	11	37	3	10	1	0	1	3	0	.270
1973	Los Angeles.....	3B	152	507	60	124	18	4	15	80	1	.245
1974	Los Angeles.....	3B	159	577	88	151	20	2	18	97	1	.262
1975	Los Angeles.....	3B	158	566	72	160	29	2	25	101	5	.283
1976	Los Angeles.....	3B	145	502	69	139	18	3	23	80	0	.277
1977	Los Angeles.....	3B	153	564	77	136	22	3	30	110	3	.241
1978	Los Angeles.....	3B	159	555	84	150	32	0	23	84	2	.270
1979	Los Angeles.....	3B	150	487	77	137	20	1	28	81	3	.281
1980	Los Angeles.....	3B	157	551	81	140	25	0	28	77	2	.254
	Totals..........		1246	4348	611	1147	185	15	191	713	17	.264

STEVE HOWE 23 6-1 180 Bats L Throws L

The pitching sensation of the 1980 season for the Dodgers . . . Voted N.L. Rookie of the Year . . . Jumped from a few weeks of Double-A ball in '79 to the major league club after beginning the spring as a non-roster player . . . Injuries to Don Stanhouse and Terry Forster accelerated the progress . . . Established a Dodgers' rookie record with 17 saves, topping Joe Black's 15 . . . Stole thunder from Bobby Castillo, who had a good year out of the bullpen from the right side . . . Born March 10, 1958, at Pontiac, Mi. . . . A standout at U. of Michigan, where his 27 victories are a school record . . . Went 6-2 with 3.13 ERA at San Antonio in pro debut . . . Won regular-season finale over Houston.

Year	Club	G	IP	W	L	Pct.	SO	BB	H	ERA
1980	Los Angeles.............	59	85	7	9	.438	39	22	83	2.65

JERRY REUSS 31 6-5 217 Bats L Throws L

After winning only 20 games the previous three years, he soared to 18-6 record and 2.52 ERA . . . Top achievement was an 8-0, no-hit victory at San Francisco, June 27 . . . Went 3-0 with three shutouts in June to earn N.L. Player-of-Month distinction . . . Got going with a 3-1 May and was 5-0 with a 2.35 ERA in August . . . Didn't start until after he went 3-0 with a 0.64 ERA in four relief appearances . . . Slow starts by Dave Goltz and Rick Sutcliffe sped up his progress . . . Born June 19, 1949, at St. Louis . . . Frustrated by lack of work with Pittsburgh after averaging 16 victories in 1973-76 . . . Pitched three scoreless innings in 1975 All-Star Game . . . N.L. shutout leader in '80 with six.

Year	Club	G	IP	W	L	Pct.	SO	BB	H	ERA
1969	St. Louis	1	7	1	0	1.000	3	3	2	0.00
1970	St. Louis	20	127	7	8	.467	74	49	132	4.11
1971	St. Louis	36	211	14	14	.500	131	109	228	4.78
1972	Houston	33	192	9	13	.409	174	83	177	4.17
1973	Houston	41	279	16	13	.552	177	117	271	3.74
1974	Pittsburgh	35	260	16	11	.593	105	101	259	3.50
1975	Pittsburgh	32	237	18	11	.621	131	78	224	2.54
1976	Pittsburgh	31	209	14	9	.609	108	51	209	3.53
1977	Pittsburgh	33	208	10	13	.435	116	71	225	4.11
1978	Pittsburgh	23	83	3	2	.600	42	23	97	4.88
1979	Los Angeles	39	160	7	14	.333	83	60	178	3.54
1980	Los Angeles	37	229	18	6	.750	111	40	193	2.52
	Totals	361	2202	133	114	.538	1255	785	2195	3.65

BOB WELCH 24 6-3 190 — Bats R Throws R

Bloomed into a standout starter after gutsy off-season battle with bottle that led to alcohol treatment . . . Was 4-0 with a 2.19 ERA in May . . . Capped month with a one-hitter against Atlanta in which he faced minimum 27 batters, rarer than no-hitter . . . Born Nov. 3, 1956, at Detroit . . . Helped to pitch L.A. to World Series in '78 as a rookie, triggering nine-game win streak with shutout of Giants . . . In celebrated duel with Reggie Jackson in Series, he struck out Yankees' slugger to save Game 2 . . . Succumbed to the pressure in '79 and was limited to 81 innings by a sore arm . . . Along with Sutton and Reuss, a solid comeback candidate . . . Was 4-0 last September, but out with injury final week.

Year	Club	G	IP	W	L	Pct.	SO	BB	H	ERA
1978	Los Angeles	23	111	7	4	.636	66	26	92	2.03
1979	Los Angeles	25	81	5	6	.455	64	32	82	4.00
1980	Los Angeles	32	214	14	9	.609	141	79	190	3.28
	Totals	80	406	26	19	.578	271	137	364	3.08

BURT HOOTON 31 6-1 200 — Bats R Throws R

Posted highest ERA in six years with Dodgers while troubled with bursitis in his shoulder, but still made big contribution with 14-8 record . . . Knuckle curve is rated best in N.L., a baffling pitch which has usually kept him among ERA leaders . . . Enjoyed finest season in '78, pitching Dodgers to World Series with 19-10, 2.71 stats . . . Has 2-2 career record in World Series . . . Born Feb. 7, 1950, at Greenville, Tex.

. . . Nicknamed Happy because of dour look, win or lose . . . Greatest pitcher in U. of Texas history, 35-3 with 1.14 ERA for All-America career . . . Holds L.A. mark of 12 straight victories in '75 . . . Particularly tough on Giants, beating them 10 in a row before a September setback.

Year	Club	G	IP	W	L	Pct.	SO	BB	H	ERA
1971	Chicago (NL).............	3	21	2	0	1.000	22	10	8	2.14
1972	Chicago (NL).............	33	218	11	14	.440	132	81	201	2.81
1973	Chicago (NL).............	42	240	14	17	.452	134	73	248	3.68
1974	Chicago (NL).............	48	176	7	11	.389	94	51	214	4.81
1975	Chi (NL)-LA..............	34	235	18	9	.667	153	68	190	3.06
1976	Los Angeles..............	33	227	11	15	.423	116	60	203	3.25
1977	Los Angeles..............	32	223	12	7	.632	153	60	184	2.62
1978	Los Angeles..............	32	236	19	10	.655	104	61	196	2.71
1979	Los Angeles..............	29	212	11	10	.524	129	63	191	2.97
1980	Los Angeles..............	34	207	14	8	.636	118	64	194	3.65
	Totals..................	320	1995	119	101	.541	1155	591	1829	3.23

Steve Howe's Rookie-of-the-Year season included 17 saves.

TOP PROSPECTS

MIKE SCIOSCIA 22 6-2 200 Bats L Throws R
With Steve Yeager and Joe Ferguson tailing off, Scioscia is the club's catcher of the present and the future . . . Performed well when called up last season, hitting and throwing better than the veterans . . . Born Nov. 27, 1958, at Upper Darby, Pa. . . . As a 20-year-old, batted .299 in Triple-A in '79 . . . Club also high on infielder-outfielder Mickey Hatcher and 19-year-old lefty reliever Fernando Valenzuela, who didn't allow a run in 18 innings with Dodgers.

MANAGER TOM LASORDA: Bounced back under pressure to direct a solid season despite numerous injuries that left the club crippled down the stretch . . . Got off on wrong foot when several veterans objected to his lineup juggling in April . . . There's no middle ground with Tommy. You either like him or not, critics feeling he is more concerned with his Hollywood hangers-on than with the business at hand . . . Let's face it, he's an extrovert who relishes the show-biz hoopla . . . He'll be out of baseball before he changes . . . Tommy's office looks like a deli after games . . . Born Sept. 22, 1927, at Norristown, Pa. . . . Was an outstanding Triple-A pitcher for Montreal, 107-57 in nine seasons, but never made it in the bigs . . . A loyal Dodger, he patiently waited for Walter Alston to retire and promptly won back-to-back pennants in 1977-78 . . . Manager of Year in '77 . . . A colorful character and a sore loser.

GREATEST TEAM

Separating the Bums of Brooklyn and the Dodgers of Los Angeles, two outstanding teams can be found. The Boys of Summer won four pennants in 1952-56, but beat the Yankees in the Series only in '55. The '53 squad went 105-49 and won the flag by 13 games, so it rates an edge despite losing in six games to the inevitable Yanks. Duke Snider and Roy Campanella broke the 40-home run barrier and Gil Hodges added 31. Carl Erskine (206) and Russ Meyer (15-5) led a talented pitching staff.

The '52 Bums had everything, too. Hodges had 32 homers and 102 RBI, Jackie Robinson batted .308, Snider belted 21 homers and batted .303 and Campanella totaled 22 homers and 97 RBI. There was no 20-game winner, but the staff was formidable with Joe Black (15-4, 2.15), Erskine (14-6, 2.70), Billy Loes (13-8, 2.70) and Preacher Roe (11-2, 3.11).

Los Angeles' most successful club was the 1963 version which won 99 games and swept the Yankees in the Series. Sandy Koufax was incredible at 25-5, 1.88 and added two wins in the Series. Don Drysdale won 19 games and reliever Ron Perranoski was 16-3, 1.67 with 21 saves. There was hitting, too. Tommy Davis was a batting champ at .326, Maury Wills batted .302 and Frank Howard supplied 28 homers.

ALL-TIME DODGER LEADERS

BATTING: Babe Herman, .393, 1930
HRs: Duke Snider, 43, 1956
RBIs: Tommy Davis, 153, 1962
STEALS: Maury Wills, 104, 1962
WINS: Joe McGinnity, 29, 1900
STRIKEOUTS: Sandy Koufax, 382, 1965

SAN DIEGO PADRES

TEAM DIRECTORY: Owner: Ray Kroc; Pres.: Ballard Smith; Dir. Baseball Operations: Jack McKeon; Dir. Business Operations: Elton Schiller; Major League Admin.: Jim Weigel; Dir. Pub. Rel.: Bob Chandler; Trav. Sec.: John Mattei; Mgr.: Frank Howard. Home: San Diego Stadium (51,362). Field distances: 330, l.f. line; 420, c.f.; 330, r.f. line. Spring training: Yuma, Ariz.

SCOUTING REPORT

HITTING: Despite the loss of Dave Winfield, the Padres could improve at the plate with the addition of Terry Kennedy and promising young hitters Broderick Perkins, Randy Bass and Luis Salazar, who impressed in September trials. Kennedy is the key, for he is regarded as the game's next catching star.

High-flying Tim Flannery gives Padres infield depth.

Continued success by Gene Richards (.301) and Jerry Mumphrey (.298) will help and Ozzie Smith is destined to break out of his rut and bat above .230. In one year, thanks in part to Jack McKeon, the Padres have changed their look and are going with a younger, faster team. Richards (61), Smith (57) and Mumphrey (52) combined for 170 steals last year and the club topped the N.L. in thefts, edging Montreal 239-237.

Salazar bears watching after batting .316 in Triple-A last season and following it up with a classy .337 mark in 44 games with San Diego. Perkins popped at a .312 clip on the Triple-A level and spurted to .370 in 43 games. Bass had 37 homers and 143 RBI in Triple-A and added three more homers and eight RBI with the Padres. Promising.

PITCHING: Rollie Fingers and Bob Shirley, both gone now, accounted for 22 of the club's 73 victories last year, so the gap will have to be filled by a flock of promising youngsters, including the quartet of Al Olmsted, John Littlefield, John Urrea and Kim Seaman, obtained from St. Louis. They were a combined 13-9 with the Cards, but are capable of much more with regular duty.

Randy Jones now seeks revival with the Mets, and veterans Rick Wise and John Curtis may be no better than .500 pitchers (they were a combined 16-16 in 1980), so young Padres' farmhands like Juan Eichelberger, Gary Lucas, Steve Mura, George Stablein and Tom Tellmann—plus John Pacella from the Mets—figure to be more prominent in the total picture, consistent with the club's commitment to youth.

FIELDING: Winfield's rifle arm undoubtedly will be missed, but Smith is a Gold Glove shortstop, Kennedy is a comer behind the plate and Richards made great strides in improving his outfield play. The club ranked a solid fourth in the N.L. at .980 last year and figures to be even better afield this season.

OUTLOOK: Rosy, but probably too early to expect a big improvement until the pitching depth is sorted out. The Padres are probably a couple of years away and how Frank Howard handles the youngsters in his maiden campaign as a manager could well determine the club's future.

There just are too many unanswered questions when so many newcomers and youngsters are thrust into front-line duty. One thing seems certain: the Padres' attitude should be greatly improved now that all the grumbling veterans are gone and Jerry Coleman, a nice guy who finished last, is back where he belongs in the broadcast booth.

SAN DIEGO PADRES 1981 ROSTER

MANAGER Frank Howard
Coaches—Chuck Estrada, Bobby Tolan, Eddie Brinkman

PITCHERS

No.	Name	1980 Club	W-L	IP	SO	ERA	B-T	Ht.	Wt.	Born
36	Armstrong, Mike	Hawaii	4-4	74	67	1.95	R-R	6-3	193	3/7/54 Glen Cove, NY
		San Diego	0-0	14	14	5.79				
51	Curtis, John	San Diego	10-8	187	71	3.51	L-L	6-2	185	3/9/48 Newton, MA
13	Eichelberger, Juan	Hawaii	7-3	77	62	3.51	R-R	6-2	195	10/21/53 St. Louis, MO
		San Diego	4-2	89	43	3.64				
62	Fireovid, Steve	Amarillo	12-6	164	106	4.72	B-R	6-2	195	6/6/57 Bryan, OH
59	Hamm, Tim	Reno	15-7	179	122	3.12	R-R	6-4	200	8/8/60 Santa Cruz, CA
63	Hawkins, Andy	Reno	13-10	171	124	4.26	R-R	6-3	200	1/21/60 Waco, TX
–	Littlefield, John	St. Louis	5-5	66	22	3.14	R-R	6-2	200	1/5/54 Covina, CA
43	Lucas, Gary	San Diego	5-8	150	85	3.24	L-L	6-5	200	11/8/54 Colton, CA
27	Mura, Steve	San Diego	8-7	169	109	3.67	R-R	6-2	188	2/12/55 New Orleans, LA
–	Olmsted, Al	Arkansas	3-4	55	41	3.27	R-L	6-2	195	3/18/57 St. Louis, MO
		Springfield	10-5	117	62	2.77				
		St. Louis	1-1	35	14	2.83				
–	Pacella, John	New York (NL)	3-4	84	68	5.14	R-R	6-2	184	9/15/56 Brooklyn, NY
41	Rasmussen, Eric	San Diego	4-11	111	50	4.38	R-R	6-3	205	3/22/52 Racine, WI
–	Seaman, Kim	Springfield	2-3	37	28	4.62	L-L	6-3	205	5/6/57 Pascagoula, MS
		St. Louis	3-2	24	10	3.38				
45	Show, Eric	Amarillo	12-6	166	144	3.74	R-R	6-1	185	5/19/56 Riverside, CA
42	Stablein, George	Hawaii	12-7	153	81	3.88	R-R	6-4	185	10/29/57 Inglewood, CA
		San Diego	0-1	12	4	3.00				
49	Tellman, Tom	Hawaii	13-5	170	83	3.23	R-R	6-4	185	3/29/54 Warren, PA
		San Diego	3-0	22	9	1.23				
–	Urrea, John	St. Louis	4-1	65	36	3.46	R-R	6-3	205	2/9/55 Los Angeles, CA
40	Wise, Rick	San Diego	6-8	154	59	3.68	R-R	6-2	195	9/13/45 Jackson, MI

CATCHERS

No.	Name	1980 Club	H	HR	RBI	Pct.	B-T	Ht.	Wt.	Born
3	Fahey, Bill	San Diego	62	1	22	.257	L-R	6-0	200	6/14/50 Detroit, MI
54	Gwosdz, Doug	Amarillo	70	7	43	.245	R-R	5-11	180	6/20/60 Houston, TX
–	Kennedy, Terry	St. Louis	63	4	34	.254	L-R	6-4	220	6/4/56 Mesa, AZ
7	Stimac, Craig	Hawaii	126	11	47	.298	R-R	6-2	185	11/18/54 Oak Park, IL
		San Diego	11	0	7	.220				
–	Swisher, Steve	St. Louis	6	0	2	.250	R-R	6-2	205	8/9/51 Parkersburg, WVA
47	Tingley, Ron	Reno	61	3	35	.299	R-R	6-2	160	5/27/59 Presque Isle, ME
INFIELDERS										
5	Bass, Randy	Denver	150	37	143	.333	L-R	6-1	210	3/13/54 Lawton, OK
		San Diego	14	3	8	.286				
30	Cash, Dave	San Diego	90	1	23	.227	R-R	5-11	172	6/11/48 Utica, NY
8	Evans, Barry	San Diego	29	1	14	.232	R-R	6-1	180	11/13/56 Atlanta, GA
		Hawaii	26	2	15	.250				
6	Flannery, Tim	Hawaii	63	1	16	.346	L-R	5-11	170	9/29/57 Tulsa, OK
		San Diego	70	0	25	.240				
–	Moreno, Jose	Tidewater	66	5	39	.280	B-R	6-0	175	11/2/57 Dominican Republic
15	Perkins, Broderick	Hawaii	136	6	65	.312	L-L	5-10	180	11/23/54 Pittsburg, CA
		San Diego	37	2	14	.370				
–	Phillips, Mike	St. Louis	30	0	7	.234	L-R	6-1	185	8/19/50 Beaumont, TX
4	Salazar, Luis	Portland	144	7	54	.315	R-R	5-9	180	5/19/56 Venezuela
		Hawaii	13	2	10	.325				
		San Diego	57	1	25	.337				
1	Smith, Ozzie	San Diego	140	0	35	.230	B-R	5-10	150	12/26/54 Mobile, AL
OUTFIELDERS										
14	Beswick, Jim	Hawaii	118	3	54	.266	B-R	6-1	175	2/12/58 Wilkinsburg, PA
21	Dade, Paul	San Diego	10	0	3	.189	R-R	6-0	195	12/7/51 Seattle, WA
		Hawaii	5	0	2	.357				
–	Edwards, Dave	Minnesota	50	2	20	.250	R-R	6-0	170	2/24/54 Los Angeles, CA
28	Mumphrey, Jerry	San Diego	168	4	59	.298	B-R	6-2	185	9/9/52 Tyler, TX
20	Turner, Jerry	San Diego	44	3	18	.288	L-L	5-9	180	1/17/54 Texarkana, AR
17	Richards, Gene	San Diego	193	4	41	.301	L-L	6-0	175	9/29/53 Monticello, SC
–	Stegman, Dave	Evansville	12	1	6	.203	R-R	5-11	190	1/30/54 Inglewood, CA
		Detroit	23	2	9	.177				

PADRE PROFILES

GENE RICHARDS 27 6-0 175 Bats L Throws L

Rebounded nicely from an off season to bat .301 and set a club record with 61 stolen bases . . . Improved dramatically afield and set a team record for outfield assists . . . Established major league mark for rookies with 56 steals in '77 . . . Also set club mark with 18 consecutive steals . . . Batted .327 in May . . . Born Sept. 12, 1953, at Monticello, S.C. . . . Reached majors in two years after short but sweet minor league career . . . California League batting (.381) and stolen base (85) king as rookie for Reno in '75 . . . Followed with .331 mark in PCL before jumping to bigs . . . Signed with Padres after South Carolina State College dropped baseball . . . Much better fielder in left now that Mumphrey is in center . . . Batted .351 in September.

Year	Club	Pos.	G	AB	R	H	2B	3B	HR	RBI	SB	Avg.
1977	San Diego......	OF-1B	146	525	79	152	16	11	5	32	56	.290
1978	San Diego......	OF-1B	154	555	90	171	26	12	4	45	37	.308
1979	San Diego......	OF	150	545	77	152	17	9	4	41	24	.279
1980	San Diego......	OF	158	642	91	193	26	8	4	41	61	.301
	Totals..........		608	2267	337	668	85	40	17	159	178	.295

JERRY MUMPHREY 28 6-2 185 Bats S Throws R

A fine off-season acquisition from Cleveland last February, he ranked as the club's most impressive newcomer . . . Batted close to .300 and stole 52 bases . . . Had a hot September to help club finish strong . . . Became full-time starter with Padres and registered career highs in most departments . . . Born Sept. 9, 1952, at Tyler, Tex. . . . Best previous season was '79, when he batted .295 as part-timer with Cards . . . Swapped to Indians for Bobby Bonds and then was shipped to San Diego for Bob Owchinko and Jim Wilhelm . . . Joined Richards and Smith to give club trio of class base stealers . . . Shored center field position . . . Batted .387 in September.

Year	Club	Pos.	G	AB	R	H	2B	3B	HR	RBI	SB	Avg.
1974	St. Louis.......	OF	5	2	2	0	0	0	0	0	0	.000
1975	St. Louis.......	OF	11	16	2	6	2	0	0	1	0	.375
1976	St. Louis.......	OF	112	384	51	99	15	5	1	26	22	.258
1977	St. Louis.......	OF	145	463	73	133	20	10	2	38	22	.287
1978	St. Louis.......	OF	125	367	41	96	13	4	2	37	14	.262
1979	St. Louis.......	OF	124	339	53	100	10	3	3	32	8	.295
1980	San Diego......	OF	160	564	61	168	24	3	4	59	52	.298
	Totals..........		682	2135	283	602	84	25	12	193	118	.282

OZZIE SMITH 26 5-10 150 **Bats R Throws R**

Created a stir when he came out publicly and said he couldn't make ends meet on $72,500 salary. Placed want-ad in paper and received job offers for supplemental income . . . Low batting average belies value to club, for he's a crack shortstop, can steal bases (57) and topped the N.L. in sacrifice hits . . . After .258 rookie season, slipped to .211 in '79, failing to collect a hit in first 32 at bats of season . . . Only played 68 games in minors, batting .303 for Walla Walla, Wash., in '77 . . . Born Dec. 16, 1954, at Mobile, Ala., also home of boyhood heroes Henry Aaron and Willie McCovey . . . Topped N.L. with 28 sacrifice bunts in '78 and was runnerup to Bob Horner for Rookie of Year honors . . . Set major league mark for assists by a shortstop last year and won Gold Glove.

Year	Club	Pos.	G	AB	R	H	2B	3B	HR	RBI	SB	Avg.
1978	San Diego......	SS	159	590	69	152	17	6	1	46	40	.258
1979	San Diego......	SS	156	587	77	124	18	6	0	27	28	.211
1980	San Diego......	SS	158	609	67	140	18	5	0	35	57	.230
	Totals..........		473	1786	213	416	53	17	1	108	125	.233

TERRY KENNEDY 24 6-4 220 **Bats L Throws R**

The biggest name the Padres snagged in the 11-player deal with the Cardinals last December . . . Never got a real chance in St. Louis, playing behind Ted Simmons . . . Batted .254 with 4 HR and 34 RBI in only 248 at-bats last season . . . Considered to be the best young receiver in the league . . . Born June 4, 1956, in Mesa, Ariz. . . . Had outstanding college career at Florida State University, where his coach was former major league infielder Woody Woodward . . . Was named Sporting News College Player of the Year in 1977 . . . With departure of Gene Tenace, Kennedy will be handed Padres' catching job . . . The son of Cubs' general manager Bob Kennedy.

Year	Club	Pos.	G	AB	R	H	2B	3B	HR	RBI	SB	Avg.
1978	St. Louis	C	10	29	0	5	0	0	0	2	0	.172
1979	St. Louis	C	33	109	11	31	7	0	2	17	0	.284
1980	St. Louis	C-OF	84	248	28	63	12	3	4	34	0	.254
	Totals..........		127	386	39	99	19	3	6	53	0	.256

BRODERICK PERKINS 26 5-10 180 Bats L Throws L

His emergence and presence of Randy Bass made Willie Montanez expendable . . . First baseman came up to stay with successive .327 and .312 season for Hawaii in PCL . . . Promoted last Aug. 11 and immediately started booming, hitting close to .400 down the stretch, including a club-high, 13-game batting streak . . . Born Nov. 23, 1954, at Pittsburg, Cal. . . . Started strong with Pads in '79, but back injury retarded progress and he was sent back to Triple-A . . . A top minor league hitter after being MVP of the West Coast Athletic Conference for St. Mary's College.

Year	Club	Pos.	G	AB	R	H	2B	3B	HR	RBI	SB	Avg.
1978	San Diego......	1B	62	217	14	52	14	1	2	33	4	.240
1979	San Diego......	1B	57	87	8	23	0	0	0	8	0	.264
1980	San Diego......	1B	43	100	18	37	9	0	2	14	2	.370
	Totals..........		162	404	40	112	23	1	4	55	6	.277

RICK WISE 35 6-2 195 Bats R Throws R

Another Ray Kroc free-agent acquisition that failed to pay dividends . . . Signed five-year, $2.1 million pact last year and then won all of six games . . . In fairness, though, injuries limited him to 27 games . . . Seemingly has been around forever, he won first game in 1964 with Phillies . . . Has also toiled for Cardinals, Red Sox and Indians . . . Had great sense of timing when he went 15-10 in option year in Cleveland . . . That earned him the fat contract with Padres . . . Born Sept. 13, 1945, in Jackson, Mich. . . . Author of 30 career shutouts . . . Was one of league's better-hitting pitchers but six-year tour of duty in A.L. made him rusty: he hit only .158 last season.

Year	Club	G	IP	W	L	Pct.	SO	BB	H	ERA
1964	Philadelphia..............	25	69	5	3	.625	39	25	78	4.04
1966	Philadelphia..............	22	99	5	6	.455	58	24	100	3.73
1967	Philadelphia..............	36	181	11	11	.500	111	45	177	3.28
1968	Philadelphia..............	30	182	9	15	.375	97	37	210	4.55
1969	Philadelphia..............	33	220	15	13	.536	144	61	215	3.23
1970	Philadelphia..............	35	220	13	14	.481	113	65	253	4.17
1971	Philadelphia..............	38	272	17	14	.548	155	70	261	2.88
1972	St. Louis.................	35	269	16	16	.500	142	71	250	3.11
1973	St. Louis.................	35	259	16	12	.571	144	59	259	3.37
1974	Boston....................	9	49	3	4	.429	25	16	47	3.86
1975	Boston....................	35	255	19	12	.613	141	72	262	3.95
1976	Boston....................	34	224	14	11	.560	93	48	218	3.54
1977	Boston....................	26	128	11	5	.688	85	28	151	4.78
1978	Cleveland.................	33	212	9	19	.321	106	59	226	4.33
1979	Cleveland.................	34	232	15	10	.600	108	68	229	3.72
1980	San Diego.................	27	154	6	8	.429	59	37	172	3.68
	Totals....................	487	3025	184	173	.515	1620	785	3108	3.68

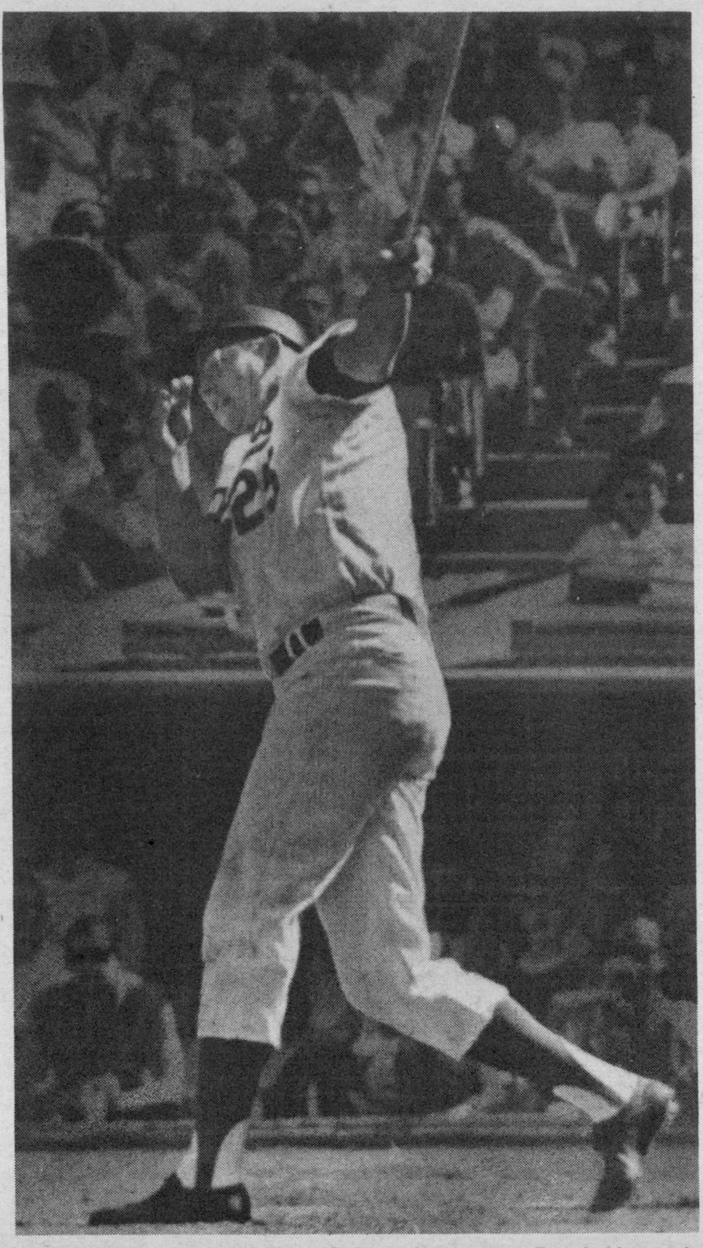

The Padres could use the HR bat of manager Frank Howard.

JOHN CURTIS 33 6-2 185 **Bats L Throws L**

Finished strong to register respectable stats following horrendous start . . . Lost five in a row while troubled by shoulder injury before All-Star break . . . Bounced back to go 3-1 with a 2.75 ERA in August . . . One of few bearded ballplayers in majors . . . Born March 9, 1948, at Newton, Mass. . . . Earned lucrative free-agent contract by going 10-9 with Giants in '79, best season since 1973 . . . Well-traveled veteran is a writer in the off-season, an essayist rather than a deadline-beater . . . Fired three no-hitters in Clemson career, going 15-3 in two years . . . Hurled U.S. to first-ever win over Cuba in Pan American Games . . . Was 4-0, 2.36 in September, salvaging season.

Year	Club	G	IP	W	L	Pct.	SO	BB	H	ERA
1970	Boston	1	2	0	0	.000	1	1	4	13.50
1971	Boston	5	26	2	2	.500	19	6	30	3.12
1972	Boston	26	154	11	8	.579	106	50	161	3.74
1973	Boston	35	221	13	13	.500	101	83	225	3.58
1974	St. Louis	33	195	10	14	.417	89	83	199	3.78
1975	St. Louis	39	147	8	9	.471	67	65	151	3.43
1976	St. Louis	37	134	6	11	.353	52	65	139	4.50
1977	San Francisco	43	77	3	3	.500	47	48	95	5.49
1978	San Francisco	46	63	4	3	.571	38	29	60	3.71
1979	San Francisco	27	121	10	9	.526	85	42	121	4.17
1980	San Diego	30	187	10	8	.556	71	67	184	3.51
	Totals	322	1327	77	80	.490	676	539	1369	3.87

TOP PROSPECTS

LUIS SALAZAR 24 5-9 180 **Bats R Throws R**

An instant sensation upon joining club in swap with Pirates for Kurt Bevacqua and Mark Lee . . . Hit in 17 of first 21 games and batted in .350-.400 range down stretch . . . Will play somewhere in club's infield this season . . . Born May 19, 1956, at Puerto LaCruz, Venezuela . . . Tougher for Randy Bass to break into lineup because of Perkins' presence at first base . . . But Bass also hit well with Pads after journeyman minor league slugger topped American Assn. with 37 homers and 143 RBI at Denver . . . Came from Expos' system in exchange for John D'Acquisto.

MANAGER FRANK HOWARD: The biggest manager (6-7, 330) in the bigs, Howard is, like predecessor Jerry Coleman, a rookie in the job . . . He did manage once before, Spokane, which finished fourth in the PCL in 1976 . . . Comes off four years as first-base coach at Milwaukee . . . Hondo was a notorious slugger (382 homers) during a 15-year major league career with the Dodgers, Washington Senators, Texas Rangers and the Tigers . . . Was N.L. Rookie of the Year with Dodgers in 1960, twice led the A.L. in homers (44 in 1968 and '70) . . . Spent a season in Japan in '74 . . . Born Aug. 4, 1936, in Columbus, Ohio, has lived with wife and six children in Green Bay, Wis. . . . Played baseball and basketball at Ohio State . . . Broke in with the Dodgers' Green Bay farm team in '58 . . . Said Jack McKeon, the Padres' new director of baseball operations: "I've seen what a good teacher he is, how players respond to him [in spring training and instructional leagues]. He has enthusiasm, charisma and is firm. I know I wouldn't want to challenge him physically."

GREATEST TEAM

Not much to choose from here, but the '78 club is the best bet with a club-high 84-78 record and a solid fourth-place finish. Youngsters Gene Richards and Dave Winfield each batted .308 and the latter smacked 24 homers and knocked in 97 runs. Gaylord Perry won the Cy Young Award with a 21-6 and a 2.72 ERA. Rollie Fingers saved a record 37 games.

Though only fourth, the '78 Padres were the best in the short history of the franchise simply because no other San Diego club ever posted a winning record. One year later, however, manager Roger Craig was relieved of duties. Baseball is a funny game.

ALL-TIME PADRE LEADERS

BATTING: Clarence Gaston, .318, 1970
HRs: Nate Colbert, 38, 1970
RBIs: Dave Winfield, 118, 1979
STEALS: Gene Richards, 61, 1980
WINS: Randy Jones, 22, 1976
STRIKEOUTS: Clay Kirby, 231, 1971

SAN FRANCISCO GIANTS

TEAM DIRECTORY: Pres.: Bob Lurie; VP-Baseball Oper.: Spec Richardson; VP-Bus. Oper.: Pat Gallagher; Exec. Asst. to Pres.: Corey Busch; Dir. Player Personnel: Bob Fontaine; Dir. Scouting-Minor League Oper.: Jack Schwarz; Dir. Publ.: Duffy Jennings; Community and PR Dir.: Stu Smith; Trav. Sec.: Ralph Nelson; Mgr.: Frank Robinson. Home: Candlestick Park (58,000). Field distances: 335, l.f. line; 410, c.f.; 325, r.f. line. Spring training: Phoenix, Ariz.

SCOUTING REPORT

HITTING: Lots of room for improvement after the club was last in the N.L. with a .244 average last season. But help appears on the way with Enos Cabell and Jerry Martin adding punch to the

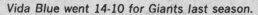

Vida Blue went 14-10 for Giants last season.

lineup and giving some protection to slugging star Jack Clark.

Another bonus could be the return to form of Mike Ivie and Rennie Stennett. Both have had big years in the past, but were nothing but a thorn in the side of departed manager Dave Bristol last season. A solid campaign by either, especially by powerful Ivie, and the expected help provided by Cabell and Martin could make the club decent at the dish. Darrell Evans and Milt May also are capable.

PITCHING: Destined to improve, especially with more plate support. The club lost 13 wins in John Montefusco, Bob Knepper and Phil Nastu, but gained 14 in Doyle Alexander, so there probably won't be a dropoff. But strong years from Vida Blue and Ed Whitson are vital to the club's continued success on the mound.

The Giants were fourth in the N.L. with a 3.56 team ERA, and most of it can be attributed to the work of Blue (2.97) and Whitson (3.10) and a bullpen which could be the division's best. With apologies to Houston, S.F. had a solid four-man bullpen of righthanders Greg Minton and Tom Griffin and lefthanders Al Holland and Gary Lavelle.

FIELDING: Not good and the prospect of a big improvement is questionable. The club is not solid down the middle, though shortstop Johnnie LeMaster has the physical tools to be an excellent fielder. Catcher May has a weak arm, second baseman Stennett has limited range and Cabell made even more errors than Evans at third last season.

OUTLOOK: Easily the most revamped N.L. West team over the winter. The Giants were busy at the winter meetings, making three trades and coming close to completing a fourth (Ken Forsch) which would have bolstered their rotation. The chemistry on the club couldn't be any worse than it was last year, so the changes can't help but have a positive impact.

The new look includes a new manager, for Bristol was stunningly dismissed during the meetings, his failure to relate to his grumbling players considered as a major factor. Frank Robinson will have a lot of possibilities, especially since the club entered spring training with an abundance of outfielders.

If only half of the new players come through and the club can avoid numerous injuries, there's no way to go but up. A pitching edge over the Braves and Padres makes the Giants the best bet among the underdogs of crashing the first division should the Reds falter.

SAN FRANCISCO GIANTS 1981 ROSTER

MANAGER Frank Robinson
Coaches—Unnamed at press time

PITCHERS

No.	Name	1980 Club	W-L	IP	SO	ERA	B-T	Ht.	Wt.	Born
–	Alexander, Doyle	Atlanta	14-11	232	114	4.19	R-R	6-3	205	9/4/50 Cordova, AL
14	Blue, Vida	San Francisco	14-10	224	129	2.97	B-L	6-0	192	7/28/49 Mansfield, LA
34	Bordley, Bill	Phoenix	4-8	111	66	5.35	L-L	6-2	200	1/9/58 Los Angeles, CA
		San Francisco	2-3	31	11	4.65				
48	Breining, Fred	Phoenix	6-13	100	84	4.14	R-R	6-4	185	11/15/55 San Francisco, CA
		San Francisco	0-0	7	3	5.14				
43	Griffin, Tom	San Francisco	5-1	108	79	2.75	R-R	6-3	210	2/22/48 Los Angeles, CA
40	Hargesheimer, Al	Shreveport	2-6	81	40	1.78	R-R	6-3	200	11/21/56 Chicago, IL
		Phoenix	1-1	17	13	4.24				
		San Francisco	4-6	75	40	4.32				
19	Holland, Al	San Francisco	5-3	82	65	1.76	R-L	5-11	213	8/16/52 Roanoke, VA
46	Lavelle, Gary	San Francisco	6-8	100	66	3.42	B-L	6-1	190	1/3/49 Scranton, PA
38	Minton, Greg	San Francisco	4-6	91	42	2.47	B-R	6-2	194	7/29/51 Lubbock, TX
17	Moffitt, Randy	San Francisco	1-1	17	10	4.76	R-R	6-3	195	10/13/48 Long Beach, CA
33	Ripley, Al	Phoenix	5-0	44	19	2.45	R-R	6-3	200	10/18/52 Norwood, MA
		San Francisco	9-10	113	65	4.14				
28	Rowland, Mike	Phoenix	5-11	140	58	4.56	R-R	6-3	205	1/31/53 Chicago, IL
		San Francisco	1-1	27	8	2.33				
50	Stember, Jeff	Shreveport	5-5	102	61	2.65	R-R	6-5	220	3/2/58 Elizabeth, NJ
		Phoenix	5-2	55	29	3.44				
		San Francisco	0-0	3	0	3.00				
32	Whitson, Ed	San Francisco	11-13	212	90	3.10	R-R	6-3	190	5/19/55 Johnson City, TN

CATCHERS

No.	Name	1980 Club	H	HR	RBI	Pct.	B-T	Ht.	Wt.	Born
–	Cummings, Bob	Clinton	103	13	79	.282	R-R	6-2	185	9/8/60 Chicago, IL
35	Littlejohn, Dennis	Phoenix	54	3	22	.320	R-R	6-2	210	10/4/54 Santa Monica, CA
		San Francisco	7	0	2	.241				
7	May, Milt	San Francisco	93	6	50	.260	L-R	6-0	190	8/1/50 Gary, IN
–	Rabb, John	Fresno	96	19	80	.243	R-R	6-1	179	6/23/60 Los Angeles, CA
	Ransom, Jeff	Shreveport	104	0	39	.264	B-R	5-11	185	11/11/60 Fresno, CA

INFIELDERS

No.	Name	1980 Club	H	HR	RBI	Pct.	B-T	Ht.	Wt.	Born
–	Cabell, Enos	Houston	167	2	55	.276	R-R	6-4	185	10/8/49 Ft. Riley, KS
41	Evans, Darrell	San Francisco	147	20	78	.264	L-R	6-2	200	5/26/47 Pasadena, CA
15	Ivie, Mike	San Francisco	69	4	25	.241	R-R	6-4	215	8/8/52 Decatur, GA
10	LeMaster, Johnny	San Francisco	87	3	31	.215	R-R	6-2	165	6/19/54 Portsmouth, OH
29	Murray, Rich	Phoenix	44	7	31	.262	R-R	6-4	205	7/6/57 Los Angeles, CA
		San Francisco	42	4	24	.216				
2	Pettini, Joe	Phoenix	97	2	32	.282	R-R	5-9	165	1/26/55 Wheeling, WV
		San Francisco	44	1	9	.232				
6	Stennett, Rennie	San Francisco	97	2	37	.244	R-R	5-11	185	4/5/51 Panama
21	Sularz, Guy	Phoenix	84	2	26	.275	R-R	5-11	165	11/7/55 Minneapolis, MN
		San Francisco	16	0	3	.246				

OUTFIELDERS

No.	Name	1980 Club	H	HR	RBI	Pct.	B-T	Ht.	Wt.	Born
22	Clark, Jack	San Francisco	124	22	82	.284	R-R	6-1	170	11/10/55 New Brighton, PA
–	Davis, Charlie	Shreveport	130	12	67	.294	B-R	6-3	195	1/17/60 Jamaica
–	Figueroa, Jesus	Wichita	4	1	3	.103	L-L	5-10	160	2/20/57 Dominican Republic
		Chicago (NL)	50	1	11	.253				
31	Herndon, Larry	San Francisco	127	8	49	.258	R-R	6-3	190	11/3/53 Sunflower, MS
–	Martin, Jerry	Chicago (NL)	112	23	73	.227	R-R	6-1	195	5/11/49 Slikerville, NJ
30	North, Bill	San Francisco	104	1	19	.251	B-R	5-11	185	5/15/48 Seattle, WA
49	Venable, Max	Phoenix	89	5	40	.286	L-R	5-10	180	6/6/57 Phoenix, AZ
		San Francisco	37	0	10	.268				
45	Whitfield, Terry	San Francisco	95	4	26	.296	L-R	6-1	197	1/12/53 Blythe, CA
9	Wohlford, Jim	San Francisco	54	1	24	.280	R-R	5-11	175	2/28/51 Visalia, CA

GIANT PROFILES

JACK CLARK 25 6-1 170 — Bats R Throws R

Heading for super season before being struck by Mark Bomback pitch and breaking bone in left hand Aug. 20 . . . Didn't play for another month, yet still managed 18 game-winning RBI . . . Critical of management for not obtaining more batting punch to protect him in lineup . . . Became a father for the first time . . . Born Nov. 10, 1955, at New Brighton, Pa., but was reared in Southern California . . . A low draft choice who made it big . . . Had a woeful April, but got on right course with .340 May, including six homers, 24 RBI . . . Has matured into a gifted all-around player . . . Set all-time Giant records in 1978 by hitting in 26 straight games and belting 46 doubles . . . Selected for All-Star Game in 1978-79.

Year	Club	Pos.	G	AB	R	H	2B	3B	HR	RBI	SB	Avg.
1975	San Francisco ...	OF-3B	8	17	3	4	0	0	0	2	1	.235
1976	San Francisco ...	OF	26	102	14	23	6	2	2	10	6	.225
1977	San Francisco ...	OF	136	413	64	104	17	4	13	51	12	.252
1978	San Francisco ...	OF	156	592	90	181	46	8	25	98	15	.306
1979	San Francisco ...	OF-3B	143	527	84	144	25	2	26	86	11	.273
1980	San Francisco ...	OF	127	437	77	124	20	8	22	82	2	.284
	Totals..........		596	2088	332	580	114	24	88	329	47	.278

TERRY WHITFIELD 28 6-1 197 — Bats L Throws R

Can't shake part-time-player label because of difficulty hitting lefthanders . . . Must be doing something right because average in four years with S.F. never below .285 . . . Off to slow start last season, but took off after All-Star break and batted above .330 during second half . . . Born Jan. 12, 1953, at Blythe, Cal. . . . Rapped as a poor clutch hitter, a claim supported by low RBI figure, yet he ranked third on the club with eight game-winning RBI . . . Valuable addition to club because of constant hustle and readiness off bench . . . Left field is best position . . . Four-sport star as prep and was Yankees' No. 1 draft pick in 1971.

Year	Club	Pos.	G	AB	R	H	2B	3B	HR	RBI	SB	Avg.
1974	New York (AL) ..	OF	2	5	0	1	0	0	0	0	0	.200
1975	New York (AL) ..	OF	28	81	9	22	1	1	0	7	1	.272
1976	New York (AL) ..	OF	1	0	0	0	0	0	0	0	0	.000
1977	San Francisco ...	OF	114	326	41	93	21	3	7	36	2	.285
1978	San Francisco ...	OF	149	488	70	141	20	2	10	32	5	.289
1979	San Francisco ...	OF	133	394	52	113	20	4	5	44	5	.287
1980	San Francisco ...	OF	118	321	38	95	16	2	4	26	4	.296
	Totals..........		545	1615	210	465	78	12	26	145	17	.288

MILT MAY 30 6-0 190 Bats L Throws R

Until he was slowed by a muscle pull in his rib cage down the stretch, veteran catcher probably was best free agent acquisition in N.L. . . . At time of injury was batting around .290 and providing plate relief for Clark . . . Gave club best hitting behind the plate since days of Tom Haller and Dick Dietz . . . Born Aug. 1, 1950, Gary, Indiana . . . Son of Pinky May, former Phillies infielder . . . Target of criticism in S.F. debut because he threw out only one baserunner in first 25 steal attempts . . . Delivered game-winning pinch-hit for Pirates against Orioles in fourth game of 1971 World Series . . . Broken ankle and collarbone plagued A.L. career.

Year	Club	Pos.	G	AB	R	H	2B	3B	HR	RBI	SB	Avg.
1970	Pittsburgh......	PH	5	4	1	2	1	0	0	2	0	.500
1971	Pittsburgh......	C	49	126	15	35	1	0	6	25	0	.278
1972	Pittsburgh......	C	57	139	12	39	10	0	0	14	0	.281
1973	Pittsburgh......	C	101	283	29	76	8	1	7	31	0	.269
1974	Houston........	C	127	405	47	117	17	4	7	54	0	.289
1975	Houston........	C	111	386	29	93	15	1	4	52	1	.241
1976	Detroit.........	C	6	25	2	7	1	0	0	1	0	.280
1977	Detroit.........	C	115	397	32	99	9	3	12	46	0	.249
1978	Detroit.........	C	105	352	24	88	9	0	10	37	0	.250
1979	Det.-Chi. (AL)...	C	71	213	24	54	15	0	7	31	0	.254
1980	San Francisco...	C	111	358	27	93	16	2	6	50	0	.260
	Totals.........		858	2688	242	703	102	11	59	343	1	.262

LARRY HERNDON 27 6-3 190 Bats R Throws R

Club patiently waiting for fleet outfielder to blossom . . . Had best chance last year, but season was marked with inconsistency at the plate . . . Still attained career highs with eight homers and 50 RBI . . . The former track star had a career-high 11 triples to lead club . . . Born Nov. 3, 1953, at Sunflower, Miss. . . . Hit safely in 24 of first 26 games following promotion from Triple-A in 1976, including 14 in a row . . . Stole 91 bases in two successive minor league seasons as a Cardinals' prospect, but hasn't been encouraged to make better use of his speed by the Giants . . . Can play all three outfield positions . . . Attended Tennessee A&I.

Year	Club	Pos.	G	AB	R	H	2B	3B	HR	RBI	SB	Avg.
1974	St. Louis.......	OF	12	1	3	1	0	0	0	0	0	1.000
1976	San Francisco...	OF	115	337	42	97	11	3	2	23	12	.288
1977	San Francisco...	OF	49	109	13	26	4	3	1	5	4	.239
1978	San Francisco...	OF	151	471	52	122	15	9	1	32	13	.259
1979	San Francisco...	OF	132	354	35	91	14	5	7	36	8	.257
1980	San Francisco...	OF	139	493	54	127	17	11	8	49	8	.258
	Totals.........		598	1765	199	464	61	31	19	145	45	.263

DARRELL EVANS 33 6-2 200 **Bats L Throws R**

Steady veteran has averaged 18-plus homers in four full years with club . . . Second to Clark in game-winning RBI with 14 . . . Made three errors in one inning during opening series at San Diego, triggering a lackluster season afield . . . May be shifted from third to first if Ivie or Murray aren't factors . . . Born May 26, 1947, at Pasadena, Cal. . . . Team captain, but a tough role because of his quiet nature . . . By hitting 41 home runs in 1973, joined Atlanta teammates Henry Aaron and Dave Johnson as only trio in major league history to hit at least 40 apiece . . . That aberration miscast Darrell as a future slugging star . . . Good eye leads to numerous walks, but he can't raise lifetime average above .250.

Year	Club	Pos.	G	AB	R	H	2B	3B	HR	RBI	SB	Avg.
1971	Atlanta.........	3B-OF	89	260	42	63	11	1	12	38	2	.242
1972	Atlanta.........	3B	125	418	67	106	12	0	19	71	4	.254
1973	Atlanta.........	3B-1B	161	595	114	167	25	8	41	104	6	.281
1974	Atlanta.........	3B	160	571	99	137	21	3	25	79	4	.240
1975	Atlanta.........	3B-1B	156	567	82	138	22	2	22	73	12	.243
1976	Atl.-S.F.	1B-3B	136	396	53	81	9	1	11	46	9	.205
1977	San Francisco ...	OF-1B-3B	144	461	64	117	18	3	17	72	9	.254
1978	San Francisco ...	3B	159	547	82	133	24	2	20	78	4	.243
1979	San Francisco ...	3B	160	562	68	142	23	2	17	70	6	.253
1980	San Francisco ...	3B	154	556	69	147	23	0	20	78	17	.264
	Totals..........		1468	5003	747	1251	189	23	204	719	73	.250

VIDA BLUE 31 6-0 192 **Bats S Throws L**

A traditionally quick starter, Vida was 6-1 with five complete games and a 2.67 ERA in May . . . Heading for 20-win season when neck-shoulder injury placed him on disabled list . . . Had to pull out after being named to All-Star Game . . . Voted No. 2 lefthander on majors' team of decade . . . Truly S.F. stopper because of penchant for braking losing streaks . . . Born July 28, 1949, at Mansfield, La. . . . Pitched no-hitter for A's against Twins in 1970 . . . Swept MVP and Cy Young awards in 1971 following first full season in bigs . . . Became instant national celebrity and cover boy . . . N.L. debut in 1978 also a success, capped by Pitcher-of-Year honors from The Sporting News . . . Has started All-Star Game for both leagues . . . After stormy '79 settled down and enjoyed a tranquil '80 campaign.

Year	Club	G	IP	W	L	Pct.	SO	BB	H	ERA
1969	Oakland	12	41	1	1	.500	24	18	49	6.21
1970	Oakland	6	39	2	0	1.000	35	12	20	2.08
1971	Oakland	39	312	24	8	.750	301	88	209	1.82
1972	Oakland	25	151	6	10	.375	111	48	117	2.80
1973	Oakland	37	264	20	9	.690	158	105	214	3.27
1974	Oakland	40	282	17	15	.531	174	98	246	3.26
1975	Oakland	39	278	22	11	.667	189	99	243	3.01
1976	Oakland	37	298	18	13	.581	166	63	268	2.35
1977	Oakland	38	280	14	19	.424	157	86	284	3.83
1978	San Francisco	35	258	18	10	.643	171	70	233	2.79
1979	San Francisco	34	237	14	14	.500	138	111	246	5.01
1980	San Francisco	31	224	14	10	.583	129	61	202	2.97
	Totals	373	2665	170	120	.586	1753	859	2331	3.12

ED WHITSON 25 6-3 190 — Bats R Throws R

Lived up to promise by becoming club's best righthanded starter following decline of John Montefusco and Ed Halicki . . . Recorded first major league shutout against Cubs in May and repeated feat against Chicago a few days later . . . Overcame 0-5 start to go 4-2 in June, square record and make All-Star squad . . . Born May 19, 1955, at Johnson City, Tenn. . . . Failed to flourish during second half because a blister retarded his progress . . . Once the top pitching prospect in the Pirates' system, he couldn't crack the Bucs' rotation and came to S.F. as part of the Bill Madlock swap . . . His development took the heat off G.M. Spec Richardson, who was criticized for the trade in '79.

Year	Club	G	IP	W	L	Pct.	SO	BB	H	ERA
1977	Pittsburgh	5	16	1	0	1.000	10	9	11	3.38
1978	Pittsburgh	43	74	5	6	.455	64	37	66	3.28
1979	Pitt.-S.F.	37	158	7	11	.389	93	75	151	4.10
1980	San Francisco	34	212	11	13	.458	90	56	222	3.10
	Totals	119	460	24	30	.444	257	177	450	3.48

GARY LAVELLE 32 6-1 190 — Bats S Throws L

Hard-throwing veteran was replaced as club's top lefty out of bullpen, but still worked the most innings in relief and registered nine saves . . . Player representative . . . Nicknamed Pudge . . . Is particularly effective against Astros and Cardinals . . . Mentioned in several rumors involving swaps to St. Louis . . . Pride wounded when Holland became southpaw bullpen ace . . . Born Jan. 3, 1949, at Scranton, Pa. . . . Topped N.L. relievers with 13 victories in 1978, the first time his ERA soared above 3.00 . . . Holds club records with 73 relief appearances and 20 saves, the latter achieved both in 1977 and in 1979 . . . Pitched 114 innings without allowing a home run in 1976-77 . . . Once threw a no-hitter in minors.

Year	Club	G	IP	W	L	Pct.	SO	BB	H	ERA
1974	San Francisco	10	17	0	3	.000	12	10	14	2.12
1975	San Francisco	65	82	6	3	.667	51	48	80	2.96
1976	San Francisco	65	110	10	6	.625	71	52	102	2.70
1977	San Francisco	73	118	7	7	.500	93	37	106	2.06
1978	San Francisco	67	98	13	10	.565	63	44	96	3.31
1979	San Francisco	70	97	7	9	.438	80	42	86	2.51
1980	San Francisco	62	100	6	8	.429	66	36	106	3.42
	Totals..................	412	622	49	46	.516	436	269	588	2.78

GREG MINTON 29 6-2 194 Bats R Throws R

Has not allowed a home run since September 1978, more than 170 innings . . . After becoming club's top righthanded reliever in '79, continued development by clinching role last year . . . Late elbow problem deprived him of goal, breaking Lavelle's saves record . . . He settled for 19 . . . One of best sinkers in baseball . . . Born July 29, 1951, at Lubbock, Tex., but reared in San Diego area . . . MVP at Mesa J.C. . . . Came to Giants from K.C. in exchange for Fran Healy, Yankees' broadcaster . . . Came to majors to stay in '79 and responded with 1.80 ERA, finishing season with 12 and two-thirds scoreless innings . . . Got big chance when illness reduced Randy Moffitt's effectiveness.

Year	Club	G	IP	W	L	Pct.	SO	BB	H	ERA
1975	San Francisco	4	17	1	1	.500	6	11	19	6.88
1976	San Francisco	10	26	0	3	.000	7	12	32	4.85
1977	San Francisco	2	14	1	1	.500	5	4	14	4.50
1978	San Francisco	11	16	0	1	.000	6	8	22	7.88
1979	San Francisco	46	80	4	3	.571	33	27	59	1.80
1980	San Francisco	68	91	4	6	.400	42	34	81	2.47
	Totals..................	141	244	10	15	.400	99	96	227	3.28

AL HOLLAND 28 5-11 213 Bats R Throws L

Would have been solid Rookie-of-Year candidate if club were a contender . . . Outstanding first-year stats after getting a taste with seven scoreless innings at end of '79 season . . . A bull-chested athlete who knows no fear . . . Challenges hitters with a live fastball . . . Entered September with a 1.15 ERA, but nagging injuries contributed to a brief slump . . . Born Aug. 16, 1952, at Roanoke, Va. . . . Came from Bucs in

Madlock deal, further proof S.F. made good long-range swap . . . A favorite of manager Bristol because of aggressive nature and desire to excel . . . Attended North Carolina A&T, where he also starred in football . . . Has a degree in recreation.

Year	Club	G	IP	W	L	Pct.	SO	BB	H	ERA
1977	Pittsburgh	2	2	0	0	.000	1	0	4	9.00
1979	San Francisco	3	7	0	0	.000	7	5	3	0.00
1980	San Francisco	54	82	5	3	.625	65	34	71	1.76
	Totals	59	91	5	3	.625	73	39	78	1.78

ENOS CABELL 31 6-4 185 — Bats R Throws R

Disappointing playoff series with Astros led to trade to Giants . . . Was mainstay in Houston for six years . . . Injuries contributed to reduction of stolen base and RBI figures last year . . . Set club record with 213 consecutive games until rib injury sidelined him . . . Born Oct. 8, 1949, at Fort Riley, Kans. . . . Reared in L.A. area, where he was a J.C. basketball and baseball star . . . As a pro rookie in '69, he won minor league batting title for Bluefield (.374) and repeated in Triple-A for Rochester (.354) in '73 . . . Averaged 37 stolen bases in 1976-79 until drop last year.

Year	Club	Pos.	G	AB	R	H	2B	3B	HR	RBI	SB	Avg.
1972	Baltimore	1B	3	5	0	0	0	0	0	1	0	.000
1973	Baltimore	1B-3B	32	47	12	10	2	0	1	3	1	.213
1974	Baltimore	1B-OF-3B-2B	80	174	24	42	4	2	3	17	5	.241
1975	Houston	OF-1B-3B	117	348	43	92	17	6	2	43	12	.264
1976	Houston	3B-1B	144	586	85	160	13	7	2	43	35	.273
1977	Houston	3B-1B-SS	150	625	101	176	36	7	16	68	42	.282
1978	Houston	3B-1B-SS	162	660	92	195	31	8	7	71	33	.295
1979	Houston	3B-1B	155	603	60	164	30	5	6	67	37	.272
1980	Houston	3B-1B	152	604	69	167	23	8	2	55	21	.276
	Totals		995	3652	486	1006	156	43	39	368	186	.275

DOYLE ALEXANDER 30 6-3 205 — Bats R Throws R

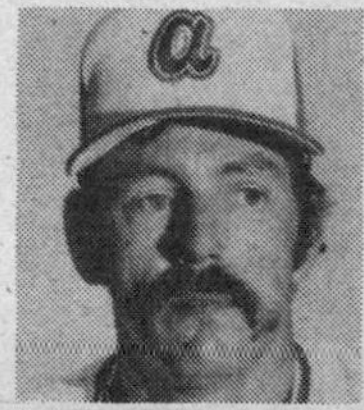

A thinking-man's pitcher and a keen student of the game . . . Enjoyed best season in Braves' debut since going 17-11 as Texas free-agent acquisition in '77 . . . Started slowly, going 0-2 in April, but rallied with 4-1 record, 2.93 ERA in June . . . Logged more than 200 innings after working only 113 in '79 . . . Born Sept. 4, 1950, at Cordova, Ala. . . . Involved in two blockbuster trades . . . Went from Dodgers to Orioles in '71 in deal that included Frank Robinson . . . Obtained by Yankees in '76 in swap that sent Rudy May, Scott McGregor and Rick Dempsey to O's . . . And now is a Giant in exchange for John Montefusco.

Year	Club	G	IP	W	L	Pct.	SO	BB	H	ERA
1971	Los Angeles	17	92	6	6	.500	30	18	105	3.82
1972	Baltimore	35	106	6	8	.429	49	30	78	2.46
1973	Baltimore	29	175	12	8	.600	63	52	169	3.84
1974	Baltimore	30	114	6	9	.400	40	43	127	4.03
1975	Baltimore	32	133	8	8	.500	46	47	127	3.05
1976	Balt.-N.Y. (AL)	30	201	13	9	.591	58	63	172	3.36
1977	Texas	34	237	17	11	.607	82	82	221	3.65
1978	Texas	31	191	9	10	.474	81	71	198	3.86
1979	Texas	23	113	5	7	.417	50	69	114	4.46
1980	Atlanta	35	232	14	11	.560	114	74	227	4.19
	Totals	296	1594	96	87	.525	613	549	1538	3.70

JERRY MARTIN 31 6-1 195 — Bats R Throws R

Contract dispute had kept this new Giant unhappy as Cub last year, but he had best power season . . . Topped the club in homers with career-high 23 . . . Poor year for average, however, after showing gradual improvement every season in bigs . . . Began power surge after joining Cubs for '79 season . . . That year doubled his previous highs with 19 homers, 73 RBI . . . Born May 11, 1949, at Columbia, S.C. . . . Was capable fill-in for Phillies early in career, belting three pinch-hit home runs in '78 and adding another in the playoffs.

Year	Club	Pos.	G	AB	R	H	2B	3B	HR	RBI	SB	Avg.
1974	Philadelphia	OF	13	14	2	3	1	0	0	1	0	.214
1975	Philadelphia	OF	57	113	15	24	7	1	2	11	2	.212
1976	Philadelphia	OF-1B	130	121	30	30	7	0	2	15	3	.248
1977	Philadelphia	OF-1B	116	215	34	56	16	3	6	28	6	.260
1978	Philadelphia	OF	128	266	40	72	13	4	9	36	9	.271
1979	Chicago (NL)	OF	150	534	74	145	34	3	19	73	2	.272
1980	Chicago (NL)	OF	141	494	57	112	22	2	23	73	8	.227
	Totals		735	1757	252	442	100	13	61	237	30	.252

TOP PROSPECTS

MAX VENABLE 23 5-10 180 — Bats L Throws R

Took over center field job in September and, barring trades, may become a regular in '81 . . . Batted in .300 area when he got his chance and also delivered at plus-.300 pace as a pinch-batter . . . Outstanding base stealer as a Dodgers' farmhand, pilfering 46 in California League in '78 . . . Born June 6, 1957, at Phoenix . . . Club also likes the glovework of infielders Joe Pettini and Guy Sularz and the pitching of Mike Rowland and Al Hargesheimer.

MANAGER FRANK ROBINSON: It was on Oct. 3, 1974, that Frank Robinson made history when he was named major league baseball's first black manager . . . But his tenure with the Cleveland Indians lasted less than two and a half seasons . . . And now he's ready for another shot . . . Bright, articulate, an acknowledged leader, Robinson is the only one in history to win MVP in both leagues . . . His 586 career home runs, including a high of 49 in 1966 when he won the Triple Crown at Baltimore, place him fourth on the all-time list, but homers were only part of his stick . . . An all-star outfielder with Cincinnati (MVP in 1961), and then with Baltimore, he later played with Los Angeles, California and Cleveland—a total of 21 seasons . . . Born in Beaumont, Tex., Aug. 31, 1935, the youngest of 10 children, he grew up in California.

GREATEST TEAM

The 1951 Giants are best remembered for Bobby Thomson's dramatic playoff homer, but the finest team for the New York franchise had to be the 1954 entry. It rates a special niche in Giants' lore not for beating Brooklyn by five games, but because it posted the World Series upset of the post-war period by sweeping the Cleveland Indians in four straight.

This was a Cleveland club which interrupted a string of Yankees' triumphs by setting an A.L. record with 111 victories. But the Giants, behind the heroics of Dusty Rhodes, convincingly won the four games, 5-2, 3-1, 6-2, 7-4. Don Mueller batted .389 in the Series, Alvin Dark .412, Hank Thompson .364 and Rhodes .667 (4-6) with two home runs.

During the regular season, Willie Mays won a batting title at .345 and had 41 homers and 110 RBI. Mueller batted .342 and Johnny Antonelli was 21-7 with a 2.29 ERA. The best of the John McGraw clubs probably was the '22 team which went 93-61 and swept the Yankees in the Series. San Francisco had only one pennant winner, the '62 squad which won a playoff series from the Dodgers before bowing to the Yankees in seven.

ALL-TIME GIANT LEADERS

BATTING: Bill Terry, .401, 1930
HRs: Willie Mays, 52, 1965
RBIs: Mel Ott, 151, 1929
STEALS: George Burns, 62, 1914
WINS: Christy Mathewson, 37, 1908
STRIKEOUTS: Christy Mathewson, 267, 1903

INSIDE THE AMERICAN LEAGUE

By JIM HAWKINS
Detroit Free Press

PREDICTED ORDER OF FINISH

East	West
Milwaukee Brewers	Texas Rangers
New York Yankees	Kansas City Royals
Baltimore Orioles	California Angels
Cleveland Indians	Oakland A's
Detroit Tigers	Chicago White Sox
Boston Red Sox	Minnesota Twins
Toronto Blue Jays	Seattle Mariners

Playoff winner: Milwaukee

EAST DIVISION

	Team	Owner / Colors	Comment	1980	Morning Line	Manager
1	**BREWERS**	Bud Selig — White, blue & gold	There's no catching them now.	W 86 L 76	9-5	Bob Rodgers
2	**YANKEES**	George Steinbrenner — Navy blue pin stripes	Class makes them constant threat.	W 103 L 59	5-2	Gene Michael
3	**ORIOLES**	Edward Bennett Williams — Black, white & orange	Pitching, jockey keep them close.	W 100 L 62	4-1	Earl Weaver
4	**INDIANS**	Steve O'Neill — Scarlet, white & blue	Game, but in too deep.	W 79 L 81	6-1	Dave Garcia
5	**TIGERS**	John E. Fetzer — Orange, white & navy blue	Just out for another airing.	W 84 L 78	10-1	Sparky Anderson
6	**RED SOX**	Mrs. Thomas Yawkey — Red, white & blue	Have beaten better, but sour now.	W 83 L 77	25-1	Ralph Houk
7	**BLUE JAYS**	Don McDougall — Blue, white & red	Should be scratched.	W 67 L 95	100-1	Bobby Mattick

BREWERS will sprint to front and stay there, fighting off challenges of the **YANKEES** and **ORIOLES**. **INDIANS** and **TIGERS** will simply be outrun. **RED SOX** will follow pack from outset while **BLUE JAYS** get left at gate.

BEER BARREL STAKES

81st Running. American League Race. Distance, 162 games, plus playoff. Purse (based on '80): $13,000 per winning player, division, up to $35,000 total per winning player, World Championship. A field of 14 entered in two divisions.

Track Record 111 Wins–Cleveland 1954

WEST DIVISION	Owner		Morning Line Manager
1 **RANGERS** Red, white & blue Overdue; will finally wake up.	Edward Chiles	1980 W 76 L 85	2-1 Don Zimmer
2 **ROYALS** Royal blue & white Will be right there with these.	Ewing Kauffman	1980 W 97 L 65	3-1 Jim Frey
3 **ANGELS** Red, white & navy blue Had their chance.	Gene Autry	1980 W 65 L 95	5-1 Jim Fregosi
4 **A's** White, green & gold Surprised everyone last time.	Roy Eisenhardt	1980 W 83 L 79	8-1 Billy Martin
5 **WHITE SOX** Navy and white Could challenge with breaks.	Bill Veeck	1980 W 70 L 90	20-1 Tony LaRussa
6 **TWINS** Scarlet, white & blue Gene Mauch knew when to get off.	Calvin Griffith	1980 W 77 L 84	50-1 John Goryl
7 **MARINERS** Blue & gold No chance, even here.	Danny Kaye-Lester Smith	1980 W 59 L 103	100-1 Maury Wills

After years of knocking at the door, **RANGERS** will finally sneak in. **ROYALS** will contend throughout, while **ANGELS** and **A's** will threaten until backstretch, then fade. **WHITE SOX** will save ground looking for chance to upset. **TWINS** and **MARINERS** will trail.

BALTIMORE ORIOLES

TEAM DIRECTORY: Chairman of the Board: Edward Bennett Williams; Pres.: Jerold C. Hoffberger; Exec. VP-GM: Hank Peters; VP: Jack Dunn III; VP: Joseph P. Hamper, Jr.; Dir. Pub. Rel.: Bob Brown; Trav. Sec.: Philip Itzoe; Mgr.: Earl Weaver. Home: Memorial Stadium (52,862). Field distances: 309, l.f. line; 385, l.c.; 405, c.f.; 385, r.c., 309, r.f. line. Spring training: Miami, Fla.

SCOUTING REPORT

HITTING: The Orioles don't terrify too many pitchers. Five teams in the league owned better batting averages last year. Five teams stole more bases. Four teams scored more runs. Three teams hit more homers. But only one team in all of baseball—the New York Yankees—won more games. Al Bumbry was among the league leaders at .318 and Ken Singleton's .304 average doesn't reflect the fact that the soft-spoken outfielder led everybody with 19 game-winning hits.

The Orioles could use another solid RBI man. They're a little lacking in righthanded power, too. But they do have Eddie Murray (.300, 32 HRs, 116 RBI) and John Lowenstein (.311). If Doug DeCinces (.249) can bounce back from his chronic back ailment and young catcher Dan Graham (.278) continues to hit, the Birds may have offense enough.

PITCHING: What a staff! "Every night," says Singleton, "we send a guy out there who's capable of throwing a shutout." Singleton has nicknames for them all. Jim Palmer (16-10) is "Cy Old." Mike Flanagan (16-13) is "Cy Young." Steve Stone (25-7) is "Cy Present." and Scott McGregor (20-8) is "Cy Future." No wonder the Birds once again won 100 games. They have, without a doubt, the best starting rotation in baseball.

And their bullpen, starring Tim Stoddard (26 saves) and Tippy Martinez (10 saves), is not bad. As a team, the Birds finished third behind Oakland and New York with a 3.64 ERA last season—in what could be considered an off-year for them. They're that good.

FIELDING: Once again last summer, there they were—atop the American League when the final fielding averages were figured. Let's see, that makes six titles in the last seven years. And in 1979, the one time they missed, they finished .001 back. The Orioles are looking for a first-rate shortstop in the mold of Mark

Cy Young winner Steve Stone was 25-7 in 1980.

Belanger, and they could use a back-up third baseman in case DeCinces' back acts up again. But in Baltimore, defense–and pitching–are the names of the game.

OUTLOOK: How could the future of a team that won 100 games the summer before appear anything but bright? Even if the Orioles did choose to stand pat during the off-season. Even if some of the key guys are getting older and others, such as Steve Stone, cannot be expected to have such sensational seasons again. The Orioles definitely have the pitching and the defense to climb to the top again. Only their offense is slightly suspect. Even so, over the years, the Birds have been the most consistent winner in the league. That's important.

BALTIMORE ORIOLES 1981 ROSTER

MANAGER Earl Weaver
Coaches—Elrod Hendricks, Ray Miller, Cal Ripken

PITCHERS

No.	Name	1980 Club	W-L	IP	SO	ERA	B-T	Ht.	Wt.	Born
52	Boddicker, Mike	Rochester	12-9	190	109	2.18	R-R	5-11	172	8/23/57 Cedar Rapids, IA
		Baltimore	0-1	7	4	6.43				
–	Carey, Brooks	Charlotte	8-7	163	78	3.70	L-L	6-1½	185	3/18/56 Key West, FL
46	Flanagan, Mike	Baltimore	16-13	251	128	4.12	L-L	6-0	195	12/16/51 Manchester, NH
21	Ford, Dave	Baltimore	1-3	70	22	4.24	R-R	6-4	200	12/29/56 Cleveland, OH
45	Jones, Larry	Rochester	13-14	180	88	4.35	R-R	6-2	195	2/6/55 Richmond, VA
30	Martinez, Dennis	Miami	0-0	12	7	0.00	R-R	6-1	183	5/14/55 Nicaragua
		Baltimore	6-4	100	42	3.96				
23	Martinez, Tippy	Baltimore	4-4	81	68	3.00	L-L	5-10	175	5/31/50 LaJunta, CO
16	McGregor, Scott	Baltimore	20-8	252	119	3.32	B-L	6-1	190	1/18/54 Inglewood, CA
22	Palmer, Jim	Baltimore	16-10	224	109	3.98	R-R	6-3	194	10/15/45 New York, NY
40	Rowe, Tom	Rochester	6-7	92	39	4.60	R-R	6-3	190	10/16/57 Bronx, NY
		Charlotte	4-2	49	35	2.76				
53	Stewart, Sammy	Baltimore	7-7	119	78	3.56	R-R	6-3	208	10/28/54 Asheville, NC
49	Stoddard, Tim	Baltimore	5-3	86	64	2.51	R-R	6-7	250	1/24/53 East Chicago, IN
32	Stone, Steve	Baltimore	25-7	251	149	3.23	R-R	5-10	175	7/14/47 Cleveland, OH

CATCHERS

No.	Name	1980 Club	H	HR	RBI	Pct.	B-T	Ht.	Wt.	Born
24	Dempsey, Rick	Baltimore	95	9	40	.262	R-R	6-0	184	9/13/49 Fayetteville, TN
37	Graham, Dan	Rochester	18	4	12	.346	L-R	6-1	212	7/19/54 Ray, AZ
		Baltimore	74	15	54	.278				
59	Huppert, Dave	Charlotte	70	3	23	.219	R-R	6-1	190	4/1/57 South Gate, CA
–	Morales, Jose	Minnesota	73	8	36	.303	R-R	6-0	195	12/30/44 St. Croix, VI

INFIELDERS

No.	Name	1980 Club	H	HR	RBI	Pct.	B-T	Ht.	Wt.	Born
7	Belanger, Mark	Baltimore	61	0	22	.228	R-R	6-2	170	6/8/44 Pittsfield, MA
2	Bonner, Bob	Rochester	113	2	41	.241	R-R	6-0	185	8/12/56 Uvalde, TX
		Baltimore	0	0	1	.000				
10	Crowley, Terry	Baltimore	67	12	50	.288	L-L	6-0	182	2/16/47 Staten Island, NY
25	Dauer, Rich	Baltimore	158	2	63	.284	R-R	6-0	177	7/27/52 San Bernardino, CA
11	DeCinces, Doug	Baltimore	122	16	64	.249	R-R	6-2	194	8/29/50 Burbank, CA
3	Garcia, Kiko	Baltimore	62	1	27	.199	R-R	5-11	178	10/14/53 Martinez, CA
6	Krenchicki, Wayne	Rochester	82	2	39	.264	L-R	6-1	175	9/17/54 Trenton, NJ
		Baltimore	2	0	0	.143				
36	Logan, Dan	Rochester	38	2	16	.195	L-L	6-6	230	7/17/56 Trion, GA
		Charlotte	80	13	57	.278				
33	Murray, Eddie	Baltimore	186	32	116	.300	B-R	6-2	197	2/24/56 Los Angeles, CA
9	Rayford, Floyd	Baltimore	4	0	1	.222	R-R	5-10	195	7/27/57 Memphis, TN
		Rochester	89	9	46	.230				
–	Ripken, Cal Jr.	Charlotte	144	25	78	.276	R-R	6-4	200	8/24/60 Havre de Grace, MD
12	Sakata, Lenn	Rochester	32	3	8	.344	R-R	5-9	160	6/8/53 Honolulu, HI
		Baltimore	16	1	9	.193				

OUTFIELDERS

No.	Name	1980 Club	H	HR	RBI	Pct.	B-T	Ht.	Wt.	Born
27	Ayala, Benny	Baltimore	45	10	33	.265	R-R	6-1	195	2/7/51 Puerto Rico
1	Bumbry, Al	Baltimore	205	9	53	.318	L-R	5-8	175	4/21/47 Fredericksburg, VA
15	Corey, Mark	Rochester	61	3	25	.230	R-R	6-2	200	11/3/55 Tucumcari, NM
		Baltimore	10	1	2	.278				
–	Dwyer, Jim	Boston	74	9	38	.285	L-L	5-10	175	1/3/50 Evergreen Park, IL
41	Hazewood, Drungo	Charlotte	130	28	80	.261	R-R	6-3	210	9/1/59 Mobile, AL
		Baltimore	0	0	0	.000				
38	Lowenstein, John	Baltimore	61	4	27	.311	L-R	6-1	180	1/27/47 Wolf Point, MT
35	Roenicke, Gary	Baltimore	71	10	28	.239	R-R	6-3	200	12/5/54 Covina, CA
29	Singleton, Ken	Baltimore	177	24	104	.304	B-R	6-4	211	6/10/47 New York, NY
–	Shelby, John	Charlotte	135	6	51	.241	R-R	6-1	175	2/23/58 Lexington, KY
34	Williams, Dallas	Rochester	143	11	54	.270	L-L	5-11	165	2/28/58 Brooklyn, NY

ORIOLE PROFILES

MIKE FLANAGAN 29 6-0 195 Bats L Throws L

Besieged by all sorts of advice as struggled through first two-thirds of 1980 season . . . Also hampered by sore shoulder . . . But never lost his sense of humor . . . "Mike is just paying the price for being the Cy Young winner," says pitching coach Ray Miller . . . Received letter from Iranian hostage William Keogh, requesting an autograph . . . Born Dec. 16, 1951, in Manchester, N.H. . . . Outstanding stuff . . . Reminds Earl Weaver of Mickey Lolich . . . Relies on heavy fastball and good curve . . . His dad was a minor league pitcher for the Red Sox and his grandfather also signed a pro contract.

Year	Club	G	IP	W	L	Pct.	SO	BB	H	ERA
1975	Baltimore................	2	10	0	1	.000	7	6	9	2.70
1976	Baltimore................	20	85	3	5	.375	56	33	83	4.13
1977	Baltimore................	36	235	15	10	.600	149	70	235	3.64
1978	Baltimore................	40	281	19	15	.559	167	87	271	4.04
1979	Baltimore................	39	266	23	9	.781	190	70	245	3.08
1980	Baltimore................	37	251	16	13	.552	128	71	278	4.12
	Totals..................	174	1128	76	53	.589	697	337	1121	3.74

SCOTT McGREGOR 27 6-1 190 Bats S Throws L

Emerged as pressure pitcher on staff in 1980 . . . Not overpowering, can't throw the ball by anyone . . . "The man's just a pitcher," says Earl Weaver. "He pitches his game, no matter what." . . . Wins with change-up, pin-point control, and heart . . . "The only way you can describe him is masterful," says Mark Belanger . . . Born Jan. 18, 1954, in Inglewood, Calif. . . . Seems to have completely recovered from sore arm that plagued him in '78-'79 . . . Acquired from Yankees in a deal that turned out great for the Orioles . . . Often compared to former Oriole star Dave McNally . . . Was teammate of George Brett in high school.

Year	Club	G	IP	W	L	Pct.	SO	BB	H	ERA
1976	Baltimore................	3	15	0	1	.000	6	5	17	3.60
1977	Baltimore................	29	114	3	5	.375	55	30	119	4.42
1978	Baltimore................	35	233	15	13	.536	94	47	217	3.32
1979	Baltimore................	27	175	13	6	.684	81	23	165	3.34
1980	Baltimore................	36	252	20	8	.714	119	58	254	3.32
	Totals..................	130	789	51	33	.607	355	163	772	3.49

JIM PALMER 35 6-3 194 Bats R Throws R

Still the ace of the staff . . . Perfectionist on the mound, believes he ought to go nine innings without making a bad pitch . . . Conducts a friendly feud with Earl Weaver . . . "See these gray hairs," says Weaver. "Every one of them has No. 22 on it." . . . "They fight like father and son, husband and wife," laughs coach Ellie Hendricks . . . Born Oct. 15, 1945, in New York City . . . Family relocated in California while he was still an infant . . . An underwear salesman—as a model . . . Continues to be hampered by bad back that has plagued him throughout his career . . . Imagines himself as a self-appointed manager . . . Is great help to other pitchers on the team.

Year	Club	G	IP	W	L	Pct.	SO	BB	H	ERA
1965	Baltimore	27	92	5	4	.556	75	56	75	3.72
1966	Baltimore	30	208	15	10	.600	147	91	176	3.46
1967	Baltimore	9	49	3	1	.750	23	20	34	2.94
1969	Baltimore	26	181	16	4	.800	123	64	131	2.34
1970	Baltimore	39	305	20	10	.667	199	100	263	2.71
1971	Baltimore	37	282	20	9	.690	184	106	231	2.68
1972	Baltimore	36	274	21	10	.677	184	70	219	2.07
1973	Baltimore	38	296	22	9	.710	158	113	225	2.40
1974	Baltimore	26	179	7	12	.368	84	69	176	3.27
1975	Baltimore	39	323	23	11	.676	193	80	253	2.09
1976	Baltimore	40	315	22	13	.629	159	84	255	2.51
1977	Baltimore	39	319	20	11	.645	193	99	263	2.91
1978	Baltimore	38	296	21	12	.636	138	97	246	2.46
1979	Baltimore	23	156	10	6	.625	67	43	144	3.29
1980	Baltimore	34	224	16	10	.615	109	74	238	3.98
	Totals	481	3499	241	132	.646	2036	1166	2929	2.74

STEVE STONE 33 5-10 175 Bats R Throws R

The major leagues' first 20-game winner last season . . . Had clause in contract which gave him $10,000 if won Cy Young Award . . . He collected . . . Reminds some of Carl Erskine . . . Refuses to throw at a hitter . . . Calls it a sign of weakness . . . "When I strike him out three times, does he throw his bat at me?" . . . At a late-season charity auction, a date with him sold for $1,300 . . . "I didn't know I was that good" . . . Born July 14, 1947, in Cleveland . . . Dramatic turn-around after 1979 season when "I was our only weakness." . . . "Everyone else was having a renaissance year and I was like Chrysler." . . . Wrote a letter to each of his teammates, thanking them for their help in 1980 . . . Signed four-year contract with Orioles as a free agent, after playing out his option with White Sox.

Year	Club	G	IP	W	L	Pct.	SO	BB	H	ERA
1971	San Francisco	24	111	5	9	.357	63	55	110	4.14
1972	San Francisco	27	124	6	8	.429	85	49	97	2.98
1973	Chicago (AL).............	36	176	6	11	.353	138	82	163	4.24
1974	Chicago (NL).............	38	170	8	6	.571	90	64	185	4.13
1975	Chicago (NL).............	33	214	12	8	.600	139	80	198	3.95
1976	Chicago (NL).............	17	75	3	6	.333	33	21	70	4.08
1977	Chicago (AL).............	31	207	15	12	.556	124	80	228	4.52
1978	Chicago (AL).............	30	212	12	12	.500	118	84	196	4.37
1979	Baltimore................	32	186	11	7	.611	96	73	173	3.77
1980	Baltimore................	37	251	25	7	.781	149	101	224	3.23
	Totals....................	305	1726	103	86	.545	1035	689	1644	3.94

RICK DEMPSEY 31 6-0 184 Bats R Throws R

Very competitive catcher . . . Will disappear into the dugout to catch a pop foul . . . Indestructible . . . "The guy loves pain," says Earl Weaver . . . Was very unhappy with fact he wasn't playing every day in '80 . . . Blamed Weaver and asked to be traded . . . "I just feel it would be better for the club to deal me now while my value is high." . . . Referred to self as "highest paid backup catcher in history" . . . Born Sept. 13, 1949, in Fayetteville, Tenn. . . . Originally signed with Twins . . . Owns an outstanding arm . . . Toured Japan with all-star team following '79 season . . . Never played regularly until the Orioles gave him the job in 1977.

Year	Club	Pos.	G	AB	R	H	2B	3B	HR	RBI	SB	Avg.
1969	Minnesota	C	5	6	1	3	1	0	0	0	0	.500
1970	Minnesota	C	5	7	1	0	0	0	0	0	0	.000
1971	Minnesota	C	6	13	2	4	1	0	0	0	0	.308
1972	Minnesota	C	25	40	0	8	1	0	0	0	0	.200
1973	New York (AL) ..	C	6	11	0	2	0	0	0	0	0	.182
1974	New York (AL) ..	C-OF	43	109	12	26	3	0	2	12	1	.239
1975	New York (AL) ..	C-OF-3B	71	145	18	38	8	0	1	11	0	.262
1976	N.Y.-Balt. (AL) ..	C-OF	80	216	12	42	2	0	0	12	1	.194
1977	Baltimore.......	C	91	270	27	61	7	4	3	34	2	.226
1978	Baltimore.......	C	136	441	41	114	25	0	6	32	7	.259
1979	Baltimore.......	C	124	368	48	88	23	0	6	41	0	.239
1980	Baltimore.......	C	119	362	51	95	26	3	9	40	3	.262
	Totals..........		711	1988	213	481	97	7	27	182	14	.242

RICH DAUER 28 6-0 177 Bats R Throws R

Worked with weights during the winter prior to the 1980 season to improve his strength . . . He didn't hit more HRs but he did blossom into one of the most valuable Orioles . . . Usually a slow starter, but a tough clutch hitter . . . Rarely strikes out . . . Especially productive with men in scoring position . . . Born July 27, 1952, in San Bernadino, Calif. . . .

Decided in April to stop swinging for the fences and concentrate on moving runners along . . . Not blessed with abundance of speed . . . Has great knack for getting in front of the ball, no matter where it is hit . . . Teammates call him "Pig Pen" . . . Can play second or third.

Year	Club	Pos.	G	AB	R	H	2B	3B	HR	RBI	SB	Avg.
1976	Baltimore.......	2B	11	39	0	4	0	0	0	3	0	.103
1977	Baltimore.......	2B-3B	96	304	38	74	15	1	5	25	1	.243
1978	Baltimore.......	2B-3B	133	459	57	121	23	0	6	46	0	.264
1979	Baltimore.......	2B-3B	142	479	63	123	20	0	9	61	0	.257
1980	Baltimore.......	2B-3B	152	557	71	158	32	0	2	63	3	.284
	Totals..........		534	1838	229	480	90	1	22	198	4	.261

DOUG DeCINCES 30 6-2 194 **Bats R Throws R**

Hobbled throughout 1980 season by a painful back injury . . . Faced major surgery over the winter . . . Refused to undergo operation so long as Orioles still had a chance in the pennant race . . . Got into many bad habits at the plate because of the pain in his back . . . Born Aug. 29, 1950, in Burbank, Calif. . . . Given impossible task of replacing Brooks Robinson at third base . . . Name is pronounced "Duh-SIN-say" . . . Very active in Special Olympics and frequently brings underprivileged or handicapped groups to the ballpark as his guests . . . Was not drafted after high school, but went to junior college to further his career.

Year	Club	Pos.	G	AB	R	H	2B	3B	HR	RBI	SB	Avg.
1973	Baltimore.......	3B-2B-SS	10	18	2	2	0	0	0	3	0	.111
1974	Baltimore.......	3B	1	1	0	0	0	0	0	0	0	.000
1975	Baltimore.......	3B-SS-2B-1B	61	167	20	42	6	3	4	23	0	.251
1976	Baltimore.......	3B-2B-SS-1B	129	440	36	103	17	2	11	42	8	.234
1977	Baltimore.......	3B-2B-1B	150	522	63	135	28	3	19	69	8	.259
1978	Baltimore.......	3B-2B	142	511	72	146	37	1	28	80	7	.286
1979	Baltimore.......	3B	120	422	67	97	27	1	16	61	5	.230
1980	Baltimore.......	3B	145	489	64	122	23	2	16	64	11	.249
	Totals..........		758	2570	324	647	138	12	94	342	39	.252

EDDIE MURRAY 25 6-2 197 **Bats S Throws R**

Got key hit after key hit to keep Orioles' pennant hopes alive in 1980 . . . Very durable, talented first baseman . . . One of 12 children . . . All four of his brothers have played or are still playing pro ball . . . Born Feb. 24, 1956, in Los Angeles . . . Played high school ball with Ozzie Smith of Padres and Darrell Jackson of Twins . . . A big hit with the Oriole fans . . . Rarely makes headlines but does his job day in and day out . . . A ballplayer's ballplayer . . . One of top-fielding first baseman in league . . . "Eddie's loaded with talent," says coach Frank Robinson. "And he's going to get better."

Year	Club	Pos.	G	AB	R	H	2B	3B	HR	RBI	SB	Avg.
1977	Baltimore.......	OF-1B	160	611	81	173	29	2	27	88	0	.283
1978	Baltimore.......	1B-3B	161	610	85	174	32	3	27	95	6	.285
1979	Baltimore.......	1B	159	606	90	179	30	2	25	99	10	.295
1980	Baltimore.......	1B	158	621	100	186	36	2	32	116	7	.300
	Totals..........		638	2448	356	712	127	9	111	398	23	.291

AL BUMBRY 33 5-8 175 Bats L Throws R

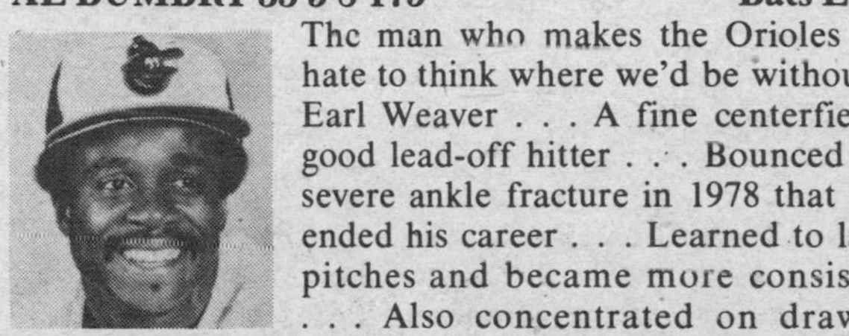

The man who makes the Orioles go . . . "I hate to think where we'd be without Al," says Earl Weaver . . . A fine centerfielder and a good lead-off hitter . . . Bounced back from severe ankle fracture in 1978 that could have ended his career . . . Learned to lay off high pitches and became more consistent hitter . . . Also concentrated on drawing more walks . . . Born April 21, 1947, in Fredricksburg, Va. . . . The fastest of the Birds . . . His return bolstered outfield defense . . . A veteran of the Vietnam War . . . Represents Orioles as an after-dinner speaker during the winter months . . . Averaged 32 points per game as a high school basketball player.

Year	Club	Pos.	G	AB	R	H	2B	3B	HR	RBI	SB	Avg.
1972	Baltimore.......	OF	9	11	5	4	0	1	0	0	1	.364
1973	Baltimore.......	OF	110	356	73	120	15	11	7	34	23	.337
1974	Baltimore.......	OF	94	270	35	63	10	3	1	19	12	.233
1975	Baltimore.......	OF-3B	114	349	47	94	19	4	2	32	16	.269
1976	Baltimore.......	OF	133	450	71	113	15	7	9	36	42	.251
1977	Baltimore.......	OF	133	518	74	164	31	3	4	41	19	.317
1978	Baltimore.......	OF	33	114	21	27	5	2	2	6	5	.237
1979	Baltimore.......	OF	148	569	80	162	29	1	7	49	37	.285
1980	Baltimore.......	OF	160	645	118	205	29	9	9	53	44	.318
	Totals..........		934	3282	524	952	153	41	41	270	199	.290

KEN SINGLETON 33 6-4 211 Bats S Throws R

Started slowly in 1980 but came on strong . . . One of the keys to Orioles last-season surge . . . Injured his back while holding Twins' pitcher Darrell Jackson during a free-for-all . . . Born June 10, 1947, in New York City . . . Rarely slips into a slump once he gets going . . . One of Birds' most productive players . . . Has fully recovered from '77 surgery on right elbow that hampered his play . . . Seldom gets the credit he deserves but says he is accustomed to anonymity . . .

Was the Mets' first pick in the January 1967 draft . . . Went to Hofstra University on a basketball scholarship.

Year	Club	Pos.	G	AB	R	H	2B	3B	HR	RBI	SB	Avg.
1970	New York (NL)..	OF	69	198	22	52	8	0	5	26	1	.263
1971	New York (NL)..	OF	115	298	34	73	5	0	13	46	0	.245
1972	Montreal	OF	142	507	78	139	23	2	14	50	5	.274
1973	Montreal	OF	162	560	100	169	26	2	23	103	2	.302
1974	Montreal	OF	148	511	68	141	20	2	9	74	5	.276
1975	Baltimore.......	OF	155	586	88	176	37	4	15	55	3	.300
1976	Baltimore.......	OF	154	544	62	151	25	2	13	70	2	.278
1977	Baltimore.......	OF	152	536	90	176	24	0	24	99	0	.328
1978	Baltimore.......	OF	149	502	67	147	21	2	20	81	0	.293
1979	Baltimore.......	OF	159	570	93	168	29	1	35	111	3	.295
1980	Baltimore.......	OF	156	583	85	177	28	3	24	104	0	.304
	Totals..........		1561	5395	786	1569	246	18	195	819	21	.291

TOP PROSPECTS

DAN GRAHAM 26 6-1 212 **Bats L Throws R**

The answer to Earl Weaver's search for a lefthanded-hitting catcher . . . Stolen from the Minnesota Twins . . . Used sparingly at first in 1980 but impressed everyone . . . Born July 19, 1954, in Ray, Ariz. . . . Went 9-for-16 with two HRs and 5 RBIs in first two games . . . Got game-winning hits his first four games in big leagues . . . Still has to improve his defense but Oriole pitchers all praised him . . . "I know I can hit."

MARK COREY 25 6-2 200 **Bats R Throws R**

Steady-hitting outfielder is knocking on the door . . . Signed with Orioles in 1976 . . . Impressive minor league credentials in spite of injuries . . . Born Nov. 3, 1955 in Tucumcari, N.M. . . . Attended Central Arizona J.C. . . . Batted .400 in Appalachian League his first year in pro ball.

MANAGER EARL WEAVER: His reputation as the smartest manager in the American League continues to grow . . . "Earl Weaver doesn't give you anything," says the Yankees' Bucky Dent . . . Agreed, after much haggling, to manage the Orioles through 1982 . . . Then, he claims, he's going to retire . . . Born Aug. 14, 1930, in St. Louis . . . Has won six division titles, four pennants and one World Series during his

12½ years in Baltimore . . . A master at making umpires mad . . . Usually gets suspended at least once each year . . . An expert at getting the most out of his players . . . His teams, in the minors and majors, have finished over .500 for 23 years in a row . . . Never played a day in the big leagues himself, but has guided the Birds to 90 or more wins 10 times . . . His hobby is gardening and he loves to entertain guests by serving the vegetables he grew himself.

GREATEST TEAM

For hitting, they had MVP Boog Powell, plus the Robinsons, Brooks and Frank. To throw the ball, they relied upon Mike Cuellar, Dave McNally and Jim Palmer, 20-game winners all. On defense, they could count on Dave Johnson, Mark Belanger, Paul Blair and, of course, Brooks.

Yes, the 1970 Orioles could do it all. And they did.

They won 108 games during the regular season, pouring it on right up until the end. Then they again swept past the Minnesota Twins in the playoffs, winning three straight.

And this time, in the World Series, the O's were sensational, avenging the previous fall's heartbreaking failure against the Mets. Brooks Robinson was at his sensational best, batting .429 and breaking the backs of the Cincinnati Reds with his incredible diving catches at third.

Then Earl Weaver, the feisty little genius who called the shots, and the rest of the Birds spent the winter taking bows. No one could say they were not well-deserved.

ALL-TIME ORIOLE LEADERS

BATTING: Ken Singleton, .328, 1977
HRs: Frank Robinson, 49, 1966
RBIs: Jim Gentile, 141, 1961
STEALS: Luis Aparicio, 57, 1964
WINS: Steve Stone, 25, 1980
STRIKEOUTS: Dave McNally, 202, 1968

BOSTON RED SOX

TEAM DIRECTORY: Pres.: Mrs. Thomas A. Yawkey; Exec. VP-GM: Haywood Sullivan; Exec. VP-Admin.: Edward (Buddy) LeRoux; Dir. Pub. Rel.: Bill Crowley; Dir. Publ.: Dick Bresciani; Trav. Sec.: Jack Rogers; Mgr.: Ralph Houk. Home: Fenway Park (33,538). Field distances: 315, l.f. line; 390, c.f.; 420, r.c. corner; 380, r.c.; 302, r.f. line. Spring training: Winter Haven, Fla.

SCOUTING REPORT

HITTING: The Red Sox keep banging the ball off Fenway Park's famous leftfield wall. But year after year they find that is not enough. The Bosox batted .283 again last season, trailing only Kansas City and Texas. And the fact that they didn't have a single hitter among the top 15 shows you the depth of the Red Sox attack. As usual, there are Fred Lynn (.301, 12 HRs and 61 RBI), Jim Rice (.294, 24 HRs, 86 RBI) and the incomparable Carl Yastrzemski (.275, 15 HRs, 50 RBI).

Tony Perez also proved he is far from finished, batting a robust .275 with 25 HRs and 105 RBI. But the big surprises were newcomers Gary Allenson (.357), Glenn Hoffman (.285) and Dave Stapleton (.321). And don't forget Jerry Remy (.313), the second baseman who had all of the rival GMs drooling during the winter trading period. It's enough to make an opposing pitcher call in sick.

PITCHING: Boston's Big Three last season was supposed to be composed of Dennis Eckersley, Mike Torrez and Bob Stanley. Instead, the top trio turned out to be named Chuck Rainey (8-3), Tom Burgmeier (5-4, 24 saves) and Steve Renko (9-9). During the winter, the Red Sox acquired Mark Clear (11-11, 9 saves) from California to bolster their bullpen, but their big guns, namely Eckersley (12-14) and Torrez (9-16), have simply got to do better if the Sox are to move upward in the standings. And Stanley must at least match last year's performance when he was 10-8 with 14 saves.

FIELDING: Only the Chicago White Sox looked shakier in the field and fumbled more often than the Red Sox did last year. The addition of Carney Lansford from the Angels is supposed to improve the Bosox at third base, where Butch Hobson committed 16 errors last year. But let's look at the record: Lansford had 19 errors in California. Only the Tigers' Tom Brookens made more. In addition, the Red Sox are going to miss Rick Burleson at shortstop. Lynn, Remy and Dwight Evans are, of course, exceptional fielders, but that still leaves a lot of holes.

OUTLOOK: The Red Sox fired Don Zimmer and hired Ralph Houk because they want a tough guy to take charge of their perennially-disappointing team. They're in for a surprise because, in spite of his reputation, The Major is basically a players' manager and a pushover. That's one reason he has always been so popular with his players, wherever he has worked. "I don't expect miracles," says Houk. And he isn't likely to get any. The Red Sox still need a couple of first-quality starting pitchers. But then who doesn't? It remains to be seen what frame of mind Lynn will be in, now that he knows the Red Sox were trying to get rid of him. And the loss of Burleson, the team leader, has got to hurt.

Jim Rice dipped to 24 HRs, 86 RBI.

BOSTON RED SOX 1981 ROSTER

MANAGER Ralph Houk
Coaches—John Pesky, Eddie Yost, Walt Hriniak, Tommy Harper, Lee Stange

PITCHERS

No.	Name	1980 Club	W-L	IP	SO	ERA	B-T	Ht.	Wt.	Born
–	Aponte, Luis	Bristol	9-1	54	43	2.50	R-R	6-0	180	7/14/54 Venezuela
		Pawtucket	6-2	49	42	2.20				
		Boston	0-0	7	1	1.29				
16	Burgmeier, Tom	Boston	5-4	99	54	2.00	L-L	5-11	180	8/2/43 St. Paul, MN
22	Campbell, Bill	Boston	4-0	41	17	4.79	R-R	6-3	190	8/9/48 Highland Park, MI
–	Clear, Mark	California	11-11	106	105	3.31	R-R	6-4	200	5/27/56 Los Angeles, CA
–	Crawford, Steve	Bristol	9-7	177	97	2.64	R-R	6-5	225	4/29/58 Pryor, OK
		Boston	2-0	32	10	3.66				
41	Drago, Dick	Boston	7-7	133	63	4.14	R-R	6-1	200	6/25/45 Toledo, OH
43	Eckersley, Dennis	Boston	12-14	198	121	4.28	R-R	6-2	190	10/3/54 Oakland, CA
–	Howard, Mike	Bristol	10-5	112	99	3.78	R-R	6-3	185	10/14/57 Portland, ME
		Pawtucket	1-5	59	35	4.58				
47	Hurst, Bruce	Pawtucket	8-6	105	56	3.94	L-L	6-3	200	3/24/58 St. George, UT
		Boston	2-2	31	16	9.00				
–	King, Jerry	Bristol	6-6	131	119	3.98	R-R	6-3	185	8/23/58 San Diego, CA
38	Lockwood, Skip	Boston	3-1	46	11	5.28	R-R	6-0	200	8/17/46 Boston, MA
31	MacWhorter, Keith	Pawtucket	7-6	123	101	2.56	R-R	6-4	185	12/30/55 Worcester, MA
		Boston	0-3	42	21	5.57				
–	Ojeda, Bob	Pawtucket	6-7	123	78	3.22	L-L	6-1	185	12/17/57 Los Angeles, CA
		Boston	1-1	26	12	6.92				
42	Rainey, Chuck	Boston	8-3	87	43	4.86	R-R	5-11	195	7/14/54 San Diego, CA
49	Remmerswaal, Win	Pawtucket	5-5	48	33	4.69	R-R	6-2	160	3/8/54 Holland
		Boston	2-1	35	20	4.63				
25	Renko, Steve	Boston	9-9	165	90	4.20	R-R	6-6	225	12/10/44 Kansas City, KA
–	Smithson, Mike	Pawtucket	5-9	99	73	2.91	L-R	6-8	200	1/1/55 Centerville, TN
46	Stanley, Bob	Boston	10-8	175	71	3.39	R-R	6-4	205	11/10/54 Portland, ME
21	Torrez, Mike	Boston	9-16	207	97	5.09	R-R	6-5	210	8/28/46 Topeka, KA
30	Tudor, John	Pawtucket	4-5	74	51	3.65	L-L	6-0	185	2/2/54 Schenectady, NY
		Boston	8-5	92	45	3.03				

CATCHERS

No.	Name	1980 Club	H	HR	RBI	Pct.	B-T	Ht.	Wt.	Born
26	Allenson, Gary	Boston	25	0	10	.357	R-R	5-11	188	2/4/55 Culver City, CA
27	Fisk, Carlton	Boston	138	18	62	.289	R-R	6-2	220	12/26/47 Bellows Falls, VT
–	Gedman, Rich	Pawtucket	82	11	29	.236	L-R	6-0	210	9/26/59 Worcester, MA
		Boston	5	0	1	.208				
–	Lickert, John	Bristol	112	3	52	.257	R-R	5-11	175	4/4/60 Pittsburgh, PA
50	Schmidt, Dave	Pawtucket	33	5	16	.229	R-R	6-1	190	12/22/56 Mesa, AZ

INFIELDERS

No.	Name	1980 Club	H	HR	RBI	Pct.	B-T	Ht.	Wt.	Born
18	Hoffman, Glen	Boston	89	4	42	.285	R-R	6-2	170	7/7/58 Orange, CA
–	Lansford, Carney	California	157	15	80	.261	R-R	6-2	195	2/7/57 San Jose, CA
5	Perez, Tony	Boston	161	25	105	.275	R-R	6-2	205	5/14/42 Cuba
2	Remy, Jerry	Boston	72	0	9	.313	L-R	5-9	165	11/8/52 Fall River, MA
26	Stapleton, Dave	Pawtucket	51	3	19	.340	R-R	6-1	170	1/16/54 Fairhope, AL
		Boston	144	7	45	.321				
–	Valdez, Julio	Pawtucket	61	4	27	.219	B-R	6-2	150	7/3/56 Dominican Republic
		Boston	5	1	4	.263				
–	Walker, Chico	Pawtucket	146	8	52	.272	B-R	5-9	170	11/25/57 Chicago, IL
		Boston	12	1	5	.211				

OUTFIELDERS

No.	Name	1980 Club	H	HR	RBI	Pct.	B-T	Ht.	Wt.	Born
24	Evans, Dwight	Boston	123	18	60	.266	R-R	6-3	205	11/3/51 Santa Monica, CA
38	Hancock, Gary	Pawtucket	52	6	19	.241	L-L	6-0	175	1/23/54 Tampa, FL
		Boston	33	4	19	.287				
19	Lynn, Fred	Boston	125	12	61	.301	L-L	6-1	190	2/3/52 Chicago, IL
–	Miller, Rick	California	113	2	38	.274	L-L	6-1	185	4/19/48 Grand Rapids, MI
–	Nichols, Reid	Pawtucket	141	4	42	.276	R-R	5-11	165	8/5/58 Ocala, FL
		Boston	8	0	3	.222				
17	Poquette, Tom			On disabled list			L-R	5-11	175	10/30/51 EauClaire, WI
14	Rice, Jim	Boston	148	24	86	.294	R-R	6-2	205	3/8/53 Anderson, SC
8	Yastrzemski, Carl	Boston	100	15	50	.275	L-R	5-11	185	8/22/39 Southampton, NY

RED SOX PROFILES

TOM BURGMEIER 37 5-11 180 Bats L Throws L

Picked up the slack when Dennis Eckersley, Bob Stanley, and Mike Torrez all faltered . . . Kept Red Sox in the pennant race for a while . . . Began his big league career in '68, but rarely made headlines until now . . . Born Aug. 2, 1943, in St. Paul . . . Developed into the dependable lefthanded reliever the Red Sox have been looking for ever since they traded Sparky Lyle . . . "I've never seen a man in such a perfect groove," said last year's pitching coach, Johnny Podres . . . Claims heavy duty doesn't bother him . . . "The more I pitch, the sharper I am." . . . Missed 15 games because of tendinitis . . . Signed with Red Sox as a free agent.

Year	Club	G	IP	W	L	Pct.	SO	BB	H	ERA
1968	California	56	73	1	4	.200	33	24	65	4.32
1969	Kansas City	31	54	3	1	.750	23	21	67	4.17
1970	Kansas City	41	68	6	6	.500	43	23	59	3.18
1971	Kansas City	67	88	9	7	.562	44	30	71	1.74
1972	Kansas City	51	55	6	2	.750	18	33	67	4.25
1973	Kansas City	6	10	0	0	.000	4	4	13	5.40
1974	Minnesota	50	92	5	3	.625	34	26	92	4.50
1975	Minnesota	46	76	5	8	.385	41	23	76	3.08
1976	Minnesota	57	115	8	1	.889	45	29	95	2.50
1977	Minnesota	61	97	6	4	.600	35	33	113	5.10
1978	Boston	35	61	2	1	.667	24	23	74	4.43
1979	Boston	44	89	3	2	.600	60	16	89	2.73
1980	Boston	62	99	5	4	.556	54	20	87	2.00
	Totals	607	977	59	43	.578	458	305	968	3.42

DICK DRAGO 35 6-1 200 Bats R Throws R

Began career as a starter but turned to bullpen five years ago . . . Returned to the starting rotation in 1980 . . . "I guess deep down you always want to be a starter" . . . His sinister appearance and his cynical outlook on life earned him the nickname "Black Dragon" . . . Born June 25, 1945, in Toledo . . . Signed with Red Sox as a free agent in 1978 and immediately became their best reliever . . . "I always felt I could be as good as Bill Campbell or Rich Gossage" . . . Lacks an overpowering fastball but does possess good slider and change-up . . . Plus, the ability to throw strikes.

Year	Club	G	IP	W	L	Pct.	SO	BB	H	ERA
1969	Kansas City	41	201	11	13	.458	108	65	190	3.76
1970	Kansas City	35	240	9	15	.375	127	72	239	3.75
1971	Kansas City	35	241	17	11	.607	109	46	251	2.99
1972	Kansas City	34	239	12	17	.414	135	51	230	3.01
1973	Kansas City	37	213	12	14	.462	98	76	252	4.23
1974	Boston	33	176	7	10	.412	90	56	165	3.48
1975	Boston	40	73	2	2	.500	43	31	69	3.82
1976	California	43	79	7	8	.467	43	31	80	4.44
1977	Cal.-Balt.	49	61	6	4	.600	35	18	71	3.39
1978	Boston	37	77	4	4	.500	42	32	71	3.04
1979	Boston	53	89	10	6	.625	67	21	85	3.03
1980	Boston	43	133	7	7	.500	63	44	127	4.13
	Totals	480	1822	104	111	.484	960	543	1830	3.57

DENNIS ECKERSLEY 26 6-2 190 — Bats R Throws R

Hampered by arm and back woes in '80 . . . Spent three days in traction and missed more than a month . . . "I almost went crazy not being able to throw" . . . On the surface, though, nothing seems to bother him . . . Born Oct. 3, 1954, in Oakland, Calif. . . . Has won in spite of his unorthodox slingshot delivery . . . Sometimes labeled a hotdog . . . Relies on his excellent fast ball plus a good sinker and slider . . . Still thinks Indians made a mistake trading him and loves to beat them, just to remind folks of that fact . . . Hurled a shutout in his first pro start.

Year	Club	G	IP	W	L	Pct.	SO	BB	H	ERA
1975	Cleveland	34	187	13	7	.650	152	90	147	2.60
1976	Cleveland	36	199	13	12	.520	200	78	155	3.44
1977	Cleveland	33	247	14	13	.519	191	54	214	3.53
1978	Boston	35	268	20	8	.714	162	71	258	2.99
1979	Boston	33	247	17	10	.630	150	59	234	2.99
1980	Boston	30	198	12	14	.462	121	44	188	4.27
	Totals	201	1346	89	64	.582	976	396	1196	3.29

STEVE RENKO 36 6-6 225 — Bats R Throws R

Began the 1980 season in the bullpen after 11 years as a starter . . . Got his chance to start again when Dennis Eckersley got hurt . . . Signed with Bosox as a free agent in 1979 but Boston fans really wanted Tommy John . . . Born Dec. 10, 1944, in Kansas City . . . Played football, basketball and baseball at the University of Kansas . . . Was a quarterback on the team that featured Gale Sayers . . . Was drafted by the Oakland Raiders but chose to sign with the Mets instead . . . Originally was a first baseman . . . Was Montreal's most consistent righthanded pitcher for six seasons.

Year	Club	G	IP	W	L	Pct.	SO	BB	H	ERA
1969	Montreal	18	103	6	7	.462	68	50	94	4.02
1970	Montreal	41	223	13	11	.542	142	104	203	4.32
1971	Montreal	40	276	15	14	.517	129	135	256	3.75
1972	Montreal	30	97	1	10	.091	66	67	96	5.20
1973	Montreal	36	250	15	11	.577	164	108	201	2.81
1974	Montreal	37	228	12	16	.429	138	81	222	4.03
1975	Montreal	31	170	6	12	.333	99	76	175	4.08
1976	Mtl.-Chi. (NL)	33	176	8	12	.400	116	46	179	3.99
1977	Chicago (NL)	13	51	2	2	.500	34	21	51	4.59
1977	Chicago (AL)	8	53	5	0	1.000	36	17	55	3.57
1978	Oakland	27	151	6	12	.333	89	67	152	4.29
1979	Boston	27	171	11	9	.550	99	53	174	4.11
1980	Boston	32	165	9	9	.500	90	56	180	4.20
	Totals	373	2114	109	125	.466	1270	881	2038	3.97

BOB STANLEY 26 6-4-205 Bats R Throws R

"He may have the best spitball in the league," claims California's Don Baylor . . . "He's the best relief pitcher in the game right now," says Ted Williams . . . Struggling as a starter, he asked Don Zimmer to send him back to the bullpen . . . And the move immediately began to pay dividends . . . Born Nov. 10, 1954, in Portland, Me. . . . Relies on a wicked sinker . . . Teammates call him "Big Foot" . . . Made the giant jump from AA ball to the big leagues four years ago . . . Was Boston's first pick in the 1974 winter draft . . . Was originally drafted by Dodgers, but didn't sign.

Year	Club	G	IP	W	L	Pct.	SO	BB	H	ERA
1977	Boston	41	151	8	7	.533	44	43	176	3.99
1978	Boston	52	142	15	2	.882	38	34	142	2.60
1979	Boston	40	217	16	12	.571	66	44	250	3.98
1980	Boston	52	175	10	8	.556	71	52	186	3.39
	Totals	185	685	49	29	.628	209	173	754	3.55

RICK MILLER 32 6-0 185 Bats L Throws L

Returned to Red Sox in the Rick Burleson deal . . . Hampered by infection in right eye that prevented him from wearing contact lenses . . . Continued to hit, even though sight in that eye is only 20-150 . . . Has always been known as an outstanding fielder . . . Only question was his ability to hit . . . Born April 19, 1948, in Grand Rapids, Mich. . . . Married to Carlton Fisk's sister . . . Signed with Angels as free agent after fleeing Boston . . . "There's no better defensive centerfielder in the AL," says Cleveland manager Dave Garcia . . . Lacks great speed but is an outstanding athlete.

Year	Club	Pos.	G	AB	R	H	2B	3B	HR	RBI	SB	Avg.
1971	Boston.........	OF	15	33	9	11	5	0	1	7	0	.333
1972	Boston.........	OF	89	98	13	21	4	1	3	15	0	.214
1973	Boston.........	OF	143	441	65	115	17	7	6	43	12	.261
1974	Boston.........	OF	114	280	41	73	8	1	5	22	13	.261
1975	Boston.........	OF	77	108	21	21	2	1	0	15	3	.194
1976	Boston.........	OF	105	269	40	76	15	3	0	27	11	.283
1977	Boston.........	OF	86	189	34	48	9	3	0	24	11	.254
1978	California.......	OF	132	475	66	125	25	4	1	37	3	.263
1979	California.......	OF	120	427	60	125	15	5	2	28	5	.293
1980	California.......	OF	129	412	52	113	14	3	2	38	7	.274
	Totals..........		1010	2732	401	728	114	28	20	256	65	.266

FRED LYNN 29 6-1 190 — Bats L Throws L

All-out style of play has resulted in numerous injuries . . . Played in 1980 All-Star Game even though he had missed the last six regular-season games because of a pulled hamstring . . . "I felt I owed it to the fans to play" . . . Reminds many of Stan Musial . . . Born Feb. 3, 1952, in Chicago . . . Went to Southern Cal on a football scholarship and played wide receiver for one year before deciding to concentrate on baseball . . . Has few peers when it comes to playing centerfield . . . Famous for his diving, tumbling catches . . . Enjoyed sensational rookie season in 1975 when he won MVP award and attracted the attention of the entire country.

Year	Club	Pos.	G	AB	R	H	2B	3B	HR	RBI	SB	Avg.
1974	Boston.........	OF	15	43	5	18	2	2	2	10	0	.419
1975	Boston.........	OF	145	528	103	175	47	7	21	105	10	.331
1976	Boston.........	OF	132	507	76	159	32	8	10	65	14	.314
1977	Boston.........	OF	129	497	81	129	29	5	18	76	2	.260
1978	Boston.........	OF	150	541	75	161	33	3	22	82	3	.298
1979	Boston.........	OF	147	531	116	177	42	1	39	122	2	.333
1980	Boston.........	OF	110	415	67	125	32	3	12	61	12	.301
	Totals..........		828	3062	523	944	217	29	124	521	43	.308

DWIGHT EVANS 29 6-3 205 — Bats R Throws R

His 1980 season started badly and went steadily downhill . . . Was benched against right-handed pitching . . . "It was just terrible . . . But the Red Sox showed their faith in him by giving him a new 5-year contract . . . And, after the All-Star break, he went on a rampage . . . Born Nov. 3, 1951, in Santa Monica, Calif. . . . Grew up in Hawaii . . . Has been hampered by injuries throughout career . . . Considered one of the better hotdogs in the league . . . Also one of the finest rightfielders . . . Has won three Gold Gloves for defensive excellence . . . Frequently among league's leading outfielders in assists and double plays.

Year	Club	Pos.	G	AB	R	H	2B	3B	HR	RBI	SB	Avg.
1972	Boston.........	OF	18	57	2	15	3	1	1	6	0	.263
1973	Boston.........	OF	119	282	46	63	13	1	10	32	5	.223
1974	Boston.........	OF	133	463	60	130	19	8	10	70	4	.281
1975	Boston.........	OF	128	412	61	113	24	6	13	56	3	.274
1976	Boston.........	OF	146	501	61	121	34	5	17	62	6	.242
1977	Boston.........	OF	73	230	39	66	9	2	14	36	4	.287
1978	Boston.........	OF	147	497	75	123	24	2	24	63	8	.247
1979	Boston.........	OF	152	489	69	134	24	1	21	58	6	.274
1980	Boston.........	OF	148	463	72	123	37	5	18	60	3	.266
	Totals..........		1064	3394	485	888	187	31	128	443	39	.262

CARL YASTRZEMSKI 41 5-11 185 Bats L Throws R

"Retire? I don't even think about it!" . . . Going on 42, still going strong . . . One of most remarkable athletes of all time . . . Continues to climb higher and higher among baseball's all-time leaders . . . "Playing baseball has always been fun for me." . . . Born Aug. 22, 1939, in Southampton, N.Y. . . . Plays that tricky leftfield wall in Fenway Park like he owns it . . . Signed by the Bosox off the campus of Notre Dame . . . Has been with the Red Sox longer than any homegrown star (Ted Williams was purchased in a minor league deal) . . . Was originally an infielder.

Year	Club	Pos.	G	AB	R	H	2B	3B	HR	RBI	SB	Avg.
1961	Boston.........	OF	148	583	71	155	31	6	11	80	6	.266
1962	Boston.........	OF	160	646	99	191	43	6	19	94	7	.296
1963	Boston.........	OF	151	570	91	183	40	3	14	68	8	.321
1964	Boston.........	OF-3B	151	567	77	164	29	9	15	67	6	.289
1965	Boston.........	OF	133	494	78	154	45	3	20	72	7	.312
1966	Boston.........	OF	160	594	81	165	39	2	16	80	8	.278
1967	Boston.........	OF	161	579	112	189	31	4	44	121	10	.326
1968	Boston.........	OF-1B	157	539	90	162	32	2	23	74	13	.301
1969	Boston.........	OF-1B	162	603	96	154	28	2	40	111	15	.255
1970	Boston.........	1B-OF	161	566	125	186	29	0	40	102	23	.329
1971	Boston.........	OF	148	508	75	129	21	2	15	70	8	.254
1972	Boston.........	OF-1B	125	455	70	120	18	2	12	68	5	.264
1973	Boston.........	1B-3B-OF	152	540	82	160	25	4	19	95	9	.296
1974	Boston.........	1B-OF	148	515	93	155	25	2	15	79	12	.301
1975	Boston.........	1B-OF	149	543	91	146	30	1	14	60	8	.269
1976	Boston.........	1B-OF	155	546	71	146	23	2	21	102	5	.267
1977	Boston.........	1B-OF	150	558	99	165	27	3	28	102	11	.296
1978	Boston.........	OF-1B	144	523	70	145	21	2	17	81	4	.277
1979	Boston.........	OF-1B	147	518	69	140	28	1	21	87	3	.270
1980	Boston.........	1B-OF	105	364	49	100	21	1	15	50	0	.275
	Totals..........		2967	10811	1689	3109	586	57	419	1663	168	.288

TONY PEREZ 38 6-2 215 **Bats R Throws R**

Like "Ol' Man River," he just keeps rolling along . . . Led the Red Sox in both home runs and RBI in '80, a remarkable feat at his age, and with all of those sluggers around him in that lineup . . . A nice guy, too . . . Born May 14, 1942, in Camaguey, Cuba . . . Has two years to go on his $1.1 million contract . . . Was a key factor in the success of Cincinnati Reds year after year during '70s . . . Seven times an All-Star with the Reds . . . Appeared in five playoffs and four World Series . . . Second in the majors during the decade of the seventies with 954 RBI.

Year	Club	Pos.	G	AB	R	H	2B	3B	HR	RBI	SB	Avg.
1964	Cincinnati	1B	12	25	1	2	1	0	0	1	0	.080
1965	Cincinnati	1B	104	281	40	73	14	4	12	47	0	.260
1966	Cincinnati	1B	99	257	25	68	10	4	4	39	1	.265
1967	Cincinnati	3B-1B-2B	156	600	78	174	28	7	26	102	0	.290
1968	Cincinnati	3B	160	625	93	176	25	7	18	92	3	.282
1969	Cincinnati	3B	160	629	103	185	31	2	37	122	4	.294
1970	Cincinnati	3B-1B	158	587	107	186	28	6	40	129	8	.317
1971	Cincinnati	3B-1B	158	609	72	164	22	3	25	91	4	.269
1972	Cincinnati	1B	136	515	64	146	33	7	21	90	4	.283
1973	Cincinnati	1B	151	564	73	177	33	3	27	101	3	.314
1974	Cincinnati	1B	158	596	81	158	28	2	28	101	1	.265
1975	Cincinnati	1B	137	511	74	144	28	3	20	109	1	.282
1976	Cincinnati	1B	139	527	77	137	32	6	19	91	10	.260
1977	Montreal	1B	154	559	71	158	32	6	19	91	4	.283
1978	Montreal	1B	148	544	63	158	38	3	14	78	2	.290
1979	Montreal	1B	132	489	58	132	29	4	13	73	2	.270
1980	Boston	1B	151	585	73	161	31	3	25	105	1	.275
	Totals.........		2313	8503	1153	2399	443	70	348	1462	48	.282

JIM RICE 28 6-2 205 **Bats R Throws R**

Spent much of 1980 season mired in worst slump of his career . . . "You know the pitchers are going to pay for that," said Don Zimmer . . . Still one of the most respected, most feared sluggers in the game . . . A one-man wrecking crew when he's hot . . . Born March 8, 1953, in Anderson, S.C. . . . Frequently at odds with the press because he refuses to speak . . . "Privacy is important to everyone" . . . Was awesome in '78 when he reigned as the A.L.'s MVP . . . Loves to play golf and can drive the ball a mile . . . Believe it or not, his best years may still lie ahead of him.

Year	Club	Pos.	G	AB	R	H	2B	3B	HR	RBI	SB	Avg.
1974	Boston.........	OF	24	67	6	18	2	1	1	13	0	.269
1975	Boston.........	OF	144	564	92	174	29	4	22	102	10	.309
1976	Boston.........	OF	153	581	75	164	25	8	25	85	8	.282
1977	Boston.........	OF	160	644	104	206	29	15	39	114	5	.320
1978	Boston.........	OF	163	677	121	213	25	15	46	139	7	.315
1979	Boston.........	OF	158	619	117	201	39	6	39	130	9	.325
1980	Boston.........	OF	124	504	81	148	22	6	24	86	8	.294
	Totals.........		926	3656	596	1124	171	55	196	669	47	.307

TOP PROSPECTS

BRUCE HURST 23 6-3 200 **Bats L Throws L**
Won a job in spring training because the Bosox were desperate for a lefthanded starter . . . Shelled his first three times out and headed for a similar fate in his fourth start when he settled down and retired 16 Tigers in a row . . . Most observers agree it's merely a matter of time before he becomes a star . . . Born March 24, 1958, in St. George, Utah . . . Was Boston's first pick in June, 1976, draft.

GARRY HANCOCK 27 6-0 175 **Bats L Throws L**
Has excellent minor league credentials . . . Problem is finding room for him in Boston outfield . . . Born Jan. 23, 1954, in Tampa . . . Was Cleveland's No. 1 pick in January, 1976 . . . Joined Boston organization in a minor-league deal.

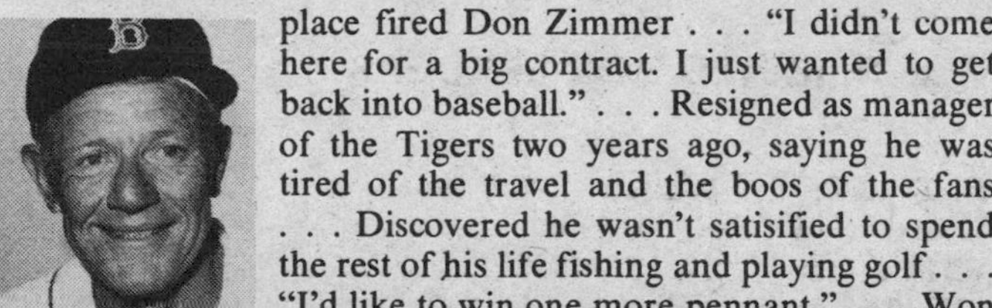

MANAGER RALPH HOUK: Coaxed out of retirement to replace fired Don Zimmer . . . "I didn't come here for a big contract. I just wanted to get back into baseball." . . . Resigned as manager of the Tigers two years ago, saying he was tired of the travel and the boos of the fans . . . Discovered he wasn't satisified to spend the rest of his life fishing and playing golf . . . "I'd like to win one more pennant." . . . Won pennants his first three seasons managing in the majors, with the Yankees in '61, '62 and '63 . . . Was offered the job of Red Sox manager in 1959 but turned it down because the Yankees promised him he would succeed Casey Stengel . . . Born Aug. 9, 1919, in Lawrence, Kan. . . . The Major . . . A battlefield hero during World War II . . . Noted as a tough boss but actually pampers his players . . . "It's not a good move, it's a great move," says Carl Yastrzemski . . . Was a back-up catcher with the Yankees as a player.

GREATEST TEAM

Frustrated after finishing second behind the Yankees in 1938, 1939, 1941, and 1942, the Boston Red Sox finally went all the way to the World Series in 1946. With the exception of three days in April, the Red Sox occupied first place all season and coasted home, 12 games ahead.

One big reason for the Bosox success was the return of superstar Ted Williams. Although still a bit rusty after spending three years in military service, Williams finished second in all three Triple Crown categories and was named the American League's MVP.

Shortstop Johnny Pesky, second baseman Bobby Doerr and centerfielder Dom DiMaggio also had great years and the addition of first baseman Rudy York gave the Sox a big boost.

However, it was the pitching of Boo Ferriss, Tex Hughson, Mickey Harris and Joe Dobson that really made possible the Red Sox' first pennant since 1918.

ALL-TIME RED SOX LEADERS

BATTING: Ted Williams, .406, 1941
HRs: Jimmy Foxx, 50, 1938
RBIs: Jimmy Foxx, 175, 1938
STEALS: Tommy Harper, 54, 1973
WINS: Joe Wood, 34, 1912
STRIKEOUTS: Joe Wood, 258, 1912

CLEVELAND INDIANS

TEAM DIRECTORY: Prin. Owner: Steve O'Neill; Pres.: Gabe Paul; VP-GM: Phillip Seghi; Treas.: Dudley S. Blossom; VP-Dir. Player Development and Scouting: Bob Quinn; Dir. Pub. Rel.: Bob DiBiasio; Trav. Sec.: Mike Seghi; Mgr.: Dave Garcia. Home: Cleveland Municipal Stadium (76,713). Field distances: 320, l.f. line; 377, l.c.; 400, c.f.; 385, r.c.; 320, r.f. line. Spring training: Tucson, Ariz.

SCOUTING REPORT

HITTING: There certainly was nothing wrong with the Indians' offense last year. As a team, the Tribe batted .277—their best effort since 1948. And there is no reason to believe they won't be able to hit that well, or better, again. A healthy Andre Thornton ought to make a big, big difference all by himself. Thornton, the Injuns' slugging first baseman and the team's premier power hit-

Joe Charboneau (23 HRs) was named Rookie of the Year.

ter, missed all of last year because of two knee operations.

Rookie of the Year Joe Charboneau must now prove last season's surprising performance was no fluke, but that should not present a problem. The big surprise last year was speedster Miguel Dilone, who has made the Indians' attack exciting. A better year from Rick Manning (.234) is a must. And the Indians are counting on second baseman Duane Kuiper to bounce back after missing most of last season with injuries. Jorge Orta, a free-agent find, has developed into a solid, everyday player.

PITCHING: No doubt about it, that is where the problem lies. The Indians featured the worst pitching in the league last year. In an effort to rectify that predicament, they outbid the Angels for veteran righthander Bert Blyleven (8-13), who had worn out his welcome in Pittsburgh. They also came up with enough cash to keep free agent Dan Spillner (16-11). Together with Len Barker (19-12), who tired during the final weeks last year but could become one of the big winners in the league, and John Denny (8-6), who was sidelined with a heel injury, they give the Tribe a solid starting staff.

But the relievers are something else—lefthander Sid Monge (3-5, 14 saves), Wayne Garland (6-9), still struggling to come back from shoulder surgery and Ross Grimsley, a better pitcher than his 4-5 record indicates. Rick Waits (13-14) will also be a factor.

FIELDING: For a change, the Indians' defense was a sight to behold last season as they climbed from a so-so seventh to second in the league behind Baltimore. Catcher Ron Hassey, in particular, proved to be a pleasant surprise. The presence of Kuiper in the middle of the infield for a full season would make the Injuns' defense—which is steady although seldom spectacular—even more dependable. Manning is one of the better centerfielders and Tom Veryzer has developed into the shortstop the Tigers always thought he could be.

OUTLOOK: A year ago, the Indians set their sights on 85 wins. That was before they lost their team leader, Kuiper, their top slugger, Thornton, and a key pitcher, Denny. Even so, they only fell six short of their goal, winning 79 games. That was only good enough for sixth place, but under the circumstances, the Indians had to be encouraged. If they can keep their key people healthy, if they can stop blowing games in the late innings, if Charboneau and Dilone can do it again, Cleveland could catch some people by surprise.

CLEVELAND INDIANS 1981 ROSTER

MANAGER Dave Garcia
Coaches—Dave Duncan, Tom McCraw, Joe Nossek, Dennis Sommers

PITCHERS

No.	Name	1980 Club	W-L	IP	SO	ERA	B-T	Ht.	Wt.	Born
39	Barker, Len	Cleveland	19-12	246	187	4.17	R-R	6-4	235	7/7/55 Ft. Knox, KY
–	Blyleven, Bert	Pittsburgh	8-13	217	169	3.82	R-R	6-3	207	4/6/51 Holland
45	Brennan, Tom	Tacoma	9-3	152	77	2.49	R-R	6-1	180	10/30/52 Chicago, IL
38	Cuellar, Bobby	Tacoma	8-3	90	55	3.30	R-R	5-11	190	8/20/52 Alice, TX
40	Denny, John	Cleveland	8-6	109	59	4.38	R-R	6-3	190	11/8/52 Prescott, AZ
17	Garland, Wayne	Cleveland	6-9	150	55	4.62	R-R	6-0	195	10/26/50 Nashville, TN
59	Glaser, Gordy	Chattanooga	6-4	101	43	2.76	R-R	6-3	185	11/19/57 Baton Rouge, LA
		Tacoma	4-3	50	7	6.48				
48	Grimsley, Ross	Montreal	2-4	41	11	6.37	L-L	6-3	200	1/7/50 Topeka, KS
		Cleveland	4-5	75	18	6.72				
43	Monge, Sid	Cleveland	3-5	94	61	3.54	B-L	6-2	195	4/11/51 Mexico
51	Narleski, Steve	Chattanooga	11-12	102	68	3.97	R-R	6-3	195	9/12/55 Camden, NJ
47	Paxton, Mike	Tacoma	6-10	135	46	5.00	R-R	5-11	190	9/3/53 Memphis, TN
61	Puryear, Nate	Tacoma			Did not play		R-R	6-4	205	7/30/54 Biloxi, MS
37	Spillner, Dan	Cleveland	16-11	194	100	5.29	R-R	6-1	190	11/27/51 Casper, WY
46	Stanton, Mike	Cleveland	1-3	86	74	5.44	R-R	6-2	200	9/25/52 St. Louis, MO
36	Waits, Rick	Cleveland	13-14	224	109	4.46	L-L	6-3	195	5/15/52 Atlanta, GA
56	Wihtol, Sandy	Tacoma	4-9	58	38	3.57	R-R	6-2	190	6/1/55 Palo Alto, CA
		Cleveland	1-0	35	20	3.60				
33	Wilkins, Eric	Tacoma	7-4	101	72	3.92	R-R	6-1	180	12/9/56 Seattle, WA

CATCHERS

No.	Name	1980 Club	H	HR	RBI	Pct.	B-T	Ht.	Wt.	Born
22	Bando, Chris	Chattanooga	141	12	73	.349	B-R	6-0	195	2/4/56 Cleveland, OH
16	Diaz, Bo	Cleveland	47	3	32	.227	R-R	5-11	190	3/23/53 Venezuela
9	Hassey, Ron	Cleveland	124	8	65	.318	L-R	6-2	195	2/27/53 Tucson, AZ
–	Sanguillen, Manny	Pittsburgh	12	0	2	.250	R-R	6-0	193	3/21/44 Panama

INFIELDERS

No.	Name	1980 Club	H	HR	RBI	Pct.	B-T	Ht.	Wt.	Born
7	Bannister, Alan	Chi (AL)-Cle	111	1	41	.283	R-R	5-11	175	9/3/51 Buena Park, CA
20	Bonilla, Juan	Tacoma	152	4	55	.303	R-R	5-9	170	2/12/56 Puerto Rico
8	Brohamer, Jack	Bos-Cle	50	2	21	.251	L-R	5-9	170	2/26/50 Maywood, CA
31	Cage, Wayne	Tacoma	126	19	89	.308	L-L	6-4	190	11/23/51 Monroe, LA
10	Dybzinski, Jerry	Cleveland	57	1	23	.230	R-R	6-2	180	7/7/55 Cleveland, OH
21	Hargrove, Mike	Cleveland	179	11	85	.304	L-L	6-0	195	10/26/49 Perryton, TX
11	Harrah, Toby	Cleveland	150	11	72	.267	R-R	6-0	180	10/26/48 Sissonville, WV
18	Kuiper, Duane	Cleveland	42	0	9	.282	L-R	6-0	175	6/19/50 Racine, WI
57	Logrande, Angelo	Chattanooga	137	25	81	.290	R-R	6-3	215	12/4/57 San Pedro, CA
12	Rosello, Dave	Cleveland	29	2	12	.248	R-R	5-11	160	6/26/50 Puerto Rico
29	Thornton, Andre	Cleveland			Did not play		R-R	6-2	205	8/13/49 Tuskegee, AL
15	Veryzer, Tom	Cleveland	97	2	28	.271	R-R	6-1	185	2/11/53 Pt. Jefferson, NY

OUTFIELDERS

No.	Name	1980 Club	H	HR	RBI	Pct.	B-T	Ht.	Wt.	Born
34	Charboneau, Joe	Cleveland	131	23	87	.289	R-R	6-2	200	6/17/55 Belvidere, IL
27	Dilone, Miguel	Wichita	20	0	2	.238	B-R	5-11	160	11/1/54 Dominican Republic
		Cleveland	180	0	40	.341				
–	Kelly, Pat	Baltimore	52	3	26	.260	L-L	6-1	194	7/30/44 Philadelphia, PA
–	Littleton, Larry	Tacoma	136	17	80	.271	R-R	6-1	185	4/3/54 Charlotte, NC
28	Manning, Rick	Cleveland	110	3	52	.234	L-R	6-1	180	9/2/54 Niagara Falls, NY
6	Orta, Jorge	Cleveland	140	10	64	.291	L-R	5-10	175	11/26/50 Mexico
26	Pagel, Karl	Wichita	50	11	32	.267	L-L	6-2	185	3/29/55 Madison, WI
		Tacoma	43	4	26	.264				

INDIAN PROFILES

LEN BARKER 25 6-4 235 Bats R Throws R

Throws the best fastball in the league, according to Angels' manager Jim Fregosi . . . Strictly a power pitcher who goes in streaks . . . However, his control is much improved . . . "I've never had better control of my pitches" . . . Flirted with no-hitters twice in 1980 . . . Went an entire game without walking anyone—a first for him . . . "Len's the most consistent pitcher we had," says manager Dave Garcia . . . Born July 7, 1955, in Fort Knox, Ky. . . . "He has all the tools to win 20 games," says Garcia . . . Long leg kick gives base runners an excellent chance to steal . . . Acquired from Texas Rangers . . . Used mainly in relief until the Indians gave him a chance to start.

Year	Club	G	IP	W	L	Pct.	SO	BB	H	ERA
1976	Texas	2	15	1	0	1.000	7	6	7	2.40
1977	Texas	15	47	4	1	.800	51	24	36	2.68
1978	Texas	29	52	1	5	.167	33	29	63	4.85
1979	Cleveland	29	137	6	6	.500	93	70	146	4.93
1980	Cleveland	36	246	19	12	.613	187	92	237	4.17
	Totals	111	497	31	24	.564	371	221	489	4.26

WAYNE GARLAND 30 6-0 195 Bats R Throws R

Encouraged by his performance in 1980 . . . Still working to bounce back after shoulder surgery . . . No pitcher has ever succesfully returned from an operation on his rotator cuff . . . "Things are definitely looking up" . . . Redesigned his delivery after surgery . . . Now throws a fastball, curve, slider, screwball and knuckleball . . . Born Oct. 26, 1950, in Nashville . . . Signed 10-year, guaranteed $2.3-million contract as free agent in 1976 . . . Could have taken money and retired after injury but was determined to pitch again . . . Indians keep hoping he can regain the form that made him a 20-game winner for the Orioles' in '76.

Year	Club	G	IP	W	L	Pct.	SO	BB	H	ERA
1973	Baltimore	4	16	0	1	.000	10	7	14	3.94
1974	Baltimore	20	91	5	5	.500	40	26	68	2.97
1975	Baltimore	29	87	2	5	.286	46	31	80	3.72
1976	Baltimore	38	232	20	7	.741	113	64	224	2.68
1977	Cleveland	38	283	13	19	.406	118	88	281	3.59
1978	Cleveland	6	30	2	3	.400	13	16	43	7.80
1979	Cleveland	18	95	4	10	.286	40	34	120	5.21
1980	Cleveland	25	150	6	9	.400	55	48	163	4.62
	Totals	178	984	52	59	.468	435	314	993	3.78

RICK WAITS 28 6-3 195 — Bats L Throws L

Senior member of Indians staff . . . Had been counted on to win 20 in '79, but lost magic touch . . . "It was simply because the hitters caught up with me." . . . Came up with screwball and slider in 1980 . . . Also made up his mind he was going to cut down on his walks . . . Born May 5, 1952, in Atlanta . . . The best national anthem singer in the big leagues . . . Has appeared on NBC's "Today Show" . . . Seems to be at his best against the Yankees when they are trying to clinch the Eastern title . . . Once pitched back-to-back no-hitters while in high school.

Year	Club	G	IP	W	L	Pct.	SO	BB	H	ERA
1973	Texas	1	1	0	0	.000	0	1	1	9.00
1975	Cleveland	16	70	6	2	.750	34	25	57	2.96
1976	Cleveland	26	124	7	9	.438	65	54	143	3.99
1977	Cleveland	37	135	9	7	.563	62	64	132	4.00
1978	Cleveland	34	230	13	15	.464	97	86	206	3.21
1979	Cleveland	34	231	16	13	.552	91	91	230	4.44
1980	Cleveland	33	224	13	14	.481	109	82	231	4.46
	Totals	181	1015	64	60	.516	458	403	1000	3.95

MIGUEL DILONE 26 5-11 160 — Bats S Throws R

Stolen from Cubs' farm system for $35,000 . . . "The kid has simply done everything for us," says Dave Garcia . . . Failed to stick with Pirates, A's or Cubs, but has found a home in Cleveland . . . Shattered the Indians' stolen-base record, which was set way back in 1917 . . . Born Dec. 1, 1954, in Santiago, D.R. . . . Nicknamed "Liebre" which means "jackrabbit" in Spanish . . . Coach Tom McCraw calls him, "our engine, our motor, our catalyst!" . . . Believes his can steal 80 bases a year . . . Claims Charley Finley ruined his confidence as a complete ballplayer by using him simply to steal . . . "I don't want to be known as a pinch runner. I want to be known as a baseball player."

Year	Club	Pos.	G	AB	R	H	2B	3B	HR	RBI	SB	Avg.
1974	Pittsburgh	OF	12	2	3	0	0	0	0	0	2	.000
1975	Pittsburgh	OF	18	6	8	0	0	0	0	0	2	.000
1976	Pittsburgh	OF	16	17	7	4	0	0	0	0	5	.235
1977	Pittsburgh	OF	29	44	5	6	0	0	0	0	12	.136
1978	Oakland	OF-3B	135	258	34	59	8	0	1	14	50	.229
1979	Oakland	OF	30	91	15	17	1	2	1	6	6	.187
1979	Chicago (NL)	OF	43	36	14	11	0	0	0	1	15	.306
1980	Cleveland	OF	132	528	82	180	30	9	0	40	61	.341
	Totals		415	982	168	277	39	11	2	61	153	.282

RON HASSEY 28 6-2 195 Bats L Throws R

One of the Indians' most pleasant surprises in 1980 . . . Much improved all-around player . . . Farm director Bob Quinn predicts he has the power to hit 15 or 20 HRs a year . . . Was platooned in '80, appearing only against right-handed pitching . . . Born Feb. 27, 1953, in Tucson . . . Has made himself into a fine receiver through plenty of hard work . . . Always could hit . . . Only question was his defense . . . Was Tribe's best clutch hitter in '80 . . . "I think I concentrate more with men on base." . . . Was not drafted until the 18th round in 1976.

Year	Club	Pos.	G	AB	R	H	2B	3B	HR	RBI	SB	Avg.
1978	Cleveland.......	C	25	74	5	15	0	0	2	9	2	.203
1979	Cleveland.......	C-1B	75	223	20	64	14	0	4	32	1	.287
1980	Cleveland.......	C-1B	130	390	43	124	18	4	8	65	0	.318
	Totals..........		230	687	68	203	32	4	14	106	3	.295

JOE CHARBONEAU 25 6-2 200 Bats R Throws R

"Super Joe" . . . Was Indians' rookie sensation in 1980 . . . As his legend grew he became the most popular player on the team . . . Even had a song written about him . . . Gained fame because of earlier odd-ball behavior but also proved himself to be a fine young hitter . . . Born June 17, 1955, in Belvedere, Ill. . . . A descendant of the French scout Touissant Charboneau, who guided explorers Lewis and Clark . . . Was traded to the Tribe after four frustrating seasons in the Phillies' farm system . . . Was a successful semi-pro boxer as a youth . . . Has been known to extract his own teeth, and sew up his own stab wounds with fishing line.

Year	Club	Pos.	G	AB	R	H	2B	3B	HR	RBI	SB	Avg.
1980	Cleveland.......	OF	131	453	76	131	17	2	23	87	2	.289

MIKE HARGROVE 31 6-0 195 Bats L Throws L

Signed a $2 million contract to stay with Tribe . . . Drives enemy pitchers crazy with his fidgeting at the plate . . . Has great concentration and bat control . . . Expert at fouling off pitches until he gets one he wants or draws a walk . . . Born Oct. 26, 1949, in Perryton, Tex. . . . One of the best lead-off hitters ever to wear an Indians uniform . . . "I can do everything a lead-off man is supposed to do except run with speed" . . . Was 577th player picked in 1972 free agent draft . . . Improved considerably in 1979 when Dave Garcia took over as Indians' manager and told him he had an everyday job.

Year	Club	Pos.	G	AB	R	H	2B	3B	HR	RBI	SB	Avg.
1974	Texas..........	1B-OF	131	415	57	134	18	6	4	66	0	.323
1975	Texas..........	1B-OF	145	519	82	157	22	2	11	62	4	.303
1976	Texas..........	1B	151	541	80	155	30	1	7	58	2	.287
1977	Texas..........	1B	153	525	98	160	28	4	18	69	2	.305
1978	Texas..........	1B	146	494	63	124	24	1	7	40	2	.251
1979	San Diego......	1B	52	125	15	24	5	0	0	8	0	.192
1979	Cleveland.......	OF-1B	100	338	60	110	21	4	10	56	2	.325
1980	Cleveland.......	1B-OF	160	589	86	179	22	2	11	85	4	.304
	Totals..........		1038	3546	541	1043	170	20	68	444	16	.294

RICK MANNING 26 6-1 180 — Bats L Throws R

Slumped badly at plate in 1980 but became better than ever defensively . . . Dave Garcia calls him the best centerfielder in the American League . . . "I saved a lot of runs, at least twice as many as I drove in" . . . Accumulated career-high number of walks . . . "If I had Mike Hargrove's discipline or he had my speed, we might have the first $2 million-a-year ballplayer" . . . Born Sept. 2, 1954, in Niagra Falls, N.Y. . . . Captain of the Indians' outfielder corps . . . Was great help to Joc Charboneau, Miguel Dilone and Jorge Orta . . . Believes he is a better CF than Fred Lynn . . . Denies his $1.4-million, 5-year contract has diminished his enthusiasm . . . "I love this game."

Year	Club	Pos.	G	AB	R	H	2B	3B	HR	RBI	SB	Avg.
1975	Cleveland.......	OF	120	480	69	137	16	5	3	35	19	.285
1976	Cleveland.......	OF	138	552	73	161	24	7	6	43	16	.292
1977	Cleveland.......	OF	68	252	33	57	7	3	5	18	9	.226
1978	Cleveland.......	OF	148	566	65	149	27	3	3	50	12	.263
1979	Cleveland.......	OF	144	560	67	145	12	2	3	51	30	.259
1980	Cleveland.......	OF	140	471	55	110	17	4	3	52	12	.234
	Totals..........		758	2881	362	759	103	24	23	249	98	.263

DUANE KUIPER 30 6-0 175 — Bats L Throws R

Stabilizing force in Indians' infield . . . Missed second half of 1980 season because of damaged knee . . . Tribe's team captain and a key cog in their attack . . . Was No. 1 pick in January 1972 draft . . . Born June 19, 1950, in Racine, Wis. . . . Good clutch hitter . . . Popular both with fans and Cleveland press . . . Once went 1,382 games without hitting a home run . . . His 1977 performance was considered by many to have been the finest defensive effort ever put forth by a Cleveland player.

Year	Club	Pos.	G	AB	R	H	2B	3B	HR	RBI	SB	Avg.
1974	Cleveland	2B	10	22	7	11	2	0	0	4	1	.500
1975	Cleveland	2B	90	346	42	101	11	1	0	25	19	.292
1976	Cleveland	2B-1B	135	506	47	133	13	6	0	37	10	.263
1977	Cleveland	2B	148	610	62	169	15	8	1	50	11	.277
1978	Cleveland	2B	149	547	52	155	18	6	0	43	4	.283
1979	Cleveland	2B	140	479	46	122	9	5	0	39	4	.255
1980	Cleveland	2B	42	149	10	42	5	0	0	9	0	.282
	Totals		714	2659	266	733	73	26	1	207	49	.276

JORGE ORTA 30 5-10 175 — Bats L Throws R

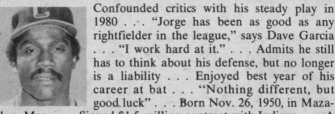

Confounded critics with his steady play in 1980 . . . "Jorge has been as good as any rightfielder in the league," says Dave Garcia . . . "I work hard at it." . . . Admits he still has to think about his defense, but no longer is a liability . . . Enjoyed best year of his career at bat . . . "Nothing different, but good luck" . . . Born Nov. 26, 1950, in Mazatlan, Mex. . . . Signed $1.5-million contract with Indians . . . A good base runner . . . Usually plays better after weather warms up . . . Seldom says much, prefers to let his bat speak for him.

Year	Club	Pos.	G	AB	R	H	2B	3B	HR	RBI	SB	Avg.
1972	Chicago (AL)	SS-2B-3B	51	124	20	25	3	1	3	11	1	.202
1973	Chicago (AL)	2B-SS	128	425	46	113	9	10	6	40	8	.266
1974	Chicago (AL)	2B-SS	139	525	73	166	31	2	10	67	9	.316
1975	Chicago (AL)	2B	140	542	64	165	26	10	11	83	16	.304
1976	Chicago (AL)	OF-3B	158	636	74	174	29	8	14	72	24	.274
1977	Chicago (AL)	2B	144	564	71	159	27	8	11	84	4	.282
1978	Chicago (AL)	2B	117	420	45	115	19	2	13	53	1	.274
1979	Chicago (AL)	2B	113	325	49	85	18	3	11	46	1	.262
1980	Cleveland	OF-2B	129	481	78	140	18	3	10	64	6	.291
	Totals		1119	4042	520	1142	180	47	89	520	70	.283

TOP PROSPECTS

CHRIS BANDO 25 6-0 195 — Bats S Throws L

Brother of Brewers' star, Sal . . . Was Indians' No. 2 pick in June 1978 draft . . . Hindered by broken leg in 1979 . . . Born Feb. 4, 1956, in Cleveland . . . Earned All-America honors at Arizona State, leading his team to the NCAA championship . . . Could be Tribe's catcher of the future.

VON HAYES 22 6-5 185 — Bats L Throws R

Long and lanky infielder . . . Picked on seventh round in June 1979 . . . Batted .511 with 17 HRs and 39 RBIs in semi-pro ball in 1979 . . . Born Aug. 31, 1958 in Stockton, Calif. . . . Was MVP in the U.S.-Japan College World Series in '79, batting .545 with 5 HRs and 23 RBIs.

MANAGER DAVE GARCIA: Third-oldest skipper in the A.L. . . . Born Sept. 15, 1920, in East St. Louis, Ill. . . . Has had a positive influence on Indians since he replaced Jeff Torborg in July of 1979 . . . Was named Indians' Man of the Year in '79 . . . Was fired earlier as manager of the California Angels because he was too quiet . . . But when he speaks, Indians listen . . . Players have responded to his no-platoon methods . . . Spent 20 years as a minor league infielder but never made it to the majors . . . Worked as player-manager for nine years before he finally hung up his glove in '58 . . . Also coached for the Padres, Angels and Indians.

GREATEST TEAM

The New York Yankees, shooting for their sixth pennant in a row, won 103 games in 1954. Most seasons that would have been more than enough. But this time, they weren't even close.

Picked to finish no higher than third before the season began, the Cleveland Indians, depending upon their incredibly deep pitching staff of Early Wynn, Bob Lemon, Mike Garcia, Bob Feller, Art Houtteman, plus relievers Ray Narleski, Don Mossi and Hal Newhouser, won a league-record 111 times.

The Indians were no slouches on offense, either. Not with Bobby Avila, Larry Doby and Al Rosen in the line-up. Avila won the batting title with a .341 average, Doby finished first with 32 HRs and 126 RBI, and Rosen chipped in 24 of the Tribe's league-leading 156 homers.

Their bubble burst in the World Series, however, as the New York Giants, led by Willie Mays and pinch-hitter Dusty Rhodes, upset the heavily favored Indians with a four-game sweep.

ALL-TIME INDIAN LEADERS

BATTING: Joe Jackson, .408, 1911
HRs: Al Rosen, 43, 1953
RBIs: Hal Trosky, 162, 1936
STEALS: Miguel Dilone, 61, 1980
WINS: Jim Bagby, 31, 1920
STRIKEOUTS: Bob Feller, 348, 1946

DETROIT TIGERS

TEAM DIRECTORY: Owner-Chairman of the Board: John Fetzer; Pres.-GM: Jim Campbell; VP-Baseball Operations: William Haase; VP-Finance: Alex Callam; Dir. Pub. Rel.: Dan Ewald; Trav. Sec.: Bill Brown; Mgr.: Sparky Anderson. Home: Tiger Stadium (54,226). Field distances: 340, l.f. line; 365, l.c.; 440, c.f.; 370, r.c.; 325, r.f. line. Spring training: Lakeland, Fla.

SCOUTING REPORT

HITTING: There is nothing wrong with the eight players the Tigers send out on the field day after day. They can hit. In fact, they scored more runs than any other team in the league last year, even though they didn't have a hitter among the top 15. Alan Trammell hit .300 and emerged as the team leader. Steve Kemp (.293, 21 HRs, 101 RBI), Lance Parrish (.286, 24 HRs, 82 RBI), Richie Hebner (.290, 12 HRs, 82 RBI) and Champ Summers (.297, 16 HRs, 60 RBI) made the Tigers a formidable force.

And Tom Brookens was a .275 surprise at third base. The Tigers are hoping Kirk Gibson, who was leading the team with nine HRs when he hurt his hand, can bounce back. If not, they have found Rick Peters, who hit .291. Aside from their lack of speed and the need for another righthanded power hitter, the Tigers are set.

PITCHING: The Tigers are still several pitchers away from being able to seriously contend. It is unlikely Kevin Saucier (7-3), acquired from Texas for shortstop Mark Wagner, or Dennis Kinney (4-6), obtained from San Diego, will be the answer. The Tigers need help in the bullpen, where Aurelio Lopez (13-6 with 21 saves) has been asked to do it alone since John Hiller left. In spite of last season's 16 wins, Jack Morris was not the ace the Tigers hoped he would be. Dan Petry (10-9) is coming and Dan Schatzeder (11-13) should get better. But that's not enough. A comeback by Mark Fidrych would, of course, solve a lot of problems.

FIELDING: Parrish tied Jim Sundberg of Texas for the league lead with 17 passed balls, and Brookens led all third basemen with 29 errors, but overall the Tigers are decent defensively. Hebner is better at first than he was at third, Lou Whitaker and Trammell are solid up the middle, and Kemp, plus either Peters or Gibson and either Summers or Al Cowens are adequate in the outfield.

Lance Parrish sparked Tiger attack with 24 homers.

OUTLOOK: A year ago, Sparky Anderson predicted his Tigers would win 90 games. The Tigers made their manager eat his words. But only by six games. Sparky isn't making any predictions this year. Perhaps that is because he now realizes exactly what he is up against. The Tigers have steadily improved year by year and now boast the nucleus of an outstanding team. But they have reached the point where they need outside help–specifically a couple of top-notch pitchers–if they are to improve their status in the standings.

DETROIT TIGERS 1981 ROSTER

MANAGER Sparky Anderson
Coaches—Gates Brown, Billy Consolo, Roger Craig, Alex Grammas, Dick Tracewski

PITCHERS

No.	Name	1980 Club	W-L	IP	SO	ERA	B-T	Ht.	Wt.	Born
41	Cappuzzello, George	Montgomery	9-9	152	121	3.26	R-L	6-0	175	1/15/54 Youngstown, OH
		Evansville	0-1	14	9	4.50				
43	Chris, Mike	Evansville	7-14	140	85	4.55	L-L	6-2	175	10/8/57 Santa Monica, CA
20	Fidrych, Mark	Evansville	6-7	117	62	3.93	R-R	6-3	175	8/14/54 Worcester, MA
		Detroit	2-3	44	16	5.73				
–	Kinney, Dennis	San Diego	4-6	83	40	4.23	L-L	6-1	170	2/26/52 Toledo, OH
29	Lopez, Aurelio	Detroit	13-6	124	97	3.77	R-R	6-0	230	10/5/48 Mexico
47	Morris, Jack	Detroit	16-15	250	112	4.18	R-R	6-3	190	5/16/55 St. Paul, MN
46	Petry, Dan	Evansville	2-0	30	16	2.73	R-R	6-4	200	11/13/58 Palo Alto, CA
		Detroit	10-9	165	88	3.93				
48	Robbins, Bruce	Evansville	2-6	58	44	4.19	L-L	6-2	190	9/10/59 Dunkirk, IN
		Detroit	4-2	52	23	6.58				
19	Rozema, Dave	Detroit	6-9	145	49	3.91	R-R	6-4	200	8/5/56 Grand Rapids, MI
49	Rucker, Dave	Evansville	7-8	92	53	3.42	L-L	6-1	185	9/1/58 San Bernadino, CA
–	Saucier, Kevin	Philadelphia	7-3	50	25	3.42	R-L	6-1	195	8/9/56 Pensacola, FL
36	Schatzeder, Dan	Detroit	11-13	193	94	4.01	L-L	6-0	195	12/1/54 Elmhurst, IL
42	Steffen, Dave	Evansville	0-0	7	3	16.71	R-R	6-3	220	12/17/58 Dearborn, MI
45	Tobik, Dave	Evansville	3-3	48	49	3.94	R-R	6-1	195	3/2/53 Euclid, OH
		Detroit	1-0	61	34	3.98				
28	Ujdur, Jerry	Evansville	9-4	115	62	3.37	R-R	6-1	195	3/5/57 Duluth, MN
		Detroit	1-0	21	8	7.71				
40	Underwood, Pat	Detroit	3-6	113	60	3.58	L-L	6-0	175	2/9/57 Kokomo, IN
44	Weaver, Roger	Evansville	3-3	37	21	3.13	R-R	6-3	200	10/6/54 Amsterdam, NY
		Detroit	3-4	64	42	4.08				
39	Wilcox, Milt	Detroit	13-11	199	97	4.48	R-R	6-2	215	4/20/50 Honolulu, HI

CATCHERS

No.	Name	1980 Club	H	HR	RBI	Pct.	B-T	Ht.	Wt.	Born
12	Castillo, Marty	Evansville	114	12	62	.251	R-R	6-1	190	1/16/57 Long Beach, CA
15	Dyer, Duffy	Detroit	20	4	11	.185	R-R	6-0	200	8/15/45 Dayton, OH
13	Parrish, Lance	Detroit	158	24	82	.286	R-R	6-3	210	6/15/56 McKeesport, PA
14	Wockenfuss, John	Detroit	102	16	65	.274	R-R	6-0	180	2/27/49 Welch, WV

INFIELDERS

No.	Name	1980 Club	H	HR	RBI	Pct.	B-T	Ht.	Wt.	Born
16	Brookens, Tom	Detroit	140	10	66	.275	R-R	5-10	170	8/10/53 Chambersburg, PA
2	Hebner, Richie	Detroit	99	12	82	.290	L-R	6-1	195	11/26/47 Boston, MA
9	Papi, Stan	Oklahoma City	10	0	3	.333	R-R	6-0	180	5/14/51 Fresno, CA
		Bos-Detroit	27	3	17	.237				
3	Trammell, Alan	Detroit	168	9	65	.300	R-R	6-0	170	2/21/58 Garden Grove, CA
1	Whitaker, Lou	Detroit	111	1	45	.233	L-R	5-11	160	5/12/57 New York, NY

OUTFIELDERS

No.	Name	1980 Club	H	HR	RBI	Pct.	B-T	Ht.	Wt.	Born
34	Brown, Darrell	Evansville	138	3	43	.277	R-R	6-0	180	10/29/55 Oklahoma City, OK
25	Corcoran, Tim	Detroit	44	3	18	.288	L-L	5-11	175	3/19/53 Glendale, CA
10	Cowens, Al	Calif-Detroit	140	6	59	.268	R-R	6-2	200	10/25/51 Los Angeles, CA
37	Filkins, Les	Montgomery	50	6	31	.287	L-L	5-11	185	9/14/56 Chicago, IL
		Evansville	81	7	38	.297				
23	Gibson, Kirk	Detroit	46	9	16	.263	L-L	6-3	210	5/28/57 Pontiac, MI
35	Jones, Lynn	Evansville	33	0	11	.273	R-R	5-9	175	1/1/53 Meadville, PA
		Detroit	14	0	6	.255				
33	Kemp, Steve	Detroit	149	21	101	.293	L-L	6-0	190	8/7/54 San Angelo, TX
27	Lentine, Jim	St. Louis	1	0	1	.100	R-R	6-0	175	7/16/54 Los Angeles, CA
		Springfield	22	1	7	.306				
		Detroit	42	1	17	.261				
32	Peters, Rick	Detroit	139	2	42	.291	B-R	5-10	160	11/21/55 Lynwood, CA
24	Summers, Champ	Detroit	103	17	60	.297	L-R	6-2	205	6/15/48 Bremerton, WA

TIGER PROFILES

JACK MORRIS 25 6-3 190 Bats R Throws R

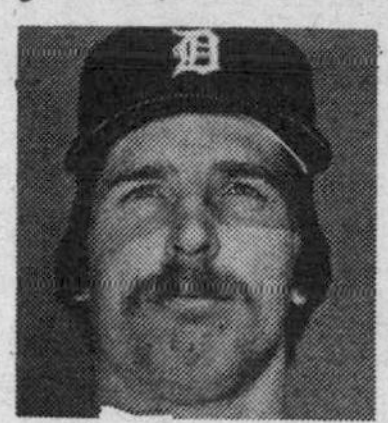

Failed to live up to his advance billing as one of the finest righthanded pitchers in the league in 1980 . . . Was briefly demoted to the bullpen . . . "At first I was pretty bitter." . . . Battles himself, frequently blows his cool when he gets into trouble . . . "Let's just say it's something I've been trying to overcome for a long time. Jack Morris is just not satisfied with Jack Morris" . . . Born May 16, 1955, in St. Paul . . . Fined $50 for pitching from a full windup instead of a stretch with Oakland's Dwayne Murphy on third base . . . Owns the best fastball on the team . . . Has been clocked at 94 mph.

Year	Club	G	IP	W	L	Pct.	SO	BB	H	ERA
1977	Detroit	7	46	1	1	.500	28	23	38	3.72
1978	Detroit	28	106	3	5	.375	48	49	107	4.33
1979	Detroit	27	198	17	7	.708	113	59	179	3.27
1980	Detroit	36	250	16	15	.516	112	87	252	4.18
	Totals	98	600	37	28	.569	301	218	576	3.87

DAN SCHATZEDER 26 6-0 195 Bats L Throws L

Acquired from Montreal in exchange for speedster Ron LeFlore prior to 1980 season . . . Got off to slow start and was hampered by sore arm . . . Finally got himself straightened out and is expected to be Tigers top lefthander this year . . . When he finally won his first game after three losses, he quipped, "Now I can walk my dog without a bodyguard" . . . Born Dec. 1, 1954, in Elmhurst, Ill. . . . Regained his fastball and his confidence during second half of the season . . . Was regarded as one of top young lefthanders in NL before the trade . . . Originally was an outfielder . . . Was used both as a starter and in relief by Montreal.

Year	Club	G	IP	W	L	Pct.	SO	BB	H	ERA
1977	Montreal	6	22	2	1	.667	14	13	16	2.45
1978	Montreal	29	144	7	7	.500	69	68	108	3.06
1979	Montreal	32	162	10	5	.667	106	59	136	2.83
1980	Detroit	32	193	11	13	.458	94	58	178	4.01
	Totals	99	521	30	26	.536	283	198	438	3.32

MILT WILCOX 30 6-2 215 Bats R Throws R

Most dependable pitcher on the staff last season . . . Injured shoulder in fight with Royals' George Brett . . . Tough competitor . . . Serves as Tigers' player rep . . . Was rumored on his way to Los Angeles Dodgers early in season . . . Born April 20, 1950, in Honolulu . . . Direct descendant of English sea captain who married Hawaiian maiden . . . Keeps statues of two Hawaiian war gods for good luck . . . Was ready to quit when Tigers rescued him from Cubs' farm system in 1975 . . . Hampered by arm ailments earlier in career . . . A hard thrower, calls his fastball "yackadoo."

Year	Club	G	IP	W	L	Pct.	SO	BB	H	ERA
1970	Cincinnati	5	22	3	1	.750	13	7	19	2.45
1971	Cincinnati	18	43	2	2	.500	21	17	43	3.35
1972	Cleveland	32	156	7	14	.333	90	72	145	3.40
1973	Cleveland	26	134	8	10	.444	82	68	143	5.84
1974	Cleveland	41	71	2	2	.500	33	24	74	4.69
1975	Chicago (NL)	25	38	0	1	.000	21	17	50	5.68
1977	Detroit	20	106	6	2	.750	82	37	96	3.65
1978	Detroit	29	215	13	12	.520	132	68	208	3.77
1979	Detroit	33	196	12	10	.545	109	73	201	4.36
1980	Detroit	32	199	13	11	.542	97	68	201	4.48
	Totals	261	1180	66	65	.504	680	451	1180	4.24

LANCE PARRISH 24 6-3 210 Bats R Throws R

Improved both at plate and behind it in 1980 . . . Still lets too many pitches get past him but has begun hitting more often with men on base . . . Was fined $200 when he destroyed a water cooler in the dugout . . . Born June 15, 1956, in McKeesport, Pa. . . . Now makes his home in Southern California . . . Regarded as one of finest young catchers in the league . . . Incredibly strong . . . Turned down football scholarship at UCLA to sign with the Tigers . . . Quiet individual, sometimes needs to be prodded to work harder . . . Once worked as a bodyguard for singer Tina Turner.

Year	Club	Pos.	G	AB	R	H	2B	3B	HR	RBI	SB	Avg.
1977	Detroit	C	12	46	10	9	2	0	3	7	0	.196
1978	Detroit	C	85	288	37	63	11	3	14	41	0	.219
1979	Detroit	C	143	493	65	136	26	3	19	65	6	.276
1980	Detroit	C	144	553	79	158	34	6	24	82	6	.286
	Totals		384	1380	191	366	73	12	60	195	12	.265

RICHIE HEBNER 33 6-1 195 — Bats L Throws R

Surprised a lot of people with his steady defensive play at third base before he was transferred to first . . . Also impressed everyone with his productive hitting . . . Sidelined late in the season because of a leg injury . . . The Tigers' clubhouse comedian . . . Claimed he misses the Johnny Carson Show now that he's in the AL . . . "Games in the American League are way too long" . . . Born Nov. 26, 1947, in Boston . . . Digs graves during the off-season . . . Traded to the Tigers from the Mets . . . Disliked New York and New Yorkers . . . "Some cities you just don't warm up to."

Year	Club	Pos.	G	AB	R	H	2B	3B	HR	RBI	SB	Avg.
1968	Pittsburgh......	PH	2	1	0	0	0	0	0	0	0	.000
1969	Pittsburgh......	3B-1B	129	459	72	138	23	4	8	47	4	.301
1970	Pittsburgh......	3B	120	420	60	122	24	8	11	46	2	.290
1971	Pittsburgh......	3B	112	388	50	105	17	8	17	67	2	.271
1972	Pittsburgh......	3B	124	427	63	128	24	4	19	72	0	.300
1973	Pittsburgh......	3B	144	509	73	138	28	1	25	74	0	.271
1974	Pittsburgh......	3B	146	550	97	160	21	6	18	68	0	.291
1975	Pittsburgh......	3B	128	472	65	116	16	4	15	57	0	.246
1976	Pittsburgh......	3B	132	434	60	108	21	3	8	51	1	.249
1977	Philadelphia.....	1B-3B-2B	118	397	67	113	17	4	18	62	7	.285
1978	Philadelphia.....	1B-3B-2B	137	435	61	123	22	3	17	71	4	.283
1979	New York (NL)..	3B-1B	136	473	54	127	25	2	10	79	3	.268
1980	Detroit.........	1B-3B	104	341	48	99	10	7	12	82	0	.290
	Totals..........		1532	5306	770	1477	248	54	178	776	23	.278

ALAN TRAMMELL 23 6-0 170 — Bats R Throws R

The Tigers' brightest young star . . . Signed 7-year, $2.8-million contract—the longest and richest in Tiger history . . . "If any player on our team deserves that kind of money, he does," says GM Jim Campbell . . . "I love this place" says Trammell . . . Born Feb. 21, 1958, in Garden Grove, Calif. . . . Plays the game with a lot of enthusiasm . . . "I'm going to keep playing as hard as I can" . . . The Tigers' team leader . . . Will do whatever is necessary to win . . . One of Sparky Anderson's favorites . . . Began playing pro ball as soon as he graduated from high school . . . Never wanted to do anything else.

Year	Club	Pos.	G	AB	R	H	2B	3B	HR	RBI	SB	Avg.
1977	Detroit.........	SS	19	43	6	8	0	0	0	0	0	.186
1978	Detroit.........	SS	139	448	49	120	14	6	2	34	3	.268
1979	Detroit.........	SS	142	460	68	127	11	4	6	50	17	.276
1980	Detroit.........	SS	146	560	107	168	21	5	9	65	12	.300
	Totals..........		446	1511	230	423	46	15	17	149	32	.280

LOU WHITAKER 23 5-11 160 — Bats L Throws R

Slumped badly at the plate last season, but continued to stand out in the field . . . Failed in his bid to replace Ron LeFlore as the Tigers' lead-off hitter . . . Many felt he became unaggressive when the Tigers told him to draw more walks . . . "He tried to be too selective," says hitting coach Gates Brown . . . Lashed back verbally at fans who booed him, but otherwise kept his cool . . . "I don't throw bats or helmets. I don't use obscene language. That just makes you look bad." . . . Born May 12, 1957, in New York City . . . Along with Alan Trammell forms heart of the Tiger infield . . . And Tigers hope to have him there for many years to come . . . Soft-spoken and introverted, can become moody at times.

Year	Club	Pos.	G	AB	R	H	2B	3B	HR	RBI	SB	Avg.
1977	Detroit.........	2B	11	32	5	8	1	0	0	2	0	.250
1978	Detroit.........	2B	139	484	71	138	12	7	3	58	7	.285
1979	Detroit.........	2B	127	423	75	121	14	8	3	42	20	.286
1980	Detroit.........	2B	145	477	68	111	19	1	1	45	8	.233
	Totals..........		422	1416	219	378	46	16	7	147	35	.267

CHAMP SUMMERS 32 6-2 205 — Bats L Throws R

Came to the Tigers from the Reds for minor league pitcher Sheldon Burnside in one of the best deals GM Jim Campbell ever made . . . "I love it here. I love the fans. Even when I go badly, they're on my side." . . . Regulars in the rightfield stands at Tiger Stadium refer to that section as "Champ's Camp" . . . Born June 15, 1948, in Bremerton, Wash. . . . Struggled for many years to find his niche as a ballplayer . . . "I know how lucky I am. I could be pumping gas" . . . Hustles all the time . . . "That's the way I have to play. Take that away and there's not much left."

Year	Club	Pos.	G	AB	R	H	2B	3B	HR	RBI	SB	Avg.
1974	Oakland........	OF	20	24	2	3	1	0	0	3	0	.125
1975	Chicago (NL)....	OF	76	91	14	21	5	1	1	16	0	.231
1976	Chicago (NL)....	OF-1B-C	83	126	11	26	2	0	3	13	1	.206
1977	Cincinnati	OF-3B	59	76	11	13	4	0	3	6	0	.171
1978	Cincinnati	OF	13	35	4	9	2	0	1	3	2	.257
1979	Cincinnati	OF-1B	27	60	10	12	2	1	1	11	0	.200
1979	Detroit.........	OF-1B	90	246	47	77	12	1	20	51	7	.313
1980	Detroit.........	OF-1B	120	347	61	103	19	1	17	60	4	.297
	Totals..........		488	1005	160	264	47	4	46	163	14	.263

STEVE KEMP 26 6-0 190 **Bats L Throws L**

Hampered by injuries in 1980 and the Tigers definitely missed his bat . . . One of the keys to their future success . . . Wanted to sign a contract that would keep him in Detroit for at least the next five years . . . Has proven himself to be a big league star . . . Born Aug. 7, 1954, in San Angelo, Tex. . . . His teammates call him "Bubs" . . . Is very proud of the fact he was the No. 1 pick in the nation in January, 1976, after he was completely ignored in the free after draft when he graduated from high school . . . An aggressive fielder although he lacks finesse.

Year	Club	Pos.	G	AB	R	H	2B	3B	HR	RBI	SB	Avg.
1977	Detroit.........	OF	151	552	75	142	29	4	18	88	3	.257
1978	Detroit.........	OF	159	582	75	161	18	4	15	79	2	.277
1979	Detroit.........	OF	134	490	88	156	26	3	26	105	5	.318
1980	Detroit.........	OF	135	508	88	149	23	3	21	101	5	.293
	Totals..........		579	2132	326	608	96	14	80	373	15	.285

KIRK GIBSON 23 6-3 210 **Bats L Throws L**

Underwent major wrist surgery to repair torn cartilage Aug. 22 . . . Tigers are hoping he can regain the form that made of one of the league's outstanding rookies before he was injured . . . Was leading the Tigers in HRs when he hurt his hand swinging at a pitch . . . Spent winter with his arm in a cast . . . Admits he might turn to football if he has problems playing baseball . . . Born May 28, 1957, in Pontiac, Mich. . . . Turned down lucrative offer from the St. Louis football Cardinals to sign $200,000 bonus contract with the Tigers . . . Could become a superstar . . . Earned All-America honors in football while at Michigan State University.

Year	Club	Pos.	G	AB	R	H	2B	3B	HR	RBI	SB	Avg.
1979	Detroit.........	OF	12	38	3	9	3	0	1	4	3	.237
1980	Detroit.........	OF	51	175	23	46	2	1	9	16	4	.263
	Totals..........		63	213	26	55	5	1	10	20	7	.258

TOP PROSPECTS

DAVE STEFFEN 22 6-3 220 **Bats R Throws R**

Injured his arm in spring training and never completely recovered . . . Otherwise he probably would have been pitching at

Tiger Stadium last season . . . Still considered one of the outstanding pitching prospects in the farm system . . . Born Dec. 17, 1958, in Dearborn, Mich. . . . Big, burly, hard-throwing righthander . . . Excelled at wrestling and football while in high school.

RICK LEACH 23 6-0 195 **Bats L Throws L**

Could be Tigers' first baseman of the future . . . Was extremely disappointed when he was not called up to Detroit in September but Tigers chose to preserve his options . . . Born May 4, 1957, in Ann Arbor, Mich. . . . Was an outstanding quarterback and outfielder at the University of Michigan . . . Tried out with the Denver Broncos, but chose pro baseball instead.

MANAGER SPARKY ANDERSON: Boldly predicted his Tigers would win 90 games in 1980, then had to eat his words . . . "The messiah didn't make it" . . . Became angry early in the season over what he considered to be unfair criticism of his relationship with his players and vowed to limit his conversations with the press to the details of that day's game . . . He soon relented, however, and began expounding again . . . "I'm me," he says . . . Born Feb. 22, 1934, in Bridgewater, S.D. . . . Rejected offers from six other clubs to sign a 5½-year contract with the Tigers in 1979 . . . He is believed to be the best-paid manager in baseball history, making more than $150,000 a year . . . On the go from morning to night . . . Never seems to run out of energy.

GREATEST TEAM

Going into the 1935 season, the Detroit Tigers were a team with a mission, a team with something to prove. The previous year, they waltzed to the American League pennant, winning 101 games, only to succumb to the St. Louis Cardinals in the World Series. In '35, they were determined to make amends.

And they did. Player-manager Mickey Cochrane, Charley Gehringer, Pete Fox and Tommy Bridges saw to that as the Tigers prevailed in the Series against the Cubs, four games to two.

That put a sudden stop to suggestions that their 1934 pennant had been a fluke.

Hank Greenberg established himself as one of premier sluggers in the game, leading the league in both home runs and RBI, before breaking his wrist in the second game of the Series.

And the pitching, provided by Schoolboy Rowe, Eldon Auker, General Crowder and Bridges was positively superb.

When the Series was over, the fans, of the city of Detroit danced in the streets until dawn. The Tigers had proved their point.

ALL-TIME TIGER LEADERS

BATTING: Ty Cobb, .420, 1911
HRs: Hank Greenberg, 58, 1938
RBIs: Hank Greenberg, 183, 1937
STEALS: Ty Cobb, 96, 1915
WINS: Denny McLain, 31, 1968
STRIKEOUTS: Mickey Lolich, 308, 1971

MILWAUKEE BREWERS

TEAM DIRECTORY: Chairman of the Board: Ed Fitzgerald; Pres.: Allan (Bud) Selig; Exec VP-GM: Harry Dalton; VP-Marketing: Richard Hackett; VP-Stadium Operation: Gabe Paul, Jr.; Admin. Asst. Scouting and Player Development: Bruce Manno; Dir. Pub. Rel.: Tom Skibosh; Mgr.: Bob (Buck) Rodgers. Home: Milwaukee County Stadium (54,187). Field distances: 320, l.f. line; 392, l.c.; 402, c.f.; 392, r.c.; 315, r.f. line. Spring training: Sun City, Ariz.

SCOUTING REPORT

HITTING: The list of the American League's leading hitters in 1980 reads like Who's Who in the Starting Lineup of the Brewers. Cecil Cooper: .352. Paul Molitor: .304. Ben Oglivie: .304. Most home runs: Oglivie, 41. Most RBI: Cooper, 122. Most doubles: Robin Yount, 49. Most total bases: Cooper, 335. And then there was Gorman Thomas, who had an off-year, merely 38 HRs and 105 RBI.

Add to that catcher Ted Simmons (.303, 21 HRs, 98 RBI) and it's easy to see why the Brewers' offense has been described as awesome. From top to bottom in the batting order, the powerful Brewers have balance that can make them positively brutal on opposing pitchers.

PITCHING: A bullpen. New manager Bob Rodgers kept saying he would give almost anything for bullpen. Now he has one. The bullpen's name is Rollie Fingers. Acquired from St. Louis along with Simmons and starting pitcher Pete Vuckovich (12-9) in a deal that can only be described as a steal (Milwaukee sent Sixto Lezcano and Lary Sorensen to the Cardinals), Fingers gives the Brewers the relief ace they have long lacked. That's doubly important because Rodgers likes to rely on his bullpen even more than his predecessor, George Bamberger, did.

Actually, as a whole, the Brewers' pitching staff performed surprisingly well last year, finishing fourth in the league. Moose Haas was 16-15 with a 3.11 ERA. He also ranked among the league leaders in a handful of other categories. And Jim Slaton, sidelined most of last season with an arm injury, showed last fall he could throw again.

FIELDING: The Brewers slipped somewhat defensively last season. But Cecil Cooper capped off an outstanding season by leading all first basemen in the league. Yount, Molitor, Thomas and

Simmons all can play the field. Perhaps the most dramatic improvement, though, has been in the fielding of Oglivie, who was a liability when he roamed the outfield in Detroit.

OUTLOOK: For years, the Brewers have had the horses. The only question was their arms. Now that they have Fingers and Vuckovich, they no longer have an excuse. The Brewers have gambled, spending $1 million merely to convince Simmons to agree to the trade, and the pressure will be on them to win. This year! "This is the best balanced club we've had in the three years I've been here," admits GM Harry Dalton. The Brewers finished 17 games back a year ago, but that figure is misleading. They faded late and they weren't really that bad. Now, they're substantially better.

Cecil Cooper led the AL in total bases (335).

MILWAUKEE BREWERS 1981 ROSTER

MANAGER Bob Rodgers
Coaches—Larry Haney, Ron Hansen, Harvey Kuenn, Cal McLish, Harry Warner

PITCHERS

No.	Name	1980 Club	W-L	IP	SO	ERA	B-T	Ht.	Wt.	Born
46	Augustine, Jerry	Milwaukee	4-3	70	22	4.50	L-L	6-0	185	7/24/52 Kewaunee, WI
48	Caldwell, Mike	Milwaukee	13-11	225	74	4.04	R-L	6-0	185	1/22/49 Tarboro, NC
23	Cleveland, Reggie	Milwaukee	11-9	154	54	3.74	R-R	6-1	200	5/23/48 Canada
–	Cocanower, Jaime	Stockton	17-5	198	132	2.18	R-R	6-4	200	2/14/57 Canal Zone
–	DiPino, Frank	Holyoke	7-0	76	58	1.30	L-L	5-10	175	10/22/56 Camillus, NY
		Vancouver	3-1	28	32	2.25				
–	Easterly, Jamie	Denver	9-8	134	105	3.64	L-L	5-10	180	2/17/53 Houston, TX
–	Fingers, Rollie	San Diego	11-9	103	69	2.80	R-R	6-3	195	8/25/46 Steubenville, OH
40	Flinn, John	Vancouver	2-3	43	28	4.40	R-R	6-1	180	9/2/54 Merced, CA
		Milwaukee	2-1	37	15	3.89				
30	Haas, Moose	Milwaukee	16-15	252	146	3.11	R-R	6-0	170	4/22/56 Baltimore, MD
47	Holdsworth, Fred	Vancouver	5-5	118	64	2.67	R-R	6-1	190	5/29/52 Detroit, MI
		Milwaukee	0-0	20	12	4.50				
–	Jones, Doug	Stockton	6-2	76	54	2.84	R-R	6-2	170	6/24/57 Lebanon, IN
		Holyoke	5-3	62	39	2.92				
		Vancouver	3-2	53	28	3.23				
45	Keeton, Rickey	Vancouver	10-4	136	51	3.31	R-R	6-2	190	3/18/57 Cincinnati, OH
		Milwaukee	2-2	28	8	4.82				
10	McClure, Bob	Milwaukee	5-8	91	47	3.07	B-L	5-11	170	4/29/53 Oakland, CA
43	Mitchell, Paul	Vancouver	5-3	49	29	3.31	R-R	6-1	195	8/19/50 Worcester, MA
		Milwaukee	5-5	89	29	3.54				
55	Olsen, Rich	Vancouver	7-6	91	64	3.96	R-R	6-0	180	6/1/57 Kailua, HI
58	Ouinones, Rene	Vancouver	7-7	103	74	3.50	R-R	6-0	180	2/19/57 Puerto Rico
41	Slaton, Jim	Milwaukee	1-1	16	4	4.50	R-R	6-0	185	6/19/50 Long Beach, CA
–	Swift, Weldon	Holyoke	11-10	179	92	3.31	R-R	6-2	200	2/17/58 Baltimore, MD
–	Vuckovich, Pete	St. Louis	12-9	222	132	3.41	R-R	6-4	220	10/27/52 Johnstown, PA

CATCHERS

No.	Name	1980 Club	H	HR	RBI	Pct.	B-T	Ht.	Wt.	Born
61	Foley, Bill	Vancouver	74	4	38	.267	R-R	6-2	210	9/2/56 Flushing, NY
59	Lake, Steve	Holyoke	84	2	43	.257	R-R	6-1	180	3/14/57 Redondo Beach, CA
21	Martinez, Buck	Milwaukee	49	3	17	.224	R-R	5-11	190	11/7/48 Redding, CA
22	Moore, Charlie	Milwaukee	93	2	30	.291	R-R	5-11	180	6/21/53 Birmingham, AL
–	Simmons, Ted	St. Louis	150	21	98	.303	B-R	6-0	200	8/9/49 Highland Park, MI
5	Yost, Ned	Vancouver	80	2	41	.309	R-R	6-1	185	8/19/55 Eureka, CA
		Milwaukee	5	0	0	.161				

INFIELDERS

No.	Name	1980 Club	H	HR	RBI	Pct.	B-T	Ht.	Wt.	Born
6	Bando, Sal	Milwaukee	50	5	31	.197	R-R	6-0	200	2/13/44 Cleveland, OH
15	Cooper, Cecil	Milwaukee	219	25	122	.352	L-L	6-2	190	12/30/49 Brenham, TX
17	Gantner, Jim	Milwaukee	117	4	40	.282	L-R	5-11	175	1/5/53 Eden, WI
–	Howell, Roy	Toronto	142	10	57	.269	L-R	6-1	190	12/18/53 Lompoc, CA
4	Molitor, Paul	Milwaukee	137	9	37	.304	R-R	6-0	175	8/22/56 St. Paul, MN
7	Money, Don	Milwaukee	74	17	46	.256	R-R	6-1	190	6/7/47 Washington, DC
8	Poff, John	Oklahoma City	140	13	90	.282	L-L	6-2	200	10/23/52 Chillicothe, OH
		Milwaukee	17	1	7	.250				
34	Romero, Ed	Vancouver	47	0	16	.273	R-R	5-11	150	12/19/57 Puerto Rico
		Milwaukee	27	1	10	.260				
19	Yount, Robin	Milwaukee	179	23	87	.293	R-R	6-1	170	9/16/55 Danville, IL

OUTFIELDERS

No.	Name	1980 Club	H	HR	RBI	Pct.	B-T	Ht.	Wt.	Born
57	Bass, Kevin	Holyoke	147	4	52	.300	B-R	6-0	180	5/12/59 Menlo Park, CA
29	Brouhard, Mark	Milwaukee	29	5	16	.232	R-R	6-1	210	5/22/56 Burbank, CA
26	Davis, Dick	Milwaukee	99	4	.30	.271	R-R	6-3	195	9/25/53 Long Beach, CA
–	Edwards, Marshall	Vancouver	139	2	68	.291	L-L	5-9	157	8/27/52 Los Angeles, CA
9	Hisle, Larry	Milwaukee	17	6	16	.282	R-R	6-2	195	5/5/47 Portsmouth, OH
24	Oglivie, Ben	Milwaukee	180	41	118	.304	L-L	6-2	170	2/11/49 Panama
20	Thomas, Gorman	Milwaukee	150	38	105	.239	R-R	6-3	205	12/12/50 Charleston, SC

BREWER PROFILES

MIKE CALDWELL 32 6-0 185 — Bats R Throws L

Fierce competitor, will do anything to beat you . . . Teammates call him "Mr. Warmth" . . . Frequently accused of throwing spitters . . . Especially effective against the Yankees . . . Struggled midway through '80 season because he was serving up home runs instead of ground balls . . . Senior citizen of the Brewers' staff . . . Born Jan. 22, 1949, in Tarboro, N.C. . . . Was originally drafted by San Diego . . . Made major league debut after only 19 games in minors . . . Hampered by elbow injury while in National League . . . Rebounded with Brewers in '78 . . . Has only average stuff, but counts on superb control.

Year	Club	G	IP	W	L	Pct.	SO	BB	H	ERA
1971	San Diego	6	7	1	0	1.000	5	3	4	0.00
1972	San Diego	42	164	7	11	.389	102	49	183	4.01
1973	San Diego	55	149	5	14	.263	86	53	146	3.74
1974	San Francisco	31	189	14	5	.737	83	63	176	2.95
1975	San Francisco	38	163	7	13	.350	57	48	194	4.80
1976	San Francisco	50	107	1	7	.125	55	20	145	4.88
1977	Cincinnati	14	25	0	0	.000	11	8	25	3.96
1977	Milwaukee	21	94	5	8	.385	38	36	101	4.60
1978	Milwaukee	37	293	22	9	.710	131	54	258	2.37
1979	Milwaukee	30	235	16	6	.727	89	39	252	3.29
1980	Milwaukee	34	225	13	11	.542	74	56	248	4.04
	Totals	358	1651	91	84	.520	731	429	1732	3.63

CECIL COOPER 31 6-2 190 — Bats L Throws L

Compiled incredible offensive statistics in 1980 . . . Unfortunately his efforts were overshadowed by George Brett . . . "I don't want people to praise me, just give me my due." . . . "He can do everything," says former manager George Bamberger. "Good hitter, good fielder, good base runner." . . . Usually collects batting stances the way some guys collect hats, but stuck basically to same one last season . . . Did move back off the plate late in the year, after watching Brett on TV . . . Born Dec. 20, 1949, in Brenham, Tex. . . . Looking at his unorthodox, wide-open stance, you'd say there is no way he can hit like that . . . Has had trouble handling high fastball in the past . . . Has strung together six solid seasons in a row . . .

An unsung star . . . Nicknamed "Coop." . . . Active in several charities in Milwaukee.

Year	Club	Pos.	G	AB	R	H	2B	3B	HR	RBI	SB	Avg.
1971	Boston	1B	14	42	9	13	4	1	0	3	1	.310
1972	Boston	1B	12	17	0	4	1	0	0	2	0	.235
1973	Boston	1B	30	101	12	24	2	0	3	11	1	.238
1974	Boston	1B	121	414	55	114	24	1	8	43	2	.275
1975	Boston	1B	106	305	49	95	17	6	14	44	1	.311
1976	Boston	1B	123	451	66	127	22	6	15	78	7	.282
1977	Milwaukee	1B	160	643	86	193	31	7	20	78	13	.300
1978	Milwaukee	1B	107	407	60	127	23	2	13	54	3	.312
1979	Milwaukee	1B	150	590	83	182	44	1	24	106	15	.308
1980	Milwaukee	1B	153	622	96	219	33	4	25	122	17	.352
	Totals		976	3592	516	1098	201	28	122	541	60	.306

TED SIMMONS 31 6-0 200 — Bats S Throws R

Became a Brewer in multi-player deal with Cards . . . Broken bone in left wrist limited him to 123 games in '79, but enjoyed a healthy '80 and starts were as good as ever . . . Had career-high 26 homers despite missing 39 games in '79 . . . Is an avid antique and art collector . . . Also dabbles in photography . . . An underrated performer since batting .304 in 1971 because he's always played in shadow of Bench . . . Born Aug. 9, 1949, at Highland Park, Mich.

Year	Club	Pos.	G	AB	R	H	2B	3B	HR	RBI	SB	Avg.
1968	St. Louis	C	2	3	0	1	0	0	0	0	0	.333
1969	St. Louis	C	5	14	0	3	0	1	0	3	0	.214
1970	St. Louis	C	82	284	29	69	8	2	3	24	2	.243
1971	St. Louis	C	133	510	64	155	32	4	7	77	1	.304
1972	St. Louis	C-1B	152	594	70	180	36	6	16	96	1	.303
1973	St. Louis	C-1B-OF	161	619	62	192	36	2	13	91	2	.310
1974	St. Louis	C-1B	152	599	66	163	33	6	20	103	0	.272
1975	St. Louis	C-1B-OF	157	581	80	193	32	3	18	100	1	.332
1976	St. Louis	C-1B-OF-3B	150	546	60	159	35	3	5	75	0	.291
1977	St. Louis	C-OF	150	516	82	164	25	3	21	95	2	.318
1978	St. Louis	C-OF	152	516	71	148	40	5	22	80	1	.287
1979	St. Louis	C	123	448	68	127	22	0	26	87	0	.283
1980	St. Louis	C-OF	145	495	84	150	33	2	21	98	1	.303
	Totals		1564	5725	736	1704	332	37	172	929	11	.298

PAUL MOLITOR 24 6-0 175 — Bats R Throws R

Was leading the league in early June with .358 average when he injured his back . . . "Hitting is something you do day by day" . . . Credits ability to run and bunt as reason he is able to avoid slumps . . . Key to Brewers' offense in spite of all the potent bats in their lineup . . . Teammates call him "The Ignitor" . . . "Paul has the best instincts of any young player I've seen in a long time," says manager Buck Rodgers . . . Born Aug. 22, 1956, in St. Paul . . . The Brewers' most eligible bachelor . . . Will beat you any way he can . . . Stunned everyone with his surprising performance as rookie in '78 . . . Can also play shortstop . . . Should be superstar for many years to come . . . Was Brewers' No. 1 pick in June, 1977 draft after All-America career at University of Minnesota . . . Arm injury in college forced him to abandon career on the mound and become an infielder.

Year	Club	Pos.	G	AB	R	H	2B	3B	HR	RBI	SB	Avg.
1978	Milwaukee......	SS-2B	125	521	73	142	26	4	6	45	30	.273
1979	Milwaukee......	2B-SS	140	584	88	188	27	16	9	62	33	.322
1980	Milwaukee......	2B-SS	111	450	81	137	29	2	9	37	34	.304
	Totals..........		376	1555	242	467	82	22	24	144	97	.300

ROBIN YOUNT 25 6-1 170 — Bats R Throws R

No longer the Brewers' boy wonder . . . Now an established, proven star . . . Reached 1,000-hit mark in 1980, making him third youngest ever to achieve that feat . . . Only Ty Cobb and Al Kaline got there sooner . . . May be best offensive shortstop in the league . . . But has also improved dramatically on defense . . . Brewers' GM Harry Dalton believes he should have been a leading candidate for MVP honors in '80 . . . Born Sept. 16, 1955, in Danville, Ill. . . . "Success hasn't hurt him a bit," says former manager George Bamberger . . . Been the Brewers' regular shortstop since age 18 . . . Has chance to become superstar . . . Could reach 3,000 hits . . . "I'm not looking that far ahead." . . . Born to play baseball.

Year	Club	Pos.	G	AB	R	H	2B	3B	HR	RBI	SB	Avg.
1974	Milwaukee......	SS	107	344	48	86	14	5	3	26	7	.250
1975	Milwaukee......	SS	147	558	67	149	28	2	8	52	12	.267
1976	Milwaukee......	SS-OF	161	638	59	161	19	3	2	54	16	.252
1977	Milwaukee......	SS	154	605	66	174	34	4	4	49	16	.288
1978	Milwaukee......	SS	127	502	66	147	23	9	9	71	16	.293
1979	Milwaukee......	SS	149	577	72	154	26	5	8	51	11	.267
1980	Milwaukee......	SS	143	611	121	179	49	10	23	87	20	.293
	Totals..........		988	3835	499	1050	193	38	57	390	98	.274

BEN OGLIVIE 32 6-2 170 — Bats L Throws L

Enjoyed finest season yet in 1980, tying Reggie Jackson for A.L. homer title . . . Says playing every day has given him confidence, but claims he is still same player he was with Red Sox and Tigers, when he was platooned . . . Much maligned as outfielder earlier, now makes many remarkable catches . . . Exciting offensive star . . . "The harder the pitcher throws the ball," says teammate Jim Slaton, "the harder he swings." . . . Broke his own team record for HRs by a left-handed hitter and also topped 100 RBIs for first time . . . Born Feb 11, 1949, in Colon, Panama . . . Was nicknamed "The Banana Man," while with the Tigers, but now known as "Spider-man." . . . Loves to read philosophy and carries his books with him on the road.

Year	Club	Pos.	G	AB	R	H	2B	3B	HR	RBI	SB	Avg.
1971	Boston.........	OF	14	38	2	10	3	0	0	4	0	.263
1972	Boston.........	OF	94	253	27	61	10	2	8	30	1	.241
1973	Boston.........	OF	58	147	16	32	9	1	2	9	1	.218
1974	Detroit.........	OF-1B	92	252	28	68	11	3	4	29	12	.270
1975	Detroit.........	OF-1B	100	332	45	95	14	1	9	36	11	.286
1976	Detroit.........	OF-1B	115	305	36	87	12	3	15	47	9	.285
1977	Detroit.........	OF	132	450	63	118	24	2	21	61	9	.262
1978	Milwaukee......	OF-1B	128	469	71	142	29	4	18	72	11	.303
1979	Milwaukee......	OF-1B	139	514	88	145	30	4	29	81	12	.282
1980	Milwaukee......	OF-1B	156	592	94	180	26	2	41	118	11	.304
	Totals.........		1028	3352	470	938	168	22	147	487	77	.280

ROLLIE FINGERS 34 6-3 195 Bats R Throws R

Moaned and groaned his way toward another solid season in 1980, edging Bruce Sutter for Fireman-of-Year honor . . . Voted top reliever of the Seventies and lost little of his effectiveness last year . . . Did lose patience, however, and accused Padres manager Jerry Coleman of incompetence . . . At winter meetings San Diego dealt him to St. Louis and then he was traded to Milwaukee . . . A strong finish kept his career ERA under 3.00 and he finished with 23 saves, a big improvement over 1979's 13 . . . Born Aug. 25, 1946, at Steubenville, Ohio . . . Shares major league record with 37 saves in '78 . . . In 33-plus innings of World Series relief for A's, registered 1.35 ERA with six saves and two wins in 16 games.

Year	Club	G	IP	W	L	Pct.	SO	BB	H	ERA
1968	Oakland...............	1	1	0	0	.000	0	1	4	36.00
1969	Oakland...............	60	119	6	7	.462	61	41	116	3.71
1970	Oakland...............	45	148	7	9	.438	79	48	137	3.65
1971	Oakland...............	48	129	4	6	.400	98	30	94	3.00
1972	Oakland...............	65	111	11	9	.550	113	33	85	2.51
1973	Oakland...............	62	127	7	8	.467	110	39	107	1.92
1974	Oakland...............	76	119	9	5	.643	95	29	104	2.65
1975	Oakland...............	75	127	10	6	.625	115	33	95	2.98
1976	Oakland...............	70	135	13	11	.542	113	40	118	2.53
1977	San Diego..............	78	132	8	9	.471	113	36	123	3.00
1978	San Diego..............	67	107	6	13	.316	72	29	84	2.52
1979	San Diego..............	54	84	9	9	.500	65	37	91	4.50
1980	San Diego..............	66	103	11	9	.550	69	32	101	2.80
	Totals..................	767	1442	101	101	.500	1103	427	1249	2.97

GORMAN THOMAS 30 6-3 205 — Bats R Throws R

Has never really gotten the credit he believes he deserves . . . "Half of my mail comes addressed to Thomas Gorman" . . . But claims that doesn't bother him . . . "I don't need my name in the paper every day as long as my name is in the lineup every day" . . . Goes wild when he puts on a uniform . . . Knows every outfield wall in the American League . . . "He's a crazy guy in his own way," says his friend, pitcher Bill Travers . . . Born Dec. 12, 1950, in Charleston, S.C. . . . Returned to Brewers after being traded to Rangers because George Bamberger wanted him to play centerfield . . . "The job is yours," Bamberger told him. "Don't lose it." . . . He didn't . . . Still strikes out a lot and slips into slumps . . . Practical joker, sticks live fish and dead frogs into teammates' socks and jocks.

Year	Club	Pos.	G	AB	R	H	2B	3B	HR	RBI	SB	Avg.
1973	Milwaukee......	OF-3B	59	155	16	29	7	1	2	11	5	.187
1974	Milwaukee......	OF	17	46	10	12	4	0	2	11	4	.261
1975	Milwaukee......	OF	121	240	34	43	12	2	10	28	4	.179
1976	Milwaukee......	OF-3B	99	227	27	45	9	2	8	36	2	.198
1978	Milwaukee......	OF	137	452	70	111	24	1	32	86	3	.246
1979	Milwaukee......	OF	156	557	97	136	29	0	45	123	1	.244
1980	Milwaukee......	OF	162	628	78	150	26	3	38	105	8	.239
	Totals..........		751	2305	332	526	111	9	137	400	27	.228

DON MONEY 33 6-1 190 — Bats R Throws R

Hobbled by injuries in 1980 . . . One of Brewers' steadiest performers when he's healthy . . . Can play wherever he's needed . . . Nicknamed "Mun" . . . Wrote book about his former teammate, Henry Aaron . . . Born June 7, 1947, in Washington, D.C. . . . Owns bar in Milwaukee with pitcher Bill Travers . . . Ranks as senior Brewer in terms of service, having spent seven years in Milwaukee.

Year	Club	Pos.	G	AB	R	H	2B	3B	HR	RBI	SB	Avg.
1968	Philadelphia.....	SS	4	13	1	3	2	0	0	2	0	.231
1969	Philadelphia.....	SS	127	450	41	103	22	2	6	42	1	.229
1970	Philadelphia.....	3B-SS	120	447	66	132	25	4	14	66	4	.295
1971	Philadelphia.....	3B-OF-2B	121	439	40	98	22	8	7	38	4	.223
1972	Philadelphia.....	3B-SS	152	536	54	119	16	2	15	52	5	.222
1973	Milwaukee......	3B-SS	145	556	75	158	28	2	11	61	22	.284
1974	Milwaukee......	3B-2B	159	629	85	178	32	3	15	65	19	.283
1975	Milwaukee......	3B-SS	109	405	58	112	16	1	15	43	7	.277
1976	Milwaukee......	3B-SS	117	439	51	117	18	4	12	62	6	.267
1977	Milwaukee......	2B-OF-3B	152	570	86	159	28	3	25	83	8	.279
1978	Milwaukee......	1B-2B-OF-SS	137	518	88	152	30	2	14	54	3	.293
1979	Milwaukee......	3B-1B-2B	92	350	52	83	20	1	6	38	1	.237
1980	Milwaukee......	3B-2B-1B	86	289	39	74	17	1	17	46	0	.256
	Totals..........		1521	5641	736	1488	276	33	157	652	80	.264

PETE VUCKOVICH 28 6-4 220 **Bats R Throws R**

Became a Card in deal that sent Ted Simmons to Milwaukee . . . Aggressive and hard-nosed . . . Had career-best 15-10 record in '79, but no shutouts . . . Posted three blankings in '80 and lowered ERA despite inferior record . . . Born Oct. 27, 1952, at Johnstown, Pa. . . . Came up with White Sox and went with expansion Toronto in '77 . . . Fired first shutout in Blue Jays' history, defeating O's Jim Palmer, 2-0 . . . Swapped to St. Louis in '78 and 2.55 ERA ranked third in N.L. . . . A baseball standout at Clarion State (Pa.) Teachers College . . . Reached bigs for good by posting 11-4 record with Denver in '75 . . . Was 3-0 in September.

Year	Club	G	IP	W	L	Pct.	SO	BB	H	ERA
1975	Chicago (AL)............	4	10	0	1	.000	5	7	17	13.50
1976	Chicago (AL)............	33	110	7	4	.636	62	60	122	4.66
1977	Toronto	53	148	7	7	.500	123	59	143	3.47
1978	St. Louis	45	198	12	12	.500	149	59	187	2.55
1979	St. Louis	34	233	15	10	.600	145	64	229	3.59
1980	St. Louis	32	222	12	9	.571	132	68	203	3.41
	Totals..................	201	921	53	43	.552	616	317	901	3.54

TOP PROSPECT

MARK BROUHARD 24 6-1 210 **Bats R Throws R**

Drafted out of Angels' farm system following '79 season . . . Led Texas League with 28 HRs, 107 RBI and .335 average in '79 . . . Born May 22, 1956, in Burbank, Calif. . . . Can play first base or outfield . . . Power hitter, noted for long HRs . . . Once hit homer that traveled 617 feet in the air and a total distance of 682 feet . . . Had to make difficult adjustment of sitting on Brewers' bench in 1980 while their proven sluggers played.

MANAGER BOB RODGERS: Named to replace George Bamberger, who decided to retire after bouncing back from open-heart surgery . . . Everyone calls him "Buck." . . . Proved himself capable when he was called upon to manage the Brewers during the first two months of the 1980 season while Bamberger was sidelined . . . Born Aug. 16, 1938, in Delaware, Ohio . . . Spent nine years as a catcher with the Angels

. . . Set record by catching 155 games as rookie in '62 . . . Never much of a hitter, better known for his defense and guile in handling pitchers . . . Compiled a 145-125 record as manager in the minors . . . Also coached for the Giants and Twins . . . Popular with his players and the press . . . Works as a glue salesman during the off-season.

GREATEST TEAM

In Milwaukee, they called them "Bambi's Bombers." And George Bamberger's 1979 Brewers could, indeed, bombard people.

Gorman Thomas led the league with 45 HRs and set a club record with 123 RBI. Sixto Lezcano smacked 28 homers and accounted for 101 runs. Cecil Cooper had 24 HRs and 106 ribbies. Ben Oglivie chipped in 29 homers, helping give the Brewers a team total of 185.

Meanwhile, second baseman Paul Molitor proved beyond a doubt that his rookie season performance was no fluke as he improved in every aspect of the game and excited Brewers fans with his aggressive style of playing.

Unfortunately, all that was not nearly enough.

The lack of a reliable stopper in the bullpen, the loss of Larry Hisle and Don Money, and inconsistent showings by pitchers such as Mike Caldwell, Jim Slaton, Bill Travers and Lary Sorensen led to the Brewers' downfall.

Nevertheless, the Brewers won 95 games and served notice all around the American League that this transplanted expansion team could no longer be ignored.

ALL-TIME BREWER LEADERS

BATTING: Cecil Cooper, .352, 1980
HRs: Gorman Thomas, 45, 1979
RBIs: Gorman Thomas, 123, 1979
STEALS: Tommy Harper, 73, 1969
WINS: Mike Caldwell, 22, 1978
STRIKEOUTS: Marty Pattin, 161, 1971

NEW YORK YANKEES

TEAM DIRECTORY: Principal Owner: George Steinbrenner III; Exec. VP: Cedric Tallis; VP-Baseball Operations: Bill Bergesch; Dir. Pub. Rel.: Larry Wahl; Trav. Sec.: Bill Kane; Mgr.: Gene Michael. Home: Yankee Stadium (57,545). Field distances: 312, l.f. line; 387, l.f.; 430, l.c.; 417, c.f.; 385, r.c.; 353, r.f.; 310, r.f. line. Spring training: Fort Lauderdale, Fla.

SCOUTING REPORT

HITTING: You have to wonder a bit about the Yankees when you see their leading hitting last year was Bob Watson at .307. Whatever happened to the Bronx Bombers? Reggie Jackson continues to carry his share of the load, hitting .300 with 41 HRs and 111 RBI last season. And Willie Randolph hit .294. Rick Cerone did a better job behind the plate than most dared hope, hitting .277 with 14 homers and 85 RBI. But Lou Piniella, while batting .287, drove in only 27 runs, and Graig Nettles hit a mere .244 with 45 RBI before his season was curtailed by hepatitis. Seven teams—five of them from the Eastern Division—outhit the Yanks last year. But now the Yanks have slugger Dave Winfield, baseball's biggest free agent ever. And at these prices ($15 million and all else), he'd better escalate his Padre figures of .276, 20 HRs, 87 RBI.

PITCHING: Even without free agents Don Sutton and Dan Spillner, who elected to sign elsewhere, the Yankees have a staff that is the envy of nearly every team in the league. They're amazing. Journeyman Rudy May was a mere 15-5 last year, with the best ERA (2.47) in the league. Ageless Tommy John won 22 and lost 9. Ron Guidry was a disappointing (only for him) 17-10. And, of course, in the bullpen, there was Goose Gossage with his 33 saves. Only Oakland outpitched the Yanks last season and many believe the ironman performance of the A's may have been something of a fluke. In contrast to the A's, the Yankees only completed 29 games—second lowest in the league. But they led all comers with 50 saves and they also shut out the competition a league-leading 15 times.

FIELDING: Utility man Larry Milbourne, acquired from Seattle, replaces Fred Stanley. Otherwise everything stays about the same. And why not? Bucky Dent led all shortstops in the league with his glove last year and Randolph is second only to Kansas City's Frank White at second base. Cerone emerged as a topflight catcher, although he was charged with 14 passed balls. Everywhere you look, the Yankees are sound.

Was Dave Winfield born to be a Yankee?

OUTLOOK: Can Gene Michael stay friends with George Steinbrenner for a full season? Can Gene Michael win 103 games? Will Dave Winfield find success in New York to match his fabulous salary? Stay tuned as the pin-striped soap opera continues. Many believe Michael may have embarked on a "Mission Impossible," trying to win a division and keep Steinbrenner happy at the same time. As Dick Howser proved last season, accomplishing the first feat doesn't necessarily assure the second. And there is certainly no guarantee that the aging Yankees will be able to win in the East again, even with the addition of Winfield. If they don't, it is a cinch Steinbrenner will not be smiling.

NEW YORK YANKEES 1981 ROSTER

MANAGER Gene Michael

Coaches—Joe Altobelli, Yogi Berra, Mike Ferraro, Charlie Lau, Jeff Torborg, Stan Williams

PITCHERS

No.	Name	1980 Club	W-L	IP	SO	ERA	B-T	Ht.	Wt.	Born
43	Bird, Doug	Columbus	6-0	48	30	2.25	R-R	6-4	180	3/5/50 Corona, CA
		New York (AL)	3-0	51	17	2.65				
–	Cochrane, Greg	Columbus	12-7	165	106	2.56	R-R	6-2	190	11/15/53 Whittier, CA
39	Davis, Ron	New York (AL)	9-3	131	65	2.95	R-R	6-4	198	8/6/55 Houston, TX
54	Gossage, Rich	New York (AL)	6-2	99	103	2.27	R-R	6-3	217	7/5/51 Colorado Springs, CO
52	Griffin, Mike	Columbus	7-2	83	47	3.47	R-R	6-5	195	6/26/57 Colusa, CA
		New York (AL)	2-4	54	25	4.83				
49	Guidry, Ron	New York (AL)	17-10	220	166	3.56	L-L	5-11	160	8/28/50 Lafayette, LA
25	John, Tommy	New York (AL)	22-9	265	78	3.43	R-L	6-3	203	5/22/43 Terre Haute, IN
53	Lollar, Tim	Columbus	2-1	49	50	2.57	L-L	6-3	200	3/17/56 Poplar Bluff, MO
		New York (AL)	1-0	32	13	3.34				
45	May, Rudy	New York (AL)	15-5	175	133	2.46	L-L	6-2	195	7/18/44 Coffeyville, KS
–	McGaffigan, Andy	Nashville	15-5	170	125	2.38	R-R	6-3	185	10/25/56 West Palm Beach, FL
–	Morgan, Mike	Ogden	6-9	115	46	5.40	R-R	6-2	200	10/8/59 Tulare, CA
–	Nelson, Gene	Ft. Lauderdale	20-3	196	130	1.97	R-R	6-0	172	12/3/60 Tampa, FL
–	Righetti, Dave	Columbus	6-10	142	139	4.63	L-L	6-3	195	11/29/58 San Jose, CA
–	Ryder, Brian	Nashville	15-9	201	134	3.04	R-R	6-6	175	2/13/60 Worcester, MA
38	Underwood, Tom	New York (AL)	13-9	187	116	3.66	L-L	5-11	185	12/22/53 Kokoma, IN
62	Welsh, Chris	Columbus	9-12	158	84	2.73	L-L	6-2	185	4/4/55 Wilmington, DE

CATCHERS

No.	Name	1980 Club	H	HR	RBI	Pct.	B-T	Ht.	Wt.	Born
10	Cerone, Rick	New York (AL)	144	14	85	.277	R-R	5-11	185	5/19/54 Newark, NJ
–	Espino, Juan	Nashville	9	0	9	.161	R-R	6-0	185	3/16/56 Dominican Republic
		Columbus	27	1	16	.209				
47	Robinson, Bruce	Columbus	80	12	48	.240	L-R	6-2	194	4/16/54 LaJolla, CA
		New York (AL)	0	0	0	.000				
24	Werth, Dennis	Columbus	20	3	15	.220	R-R	6-1	201	12/29/52 Lincoln, IL
		New York (AL)	20	3	12	.308				

INFIELDERS

No.	Name	1980 Club	H	HR	RBI	Pct.	B-T	Ht.	Wt.	Born
–	Balboni, Steve	Nashville	157	34	122	.301	R-R	6-3	225	1/16/57 Brockton, MA
20	Dent, Bucky	New York (AL)	128	5	52	.262	R-R	5-11	184	11/25/51 Savannah, GA
–	Milbourne, Larry	Seattle	68	0	26	.264	B-R	6-0	155	2/14/51 Port Norris, NJ
9	Nettles, Graig	New York (AL)	79	16	45	.244	L-R	6-0	187	8/20/44 San Diego, CA
30	Randolph, Willie	New York (AL)	151	7	46	.294	R-R	5-11	163	7/6/54 Holly Hill, SC
27	Rodriguez, Aurelio	San Diego	35	2	13	.200	R-R	5-11	180	12/28/47 Mexico
		New York (AL)	36	3	14	.220				
–	Santana, Rafael	Nashville	64	0	20	.233	R-R	6-1	156	1/31/58 Dominican Republic
		Ft. Lauderdale	38	1	17	.226				
21	Soderholm, Eric	New York (AL)	79	11	35	.287	R-R	5-11	202	9/24/48 Cortland, NY
12	Spencer, Jim	New York (AL)	61	13	43	.236	L-L	6-2	205	7/30/47 Hanover, PA
–	Tabler, Pat	Nashville	142	16	83	.296	R-R	6-3	185	2/2/58 Hamilton, OH
28	Watson, Bob	New York (AL)	144	13	68	.307	R-R	6-2	212	4/10/46 Los Angeles, CA

OUTFIELDERS

No.	Name	1980 Club	H	HR	RBI	Pct.	B-T	Ht.	Wt.	Born
13	Brown, Bobby	New York (AL)	107	14	47	.260	B-R	6-1	198	5/24/54 Norfolk, VA
17	Gamble, Oscar	New York (AL)	54	14	50	.278	L-R	5-11	187	12/20/49 Ramer, AL
44	Jackson, Reggie	New York (AL)	154	41	111	.300	L-L	6-0	206	5/18/46 Wyncote, PA
22	Jones, Ruppert	New York (AL)	73	9	42	.223	L-L	5-10	171	3/12/55 Dallas, TX
46	Lefebvre, Joe	Columbus	55	10	26	.278	L-R	5-10	170	2/22/56 Concord, NH
		New York (AL)	34	8	21	.227				
–	McGee, Willie	Nashville	63	1	22	.283	R-R	6-0	160	11/2/58 San Francisco, CA
2	Murcer, Bobby	New York (AL)	80	13	57	.269	L-R	5-11	185	5/20/46 Oklahoma City, OK
14	Piniella, Lou	New York (AL)	92	2	27	.287	R-R	6-2	199	8/28/43 Tampa, FL
56	Wilborn, Ted	Nashville	123	6	63	.270	B-R	6-0	170	12/16/58 Waco, TX
		New York (AL)	2	0	1	.250				
31	Winfield, Dave	San Diego	154	20	87	.276	R-R	6-6	220	10/3/51 St. Paul, MN

YANKEE PROFILES

RICH GOSSAGE 29 6-3 217 Bats R Throws R

Sensational during second half of the season . . . May have been the Most Valuable Yankee . . . Signed $2.75 million contract with Yanks as a free agent, but has been worth his weight in gold . . . Hitters quake at his sight . . . Thrives on pressure . . . Fastball regularly clocked at 96 m.p.h. . . . Born July 5, 1951, in Colorado Springs . . . Won't soon forget the three run homer he served up to George Brett to give Kansas City the pennant . . . Friends and foes alike call him "Goose" . . . Had always been a starter until White Sox sent him to bullpen . . . "The more I did it, the more I loved it," he says, when asked about pitching in relief . . . "I couldn't go nine anymore."

Year	Club	G	IP	W	L	Pct.	SO	BB	H	ERA
1972	Chicago (AL)	36	80	7	1	.875	57	44	72	4.28
1973	Chicago (AL)	20	50	0	4	.000	33	37	57	7.38
1974	Chicago (AL)	39	89	4	6	.400	64	47	92	4.15
1975	Chicago (AL)	62	142	9	8	.529	130	70	99	1.84
1976	Chicago (AL)	31	224	9	17	.346	135	90	214	3.94
1977	Pittsburgh	72	133	11	9	.550	151	49	78	1.62
1978	New York (AL)	63	134	10	11	.476	122	59	87	2.01
1979	New York (AL)	36	58	5	3	.625	41	19	48	2.64
1980	New York (AL)	64	99	6	2	.750	103	37	74	2.27
	Totals	423	1009	61	61	.500	836	352	821	3.06

RON GUIDRY 30 5-11 160 Bats L Throws L

Continues to struggle to regain the fabulous form that made him baseball's premier pitcher in '78 . . . Blames '80 woes on a "flat" slider . . . There's nothing wrong with his arm or his willingness to work . . . When he had problems as a starter, he demoted himself to the bullpen to work them out . . . "When you throw good pitches and nothing happens, you begin to wonder about yourself." . . . Still one of the most respected pitchers in the game . . . Born Aug. 28, 1950, in Lafayette, La. . . . Owns the best slider in the A.L. as a well as a blazing fastball . . . "Guidry hits your bat, you don't hit him," says

Seattle's Tom Paciorek . . . Was bombed in opening game of playoffs against Royals and never got another chance.

Year	Club	G	IP	W	L	Pct.	SO	BB	H	ERA
1975	New York (AL)	10	16	0	1	.000	15	9	15	3.38
1976	New York (AL)	20	16	0	0	.000	12	4	20	5.63
1977	New York (AL)	31	211	16	7	.696	176	65	174	2.82
1978	New York (AL)	35	274	25	3	.893	248	72	187	1.74
1979	New York (AL)	33	236	18	8	.692	201	71	203	2.78
1980	New York (AL)	37	220	17	10	.630	166	80	215	3.56
	Totals	166	973	76	29	.724	818	301	814	2.73

TOM UNDERWOOD 27 5-11 185 **Bats R Throws L**

Found baseball fun again in 1980 . . . "I enjoy this because the games mean something." . . . His goal in '80 was to even his lifetime record at .500, but he didn't quite make it . . . Always maintained he was a better pitcher than his record indicated while he was with Toronto . . . Won six in a row for first time in his career . . . Has excellent curve and a decent fastball, too . . . Born Dec. 22, 1953, in Kokomo, Ind. . . . Brother, Pat, pitches for Tigers . . . Insists he is not a strikeout pitcher, but admits, "I get my share." . . . Also can come in from the bullpen to relieve . . . Was once No. 2 pick of Philadelphia Phillies.

Year	Club	G	IP	W	L	Pct.	SO	BB	H	ERA
1974	Philadelphia..............	7	13	1	0	1.000	8	5	15	4.85
1975	Philadelphia..............	35	219	14	13	.519	123	84	221	4.15
1976	Philadelphia..............	33	156	10	5	.667	94	63	154	3.52
1977	Phil.-St. L................	33	133	9	11	.450	86	75	148	5.01
1978	Toronto	31	198	6	14	.300	140	87	201	4.09
1979	Toronto	33	227	9	16	.360	127	95	213	3.69
1980	New York (AL)	38	187	13	9	.591	116	66	163	3.66
	Totals	210	1133	62	68	.477	694	475	1115	3.99

TOMMY JOHN 37 6-3 203 **Bats R Throws R**

Reached 200 career win plateau in '80 and immediately began looking forward to victory No. 300 . . . "That will mean pitching for six more years and I think I can do it." . . . "I'll be back until the hitters force me to retire." . . . Won seven in row at start of season, but then he always gets off to a good beginning . . . "I work hard all winter. I throw every day." . . . Born May 5, 1943, in Terre Haute, Ind. . . . Sinker ball specialist . . . Started third and final game of A.L. playoff against Royals . . . The "Bionic Man." . . . His career was apparently over when doctors transplanted a tendon from his right forearm to his left elbow in '74 . . . One of few free agent pitchers who has earned his keep.

Year	Club	G	IP	W	L	Pct.	SO	BB	H	ERA
1963	Cleveland	6	20	0	2	.000	9	6	23	2.25
1964	Cleveland	25	94	2	9	.182	65	35	97	3.93
1965	Chicago (AL)	39	184	14	7	.667	126	58	162	3.03
1966	Chicago (AL)	34	223	14	11	.560	138	57	195	2.62
1967	Chicago (AL)	31	178	10	13	.435	110	47	143	2.48
1968	Chicago (AL)	25	177	10	5	.667	117	49	135	1.98
1969	Chicago (AL)	33	232	9	11	.450	128	90	230	3.26
1970	Chicago (AL)	37	269	12	17	.414	138	101	253	3.28
1971	Chicago (AL)	38	229	13	16	.448	131	58	244	3.62
1972	Los Angeles	29	187	11	5	.688	117	40	172	2.89
1973	Los Angeles	36	218	16	7	.696	116	50	202	3.10
1974	Los Angeles	22	153	13	3	.813	78	42	133	2.59
1975	Los Angeles					Did Not Play				
1976	Los Angeles	31	207	10	10	.500	91	61	207	3.09
1977	Los Angeles	31	220	20	7	.741	123	50	225	2.78
1978	Los Angeles	33	213	17	10	.630	124	53	230	3.30
1979	New York (AL)	37	276	21	9	.700	111	65	268	2.97
1980	New York (AL)	36	265	22	9	.710	78	56	270	3.43
	Totals	523	3345	214	151	.586	1800	918	3189	3.02

RICK CERONE 26 5-11 185 Bats R Throws R

Called upon to fill the position left vacant by the tragic death of Thurman Munson and did remarkably well . . . Was one of the most valuable players on the team . . . Extremely productive at the plate and an iron man behind it . . . Throws as well as any catcher in the league . . . Born May 19, 1954, in Newark, N.J. . . . Three times Tiger manager Sparky Anderson walked Graig Nettles with first base open to pitch to Rick and three times Rick came through with clutch hits, two singles and a grand slam . . . Several days later, Toronto manager Bobby Mattick made the same mistake with the same result . . . When will they ever learn? . . . Was No. 1 draft pick of Indians in 1974 . . . Acquired by Yanks in trade with Toronto.

Year	Club	Pos.	G	AB	R	H	2B	3B	HR	RBI	SB	Avg.
1975	Cleveland	C	7	12	1	3	1	0	0	0	0	.250
1976	Cleveland	C	7	16	1	2	0	0	0	1	0	.125
1977	Toronto	C	31	100	7	20	4	0	1	10	0	.200
1978	Toronto	C	88	282	25	63	8	2	3	20	0	.223
1979	Toronto	C	136	469	47	112	27	4	7	61	1	.239
1980	New York (AL)	C	147	519	70	144	30	4	14	85	1	.277
	Totals		416	1398	151	344	70	10	25	177	2	.246

REGGIE JACKSON 34 6-0 206 Bats L Throws L

Finally found peace in 1980 . . . Much happier man now that Billy Martin is gone . . . Continues to move upwards in baseball's all-time HR parade . . . "Reggie's such a money player, he gets himself psyched up," says Tom Underwood . . . Nevertheless, watched World Series on TV for second year in a row . . . Born May 18, 1946, in Wyncote, Pa. . . . Next goal is 500 career homers . . . "He's never cheated and he never cheats the fans," says rival pitcher Ed Farmer of the Chisox . . . Frequently rises to occasion after being knocked down . . . Recalls hitting "seven or eight" HRs in that situation . . . Has emerged as a true team leader . . . Has chance to become first player to sign multimillion-dollar contracts as a free agent twice in his career.

Year	Club	Pos.	G	AB	R	H	2B	3B	HR	RBI	SB	Avg.
1967	Kansas City.....	OF	35	118	13	21	4	4	1	6	1	.178
1968	Oakland........	OF	154	553	82	138	13	6	29	74	14	.250
1969	Oakland........	OF	152	549	123	151	36	3	47	118	13	.275
1970	Oakland........	OF	149	426	57	101	21	2	23	66	26	.237
1971	Oakland........	OF	150	567	87	157	29	3	32	80	16	.277
1972	Oakland........	OF	135	499	72	132	25	2	25	75	9	.265
1973	Oakland........	OF	151	539	99	158	28	2	32	117	22	.293
1974	Oakland........	OF	148	506	90	146	25	1	29	93	25	.289
1975	Oakland........	OF	157	593	91	150	39	3	36	104	17	.253
1976	Baltimore.......	OF	134	498	84	138	27	2	27	91	28	.277
1977	New York (AL)..	OF	146	525	93	150	39	2	32	110	17	.286
1978	New York (AL)..	OF	139	511	82	140	13	5	27	97	14	.274
1979	New York (AL)..	OF	131	465	78	138	24	2	29	89	9	.297
1980	New York (AL)..	OF	143	514	94	154	22	4	41	111	1	.300
	Totals.........		1924	6863	1145	1874	345	41	410	1231	212	.273

WILLIE RANDOLPH 26 5-11 163 Bats R Throws R

Very, very steady . . . Probably Yanks' best all-around player in '80 . . . Seldom makes headlines, just gets the job done . . . Holds together the infield defense . . . No slouch at the plate, either . . . An ideal lead-off man . . . Often sets the stage for the sluggers who follow . . . Would like to steal 50 bases a year . . . Born July 6, 1954, in Holly Hill, S.C. . . . Blamed slow start in '80 on players' strike . . . A fierce competitor . . . Latest in long line of outstanding Yankee second basemen that includes Tony Lazzeri, Joe Gordon and Bobby Richardson . . . Acquired from Pittsburgh, where he was considered a top prospect.

Year	Club	Pos.	G	AB	R	H	2B	3B	HR	RBI	SB	Avg.
1975	Pittsburgh	2B-3B	30	61	9	10	1	0	0	3	1	.164
1976	New York (AL) ..	2B	125	430	59	115	15	4	1	40	37	.267
1977	New York (AL) ..	2B	147	551	91	151	28	11	4	40	13	.274
1978	New York (AL) ..	2B	134	499	87	139	18	6	3	42	36	.279
1979	New York (AL) ..	2B	153	574	98	155	15	13	5	61	33	.270
1980	New York (AL) ..	2B	138	513	99	151	23	7	7	46	30	.294
	Totals..........		627	2628	443	721	100	41	20	232	150	.274

RUDY MAY 36 6-2 195 Bats L Throws L

Another free agent pitcher who made good for the Yanks . . . Signed after playing out his option in Montreal . . . Was extremely consistent, rarely allowing any game to get out of hand . . . Called upon to pitch second game of playoff, but one bad inning proved to be his downfall . . . His friends call him "Dude" . . . Born July 18, 1944, in Coffeyville, Kan. . . . Originally signed with Twins in 1963 . . . Quickly bounced to White Sox, Phillies and Angels before reaching big leagues in '65 . . . Allowed just one hit against Tigers and Denny McLain in his big league debut, but didn't get the decision.

Year	Club	G	IP	W	L	Pct.	SO	BB	H	ERA
1965	California...............	30	124	4	9	.308	76	78	111	3.92
1969	California...............	43	180	10	13	.435	133	66	142	3.45
1970	California...............	38	209	7	13	.350	164	81	190	4.00
1971	California...............	32	208	11	12	.478	156	87	160	3.03
1972	California...............	35	205	12	11	.522	169	82	162	2.94
1973	California...............	34	185	7	17	.292	134	80	177	4.38
1974	Cal.-N.Y. (AL)	35	141	8	5	.615	102	58	104	3.19
1975	New York (AL)	32	212	14	12	.538	145	99	179	3.06
1976	N.Y.-Balt. (AL)	35	220	15	10	.600	109	70	205	3.72
1977	Baltimore................	37	252	18	14	.563	105	78	243	3.61
1978	Montreal	27	144	8	10	.444	87	42	141	3.88
1979	Montreal	33	94	10	3	.769	67	31	88	2.30
1980	New York (AL)	41	175	15	5	.750	133	39	144	2.47
	Totals..................	452	2349	139	134	.509	1580	891	2046	3.41

BOBBY MURCER 34 5-11 185 Bats L Throws R

Has been a big disappointment since his return . . . Was not happy with his role early in 1980 season, and said so . . . "He bitched," admits Gene Michael, "but at least when he got his chance, he did something about it." . . . Usually plays only against righthanded pitchers . . . Wants to be in there every day . . . Born May 20, 1946, in Oklahoma City . . . Had some great years as a Yankee before he was traded away . . . Was discovered by Tom Greenwade, the same scout who signed Mickey Mantle . . . Never became the full-fledged superstar he was at first billed to be.

Year	Club	Pos.	G	AB	R	H	2B	3B	HR	RBI	SB	Avg.
1965	New York (AL) ..	SS	11	37	2	9	0	1	1	4	0	.243
1966	New York (AL) ..	SS	21	69	3	12	1	1	0	5	2	.174
1967	New York (AL) ..		In Military Service									
1968	New York (AL) ..		In Military Service									
1969	New York (AL) ..	OF-3B	152	564	82	146	24	4	26	82	7	.259
1970	New York (AL) ..	OF	159	581	95	146	23	3	23	78	15	.251
1971	New York (AL) ..	OF	146	529	94	175	25	6	25	94	14	.331
1972	New York (AL) ..	OF	153	585	102	171	30	7	33	96	11	.292
1973	New York (AL) ..	OF	160	616	83	187	29	2	22	95	6	.304
1974	New York (AL) ..	OF	156	606	69	166	25	4	10	88	14	.274
1975	San Francisco ...	OF	147	526	80	157	29	4	11	91	9	.298
1976	San Francisco ...	OF	147	533	73	138	20	2	23	90	12	.259
1977	Chicago (NL)....	OF-2B-SS	154	554	90	147	18	3	27	89	16	.265
1978	Chicago (NL)....	OF	146	499	66	140	22	6	9	64	14	.281
1979	Chicago (NL)....	OF	58	190	22	49	4	1	9	22	2	.258
1979	New York (AL) ..	OF	74	264	42	72	12	0	8	33	1	.273
1980	New York (AL) ..	OF	100	297	41	80	9	1	13	57	2	.269
	Totals..........		1784	6450	944	1795	271	45	238	988	123	.278

BOB WATSON 34 6-2 212

Bats R Throws R

The Yanks would have been hurting without him . . . Signed as a free agent after Bosox let him walk away . . . Was leading Yankee hitter among the regulars . . . Spent his entire career in Astros organization before he was traded to Red Sox amidst a contract dispute . . . Was one of most consistent hitters in Houston history . . . Born April 10, 1946, in Los Angeles . . . Once drove in runs in nine consecutive games . . . Began career as catcher, but moved to outfield, and later to first base . . . Can also DH, of course . . . Extremely durable . . . Rarely gets hurt . . . Was a sergeant in the Marine Corps.

Year	Club	Pos.	G	AB	R	H	2B	3B	HR	RBI	SB	Avg.
1969	Houston........	OF-1B-C	20	40	3	11	3	0	0	3	0	.275
1970	Houston........	1B-C-OF	97	327	48	89	19	2	11	61	1	.272
1971	Houston........	OF-1B	129	468	49	135	17	3	9	67	0	.288
1972	Houston........	OF-1B	147	548	74	171	27	4	16	86	1	.312
1973	Houston........	OF-1B-C	158	573	97	179	24	3	16	94	1	.312
1974	Houston........	OF-1B	150	524	69	156	19	4	11	67	3	.298
1975	Houston........	1B-OF	132	485	67	157	27	1	18	85	3	.324
1976	Houston........	1B	157	585	76	183	31	3	16	102	3	.313
1977	Houston........	1B	151	554	77	160	38	6	22	110	5	.289
1978	Houston........	1B	139	461	51	133	25	4	14	79	3	.289
1979	Houston........	1B	49	163	15	39	4	0	3	18	0	.239
1979	Boston..........	1B	84	312	48	105	19	4	13	53	3	.337
1980	New York (AL) ..	1B	130	469	62	144	25	3	13	68	2	.307
	Totals..........		1595	5664	750	1697	285	37	165	903	5	.300

DAVE WINFIELD 29 6-6 220 **Bats R Throws R**

Ended bidding contest by signing 10-year, $15-million Yankee pact with clauses that could bring contract value to $25 million . . . Endured frustrating 1980 season following pay demands that were deemed atrocious by many San Diego fans . . . Booed at home games . . . Average and power figures slipped following banner '79 season in which he topped N.L. with 118 RBI despite little help in the lineup . . . Still had 20 homers and 87 RBI, good for many players, but not a superstar . . . Born Oct. 3, 1951, at St. Paul, Minn. . . . Known for philanthropic deeds, has set up a foundation to do charitable work for underprivileged youth . . . Tremendous career as college athlete at U. of Minnesota . . . Was MVP of College World Series and was drafted by three pro teams: Padres, Vikings (NFL) and Utah (ABA).

Year	Club	Pos.	G	AB	R	H	2B	3B	HR	RBI	SB	Avg.
1973	San Diego......	OF-1B	56	141	9	39	4	1	3	12	0	.277
1974	San Diego......	OF	145	498	57	132	18	4	20	75	9	.265
1975	San Diego......	OF	143	509	74	136	20	2	15	76	23	.267
1976	San Diego......	OF	137	492	81	139	26	4	13	69	26	.283
1977	San Diego......	OF	157	615	104	169	29	7	25	92	16	.275
1978	San Diego......	OF-1B	158	587	88	181	30	5	24	97	21	.308
1979	San Diego......	OF	159	597	97	184	27	10	34	118	15	.308
1980	San Diego......	OF	162	558	89	154	25	6	20	87	23	.276
	Totals..........		1117	3997	599	1134	179	39	154	626	133	.284

TOP PROSPECTS

DENNIS WERTH 28 6-1 201 **Bats R Throws R**

Batted .308 in 39 games with Yanks in '80 . . . May be a late bloomer whose time has finally come . . . Has put together outstanding minor league statistics, year after year . . . Originally a catcher, but has been converted to first base . . . Born Dec. 29, 1952, in Lincoln, Ill. . . . Hits with power but is also sound defensively at first.

MIKE MORGAN 21 6-2 200 **Bats R Throws R**

Came to Yankees from A's in deal that originally involved Brian Doyle as well as Fred Stanley . . . Already has three minor league seasons behind him . . . Was No. 4 overall draft pick in June 1978 draft . . . Made major league debut a few days after he graduated from high school . . . Pitched a complete game against the Orioles, but lost . . . Born Oct. 10, 1959, in Tulare, Calif. . . . Still learning and still young . . . Could be outstanding.

MANAGER GENE MICHAEL: The seventh Yankee manager in the last eight years . . . Stepped into George Steinbrenner's hot seat when Dick Howser "resigned" last November . . . Only previous managerial experience came in 1979, when he guided Yankee farm club at Columbus to International League championship . . . Was Yankee general manager last year . . . Broke into majors with Pittsburgh in 1966 and spent majority of ten-year career with Yanks as utility infielder . . . Born June 2, 1938, in Kent, Ohio . . . Once said that he felt his future was in the front office rather than in uniform as a manager, but Steinbrenner persuaded him to sign three-year contract to manage . . . If he fulfills pact, he'll set longetivity record for a Steinbrenner manager . . . "I'm no yes man," he said when he was named, but that attitude may change when the phone calls from on high start coming in April.

GREATEST TEAM

Babe Ruth. Lou Gehrig. Bob Meusel. Tony Lazzeri. Earle Combs. Need one say more?

How about Waite Hoyt, Wilcy Moore, Herb Pennock, Urban Shocker and Dutch Ruether?

Still not convinced? Well, throw in Mark Koenig, Joe Dugan, and a manager named Miller Huggins.

No doubt about it: The 1927 Yankees were not only the finest bunch of ballplayers ever to represent the city of New York, they were probably the best team ever put together anywhere.

They breezed to the American League pennant, taking over first place on Opening Day and staying there until the end of the season. They won 110 games, losing only 44. And they finished a record 19 lengths ahead of the runnerup Philadelphia Athletics.

In a word, they were awesome. And they didn't slow down when they reached the World Series, wiping out the Pittsburgh Pirates in four straight.

ALL-TIME YANKEE LEADERS

BATTING: Babe Ruth, .393, 1923
HRs: Roger Maris, 61, 1961
RBIs: Lou Gehrig, 184, 1931
STEALS: Fred Maisel, 74, 1914
WINS: Jack Chesbro, 41, 1904
STRIKEOUTS: Ron Guidry, 248, 1978

Without Gossage, Yanks' Goose would be cooked.

TORONTO BLUE JAYS

TEAM DIRECTORY: Chairman of the Board: R. Howard Webster; Pres.: Peter Bavasi; VP-Baseball Operations: Pat Gillick; VP-Business Operations: Paul Beeston; Dir. Pub. Rel.: Howard Starkman; Trav. Sec.: Ken Carson; Mgr.: Bobby Mattick; Home: Exhibition Stadium (43,737). Field distances: 330, l.f. line; 375, l.c.; 400, c.f.; 375, r.c.; 330, r.f. line. Spring training: Dunedin, Fla.

SCOUTING REPORT

HITTING: You at least have to give the Blue Jays credit for being consistent. For the second year in a row, they batted .251, the second-lowest average in the league. Continuing to look on the bright side, Alfredo Griffin (.254) tied Willie Wilson for the league lead in triples with 15. And John Mayberry was 11th in walks with 77.

Mayberry (.248, 30 HRs, 82 RBI), along with Barry Bonnell (.268, 13 HRs, 56 RBI), Otto Velez (.269, 20 HRs, 62 RBI) and Al Woods (.300, 15 HRs, 47 RBI) will again have to provide most of the punch. And Damaso Garcia made his presence felt last season with a .278 average. But most of the other numbers were disappointing, including Rick Bosetti's .213.

PITCHING: The Blue Jays climbed from last to ninth in team ERA with a 4.19 mark, outpitching Detroit, Boston, Seattle, California and Cleveland. Even so, the Jays need help. Righthanded help. And lefthanded help. They are hoping Paul Mirabella (5-12) can provide some of the latter. Jim Clancy (13-16) did crack the top ten last year with his 3.30 ERA and Dave Steib was 12-15, but after that, it was usually pot luck. In fact, even the now-traded Bob Bailor, the versatile utilityman, was called upon to pitch in three games. And how much help can they expect from Roy Lee Jackson (1-7, 4.18 ERA), the Mets' pitcher who came in the Bailor exchange?

FIELDING: They say you begin to build a defense by stationing dependable players up the middle. If that's true, the Jays are headed in the right direction. In second baseman Garcia and shortstop Griffin, both of whom are only 23, they have one of the finest young double-play combinations in the game. In fact, the Jays tied the Boston Red Sox for the league lead with 206 double plays last year. And if Bosetti recovers from a busted arm, the Jays will again feature one of the better centerfielders in the game. What they desperately need now is a catcher. Even so,

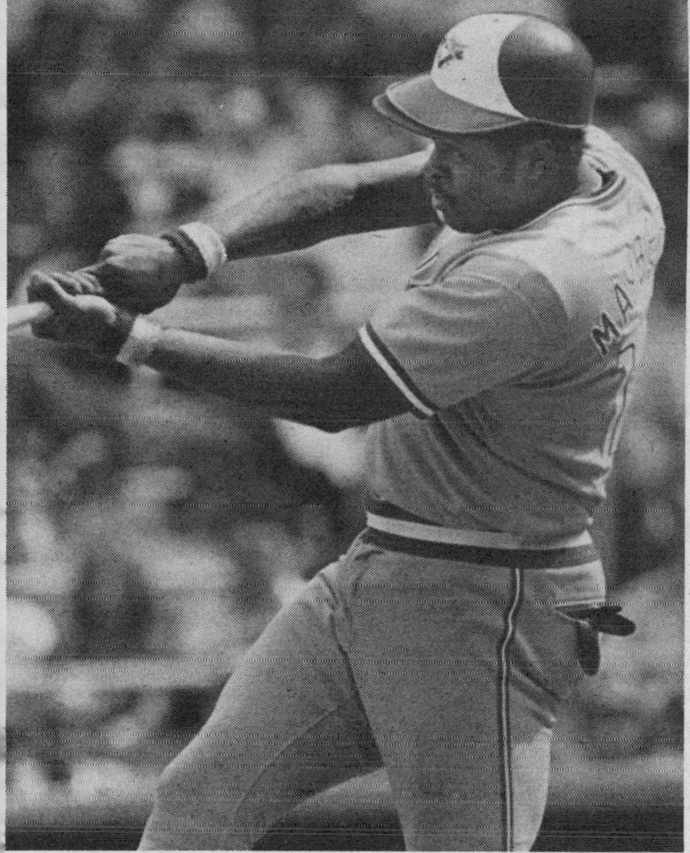

John Mayberry has had eight 20-homer seasons.

Toronto did finish third in the league in fielding last season, trailing only Baltimore and Cleveland.

OUTLOOK: It is, indeed, hard to imagine the Blue Jays advancing anywhere in the American League East in the near future. The competition is simply too keen. Slowly but surely, the Jays seem to be improving, but they still have a long way to go, even to reach sixth place. They have tried changing players, they have tried changing managers. Now they have to try being patient. After four last-place finishes in four years in the league, with No. 5 inevitably ahead, it is a lot to ask.

TORONTO BLUE JAYS 1981 ROSTER

MANAGER Bob Mattick
Coaches—Bobby Doerr, John Felske, Al Widmar, Denis Menke, Jimmy Williams

PITCHERS

No.	Name	1980 Club	W-L	IP	SO	ERA	B-T	Ht.	Wt.	Born
46	Barlow, Mike	Syrause	3-2	51	26	4.59	L-R	6-5	215	4/30/48 Stamford, NY
		Toronto	3-1	55	19	4.09				
18	Clancy, Jim	Toronto	13-16	251	152	3.30	R-R	6-4	180	12/18/55 Chicago, IL
36	Garvin, Jerry	Toronto	4-7	83	52	2.28	L-L	6-3	195	10/21/55 Oakland, CA
47	Huffman, Phil	Syracuse	3-9	93	47	3.97	R-R	6-2	180	6/20/58 Freeport, TX
–	Jackson, Roy Lee	Tidewater	3-5	78	56	2.31	R-R	6-2	195	5/1/54 Opilika, AL
		New York (NL)	1-7	71	58	4.18				
48	Leal, Luis	Syracuse	6-5	110	76	3.27	R-R	6-3	205	3/21/57 Venezuela
		Toronto	3-4	60	26	4.50				
50	McLaughlin, Joey	Toronto	6-9	136	70	4.50	R-R	6-2	205	7/11/56 Tulsa, OK
42	Mirabella, Paul	Syracuse	1-2	31	23	2.61	L-L	6-2	195	3/20/54 Belleville, NJ
		Toronto	5-12	131	53	4.33				
–	Puleo, Charlie	Knoxville	8-7	108	97	2.83	R-R	6-3	190	2/7/55 Glen Ridge, NJ
35	Santana, Rafael	Knoxville	0-7	83	63	3.90	R-R	6-1	165	3/4/58 Dominican Republic
21	Schrom, Ken	Salt Lake City	0-1	23	11	7.94	R-R	6-2	195	11/23/54 Graneville, ID
		Syracuse	0-2	46	31	3.58				
		Toronto	1-0	31	13	5.23				
37	Stieb, Dave	Toronto	12-15	243	108	3.71	R-R	6-1	185	7/22/57 Santa Ana, CA
40	Todd, Jackson	Syracuse	7-9	153	118	3.41	R-R	6-2	190	11/20/51 Tulsa, OK
		Toronto	5-2	85	44	4.02				
23	Willis, Mike	Syracuse	7-4	69	48	2.48	L-L	6-2	200	12/26/50 Oklahoma City, OK
		Toronto	2-1	26	14	1.73				

CATCHERS

No.	Name	1980 Club	H	HR	RBI	Pct.	B-T	Ht.	Wt.	Born
8	Davis, Bob	Toronto	47	4	19	.216	R-R	6-0	190	3/1/52 Pryor, OK
5	Milner, Brian	Kinston	116	6	71	.257	R-R	6-2	200	11/17/59 Fort Worth, TX
27	Petralli, Gene	Knoxville	109	3	38	.285	B-R	6-1	180	9/25/59 Sacramento, CA
12	Whitt, Ernie	Toronto	70	6	34	.237	L-R	6-2	200	6/13/52 Detroit, MI

INFIELDERS

No.	Name	1980 Club	H	HR	RBI	Pct.	B-T	Ht.	Wt.	Born
2	Ainge, Dan	Syracuse	72	2	17	.244	R-R	6-4	175	3/17/59 Eugene, OR
		Toronto	27	0	4	.243				
7	Garcia, Damaso	Toronto	151	4	46	.278	R-R	6-0	165	2/7/57 Dominican Republic
4	Griffin, Alfredo	Toronto	166	2	41	.254	B-R	5-11	160	3/10/57 Dominican Republic
–	Hernandez, Pedro	Knoxville	120	4	43	.283	R-R	6-1	160	4/4/59 Dominican Republic
16	Iorg, Garth	Syracuse	40	1	14	.299	R-R	5-11	165	10/12/54 Arcata, CA
		Toronto	55	2	14	.248				
10	Mayberry, John	Toronto	124	30	82	.248	L-L	6-3	220	2/18/50 Detroit, MI
17	Ramos, Domingo	Syracuse	80	4	27	.251	R-R	5-10	154	3/29/58 Dominican Republic
		Toronto	2	0	0	.125				
26	Upshaw, Willie	Syracuse	91	9	52	.254	L-L	6-0	185	4/27/57 Blanco, TX
		Toronto	13	1	5	.213				

OUTFIELDERS

No.	Name	1980 Club	H	HR	RBI	Pct.	B-T	Ht.	Wt.	Born
29	Barfield, Jesse	Knoxville	104	14	65	.240	R-R	6-1	170	10/29/59 Joliet, IL
9	Bonnell, Barry	Toronto	124	13	56	.268	R-R	6-3	200	10/27/53 Milford, OH
22	Bosetti, Rick	Toronto	40	4	18	.213	R-R	5-11	185	8/5/53 Redding, CA
49	Hodgson, Paul	Knoxville	44	5	26	.235	R-R	6-2	190	4/14/60 Canada
		Kinston	77	7	39	.352				
		Toronto	9	1	5	.220				
15	Moseby, Lloyd	Syracuse	47	3	19	.322	L-R	6-3	200	11/5/59 Portland, AR
		Toronto	89	9	46	.229				
19	Velez, Otto	Toronto	96	20	62	.269	R-R	6-0	195	11/20/50 Puerto Rico
20	Woods, Al	Toronto	112	15	47	.300	L-L	6-3	200	8/8/53 Oakland, CA

BLUE JAY PROFILES

JIM CLANCY 25 6-4 180 Bats R Throws R

One of the few bright spots on the Blue Jays pitching staff last season . . . Jays have been expected big things from him ever since they made him their first-round pick from the Rangers in the expansion draft . . . "He's got the kind of arm you can build a franchise on," says Whitey Herzog . . . Born Dec. 18, 1955, in Chicago . . . Credits pitching coach Al Widmar with changing his style . . . Relies on a 90 mph fastball and a slider . . . Is also working on a change-up . . . "I'm more confident now than I've ever been." . . . Struck out career-high 11 batters against Chicago.

Year	Club	G	IP	W	L	Pct.	SO	BB	H	ERA
1977	Toronto	13	77	4	9	.308	44	47	80	5.03
1978	Toronto	31	194	10	12	.455	106	91	199	4.08
1979	Toronto	12	64	2	7	.222	33	31	65	5.48
1980	Toronto	34	251	13	16	.448	152	128	217	3.30
	Totals	90	586	29	44	.397	335	297	561	4.02

JERRY GARVIN 25 6-3 195 Bats L Throws L

Bounced back from a disastrous 1979 season to become the most dependable member of the Jays' bullpen . . . Says increased use of his fastball and new-found ability to stay ahead of the hitters is responsible for improvement . . . Previously relied on his forkball . . . Born Oct. 21, 1955, in Oakland . . . Many people thought he couldn't pitch in relief because his arm wouldn't snap back quickly enough . . . But Bobby Mattick said, "Let's give it a try." . . . Was the second player grabbed by the Jays in the expansion draft . . . Began his career with the Twins.

Year	Club	G	IP	W	L	Pct.	SO	BB	H	ERA
1977	Toronto	34	245	10	18	.357	127	85	247	4.19
1978	Toronto	26	145	4	12	.250	67	48	189	5.52
1979	Toronto	8	23	0	1	.000	14	10	15	2.74
1980	Toronto	61	83	4	7	.364	52	27	70	2.28
	Totals	129	496	18	38	.321	260	170	521	4.19

JOEY McLAUGHLIN 24 6-2 205 **Bats R Throws R**

Acquired from the Braves to bolster the bullpen but also used as starter . . . "It doesn't matter to me" . . . Made rather inauspicious big league debut, yielding a single, two walks and two homers in one-third of an inning against Philadelphia . . . Born July 11, 1956, in Tulsa, Okla. . . . Was used both as a starter and a reliever while in minor leagues . . . Came to Jays along with Barry Bonnell in deal that sent Chris Chambliss and Luis Gomez to Atlanta.

Year	Club	G	IP	W	L	Pct.	SO	BB	H	ERA
1977	Atlanta	3	6	0	0	.000	0	3	10	15.00
1979	Atlanta	37	69	5	3	.625	40	34	54	2.48
1980	Toronto	55	136	6	9	.400	70	53	159	4.50
	Totals	95	211	11	12	.478	110	90	223	4.14

DAVE STEIB 23 6-1 185 **Bats R Throws R**

Pitched extremely well early in the season even though he held out in the spring and was eight days late reporting to camp . . . "I should be compensated for what I do on the field and not on my length of service" . . . Forced Jays to renew his contract . . . Made it to majors after spending less than one season in minors . . . Born July 22, 1957, in Santa Ana, Calif. . . . An outfielder in college, he volunteered to pitch one day when his Southern Illinois team got into trouble . . . A fine fielder . . . Signed a $25,000 bonus to sign with Blue Jays . . . Could be future ace of the staff.

Year	Club	G	IP	W	L	Pct.	SO	BB	H	ERA
1979	Toronto	18	129	8	8	.500	52	48	139	4.33
1980	Toronto	34	243	12	15	.444	108	83	232	3.70
	Totals	52	372	20	23	.465	160	131	371	3.92

DAMASO GARCIA 23 6-0 165 **Bats R Throws R**

Bobby Mattick calls him "A mini-Manny Sanguillen" . . . Among the top rookies in the league last year . . . An outstanding fielder . . . Acquired from the Yankees in trade that sent Tom Underwood and Rick Cerone to New York . . . Born Feb. 7, 1957, in Moca, D.R. . . . Was a soccer star in high school and college . . . Rod Carew was his boyhood hero

. . . Can play either second base or shortstop . . . Was once considered one of the top prospects in the Yankee farm system but got his chance with Toronto . . . Good speed on the basepaths.

Year	Club	Pos.	G	AB	R	H	2B	3B	HR	RBI	SB	Avg.
1978	New York (AL) . .	SS-2B	18	41	5	8	0	0	0	1	1	.195
1979	New York (AL) . .	SS-3B	11	38	3	10	1	0	0	4	2	.263
1980	Toronto	2B-SS-3B	140	543	50	151	30	7	4	46	13	.278
	Totals.		169	622	58	169	31	7	4	51	16	.272

ALREDO GRIFFIN 24 5-11 160 — Bats S Throws R

"He's the spark who turns things on for us," says Bobby Mattick . . . Enjoyed a 14-game hitting streak . . . "He's handling the bat better, he seems more confident, and he's running better," says Mattick . . . Born March 10, 1957, in Santo Domingo, D.R. . . . Average has climbed steadily since he began choking up on the bat . . . Broke Bob Bailor's club stolen-base record in '79 . . . A line-drive hitter in the mold of Matty Alou . . . One of the most exciting young players in the game today . . . Should continue to improve . . . Shared 1970 AL Rookie-of-the-Year award with Twins' John Castino . . . Hit first pitch thrown to him in the big leagues for a single.

Year	Club	Pos.	G	AB	R	H	2B	3B	HR	RBI	SB	Avg.
1976	Cleveland.	SS	12	4	0	1	0	0	0	0	0	.250
1977	Cleveland.	SS	14	41	5	6	1	0	0	3	2	.146
1978	Cleveland.	SS	5	4	1	2	1	0	0	0	0	.500
1979	Toronto	SS	153	624	81	179	22	10	2	31	20	.287
1980	Toronto	SS	155	653	63	166	26	15	2	41	18	.254
	Totals.		339	1326	150	354	50	25	4	75	40	.267

JOHN MAYBERRY 31 6-3 220 — Bats L Throws L

Broke the club record with a 17-game hitting streak . . . Still one of the most dangerous sluggers in the league when he's in the groove . . . Never quite became the superstar some people expected him to be . . . Born Feb. 28, 1949, in Detroit . . . Went to high school with Willie Horton . . . Was also an outstanding basketball player . . . Has been one of the most consistently productive first basemen in the the game during the past decade . . . Also a fine fielder . . . Was Houston's No. 1 pick in the 1967 free agent draft.

Year	Club	Pos.	G	AB	R	H	2B	3B	HR	RBI	SB	Avg.
1968	Houston........	1B	4	9	0	0	0	0	0	0	0	.000
1969	Houston........	PH	5	4	0	0	0	0	0	0	0	.000
1970	Houston........	1B	50	148	23	32	3	2	5	14	1	.216
1971	Houston........	1B	46	137	16	25	0	1	7	14	0	.182
1972	Kansas City.....	1B	149	503	65	150	24	3	25	100	0	.298
1973	Kansas City.....	1B	152	510	87	142	20	2	26	100	3	.278
1974	Kansas City.....	1B	126	427	63	100	13	1	22	69	4	.234
1975	Kansas City.....	1B	156	554	95	161	38	1	34	106	5	.291
1976	Kansas City.....	1B	161	594	76	138	22	2	13	95	3	.232
1977	Kansas City.....	1B	153	543	73	125	22	1	23	82	1	.230
1978	Toronto	1B	152	515	51	129	15	2	22	70	1	.250
1979	Toronto	1B	137	464	61	127	22	1	21	74	1	.274
1980	Toronto	1B	149	501	62	124	19	2	30	82	0	.248
	Totals..........		1440	4909	672	1253	198	18	228	806	19	.255

OTTO VELEZ 30 6-0 195 Bats R Throws R

Stopped taking batting practice and started hitting . . . "I like to go to home plate feeling strong" . . . Matched A.L. record with four HRs and 10 RBI in doubleheader against Cleveland . . . "I think that was the greatest moment for me" . . . Born Nov. 29, 1950, in Ponce, Puerto Rico . . . Replaced Rico Carty as the Jays' DH . . . Had never been given a chance to play regularly . . . "I'm not saying I can hit 30 HRs, but I would like to have 500 at-bats" . . . Appeared destined for certain stardom when he broke in with the Yankees.

Year	Club	Pos.	G	AB	R	H	2B	3B	HR	RBI	SB	Avg.
1973	New York (AL) ..	OF	23	77	9	15	4	0	2	7	0	.195
1974	New York (AL) ..	1B-OF-3B	27	67	9	14	1	1	2	10	0	.209
1975	New York (AL) ..	1B	6	8	0	2	0	0	0	1	0	.250
1976	New York (AL) ..	1B-OF-3B	49	94	11	25	6	0	2	10	0	.266
1977	Toronto	OF	120	360	50	92	19	3	16	62	4	.256
1978	Toronto	OF-1B	91	248	29	66	14	2	9	38	1	.266
1979	Toronto	OF-1B	99	274	45	79	21	0	15	48	0	.288
1980	Toronto	OF-1B	104	357	54	96	12	3	20	62	0	.269
	Totals..........		519	1485	207	389	77	9	66	238	5	.262

TOP PROSPECTS

COLIN McLAUGHLIN 21 6-6 205 Bats S Throws R

The top pick in the nation in the January 1980 free agent draft . . . Born June 9, 1959, in Winchester, Mass. . . . Played basketball and soccer and ran cross country in addition to participating in baseball in high school . . . Later starred at the University of Connecticut, compiling a 12-2 record with a 2.51 ERA as a freshman.

LLOYD MOSEBY 21 6-3 200 **Bats L Throws R**
Picked right behind Bob Horner of Atlanta in June 1978 . . . A power-hitting outfielder, knocked in 84 runs and belted 18 HRs in his first full season in pro ball . . . Born Nov. 5, 1959, in Portland, Ark. . . . Was high school All-America in baseball and basketball . . . Tried out for his Little League team as a catcher but was cut.

MANAGER BOBBY MATTICK: Oldest manager in the league . . . Rehired in spite of Blue Jays' sloppy play in 1980 . . . "We don't do things like some other teams," says Peter Bavasi. "Instead of firing the manager and patting the players on the head, we fire some players and rehire the manager." . . . Born Dec. 5, 1915, in Sioux City, Iowa . . . Batted .233 as a player in the big leagues before his career was cut short by a serious eye injury . . . Was working as the Blue Jays' chief scout when he was named manager . . . Among the eventual stars he signed and developed as a scout were Frank Robinson, Vada Pinson, Curt Flood, Jim Maloney, Tommy Harper, Dave Giusti, Rusty Staub, Darrell Porter, Gorman Thomas, Sixto Lezcano, Bobby Grich, Don Baylor, Gary Carter, Ellis Valentine and Warren Cromartie . . . He could use a few of those guys now.

GREATEST TEAM

The Blue Jays were brand new in 1977. And, as expected, their victories were few.

Nevertheless, in Toronto, the '77 season was undeniably a success.

Although they had the poorest record of any team in baseball, winning only 54 of 161 games, they attracted 1,701,039 fans to Exhibition Stadium—a record for a first-year expansion team.

No longer was there any doubt that big league baseball belonged in Canada.

It wasn't all doom and gloom on the field, either.

Bob Bailor, the Blue Jays' No. 1 pick in the expansion draft, batted an impressive .310—the best average ever by a player on a first-year expansion team.

Other bright spots included Roy Howell (.302) and outfielder Alvis Woods (.284).

No one was predicting a pennant in the near future. Everyone in the Blue Jays' organization admitted such success would take time.

But no one was complaining about the way the Blue Jays had begun.

ALL-TIME BLUE JAY LEADERS

BATTING: Bob Bailor, .310, 1977
HRs: John Mayberry, 30, 1980
RBIs: John Mayberry, 82, 1980
STEALS: Alfredo Griffin, 20, 1979
WINS: Dave Lemanczyk, 13, 1977
Jim Clancy, 13, 1980
STRIKEOUTS: Jim Clancy, 152, 1980

Shortstop Alfredo Griffin is Blue Jays' catalyst.

CALIFORNIA ANGELS

TEAM DIRECTORY: Chairman of the Board-Pres.: Gene Autry; VP-Asst. Chairman of the Board: Red Patterson; VP-GM: Buzzy Bavasi; Dir. Pub. Rel.: Tom Seeberg; Mgr.: Jim Fregosi. Home: Anaheim Stadium (69,000). Field distances: 333, l.f. line; 386, l.c.; 404, c.f.; 386, r.c.; 333, r.f. line. Spring training: Palm Springs, Cal.

SCOUTING REPORT

HITTING: Although he finished a distant fifth behind George Brett in the batting race, Rod Carew (.331) was one of the few Angel hitters who earned his pay last year. That .331 mark, in fact, was the highest in club history. Jason Thompson batted .317 and smacked 17 HRs after coming over from the Tigers where he was unhappy, but the problem may be finding some place for him to play.

Don Baylor was hobbled much of the year with painful inju-

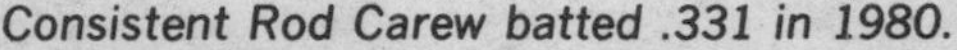

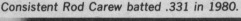

Consistent Rod Carew batted .331 in 1980.

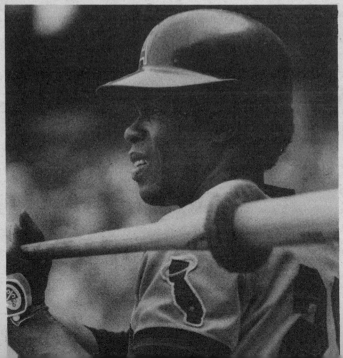

ries and is a key to the comeback California hopes to achieve this year. Bobby Grich (.271) was, perhaps, the most consistent Angel last year. The addition of Rick Burleson and Butch Hobson will help some, but the Angels still must figure out how to hit right-handed pitching. Last year they were 43-67 against righthanders.

PITCHING: Only the Indians looked worse on the mound than the Angels did last year. No staff in the league completed fewer games than the Angels' 22. As a group the Angels' starters were 37-75. To solve that problem, Gene Autry dipped into his bottomless saddlebag again and signed free agents Geoff Zahn (a 33-year-old lefthander with a 59-67 record, lifetime) and young John D'Acquisto (2-5 with 3 saves last year). That isn't enough.

Bruce Kison (3-6), who was supposed to make the fans forget Nolan Ryan, may never pitch again and Frank Tanana (11-12) can no longer win consistently. When the hero of your pitching staff is Andy Hassler (5-1, with 10 saves) you're in big trouble. Meanwhile, the Angels keep hoping Dave Frost's back problems are behind him and kids like Ralph Botting, Bob Ferris, Jim Dorsey and Dave Schuler can come through.

FIELDING: The Angels were in dire need of a shortstop, and they got a very good one in Rick Burleson. Three times an All-Star, Burleson is one of the best in the business and a team leader to boot. The Angels may also have improved themselves at third base where Butch Hobson replaces Carney Lansford. Neither man can carry Brooks Robinson's glove. Elsewhere, the Angels are adequate and their pitching staff needs all of the help it can get.

OUTLOOK: Are the Angels jinxed? It certainly is beginning to look that way. Once again last year, the Angels were beset by an incredible array of crippling injuries—and it showed in the standings. At one point, manager Jim Fregosi, who himself has ulcers, ordered his troops not to get hurt anymore. "I told them, 'There's no more room on the disabled list,' " he recalls. "I said, 'If anybody else gets hurt, we'll have to do what they do to horses—shoot them.' "

Unfortunately it was not funny. Many feel the Angels' refusal to renegotiate with Nolan Ryan may have undermined the morale of the team. "When he left," says Baylor, "the backbone of the staff dissolved." Whatever the explanation, the Angels have spent millions signing free agents and have accomplished little. Without a dependable pitching staff, they don't appear able to make amends this year.

CALIFORNIA ANGELS 1981 ROSTER

MANAGER Jim Fregosi
Coaches—Bobby Knoop, Preston Gomez, Tom Morgan, Bob Clear, Jimmy Reese, Merv Rettenmund

PITCHERS

No.	Name	1980 Club	W-L	IP	SO	ERA	B-T	Ht.	Wt.	Born
46	Aase, Don	California	8-13	175	74	4.06	R-R	6-3	195	9/8/54 Orange, CA
33	Barr, Jim	California	1-4	68	22	5.56	R-R	6-3	215	2/10/48 Lynwood, CA
48	Botting, Ralph	S. Lake City	15-8	173	87	5.57	L-L	6-0	195	5/12/55 Houlton, ME
		California	0-3	26	12	5.88				
–	Brown, Steve	El Paso	14-12	209	130	3.65	R-R	6-5	200	2/12/57 San Francisco, CA
–	D'Acquisto, John	SD-Mont.	2-5	88	59	3.38	R-R	6-3	205	12/24/51 San Diego, CA
43	Dorsey, Jim	S. Lake City	14-7	173	109	4.01	R-R	6-2	190	8/2/55 Chicago, IL
		California	1-2	16	8	9.00				
–	Eddy, Steve	S. Lake City	8-12	158	45	5.53	R-R	6-2	185	8/21/57 Sterling, IL
37	Frost, Dave	California	4-8	78	28	5.31	R-R	6-6	235	11/17/52 Long Beach, CA
41	Hassler, Andy	Pittsburgh	0-0	12	4	3.75	L-L	6-5	215	10/18/51 Texas City, TX
		California	5-1	83	75	2.49				
24	Kison, Bruce	California	3-6	73	28	4.93	R-R	6-4	173	2/8/50 Pasco, WA
42	Knapp, Chris	California	2-11	117	46	6.15	R-R	6-5	200	9/16/53 Cherry Point, NC
17	LaRoche, Dave	California	3-5	128	89	4.08	L-L	6-2	195	5/14/48 Colorado Springs, CO
27	Martinez, Fred	California	7-9	149	57	4.53	R-R	6-3	190	3/15/57 Los Angeles, CA
39	Montague, John	California	4-2	74	22	5.11	R-R	6-2	205	9/12/47 Newport News, VA
47	Schuler, Dave	S. Lake City	11-4	71	42	2.28	R-L	6-4	211	10/4/53 Framingham, MA
		California	0-1	13	7	3.46				
40	Tanana, Frank	California	11-12	204	113	4.15	L-L	6-3	195	7/3/53 Detroit, MI
–	Witt, Mike	El Paso	5-5	70	39	5.81	R-R	6-7	185	8/20/60 Fullerton, CA
		Salinas	7-3	90	76	2.10				
–	Zahn, Geoff	Minnesota	14-18	233	96	4.40	L-L	6-0	175	12/19/46 Baltimore, MD

CATCHERS

No.	Name	1980 Club	H	HR	RBI	Pct.	B-T	Ht.	Wt.	Born
–	Bishop, Mike	S. Lake City	11	1	7	.344	R-R	6-2	188	11/5/58 Santa Maria, CA
		El Paso	159	33	104	.325				
23	Donohue, Tom	California	41	2	14	.188	R-R	6-0	195	11/15/52 Westbury, NY
9	Downing, Brian	California	27	2	25	.290	R-R	5-10	200	10/9/50 Los Angeles, CA
–	Harper, Brian	El Paso	114	12	66	.285	R-R	6-2	195	10/16/59 Los Angeles, CA
8	Skaggs, Dave	Balt-Cal	14	1	9	.197	R-R	6-2	205	6/12/51 Santa Monica, CA

INFIELDERS

No.	Name	1980 Club	H	HR	RBI	Pct.	B-T	Ht.	Wt.	Born
–	Bertoni, Jeff	S. Lake City	85	4	43	.287	R-R	6-2	180	8/3/55 Bakersfield, CA
–	Burleson, Rick	Boston	179	8	51	.278	R-R	5-10	160	4/29/51 Lynwood, CA
19	Campaneris, Bert	California	53	2	18	.252	R-R	5-10	160	3/9/42 Cuba
29	Carew, Rod	California	179	3	59	.331	L-R	6-0	182	10/1/45 Panama
4	Grich, Bobby	California	135	14	62	.271	R-R	6-2	190	1/15/49 Muskegon, MI
18	Harris, John	S. Lake City	172	17	98	.333	L-L	6-3	215	9/13/54 Portland, OR
		California	12	2	7	.293				
–	Hobson, Butch	Boston	74	11	39	.228	R-R	6-1	190	8/17/51 Tuscaloosa, AL
2	Patek, Fred	California	72	5	34	.264	R-R	5-6	150	10/9/44 Oklahoma City, OK
–	Sconiers, Daryl	El Paso	187	15	87	.370	L-L	6-2	185	10/3/58 San Bernardino, CA
33	Thompson, Jason	Det-Cal	126	21	90	.288	L-L	6-4	220	7/6/54 Hollywood, CA
31	Thon, Dickie	S. Lake City	61	2	28	.394	R-R	5-11	150	6/20/58 South Bend, IN
		California	68	0	15	.255				

OUTFIELDERS

No.	Name	1980 Club	H	HR	RBI	Pct.	B-T	Ht.	Wt.	Born
25	Baylor, Don	California	85	5	51	.250	R-R	6-1	195	6/28/49 Austin, TX
–	Beniquez, Juan	Seattle	54	6	21	.228	R-R	5-11	165	5/13/50 San Sebastian, PR
–	Brunansky, Tom	S. Lake City	11	1	8	.344	R-R	6-4	205	8/20/60 Covina, CA
		El Paso	160	24	97	.323				
32	Clark, Bobby	S. Lake City	39	4	21	.345	R-R	6-0	190	6/13/55 Sacramento, CA
		California	60	5	23	.230				
15	Ford, Dan	California	63	7	26	.279	R-R	6-1	185	5/19/52 Los Angeles, CA
20	Harlow, Larry	California	83	4	27	.276	L-L	6-2	176	11/13/51 Colorado Springs, CO
14	Kubski, Gil	S. Lake City	146	8	54	.307	L-R	6-3	185	10/12/54 Longview, TX
		California	16	0	6	.254				
26	Rudi, Joe	California	88	16	53	.237	R-R	6-2	200	9/7/46 Modesto, CA

ANGELS PROFILES

DON BAYLOR 31 6-1 195 Bats R Throws R

Hampered by injuries in 1980 after banner season in '79 . . . Played more than a month with a busted hand . . . When he came back, he lacked his old pop at the plate . . . Booed by the fans and the Angels' front office . . . "There's nothing I can do." . . . Born June 28, 1949, in Austin, Tex. . . . A great competitor, comes to play . . . Rivals say "He'll beat you any way he can." . . . Will even fake a leg injury, then try to steal . . . "He's a man's man," says sportscaster Dick Enberg . . . Earl Weaver informed him early in his career that he could be the MVP by 1978 . . . Weaver only missed by one year . . . Has finally been recognized as an outstanding player, although he has been one for several years.

Year	Club	Pos.	G	AB	R	H	2B	3B	HR	RBI	SB	Avg.
1970	Baltimore	OF	8	17	4	4	0	0	0	4	1	.235
1971	Baltimore	OF	1	2	0	0	0	0	0	1	0	.000
1972	Baltimore	OF-1B	102	319	33	81	13	3	11	38	24	.254
1973	Baltimore	OF-1B	118	405	64	116	20	4	11	51	32	.286
1974	Baltimore	OF-1B	137	489	66	133	22	1	10	59	29	.272
1975	Baltimore	OF-1B	145	524	79	148	21	6	25	76	32	.282
1976	Oakland	OF-1B	157	595	85	147	25	1	15	68	52	.247
1977	California	OF-1B	154	561	87	141	27	0	25	75	26	.251
1978	California	OF-1B	158	591	103	151	26	0	34	99	22	.255
1979	California	OF-1B	162	628	120	186	33	3	36	139	22	.296
1980	California	OF-1B	90	340	39	85	12	2	5	51	6	.250
	Totals		1252	4472	680	1192	199	20	172	661	246	.267

GEOFF ZAHN 34 6-0 175 Bats L Throws L

Won a $200,000 contract when he took the Twins to arbitration prior to 1980 season . . . And then signed $1 million, three-year contract with Angels after playing out option . . . Had been released by Cubs in 1976 and signed for paltry $38,000 with Minnesota . . . Pitched better last year than his 14-18 record indicates . . . "It definitely was a weird season for me." . . . Relies mainly on sinking fastball . . . Born Dec. 19, 1946, in Baltimore . . . Has pleasant sense of humor but, unlike many lefthanders, he's no flake . . . Deeply religious . . .

Was star at University of Michigan . . . Was one of winningest lefthanders in Twins' history.

Year	Club	G	IP	W	L	Pct.	SO	BB	H	ERA
1973	Los Angeles	6	13	1	0	1.000	9	2	5	1.38
1974	Los Angeles	21	80	3	5	.375	33	16	78	2.03
1975	L.A.-Chi. (NL)	18	66	2	8	.200	22	31	69	4.64
1976	Chicago (NL)	3	8	0	1	.000	4	2	16	11.25
1977	Minnesota	34	198	12	14	.462	88	66	234	4.68
1978	Minnesota	35	252	14	14	.500	106	81	260	3.04
1979	Minnesota	26	169	13	7	.650	58	41	181	3.57
1980	Minnesota	38	233	14	18	.438	96	66	273	4.40
	Totals	181	1019	59	67	.468	416	305	1116	3.82

DAVE LaROCHE 32 6-2 195 — Bats L Throws L

Pressed into service as a starting pitcher, broke team mark for most games set by Nolan Ryan . . . Born May 14, 1948, in Colorado Springs . . . Was outstanding reliever in '78 but plagued by bad luck in '79 . . . Depends mainly on his fastball . . . Came up through Angels' farm system but was traded to Minnesota . . . Bounced from Twins to Cubs to Indians before returning to Angels . . . Twice has been named to A.L. All-Star team.

Year	Club	G	IP	W	L	Pct.	SO	BB	H	ERA
1970	California	38	50	4	1	.800	44	21	41	3.42
1971	California	56	72	5	1	.833	63	27	55	2.50
1972	Minnesota	62	95	5	7	.417	79	39	72	2.84
1973	Chicago (NL)	45	54	4	1	.800	34	29	55	5.83
1974	Chicago (NL)	49	92	5	6	.455	49	47	103	4.79
1975	Cleveland	61	82	5	3	.625	94	57	61	2.20
1976	Cleveland	61	96	1	4	.200	104	49	57	2.25
1977	Clev.-Cal.	59	100	8	7	.533	79	44	79	3.51
1978	California	59	96	10	9	.526	70	48	73	2.81
1979	California	53	86	7	11	.389	59	32	107	5.55
1980	California	52	128	3	5	.375	89	39	122	4.08
	Totals	595	951	57	55	.509	764	432	825	3.57

FRANK TANANA 27 6-3 195 — Bats L Throws L

No longer Fast Frankie, the overpowering pitcher . . . Now must survive on finesse . . . His fastball now in 88 mph range . . . Grew angry when he was banished to the bullpen . . . "I'm a pawn in a chess game. I'm not the king, just part of the game." . . . Rejected the Angels' appeal that he go to Salt Lake City to get his act together . . . "They have given up on me and I don't understand why!" . . . Born July 3, 1953, in Detroit . . . Pitched better late in season . . . "I decided to have some fun. I went back to being my old self." . . . Claims all he needs is to get his old confidence back.

Year	Club	G	IP	W	L	Pct.	SO	BB	H	ERA
1973	California................	4	26	2	2	.500	22	8	20	3.12
1974	California................	39	269	14	19	.424	180	77	262	3.11
1975	California................	34	257	16	9	.640	269	73	211	2.63
1976	California................	34	288	19	10	.655	261	73	212	2.44
1977	California................	31	241	15	9	.625	205	61	201	2.54
1978	California................	33	239	18	12	.600	137	60	239	3.65
1979	California................	18	90	7	5	.583	46	25	93	3.90
1980	California................	32	204	11	12	.478	113	45	223	4.15
	Totals..................	225	1614	102	78	.567	1233	422	1461	3.08

BOBBY GRICH 32 6-2 190 Bats R Throws R

Sat down and had a talk with himself after slow start . . . "I told myself, 'It looks like you're gone if you don't have a good second half.' " . . . Then he went on a batting binge, getting 5 HRs and 16 RBI in July to hike his batting average 28 points . . . Born Jan. 15, 1949, in Muskegon, Mich. . . . Owns a luxurious condominium in Belmont Shores, Calif., and another in Palm Springs . . . "I don't want to be traded" . . . Occasionally bothered by stiffness in his back but still a fine fielder . . . "I still enjoy playing and the travel" . . . Would like to play three more years . . . Firm believer in "The Power of Positive Thinking." . . . Has converted one of his bedrooms into a weight room so he can work out at home.

Year	Club	Pos.	G	AB	R	H	2B	3B	HR	RBI	SB	Avg.
1970	Baltimore.......	SS-2B-3B	30	95	11	20	1	3	0	8	1	.211
1971	Baltimore.......	SS-2B	7	30	3	9	0	0	1	6	1	.300
1972	Baltimore.......	SS-2B-1B-3B	133	460	66	128	21	3	12	50	13	.278
1973	Baltimore.......	2B	162	581	82	146	29	7	12	50	17	.251
1974	Baltimore.......	2B	160	582	92	152	29	6	19	82	17	.261
1975	Baltimore.......	2B	150	524	81	136	26	4	13	57	14	.262
1976	Baltimore.......	2B-3B	144	518	93	138	31	4	13	54	14	.266
1977	California.......	SS	52	181	24	44	6	0	7	23	6	.243
1978	California.......	2B	144	487	68	122	16	2	6	42	4	.251
1979	California.......	2B	153	534	78	157	30	5	30	101	1	.294
1980	California.......	2B	150	498	60	135	22	2	14	62	3	.271
	Totals..........		1285	4490	663	1187	211	36	127	534	91	.264

ROD CAREW 35 6-0 182 Bats L Throws R

Stopped talking to press in 1980 because he felt he was getting too much blame for collapse of the Angels . . . Has been hampered by injuries since coming to California . . . Seven-times the A.L. batting king . . . Described as "Picasso at the plate." . . . Born Oct. 1, 1945, in Gatun, Panama Canal Zone . . . Has the uncanny ability to stroke the ball just out of the reach of fielders . . . Also an excellent bunter which helps him avoid slumps . . . Was named the top hitter of the seventies, compiling a .343 average during that decade . . . May lead the league in unpublicized hospital visits . . . "I could always hit a baseball." . . . Was A.L. Rookie of the Year with Twins in 1967 and MVP in '77 . . . Would like to get 3,000 hits . . . "I enjoy playing."

Year	Club	Pos.	G	AB	R	H	2B	3B	HR	RBI	SB	Avg.
1967	Minnesota	2B	137	514	66	150	22	7	8	51	5	.292
1968	Minnesota	2B-SS	127	461	46	126	27	2	1	42	12	.273
1969	Minnesota	2B	123	458	79	152	30	4	8	56	19	.332
1970	Minnesota	2B-1B	51	191	27	70	12	3	4	28	4	.366
1971	Minnesota	2B-3B	147	577	88	177	16	10	2	48	6	.307
1972	Minnesota	2B	142	535	61	170	21	6	0	51	12	.318
1973	Minnesota	2B	149	580	98	203	30	11	6	62	41	.350
1974	Minnesota	2B	153	599	86	218	30	5	3	55	38	.364
1975	Minnesota	2B-1B	143	535	89	192	24	4	14	80	35	.359
1976	Minnesota	1B-2B	156	605	97	200	29	12	9	90	49	.331
1977	Minnesota	1B-2B	155	616	128	239	38	16	14	100	23	.388
1978	Minnesota	1B-2B-OF	152	564	85	188	26	10	5	70	27	.333
1979	California	1B	110	409	78	130	15	3	3	44	18	.318
1980	California	1B	144	540	74	179	34	7	3	59	23	.331
	Totals		1889	7184	1102	2394	354	100	80	836	312	.333

LARRY HARLOW 29 6-2 176 Bats L Throws L

Did a Clark Kent routine in 1980, a transformation that makes him a strong man with bulging chest and biceps . . . "I took up weight-lifting." . . . That decision may have saved his career . . . Now much more powerful . . . Usually gets off to a fast start . . . Born Nov. 13, 1951, in Colorado Springs . . . Tried to develop "inside-out swing," to help him handle high pitches . . . "Defense is my strong point." . . . Can play all three outfield positions . . . Has been striving to achieve consistency at the plate . . . Acquired from Baltimore Orioles.

Year	Club	Pos.	G	AB	R	H	2B	3B	HR	RBI	SB	Avg.
1975	Baltimore	OF	4	3	1	1	0	0	0	0	0	.333
1977	Baltimore	OF	46	48	4	10	0	1	0	0	6	.208
1978	Baltimore	OF	147	460	67	112	25	1	8	26	14	.243
1979	Balt.-Cal.	OF	100	200	27	48	9	2	0	15	2	.240
1980	California	OF	109	301	47	83	13	4	4	27	3	.276
	Totals		406	1012	146	254	47	8	12	68	25	.251

JASON THOMPSON 26 6-4 220 Bats L Throws L

Found happiness after trade to Angels by Tigers in late May . . . Also began to hit with gusto . . . Was offered uniform No. 30, the same number he wore with the Tigers, but asked for No. 22 instead . . . Pointed out No. 30 had been worn with distinction in California for a number of years by a fellow named Nolan Ryan . . . Born July 6, 1954, in Hollywood, Calif. . . . A solid, all-around performer for Angels . . . "In Detroit, they always wanted me to pull, be a power hitter. That's not my style." . . . Angels' owner Gene Autry had always regretted fact his team let Thompson, a home-grown player, get away . . . Was completely ignored by the Central Scouting Bureau while in college . . . Can play 1B or DH.

Year	Club	Pos.	G	AB	R	H	2B	3B	HR	RBI	SB	Avg.
1976	Detroit.........	1B	123	412	45	90	12	1	17	54	2	.218
1977	Detroit.........	1B	158	585	87	158	24	5	31	105	0	.270
1978	Detroit.........	1B	153	589	79	169	25	3	26	96	0	.287
1979	Detroit.........	1B	145	492	58	121	16	1	20	79	2	.246
1980	Det.-Calif.	1B	138	438	69	126	19	0	21	90	2	.288
	Totals..........		717	2516	338	664	96	10	115	424	6	.264

RICK BURLESON 29 5-10 160 Bats R Throws R

May be best all-around shortstop in the league . . . Traded to Angels when Red Sox felt he would play out option with them . . . Didn't get the publicity of Jim Rice or Fred Lynn or Yaz, but gets the job done . . . Born April 29, 1951, in Lynwood, Calif. . . . Was hitting .203 on May 1. Then went on a tear, raising average to .277 . . . Went 5-for-6 against A's–the first Boston player ever to enjoy a five-hit game . . . A tremendous competitor . . . "Every time he makes an out, he looks like he wants to eat the bat," said Don Zimmer . . . Has a knack for being in the right place at the right time . . . Gets to many balls other shortstops can't touch . . . Known as "The Rooster" because of his aggressive nature.

Year	Club	Pos.	G	AB	R	H	2B	3B	HR	RBI	SB	Avg.
1974	Boston.........	SS-2B-3B	114	384	36	109	22	0	4	44	3	.284
1975	Boston.........	SS	158	580	66	146	25	1	6	62	8	.252
1976	Boston.........	SS	152	540	75	157	27	1	7	42	14	.291
1977	Boston.........	SS	154	663	80	194	36	7	3	52	13	.293
1978	Boston.........	SS	145	626	75	155	32	5	5	49	8	.248
1979	Boston.........	SS	153	627	93	174	32	5	5	60	9	.278
1980	Boston.........	SS	155	644	89	179	29	2	8	51	12	.278
	Totals..........		1031	4064	514	1114	203	21	38	360	67	.274

JOE RUDI 34 6-2 200 Bats R Throws R

Hit in 1980 like he did in World Championship years with the A's . . . Credits his yogurt diet with his improvement . . . "Once you have a little yogurt, you can't eat much more" . . . Gentleman Joe . . . Born Sept. 7, 1946, in Modesto, Calif. . . . Former batting coach Deron Johnson told him to move closer to plate . . . That helped . . . "I don't think he realized how quick his bat is," said Johnson . . . Signed with Angels as free agent in winter of '76 but was soon befelled by injury . . . One of the hardest workers on the team . . . Has hit a dozen grand slams–tops among all active players in the league . . . Has excellent ratio of RBI-per-times-at-bat.

Year	Club	Pos.	G	AB	R	H	2B	3B	HR	RBI	SB	Avg.
1967	Kansas City	1B-OF	19	43	4	8	2	0	0	1	0	.186
1968	Oakland	OF	68	181	10	32	5	1	1	12	1	.177
1969	Oakland	OF-1B	35	122	10	23	3	1	2	6	1	.189
1970	Oakland	OF-1B	106	350	40	108	23	2	11	42	3	.309
1971	Oakland	OF-1B	127	513	62	137	23	4	10	52	3	.267
1972	Oakland	OF-1B	147	593	94	181	32	9	19	75	3	.305
1973	Oakland	OF-1B	120	437	53	118	25	1	12	66	0	.270
1974	Oakland	OF-1B	158	593	73	174	39	4	22	99	2	.293
1975	Oakland	1B-OF	126	468	66	130	26	6	21	75	2	.278
1976	Oakland	OF-1B	130	500	54	135	32	3	13	94	6	.270
1977	California	OF	64	242	48	64	13	2	13	53	1	.264
1978	California	OF-1B	133	497	58	127	27	1	17	79	2	.256
1979	California	OF-1B	90	330	35	80	11	3	11	61	0	.242
1980	California	OF-1B	104	372	42	88	17	1	16	53	1	.237
	Totals		1427	5241	649	1405	278	38	168	768	25	.268

TOP PROSPECT

BOBBY CLARK 25 6-0 190 **Bats R Throws R**

Seems destined for future stardom . . . Combines speed and power . . . "Watch the pop in his bat," says Jim Fregosi . . . Almost won a job last spring . . . Born June 13, 1955, in Sacramento, Cal. . . . Outstanding hitter in minor leagues . . . A centerfielder in the minors, can also play left . . . "All I want to do is contribute and I feel I'm ready to do that."

MANAGER JIM FREGOSI: Rumored to be in serious trouble when Angels collapsed in 1980 . . . Yet managed to keep his sense of humor . . . When he found out Angels had enlarged his office while the team was on the road, he quipped, "Either they think I'm doing a helluva job or they're looking for a fatter manager." . . . Born April 4, 1942, in San Francisco . . . Guided Angels to Western Division title in '79 despite a rash of 47 injuries . . . Had to use 81 different lineups

. . . Personally has had to battle serious stomach problems . . . "I advocate togetherness" . . . "He's the best young manager I've ever seen," says Sparky Anderson . . . Spent 18 seasons in the big leagues as a player, achieving his greatest glory while with Angels . . . Has long been a favorite of owner Gene Autry . . . Began thinking about becoming a manger when he was 22.

GREATEST TEAM

All of the millions California Angels owner Gene Autry had invested in free agents finally paid dividends in 1979. But those rewards didn't come easily.

Perennial batting champ Rod Carew, acquired from the Minnesota Twins during the off-season, got hurt. So did Dan Ford, Rick Miller and Frank Tanana.

Of the pitchers, only Nolan Ryan, Dave Frost and rookie Mark Clear enjoyed respectable years.

But, in spite of all of that adversity, the Angels finally finished first for the first time in the American League West.

They did so because Don Baylor put together a sensational season, batting .296 with 36 HRs, 139 RBI, and 22 stolen bases to reign as the AL's MVP.

They won because of Bobby Grich and Brian Downing, Willie Mays Aikens, Carney Lansford and Dan Ford.

And they won because manager Jim Fregosi, in his first full season on the job, keep himself and his ballclub cool in spite of 47 injuries and an unsightly 4.34 team ERA.

ALL-TIME ANGEL LEADERS

BATTING: Rod Carew, .331, 1980
HRs: Leon Wagner, 37, 1962
Bobby Bonds, 37, 1977
RBIs: Don Baylor, 139, 1979
STEALS: Mickey Rivers, 70, 1975
WINS: Clyde Wright, 22, 1970
Nolan Ryan, 22, 1974
TRIKEOUTS: Nolan Ryan, 383, 1973

CHICAGO WHITE SOX

(Editor's note: Efforts to achieve an approved sale of the White Sox were continuing at press time.)

TEAM DIRECTORY: Pres.: Bill Veeck; VP: Roland Hemond; Bus. Mgr.: Rudy Schaffer; Dir. Player Development: Paul Richards; Pub. Rel.: Chuck Shriver; Trav. Sec.: Glen Rosenbaum; Mgr.: Tony LaRussa. Home: Comiskey Park (44,492). Field distances: 352, l.f. line; 375, l.c.; 445, c.f.; 375, r.c.; 352, r.f. line. Spring training: Sarasota, Fla.

SCOUTING REPORT

HITTING: Reserve outfielder Wayne Nordhagen summed it up best. "Remember," he said, "we're not the 1927 Yankees." That's for sure. The White Sox, who outhit only Toronto and Seattle last season, did make an effort to juice up their offense during the winter, signing free-agent speedster Ron LeFlore. LeFlore stole more bases (97) than the entire Chisox team (66) last year and he will put some life in their attack.

He may also make life miserable for manager Tony LaRussa with his off-the-field shenanigans. The Expos, who let LeFlore go, claimed he caused more problems than he solved. But the White Sox scored fewer runs than any team in the league last year and they are willing to try anything to alter that statistic. Chet Lemon (.292, 11 HRs, 51 RBI) and Lamar Johnson (.277, 13 HRs, 81 RBI) will again have to provide most of the muscle.

PITCHING: "We have the best pitching staff in baseball," lamented Sox owner Bill Veeck. "They just don't get the chance to pitch against the White Sox." Indeed, the White Sox hurlers are good. And young. Britt Burns (15-13 with a 2.84 ERA) is one of most promising young lefthanders in the league. In addition, the Chisox still have Ken Kravec (3-6), Mike Proly (5-10), Steve Trout (9-16), Dick Dotson (12-10) and Lamarr Hoyt (9-3).

Given better support, their numbers would undoubtedly be better. In the bullpen, the White Sox will again rely upon rejuvenated Ed Farmer, who was 7-9 with 30 saves last season. Remember: Good pitching is supposed to beat good hitting every time.

FIELDING: Aside from the diving stops of first baseman Mike Squires, the White Sox did little to brag about defensively last year. The signing of free-agent catcher Jim Essian will help

Ron LeFlore will add speed to the White Sox attack.

some, but LeFlore won't improve things in the outfield. The White Sox, who led the league by a mile with 171 errors last year, remain weak up the middle, where it hurts the most.

OUTLOOK: Given a half-dozen dependable everyday players, the White Sox would undoubtedly be in contention. But without them, it will be a struggle to finish fifth again this year. The pitching is willing, but the support, both offensively and defensively, remains weak. And one has to wonder how LaRussa will handle LeFlore. One also has to wonder about the future of this franchise. Bill Veeck wanted to sell, claiming he couldn't cope with today's skyrocketing prices. But the league rejected Edward DeBartolo's bid to buy the club. So where does that leave Veeck? Certainly not any richer than he was last fall when he tried to sell. And where does that leave the White Sox? Certainly not much better off than they were a year ago.

CHICAGO WHITE SOX 1981 ROSTER

MANAGER Tony LaRussa

Coaches—Loren Babe, Orlando Cepeda, Art Kusnyer, Minnie Minoso, Vada Pinson, Ron Schueler, Bobby Winkles

PITCHERS

No.	Name	1980 Club	W-L	IP	SO	ERA	B-T	Ht.	Wt.	Born
52	Barnes, Richard	Iowa	3-12	123	59	5.08	R-L	6-4	180	7/11/59 Palm Beach, FL
–	Barnicle, Theodore	Glens Falls	5-2	67	40	4.43	R-L	6-0	175	11/20/53 Boston, MA
		Iowa	5-0	37	34	3.41				
46	Barrios, Francisco	Chicago (AL)	1-1	16	2	5.06	R-R	6-3	195	6/10/53 Mexico
		Appleton	2-0	13	5	0.69				
		Iowa	0-0	3	0	15.00				
30	Baumgarten, Ross	Chicago (AL)	2-12	136	66	3.44	L-L	6-1	180	5/27/55 Highland Park, IL
40	Burns, Britt	Chicago (AL)	15-13	238	133	2.84	R-L	6-5	215	6/8/59 Houston, TX
49	Dotson, Richard	Chicago (AL)	12-10	198	109	4.27	R-R	6-0	185	1/10/59 Cincinnati OH
–	Eduardo, Hector	Springfield	8-13	148	108	5.35	R-R	6-6	184	4/10/54 Dominican Republic
22	Farmer, Ed	Chicago (AL)	7-9	100	54	3.33	R-R	6-5	205	10/18/49 Evergreen Park, IL
–	Hickey, Kevin	Glens Falls	9-7	169	80	4.31	L-L	6-1	170	12/25/57 Chicago, IL
36	Hoffman, Guy	Iowa	6-3	75	56	3.60	L-L	5-9	175	7/9/56 Ottawa, IL
		Chicago (AL)	1-0	38	24	2.61				
31	Hoyt, Dewey	Iowa	5-2	62	36	2.90	R-R	6-3	190	1/1/55 Columbia, SC
		Chicago (AL)	9-3	112	55	4.58				
27	Kravec, Ken	Chicago (AL)	3-6	82	37	6.91	L-L	6-2	185	7/29/51 Cleveland, OH
24	Proly, Mike	Chicago (AL)	5-10	147	66	3.06	R-R	6-0	185	12/15/50 Jamaica, NY
35	Robinson, Dewey	Iowa	5-5	73	58	2.84	R-R	6-0	180	4/28/55 Evanston, IL
		Chicago (AL)	1-1	35	28	3.09				
–	Teutsch, Mark	Glens Falls	13-6	119	67	3.25	R-R	6-1	175	8/25/57 Plainfield, NJ
33	Trout, Steve	Chicago (AL)	9-16	200	89	3.69	L-L	6-4	195	7/20/57 Detroit, MI

CATCHERS

No.	Name	1980 Club	H	HR	RBI	Pct.	B-T	Ht.	Wt.	Born
38	Borgmann, Glenn	Iowa	67	6	36	.315	R-R	6-2	210	5/25/50 Paterson, NJ
		Chicago (AL)	19	2	14	.218				
19	Colbern, Mike	Iowa	66	8	34	.246	R-R	6-3	205	4/19/55 Santa Monica, CA
–	Essian, Jim	Oakland	66	5	29	.232	R-R	6-1	190	1/2/51 Detroit, MI
17	Foley, Marvis	Chicago (AL)	29	4	15	.212	L-R	6-0	195	8/29/53 Stanford, KY
		Glens Falls	19	1	9	.333				
		Iowa	16	3	9	.211				
6	Seilheimer, Rick	Glens Falls	60	9	46	.260	L-R	5-11	186	7/30/60 Brenham, TX
		Chicago (AL)	11	1	3	.212				

INFIELDERS

No.	Name	1980 Club	H	HR	RBI	Pct.	B-T	Ht.	Wt.	Born
–	Bernazard, Tony	Montreal	41	5	18	.224	B-R	5-9	164	8/24/56 Puerto Rico
13	Chappas, Harry	Chicago (AL)	8	0	2	.160	B-R	5-4	150	10/26/57 Mt. Ranier, MD
		Iowa	51	2	22	.206				
21	Cruz, Todd	Cal-Chi (AL)	79	3	23	.237	R-R	6-0	175	11/23/55 Highland Park, MI
23	Johnson, Lamar	Chicago (AL)	150	13	81	.277	R-R	6-2	225	9/2/50 Bessemer, AL
12	Morrison, Jim	Chicago (AL)	171	15	57	.283	R-R	5-11	178	9/23/52 Pensacola, FL
26	Mullins, Francis	Glens Falls	62	12	39	.300	R-R	6-0	180	5/14/57 Oakland, CA
		Iowa	51	6	35	.254				
		Chicago (AL)	12	0	3	.194				
11	Pryor, Greg	Chicago (AL)	81	1	29	.240	R-R	6-0	175	10/2/49 Marietta, OH
25	Squires, Mike	Chicago (AL)	97	2	33	.283	L-L	5-11	185	3/5/52 Kalamazoo, MI

OUTFIELDERS

No.	Name	1980 Club	H	HR	RBI	Pct.	B-T	Ht.	Wt.	Born
3	Baines, Harold	Chicago (AL)	125	13	49	.255	L-L	6-2	175	3/15/59 Easton, MD
32	Bosley, Thad	Chicago (AL)	33	2	14	.224	L-L	6-3	175	9/17/56 Oceanside, CA
7	Johnson, Randall	Glens Falls	80	25	70	.282	L-L	6-2	195	8/15/58 Miami, FL
		Chicago (AL)	4	0	3	.200				
		Iowa	14	1	8	.233				
47	Kuntz, Rusty	Iowa	99	11	54	.292	R-R	6-3	190	2/4/55 Orange, CA
		Chicago (AL)	14	0	3	.226				
–	LeFlore, Ron	Montreal	134	4	39	.257	R-R	6-0	200	6/16/52 Detroit, MI
44	Lemon, Chet	Chicago (AL)	150	11	51	.292	R-R	6-0	190	2/12/55 Jackson, MS
5	Molinaro, Bob	Chicago (AL)	100	5	36	.291	L-R	6-0	180	5/21/50 Newark, NJ
34	Moore, Junior	Iowa	29	3	22	.284	R-R	5-11	185	1/25/53 Waskom, TX
		Chicago (AL)	31	1	10	.256				
20	Nordhagen, Wayne	Chicago (AL)	115	15	59	.277	R-R	6-2	195	7/4/48 Thief River Falls, MN
18	Pruitt, Ron	Clev-Chi (AL)	32	2	15	.302	R-R	6-0	185	10/21/51 Flint, MI
48	Sutherland, Leon	Iowa	95	2	23	.260	L-L	5-10	165	4/6/58 Cuba
		Chicago (AL)	23	0	5	.258				

WHITE SOX PROFILES

BRITT BURNS 21 6-5 215 — Bats R Throws L

"It's still hard to believe he's come so far so fast," says Tony LaRussa . . . Made major league debut in 1978, two months after he graduated from high school . . . Has fine fastball . . . "He's the best-looking young lefthander I've seen in a long while," says Boston's Dwight Evans. "He doesn't know how good he is." . . . Born June 8, 1959, in Houston . . . May be the hardest thrower in AL since Terry Forster was healthy . . . A prolific eater . . . Once won 18 in a row while in high school . . . His ERA was 0.12 during that streak . . . Was Sox' third pick in June 1978 draft . . . Definitely a strikeout pitcher . . . Given first name is Robert.

Year	Club	G	IP	W	L	Pct.	SO	BB	H	ERA
1978	Chicago (AL)............	2	8	0	2	.000	3	3	14	12.38
1979	Chicago (AL)............	6	5	0	0	.000	2	1	10	5.40
1980	Chicago (AL)............	34	238	15	13	.536	133	63	213	2.84
	Totals..................	42	251	15	15	.500	138	67	237	3.19

ED FARMER 31 6-5 205 — Bats R Throws R

Embroiled in controversy following his on-the-field fight with Tigers' Al Cowens . . . Cowens charged the mound and Farmer filed assault charges . . . Warrant was later dropped after two men shook hands at home plate . . . Was Sox relief sensation until he was slowed at mid-season by a kidney disorder . . . Born Oct. 18, 1949, in Chicago . . . Was once known as "Eatin' Ed," but has shed that carefree attitude . . . Rarely smiles any more . . . A series of misfortunes has matured him . . . Has pitched for seven teams in his roller-coaster career and been rejected by six . . . Seems to have found home and happiness in Chicago . . . His favorite spectator sport is hockey.

Year	Club	G	IP	W	L	Pct.	SO	BB	H	ERA
1971	Cleveland................	43	79	5	4	.556	48	41	77	4.33
1972	Cleveland................	46	61	2	5	.286	33	27	51	4.43
1973	Cleve-Det................	40	62	3	2	.600	38	32	77	4.94
1974	Philadelphia.............	14	31	2	1	.667	20	27	41	8.42
1977	Baltimore................	1	0	0	0	.000	0	1	1	—
1978	Milwaukee................	3	11	1	0	1.000	6	4	7	0.82
1979	Texas-Chi (AL)...........	53	114	5	7	.412	73	53	96	3.00
1980	Chicago (AL).............	64	100	7	9	.438	54	56	92	3.33
	Totals...................	264	458	25	28	.472	272	241	442	4.09

MIKE PROLY 30 6-0 185 **Bats R Throws R**

Got reputation as a head-hunter after he hit two batters in two weeks . . . "He's not a bad actor," insists Tony LaRussa, "he's just a good competitor." . . . Paid his dues, spending eight years in pro ball . . . Was with Cardinals and Twins before joining Chisox as a free agent . . . Stopped Bosox on six hits in first big league start . . . Born Dec. 15, 1950, in Jamaica, N.Y. . . . Can either start or relieve, depending upon the situation . . . Has been hindered by injuries since joining Sox.

Year	Club	G	IP	W	L	Pct.	SO	BB	H	ERA
1976	St. Louis	14	17	1	0	1.000	4	6	21	3.71
1978	Chicago (AL)	14	66	5	2	.714	19	12	63	2.73
1979	Chicago (AL)	38	88	3	8	.273	32	40	89	3.89
1980	Chicago (AL)	62	147	5	10	.333	56	58	136	3.06
	Totals	128	318	14	20	.412	111	116	309	3.25

JIM ESSIAN 30 6-1 190 **Bats R Throws R**

Signed four-year contract worth over a million dollars after playing out option with A's . . . Had best major-league season with White Sox back in 1977, when he batted .273 with 10 HRs and 44 RBI . . . Slumped to .232 last year, but got big pact in free-agent draft because catchers are in great demand . . . Made big-league debut with Phillies back in 1972 . . . Can also fill in at first and third base . . . Born Jan. 21, 1951, in Detroit . . . Hard to strike out: he whiffed only 17 times in 285 at-bats last season.

Year	Club	Pos.	G	AB	R	H	2B	3B	HR	RBI	SB	Avg.
1973	Philadelphia	C	2	3	0	0	0	0	0	0	0	.000
1974	Philadelphia	C-1B-3B	17	20	1	2	0	0	0	0	0	.100
1975	Philadelphia	C	2	1	1	1	0	0	0	1	0	1.000
1976	Chicago (AL)	C-1B-3B	78	199	20	49	7	0	0	21	2	.246
1977	Chicago (AL)	C-3B	114	322	50	88	18	2	10	44	1	.273
1978	Oakland	C-1B-2B	126	278	21	62	9	1	3	26	2	.223
1979	Oakland	C-1B-3B	98	313	34	76	16	0	8	40	0	.243
1980	Oakland	C-1B-3B	87	285	19	66	11	0	5	29	1	.232
	Totals		524	1421	146	342	61	3	26	161	6	.241

LAMAR JOHNSON 30-6-2 225 **Bats R Throws R**

Chisox' lone legitimate slugger . . . Named A.L. Player of the Month in April . . . Once sang the national anthem before a game . . . Says having Chet Lemon batting behind him has helped his hitting . . . Got off to awesome start in '80 . . . Was leading league in five power categories and was close in a couple of others . . . Born Sept. 2, 1950, in Bessemer,

Ala. . . . Always has hit for average but RBIs have been lacking until now . . . Had never seen a major league game until he played in one . . . Feasted on Oriole pitching in '80 . . . Spent seven seasons in minors waiting for Dick Allen and Jim Spencer to move out of the way.

Year	Club	Pos.	G	AB	R	H	2B	3B	HR	RBI	SB	Avg.
1974	Chicago (AL)....	1B	10	29	1	10	0	0	0	2	0	.345
1975	Chicago (AL)....	1B	8	30	2	6	3	0	1	1	0	.200
1976	Chicago (AL)....	1B-OF	82	222	29	71	11	1	4	33	2	.320
1977	Chicago (AL)....	1B	118	374	52	113	12	5	18	65	1	.302
1978	Chicago (AL)....	1B	148	498	52	136	23	2	8	72	6	.273
1979	Chicago (AL)....	1B	133	479	60	148	29	1	12	74	8	.309
1980	Chicago (AL)....	1B	147	541	51	150	26	3	13	81	2	.277
	Totals..........		646	2173	247	634	104	12	56	328	19	.292

CHET LEMON 26 6-0 190 Bats R Throws R

Did not look like his old familiar self at the plate in '80 . . . "I need to find direction." . . . A fanatic during batting practice . . . "It takes a lot of work to get me going." . . . Some feel he may have been pressing because he is the Sox' only bona fide star . . . Born Feb. 12, 1955, in Jackson, Miss. . . . "Maybe subconsciously, my juices were flowing too much." . . . Thrived when elevated to lead-off spot late in the season . . . "I've got to stay within myself." . . . Was track and football star as well as baseball standout in high school . . . A's No. 1 draft pick in 1972.

Year	Club	Pos.	G	AB	R	H	2B	3B	HR	RBI	SB	Avg.
1975	Chicago (AL)....	3B-OF	9	35	2	9	2	0	0	1	1	.257
1976	Chicago (AL)....	OF	132	451	46	111	15	5	4	38	13	.246
1977	Chicago (AL)....	OF	150	553	99	151	38	4	19	67	8	.273
1978	Chicago (AL)....	OF	105	357	51	107	24	6	13	55	5	.300
1979	Chicago (AL)....	OF	148	556	79	177	44	2	17	86	7	.318
1980	Chicago (AL)....	OF	147	514	76	150	32	6	11	51	6	.292
	Totals..........		691	2466	353	705	155	23	64	298	40	.286

JIM MORRISON 28 5-11 178 Bats R Throws R

Good RBI man . . . Once went 0-for-31 while with Phillies . . . How did he break out of the slump? "I didn't. They took me out of the lineup for life." . . . Goes into each game with intense mental preparedness . . . Drilled in ribs by Yankees' Ron Guidry, he trapped the ball against his side with his arm and fired it back to the pitcher as he trotted to first . . . Born Sept. 23, 1952, in Pensacola, Fla. . . . Put sign "E-4" above his locker to remind himself of his stupid mistakes . . . Teammates call him "Iron Man." . . . "You can see the intensity in his eyes 20 minutes before a game and 20 minutes after," rivals say.

Year	Club	Pos.	G	AB	R	H	2B	3B	HR	RBI	SB	Avg.
1977	Philadelphia.....	3B	5	7	3	3	0	0	0	1	0	.429
1978	Philadelphia.....	2B-3B	53	108	12	17	1	1	3	10	1	.157
1979	Chicago (AL)....	2B-3B	67	240	38	66	14	0	14	35	11	.275
1980	Chicago (AL)....	2B-3B	162	604	66	171	40	0	15	57	9	.283
	Totals..........		287	959	119	257	55	1	32	103	21	.268

GREG PRYOR 31 6-0 175 Bats R Throws R

Opened season at shortstop, later moved to third . . . Finally found niche as utility player . . . "He's a man who has the rare ability to play three positions well," says Tony LaRussa . . . But he's not satisfied with that role . . . "If this were a world championship team I might look at it in a different light." . . . Born Oct. 2, 1949, in Marietta, Ohio . . . "I don't have great speed, but I'm sneaky." . . . Believes in himself as a clutch player . . . "I've proved I can play adequate shortstop." . . . Was two-time All-American in college . . . His father once played football for the Baltimore Colts.

Year	Club	Pos.	G	AB	R	H	2B	3B	HR	RBI	SB	Avg.
1976	Texas..........	2B-3B-SS	5	8	2	3	0	0	0	1	0	.375
1978	Chicago (AL)....	2B-SS-3B	82	222	27	58	11	0	2	15	3	.261
1979	Chicago (AL)....	SS-2B-3B	143	476	60	131	23	3	3	34	3	.275
1980	Chicago (AL)....	SS-2B-3B	122	338	32	81	18	4	1	29	2	.240
	Totals..........		352	1044	121	273	52	7	6	79	8	.261

MIKE SQUIRES 29 5-11 185 Bats L Throws L

Fast becoming famous for his diving catches at first base . . . Also displaying encouraging ability with the bat . . . Wasn't drafted until the 18th round after career at Western Michigan University . . . Born March 5, 1952, in Kalamazoo, Mich. . . . Set all sorts of fielding records while in minors . . . Once went 76 games without an error . . . Also had 33-game hitting streak in minors . . . Enjoyed banner night against Tigers in '79, with double and three singles . . . Can also steal a base when needed.

Year	Club	Pos.	G	AB	R	H	2B	3B	HR	RBI	SB	Avg.
1975	Chicago (AL)....	1B	20	65	5	15	0	0	0	4	3	.231
1977	Chicago (AL)....	1B	3	3	0	0	0	0	0	0	0	.000
1978	Chicago (AL)....	1B	46	150	25	42	9	2	0	19	4	.280
1979	Chicago (AL)....	1B-OF	122	295	44	78	10	1	2	22	15	.264
1980	Chicago (AL)....	1B-OF	131	343	38	97	11	3	2	33	8	.283
	Totals..........		322	856	112	232	30	6	4	78	30	.271

RON LeFLORE 30 6-0 200 Bats R Throws R

Signed multi-year $2.4 million pact after playing out option with Expos . . . Batted a mere .257 last year after .297 career mark in A.L., yet reached stolen base heights by swiping 97 to win blazing battle with Omar Moreno for N.L. honors . . . Credits synthetic turfs in league with giving him better acceleration . . . Salary request led to exodus from Detroit and free-agent declaration in Montreal . . . Born June 16, 1950, at Detroit . . . Learned to play game in prison . . . Tigers' Player of Year 1977-79 . . . Played only 134 minor league games before reaching bigs in '74 . . . Became superstar in '76 with .316 average, 58 steals . . . Had 30-game batting streak that year, longest in A.L. in 26 years . . . A.L. stolen base king in '78 . . . Broken hand limited him to base-running down the stretch in '80.

Year	Club	Pos.	G	AB	R	H	2B	3B	HR	RBI	SB	Avg.
1974	Detroit.........	OF	59	254	37	66	8	1	2	13	23	.260
1975	Detroit.........	OF	136	550	66	142	13	6	8	37	28	.258
1976	Detroit.........	OF	135	544	93	172	23	8	4	39	58	.316
1977	Detroit.........	OF	154	652	100	212	30	10	16	57	39	.325
1978	Detroit.........	OF	155	666	126	198	30	3	12	62	68	.297
1979	Detroit.........	OF	148	600	110	180	22	10	9	57	78	.300
1980	Montreal	OF	139	521	95	134	21	11	4	39	97	.257
	Totals.........		926	3787	627	1104	147	49	55	304	391	.292

TOP PROSPECTS

RICKY SEILHEIMER 20 5-11 186 Bats L Throws R

Chicago's catcher of the future . . . Has strong arm, but must learn to get rid of ball quicker . . . Spent six weeks with White Sox in '80 . . . "I'll be back." . . . Born Aug. 30, 1960, in Brenham, Tex. . . . Batted .212 in 20-game trial . . . Threw out only two of 30 runners . . . Sox No. 1 pick in June, 1979 . . . Planned to work on throwing during Instructional League.

LEON SUTHERLAND 22 5-10 165 Bats L Throws L

Summoned from Iowa in mid-August to inject spark of speed into somnolent Sox' attack . . . A 9.7 sprinter . . . Went 5-for-8 in first two games in big leagues . . . Born April 6, 1958, in Santiago, Cuba . . . Leading candidate for Sox' lead-off spot . . . Twice spoiled no-hit bids with late-inning hits . . . Stroked second pitch he saw in big leagues for a single.

MANAGER TONY LaRUSSA: The only lawyer managing in the major leagues . . . No less of an authority than Hall of Famer Al Lopez predicts someday Tony will be a big success as a manager . . . As a rookie manager in the minor leagues, he led Knoxville to the Southern League title by 14½ games . . . Promoted midway through the '79 season when Don Kessinger abruptly resigned . . . Born Oct. 4, 1944, in Tampa . . . Made pro debut as a player with Kansas City organization in 1962 . . . Saw service with Royals, Braves, Cubs and A's but spent most of his playing career in the minors . . . "My No. 1 goal is to build a championship." . . . Also managed in the winter leagues to learn his trade.

GREATEST TEAM

For four decades, the Chicago White Sox had known little but disappointment, distress and defeat. Then, in 1959, the Go-Go Sox finally did more than a few things right.

Led by MVP Nellie Fox, Luis Aparicio, 22-game winner Early Wynn, as well as Jim Landis, Sherm Lollar and relievers Gerry Staley and Turk Lown, the White Sox literally ran all the way to their first World Series since the appearance of the infamous Black Sox in 1919.

With wily Bill Veeck in the front office, and veteran Al Lopez calling the shots on the field, the upstart Chisox, who had been given little or no chance when the season began, ended the New York Yankees' stranglehold on the American League pennant.

Unfortunately, when they reached the World Series, their high-octane offense ran out of gas, as Los Angeles Dodgers' catcher John Roseboro and relief ace Larry Sherry spoiled what up to then had been a dream season for the White Sox.

ALL-TIME WHITE SOX LEADERS

BATTING: Luke Appling, .388, 1936
HRs: Dick Allen, 37, 1972
RBIs: Zeke Bonura, 138, 1936
STEALS: Wally Moses, 56, 1943
Luis Aparicio, 56, 1959
WINS: Ed Walsh, 40, 1908
STRIKEOUTS: Ed Walsh, 269, 1908

KANSAS CITY ROYALS

TEAM DIRECTORY: Pres.: Ewing Kauffman; VP-GM: Joe Burke; VP-Administration: Spencer Robinson; VP-Player Personnel: John Schuerholz; VP-Controller: Dale Rohr; Dir. Pub. Rel.: Dean Vogelaar; Trav. Sec.: Bill Beck; Mgr.: Jim Frey. Home: Royals Stadium (40,628). Field distances: 330, l.f. line; 385, l.c.; 410, c.f.; 385, r.c.; 330, r.f. line. Spring training: Fort Myers, Fla.

SCOUTING REPORT

HITTING: It's difficult to find fault with an attack that includes baseball's best hitter, George Brett (.390), and the game's most

George Brett can beat you with his glove, too.

exciting player, Willie Wilson (230 hits, 133 runs, 79 SB). No wonder the Royals were the top-hitting team in the league with a .286 average last season. In 30 years, no team had put on a show like that. The Royals also led the league in stolen bases with 185. And they were only shut out five times, the lowest such total in the league.

In addition to Brett, whose average was the best since Ted Williams hit .406 four decades ago, and Wilson (.326), the Royals feature John Wathan (.305), World Series hero Willie Aikens (.278, 20 HRs, 98 RBI), Clint Hurdle (.294) and Hal McRae (.297). With a lineup like that, the Royals will hardly miss Darrell Porter.

PITCHING: Kansas City's pitchers rarely overpower people. Usually they are not even particularly impressive. But they win. And with the Royals' offense you don't have to be Cy Young every night. Larry Gura (18-10), Rich Gale (13-9), Dennis Leonard (20-11), Renie Martin (10-10) and Paul Splittorff (14-11) are seldom spectacular.

But, with the help of Dan Quisenberry (12-7 plus 33 saves), they seem to get the job done more often than not. The Royals would like more pitching. They are the first to admit that. But they believe they can continue to get by until somebody better comes along.

FIELDING: The Royals finished in the middle of the pack defensively last year. But they remain fundamentally sound. Frank White is in a class by himself at second base and U.L. Washington is no slouch at short. Amos Otis is still one of the best in the outfield. That gives the Royals strength up the middle. And there is nothing wrong with the way Brett and Aikens play the field, either.

OUTLOOK: After coming so close last year, the Royals are more determined to go all the way. They overcame one stumbling block last October when they finally got by the New York Yankees. And last year's experience should make them a better ballclub, if they can get into the World Series again. However, that won't be easy. Brett can hardly be expected to hit .390 again and Wilson will be hard-pressed to match last season's sensational statistics. Meanwhile, Otis is unhappy about the proposed transfer of Wilson to centerfield, Wathan has to prove he can fill Porter's shoes for a full season, and Quisenberry still has to do it again.

KANSAS CITY ROYALS 1981 ROSTER

MANAGER Jim Frey
Coaches—Billy Connors, Gordy MacKenzie, Jose Martinez, Jim Schaffer

PITCHERS

No.	Name	1980 Club	W-L	IP	SO	ERA	B-T	Ht.	Wt.	Born
25	Brett, Ken	Omaha	0-0	9	2	4.00	L-L	5-11	190	9/18/48 Brooklyn, NY
		Kansas City	0-0	13	4	0.00				
28	Chamberlain, Craig	Kansas City	0-1	9	3	7.00	R-R	6-1	190	2/2/57 Hollywood, CA
		Omaha	11-10	170	81	4.76				
31	Christensen, Gary	Kansas City	3-0	31	16	5.23	L-L	6-5	212	5/5/53 Mineola, NY
		Omaha	2-4	41	37	2.41				
38	Gale, Rich	Kansas City	13-9	191	97	3.91	R-R	6-7	225	1/19/54 Littleton, NH
32	Gura, Larry	Kansas City	18-10	283	113	2.96	L-L	6-1	185	11/26/47 Joliet, IL
50	Jones, Mike	Jacksonville	13-6	158	116	3.87	L-L	6-5	226	7/30/59 Rochester, NY
		Kansas City	0-1	5	2	10.80				
—	Laskey, Bill	Omaha	5-8	145	77	4.16	R-R	6-5	190	12/20/57 Toledo, OH
22	Leonard, Dennis	Kansas City	20-11	280	155	3.79	R-R	6-1	190	5/8/51 Brooklyn, NY
27	Martin, Renie	Kansas City	10-10	137	68	4.40	R-R	6-4	185	8/30/55 Dover, DE
49	Morley, Mike	Omaha	2-2	38	14	3.08	B-L	5-11	181	1/18/59 Lansing, MI
29	Quisenberry, Dan	Kansas City	12-7	128	37	3.09	R-R	6-2	180	2/7/54 Santa Monica, CA
34	Splittorff, Paul	Kansas City	14-11	204	53	4.15	L-L	6-3	210	10/8/46 Evansville, IN
21	Twitty, Jeff	Omaha	6-3	48	24	1.88	L-L	6-2	180	11/10/57 Lancaster, SC
		Kansas City	2-1	22	9	6.14				

CATCHERS

No.	Name	1980 Club	H	HR	RBI	Pct.	B-T	Ht.	Wt.	Born
13	Gaudet, Jim	Evansville	10	0	2	.185	R-R	6-0	185	6/3/55 New Orleans, LA
		Omaha	67	4	29	.277				
9	Quirk, Jamie	Kansas City	45	5	21	.276	L-R	6-4	200	10/22/54 Whittier, CA
12	Wathan, John	Kansas City	138	6	58	.305	R-R	6-2	205	10/4/49 Cedar Rapids, IO

INFIELDERS

No.	Name	1980 Club	H	HR	RBI	Pct.	B-T	Ht.	Wt.	Born
24	Aikens, Willie	Kansas City	151	20	98	.278	L-R	6-2	220	10/14/54 Seneca, SC
23	Barranca, German	Omaha	69	3	26	.226	L-R	6-0	175	10/19/56 Mexico
		Kansas City	0	0	0	.000				
5	Brett, George	Kansas City	175	24	118	.390	L-R	6-0	200	5/15/53 Glendale, WVA
17	Castillo, Manny	Omaha	173	6	70	.289	B-R	5-9	160	4/1/57 Dominican Republic
		Kansas City	2	0	0	.200				
7	Chalk, Dave	Kansas City	42	1	20	.251	R-R	5-10	170	8/30/50 Del Rio, TX
53	Concepcion, Onex	Jacksonville	88	12	44	.322	R-R	5-6	160	10/5/58 Puerto Rico
		Omaha	59	4	34	.281				
		Kansas City	2	0	2	.133				
51	Heath, Kelly	Omaha	46	3	22	.253	R-R	5-7	155	9/4/57 Plattsburg, NY
		Jacksonville	63	5	27	.307				
—	Ireland, Tim	Omaha	133	12	63	.296	R-R	6-0	180	3/14/53 Oakland, CA
—	Johnson, Ronald	Jacksonville	139	23	104	.270	R-R	6-2	223	3/23/56 Long Beach, CA
—	May, Lee	Baltimore	54	7	31	.243	R-R	6-3	205	3/23/43 Birmingham, AL
18	Mulliniks, Rance	Kansas City	14	0	6	.259	L-R	6-0	170	1/15/56 Tulare, CA
52	Phelps, Ken	Omaha	130	23	72	.294	L-L	6-1	209	8/6/54 Seattle, WA
		Kansas City	0	0	0	.000				
1	Terrell, Jerry	Kansas City	1	0	0	.063	R-R	6-0	170	7/13/46 Waseca, MN
		Omaha	47	2	21	.288				
30	Washington, U.L.	Kansas City	150	6	53	.273	B-R	5-11	175	10/27/53 Atoka, OK
20	White, Frank	Kansas City	148	7	60	.264	R-R	5-11	170	9/4/50 Greenville, MS

OUTFIELDERS

No.	Name	1980 Club	H	HR	RBI	Pct.	B-T	Ht.	Wt.	Born
—	Garcia, Daniel	Omaha	130	1	49	.320	L-L	6-1	182	4/29/54 Brooklyn, NY
10	Hurdle, Clint	Kansas City	116	10	60	.294	L-R	6-3	195	7/30/57 Big Rapids, MI
11	McRae, Hal	Kansas City	145	14	83	.297	R-R	5-11	180	7/10/46 Avon Park, FL
—	Motley, Darryl	Ft. Myers	36	5	24	.310	R-R	5-9	196	1/21/60 Muskogee, OK
		Jacksonville	58	5	31	.319				
26	Otis, Amos	Kansas City	99	10	53	.251	R-R	5-11	166	4/26/47 Mobile, AL
6	Wilson, Willie	Kansas City	230	3	49	.326	B-R	6-3	190	7/9/55 Montgomery, AL

ROYAL PROFILES

DENNIS LEONARD 29 6-1 190 Bats R Throws R

One of most consistent winners in the league, even though he rarely gets credit for it . . . Mixes fine fastball, slider and curve and has good control of all . . . Beat Yankees in second game of playoff . . . Also won key game against Phillies in World Series . . . Put together a string of 23 scoreless innings in a row during regular season . . . Born May 8, 1951, in Brooklyn . . . Led the league in starts (38) in 1980 . . . Also ranked in Top 10 in innings pitched, shutouts and strikeouts . . . Was 13-4 after the All-Star break, and a key factor in Royals' drive to the division title . . . One of only two pitchers in league (Tommy John is the other) to win 20 or more in three of past four seasons.

Year	Club	G	IP	W	L	Pct.	SO	BB	H	ERA
1974	Kansas City..............	5	22	0	4	.000	8	12	28	5.32
1975	Kansas City..............	32	212	15	7	.682	146	90	212	3.78
1976	Kansas City..............	35	259	17	10	.630	150	70	247	3.51
1977	Kansas City..............	38	293	20	12	.625	244	79	246	3.04
1978	Kansas City..............	40	295	21	17	.553	183	78	283	3.33
1979	Kansas City..............	32	236	14	12	.538	126	56	226	4.08
1980	Kansas City..............	38	280	20	11	.645	155	80	271	3.79
	Totals..................	220	1597	107	73	.594	1012	465	1513	3.58

DAN QUISENBERRY 27 6-2 180 Bats R Throws R

The man who made the Royals' bullpen respectable during the regular season . . . Didn't fare nearly so well against the Phillies during the World Series—although he did lead his team in clever quips . . . "Quis" . . . A straight-arrow: Doesn't drink, smoke or swear . . . Made a bet with Clint Hurdle that he could go the entire season without cussing . . . Born Feb. 7, 1954, in Santa Monica, Calif. . . . Throws submarine-style, a la Kent Tekulve . . . Specializes in throwing ground balls . . . Worked with Tekulve during spring training . . . "He taught me to keep my body down, my weight on my back foot." . . . Threw overhanded until late in his college career . . . "I threw like every other kid." . . . Ignored in draft, but signed with Royals as a free agent.

Year	Club	G	IP	W	L	Pct.	SO	BB	H	ERA
1979	Kansas City..............	32	40	3	2	.600	13	7	42	3.15
1980	Kansas City..............	75	128	12	7	.632	37	27	129	3.09
	Totals..................	107	168	15	9	.625	50	34	171	3.11

JOHN WATHAN 31 6-2 205 — Bats R Throws R

One of Royals' unsung heroes in '80 . . . Did a remarkable job as Darrell Porter's replacement . . . Nicknamed "Duke" because of his imitations of actor John Wayne . . . Caught career-high 40 games in a row while Porter was out . . . Many thought he should have been behind the plate more during the World Series . . . Born Oct. 4, 1949, in Cedar Rapids, Ia. . . . Was Royals' No. 1 pick in January 1971 draft . . . Helped out in outfield, at first base, and as DH, after Porter's return . . . Credited with helping young pitchers mature . . . Among leading candidates for comeback of the year.

Year	Club	Pos.	G	AB	R	H	2B	3B	HR	RBI	SB	Avg.
1976	Kansas City.....	C-1B	27	42	5	12	1	0	0	5	0	.286
1977	Kansas City.....	C-1B	55	119	18	39	5	3	2	21	2	.328
1978	Kansas City.....	1B-C	67	190	19	57	10	1	2	28	2	.300
1979	Kansas City.....	1B-C-OF	90	199	26	41	7	3	2	28	2	.206
1980	Kansas City.....	1B-OF-C	126	453	57	138	14	7	6	58	17	.305
	Totals..........		365	1003	125	287	37	14	12	140	23	.286

GEORGE BRETT 27 6-0 200 — Bats L Throws R

The Man Who Almost Hit .400 . . . Went on an incredible batting spree after All-Star break . . . MVP . . . Probably best all-around hitter in the game . . . "I've seen Dave Parker and I've seen Dave Winfield, and George Brett is the best player in baseball," says Cardinals' manager Whitey Herzog, who used to manage the Royals . . . Won the AL playoff clincher with a three-run homer off Rich Gossage . . . Born May 15, 1953, in Glen Dale, W. Va. . . . Hampered by painful, well-publicized case of hemorrhoids during the World Series . . . When he's not hitting, often grabs a bat and beats a garbage can . . . "I'd rather play in a close game. When the game is on the line I have more concentration." . . . Nicknamed "Mullet." . . . "The man is going to go as far as any man can," says Clint Hurdle.

Year	Club	Pos.	G	AB	R	H	2B	3B	HR	RBI	SB	Avg.
1973	Kansas City.....	3B	13	40	2	5	2	0	0	0	0	.125
1974	Kansas City.....	3B-SS	133	457	49	129	21	5	2	47	8	.282
1975	Kansas City.....	3B-SS	159	634	84	195	35	13	11	89	13	.308
1976	Kansas City.....	3B-SS	159	645	94	215	34	14	7	67	21	.333
1977	Kansas City.....	3B-SS	139	564	105	176	32	13	22	88	14	.312
1978	Kansas City.....	3B-SS	128	510	79	150	45	8	9	62	23	.294
1979	Kansas City.....	3B-1B	154	645	119	212	42	20	23	107	17	.329
1980	Kansas City.....	3B	117	449	87	175	33	9	24	118	15	.390
	Totals..........		1002	3944	619	1257	244	82	98	578	111	.319

WILLIE AIKENS 26 6-2 220 **Bats L Throws R**

World Series hero, even though Royals lost to Phils . . . Hammered four home runs—one short of Reggie Jackson's record . . . Only man ever to hit two homers in two separate games of same Series . . . Full name: Willie Mays Aikens . . . So named because he was born shortly after Willie Mays' great catch in 1954 World Series . . . Would prefer people didn't use his middle name, though . . . Born Oct. 14, 1954, in Seneca, S.C. . . . Says his stuttering made life miserable as a youth . . . But showed his class and maturity in addressing the press during Series . . . Knee surgery during off-season reduced his effectiveness in '80 . . . Never too fast, now one of the slowest men in major leagues . . . A perfectionist, sometimes tries too hard . . . A streak hitter, capable of carrying a whole club when he's hot.

Year	Club	Pos.	G	AB	R	H	2B	3B	HR	RBI	SB	Avg.
1977	California.......	1B	42	91	5	18	4	0	0	6	1	.198
1979	California.......	1B	116	379	59	106	18	0	21	81	1	.280
1980	Kansas City.....	1B	151	543	70	151	24	0	20	98	1	.278
	Totals..........		309	1013	134	275	46	0	41	185	3	.271

FRANK WHITE 30 5-11 170 **Bats R Throws R**

Stole the show during the World Series with his superlative fielding, even though he didn't hit a lick . . . The best fielding second baseman in the game. Period . . . Was discovered at tryout for Royals' ill-fated baseball academy . . . Has been a major factor in the development of shortstop U.L. Washington . . . Born Sept. 4, 1950, in Greenville, Miss. . . . Has outstanding range and speed . . . Had one of his best years ever at the plate in '80 . . . Made only four errors after All-Star break, and none during final 35 games . . . Never played baseball in high school because his school didn't have a team.

Year	Club	Pos.	G	AB	R	H	2B	3B	HR	RBI	SB	Avg.
1973	Kansas City.....	SS-2B	51	139	20	31	6	1	0	5	3	.223
1974	Kansas City.....	2B-SS-3B	99	204	19	45	6	3	1	18	3	.221
1975	Kansas City.....	2B-3B-SS-C	111	304	43	76	10	2	7	36	11	.250
1976	Kansas City.....	2B-SS	152	446	39	102	17	6	2	46	20	.229
1977	Kansas City.....	2B-SS	152	474	59	116	21	5	5	50	23	.245
1978	Kansas City.....	2B	143	461	66	127	24	6	7	50	13	.275
1979	Kansas City.....	2B	127	467	73	124	26	4	10	48	28	.266
1980	Kansas City.....	2B	154	560	70	148	22	5	7	60	19	.264
	Totals..........		989	3055	389	769	132	32	39	313	120	.252

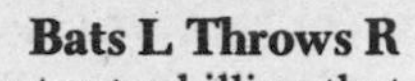

CLINT HURDLE 23 6-3 195 Bats L Throws R

Finally beginning to live up to star billing that was heaped upon him as a 19-year-old rookie phenom in 1977 . . . Hit .375 during playoff sweep over Yankees but was upset because he was platooned during World Series . . . Cocky, gregarious guy . . . Fun to be around . . . Believes he may have tried too hard to please first batting coach Charley Lau, then manager Whitey Herzog . . . "Everybody had an answer, but nobody had THE answer." . . . Booed during first two seasons . . . Born July 30, 1957, in Big Rapids, Mich. . . . Royals' No. 1 pick in June, 1975 . . . Just wants to be accepted as a bona fide big league star . . . "I am what I am."

Year	Club	Pos.	G	AB	R	H	2B	3B	HR	RBI	SB	Avg.
1977	Kansas City.....	OF	9	26	5	8	0	0	2	7	0	.308
1978	Kansas City.....	OF-3B-1B	133	417	48	110	25	5	7	56	1	.264
1979	Kansas City.....	OF-3B	59	171	16	41	10	3	3	30	0	.240
1980	Kansas City.....	OF	130	395	50	116	31	2	10	60	0	.294
	Totals..........		331	1009	119	275	66	10	22	153	1	.273

HAL McRAE 34 5-11 180 Bats R Throws R

Ended season expecting to be traded . . . "I just think they feel they can do without me." . . . Wanted Royals to renegotiate his $225,-000-a-year contract . . . They wouldn't . . . "I know I can hit." . . . Spends most of the game in the locker room, concentrating, when he's the DH . . . "I think about what I've got to do at the plate." . . . Born July 10, 1946, in Avon Park, Fla. . . . Intense competitor and an aggressive agitator in the clubhouse . . . Has been called a "dirty player," because he doesn't hesitate to bowl over opposing players who get in his way . . . One of 11 children . . . One of A.L.'s most productive DHs.

Year	Club	Pos.	G	AB	R	H	2B	3B	HR	RBI	SB	Avg.
1968	Cincinnati	2B	17	51	1	10	1	0	0	2	1	.196
1970	Cincinnati	OF-3B-2B	70	165	18	41	6	1	8	23	0	.248
1971	Cincinnati	OF	99	337	39	89	24	2	9	34	3	.264
1972	Cincinnati	OF-3B	62	97	9	27	4	0	5	26	0	.278
1973	Kansas City.....	OF-3B	106	338	36	79	18	3	9	50	2	.234
1974	Kansas City.....	OF-3B	148	539	71	167	36	4	15	88	11	.310
1975	Kansas City.....	OF-3B	126	480	58	147	38	6	5	71	11	.306
1976	Kansas City.....	OF	149	527	75	175	34	5	8	73	22	.332
1977	Kansas City.....	OF	162	641	104	191	54	11	21	92	18	.298
1978	Kansas City.....	OF	156	623	90	170	39	5	16	72	17	.273
1979	Kansas City.....	DH	101	393	55	113	32	4	10	74	5	.288
1980	Kansas City.....	DH	124	489	73	145	39	5	14	83	10	.297
	Totals..........		1319	4680	629	1354	325	46	120	686	100	.289

WILLIE WILSON 25 6-3 190 **Bats S Throws R**

The most exciting player in the league . . . Can manufacture runs all by himself . . . The fastest man in the game, and maybe the quickest who ever played . . . Yet prefers to be known as a hitter and a complete player rather than merely as a base stealer . . . Went to bat 705 times in 1980—a major league record . . . Became only second switch hitter in history to collect 100 hits from each side of the plate . . . Set A.L. record for singles with 184 . . . Born July 9, 1955, in Montgomery, Ala. . . . Set another record he's not particularly proud of by striking out 12 times in the World Series . . . "I've never seen anything like him turning second," says Boston's Dwight Evans . . . Manager Jim Frey likens him to Babe Ruth . . . "The crowd starts buzzing in anticipation of what he might do, three batters ahead." . . . Hates to sign autographs . . . "In high school when we were bad we were punished by having to write our names 100 times."

Year	Club	Pos.	G	AB	R	H	2B	3B	HR	RBI	SB	Avg.
1976	Kansas City.....	OF	12	6	0	1	0	0	0	0	2	.167
1977	Kansas City.....	OF	13	34	10	11	2	0	0	1	6	.324
1978	Kansas City.....	OF	127	198	43	43	8	2	0	16	46	.217
1979	Kansas City.....	OF	154	588	113	185	18	13	6	49	83	.315
1980	Kansas City.....	OF	161	705	133	230	28	15	3	49	79	.326
	Totals.........		467	1531	299	470	56	30	9	115	216	.307

LEE MAY 38 6-3 205 **Bats R Throws R**

The Big Bopper moves on again . . . Signed on with Royals after playing out option in Baltimore . . . Orioles used him almost strictly as DH last two years . . . Home runs have declined steadily last three years, but he has hit 351 . . . Has had home run in all 29 big league parks he's played in . . . Born March 23, 1943, in Birmingham, Ala. . . . Brother of ex-major leaguer Carlos . . . Needs only 13 hits to reach 2,000 mark . . . A quiet man who is still dangerous with the bat . . . Royals hope there's one good year left in him.

Year	Club	Pos.	G	AB	R	H	2B	3B	HR	RBI	SB	Avg.
1965	Cincinnati	PH	5	4	1	0	0	0	0	0	0	.000
1966	Cincinnati	1B	25	75	14	25	5	1	2	10	0	.333
1967	Cincinnati	1B-OF	127	438	54	116	29	2	12	57	4	.265
1968	Cincinnati	1B-OF	146	559	78	162	32	1	22	80	4	.290
1969	Cincinnati	1B-OF	158	607	85	169	32	3	38	110	5	.278
1970	Cincinnati	1B	153	605	78	153	34	2	34	94	1	.253
1971	Cincinnati	1B	147	553	85	154	17	3	39	98	3	.278
1972	Houston........	1B	148	592	87	168	31	2	29	98	3	.284
1973	Houston........	1B	148	545	65	147	24	3	28	105	1	.270
1974	Houston........	1B	152	556	59	149	26	0	24	85	1	.268
1975	Baltimore.......	1B	146	580	67	152	28	3	20	99	1	.262
1976	Baltimore.......	1B	148	530	61	137	17	4	25	109	4	.258
1977	Baltimore.......	1B	150	585	75	148	15	2	27	99	2	.253
1978	Baltimore.......	1B	148	556	56	137	16	1	25	80	5	.246
1979	Baltimore.......	1B	124	456	59	116	15	0	19	69	3	.254
1980	Baltimore.......	1B	78	222	20	54	10	2	7	31	2	.243
	Totals..........		2003	7463	944	1987	332	29	351	1224	39	.266

TOP PROSPECTS

JIM GAUDET 25 6-0 185 **Bats R Throws R**

May be heir-apparent to Darrell Porter behind the plate . . . Has made steady progress through minor league system because the Royals were in no rush . . . Excellent defensive catcher, with a strong arm . . . Born June 3, 1955, in New Orleans . . . Enemy runners are reluctant to take off when he's behind the plate.

JEFF TWITTY 23 6-2 180 **Bats L Throws L**

The Royals thought enough of him to carry him on their playoff and World Series rosters . . . A sinkerball pitcher with outstanding control . . . Born Nov. 10, 1957, in West Columbia, S.C. . . . Opened 1980 season at Omaha, but called up to big leagues three times . . . Starred at University of South Carolina.

MANAGER JIM FREY: Mild-mannered and bespectacled . . . Looks more like a high school math teacher than a big league manager . . . Nevertheless, guided Royals to the World Series as a rookie . . . Can be tough and direct in dealing with his players . . . "When there's something to say, I think I ought to say it." . . . Spent 16 years in Orioles' organization, 10 of those as a coach . . . "Frey can look you in the eye and lie better than any man I've ever met," says Earl Weaver. "He will beat you any way he can." . . . Born May 26, 1931, in

Cleveland . . . Went to high school with former Boston manager Don Zimmer . . . Phillies' Pete Rose went there, too . . . Spent 14 years as an outfielder in the minor leagues, but never reached the majors.

GREATEST TEAM

Four times, the Kansas City Royals had marched to the top spot in the American League West. Three times, the New York Yankees had sent them home, empty-handed and hurt. Finally, in 1980, the Royals found out how it felt to reach the World Series.

And you could not have found a more deserving team in the American League.

Led by George Brett, who had visions of batting .400 until the final week of the season, and Willie Wilson, who ran wild on the base paths, and Dennis Leonard, who again won 20 games, and Dan Quisenberry, the new-found relief ace, the Royals romped in the A.L. West, finishing 14 games in front.

But then, the Royals were already accustomed to dominating their division. The 1980 season suddenly became oh, so, sweet and special when the Royals swept the hated, haughty Yankees in three straight in the playoffs.

For the Royals, and their faithful fans, that was the ultimate. It was almost enough to make them forget they failed in the World Series against the Philadelphia Phillies.

ALL-TIME ROYAL LEADERS

BATTING: George Brett, .390, 1980
HRs: John Mayberry, 34, 1975
RBIs: George Brett, 118, 1980
STEALS: Willie Wilson, 83, 1979
WINS: Steve Busby, 22, 1974
STRIKEOUTS: Dennis Leonard, 244, 1977

MINNESOTA TWINS

TEAM DIRECTORY: Chairman of the Board-Pres.: Calvin Griffith; VP-Asst. Treas.: Thelma Griffith Hayes; VP-Sec. Treas.: Clark Griffith; VP: Bruce Haynes; VP: James Robertson; VP: William Robertson; VP: George Brophy; Dir. Pub. Rel.: Tom Mee; VP-Trav. Sec.: Howard T. Fox, Jr.; Mgr.: Johnny Goryl. Home: Metropolitan Stadium (45,919). Field distances: 343, l.f. line; 406, l.c.; 402, c.f.; 410, r.c.; 330, r.f. Spring training: Orlando, Fla.

SCOUTING REPORT

HITTING: Twins owner Calvin Griffith remembers the good old days when the Twins featured the likes of Harmon Kille-

Ken Landreaux batted at solid .281 clip for Twins.

brew, Tony Oliva, Bob Allison and Don Mincher. "I wish I had one of those fellows now," says Griffith. Unfortunately, Roy Smalley (.278) is the closest thing the Twins have to a home run hitter. And he only smacked a dozen last year.

Switch-hitting catcher Butch Wynegar (.255) has not blossomed into the slugger the Twins once hoped he would be and Ron Jackson (.265) was a big disappointment last year. Ken Landreaux hit .281, but drove in only 62 runs. What the Twins need is a solid RBI man, preferably one who hits righthanded. However, such fellows are hard to find, especially when you don't have a lot to trade. So all Calvin Griffith can do is dream.

PITCHING: Once again, free agency has cost the Twins a key player. This time it was 14-game winner Geoff Zahn, a steady although not spectacular lefthander, who fled to sign with the California Angels. The addition of Byron McLaughlin (3-6), acquired in trade from Seattle for Willie Norwood, will hardly begin to offset the loss of Zahn. Doug Corbett (8-6) was a pleasant surprise, as was Tiger reject Fernando Arroyo (6-6). Veteran Jerry Koosman (16-13) continues to win, Darrell Jackson (9-9) still could develop into a top-notch lefthander, and Roger Erickson pitched far better last season than his 7-13 record suggests.

FIELDING: Rob Wilfong led all second baseman in the league with a .995 average afield, committing only three errors. So much for the good news. Now, the bad. Much of the time, Rick Sofield, Hosken Powell and Bombo Rivera appeared to be waging wars with routine fly balls. Third baseman John Castino committed 18 errors–the fourth-highest total in the league. And Roy Smalley was guilty of 17 miscues at short. Not outrageous figures, certainly, but nothing to be particularly proud of or win a pennant with, either.

OUTLOOK: 1980 was supposed to be the season the Twins finally matured and became bona fide contenders. Some people even picked them to win their division. Instead, the Twins stumbled and settled for third. That convinced manager Gene Mauch, the perfectionist, he had seen enough. He packed his bags and went home, still without a pennant to his credit. Mauch's temporary replacement, John Goryl, did such a fine job in September, the Twins gave him the job permanently. Now Goryl will get a chance to find out, first hand, how Gene Mauch felt.

MINNESOTA TWINS 1981 ROSTER

MANAGER John Goryl

Coaches—Karl Kuehl, Camilo Pascual, Billy Gardner, Rick Stelmaszek

PITCHERS

No.	Name	1980 Club	W-L	IP	SO	ERA	B-T	Ht.	Wt.	Born
30	Arroyo, Fernando	Toledo	6-1	72	36	1.63	R-R	6-2	190	3/21/52 Sacramento, CA
		Minnesota	6-6	92	27	4.70				
23	Corbett, Doug	Minnesota	8-6	136	89	1.99	R-R	6-1	185	11/4/52 Sarasota, FL
19	Erickson, Roger	Minnesota	7-13	191	97	3.25	R-R	6-3	190	8/30/56 Springfield, IL
37	Felton, Terry	Minnesota	0-3	18	14	7.00	R-R	6-2	185	10/29/57 Texarkana, TX
		Toledo	7-8	146	100	4.01				
39	Havens, Brad	Visalia	14-9	–	179	3.32	L-L	6-1	180	11/17/59 Royal Oak, MI
31	Jackson, Darrell	Minnesota	9-9	172	90	3.87	L-L	5-10	150	4/3/56 Los Angeles, CA
36	Koosman, Jerry	Minnesota	16-13	225	149	4.04	R-L	6-2	218	12/23/43 Appleton, MN
40	Kromy, Ted	Visalia	12-12	–	113	3.44	R-R	6-2	173	7/2/59 Spring Lake Park, MN
–	McLaughlin, Byron	Seattle	3-6	91	41	6.82	R-R	6-1	175	9/29/55 Van Nuys, CA
17	Redfern, Pete	Minnesota	7-7	105	73	4.54	R-R	6-2	190	8/25/54 Glendale, CA
46	Sarmiento, Wally	Toledo	6-6	85	39	2.65	R-R	6-0	160	11/25/58 Venezuela
22	Verhoeven, John	Minnesota	3-4	100	42	3.96	R-R	6-5	207	7/3/53 Mission Viejo, CA
20	Veselic, Bob	Toledo	11-8	174	105	3.36	R-R	6-0	182	9/27/55 Walnut, CA
		Minnesota	0-0	4	2	4.50				
28	Williams, Al	Toledo	9-3	107	59	2.10	R-R	6-4	190	5/7/54 Venezuela
		Minnesota	6-2	77	35	3.51				

CATCHERS

No.	Name	1980 Club	H	HR	RBI	Pct.	B-T	Ht.	Wt.	Born
11	Butera, Sal	Minnesota	23	0	2	.271	R-R	6-0	189	9/25/52 Bohemia, NY
48	Smith, Ray	Toledo	109	0	46	.274	R-R	6-1	185	9/18/55 Vista, CA
16	Wynegar, Butch	Minnesota	124	5	57	.255	B-R	6-0	195	3/14/56 York, PA

INFIELDERS

No.	Name	1980 Club	H	HR	RBI	Pct.	B-T	Ht.	Wt.	Born
–	Baker, Chuck	Hawaii	129	9	45	.273	R-R	5-11	175	12/6/52 Seattle, WA
		San Diego	3	0	0	.100				
2	Castino, John	Minnesota	165	13	64	.302	R-R	5-11	175	10/23/54 Evanston, IL
21	Faedo, Lenny	Orlando	105	6	26	.240	R-R	6-0	170	5/13/60 Tampa, FL
		Minnesota	2	0	0	.250				
25	Goodwin, Danny	Minnesota	23	1	11	.200	L-R	6-1	203	9/2/53 St. Louis, MO
15	Jackson, Ron	Minnesota	105	5	42	.265	R-R	6-0	217	5/9/53 Birmingham, AL
14	Mackanin, Pete	Minnesota	85	4	35	.266	R-R	6-2	196	8/1/51 Chicago, IL
5	Smalley, Roy	Minnesota	135	12	63	.278	B-R	6-1	190	10/25/52 Los Angeles, CA
1	Vega, Jesus	Toledo	139	14	79	.303	R-R	6-1	190	10/14/55 Puerto Rico
		Minnesota	5	0	4	.167				
49	Walker, Johnnie	Toledo	124	1	48	.255	B-R	5-11	165	5/7/58 Sacramento, CA
50	Washington, Ron	Toledo	117	3	36	.287	R-R	5-11	160	4/29/52 New Orleans, LA
7	Wilfong, Rob	Minnesota	103	8	45	.248	L-R	6-1	185	9/1/53 Pasadena, CA

OUTFIELDERS

No.	Name	1980 Club	H	HR	RBI	Pct.	B-T	Ht.	Wt.	Born
8	Adams, Glenn	Minnesota	75	6	38	.286	L-R	6-0	188	10/4/47 Northbridge, MA
51	Engle, Dave	Toledo	150	7	73	.307	R-R	6-3	210	11/30/56 Manhattan Beach, CA
52	Funderburk, Mark	Orlando	131	25	87	.250	R-R	6-4	226	5/16/57 Charlotte, NC
18	Johnston, Greg	Toledo	150	14	66	.296	L-L	6-0	175	2/12/55 Los Angeles, CA
		Minnesota	5	0	1	.185				
44	Landreaux, Ken	Minnesota	136	7	62	.281	L-R	5-11	170	12/22/54 Los Angeles, CA
10	Powell, Hosken	Minnesota	127	6	35	.262	L-L	6-1	185	5/14/55 Salem, AL
9	Rivera, Bombo	Minnesota	25	3	10	.221	R-R	5-10	192	8/2/52 Puerto Rico
12	Sofield, Rick	Minnesota	103	9	49	.247	L-R	6-1	193	12/16/56 Cheyenne, WY
32	Ward, Gary	Toledo	140	13	66	.282	R-R	6-2	207	12/6/53 Los Angeles, CA
		Minnesota	19	1	10	.463				

TWIN PROFILES

DOUG CORBETT 28 6-1 185 Bats R Throws R

Pitched far better than anyone dared dream or hope in 1980 . . . One of top rookies in the league in spite of advanced age . . . Spent five years buried in the Reds' farm system . . . Claims no one ever told him he even had a chance to pitch in the big leagues . . . Born Nov. 14, 1952, in Sarasota, Fla. . . . Had five good minor league seasons in a row . . . "My record speaks for itself." . . . Twins claimed him for $25,000 on the advice of former manager Cal Ermer . . . Can strike out enemy hitters or coax them to hit ground balls . . . Rarely blows a lead . . . Once starred at University of Florida . . . Originally signed with Royals . . . Has been a reliever throughout his career.

Year	Club	G	IP	W	L	Pct.	SO	BB	H	ERA
1980	Minnesota	73	136	8	6	.571	89	42	102	1.99

DARRELL JACKSON 24 5-10 150 Bats S Throws L

Answer to Twins' long search for another capable lefty . . . "All Jackson lacks is composure," former manager Gene Mauch once remarked . . . Finally gained control of himself in 1980 . . . Born April 3, 1956, in Los Angeles . . . Played high school ball with San Diego's Ozzie Smith and Baltimore's Eddie Murray . . . Starred on sandlots with Chet Lemon of Chicago . . . Slender build reminds some of former Twin lefty Tom Hall . . . Participated in three College World Series while at Arizona State . . . A serious hand injury while in college threatened to end his pro career before it got started . . . One of few players to reach big leagues in their first professional season.

Year	Club	G	IP	W	L	Pct.	SO	BB	H	ERA
1978	Minnesota	19	92	4	6	.400	54	48	89	4.50
1979	Minnesota	24	69	4	4	.500	43	26	89	4.30
1980	Minnesota	32	172	9	9	.500	90	69	161	3.87
	Totals..................	75	333	17	19	.472	187	143	339	4.14

ROGER ERICKSON 24 6-3 190 Bats R Throws R

Was Twins' best pitcher in 1980 in spite of his disappointing record . . . Time and time again he was the victim of poor support . . . "When he pitches, we just don't hit," says pitching coach Camilo Pascual . . . Born Aug. 30, 1956, in Springfield, Ill. . . . Underwent elbow surgery after '79 season . . . The more he pitched in '80, the better he got . . . "The zip is back on Roger's fastball," says catcher Butch Wynegar . . . No longer reluctant to throw his breaking pitches . . . Could be ready to become Twins' ace.

Year	Club	G	IP	W	L	Pct.	SO	BB	H	ERA
1978	Minnesota	37	266	14	13	.519	121	79	268	3.96
1979	Minnesota	24	123	3	10	.231	47	48	154	5.63
1980	Minnesota	32	191	7	13	.350	97	56	198	3.25
	Totals	93	580	24	36	.400	265	183	620	4.08

JERRY KOOSMAN 37 6-2 218 Bats R Throws L

Tied club record by striking out 15 in a game . . . Measures success in number of caps and sweatshirts he goes through in a game . . . On a hot night, he'll use four caps and five sweatshirts . . . Turned out to be a steal for the Twins after he forced Mets to trade him to Minnesota . . . Born Dec. 23, 1943, in Appleton, Minn. . . . Makes his home in Twin Cities area and soon became a favorite of the fans . . . Boasts one of the best pickoff moves in the business . . . Signed with Mets instead of the Twins in '64 because the Mets offered him $200 more . . . A real pro . . . Has been a big help to the younger pitchers on the Twins' staff.

Year	Club	G	IP	W	L	Pct.	SO	BB	H	ERA
1967	New York (NL)	9	22	0	2	.000	11	19	22	6.14
1968	New York (NL)	35	264	19	12	.613	178	69	221	2.08
1969	New York (NL)	32	241	17	9	.654	180	68	187	2.28
1970	New York (NL)	30	212	12	7	.632	118	71	189	3.14
1971	New York (NL)	26	166	6	11	.353	96	51	160	3.04
1972	New York (NL)	34	163	11	12	.478	147	52	155	4.14
1973	New York (NL)	35	263	14	15	.483	156	76	234	2.84
1974	New York (NL)	35	265	15	11	.577	188	85	258	3.36
1975	New York (NL)	36	240	14	13	.519	173	98	234	3.41
1976	New York (NL)	34	247	21	10	.677	200	66	205	2.70
1977	New York (NL)	32	227	8	20	.286	192	81	195	3.49
1978	New York (NL)	38	235	3	15	.167	160	84	221	3.75
1979	Minnesota	37	264	20	13	.606	157	83	268	3.38
1980	Minnesota	38	243	16	13	.552	149	69	252	4.04
	Totals	451	3052	176	163	.519	2105	972	2801	3.19

BUTCH WYNEGAR 25 6-0 195 Bats S Throws R

Red-hot before the All-Star Game, but slumped during second half . . . A rarity: A catcher who can bat lead-off . . . Has all the tools except good speed . . . Could probably hit 30 HRs a year if he decided to swing for the fences . . . The next Johnny Bench . . . Born March 14, 1956, in York, Pa. . . . Keeps getting better and better . . . Has outstanding arm . . . Has already spent five full years in the bigs . . . Began switch-hitting at age 9 to imitate his idol, Mickey Mantle . . . Now the Twins are glad he did.

Year	Club	Pos.	G	AB	R	H	2B	3B	HR	RBI	SB	Avg.
1976	Minnesota	C	149	534	58	139	21	2	10	69	0	.260
1977	Minnesota	C-3B	144	532	76	139	22	3	10	79	2	.261
1978	Minnesota	C-3B	135	454	36	104	22	1	4	45	1	.229
1979	Minnesota	C	149	504	74	136	20	0	7	57	2	.270
1980	Minnesota	C	146	486	61	124	18	3	5	57	3	.255
	Totals..........		723	2510	305	642	103	9	36	307	8	.256

JOHN CASTINO 26 5-11 175 Bats R Throws R

Proved his Rookie of the Year performance in 1979 was no fluke . . . Also made remarkable improvement at the plate . . . A hustler, on the go all the time . . . Fiestiest of the Twins . . . When he loses his temper, watch out! . . . Born Oct. 23, 1954, in Evanston, Ill. . . . Sparkplug on an often comatose team . . . "John has one pace, all-out," says former manager Gene Mauch . . . Admits he was "something of a rowdy," at Rollins College . . . One of many born-again Christians on Twins' team . . . "Being a Christian has changed my life tremendously." . . . Has been compared to Brooks Robinson but that may be a bit far-fetched.

Year	Club	Pos.	G	AB	R	H	2B	3B	HR	RBI	SB	Avg.
1979	Minnesota	3B	148	393	49	112	13	8	5	52	5	.285
1980	Minnesota	3B	150	546	67	165	17	7	13	64	7	.302
	Totals..........		298	939	116	277	30	15	18	116	12	.295

ROY SMALLEY 28 6-1 190 Bats S Throws R

Failed to match stellar 1979 showing, but still one of the keys to Twins' attack . . . May become better ballplayer now that he no longer has added burden of playing for his uncle, Gene Mauch . . . Oversized for a shortstop . . . Born Oct. 25, 1952, in Los Angeles . . . Does not possess great range, even though he did set an A.L. record with 572 assists in '79

. . . Plays closer to second base than just about any shortstop in the game . . . Has been lifting weights for three years to build up his strength . . . "Playing shortstop is very important to me. I like being in the middle of all those plays." . . . Reads at least one book a month during the season.

Year	Club	Pos.	G	AB	R	H	2B	3B	HR	RBI	SB	Avg.
1975	Texas..........	SS-2B-C	78	250	22	57	8	0	3	33	4	.228
1976	Texas-Minnesota.	SS-2B	144	513	61	133	18	3	3	44	2	.259
1977	Minnesota......	SS	150	584	93	135	21	5	6	56	5	.231
1978	Minnesota......	SS	158	586	80	160	31	3	19	77	2	.273
1979	Minnesota......	SS-1B	162	621	94	168	28	3	24	95	2	.271
1980	Minnesota......	SS	133	486	64	135	24	1	12	63	3	.278
	Totals..........		825	3040	414	788	130	15	67	368	18	.259

KEN LANDREAUX 26 5-11 170 Bats L Throws R

Put together impressive 31-game hitting streak, tops in league in 1980 . . . Calls himself "K.T." . . . "K.T. is an uneducated guess as how to abbreviate my first name." . . . Claims only way to play leftfield in Metropolitan Stadium is "on a cloudy day with the stands empty." . . . "I say outrageous things once in a while to spice up conversations." . . . Born Dec. 22, 1954, in Los Angeles . . . Plays with a flair . . . Fined for wearing his trousers too low, hiding the team insignia on his socks . . . Was also fined for failing to hustle . . . One of the better defensive outfielders in the league . . . "I know what I'm doing. I've been playing since I was six years old."

Year	Club	Pos.	G	AB	R	H	2B	3B	HR	RBI	SB	Avg.
1977	California.......	OF	23	76	6	19	5	1	0	5	1	.250
1978	California.......	OF	93	260	37	58	7	5	5	23	7	.223
1979	Minnesota......	OF	151	564	81	172	27	5	15	83	10	.305
1980	Minnesota......	OF	129	484	56	136	23	11	7	62	8	.281
	Totals..........		396	1384	180	385	62	22	27	173	26	.278

RICK SOFIELD 24 6-1 193 Bats L Throws R

One of premier hotdogs in A.L. . . . Twins' only No. 1 draft pick to make it good . . . "They stick with you longer as a No. 1 pick but they also lose their temper more quickly when you don't perform." . . . Unpredictable outfielder . . . Born Dec. 16, 1956, in Cheyenne, Wyo. . . . Got his chance when Hosken Powell suffered a broken wrist at start of '79 season . . . Made the most of opportunity . . . Was All-American in high school in football and baseball . . . Turned down football scholarship at University of Michigan because he would have had to compete at quarterback with Rick Leach.

Year	Club	Pos.	G	AB	R	H	2B	3B	HR	RBI	SB	Avg.
1979	Minnesota......	OF	35	93	8	28	5	0	0	12	2	.301
1980	Minnesota......	OF	131	417	52	103	18	4	9	49	4	.247
	Totals..........		166	510	60	131	23	4	9	61	6	.257

TOP PROSPECTS

DAVE ENGLE 24 6-3 210 **Bats R Throws R**

Made big jump from Class A to AAA in '79 . . . Has good power and could give Twins home run threat they lack . . . Can play outfield or DH . . . Born Nov. 30, 1956, in San Diego . . . A third baseman in college but was switched to catcher by Angels . . . Traded to Twins as partial payment for Rod Carew.

MARK FUNDERBURK 23 6-4 226 **Bats R Throws R**

Big, power-hitting first baseman . . . Voted "Most Dangerous Hitter" in California League in '79 . . . Born May 16, 1957, in Charlotte, N.C. . . . Originally an outfielder, moved to 1B after signing with the Twins . . . Could become awesome slugger.

MANAGER JOHN GORYL: Named to replace Gene Mauch on interim basis, and later signed for 1981 season . . . Sought to create "a looser atmosphere" and "better communications," on the team . . . Mauch always snorted at the idea of communicating with his players . . . "Don't talk—play," was his motto . . . Goryl's different . . . Born Oct. 21, 1933, in Lonsdale, R.I. . . . Spent 12 years managing in the minors for the Twins . . . Also served as third base coach, beginning in '79 . . . Impressed people with his aggressive style and his baseball instincts . . . Played in big leagues for the Cubs and the Twins . . . Nicknamed "Groucho."

GREATEST TEAM

Joe Cronin, the 27-year-old shortstop, was also the manager. The batting order included such solid hitters as Joe Kuhel, Goose Goslin, and Heinie Manush. General Crowder and Earl Whitehill were around to handle the pitching.

And the 1933 Washington Senators, forerunners of today's Minnesota Twins, romped to the American League title.

From mid-season on, the Senators were never in trouble as Cronin, who also batted .309, demonstrated as a rookie manager that he could handle people in addition to swinging a potent bat.

Off-season deals proved particularly helpful as Goslin, outfielder Fred Schulte, catcher Luke Sewell, and pitchers Walter Stewart, Jack Russell and Whitehill all played key roles.

The Senators were favored going into the World Series against New York, but managed to win only one game as Bill Terry's Giants romped behind pitcher Carl Hubbell and hot-hitting Mel Ott.

ALL-TIME TWIN LEADERS

BATTING: Rod Carew, .388, 1977
HRs: Harmon Killebrew, 49, 1964, 1969
RBIs: Harmon Killebrew, 140, 1969
STEALS: Rod Carew, 49, 1976
WINS: Jim Kaat, 25, 1966
STRIKEOUTS: Bert Blyleven, 258, 1973

OAKLAND A's

TEAM DIRECTORY: Pres.: Roy Eisenhardt; Exec. VP: Wally Haas; VP: Carl Finley; Dir. Minor League Operations: Walt Jocketty; Dir. Publ.-Trav. Sec.: Mickey Morabito; Mgr.: Billy Martin. Home: Oakland Coliseum (50,000). Field distances: 330, l.f. line; 375, l.c.; 400, c.f.; 375, r.c.; 330, r.f. line. Spring training: Scottsdale, Ariz.

SCOUTING REPORT

HITTING: When they get on base, the A's have the speed to drive opponents batty. They stole 175 bases last summer, second only to Kansas City. Rickey Henderson (.303 with 100 SB) and Dwayne Murphy (.274, 26 SB) can both fly. The A's' problem, except for Henderson, is getting on base. Oakland was shut out 13 times last year. Only the lowly Mariners were blanked more often.

The A's' big need, admittedly, is a power hitter, preferably a righthander to help out Tony Armas. And they did pick up veteran Cliff Johnson, an old friend of Billy Martin, during the off-season. But a .235 hitter isn't going to solve the A's' woes. Only Toronto and Seattle owned lower batting averages than the A's last year, and unfortunately, you can't steal first base.

PITCHING: If only Oakland had a bullpen. The amazing A's shattered the modern major-league record by completing 94 games last year–nearly twice as many as the Milwaukee Brewers, their closest challengers. Ironmen Rick Langford (28 CG), Mike Norris (24) and Matt Keough (20) were indefatigable. They were also surprisingly successful. Norris was 22-9 and a bona fide Cy Young Award candidate, Langford was 19-12, and Keough was 16-13.

As a group, the A's led the league with a 3.46 ERA. And those pitchers were the reason the A's were able to climb to second in the West. Meanwhile, back in the bullpen, Billy Martin was wondering, "What bullpen?" Led by Bob Lacey, Oakland's relievers finished last in the league, saving only 13 games.

FIELDING: Henderson, Murphy and Armas combine to give the A's one of the finest outfields in the league. Together the trio was credited with 45 assists last season–tops in the AL. All three can catch, and all three can throw. Where the A's are hurting is in the infield. They completed far fewer double plays (115) than any other club. Fine pitching was partly responsible for that, of

Placid Billy Martin guided Oakland to second place.

course, but the A's' defenders were not without fault. Oakland is hoping the acquisition of ex-Yankees Fred Stanley and Brian Doyle—two more of Billy's old buddies—will help solidify the infield.

OUTLOOK: Can Billy Martin do it again? Can he work his magic two years in a row? Or will he begin to wear out his welcome, as he has done in Minnesota and Detroit and Texas and New York? The A's looked like a different club last year under Billy. Hitting, pitching, defense—in every aspect of the game they improved. But they are still a team based primarily on terrific speed and the perseverance of their starting pitchers. What toll will all of those innings last year take on the arms of Langford, Norris and Keough? Who in the bullpen can help them out? And who is going to drive in the runs when those speedsters get on base? Not Billy Martin, that's for sure.

OAKLAND A'S 1981 ROSTER

MANAGER Billy Martin

Coaches—Clete Boyer, Art Fowler, George Mitterwald, Lee Walls, Jackie Moore

PITCHERS

No.	Name	1980 Club	W-L	IP	SO	ERA	B-T	Ht.	Wt.	Born
55	Atherton, Keith	West Haven	11-12	190	117	4.12	R-R	6-3	190	2/19/59 Mathews, VA
59	Beard, Dave	Ogden	7-8	97	110	6.40	L-R	6-5	190	10/2/59 Atlanta, GA
		Oakland	0-1	16	12	3.38				
28	Bordi, Rich	West Haven	4-6	76	49	4.14	R-R	6-7	210	4/18/59 San Francisco, CA
		Oakland	0-0	2	0	4.50				
53	Camacho, Ernie	Ogden	5-3	64	58	3.94	R-R	6-1	180	2/1/56 Salinas, CA
		Oakland	0-0	12	9	6.75				
37	Conroy, Tim	West Haven	8-15	141	72	6.45	L-L	6-0	180	4/3/60 Monroeville, PA
33	Hamilton, Dave	Ogden	0-1	31	25	3.48	L-L	6-0	190	12/13/47 Seattle, WA
		Oakland	0-3	30	23	11.40				
38	Jones, Jeff	Oakland	1-3	44	34	2.86	R-R	6-3	210	7/29/56 Detroit, MI
27	Keough, Matt	Oakland	16-13	250	121	2.92	R-R	6-2	175	7/3/55 Pomona, CA
50	Kingman, Brian	Oakland	8-20	211	116	3.84	R-R	6-1	190	7/27/54 Los Angeles, CA
34	Lacey, Bob	Oakland	3-2	80	45	2.93	R-L	6-4	190	8/25/53 Fredericksburgh, VA
22	Langford, Rick	Oakland	19-12	290	102	3.26	R-R	6-0	180	3/20/52 Farmville, VA
54	McCatty, Steve	Oakland	14-14	222	114	3.85	R-R	6-3	200	3/20/54 Detroit, MI
32	Minetto, Craig	Ogden	3-2	41	35	4.61	L-L	6-0	185	4/25/54 Stockton, CA
		Oakland	0-2	8	5	7.88				
49	Moore, Bob	West Haven	0-4	23	7	9.00	R-R	6-4	190	11/8/58 Sweetwater, LA
		Modesto	4-6	109	72	4.62				
17	Norris, Mike	Oakland	22-9	284	180	2.54	R-R	6-2	172	3/19/55 San Francisco, CA
30	Wirth, Alan	Ogden	6-9	111	45	6.32	R-R	6-5	190	12/8/56 Mesa, AZ
		Oakland	0-0	2	1	4.50				

CATCHERS

No.	Name	1980 Club	H	HR	RBI	Pct.	B-T	Ht.	Wt.	Born
25	Dempsey, Pat	Ogden	120	2	41	.318	R-R	6-4	185	10/23/56 Encino, CA
48	Heath, Mike	Oakland	74	1	33	.243	R-R	5-11	176	2/5/55 Tampa, FL
–	Johnson, Cliff	Cleveland	40	6	28	.230	R-R	6-4	225	7/22/47 San Antonio, TX
		Chicago (NL)	46	10	34	.235				
26	Meyer, Scott	West Haven	88	7	45	.243	R-R	6-1	195	8/19/57 Midlothian, IL
5	Newman, Jeff	Oakland	102	15	56	.233	R-R	6-2	218	9/11/48 Ft. Worth, TX

INFIELDERS

No.	Name	1980 Club	H	HR	RBI	Pct.	B-T	Ht.	Wt.	Born
19	Cox, Jeff	Ogden	79	0	21	.288	R-R	5-11	170	11/9/55 Los Angeles, CA
		Oakland	36	0	9	.213				
–	Doyle, Brian	New York (AL)	13	1	5	.173	L-R	5-10	170	1/26/54 Glasgow, KY
7	Edwards, Mike	Oakland	14	0	3	.237	R-R	5-10	172	8/27/52 Ft. Lewis, WA
10	Gross, Wayne	Oakland	103	14	61	.281	L-R	6-2	205	1/14/52 Riverside, CA
12	Klutts, Mickey	Oakland	53	4	21	.269	R-R	5-11	189	9/30/54 Montebello, CA
39	McKay, Dave	Oakland	72	1	29	.244	B-R	6-0	195	3/14/50 Canada
24	Moore, Kelvin	Ogden	130	25	100	.282	R-L	6-1	195	9/26/57 Leroy, AL
8	Picciolo, Rob	Oakland	65	5	18	.240	R-R	6-2	185	2/4/53 Santa Monica, CA
13	Revering, Dave	Oakland	109	15	62	.290	L-R	6-4	205	2/12/53 Roseville, CA
–	Stanley, Fred	New York (AL)	18	0	5	.209	R-R	5-11	167	8/13/47 Farhamville, OH

OUTFIELDERS

No.	Name	1980 Club	H	HR	RBI	Pct.	B-T	Ht.	Wt.	Born
11	Armas, Tony	Oakland	175	35	109	.279	R-R	5-11	198	7/12/53 Venezuela
16	Davis, Mike	Ogden	21	1	14	.304	L-L	6-2	165	6/11/59 San Diego, CA
		Oakland	20	1	8	.211				
14	Grandas, Bob	Ogden	86	4	54	.277	R-R	6-1	190	4/4/57 Flint, MI
35	Henderson, Rickey	Oakland	179	9	53	.303	R-L	5-10	178	12/25/58 Chicago, IL
21	Murphy, Dwayne	Oakland	157	13	68	.274	L-R	6-1	190	3/18/55 Merced, CA
6	Page, Mitchell	Oakland	85	17	51	.244	L-R	6-2	205	3/1/53 Compton, CA
47	Patterson, Mike	West Haven	103	15	50	.263	R-R	5-10	170	1/16/58 Los Angeles, CA
		Ogden	17	1	5	.304				

A'S PROFILES

RICK LANGFORD 29 6-0 180 — Bats R Throws R

Reeled off 22 complete games in a row–a most remarkable feat . . . "I have never set any goals in my life." . . . Obtained from Pirates in major nine-player swap in spring of 1977 . . . Says experience acquired in bullpen has helped make him a successful starter . . . Also completed 10 in a row in 1979 . . . Born March 20, 1952, in Farmville, Va. . . . Toured Japan with a team of major league all-stars following 1979 season . . . A strikeout pitcher . . . Moved up rapidly through Pirates' farm system . . . But big chance came when he was traded to A's . . . Pirates considered making him an outfielder when he signed in '73 . . . The A's are sure glad they didn't.

Year	Club	G	IP	W	L	Pct.	SO	BB	H	ERA
1976	Pittsburgh	12	23	0	1	.000	17	14	27	6.26
1977	Oakland	37	208	8	19	.296	141	73	223	4.02
1978	Oakland	37	176	7	13	.350	92	56	169	3.43
1979	Oakland	34	219	12	16	.429	101	57	233	4.27
1980	Oakland	35	290	19	12	.613	102	64	276	3.26
	Totals	155	916	46	61	.430	453	264	928	3.78

STEVE McCATTY 27 6-3 200 — Bats R Throws R

Plagued by tough luck in 1980 . . . Relies on blazing fastball . . . Keeps his teammates in stitches with his sharp wit . . . Was outstanding catcher and first baseman while in high school . . . Born March 20, 1954, in Detroit . . . Aggressive go-getter, likes to challenge hitters . . . Ignored in draft, signed with A's as free agent in June 1973 . . . Has been used both as a starter and in relief . . . First reached big leagues in '77 but didn't notch first win until May 1, 1979, the day after he had been recalled from minors.

Year	Club	G	IP	W	L	Pct.	SO	BB	H	ERA
1977	Oakland	4	14	0	0	.000	9	7	16	5.14
1978	Oakland	9	20	0	0	.000	10	9	26	4.50
1979	Oakland	31	186	11	12	.478	87	80	207	4.21
1980	Oakland	33	222	14	14	.500	114	99	202	3.85
	Totals	77	442	25	26	.490	220	195	451	4.07

DAVE REVERING 29 6-4 205 Bats L Throws R

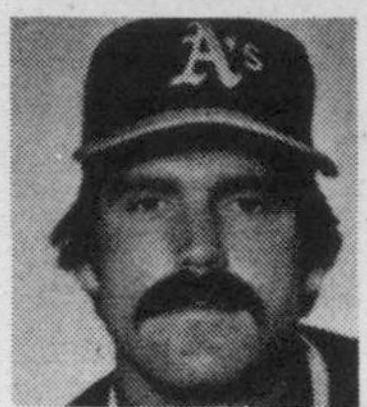

Has worked hard to improve his batting technique . . . Now hits ball to leftfield more often . . . Was platooned, playing only against righthanders . . . Credits frequent presence of Rickey Henderson and Dwayne Murphy on base paths with his improved performance in 1980 . . . Born Feb. 12, 1953, in Roseville, Calif. . . . Works for a TV station during the off-season . . . Blames former manager Sparky Anderson because he never got a chance to play with Reds, in spite of outstanding minor league record . . . A free spirit . . . Was Cincinnati's seventh pick in 1971 draft.

Year	Club	Pos.	G	AB	R	H	2B	3B	HR	RBI	SB	Avg.
1978	Oakland	1B	152	521	48	141	21	3	16	46	0	.271
1979	Oakland	1B	125	472	63	136	25	5	19	77	1	.288
1980	Oakland	1B	106	376	48	109	21	5	15	62	1	.290
	Totals		383	1369	159	386	67	13	50	185	2	.282

DWAYNE MURPHY 26 6-1 190 Bats L Throws R

Underrated outfielder . . . Excellent No. 2 hitter behind Rickey Henderson . . . "He'll be a .300 hitter as soon as he learns how to bunt," predicts coach Lee Walls . . . Played winter ball in Venezuela under direction of Felipe Alou . . . Born March 18, 1955, in Merced, Cal. . . . Studies the martial arts during the off-season and has earned his yellow belt . . . "I fought in a couple of tournaments and got my butt kicked." . . . Was not picked by A's until 12th round of June 1973 draft . . . His performance has been a pleasant surprise . . . Has a good eye, gets a lot of walks.

Year	Club	Pos.	G	AB	R	H	2B	3B	HR	RBI	SB	Avg.
1978	Oakland	OF	60	52	15	10	2	0	0	5	0	.192
1979	Oakland	OF	121	388	57	99	10	4	11	40	15	.255
1980	Oakland	OF	159	573	86	157	18	2	13	68	26	.274
	Totals		340	1013	158	266	30	6	24	113	41	.263

RICKEY HENDERSON 22 5-10 178 Bats R Throws L

Loves to run and steal . . . Speciality is a belly-flop slide . . . Admired Lou Brock and Maury Wills . . . Works well with Dwayne Murphy, the A's No. 2 hitter . . . Broke Ty Cobb's A.L. record for stolen bases (96), set in 1915 . . . Runs with reckless abandon, but knows what he's doing . . . Born Dec. 25, 1958, in Chicago . . . Now makes his home in

Oakland . . . Was A's fourth pick in 1976 draft . . . Also a fine defensive outfielder . . . Hit over .300 three years in a row in minors . . . Stole seven bases in one game while with Fresno . . . Received more than two dozen offers of college football scholarships, but chose to play pro baseball instead.

Year	Club	Pos.	G	AB	R	H	2B	3B	HR	RBI	SB	Avg.
1979	Oakland........	OF	89	351	49	96	13	3	1	26	33	.274
1980	Oakland........	OF	158	591	111	179	22	4	9	53	100	.303
	Totals..........		247	942	160	275	35	7	10	79	133	.292

TONY ARMAS 27 5-11 198 Bats R Throws R

Owns one of the strongest arms in the AL . . . Has become a hero on Oakland because of tape-measure HRs . . . Injury prone in past . . . Kept running into outfield walls . . . "Last year I was more careful." . . . Switched to lighter bat on advice of coach Felipe Alou . . . Born July 12, 1953, at Anzoatequi, Ven. . . . Aggressive hitter, comes out swinging . . . Great at breaking up double plays . . . Finally getting the chance to show what he can do . . . Obtained from Pirates . . . Full name: Antonio Rafael Armas . . . Moved back in batter's box in '80 and change paid off.

Year	Club	Pos.	G	AB	R	H	2B	3B	HR	RBI	SB	Avg.
1976	Pittsburgh......	OF	4	6	0	2	0	0	0	1	0	.333
1977	Oakland........	OF	118	363	26	87	8	2	13	53	1	.240
1978	Oakland........	OF	91	239	17	51	6	1	2	13	1	.213
1979	Oakland........	OF	80	278	29	69	9	3	11	34	1	.248
1980	Oakland........	OF	158	628	87	175	18	8	35	109	5	.279
	Totals..........		451	1514	159	384	41	14	61	210	8	.254

MITCHELL PAGE 29 6-2 205 Bats L Throws R

Another top player the A's got from Pirates in that nine-player spring swap that sent Phil Garner to Pittsburgh in 1977 . . . Might never have reached majors if Pirates hadn't traded him . . . But has since proven himself to be a bona fide big leaguer . . . Born Oct. 15, 1951, in Compton, Cal. . . . Can play first base, outfield or DH . . . A solid hitter . . . Can also run, although his job is driving other A's home . . . Was immediate sensation when he joined the A's in '77 . . . At odds with Charley Finley over his salary, he may find happiness now.

Year	Club	Pos.	G	AB	R	H	2B	3B	HR	RBI	SB	Avg.
1977	Oakland........	OF	145	501	85	154	28	8	21	75	42	.307
1978	Oakland........	OF	147	516	62	147	25	7	17	70	23	.285
1979	Oakland........	OF	133	478	51	118	11	2	9	42	17	.247
1980	Oakland........	OF	110	348	58	85	10	4	17	51	14	.244
	Totals..........		535	1843	256	504	74	21	64	238	96	.273

WAYNE GROSS 29 6-2 205 **Bats L Throws R**

Had best year in 1977 when he was named to All-Star team . . . Set major league record by starting three triple plays in '79 . . . Born Jan. 14, 1952, in Riverside, Cal. . . . Was picked on sixth round in June 1973 free agent draft . . . First reached big leagues with A's in '76 . . . Got pinch-hit single in second game . . . Can play first base, third or outfield . . . Excellent all-around athlete . . . A product of Cal Poly at Pomona, where he starred in football and baseball.

Year	Club	Pos.	G	AB	R	H	2B	3B	HR	RBI	SB	Avg.
1976	Oakland........	1B-OF	10	18	0	4	0	0	0	1	0	.222
1977	Oakland........	3B-1B	146	485	66	113	21	1	22	63	5	.233
1978	Oakland........	3B-1B	118	285	18	57	10	2	7	23	0	.200
1979	Oakland........	3B-1B-OF	138	442	54	99	19	1	14	50	4	.224
1980	Oakland........	3B-1B	113	366	45	103	20	3	14	61	5	.281
	Totals..........		525	1596	183	376	70	7	57	198	14	.236

JEFF NEWMAN 32 6-2 218 **Bats R Throws R**

Purchased from Indians following '75 season . . . A bona fide slugger . . . Was so disgusted he was going to quit when Indians got rid of him . . . Spent almost eight seasons in minor leagues . . . Finally got opportunity to show what he could do with A's in '76 . . . Born Sept. 11, 1948, in Fort Worth, Tex. . . . Has a degree from Texas Christian University . . . Was All-America twice while in college . . . Was A's only All-Star in '79 . . . Can catch or play first base . . . Has always been outstanding defensive catcher . . . Shows surprising power at times.

Year	Club	Pos.	G	AB	R	H	2B	3B	HR	RBI	SB	Avg.
1976	Oakland........	C	43	77	5	15	4	0	0	4	0	.195
1977	Oakland........	C-P	94	162	17	36	9	0	4	15	2	.222
1978	Oakland........	C-1B	105	268	25	64	7	1	9	32	0	.239
1979	Oakland........	C-1B-3B	143	516	53	119	17	2	22	71	2	.231
1980	Oakland........	C-1B-OF	127	438	37	102	19	1	15	56	3	.233
	Totals..........		512	1461	137	336	56	4	50	178	7	.230

MIKE NORRIS 26 6-2 172 **Bats R Throws R**

A's No. 1 pick, way back in January 1973 draft . . . Spent six years in minors before reaching big leagues to stay . . . Became 35th pitcher to throw shutout in his big league debut when he tossed three-hitter against White Sox on April 10, 1975 . . . But underwent surgery to remove calcium deposits in his elbow three weeks later . . . Born March 19, 1955, in San

Francisco . . . Was outstanding three-sport athlete in high school . . . Has displayed steady improvement in his battle to bounce back from elbow surgery.

Year	Club	G	IP	W	L	Pct.	SO	BB	H	ERA
1975	Oakland	4	17	1	0	1.000	5	8	6	0.00
1976	Oakland	24	96	4	5	.444	44	56	91	4.78
1977	Oakland	16	77	2	7	.222	35	31	77	4.79
1978	Oakland	14	49	0	5	.000	36	35	46	5.51
1979	Oakland	29	146	5	8	.385	96	94	146	4.81
1980	Oakland	33	284	22	9	.710	180	83	215	2.54
	Totals	120	669	34	34	.500	396	307	581	3.77

Mike Norris (r.), 22-game winner, with Rick Langford.

MANAGER BILLY MARTIN: Set major league record in 1980 when he had three biographies on the bookshelves . . . Also did a remarkable job with the A's on the field . . . Attendance in Oakland increased by more than 500,000 and much of the credit for that must go to the manager, who brought new excitement and enthusiasm to the area . . . Born May 16, 1928, in Berkeley, Calif. . . . His mother still

lives there . . . Has bounced from Minnesota to Detroit to Texas to New York as a manager, but has been successful everywhere he's been . . . Inevitably has been fired for his off-the-field antics—not for the way he runs his baseball team . . . Considered one of the best in the business . . . A scrapper as a player, was a member of six pennant winners while with the Yankees in the 1950s.

GREATEST TEAM

With all due respect to Reggie Jackson, Catfish Hunter, Sal Bando and the rest of those outstanding A's who made Oakland the baseball capital of the world and Charley Finley its king in the early 1970's, the best team that ever wore Athletics' uniforms called the city of Philadelphia home.

The year was 1929, and Connie Mack's club featured the likes of Jimmie Foxx, Al Simmons, Mickey Cochrane, George Earnshaw and Lefty Grove.

The Athletics, their spirits buoyed and their confidence reinforced by an early three-game sweep of the rival Yankees, soon left the rest of the American League wallowing in their wake.

They won 104 games and at the season's end there was serious debate as to whether or not this was the greatest team ever to represent the A.L.

Then, just to prove their regular-season performance had not been a fluke, the Athletics wiped out the Chicago Cubs of Hack Wilson and Rogers Hornsby four games to one in the World Series.

ALL-TIME A's LEADERS

BATTING: Napoleon Lajoie, .422, 1901
HRs: Jimmie Foxx, 58, 1932
RBIs: Jimmie Foxx, 169, 1932
STEALS: Rickey Henderson, 100, 1980
WINS: John Coombs, 31, 1910
Lefty Grove, 31, 1931
STRIKEOUTS: Rube Waddell, 349, 1904

SEATTLE MARINERS

TEAM DIRECTORY: Pres.: Dan O'Brien; Exec. Dir.: Kip Horsburgh; Dir. Business: Jeff Odenwald; Dir. Marketing: Jack Carvalho; Dir. Pub. Rel.: Randy Adamack; Mgr.: Maury Wills. Home: Kingdome (59,438). Field distances: 316, l.f. line; 365, l.c.; 410, c.f.; 365, r.c.; 316, r.f. line. Spring training: Tempe, Ariz.

SCOUTING REPORT

HITTING: A year ago, things were definitely looking up in the Kingdome. The expansion Mariners had outhit both the Orioles

Richie Zisk should enjoy hitting in the cozy Kingdome.

and the Yankees the year before and Seattle seemed to be on its way. Then the roof caved in and the Mariners fell back to the bottom of the heap, batting an anemic .248.

Aside from Bruce Bochte (.300, 13 HRs, 78 RBI) and Danny Meyer (.275, 11 HRs, 71 RBI), the offense gave Seattle fans little reason to applaud. Willie Horton, since traded, slumped to .221 with only 36 RBI. Julio Cruz hit a mere .209. The addition of catcher Brad Gulden should help. Last year, as a group, Mariner catchers Jerry Narron, Larry Cox, Bob Stinson and Marc Hill batted a mere .207.

The Mariners have also added veteran sluggers Jeff Burroughs (.263, 13 HRs, 51 RBI) and Richie Zisk (.290, 19 HRs, 77 RBI) along with Willie Norwood (.164). In that ballpark, both Burroughs and Zisk could have big years.

PITCHING: Seattle's pitchers must be doing something right. Most of the other teams would be interested in having one or more of them on their side. Floyd Bannister and Shane Rawley were among the most frequently-mentioned names during the annual winter trading session. Still, in Seattle, those pitchers continue to struggle. Only the Angels and Indians compiled higher ERAs than the Mariners' mark of 4.38 last year as Seattle's pitchers served up a league-leading 159 home runs. Rawley, 7-7 with 13 saves, is a respected reliever and Bannister (9-13) should continue to improve. In Steve Finch, Ken Clay, Jerry Don Gleaton and Brian Allard, all from the Rangers, the Mariners are grasping at straws.

FIELDING: You name the position, and chances are the Mariners could probably use improvement there. Bochte is adequate at first, and so are outfielders Joe Simpson and Meyer. But Ted Cox is a liability at third. The Mariners are hoping Gulden will take over as their No. 1 catcher, but they are resigned to the fact they can't possibly hope to plug every existing hole at once.

OUTLOOK: Bleak. "Give me a last-place club and after three years we'll be strong in contention," Maury Wills once predicted. "And by the fourth year, we'll go all the way." Now Wills gets an opportunity to back up those words. It won't be easy. A year ago, the Mariners were billed as the best third-year expansion team in history. Now, they're a mess. They need pitching, hitting, defense, everything. Most of all, they may need more money. Financially, the front office is in bad shape and the American League has indicated it may have to help find new owners with fresh bankrolls.

SEATTLE MARINERS 1981 ROSTER

MANAGER Maury Wills

Coaches—Wes Stock, Frank Funk, Tommy Davis, Cananea Reyes

PITCHERS

No.	Name	1980 Club	W-L	IP	SO	ERA	B-T	Ht.	Wt.	Born
17	Abbott, Glenn	Seattle	12-12	215	78	4.10	R-R	6-0	200	2/16/51 Little Rock, AR
–	Allard, Brian	Charleston	8-8	152	68	3.14	R-R	6-2	185	1/3/58 Spring Valley, IL
		Texas	0-1	14	10	5.65				
–	Andersen, Larry	Portland	5-7	93	65	1.74	R-R	6-3	180	5/16/53 Portland, OR
25	Anderson, Rick	Spokane	6-0	80	65	3.26	R-R	6-2	210	12/25/53 Inglewood, CA
		Seattle	0-0	10	7	3.60				
38	Bannister, Floyd	Seattle	9-13	218	155	3.47	L-L	6-1	190	6/10/55 Pierre, SD
45	Beattie, Jim	Seattle	5-15	187	67	4.86	R-R	6-6	205	7/4/54 Hampton, VA
46	Biercevicz, Greg	Spokane	10-9	126	60	4.93	R-R	6-1	185	10/21/55 Derby, CT
48	Clark, Bryan	Spokane	2-5	41	19	5.27	L-L	6-2	185	7/12/56 Madera, CA
		Lynn	9-5	116	96	3.10				
16	Clay, Ken	Columbus	9-4	138	77	1.96	R-R	6-2	195	4/6/54 Lynchburg, VA
		Texas	2-3	43	17	4.60				
24	Dressler, Rob	Seattle	4-10	149	50	3.99	R-R	6-3	195	2/2/54 Portland, OR
30	Finch, Steve	Charleston	7-6	116	52	7.19	R-R	6-3	160	3/9/58 Escondido, CA
27	Gleaton, Jerry Don	Tulsa	13-7	178	138	3.63	L-L	6-3	215	9/14/57 Brownwood, TX
60	Heaverlo, Dave	Seattle	6-3	79	42	3.87	R-R	6-1	195	8/25/50 Ellensburg, WA
20	Parrott, Mike	Seattle	1-16	94	53	7.28	R-R	6-4	205	12/6/54 Oxnard, CA
		Spokane	1-2	22	13	0.82				
41	Rawley, Shane	Seattle	7-7	114	68	3.32	L-L	6-0	175	7/27/55 Racine, WI
44	Sarmiento, Manny	Spokane	8-7	63	66	3.00	R-R	5-11	170	2/2/56 Venezuela
		Seattle	0-1	15	15	3.60				
–	Stoddard, Bob	Spokane	4-9	124	84	4.94	R-R	6-1	190	3/8/57 San Jose, CA

CATCHERS

No.	Name	1980 Club	H	HR	RBI	Pct.	B-T	Ht.	Wt.	Born
–	Gulden, Brad	Columbus	8	2	10	.157	L-R	5-11	182	6/10/56 New Ulm, MN
		Nashville	71	6	47	.237				
		New York (AL)	1	1	2	.333				
–	Mercado, Orlando	Lynn	101	11	71	.255	R-R	6-0	180	11/7/61 Puerto Rico
3	Narron, Jerry	Spokane	66	9	18	.283	L-R	6-3	205	1/15/56 Goldsboro, NC
		Seattle	21	4	18	.196				
–	Valle, Dave	San Jose	126	12	70	.293	R-R	6-3	205	10/30/60 Bayside, NY

INFIELDERS

No.	Name	1980 Club	H	HR	RBI	Pct.	B-T	Ht.	Wt.	Born
4	Anderson, Jim	Seattle	72	8	30	.227	R-R	6-0	170	2/23/57 Los Angeles, CA
23	Bochte, Bruce	Seattle	156	13	78	.300	L-L	6-3	200	11/12/50 Pasadena, CA
10	Cox, Ted	Seattle	60	2	23	.243	R-R	6-3	195	1/24/55 Midwest City, OK
6	Cruz, Julio	Seattle	88	2	16	.209	B-R	5-9	160	12/2/54 Brooklyn, NY
15	Edler, Dave	Spokane	132	10	72	.288	R-R	6-0	185	8/5/56 Yakima, WA
		Seattle	20	3	9	.225				
–	Guerrero, Mario	Oakland	91	2	23	.239	R-R	5-10	155	9/28/49 Dominican Republic
–	Maler, Jim	Spokane	122	9	59	.268	R-R	6-4	230	8/16/58 New York, NY

OUTFIELDERS

No.	Name	1980 Club	H	HR	RBI	Pct.	B-T	Ht.	Wt.	Born
22	Allen, Kim	Spokane	128	1	41	.294	R-R	5-11	175	4/5/53 Fontana, CA
		Seattle	51	0	3	.235				
–	Burroughs, Jeff	Atlanta	73	13	51	.263	R-R	6-0	200	3/7/51 Long Beach, CA
19	Craig, Rod	Seattle	57	3	20	.238	B-R	6-1	195	1/12/58 Los Angeles, CA
		Spokane	39	1	15	.298				
42	Henderson, Dave	Spokane	85	7	50	.279	R-R	6-2	210	7/21/58 Dos Palos, CA
51	Hobbs, Rod	Lynn	89	9	40	.221	R-R	6-3	190	5/13/59 Seattle, WA
7	Meyer, Dan	Seattle	146	11	71	.275	L-R	5-11	180	8/3/52 Hamilton, OH
–	Nanni, Tito	San Jose	38	3	23	.199	L-L	6-4	220	12/3/59 Philadelphia, PA
		Wausau	60	12	38	.254				
–	Norwood, Willie	Toledo	38	8	22	.275	R-R	6-0	193	11/7/50 Green County, AL
		Minnesota	12	1	8	.164				
14	Paciorek, Tom	Seattle	114	15	59	.273	R-R	6-4	210	11/2/46 Detroit, MI
18	Simpson, Joe	Seattle	91	3	34	.249	L-L	6-3	175	12/31/51 Purcell, OK
22	Zisk, Richie	Texas	130	19	77	.290	R-R	6-1	205	2/6/49 Brooklyn, NY

MARINER PROFILES

FLOYD BANNISTER 25 6-1 190 Bats L Throws L

Strong second-half pitcher . . . Usually gets better as season progresses . . . Acquired by M's in 1978 trade for Craig Reynolds . . . Was first player in nation picked in June 1976 draft, after outstanding career at Arizona State . . . Pitched just seven games in Houston farm system before making his major league debut with Astros in '77 . . . Born June 10, 1955, in Pierre, S.D. . . . Seems to be at his best while pitching inside the Dome . . . Toured Japan with team of major league all-stars following '79 season . . . Determined to be successful because friends and family live in Seattle suburb.

Year	Club	G	IP	W	L	Pct.	SO	BB	H	ERA
1977	Houston................	24	143	8	9	.471	112	68	138	4.03
1978	Houston................	28	110	3	9	.250	94	63	120	4.83
1979	Seattle.................	30	182	10	15	.400	115	68	185	4.05
1980	Seattle.................	32	218	9	13	.409	155	66	200	3.47
	Totals..................	114	653	30	46	.395	476	265	643	3.98

DAVE HEAVERLO 30 6-1 195 Bats R Throws R

Purchased from A's on Opening Day . . . Arrived in Seattle in fifth inning and was on the mound in the eighth . . . Mariners won and he recorded his first save . . . Acquired to be long reliever, but stepped in as righthanded short man . . . Born Aug. 25, 1950, in Ellensburg, Wash. . . . Clubhouse comic . . . "Baseball's not going to give me ulcers." . . . Shaved his head, wears wigs or ghoulish masks . . . Grew accustomed to internal turmoil in San Francisco and Oakland . . . Had reputation for not being able to hold a lead . . . "I'm out to prove to myself as well as to others that they have been wrong about me."

Year	Club	G	IP	W	L	Pct.	SO	BB	H	ERA
1975	San Francisco...........	42	64	3	1	.750	35	31	62	2.39
1976	San Francisco...........	61	75	4	4	.500	40	15	85	4.44
1977	San Francisco...........	56	99	5	1	.833	58	21	92	2.55
1978	Oakland................	69	130	3	6	.333	71	41	141	3.25
1979	Oakland................	62	86	4	11	.267	40	42	97	4.19
1980	Seattle.................	60	79	6	3	.667	42	35	75	3.87
	Totals..................	350	533	25	26	.490	286	185	552	3.43

SHANE RAWLEY 25 6-0 175 **Bats L Throws L**

Teammates taped sign that said "Goose Rawley" above his locker . . . One of the best relievers in the league . . . Used by Maury Wills in all situations, not just against left-handed hitting . . . "I'm trying to find out if he can handle that type of responsibility," says Wills . . . Confidence grew with arrival of new manager . . . Born July 27, 1955, in Racine, Wis. . . . Obtained in trade with Reds for outfielder Dave Collins . . . Is learning to fly airplanes in his spare time . . . Was Montreal's No. 2 pick in June 1974 . . . Doesn't yield many home runs.

Year	Club	G	IP	W	L	Pct.	SO	BB	H	ERA
1978	Seattle	52	111	4	9	.308	66	51	114	4.14
1979	Seattle	48	84	5	9	.357	48	40	88	3.86
1980	Seattle	59	114	7	7	.500	68	63	103	3.32
	Totals	159	309	16	25	.390	182	154	305	3.76

JIM ANDERSON 24 6-0 170 **Bats R Throws R**

Acquired from Angels to play shortstop . . . Soon shoved Mario Mendoza to the bench . . . Was All-American in high school . . . Was headed for Southern Cal to play football when Angels convinced him to try pro baseball instead . . . Was key factor in Angels' drive to division title in '79 . . . Can also play third or catch if needed . . . Born Feb. 23, 1957, in Los Angeles . . . Fine fielder . . . Batted .289 with 20 stolen bases and led Pioneer League in fielding his first season in pro ball . . . Best offensive effort came in 1977 at El Paso when he hit .285 with 18 HRs and 73 RBIs.

Year	Club	Pos.	G	AB	R	H	2B	3B	HR	RBI	SB	Avg.
1978	California	2B-SS	48	108	6	21	7	0	0	7	0	.194
1979	California	SS-3B-2B-C	96	234	33	58	13	1	3	23	3	.248
1980	Seattle	2B-SS-3B	116	317	46	72	7	0	8	30	2	.227
	Totals		260	659	85	151	27	1	11	60	5	.229

RICHIE ZISK 32 6-1 205 **Bats R Throws R**

Had not given the Rangers the sock they hoped for when they signed him as a free agent in November 1977 . . . And now he's a Mariner after waiving no-trade clause . . . A streak hitter . . . When he's hot, he's really hot . . . Can carry a club all by himself . . . Born Feb. 6, 1949, in Brooklyn . . . Can hit prodigious home runs . . . Once drove in runs in 10 games in a row while with Pittsburgh . . . Twice an All-Star . . . Attended Seton Hall U.

Year	Club	Pos.	G	AB	R	H	2B	3B	HR	RBI	SB	Avg.
1971	Pittsburgh......	OF	7	15	2	3	1	0	1	2	0	.200
1972	Pittsburgh......	OF	17	37	4	7	3	0	0	4	0	.189
1973	Pittsburgh......	OF	103	333	44	108	23	7	10	54	0	.324
1974	Pittsburgh......	OF	149	536	75	168	30	3	17	100	1	.313
1975	Pittsburgh......	OF	147	504	69	146	27	3	20	75	0	.290
1976	Pittsburgh......	OF	155	581	91	168	35	2	21	89	1	.289
1977	Chicago (AL)....	OF	141	531	78	154	17	6	30	101	0	.290
1978	Texas..........	OF	140	511	68	134	19	1	22	85	3	.262
1979	Texas..........	OF	144	503	69	132	21	1	18	64	1	.262
1980	Texas..........	OF	135	448	48	130	17	1	19	77	0	.290
	Totals..........		1138	3999	548	1150	193	24	158	651	6	.288

BRUCE BOCHTE 30 6-3 200 — Bats L Throws L

Lifted weights all winter to improve his strength, but injured his shoulder in the process . . . Quiet guy, rarely sets goals . . . Seattle's player rep and the team leader . . . Has been critical of the shabby condition of the Kingdome turf . . . Born Nov. 12, 1950, in Pasadena, Calif. . . . Makes his home in Seattle year-around . . . Was Angels' second pick in June 1972 draft . . . Signed with Mariners as a free agent . . . Was outfielder in minors but now used as DH or first baseman . . . Good speed, doesn't hesitate to go for the extra base . . . Was only Mariner at 1979 All-Star Game in Seattle.

Year	Club	Pos.	G	AB	R	H	2B	3B	HR	RBI	SB	Avg.
1974	California.......	OF-1B	57	196	24	53	4	1	5	26	6	.270
1975	California.......	1B	107	375	41	107	19	3	3	48	3	.285
1976	California.......	OF-1B	146	466	53	120	17	1	2	49	4	.258
1977	Cal.-Cle.........	OF-1B	137	492	64	148	23	1	7	51	6	.301
1978	Seattle.........	OF-1B	140	486	58	128	25	3	11	51	3	.263
1979	Seattle.........	1B	150	554	81	175	38	6	16	100	2	.316
1980	Seattle.........	1B-OF	148	520	62	156	34	4	13	78	2	.300
	Totals..........		885	3089	383	887	160	19	57	403	26	.287

JULIO CRUZ 26 5-9 160 — Bats S Throws R

May be best second baseman in A.L. when it comes to turning the double play . . . Taught to straddle the bag by M's coach Bill Mazeroski, the former Pirate star . . . Nevertheless, disgusted with 1980 performance . . . "I'm not contributing to the team." . . . Had run-ins with former manager Darrell Johnson over wearing blue jeans and playing his tape recorder . . . Became new manager Maury Wills' pet project . . . Born Dec. 2, 1954, in Brooklyn . . . "Cruz could be the All-Star second baseman," predicts Wills, "and I mean a perennial All-Star." . . . Has speed, agility, quickness and strength . . . A ton of raw talent . . . Needs to get on base more often . . . Stole 17 bases in a row.

Year	Club	Pos.	G	AB	R	H	2B	3B	HR	RBI	SB	Avg.
1977	Seattle.........	2B	60	199	25	51	3	1	1	7	15	.256
1978	Seattle.........	2B SS	147	550	77	129	14	1	1	25	59	.235
1979	Seattle.........	2B	107	414	70	112	16	2	1	29	49	.271
1980	Seattle.........	2B	119	422	66	88	9	3	2	16	45	.209
	Totals..........		433	1585	238	380	42	7	5	77	168	.240

DANNY MEYER 28 5-11 180 Bats L Throws R

Moved from third base to leftfield as former manager Darrell Johnson sought to put more punch into attack . . . Got five hits in one game to tie club record—and he got them against his former teammates, the Tigers . . . Born Aug. 3, 1952, in Hamilton, Ohio . . . Was a first-round pick in the expansion draft . . . Was once one of the brightest prospects in the Tigers' farm system after batting .396 his first year in pro ball . . . But never really established himself in Detroit . . . Has also played first base and second in his quest to find a permanent position . . . A friendly, personable guy.

Year	Club	Pos.	G	AB	R	H	2B	3B	HR	RBI	SB	Avg.
1974	Detroit.........	OF	13	50	5	10	1	1	3	7	1	.200
1975	Detroit.........	OF-1B	122	470	56	111	17	3	8	47	8	.236
1976	Detroit.........	OF-1B	105	294	37	74	8	4	2	16	10	.252
1977	Seattle.........	1B	159	582	75	159	24	4	22	90	11	.273
1978	Seattle.........	1B-OF	123	444	38	101	18	1	8	56	7	.227
1979	Seattle.........	3B-OF-1B	144	525	72	146	21	7	20	74	11	.278
1980	Seattle.........	OF-1B-3B	146	531	56	146	25	6	11	71	8	.275
	Totals..........		812	2896	339	747	114	26	74	361	56	.258

TOM PACIOREK 34 6-4 210 Bats R Throws R

Has found a home with the Mariners . . . The day he arrived he boarded the team bus and blurted out, "Am I ever glad to be here." . . . And Mariners have been happy to have him—especially his bat . . . Knows he's no wizard on defense . . . Born Nov. 2, 1946, in Detroit . . . Was two-time baseball All-American at University of Houston . . . Was good enough at football to be drafted on the ninth round by the Dolphins . . .

Comes from a very athletic family . . . Has good power . . . Was originally drafted by the Dodgers . . . Had outstanding minor league career but didn't reach majors to stay until 1973.

Year	Club	Pos.	G	AB	R	H	2B	3B	HR	RBI	SB	Avg.
1970	Los Angeles.....	OF	8	9	2	2	1	0	0	0	0	.222
1971	Los Angeles.....	OF	2	2	0	1	0	0	0	1	0	.500
1972	Los Angeles.....	OF-1B	11	47	4	12	4	0	1	6	1	.255
1973	Los Angeles.....	OF-1B	96	195	26	51	8	0	5	18	3	.262
1974	Los Angeles.....	OF-1B	85	175	23	42	8	6	1	24	1	.240
1975	Los Angeles.....	OF	62	145	14	28	8	0	1	5	4	.193
1976	Atlanta.........	OF-1B-3B	111	324	39	94	10	4	4	36	2	.290
1977	Atlanta.........	1B-OF-3B	72	155	20	37	8	0	3	15	1	.239
1978	Atlanta.........	OF-1B	5	9	2	3	0	0	0	0	0	.333
1978	Seattle.........	1B	70	251	32	75	20	3	4	30	2	.299
1979	Seattle.........	OF-1B	103	310	38	89	23	4	6	42	6	.287
1980	Seattle.........	OF-1B	126	418	44	114	19	1	15	59	3	.273
	Totals..........		751	2040	244	548	109	18	40	236	23	.269

TOP PROSPECTS

DAVE VALLE 20 6-3 205 **Bats R Throws R**

Outstanding defensive catcher . . . Seattle's No. 2 pick in June 1978 draft . . . Born Oct. 30, 1960, in Bayside, N.Y. . . . His brother, John, is an outfielder in Reds' farm system . . . Led Northwest League in putouts and double plays his first season in pro ball.

DAVE HENDERSON 22 6-2 210 **Bats R Throws R**

Power-hitting outfielder . . . Mariners' No. 1 pick in June 1977 draft . . . Was voted "Best Defensive Outfielder" and "Outfielder With the Best Arm," in California League in 1979 . . . Also an excellent hitter . . . Born July 21, 1958, in Dos Palos, Calif. . . . Could be a star soon if he continues to improve.

MANAGER MAURY WILLS: The third black to manage in the majors . . . Succeeded Darrell Johnson in August 1980 . . . Immediately began laying down the law . . . Put the Mariners through a late-season spring training, working on basics such as bunting, base running and fielding . . . "I'm not worried about winning and losing. I just want us to play well. When we lose, I want us to lose in a major league fashion." . . . Born Oct. 2, 1932, in Washington, D.C. . . . Sought to im-

Bruce Bochtc owns Mariner batting record (.316).

prove communications and teach the Mariners not to beat themselves . . . "I'm going to be honest, fair and patient." . . . Only experience as a manager came in Mexican League . . . Retired as a player in 1972 after outstanding career as record-setting base-runner . . . Spent six years as an NBC broadcaster . . . "I haven't been away from the game." . . . Turned down a chance to manage the Giants in '77 because he thought he preferred broadcasting.

GREATEST TEAM

Throughout the American League in 1979, knowledgeable people began looking at the Seattle Mariners with new respect.

Although the Mariners finished sixth, outdistancing only the inept Oakland A's, they won a team record 67 games under manager Darrell Johnson.

Willie Horton, the M's rejuvenated 36-year-old designated hitter, broke records by smashing 29 homers and knocking in 106 runs. Bruce Bochte batted .316 and also contributed 100 RBI.

Righthander Mike Parrott won 14 games and completed 13 of his starts—both all-time highs for a Seattle pitcher. Rick Honeycutt and Floyd Bannister also reached double figures on the mound.

What's more, the Mariners might even have fared much better if they had not lost both relief ace Shane Rawley and second baseman Julio Cruz for two months because of thumb injuries.

All around the league, folks were referring to the '79 Mariners as "the best third-year expansion team ever."

ALL-TIME MARINER LEADERS

BATTING: Bruce Bochte, .316, 1979
HRs: Willie Horton, 29, 1979
RBIs: Willie Horton, 106, 1979
STEALS: Julio Cruz, 59, 1978
WINS: Mike Parrott, 14, 1979
STRIKEOUTS: Floyd Bannister, 155, 1980

TEXAS RANGERS

TEAM DIRECTORY: Chairman of the Board: Eddie Chiles; Exec. VP: Eddie Robinson; Exec. VP: Samuel G. Meason; Farm Dir.: Joe Klein; News Media Dir.: Burt Hawkins; Trav. Sec.: Dan Schimek; Mgr.: Don Zimmer. Home: Arlington Stadium (41,097). Field distances: 330, l.f. line; 370, l.c.; 400, c.f.; 370, r.c.; 330, r.f. line. Spring training: Pompano Beach, Fla.

SCOUTING REPORT

HITTING: When Mickey Rivers and Bump Wills are both healthy and in the lineup, the Rangers believe they boast the

Improved bunting helped Mickey Rivers achieve .333 average.

most potent one-two punch at the top of any batting order in the league. And they may be right. Certainly, their numbers (Rivers: .333, 60 RBI, 18 stolen bases, and Wills: .263, 58 RBI, 34 SB) are nothing to sneer at. Behind them, they have Al Oliver (.319), Buddy Bell (.329) and Jim Sundberg (.273). It's an explosive offense that ranked second in the league with a .284 average, right behind division winner Kansas City, last year.

PITCHING: Continues to be the Rangers' Achilles heel. Danny Darwin (13-4) is the star on the sluggish staff that includes veterans Doc Medich (14-11), Jon Matlack (10-10) and Fergie Jenkins (12-10). Rick Honeycutt (10-17), obtained from Seattle, might help. Jenkins, who has had problems with Canadian customs officials, may encounter trouble closer to home. Fergie was dumped in Boston several years back because he couldn't get along with the manager. The Boston manager's name was Don Zimmer. Hello, Don. Hello, Fergie. The Rangers are counting on big things from John Henry Johnson and Steve Comer but the key may be reliever Jim Kern, who was a wretched 3-11 with only two saves last year. With Sparky Lyle gone, it is now up to Kern.

FIELDING: The Rangers' No. 1 need was a shortstop. They never denied that. And they think they got the guy who can do the job in Mark Wagner, a bench-warmer with the Tigers. If not, the job will belong to Mario Mendoza, who made 19 errors in 114 games with Seattle last year. Only the White Sox had a worse fielding average than the Rangers last season–in spite of the presence of catcher Sundberg and third baseman Bell, who are two of the best. Obviously, somebody else is not doing the job. Merely changing shortstops won't improve everything.

OUTLOOK: Don Zimmer has one year to try to do what Pat Corrales couldn't do in three. His first task is to hope and pray his Rangers stay healthy. Depth was supposed to be their strong suit, but a barrage of injuries left the team in shambles last year. In addition, there was dissension in the clubhouse after the front office decided to dump Corrales and keep GM Eddie Robinson, who is not particularly popular with the players. The Rangers' biggest problem over the years though, has been the months of July and August. If they can ever get to September, healthy and still in contention, they could make things interesting.

TEXAS RANGERS 1981 ROSTER

MANAGER Don Zimmer

Coaches—Jackie Brown, Tommy Helms, Darrell Johnson, Fred Koenig, Wayne Terwilliger

PITCHERS

No.	Name	1980 Club	W-L	IP	SO	ERA	B-T	Ht.	Wt.	Born
46	Babcock, Bob	Charleston	6-3	65	59	1.52	R-R	6-5	190	8/25/49 New Castle, PA
		Texas	1-2	23	15	4.70				
29	Butcher, John	Charleston	10-7	152	71	3.32	B-R	6-4	185	3/8/57 Glendale, CA
		Texas	2-2	35	27	4.11				
11	Comer, Steve	Texas	2-4	42	9	7.93	B-R	6-3	207	1/13/54 Minneapolis, MN
		Tulsa	1-2	14	8	6.28				
44	Darwin, Danny	Texas	13-4	110	104	2.62	R-R	6-3	190	10/25/55 Bonham, TX
35	Devine, Adrian	Texas	1-1	28	8	4.82	R-R	6-4	205	12/2/51 Galveston, TX
40	Honeycutt, Rick	Seattle	10-17	203	79	3.95	L-L	6-1	190	6/29/54 Chattanooga, TN
		Texas	0-0	7	2	2.57				
49	Hough, Charlie	Los Angeles	1-3	32	25	5.63	R-R	6-2	190	1/5/48 Honolulu, HI
		Texas	2-2	61	47	3.98				
31	Jenkins, Ferguson	Texas	12-12	198	129	3.77	R-R	6-5	210	12/13/43 Chatham, Ontario
38	Johnson, John Henry	Charleston	3-9	77	55	3.86	L-L	6-2	185	8/21/56 Houston, TX
		Texas	2-2	39	44	2.31				
43	Kainer, Don	Charleston	9-7	138	66	2.87	R-R	6-2	205	9/3/55 Houston, TX
		Texas	0-0	20	10	1.80				
34	Kern, Jim	Texas	3-11	63	40	4.86	R-R	6-5	205	3/15/49 Gladwin, MI
28	Lewallyn, Dennis	Albuquerque	15-2	127	58	2.13	R-R	6-4	195	8/11/53 Pensacola, FL
		Texas	0-0	6	1	7.50				
32	Matlack, Jon	Texas	10-10	235	142	3.68	L-L	6-3	200	1/19/50 West Chester, PA
33	Medich, Doc	Texas	14-11	204	91	3.93	R-R	6-5	227	12/9/48 Aliquippa, PA
26	Rajsich, Dave	Texas	2-1	48	35	6.00	L-L	6-5	180	9/28/51 Youngstown, OH
		Charleston	0-0	4	3	9.00				
15	Whitehouse, Len	Tulsa	3-2	48	38	5.44	L-L	5-11	175	9/10/57 Burlington, VT
		Charleston	8-9	99	64	4.27				

CATCHERS

No.	Name	1980 Club	H	HR	RBI	Pct.	B-T	Ht.	Wt.	Born
5	Cox, Larry	Seattle	49	4	20	.202	R-R	5-11	190	9/11/47 Bluffton, OH
9	Ellis, John	Texas	43	1	23	.236	R-R	6-2	210	8/21/48 New London, CT
8	Johnson, Bobby	Tulsa	93	13	70	.242	R-R	6-3	195	7/31/59 Dallas, TX
		Charleston	5	0	3	.147				
10	Sundberg, Jim	Texas	138	10	63	.273	R-R	6-0	196	5/18/51 Galesburg, IL

INFIELDERS

No.	Name	1980 Club	H	HR	RBI	Pct.	B-T	Ht.	Wt.	Born
25	Bell, Buddy	Texas	161	17	83	.329	R-R	6-2	185	8/27/51 Pittsburgh, PA
21	Duran, Dan	Charleston	110	13	71	.276	L-L	5-11	190	3/16/54 Palo Alto, CA
7	Holt, Roger	Columbus	81	3	35	.213	B-R	5-11	165	4/8/56 Daytona Beach, FL
		New York (AL)	1	0	1	.167				
11	Mendoza, Mario	Seattle	68	2	14	.245	R-R	5-11	187	12/26/50 Mexico
4	Norman, Nelson	Texas	7	0	1	.219	B-R	6-2	160	5/23/58 Dominican Republic
		Charleston	24	0	5	.242				
18	Putnam, Pat	Texas	108	13	55	.263	L-R	6-1	214	12/3/53 Bethel, VT
2	Richardt, Mike	Charleston	136	12	46	.279	R-R	6-0	170	5/24/58 Los Angeles, CA
		Texas	16	0	8	.225				
3	Tolleson, Wayne	Tulsa	124	1	30	.274	B-R	5-9	160	11/22/55 Spartanburg, SC
–	Wagner, Mark	Detroit	17	0	3	.236	R-R	6-1	175	3/4/54 Conneaut, OH
1	Wills, Bump	Texas	152	5	58	.263	B-R	5-9	177	7/27/52 Washington, DC

OUTFIELDERS

No.	Name	1980 Club	H	HR	RBI	Pct.	B-T	Ht.	Wt.	Born
6	Grubb, John	Texas	76	9	32	.277	L-R	6-3	188	8/4/48 Richmond, VA
53	Horton, Willie	Seattle	74	8	36	.221	R-R	5-10	210	10/18/42 Arno, VA
24	Lisi, Rick	Charleston	113	14	65	.245	R-R	6-0	175	3/17/56 Nova Scotia
19	Norris, Jim	Texas	43	0	16	.247	L-L	5-10	175	12/20/48 Brooklyn, NY
0	Oliver, Al	Texas	209	19	117	.319	L-L	6-1	203	10/14/46 Portsmouth, OH
17	Rivers, Mickey	Texas	210	7	60	.333	L-L	5-10	162	10/30/48 Miami, FL
8	Roberts, Leon	Seattle	94	10	33	.251	R-R	6-3	200	1/22/51 Vicksburg, MI
5	Sample, Billy	Texas	50	4	19	.260	R-R	5-9	175	4/2/55 Roanoke, VA

RANGER PROFILES

DANNY DARWIN 25 6-3 190 Bats R Throws R

Became the Rangers' relief ace in 1980 when Jim Kern and Sparky Lyle both faltered . . . But he belongs in the starting rotation . . . Had a 4-1 record and a 2.13 ERA when he busted his hand in a fight with fans outside Chicago's Comiskey Park . . . Spent three weeks on the disabled list . . . Born Oct. 25, 1955, in Bonham, Tex. . . . His fastball has been clocked at 94 mph . . . Strictly a power pitcher . . . Ignored by everyone in January 1976 draft . . . Nevertheless attracted 30 major league scouts while pitching in junior college . . . Signed with Rangers for sizeable bonus.

Year	Club	G	IP	W	L	Pct.	SO	BB	H	ERA
1978	Texas	3	9	1	0	1.000	8	1	11	4.00
1979	Texas	20	78	4	4	.500	58	30	50	4.04
1980	Texas	53	110	13	4	.765	104	50	98	2.62
	Totals	76	197	18	8	.692	170	81	159	3.24

JIM KERN 31 6-5 205 Bats R Throws R

Didn't do the job in 1980 . . . A major disappointment and one of the main reasons the Rangers faltered . . . As recently as the spring of '79, kept telling Pat Corrales he would be better in the starting rotation . . . Corrales didn't listen . . . "Why pitch nine innings when you can be just as famous pitching two?" . . . Born March 15, 1949, in Gladwin, Mich. . . . Called "Emu" . . . Claims his reputation as a wild man improves the already impressive velocity of his fastball, "at least in the hitters' minds." . . . "I like the scraggly look." . . . Has become more effective since he developed an off-speed pitch.

Year	Club	G	IP	W	L	Pct.	SO	BB	H	ERA
1974	Cleveland	4	15	0	1	.000	11	14	16	4.80
1975	Cleveland	13	72	1	2	.333	55	45	60	3.75
1976	Cleveland	50	118	10	7	.588	111	50	91	2.36
1977	Cleveland	60	92	8	10	.444	91	47	85	3.42
1978	Cleveland	58	99	10	10	.500	95	58	77	3.09
1979	Texas	71	143	13	5	.722	136	62	99	1.57
1980	Texas	38	63	3	11	.214	40	45	65	4.86
	Totals	294	602	45	46	.495	539	321	493	2.95

FERGIE JENKINS 37 6-5 210 **Bats R Throws R**

Arrested in Toronto after small amount of drugs was found in his luggage . . . Suspended by Bowie Kuhn, then reinstated by order of the court . . . Fourth pitcher in history to win 100 or more games in both leagues . . . Passed Bob Gibson as all-time winningest black or Latin pitcher in the big leagues . . . Born Dec. 13, 1943, in Chatham, Ontario . . . Angry at Rangers much of the year for refusing to renegotiate his contract . . . "Ten years from now, nobody is going to remember Fergie Jenkins." . . . Reaching 250 wins is the only record that really means anything to him . . . "That's something I've dreamed about and worked toward." . . . Owns a farm in Canada where he makes his home.

Year	Club	G	IP	W	L	Pct.	SO	BB	H	ERA
1965	Philadelphia	7	12	2	1	.667	10	2	7	2.25
1966	Phil.-Chi. (NL)	61	184	6	8	.429	150	52	150	3.33
1967	Chicago (NL)	38	289	20	13	.606	236	83	230	2.80
1968	Chicago (NL)	40	308	20	15	.571	260	65	255	2.63
1969	Chicago (NL)	43	311	21	15	.583	273	71	284	3.21
1970	Chicago (NL)	40	313	22	16	.579	274	60	265	3.39
1971	Chicago (NL)	39	325	24	13	.649	263	37	304	2.77
1972	Chicago (NL)	36	289	20	12	.625	184	62	253	3.21
1973	Chicago (NL)	38	271	14	16	.467	170	57	267	3.89
1974	Texas	41	328	25	12	.676	225	45	286	2.83
1975	Texas	37	270	17	18	.486	157	56	261	3.93
1976	Boston	30	209	12	11	.522	142	43	201	3.27
1977	Boston	28	193	10	10	.500	105	36	190	3.68
1978	Texas	34	249	18	8	.692	157	41	228	3.04
1979	Texas	37	259	16	14	.533	164	81	252	4.07
1980	Texas	29	198	12	12	.500	129	52	190	3.77
	Totals	578	4008	259	194	.572	2899	843	3623	3.28

BUDDY BELL 29 6-2 185 **Bats R Throws R**

Played best third base of his life in 1980 . . . Unfortunately, he was overshadowed by fellow third baseman George Brett of Kansas City . . . Doesn't make a lot of noise but hustles all the time . . . "You look at Buddy Bell in all categories," observes coach Frank Lucchesi, "You look at the pluses and minuses, and you can't find a minus in him." . . . Born Aug. 27, 1951, in Pittsburgh . . . Son of ex-major league outfielder Gus Bell . . . Hampered by painful back ailment much of last season . . . Thrives on Boston pitching . . . Best third baseman the Rangers have ever employed . . . Dependable in the clutch . . . Ignored in the free agent draft until the 16th round . . . An underrated performer.

Year	Club	Pos.	G	AB	R	H	2B	3B	HR	RBI	SB	Avg.
1972	Cleveland.......	OF-3B	132	466	49	119	21	1	9	36	5	.255
1973	Cleveland.......	3B-OF	156	631	86	169	23	7	14	59	7	.268
1974	Cleveland.......	3B	116	423	51	111	15	1	7	46	1	.262
1975	Cleveland.......	3B	153	553	66	150	20	4	10	59	6	.271
1976	Cleveland.......	3B-1B	159	604	75	170	26	2	7	60	3	.281
1977	Cleveland.......	3B-OF	129	479	64	140	23	4	11	64	1	.292
1978	Cleveland.......	3B	142	556	71	157	27	8	6	62	1	.282
1979	Texas..........	3B-SS	162	670	89	200	42	3	18	101	5	.299
1980	Texas..........	3B	129	490	76	161	24	4	17	83	3	.329
	Totals..........		1278	4872	627	1377	221	34	99	570	32	.283

PAT PUTNAM 27 6-1 214 **Bats L Throws R**

Oriole manager Earl Weaver believes he may be superstar someday . . . Grew a mustache to hide 25 stitches above his upper lip after he caught a ground ball with his face . . . Eats dog biscuits, and imitates Shamu the Whale in whirlpool . . . Born Dec. 3, 1953, in Bethel, Vt. . . . Has only spent two full years in the majors . . . Was Sporting News Rookie of the Year in '79 . . . A prolific pinch hitter when he isn't playing regularly . . . Has improved considerably at first base . . . An awesome slugger while in the minor leagues . . . Was Minor League Player of the Year in '76.

Year	Club	Pos.	G	AB	R	H	2B	3B	HR	RBI	SB	Avg.
1977	Texas..........	1B	11	26	3	8	4	0	0	3	0	.308
1978	Texas..........	1B	20	46	4	7	1	0	1	2	0	.152
1979	Texas..........	1B	139	426	57	118	19	2	18	64	1	.277
1980	Texas..........	1B	147	410	42	108	16	2	13	55	0	.263
	Totals..........		317	908	106	241	40	4	32	124	1	.265

BUMP WILLS 28 5-9 177 **Bats R Throws L**

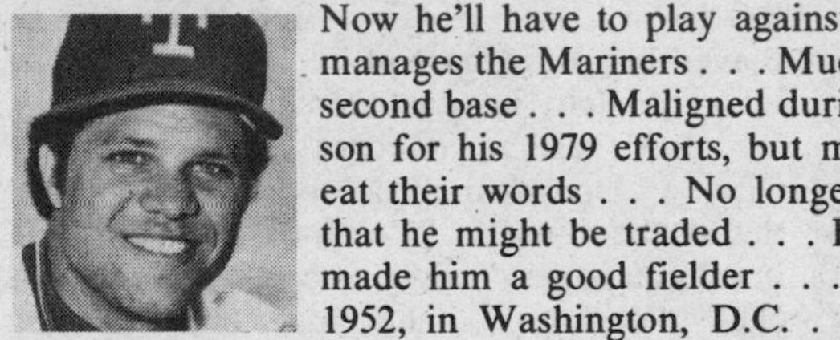

Now he'll have to play against his dad, who manages the Mariners . . . Much improved at second base . . . Maligned during the off-season for his 1979 efforts, but made his critics eat their words . . . No longer is there talk that he might be traded . . . Hard work has made him a good fielder . . . Born July 27, 1952, in Washington, D.C. . . . Good base stealer . . . Swiped more bases (115) in his first three seasons than did his famous father . . . But Maury stole 104 in his fourth year . . . Was Texas' No. 1 choice in January 1975 draft . . . Moved through Rangers' farm system in two years . . . Was rookie standout in '77.

Year	Club	Pos.	G	AB	R	H	2B	3B	HR	RBI	SB	Avg.
1977	Texas..........	2B	152	541	87	155	28	6	9	62	28	.287
1978	Texas..........	2B	157	539	78	135	17	4	9	57	52	.250
1979	Texas..........	2B	146	543	90	148	21	3	5	46	35	.273
1980	Texas..........	2B	146	578	102	152	31	5	5	58	34	.263
	Totals..........		601	2201	357	590	97	18	28	223	149	.268

AL OLIVER 34 6-1 203 Bats L Throws L

Prides himself on his ability to consistently hit .300 . . . "I've tried to be consistent in my career." . . . Got 2,000th hit during season . . . Says presence of Mickey Rivers and Bump Wills on the basepaths was responsible for his RBI increase in 1980 . . . "I don't think there's a better one-two combination in baseball." . . . Born Oct. 14, 1946, in Portsmouth, Ohio . . . Moved from leftfield to rightfield, back to left . . . Pat Corrales admitted first move was a mistake . . . "I believe I've earned the right to be put in one position and left there." . . . Got batting tip from former girl friend who told him he was lunging at plate . . . "I've paid my dues in this game and I've done my job." . . . Wears gold necklace with name "Scoop" —in minors he played first base and excelled at digging low throws out of the dirt.

Year	Club	Pos.	G	AB	R	H	2B	3B	HR	RBI	SB	Avg.
1968	Pittsburgh......	OF	4	8	1	1	0	0	0	0	0	.125
1969	Pittsburgh......	1B-OF	129	463	55	132	19	2	17	70	8	.285
1970	Pittsburgh......	OF-1B	151	551	63	149	33	5	12	83	1	.270
1971	Pittsburgh......	OF-1B	143	529	69	149	31	7	14	64	4	.282
1972	Pittsburgh......	OF-1B	140	565	88	176	27	4	12	89	2	.312
1973	Pittsburgh......	OF-1B	158	654	90	191	38	7	20	99	6	.292
1974	Pittsburgh......	OF-1B	147	617	96	198	38	12	11	85	10	.321
1975	Pittsburgh......	OF-1B	155	628	90	176	39	8	18	84	4	.280
1976	Pittsburgh......	OF-1B	121	443	62	143	22	5	12	61	6	.323
1977	Pittsburgh......	OF	154	568	75	175	29	6	19	82	13	.308
1978	Texas..........	OF	133	525	65	170	35	5	14	89	8	.324
1979	Texas..........	OF	136	492	69	159	28	4	12	76	4	.323
1980	Texas..........	OF	163	656	96	209	43	3	19	117	5	.319
	Totals..........		1734	6699	919	2028	382	68	180	999	71	.303

MICKEY RIVERS 32 5-10 162 Bats L Throws L

Enjoyed best season of his career in 1980 . . . Found happiness at last in Texas . . . Says that's because Pat Corrales promised to leave him alone . . . "They've let me relax." . . . No longer the base-stealing threat he once was, but still can run . . . Born Oct. 30, 1948, in Miami . . . Following a road trip to New York, he boarded the team bus in Texas and rode all the way to Arlington Stadium before he remembered he had left his car parked at the airport when the team left town . . . Combines with Bump Wills to put spark into Rangers' offense.

Year	Club	Pos.	G	AB	R	H	2B	3B	HR	RBI	SB	Avg.
1970	California.......	OF	17	25	6	8	2	0	0	3	1	.320
1971	California.......	OF	78	268	31	71	12	2	1	12	13	.265
1972	California.......	OF	58	159	18	34	6	2	0	7	4	.214
1973	California.......	OF	30	129	26	45	6	4	0	16	8	.349
1974	California.......	OF	118	466	69	133	19	11	3	31	30	.285
1975	California.......	OF	155	615	70	175	17	13	1	53	70	.285
1976	New York (AL)..	OF	137	590	95	184	31	8	8	67	43	.312
1977	New York (AL)..	OF	138	565	79	184	18	5	12	69	22	.326
1978	New York (AL)..	OF	141	559	78	148	25	8	11	48	25	.265
1979	NY (AL)-Texas...	OF	132	533	72	156	27	8	9	50	10	.293
1980	Texas..........	OF	147	630	96	210	32	6	7	60	18	.333
	Totals..........		1151	4539	640	1348	195	67	52	416	244	.297

JIM SUNDBERG 29 6-0 196 — Bats R Throws R

Regarded by many knowledgeable observers as the best defensive catcher in the game . . . Certainly tops in AL . . . Very durable, a necessity at that key position . . . Reached majors after only one season in minor leagues . . . Twice an All-Star . . . Nicknamed Sunny . . . Born May 18, 1951, in Galesburg, Ill. . . . Once entered a game to pinch run for speedster Bump Wills . . . Enemy runners have learned to keep their eyes open when on first base . . . He loves to pick them off . . . Always an excellent receiver, has developed into a decent hitter . . . Once put together a 22-game hitting streak.

Year	Club	Pos.	G	AB	R	H	2B	3B	HR	RBI	SB	Avg.
1974	Texas..........	C	132	368	45	91	13	3	3	36	2	.247
1975	Texas..........	C	155	472	45	94	9	0	6	36	3	.199
1976	Texas..........	C	140	448	33	102	24	2	3	34	0	.228
1977	Texas..........	C	149	453	61	132	20	3	6	65	2	.291
1978	Texas..........	C	149	518	54	144	23	6	6	58	2	.278
1979	Texas..........	C	150	495	50	136	23	4	5	64	3	.275
1980	Texas..........	C	151	505	59	138	24	1	10	63	2	.273
	Totals..........		1026	3259	347	837	136	19	39	356	14	.257

RICK HONEYCUTT 26 6-1 190 — Bats L Throws L

Came from Mariners in multi-player trade that saw departure of Richie Zisk . . . Got off to great start in '80 after Mariner pitching coach Wes Stock told him, "I can see you have no confidence, but we have confidence in you. Take the ball and pitch." . . . Born June 29, 1954, in Chattanooga, Tenn. . . . "Last year I was sure of myself. I've grown up as a starter."

. . . Credits his baby daughter Holli with much of his improvement . . . "She gave me more responsibility, helped me settle down. I have to earn for three now." . . . His big break came when Pirates sent him to Scattle . . . Probably would still be toiling in Pirates' farm system . . . Played first base while not pitching in the minor leagues.

Year	Club	G	IP	W	L	Pct.	SO	BB	H	ERA
1977	Seattle.................	10	29	0	1	.000	17	11	26	4.34
1978	Seattle.................	26	134	5	11	.313	50	49	150	4.90
1979	Seattle.................	33	194	11	12	.478	83	67	201	4.04
1980	Seattle.................	30	203	10	17	.370	79	60	221	3.95
	Totals.................	99	560	26	41	.388	229	187	598	4.23

TOP PROSPECTS

JERRY GLEATON 23 6-3 215 **Bats L Throws L**

Rangers' No. 1 pick in June 1979 draft . . . Posted 13-1 record and 1.94 ERA as junior at University of Texas . . . All-American . . . Born Sept. 14, 1957, in Brownwood, Tex. . . . Can hit, too . . . Batted over .300 as outfielder and DH in college . . . Made big league debut with Rangers in '79, after only five games in minors.

BOBBY JOHNSON 21 6-3 195 **Bats R Throws R**

Has all the tools needed to become a fine major league catcher . . . Strong arm, good hands, quick release, and good power in his bat . . . Born July 31, 1959, in Dallas . . . His uncle is former Cubs' great Ernie Banks.

MANAGER DON ZIMMER: Hired by Rangers after he was bounced in Boston . . . The Rangers' 10th manager in 10 years . . . Texas GM Eddie Robinson calls him "the best manager available." . . . Vowed he would not accept a one-year contract, but changed his mind . . . Born Jan. 17, 1931 in Cincinnati . . . Could have joined Yankees as third base coach but wanted to manage again . . . Replaced Pat Corrales, who played for him in San Diego . . . "A manager has

to be lucky." . . . Owns one of best records of any manager in baseball in recent years . . . A friendly, good-natured guy who is frequently praised for his honesty . . . Was once the most promising young player in the Brooklyn Dodgers' talent-laden farm system . . . A couple of near-tragic beanings curtailed what could have been a brilliant career . . . Keeps the race tracks busy on his days off.

GREATEST TEAM

In the spring of 1974, new manager Billy Martin put himself squarely on the spot.

"We will win," he promised. "We will contend. We will draw a million fans."

And, all around the American League, you could hear the snickers.

But when the dust settled and the season ended, there were the Texas Rangers, in second place in the American League West, a mere five games behind the Oakland A's. What's more, the Rangers had been in the race right up until the very end.

And the attendance? The Rangers had, indeed, topped the magic million mark, doubling their turnout of the previous year.

Billy Martin had kept his word.

Of course, the efforts of Fergie Jenkins, reliever Steve Foucault, Jim Bibby, MVP Jeff Burroughs, and Rookie of the Year Mike Hargrove were what really made the Rangers' remarkable about-face possible.

ALL-TIME RANGER LEADERS

BATTING: Mickey Rivers, .333, 1980
HRs: Jeff Burroughs, 30, 1973
RBIs: Jeff Burroughs, 118, 1974
STEALS: Bump Wills, 52, 1978
WINS: Ferguson Jenkins, 25, 1974
STRIKEOUTS: Gaylord Perry, 233, 1975

ALL-TIME MAJOR LEAGUE RECORDS

National	American
Batting (Season)	
Average	
.438 Hugh Duffy, Boston, 1894	.422 Napoleon Lajoie, Phila., 1901
.424 Rogers Hornsby, St. Louis, 1924	
At Bat	
699 Dave Cash, Phila., 1975	692 Bobby Richardson, N.Y., 1962
Runs	
196 William Hamilton, Phila., 1894	177 Babe Ruth, New York, 1921
158 Chuck Klein, Phila., 1930	
Hits	
254 Frank J. O'Doul, Phila., 1929	257 George Sisler, St. Louis, 1920
254 Bill Terry, New York, 1930	
Doubles	
64 Joseph M. Medwick, St. L., 1936	67 Earl W. Webb, Boston, 1931
Triples	
36 J. Owen Wilson, Pitts., 1912	26 Joseph Jackson, Cleve., 1912
	26 Samuel Crawford, Detroit, 1914
Home Runs	
56 Hack Wilson, Chicago, 1930	61 Roger Maris, New York, 1961 (162-game schedule)
	60 Babe Ruth, New York, 1927
Runs Batted in	
190 Hack Wilson, Chicago, 1930	184 Lou Gehrig, New York, 1931
Stolen Bases	
118 Lou Brock, St. Louis, 1974	96 Ty Cobb, Detroit, 1915
Bases on Balls	
148 Eddie Stanky, Brooklyn, 1945	170 Babe Ruth, New York, 1923
148 Jim Wynn, Houston, 1969	
Strikeouts	
189 Bobby Bonds, S.F., 1970	175 Dave Nicholson, Chicago, 1963
Pitching (Season)	
Games	
106 Mike Marshall, L.A., 1974	88 Wilbur Wood, Chicago, 1968
Innings Pitched	
434 Joseph J. McGinnity, N.Y., 1903	464 Edward Walsh, Chicago, 1908
Victories	
41 Jack Chesbro, New York, 1904	37 Christy Mathewson, N.Y., 1908
Losses	
29 Victor Willis, Boston, 1905	26 John Townsend, Wash., 1904
	26 Robert Groom, Wash., 1909
Strikeouts	
(Lefthander)	
382 Sandy Koufax, Los Angeles, 1965	343 Rube Waddell, Phila., 1904
(Righthander)	
303 J.R. Richard, Houston, 1978	383 Nolan Ryan, Cal., 1973
Bases on Balls	
185 Sam Jones, Chicago, 1955	208 Bob Feller, Cleveland, 1938
Earned-Run Average (Minimum 200 Innings)	
1.12 Bob Gibson, St. L., 1968	1.01 Hubert Leonard, Boston, 1914
Shutouts	
16 Grover C. Alexander, Phila., 1916	13 John W. Coombs, Phila., 1910

MAJOR LEAGUE YEAR-BY-YEAR LEADERS

NATIONAL LEAGUE MVP

Year	Player, Club
1931	Frank Frisch, St. Louis Cardinals
1932	Chuck Klein, Philadelphia Phillies
1933	Carl Hubbell, New York Giants
1934	Dizzy Dean, St. Louis Cardinals
1935	Gabby Hartnett, Chicago Cubs
1936	Carl Hubbell, New York Giants
1937	Joe Medwick, St. Louis Cardinals
1938	Ernie Lombardi, Cincinnati Reds
1939	Buck Walters, Cincinnati Reds
1940	Frank McCormick, Cincinnati Reds
1941	Dolph Camilli, Brooklyn Dodgers
1942	Mort Cooper, St. Louis Cardinals
1943	Stan Musial, St. Louis Cardinals
1944	Marty Marion, St. Louis Cardinals
1945	Phil Cavaretta, Chicago Cubs
1946	Stan Musial, St. Louis Cardinals
1947	Bob Elliott, Boston Braves
1948	Stan Musial, St. Louis Cardinals
1949	Jackie Robinson, Brooklyn Dodgers
1950	Jim Konstanty, Philadelphia Phillies
1951	Roy Campanella, Brooklyn Dodgers
1952	Hank Sauer, Chicago Cubs
1953	Roy Campanella, Brooklyn Dodgers
1954	Willie Mays, New York Giants
1955	Roy Campanella, Brooklyn Dodgers
1956	Don Newcombe, Brooklyn Dodgers
1957	Hank Aaron, Milwaukee Braves
1958	Ernie Banks, Chicago Cubs
1959	Ernie Banks, Chicago Cubs
1960	Dick Groat, Pittsburgh Pirates

Year	Player, Club
1961	Frank Robinson, Cincinnati Reds
1962	Maury Wills, Los Angeles Dodgers
1963	Sandy Koufax, Los Angeles Dodgers
1964	Ken Boyer, St. Louis Cardinals
1965	Willie Mays, San Francisco Giants
1966	Roberto Clemente, Pittsburgh Pirates
1967	Orlando Cepeda, St. Louis Cardinals
1968	Bob Gibson, St. Louis Cardinals
1969	Willie McCovey, San Francisco Giants
1970	Johnny Bench, Cincinnati Reds
1971	Joe Torre, St. Louis Cardinals
1972	Johnny Bench, Cincinnati Reds
1973	Pete Rose, Cincinnati Reds
1974	Steve Garvey, Los Angeles Dodgers
1975	Joe Morgan, Cincinnati Reds
1976	Joe Morgan, Cincinnati Reds
1977	George Foster, Cincinnati Reds
1978	Dave Parker, Pittsburgh Pirates
1979	Keith Hernandez, St. Louis Cardinals
	Willie Stargell, Pittsburgh Pirates
1980	Mike Schmidt, Philadelphia Phillies

AMERICAN LEAGUE MVP

Year	Player, Club
1931	Lefty Grove, Philadelphia Athletics
1932	Jimmy Foxx, Philadelphia Athletics
1933	Jimmy Foxx, Philadelphia Athletics
1934	Mickey Cochrane, Detroit Tigers
1935	Hank Greenberg, Detroit Tigers
1936	Lou Gehrig, New York Yankees
1937	Charley Gehringer, Detroit Tigers
1938	Jimmy Foxx, Boston Red Sox
1939	Joe DiMaggio, New York Yankees
1940	Hank Greenberg, Detroit Tigers
1941	Joe DiMaggio, New York Yankees
1942	Joe Gordon, New York Yankees
1943	Spud Chandler, New York Yankees
1944	Hal Newhouser, Detroit Tigers
1945	Hal Newhouser, Detroit Tigers
1946	Ted Williams, Boston Red Sox
1947	Joe DiMaggio, New York Yankees

Year	Player, Club
1948	Lou Boudreau, Cleveland Indians
1949	Ted Williams, Boston Red Sox
1950	Phil Rizzuto, New York Yankees
1951	Yogi Berra, New York Yankees
1952	Bobby Shantz, Philadelphia Athletics
1953	Al Rosen, Cleveland Indians
1954	Yogi Berra, New York Yankees
1955	Yogi Berra, New York Yankees
1956	Mickey Mantle, New York Yankees
1957	Mickey Mantle, New York Yankees
1958	Jackie Jensen, Boston Red Sox
1959	Nellie Fox, Chicago White Sox
1960	Roger Maris, New York Yankees
1961	Roger Maris, New York Yankees
1962	Mickey Mantle, New York Yankees
1963	Elston Howard, New York Yankees
1964	Brooks Robinson, Baltimore Orioles
1965	Zolio Versalles, Minnesota Twins
1966	Frank Robinson, Baltimore Orioles
1967	Carl Yastrzemski, Boston Red Sox
1968	Dennis McLain, Detroit Tigers
1969	Harmon Killebrew, Minnesota Twins
1970	Boog Powell, Baltimore Orioles
1971	Vida Blue, Oakland A's
1972	Dick Allen, Chicago White Sox
1973	Reggie Jackson, Oakland A's
1974	Jeff Burroughs, Texas Rangers
1975	Fred Lynn, Boston Red Sox
1976	Thurman Munson, New York Yankees
1977	Rod Carew, Minnesota Twins
1978	Jim Rice, Boston Red Sox
1979	Don Baylor, California Angels
1980	George Brett, Kansas City Royals

NATIONAL LEAGUE
Batting Champions

Year	Player, Club	Avg.
1876	Roscoe Barnes, Chicago	.403
1877	James White, Boston	.385
1878	Abner Dalrymple, Milwaukee	.356
1879	Cap Anson, Chicago	.407
1880	George Gore, Chicago	.365
1881	Cap Anson, Chicago	.399
1882	Dan Brouthers, Buffalo	.367
1883	Dan Brouthers, Buffalo	.371
1884	Jim O'Rourke, Buffalo	.350
1885	Roger Connor, New York	.371
1886	Mike Kelly, Chicago	.388
1887	Cap Anson, Chicago	.421
1888	Cap Anson, Chicago	.343
1889	Dan Brouthers, Boston	.373
1890	Jack Glassock, New York	.336
1891	Billy Hamilton, Philadelphia	.338
1892	Cupid Childs, Cleveland	.335
	Dan Brouthers, Brooklyn	.335
1893	Hugh Duffy, Boston	.378
1894	Hugh Duffy, Boston	.438
1895	Jesse Burkett, Cleveland	.423
1896	Jesse Burkett, Cleveland	.410
1897	Willie Keeler, Baltimore	.432
1898	Willie Keeler, Baltimore	.379
1899	Ed Delahanty, Philadelphia	.408
1900	Honus Wagner, Pittsburgh	.380
1901	Jesse Burkett, St. Louis Cardinals	.382
1902	C.H. Beaumont, Pittsburgh Pirates	.357
1903	Honus Wagner, Pittsburgh Pirates	.355
1904	Honus Wagner, Pittsburgh Pirates	.349
1905	J. Seymour Bentley, Cincinnati Reds	.377
1906	Honus Wagner, Pittsburgh Pirates	.339
1907	Honus Wagner, Pittsburgh Pirates	.350
1908	Honus Wagner, Pittsburgh Pirates	.354
1909	Honus Wagner, Pittsburgh Pirates	.339
1910	Sherwood Magee, Philadelphia Phillies	.331
1911	Honus Wagner, Pittsburgh Pirates	.334
1912	Heinie Zimmerman, Chicago Cubs	.372
1913	Jake Daubert, Brooklyn Dodgers	.350

Year	Player, Club	Avg.
1914	Jake Daubert, Brooklyn Dodgers	.329
1915	Larry Doyle, New York Giants	.320
1916	Hal Chase, Cincinnati Reds	.339
1917	Edd Roush, Cincinnati Reds	.341
1918	Zack Wheat, Brooklyn Dodgers	.335
1919	Edd Roush, Cincinnati Reds	.321
1920	Rogers Hornsby, St. Louis Cardinals	.370
1921	Rogers Hornsby, St. Louis Cardinals	.397
1922	Rogers Hornsby, St. Louis Cardinals	.401
1923	Rogers Hornsby, St. Louis Cardinals	.384
1924	Rogers Hornsby, St. Louis Cardinals	.424
1925	Rogers Hornsby, St. Louis Cardinals	.403
1926	Bubbles Hargrave, Cincinnati Reds	.353
1927	Paul Waner, Pittsburgh Pirates	.380
1928	Rogers Hornsby, Boston Braves	.387
1929	Lefty O'Doul, Philadelphia Phillies	.398
1930	Bill Terry, New York Giants	.401
1931	Chick Hafey, St. Louis Cardinals	.349
1932	Lefty O'Doul, Brooklyn Dodgers	.368
1933	Chuck Klein, Philadelphia Phillies	.368
1934	Paul Waner, Pittsburgh Pirates	.362
1935	Arky Vaughn, Pittsburgh Pirates	.385
1936	Paul Waner, Pittsburgh Pirates	.373
1937	Joe Medwick, St. Louis Cardinals	.374
1938	Ernie Lombardi, Cincinnati Reds	.342
1939	Johnny Mize, St. Louis Cardinals	.349
1940	Debs Garms, Pittsburgh Pirates	.355
1941	Pete Reiser, Brooklyn Dodgers	.343
1942	Ernie Lombardi, Boston Braves	.330
1943	Stan Musial, St. Louis Cardinals	.330
1944	Dixie Walker, Brooklyn Dodgers	.357
1945	Phil Cavarretta, Chicago Cubs	.355
1946	Stan Musial, St. Louis Cardinals	.365
1947	Harry Walker, St. L. Cardinals-Phila. Phillies	.363
1948	Stan Musial, St. Louis Cardinals	.376
1949	Jackie Robinson, Brooklyn Dodgers	.342
1950	Stan Musial, St. Louis Cardinals	.346
1951	Stan Musial, St. Louis Cardinals	.355
1952	Stan Musial, St. Louis Cardinals	.336
1953	Carl Furillo, Brooklyn Dodgers	.344
1954	Willie Mays, New York Giants	.345
1955	Richie Ashburn, Philadelphia Phillies	.338
1956	Hank Aaron, Milwaukee Braves	.328
1957	Stan Musial, St. Louis Cardinals	.351

Year	Player, Club	Avg.
1958	Richie Ashburn, Philadelphia Phillies	.350
1959	Hank Aaron, Milwaukee Braves	.328
1960	Dick Groat, Pittsburgh Pirates	.325
1961	Roberto Clemente, Pittsburgh Pirates	.351
1962	Tommy Davis, Los Angeles Dodgers	.346
1963	Tommy Davis, Los Angeles Dodgers	.326
1964	Roberto Clemente, Pittsburgh Pirates	.339
1965	Roberto Clemente, Pittsburgh Pirates	.329
1966	Matty Alou, Pittsburgh Pirates	.342
1967	Roberto Clemente, Pittsburgh Pirates	.357
1968	Pete Rose, Cincinnati Reds	.335
1969	Pete Rose, Cincinnati Reds	.348
1970	Rico Carty, Atlanta Braves	.366
1971	Joe Torre, St. Louis Cardinals	.363
1972	Billy Williams, Chicago Cubs	.333
1973	Pete Rose, Cincinnati Reds	.338
1974	Ralph Garr, Atlanta Braves	.353
1975	Bill Madlock, Chicago Cubs	.354
1976	Bill Madlock, Chicago Cubs	.339
1977	Dave Parker, Pittsburgh Pirates	.338
1978	Dave Parker, Pittsburgh Pirates	.334
1979	Keith Hernandez, St. Louis Cardinals	.344
1980	Bill Buckner, Chicago Cubs	.324

AMERICAN LEAGUE

Batting Champions

Year	Player, Club	Avg.
1901	Napoleon Lajoie, Philadelphia Athletics	.422
1902	Ed Delahanty, Washington Senators	.376
1903	Napoleon Lajoie, Cleveland Indians	.355
1904	Napoleon Lajoie, Cleveland Indians	.381
1905	Elmer Flick, Cleveland Indians	.306
1906	George Stone, St. Louis Browns	.358
1907	Ty Cobb, Detroit Tigers	.350
1908	Ty Cobb, Detroit Tigers	.324
1909	Ty Cobb, Detroit Tigers	.377
1910	Ty Cobb, Detroit Tigers	.385
1911	Ty Cobb, Detroit Tigers	.420
1912	Ty Cobb, Detroit Tigers	.410
1913	Ty Cobb, Detroit Tigers	.390
1914	Ty Cobb, Detroit Tigers	.368
1915	Ty Cobb, Detroit Tigers	.370
1916	Tris Speaker, Cleveland Indians	.386
1917	Ty Cobb, Detroit Tigers	.383
1918	Ty Cobb, Detroit Tigers	.382
1919	Ty Cobb, Detroit Tigers	.384
1920	George Sisler, St. Louis Browns	.407
1921	Harry Heilmann, Detroit Tigers	.393
1922	George Sisler, St. Louis Browns	.420
1923	Harry Heilmann, Detroit Tigers	.398
1924	Babe Ruth, New York Yankees	.378
1925	Harry Heilmann, Detroit Tigers	.393
1926	Heinie Manush, Detroit Tigers	.377
1927	Harry Heilmann, Detroit Tigers	.398
1928	Goose Goslin, Washington Senators	.379
1929	Lew Fonseca, Cleveland Indians	.369
1930	Al Simmons, Philadelphia Athletics	.381
1931	Al Simmons, Philadelphia Athletics	.390
1932	David Alexander, Detroit Tigers-Boston Red Sox	.367
1933	Jimmy Foxx, Philadelphia Athletics	.356
1934	Lou Gehrig, New York Yankees	.365
1935	Buddy Myer, Washington Senators	.349
1936	Luke Appling, Chicago White Sox	.388
1937	Charlie Gehringer, Detroit Tigers	.371
1938	Jimmy Foxx, Boston Red Sox	.349
1939	Joe DiMaggio, New York Yankees	.381
1940	Joe DiMaggio, New York Yankees	.352

Year	Player, Club	Avg.
1941	Ted Williams, Boston Red Sox	.406
1942	Ted Williams, Boston Red Sox	.356
1943	Luke Appling, Chicago White Sox	.328
1944	Lou Boudreau, Cleveland Indians	.327
1945	Snuffy Stirnweiss, New York Yankees	.309
1946	Mickey Vernon, Washington Senators	.353
1947	Ted Williams, Boston Red Sox	.343
1948	Ted Williams, Boston Red Sox	.369
1949	George Kell, Detroit Tigers	.343
1950	Billy Goodman, Boston Red Sox	.354
1951	Ferris Fain, Philadelphia Athletics	.344
1952	Ferris Fain, Philadelphia Athletics	.327
1953	Mickey Vernon, Washington Senators	.337
1954	Bobby Avila, Cleveland Indians	.341
1955	Al Kaline, Detroit Tigers	.340
1956	Mickey Mantle, New York Yankees	.353
1957	Ted Williams, Boston Red Sox	.388
1958	Ted Williams, Boston Red Sox	.328
1959	Harvey Kuenn, Detroit Tigers	.353
1960	Pete Runnels, Boston Red Sox	.320
1961	Norm Cash, Detroit Tigers	.361
1962	Pete Runnels, Boston Red Sox	.326
1963	Carl Yastrzemski, Boston Red Sox	.321
1964	Tony Oliva, Minnesota Twins	.323
1965	Tony Oliva, Minnesota Twins	.321
1966	Frank Robinson, Baltimore Orioles	.316
1967	Carl Yastrzemski, Boston Red Sox	.326
1968	Carl Yastrzemski, Boston Red Sox	.301
1969	Rod Carew, Minnesota Twins	.332
1970	Alex Johnson, California Angels	.329
1971	Tony Oliva, Minnesota Twins	.337
1972	Rod Carew, Minnesota Twins	.318
1973	Rod Carew, Minnesota Twins	.350
1974	Rod Carew, Minnesota Twins	.364
1975	Rod Carew, Minnesota Twins	.359
1976	George Brett, Kansas City Royals	.333
1977	Rod Carew, Minnesota Twins	.388
1978	Rod Carew, Minnesota Twins	.333
1979	Fred Lynn, Boston Red Sox	.333
1980	George Brett, Kansas City Royals	.390

NATIONAL LEAGUE

Home Run Leaders

Year	Player, Club	HRs
1900	Herman Long, Boston	12
1901	Sam Crawford, Cincinnati Reds	16
1902	Tom Leach, Pittsburgh Pirates	6
1903	Jim Sheckard, Brooklyn Dodgers	9
1904	Harry Lumley, Brooklyn Dodgers	9
1905	Fred Odwell, Cincinnati Reds	9
1906	Tim Jordan, Brooklyn Dodgers	12
1907	Dave Brian, Boston	10
1908	Tim Jordan, Brooklyn Dodgers	12
1909	Jim Murray, New York Giants	7
1910	Fred Beck, Boston	10
	Frank Schulte, Chicago Cubs	10
1911	Frank Schulte, Chicago Cubs	21
1912	Heinie Zimmerman, Chicago Cubs	14
1913	Gavvy Cravath, Philadelphia Phillies	19
1914	Gavvy Cravath, Philadelphia Phillies	19
1915	Gavvy Cravath, Philadelphia Phillies	24
1916	Dave Robertson, New York Giants	12
	Cy Williams, Chicago Cubs	12
1917	Gavvy Cravath, Philadelphia Phillies	12
	Dave Robertson, New York Giants	12
1918	Gavvy Cravath, Philadelphia Phillies	8
1919	Gavvy Cravath, Philadelphia Phillies	12
1920	Cy Williams, Philadelphia Phillies	15
1921	George Kelly, New York Giants	23
1922	Rogers Hornsby, St. Louis Cardinals	39
1923	Cy Williams, Philadelphia Phillies	41
1924	Jack Fournier, Brooklyn Dodgers	27
1925	Rogers Hornsby, St. Louis Cardinals	39
1926	Hack Wilson, Chicago Cubs	21
1927	Cy Williams, Philadelphia Phillies	30
	Hack Wilson, Chicago Cubs	30
1928	Jim Bottomley, St. Louis Cardinals	31
	Hack Wilson, Chicago Cubs	31
1929	Chuck Klein, Philadelphia Phillies	43
1930	Hack Wilson, Chicago Cubs	56
1931	Chuck Klein, Philadelphia Phillies	31
1932	Chuck Klein, Philadelphia Phillies	38
	Mel Ott, New York Giants	38
1933	Chuck Klein, Philadelphia Phillies	43

Year	Player, Club	HRs
1934	Rip Collins, St. Louis Cardinals	35
	Mel Ott, New York Giants	35
1935	Wally Berger, Boston Braves	34
1936	Mel Ott, New York Giants	33
1937	Joe Medwick, St. Louis Cardinals	31
	Mel Ott, New York Giants	31
1938	Mel Ott, New York Giants	36
1939	Johnny Mize, St. Louis Cardinals	28
1940	Johnny Mize, St. Louis Cardinals	43
1941	Dolph Camilli, Brooklyn Dodgers	34
1942	Mel Ott, New York Giants	30
1943	Bill Nicholson, Chicago Cubs	29
1944	Bill Nicholson, Chicago Cubs	33
1945	Tommy Holmes, Boston Braves	28
1946	Ralph Kiner, Pittsburgh Pirates	23
1947	Ralph Kiner, Pittsburgh Pirates	51
	Johnny Mize, New York Giants	51
1948	Ralph Kiner, Pittsburgh Pirates	40
	Johnny Mize, New York Giants	40
1949	Ralph Kiner, Pittsburgh Pirates	54
1950	Ralph Kiner, Pittsburgh Pirates	47
1951	Ralph Kiner, Pittsburgh Pirates	42
1952	Ralph Kiner, Pittsburgh Pirates	37
	Hank Sauer, Chicago Cubs	37
1953	Eddie Mathews, Milwaukee Braves	47
1954	Ted Kluszewski, Cincinnati Reds	49
1955	Willie Mays, New York Giants	51
1956	Duke Snider, Brooklyn Dodgers	43
1957	Hank Aaron, Milwaukee Braves	44
1958	Ernie Banks, Chicago Cubs	47
1959	Eddie Mathews, Milwaukee Braves	46
1960	Ernie Banks, Chicago Cubs	41
1961	Orlando Cepeda, San Francisco Giants	46
1962	Willie Mays, San Francisco Giants	49
1963	Hank Aaron, Milwaukee Braves	44
	Willie McCovey, San Francisco Giants	44
1964	Willie Mays, San Francisco Giants	47
1965	Willie Mays, San Francisco Giants	52
1966	Hank Aaron, Atlanta Braves	44
1967	Hank Aaron, Atlanta Braves	39
1968	Willie McCovey, San Francisco Giants	36
1969	Willie McCovey, San Francisco Giants	45
1970	Johnny Bench, Cincinnati Reds	45
1971	Willie Stargell, Pittsburgh Pirates	48

Year	Player, Club	HRs
1972	Johnny Bench, Cincinnati Reds	40
1973	Willie Stargell, Pittsburgh Pirates	44
1974	Mike Schmidt, Philadelphia Phillies	36
1975	Mike Schmidt, Philadelphia Phillies	38
1976	Mike Schmidt, Philadelphia Phillies	38
1977	George Foster, Cincinnati Reds	52
1978	George Foster, Cincinnati Reds	40
1979	Dave Kingman, Chicago Cubs	48
1980	Mike Schmidt, Philadelphia Phillies	48

AMERICAN LEAGUE
Home Run Leaders

Year	Player, Club	HRs
1901	Napoleon Lajoie, Philadelphia Athletics	13
1902	Ralph Seybold, Philadelphia Athletics	16
1903	John Freeman, Boston Red Sox	13
1904	Harry Davis, Philadelphia Athletics	10
1905	Harry Davis, Philadelphia Athletics	8
1906	Harry Davis, Philadelphia Athletics	12
1907	Harry Davis, Philadelphia Athletics	8
1908	Sam Crawford, Detroit Tigers	7
1909	Ty Cobb, Detroit Tigers	9
1910	Garland Stahl, Boston Red Sox	10
1911	Home Run Baker, Philadelphia Athletics	9
1912	Home Run Baker, Philadelphia Athletics	10
1913	Home Run Baker, Philadelphia Athletics	12
1914	Home Run Baker, Philadelphia Athletics	8
	Sam Crawford, Detroit Tigers	8
1915	Bob Roth, Cleveland Indians	7
1916	Wally Pipp, New York Yankees	12
1917	Wally Pipp, New York Yankees	9
1918	Babe Ruth, Boston Red Sox	11
	Clarence Walker, Philadelphia Athletics	11
1919	Babe Ruth, Boston Red Sox	29
1920	Babe Ruth, New York Yankees	54
1921	Babe Ruth, New York Yankees	59
1922	Ken Williams, St. Louis Browns	39
1923	Babe Ruth, New York Yankees	43

Year	Player, Club	HRs
1924	Babe Ruth, New York Yankees	46
1925	Bob Meusel, New York Yankees	33
1926	Babe Ruth, New York Yankees	47
1927	Babe Ruth, New York Yankees	60
1928	Babe Ruth, New York Yankees	54
1929	Babe Ruth, New York Yankees	46
1930	Babe Ruth, New York Yankees	49
1931	Babe Ruth, New York Yankees	46
	Lou Gehrig, New York Yankees	46
1932	Jimmy Foxx, Philadelphia Athletics	58
1933	Jimmy Foxx, Philadelphia Athletics	48
1934	Lou Gehrig, New York Yankees	49
1935	Hank Greenberg, Detroit Tigers	36
	Jimmy Foxx, Philadelphia Athletics	36
1936	Lou Gehrig, New York Yankees	49
1937	Joe DiMaggio, New York Yankees	49
1938	Hank Greenberg, Detroit Tigers	46
1939	Jimmy Foxx, Boston Red Sox	35
1940	Hank Greenberg, Detroit Tigers	41
1941	Ted Williams, Boston Red Sox	37
1942	Ted Williams, Boston Red Sox	36
1943	Rudy York, Detroit Tigers	34
1944	Nick Etten, New York Yankees	22
1945	Vern Stephens, St. Louis Browns	24
1946	Hank Greenberg, Detroit Tigers	44
1947	Ted Williams, Boston Red Sox	32
1948	Joe DiMaggio, New York Yankees	39
1949	Ted Williams, Boston Red Sox	43
1950	Al Rosen, Cleveland Indians	37
1951	Gus Zernial, Philadelphia Athletics	33
1952	Larry Doby, Cleveland Indians	32
1953	Al Rosen, Cleveland Indians	43
1954	Larry Doby, Cleveland Indians	32
1955	Mickey Mantle, New York Yankees	37
1956	Mickey Mantle, New York Yankees	56
1957	Roy Sievers, Washington Senators	42
1958	Mickey Mantle, New York Yankees	42
1959	Rocky Colavito, Cleveland Indians	42
	Harmon Killebrew, Washington Senators	42
1960	Mickey Mantle, New York Yankees	40
1961	Roger Maris, New York Yankees	61
1962	Harmon Killebrew, Minnesota Twins	48
1963	Harmon Killebrew, Minnesota Twins	45
1964	Harmon Killebrew, Minnesota Twins	49

Year	Player, Club	HRs
1965	Tony Conigliaro, Boston Red Sox	32
1966	Frank Robinson, Baltimore Orioles	49
1967	Carl Yastrzemski, Boston Red Sox	44
	Harmon Killebrew, Minnesota Twins	44
1968	Frank Howard, Washington Senators	44
1969	Harmon Killebrew, Minnesota Twins	49
1970	Frank Howard, Washington Senators	44
1971	Bill Melton, Chicago White Sox	33
1972	Dick Allen, Chicago White Sox	37
1973	Reggie Jackson, Oakland A's	32
1974	Dick Allen, Chicago White Sox	32
1975	George Scott, Milwaukee Brewers	36
	Reggie Jackson, Oakland A's	36
1976	Graig Nettles, New York Yankees	32
1977	Jim Rice, Boston Red Sox	39
1978	Jim Rice, Boston Red Sox	46
1979	Gorman Thomas, Milwaukee Brewers	45
1980	Ben Oglivie, Milwaukee Brewers	41
	Reggie Jackson, New York Yankees	41

CY YOUNG AWARD WINNERS

(Prior to 1967 only one pitcher won an overall major league award.)

Year	Player, Club
1956	Don Newcombe, Brooklyn Dodgers
1957	Warren Spahn, Milwaukee Braves
1958	Bob Turley, New York Yankees
1959	Early Wynn, Chicago White Sox
1960	Vernon Law, Pittsburgh Pirates
1961	Whitey Ford, New York Yankees
1962	Don Drysdale, Los Angeles Dodgers
1963	Sandy Koufax, Los Angeles Dodgers
1964	Dean Chance, Los Angeles Angels
1965	Sandy Koufax, Los Angeles Dodgers
1966	Sandy Koufax, Los Angeles Dodgers

AMERICAN LEAGUE

Year	Player, Club
1967	Jim Lonborg, Boston Red Sox
1968	Dennis McLain, Detroit Tigers
1969	Mike Cuellar, Baltimore Orioles
	Dennis McLain, Detroit Tigers
1970	Jim Perry, Minnesota Twins
1971	Vida Blue, Oakland A's
1972	Gaylord Perry, Cleveland Indians
1973	Jim Palmer, Baltimore Orioles
1974	Jim Hunter, Oakland A's
1975	Jim Palmer, Baltimore Orioles
1976	Jim Palmer, Baltimore Orioles
1977	Sparky Lyle, New York Yankees
1978	Ron Guidry, New York Yankees
1979	Mike Flanagan, Baltimore Orioles
1980	Steve Stone, Baltimore Orioles

NATIONAL LEAGUE

Year	Player, Club
1967	Mike McCormick, San Francisco Giants
1968	Bob Gibson, St. Louis Cardinals
1969	Tom Seaver, New York Mets
1970	Bob Gibson, St. Louis Cardinals
1971	Ferguson Jenkins, Chicago Cubs
1972	Steve Carlton, Philadelphia Phillies
1973	Tom Seaver, New York Mets
1974	Mike Marshall, Los Angeles Dodgers
1975	Tom Seaver, New York Mets
1976	Randy Jones, San Diego Padres
1977	Steve Carlton, Philadelphia Phillies
1978	Gaylord Perry, San Diego Padres
1979	Bruce Sutter, Chicago Cubs
1980	Steve Carlton, Philadelphia Phillies

NATIONAL LEAGUE
Rookie of Year

Year	Player, Club
1947	Jackie Robinson, Brooklyn Dodgers
1948	Al Dark, Boston Braves
1949	Don Newcombe, Brooklyn Dodgers
1950	Sam Jethroe, Boston Braves
1951	Willie Mays, New York Giants
1952	Joe Black, Brooklyn Dodgers
1953	Junior Gilliam, Brooklyn Dodgers
1954	Wally Moon, St. Louis Cardinals
1955	Bill Virdon, St. Louis Cardinals
1956	Frank Robinson, Cincinnati Reds
1957	Jack Sanford, Philadelphia Phillies
1958	Orlando Cepeda, San Francisco Giants
1959	Willie McCovey, San Francisco Giants
1960	Frank Howard, Los Angeles Dodgers
1961	Billy Williams, Chicago Cubs
1962	Kenny Hubbs, Chicago Cubs
1963	Pete Rose, Cincinnati Reds
1964	Richie Allen, Philadelphia Phillies
1965	Jim Lefebvre, Los Angeles Dodgers
1966	Tommy Helms, Cincinnati Reds
1967	Tom Seaver, New York Mets
1968	Johnny Bench, Cincinnati Reds
1969	Ted Sizemore, Los Angeles Dodgers
1970	Carl Morton, Montreal Expos
1971	Earl Williams, Atlanta Braves
1972	Jon Matlack, New York Mets
1973	Gary Matthews, San Francisco Giants
1974	Bake McBride, St. Louis Cardinals
1975	John Montefusco, San Francisco Giants
1976	Pat Zachry, Cincinnati Reds
	Butch Metzger, San Diego Padres
1977	Andre Dawson, Montreal Expos
1978	Bob Horner, Atlanta Braves
1979	Rick Sutcliffe, Los Angeles Dodgers
1980	Steve Howe, Los Angeles Dodgers

AMERICAN LEAGUE
Rookie of Year

Year	Player, Club
1949	Roy Sievers, St. Louis Browns
1950	Walt Dropo, Boston Red Sox
1951	Gil McDougald, New York Yankees
1952	Harry Byrd, Philadelphia Athletics
1953	Harvey Kuenn, Detroit Tigers
1954	Bob Grim, New York Yankees
1955	Herb Score, Cleveland Indians
1956	Luis Aparicio, Chicago White Sox
1957	Tony Kubek, New York Yankees
1958	Albie Pearson, Washington Senators
1959	Bob Allison, Washington Senators
1960	Ron Hansen, Baltimore Orioles
1961	Don Schwall, Boston Red Sox
1962	Tom Tresh, New York Yankees
1963	Gary Peters, Chicago White Sox
1964	Tony Oliva, Minnesota Twins
1965	Curt Blefary, Baltimore Orioles
1966	Tommie Agee, Chicago White Sox
1967	Rod Carew, Minnesota Twins
1968	Stan Bahnsen, New York Yankees
1969	Lou Piniella, Kansas City Royals
1970	Thurman Munson, New York Yankees
1971	Chris Chambliss, Cleveland Indians
1972	Carlton Fisk, Boston Red Sox
1973	Al Bumbry, Baltimore Orioles
1974	Mike Hargrove, Texas Rangers
1975	Fred Lynn, Boston Red Sox
1976	Mark Fidrych, Detroit Tigers
1977	Eddie Murray, Baltimore Orioles
1978	Lou Whitaker, Detroit Tigers
1979	John Castino, Minnesota Twins
	Alfredo Griffin, Toronto Blue Jays
1980	Joe Charboneau, Cleveland Indians

WORLD SERIES WINNERS

Year	A. L. Champion	N. L. Champion	World Series Winner
1903	Boston Red Sox	Pittsburgh Pirates	Boston, 5-3
1905	Philadelphia Athletics	New York Giants	New York, 4-1
1906	Chicago White Sox	Chicago Cubs	Chicago (AL), 4-2
1907	Detroit Tigers	Chicago Cubs	Chicago, 4-0-1
1908	Detroit Tigers	Chicago Cubs	Chicago, 4-1
1909	Detroit Tigers	Pittsburgh Pirates	Pittsburgh, 4-3
1910	Philadelphia Athletics	Chicago Cubs	Philadelphia, 4-1
1911	Philadelphia Athletics	New York Giants	Philadelphia, 4-2
1912	Boston Red Sox	New York Giants	Boston, 4-3-1
1913	Philadelphia Athletics	New York Giants	Philadelphia, 4-1
1914	Philadelphia Athletics	Boston Braves	Boston, 4-0
1915	Boston Red Sox	Philadelphia Phillies	Boston, 4-1
1916	Boston Red Sox	Brooklyn Dodgers	Boston, 4-1
1917	Chicago White Sox	New York Giants	Chicago, 4-2
1918	Boston Red Sox	Chicago Cubs	Boston, 4-2
1919	Chicago White Sox	Cincinnati Reds	Cincinnati, 5-2
1920	Cleveland Indians	Brooklyn Dodgers	Cleveland, 5-2
1921	New York Yankees	New York Giants	New York (NL), 5-3
1922	New York Yankees	New York Giants	New York (NL), 4-0-1
1923	New York Yankees	New York Giants	New York (AL), 4-2
1924	Washington Senators	New York Giants	Washington, 4-2
1925	Washington Senators	Pittsburgh Pirates	Pittsburgh, 4-3
1926	New York Yankees	St. Louis Cardinals	St. Louis, 4-3
1927	New York Yankees	Pittsburgh Pirates	New York, 4-0
1928	New York Yankees	St. Louis Cardinals	New York, 4-0
1929	Philadelphia Athletics	Chicago Cubs	Philadelphia, 4-2
1930	Philadelphia Athletics	St. Louis Cardinals	Philadelphia, 4-2
1931	Philadelphia Athletics	St. Louis Cardinals	St. Louis, 4-3
1932	New York Yankees	Chicago Cubs	New York, 4-0
1933	Washington Senators	New York Giants	New York, 4-1
1934	Detroit Tigers	St. Louis Cardinals	St. Louis, 4-3
1935	Detroit Tigers	Chicago Cubs	Detroit, 4-2
1936	New York Yankees	New York Giants	New York (AL), 4-2
1937	New York Yankees	New York Giants	New York (AL), 4-1
1938	New York Yankees	Chicago Cubs	New York, 4-0
1939	New York Yankees	Cincinnati Reds	New York, 4-0
1940	Detroit Tigers	Cincinnati Reds	Cincinnati, 4-3
1941	New York Yankees	Brooklyn Dodgers	New York, 4-1
1942	New York Yankees	St. Louis Cardinals	St. Louis, 4-1
1943	New York Yankees	St. Louis Cardinals	New York, 4-1
1944	St. Louis Browns	St. Louis Cardinals	St. Louis (NL), 4-2
1945	Detroit Tigers	Chicago Cubs	Detroit, 4-3
1946	Boston Red Sox	St. Louis Cardinals	St. Louis, 4-3
1947	New York Yankees	Brooklyn Dodgers	New York, 4-3
1948	Cleveland Indians	Boston Braves	Cleveland, 4-2
1949	New York Yankees	Brooklyn Dodgers	New York, 4-1
1950	New York Yankees	Philadelphia Phillies	New York, 4-0

Year	A. L. Champion	N. L. Champion	World Series Winner
1951	New York Yankees	New York Giants	New York (AL), 4-2
1952	New York Yankees	Brooklyn Dodgers	New York, 4-3
1953	New York Yankees	Brooklyn Dodgers	New York, 4-2
1954	Cleveland Indians	New York Giants	New York, 4-0
1955	New York Yankees	Brooklyn Dodgers	Brooklyn, 4-3
1956	New York Yankees	Brooklyn Dodgers	New York, 4-3
1957	New York Yankees	Milwaukee Braves	Milwaukee, 4-3
1958	New York Yankees	Milwaukee Braves	New York, 4-3
1959	Chicago White Sox	Los Angeles Dodgers	Los Angeles, 4-2
1960	New York Yankees	Pittsburgh Pirates	Pittsburgh, 4-3
1961	New York Yankees	Cincinnati Reds	New York, 4-1
1962	New York Yankees	San Francisco Giants	New York, 4-3
1963	New York Yankees	Los Angeles Dodgers	Los Angeles, 4-0
1964	New York Yankees	St. Louis Cardinals	St. Louis, 4-3
1965	Minnesota Twins	Los Angeles Dodgers	Los Angeles, 4-3
1966	Baltimore Orioles	Los Angeles Dodgers	Baltimore, 4-0
1967	Boston Red Sox	St. Louis Cardinals	St. Louis, 4-3
1968	Detroit Tigers	St. Louis Cardinals	Detroit, 4-3
1969	Baltimore Orioles	New York Mets	New York, 4-1
1970	Baltimore Orioles	Cincinnati Reds	Baltimore, 4-1
1971	Baltimore Orioles	Pittsburgh Pirates	Pittsburgh, 4-3
1972	Oakland A's	Cincinnati Reds	Oakland, 4-3
1973	Oakland A's	New York Mets	Oakland, 4-3
1974	Oakland A's	Los Angeles Dodgers	Oakland, 4-1
1975	Boston Red Sox	Cincinnati Reds	Cincinnati, 4-3
1976	New York Yankees	Cincinnati Reds	Cincinnati, 4-0
1977	New York Yankees	Los Angeles Dodgers	New York, 4-2
1978	New York Yankees	Los Angeles Dodgers	New York, 4-2
1979	Baltimore Orioles	Pittsburgh Pirates	Pittsburgh, 4-3
1980	Kansas City Royals	Philadelphia Phillies	Philadelphia, 4-2

1980 WORLD SERIES

PHILADELPHIA PHILLIES

Batter	AVG	G	AB	R	H	2B	3B	HR	RBI	GW RBI	BB	SO	SH	SF	HB	SB	CS	E
Boone	.412	6	17	3	7	2	0	0	4	0	4	0	0	1	0	0	0	0
Bowa, L.	.316		19	2	6	0	0	0	1	0	0	0	0	0	0	3	0	0
Bowa, R	.600		5	1	3	1	0	0	1	0	0	0	0	0	0	0	0	0
Bowa, T.	.375	6	24	3	9	1	0	0	2	0	0	0	0	0	0	3	0	0
Gross	.000	4	2	0	0	0	0	0	0	0	0	0	1	0	0	0	0	0
Luzinski	.000	3	9	0	0	0	0	0	0	0	1	5	0	0	1	0	0	0
Maddox	.227	6	22	1	5	2	0	0	1	0	1	3	0	1	0	0	0	0
McBride	.304	6	23	3	7	1	0	1	5	1	2	1	0	0	0	0	1	0
Moreland	.333	3	12	1	4	0	0	0	1	0	0	1	1	0	0	0	0	0
Rose, L	.313		16	2	5	1	0	0	1	0	2	2	0	0	1	0	0	0
Rose, R	.143		7	0	1	0	0	0	0	0	0	0	0	0	0	0	1	0
Rose, T	.261	6	23	2	6	1	0	0	1	0	2	2	0	0	1	0	1	0
Schmidt	.381	6	21	6	8	1	0	2	7	2	4	3	0	1	0	0	0	0
Smith	.263	6	19	2	5	1	0	0	1	0	1	1	0	0	0	0	1	0
Trillo	.217	6	23	4	5	2	0	0	2	1	0	0	0	1	0	0	0	1
Unser	.500	3	6	2	3	2	0	0	2	0	0	1	0	0	0	0	0	0
DH Hitters	.174		23	1	4	0	0	0	1	0	0	5	1	0	1	0	0	0
PH Hitters	.667		3	2	2	2	0	0	2	0	0	0	1	0	0	0	0	0
Others	.000		0	0	0	0	0	0	0	0	0	0	0	0	0	0	0	1
TOTALS	.294		201	27	59	13	0	3	26	4	15	17	2	4	2	3	3	2

Pitcher	W	L	ERA	G	GS	CG	SHO	SV	IP	H	R	ER	HR	BB	SO	HB	WP
Brusstar, R	0	0	.00	1	0	0	0	0	2.1	0	0	0	0	1	0	0	0
Bystrom, R	0	0	5.40	1	1	0	0	0	5.0	10	3	3	1	1	4	0	0
Carlton, L	2	0	2.40	2	2	0	0	0	15.0	14	5	4	0	9	17	0	1
Christenson, R	0	1	1.08	1	1	0	0	0	.1	5	4	4	1	0	0	0	0
McGraw, L	1	1	1.17	4	0	0	0	2	7.2	7	1	1	0	8	10	0	0
Noles, R	0	0	1.93	1	0	0	0	0	4.2	5	1	1	1	2	6	0	0
Reed, R	0	0	.00	2	0	0	0	1	2.0	2	0	0	0	0	2	0	0
Ruthven, R	0	0	3.00	1	1	0	0	0	9.0	9	3	3	2	0	7	0	0
Saucier, L	0	0	.00	1	0	0	0	0	.2	0	0	0	0	2	0	0	1
Walk, R	1	0	7.71	1	1	0	0	0	7.0	8	6	6	3	3	3	0	1
TOTALS	4	2	3.68	15	6	0	0	3	53.2	60	23	22	8	26	49	0	3

GAME SUMMARIES

GAME 1
at PHILADELPHIA
Tuesday, October 14

Kansas City 0 2 2 0 0 0 0 2 0 — 6 9 1
Philadelphia . . 0 0 5 1 1 0 0 0 x — 7 11 0
LEONARD, Martin (4), Quisenberry (8) and Porter,
WALK, McGraw (8) and Boone.
HR: Kansas City (3)—Otis, Aikens (2);
Philadelphia (1)—McBride
T—3:01, A—65,791

GAME 2
at PHILADELPHIA
Wednesday, October 15

Kansas City . . 0 0 0 0 0 1 3 0 0 — 4 11 0
Philadelphia . . 0 0 0 0 2 0 0 4 x — 6 8 1
Gura, QUISENBERRY (7) and Wathan;
CARLTON, Reed (9) and Boone.
HR: none
T—3:01, A—65,775

GAME 3
at KANSAS CITY
Friday, October 17

Philadelphia . 0 1 0 0 1 0 0 1 0 0 — 3 14 0
Kansas City . 1 0 0 1 0 0 1 0 0 1 — 4 11 0
Ruthven, MC GRAW (10) and Boone;
Gale, Martin (5), QUISENBERRY (8) and Porter.
HR: Philadelphia (1)—Schmidt;
Kansas City (2)—G. Brett, Otis
T—3:19, A—42,380

KANSAS CITY ROYALS

Batter	AVG	G	AB	R	H	2B	3B	HR	RBI	GW RBI	BB	SO	SH	SF	HB	SB	CS	E
Aikens	.400	6	20	5	8	0	1	4	8	1	6	8	0	0	0	0	0	2
Brett	.375	6	24	3	9	2	1	1	3	1	2	4	0	0	0	1	0	1
Cardenal	.200	4	10	0	2	0	0	0	0	0	0	3	0	0	0	0	0	0
Chalk	.000	1	0	1	0	0	0	0	0	0	1	0	0	0	0	1	0	0
Concepcion	.000	3	0	0	0	0	0	0	0	0	0	0	0	0	0	0	0	0
Hurdle	.417	4	12	1	5	1	0	0	0	0	2	1	0	0	0	1	0	0
LaCock	.000	1	0	0	0	0	0	0	0	0	0	0	0	0	0	0	0	0
McRae	.375	6	24	3	9	3	0	0	1	0	2	2	0	0	0	0	0	0
Otis	.478	6	23	4	11	2	0	3	7	0	3	3	0	0	0	0	0	0
Porter	.143	5	14	1	2	0	0	0	0	0	3	4	0	0	0	0	0	0
Washington, L.	.250		12	1	3	0	0	0	1	0	0	0	0	1	0	0	0	1
Washington, R	.300		10	0	3	0	0	0	1	0	0	6	1	1	0	0	1	0
Washington, T.	.273	6	22	1	6	0	0	0	2	0	0	6	1	2	0	0	1	1
Wathan	.286	3	7	1	2	0	0	0	1	0	2	1	0	1	0	0	0	0
White	.080	6	25	0	2	0	0	0	0	0	1	5	1	0	0	1	0	2
Wilson, L	.188		16	1	3	1	0	0	0	0	0	5	0	0	0	0	0	0
Wilson, R	.100		10	2	1	0	0	0	0	0	4	7	0	0	0	2	0	0
Wilson, T	.154	6	26	3	4	1	0	0	0	0	4	12	0	0	0	2	0	0
DH Hitters	.375		24	3	9	3	0	0	1	0	2	2	0	0	0	0	0	0
PH Hitters	.000		3	0	0	0	0	0	0	0	0	1	0	0	0	0	0	0
Others	.000		0	0	0	0	0	0	0	0	0	0	0	0	0	0	0	1
TOTALS	.290		207	23	60	9	2	8	22	2	26	49	2	3	0	6	1	7

Pitcher	W	L	ERA	G	GS	CG	SHO	SV	IP	H	R	ER	HR	BB	SO	HB	WP
Gale, R	0	1	4.26	2	2	0	0	0	6.1	11	4	3	1	4	4	0	0
Gura, L	0	0	2.19	2	2	0	0	0	12.1	8	4	3	1	3	4	0	0
Leonard, R	1	1	6.75	2	2	0	0	0	10.2	15	9	8	1	2	5	1	1
Martin, R	0	0	2.79	3	0	0	0	0	9.2	11	3	3	0	3	2	1	0
Pattin, R	0	0	.00	1	0	0	0	0	1.0	0	0	0	0	0	2	0	0
Quisenberry, R	1	2	5.23	6	0	0	0	1	10.1	10	6	6	0	3	0	0	0
Splittorff, L	0	0	5.40	1	0	0	0	0	1.2	4	1	1	0	0	0	0	0
TOTALS	2	4	4.15	17	6	0	0	1	52.0	59	27	24	3	15	17	2	1

GAME 4
at KANSAS CITY
Saturday, October 18

				R	H	E
Philadelphia	0 1 0	0 0 0	1 1 0	3	10	1
Kansas City	4 1 0	0 0 0	0 0 x	5	10	2

CHRISTENSON, Noles (1), Saucier (6), Brusstar (6) and Boone, LEONARD, Quisenberry (8) and Porter.
HR: Kansas City (2)–Aikens
T–2:37, A 42,363

GAME 5
at KANSAS CITY
Sunday, October 19

				R	H	E
Philadelphia	0 0 0	2 0 0	0 0 2	4	7	0
Kansas City	0 0 0	0 1 2	0 0 0	3	12	2

Bystrom, Reed (6), MC GRAW (7) and Boone; Gura, QUISENBERRY (7) and Porter.
HR: Philadelphia (1)–Schmidt;
Kansas City (1)–Otis
T–2:51, A–42,369

GAME 6
at PHILADELPHIA
Tuesday, October 21

				R	H	E
Kansas City	0 0 0	0 0 0	0 1 0	1	7	2
Philadelphia	0 0 2	0 1 1	0 0 x	4	9	0

GALE, Martin (3), Splittorff (5), Pattin (7), Quisenberry (8) and Wathan; CARLTON, McGraw (8) and Boone.
HR: none
T–3:00, A–65,838

OFFICIAL 1980 AMERICAN LEAGUE AVERAGES

compiled by

SPORTS INFORMATION CENTER

STANDING OF CLUBS AT CLOSE OF 1980 SEASON

AMERICAN LEAGUE WEST	Won	Lost	Pct.	Games Behind
Kansas City	97	65	.599	
Oakland	83	79	.512	14
Minnesota	77	84	.478	19½
Texas	76	85	.472	20½
Chicago	70	90	.438	26
California	65	95	.406	31
Seattle	59	103	.364	38

AMERICAN LEAGUE EAST	Won	Lost	Pct.	Games Behind
New York	103	59	.636	
Baltimore	100	62	.617	3
Milwaukee	86	76	.531	17
Boston	83	77	.5187	19
Detroit	84	78	.5185	19
Cleveland	79	81	.494	23
Toronto	67	95	.414	36

CHAMPIONSHIP SERIES: Kansas City defeated New York 3 games to 0

BATTING

TOP FIFTEEN QUALIFIERS FOR BATTING CHAMPIONSHIP

(Rankings Based on 502 or More Plate Appearances)

*Bats Lefthanded †Switch Hitter

Batter and Club	AVG	G	AB	R	H	TB	2B	3B	HR	RBI	GW RBI	TBB	IBB	SO	SH	SF	HB	SB	CS	GI DP	SLG	OBP
Brett, George, K.C.*	.390	117	449	87	175	298	33	9	24	118	14	58	16	22	0	7	1	15	6	11	.664	.461
Cooper, Cecil, Milw.*	.352	153	622	96	219	335	33	4	25	122	11	39	15	42	7	8	2	17	6	16	.539	.392
Dilone, Miguel, Clev.†	.341	132	528	82	180	228	30	9	0	40	5	28	1	45	6	2	2	61	18	7	.432	.376
Rivers, Mickey, Tex.*	.333	147	630	96	210	275	32	6	7	60	5	20	1	34	6	4	1	18	7	4	.437	.355
Carew, Rod, Calif.*	.331	144	540	74	179	236	34	7	3	59	8	59	7	38	9	3	1	23	15	15	.437	.398
Bell, Buddy, Tex	.329	129	490	76	161	244	24	4	17	83	10	40	11	39	4	0	0	3	1	16	.498	.379
Wilson, Willie, K.C.†	.326	161	705	133	230	297	28	15	3	49	4	28	3	81	5	1	6	79	10	4	.421	.357
Oliver, Al, Tex.*	.319	163	656	96	209	315	43	3	19	117	16	39	9	47	1	8	5	5	7	14	.480	.361
Bumbry, Al, Balt.*	.318	160	645	118	205	279	29	9	9	53	5	78	8	75	9	3	3	44	11	9	.433	.394
Watson, Bob, N.Y.	.307	130	469	62	144	214	25	3	13	68	11	48	5	56	1	6	1	2	1	20	.456	.373
Wathan, John, K.C.	.305	126	453	57	138	184	14	7	6	58	5	50	6	42	3	1	3	17	3	19	.406	.377
Molitor, Paul, Milw	.304	111	450	81	137	197	29	2	9	37	2	48	4	48	6	5	3	34	7	9	.438	.375
Oglivie, Ben, Milw.*	.304	156	592	94	180	333	26	2	41	118	12	54	19	71	0	9	5	11	9	5	.563	.367
Hargrove, Mike, Clev.*	.304	160	589	86	179	238	22	2	11	85	12	111	10	36	2	10	8	4	2	22	.404	.421
Singleton, Ken, Balt.†	.304	156	583	85	177	283	28	3	24	104	19	92	1	94	0	4	1	0	2	19	.485	.399

INDIVIDUAL BATTING

(All Players Listed Alphabetically)

*Bats Lefthanded †Switch Hitter

Batter and Club	AVG	G	AB	R	H	TB	2B	3B	HR	RBI	GW RBI	TBB	IBB	SO	SH	SF	HB	SB	CS	GI DP	SLG	OBP
Adams, Glenn, Minn.*	.286	99	262	32	75	108	11	2	6	38	5	15	1	26	6	4	0	2	4	11	.412	.325
Aikens, Willie, K.C.*	.278	151	543	70	151	235	24	0	20	98	13	64	3	88	0	9	7	1	0	23	.433	.362
Ainge, Dan, Tor	.243	38	111	11	27	35	6	1	0	4	0	2	0	29	1	0	1	3	0	3	.315	.263
Alexander, Gary, Clev	.225	76	173	22	40	64	7	1	5	31	2	17	1	52	0	3	0	0	4	9	.360	.292
Allen, Kim, Sea	.235	23	51	9	12	15	3	0	0	3	0	8	2	3	2	0	1	10	3	1	.294	.360
Allenson, Gary, Bos.	.357	36	70	9	25	31	6	0	0	10	0	13	0	11	1	1	0	2	2	1	.443	.458
Alston, Dell, Clev.*	.222	52	54	11	12	17	1	2	0	9	0	5	2	7	1	2	2	2	4	1	.315	.311
Anderson, Jim, Sea	.227	116	317	46	72	103	7	0	8	30	2	27	1	39	6	2	3	2	4	5	.325	.284
Armas, Tony, Oak	.279	158	623	87	175	314	18	8	35	109	11	29	4	128	2	5	2	5	3	22	.500	.313
Ashford, Tucker, Tex.	.125	15	32	2	4	4	0	0	0	3	0	3	0	3	0	0	0	0	0	1	.125	.200
Ault, Doug, Tor	.194	64	144	12	28	44	5	1	3	15	0	14	0	23	0	1	2	0	1	3	.306	.275
Ayala, Benny, Balt	.265	76	170	28	45	85	8	1	10	33	3	19	3	21	0	2	0	0	0	4	.500	.339

*Bats Lefthanded †Switch Hitter

Batter and Club	AVG	G	AB	R	H	TB	2B	3B	HR	RBI	GW RBI	IBB	IBB	SO	SH	SF	HB	SB	CS	GI DP	SLG	OBP
Bailor, Bob, Tor.	.236	117	347	44	82	103	14	2	1	16	3	36	3	34	2	1	2	12	8	5	.297	.312
Baines, Harold, Chgo.*	.255	141	491	55	125	199	23	6	13	49	3	19	7	65	2	5	1	2	4	15	.405	.284
Bando, Sal, Milw	.197	78	254	28	50	79	12	1	5	31	5	29	2	35	3	4	1	5	3	7	.311	.282
Bannister, Alan, Chgo.-Clev	.283	126	392	57	111	145	23	4	1	41	4	40	6	41	6	5	0	14	4	9	.370	.350
Barranca, German, K.C.*	—	7	0	3	0	0	0	0	0	0	0	0	0	0	0	0	0	0	0	0	—	—
Baylor, Don, Calif.	.250	90	340	39	85	116	12	2	5	51	4	24	4	32	0	5	11	6	6	9	.341	.320
Belanger, Mark, Balt	.228	113	268	37	61	74	7	3	0	22	1	12	0	25	11	0	0	6	3	1	.276	.261
Bell, Buddy, Tex	.329	129	490	76	161	244	24	4	17	83	10	40	11	39	4	0	0	3	1	16	.498	.379
Bell, Kevin, Chgo	.178	92	191	16	34	46	5	2	1	11	1	29	1	37	2	2	0	0	0	3	.241	.286
Beniquez, Juan, Sea.	.228	70	237	26	54	82	10	0	6	21	2	17	0	25	3	1	0	2	3	10	.346	.280
Blair, Paul, N.Y	.000	12	2	2	0	0	0	0	0	0	0	0	0	0	0	0	0	0	0	0	.000	.000
Bochte, Bruce, Sea.*	.300	148	520	62	156	237	34	4	13	78	10	72	13	81	4	7	0	2	3	16	.456	.385
Bonnell, Barry, Tor	.268	130	463	55	124	193	22	4	13	56	9	37	2	59	3	4	2	3	4	14	.417	.325
Bonner, Bob, Balt.	.000	4	4	1	0	0	0	0	0	1	0	0	0	0	0	0	0	0	0	0	.000	.000
Borgmann, Glenn, Chgo	.218	32	87	10	19	27	2	0	2	14	2	14	0	9	0	2	0	0	0	1	.310	.327
Bosetti, Rick, Tor.	.213	53	188	24	40	61	7	1	4	18	2	15	1	29	1	1	2	4	6	2	.324	.278
Bosley, Thad, Chgo.*	.224	70	147	12	33	41	2	0	2	14	2	10	3	27	4	1	0	3	2	5	.279	.274
Bowen, Sam, Bos	.154	7	13	0	2	2	0	0	0	0	0	2	0	3	0	0	0	1	0	0	.154	.267
Brant, Marshall, N.Y	.000	3	6	0	0	0	0	0	0	0	0	0	0	3	0	0	0	0	0	0	.000	.000
Braun, Steve, K.C.-Tor.*	.205	51	78	4	16	21	2	0	1	10	3	10	1	7	0	0	0	0	0	2	.269	.295
Brett, George, K.C.*	.390	117	449	87	175	298	33	9	24	118	14	58	16	22	0	7	1	15	6	11	.664	.461
Brohamer, Jack, Bos.-Clev.*	.251	74	199	18	50	65	7	1	2	21	2	18	4	9	4	2	0	0	1	7	.327	.313
Brookens, Tom, Det	.275	151	509	64	140	213	25	9	10	66	9	32	3	71	2	7	1	13	11	10	.418	.319
Brouhard, Mark, Milw	.232	45	125	17	29	50	6	0	5	16	3	7	0	24	0	0	1	1	0	3	400	.278
Brown, Bobby, N.Y.†	.260	137	412	65	107	171	12	5	14	47	5	29	4	82	2	3	0	27	8	8	.415	.308
Bumbry, Al, Balt.*	.318	160	645	118	205	279	29	9	9	53	5	78	8	75	9	3	3	44	11	9	.433	.394
Burleson, Rick, Bos.	.278	155	644	89	179	236	29	2	8	51	6	62	0	51	6	4	2	12	13	24	.366	.343
Butera, Sal, Minn	.271	34	85	4	23	24	1	0	0	2	0	3	0	6	1	1	1	0	0	4	.282	.303
Campaneris, Bert, Calif.	.252	77	210	32	53	69	8	1	2	18	2	14	0	33	7	2	1	10	5	4	.329	.302
Cannon, J.J., Tor.*	.080	70	50	16	4	4	0	0	0	4	0	0	0	14	0	0	1	2	2	0	.080	.098
Cardenal, Jose, K.C	.340	25	53	8	18	20	2	0	0	5	1	5	0	5	0	3	0	0	0	0	.377	.397
Carew, Rod, Calif.*	.331	144	540	74	179	236	34	7	3	59	8	59	7	38	9	3	1	23	15	15	.437	.398
Castillo, Manny, K.C.†	.200	7	10	1	2	2	0	0	0	0	0	0	0	0	0	0	0	0	0	0	.200	.200
Castino, John, Minn	.302	150	546	67	165	235	17	7	13	64	3	29	1	67	21	3	0	7	5	15	.430	.337
Cerone, Rick, N.Y	.277	147	519	70	144	224	30	4	14	85	10	32	2	56	8	10	6	1	3	14	.432	.327
Chalk, Dave, K.C	.251	69	167	19	42	57	10	1	1	20	1	18	0	27	0	3	2	1	1	5	.341	.332
Chappas, Harry, Chgo.†	.160	26	50	6	8	10	2	0	0	2	1	4	0	10	1	0	1	0	2	0	.200	.236
Charboneau, Joe, Clev	.289	131	453	76	131	221	17	2	23	87	8	49	0	70	1	6	3	2	4	24	.488	.362
Clark, Bob, Calif	.230	78	261	26	60	87	10	1	5	23	4	11	0	42	1	0	2	0	1	7	.333	.266

Cliburn, Stan, Calif	.179	54	56	7	10	18	2	0	2	6	1	3	0	9	0	1	0	0	0	1	.321	.220
Concepcion, Onix, K.C.	.133	12	15	1	2	2	0	0	0	2	0	0	0	1	0	0	0	0	0	1	.133	.133
Cooper, Cecil, Milw.*	.352	153	622	96	219	335	33	4	25	122	11	39	15	42	7	8	2	17	6	16	.539	.392
Corcoran, Tim, Det.*	.288	84	153	20	44	62	7	1	3	18	0	22	2	10	0	1	1	0	2	4	.406	.381
Corey, Mark, Balt	.278	36	36	7	10	15	2	0	1	2	0	5	0	7	0	0	0	0	1	0	.417	.366
Cosey, Ray, Oak.*	.111	9	9	0	1	1	0	0	0	0	0	0	0	0	0	0	0	0	0	0	.111	.111
Cowens, Al, Calif.-Det	.268	142	522	69	140	184	20	3	6	59	6	49	5	61	7	4	2	6	8	8	.352	.333
Cox, Jeff, Oak.	.213	59	169	20	36	39	3	0	0	9	2	14	0	23	11	0	0	8	5	2	.231	.273
Cox, Larry, Sea	.202	105	243	18	49	71	6	2	4	20	2	19	0	36	9	0	0	1	2	9	.292	.260
Cox, Ted, Sea	.243	83	247	17	60	75	9	0	2	23	2	19	3	25	1	2	0	0	0	8	.304	.297
Craig, Rodney, Sea.†	.238	70	240	30	57	83	15	1	3	20	1	17	3	35	5	0	2	3	6	5	.346	.293
Crowley, Terry, Balt.*	.288	92	233	33	67	111	8	[illegible]	12	50	7	29	2	21	2	2	0	0	0	8	.476	.366
Cruz, Julio, Sea.†	.209	119	422	66	88	109	9	3	2	16	2	59	0	49	13	2	1	45	7	6	.258	.307
Cruz, Todd, Calif.-Chgo	.237	108	333	28	79	104	14	1	3	23	3	14	1	62	6	1	2	2	1	5	.312	.272
Cubbage, Mike, Minn.*	.246	103	285	29	70	103	9	0	8	42	8	23	4	37	6	3	1	0	1	4	.361	.304
Dauer, Rich, Balt	.284	152	557	71	158	196	32	0	2	63	6	46	1	19	6	6	3	3	2	22	.352	.342
Davis, Bob, Tor	.216	91	218	18	47	70	11	0	4	19	1	12	0	25	9	0	1	0	0	9	.321	.260
Davis, Dick, Milw	.271	106	365	50	99	141	26	2	4	30	4	11	0	42	0	2	3	5	3	8	.386	.298
Davis, Mike, Oak.*	.211	51	95	11	20	27	2	1	1	8	1	7	0	14	4	1	0	2	1	2	.284	.265
Davis, Odie, Tex.	.125	17	8	0	1	1	0	0	0	0	0	0	0	2	0	0	0	0	0	0	.125	.125
Davis, Ron, N.Y.	.000	53	1	0	0	0	0	0	0	0	0	0	0	1	0	0	0	0	0	0	.000	.000
DeCinces, Doug, Balt	.249	145	489	64	122	197	23	2	16	64	11	49	5	83	4	4	3	11	6	20	.403	.322
Dempsey, Rick, Balt	.262	119	362	51	95	154	26	3	9	40	2	36	1	45	4	1	3	3	1	11	.425	.334
Dent, Bucky, N.Y.	.262	141	489	57	128	173	26	2	5	52	5	48	1	37	9	5	2	0	3	6	.354	.330
Detherage, Bob, K.C	.308	20	26	2	8	13	2	0	1	7	0	1	0	4	0	0	0	1	1	0	.500	.333
Diaz, Bo, Clev	.227	76	207	15	47	71	11	2	3	32	4	7	3	27	5	2	0	1	0	12	.343	.252
Dilone, Miguel, Clev.†	.341	132	528	82	180	228	30	9	0	40	5	28	1	45	6	2	2	61	18	7	.432	.376
Donohue Tom, Calif.	.188	84	218	18	41	53	4	1	2	14	1	7	0	63	3	1	1	5	1	0	.243	.217
Dotson, Richard, Chgo	—	36	0	0	0	0	0	0	0	0	0	0	0	0	[illegible]	0	0	0	0	0	—	—
Downing Brian, Calif.	.290	30	93	5	27	39	6	0	2	25	4	12	1	12	[illegible]	2	0	0	2	5	.419	.371
Doyle, Brian, N.Y.*	.173	34	75	8	13	17	1	0	1	5	0	6	0	7	[illegible]	0	0	1	1	1	.227	.235
Drago, Dick, Bos	.000	43	1	0	0	0	0	0	0	0	0	0	0	0	[illegible]	0	0	0	0	0	.000	.000
Dwyer, Jim, Bos.*	.285	93	260	41	74	114	11	1	9	38	7	28	5	23	1	1	2	3	2	4	.438	.359
Dybzinski, Jerry, Clev	.230	114	248	32	57	73	11	1	1	23	4	13	0	35	14	1	2	4	1	5	.294	.274
Dyer, Duffy, Det	.185	48	108	11	20	33	1	0	4	11	0	13	1	34	5	0	0	0	0	3	.306	.273
Edler, Dave, Sea.	.225	28	89	11	20	30	1	0	3	9	2	8	1	16	2	0	0	2	3	3	.337	.289
Edwards Dave, Minn	.250	81	208	26	50	67	9	1	2	20	3	12	1	51	[illegible]	1	1	2	1	6	.335	.296
Edwards Mike, Oak	.237	46	59	10	14	14	0	0	0	3	0	1	0	5	3	0	0	1	1	1	.237	.250
Elliott, Randy, Oak.	.128	14	39	4	5	8	3	0	0	1	0	1	0	13	0	0	0	0	0	1	.205	.150
Ellis, John, Tex	.236	73	182	12	43	57	9	1	1	23	2	14	1	23	0	3	1	3	0	6	.313	.294
Erickson, Roger, Minn	—	33	0	0	0	0	0	0	0	0	0	0	0	0	0	0	0	0	0	0	—	—

*Bats Lefthanded †Switch Hitter

Batter and Club	AVG	G	AB	R	H	TB	2B	3B	HR	RBI	GW RBI	IBB	IBB	SO	SH	SF	HB	SB	CS	GI DP	SLG	OBP
Essian, Jim, Oak.	.232	87	285	19	66	92	11	0	5	29	4	30	0	18	3	3	0	1	3	14	.323	.305
Evans, Dwight, Bos	.266	148	463	72	123	224	37	5	18	60	3	64	6	98	6	4	5	3	1	5	.484	.361
Faedo, Lenny, Minn	.250	5	8	1	2	3	1	0	0	0	0	0	0	0	1	0	0	0	0	0	.375	.250
Fidrych, Mark, Det	--	10	0	0	0	0	0	0	0	0	0	0	0	0	0	0	0	0	0	0	--	--
Fisk, Carlton, Bos.	.289	131	478	73	138	223	25	3	18	62	5	36	6	62	0	3	13	11	5	12	.467	.365
Flanagan, Mike, Balt.*	--	40	0	0	0	0	0	0	0	0	0	0	0	0	0	0	0	0	0	0	--	--
Foley, Marvis, Chgo*	.212	68	137	14	29	46	5	0	4	15	3	9	3	22	1	4	2	0	0	0	.336	.270
Ford, Dan, Calif.	.279	65	226	22	63	95	11	0	7	26	0	19	1	45	1	1	2	0	1	15	.420	.340
Frias, Pepe, Tex	.242	116	227	27	55	62	5	1	0	10	1	4	0	23	12	2	1	5	1	8	.273	.259
Gamble, Oscar, N.Y.*	.278	78	194	40	54	110	10	2	14	50	2	28	4	21	0	3	4	2	0	2	.567	.381
Gantner, Jim, Milw.*	.282	132	415	47	117	156	21	3	4	40	5	30	5	29	8	3	1	11	10	8	.376	.332
Garcia, Damaso, Tor	.278	140	543	50	151	207	30	7	4	46	4	12	2	55	4	3	3	13	13	14	.381	.297
Garcia, Kiko, Balt.	.199	111	311	27	62	73	8	0	1	27	2	24	0	57	3	2	0	8	4	11	.235	.257
Garr, Ralph, Calif.*	.190	21	42	5	8	9	1	0	0	3	0	4	2	6	0	0	0	0	0	0	.214	.261
Gedman, Rich, Bos.*	.208	9	24	2	5	5	0	0	0	1	0	0	0	5	0	0	0	0	0	1	.208	.208
Gibson, Kirk, Det.*	.263	51	175	23	46	77	2	1	9	16	1	10	0	45	1	2	1	4	7	0	.440	.306
Gonzales, Dan, Det.*	.143	2	7	1	1	1	0	0	0	0	0	0	0	1	0	0	0	0	0	0	.143	.143
Gonzalez, Orlando, Oak.*	.243	25	70	10	17	17	0	0	0	1	0	9	0	8	1	0	0	0	2	0	.243	.329
Goodwin, Danny, Minn.*	.200	55	115	12	23	31	5	0	1	11	2	17	0	32	1	1	0	0	0	4	.270	.303
Graham, Dan, Balt.*	.278	86	266	32	74	128	7	1	15	54	5	14	0	40	1	4	0	0	0	4	.481	.314
Gray, Gary, Clev	.148	28	54	4	8	15	1	0	2	4	1	3	1	13	0	0	0	0	0	2	.278	.193
Grich, Bobby, Calif.	.271	150	498	60	135	203	22	2	14	62	5	84	2	108	5	5	4	3	7	16	.408	.381
Griffin, Alfredo, Tor.†	.254	155	653	63	166	228	26	15	2	41	2	24	2	58	10	5	4	18	23	8	.349	.285
Gross, Wayne, Oak.*	.281	113	366	45	103	171	20	3	14	61	4	44	9	39	2	6	1	5	3	2	.467	.360
Grubb, John, Tex.*	.277	110	274	40	76	117	12	1	9	32	6	42	5	35	2	3	2	2	3	11	.427	.377
Guerrero, Mario, Oak.	.239	116	381	32	91	117	16	2	2	23	5	19	2	32	7	6	1	3	3	15	.307	.277
Gulden, Brad, N.Y.*	.333	2	3	1	1	4	0	0	1	2	0	0	0	0	0	0	0	0	0	0	1.333	.333
Hancock, Garry, Bos.*	.287	46	115	9	33	51	6	0	4	19	3	3	0	11	0	2	0	0	3	1	.443	.305
Hargrove, Mike, Clev.*	.304	160	589	86	179	238	22	2	11	85	12	111	10	36	2	10	8	4	2	22	.404	.421
Harlow, Larry, Calif.*	.276	109	301	47	83	116	13	4	4	27	3	48	1	61	4	1	1	3	2	10	.385	.377
Harrah, Toby, Clev	.267	160	561	100	150	213	22	4	11	72	6	98	3	60	2	7	7	17	2	16	.380	.383
Harrelson, Bud, Tex.†	.272	87	180	26	49	58	6	0	1	9	1	29	0	23	10	0	0	4	4	3	.322	.373
Harris, John, Calif.*	.293	19	41	8	12	23	5	0	2	7	0	7	0	4	0	1	0	0	1	2	.561	.396
Harris, Vic, Milw.†	.213	34	89	8	19	28	4	1	1	7	1	12	0	13	1	1	0	4	1	1	.316	.307
Hart, Mike, Tex.†	.250	5	4	1	1	1	0	0	0	0	0	1	0	1	0	0	0	0	0	0	.250	.400
Hassey, Ron, Clev.*	.318	130	390	43	124	174	18	4	8	65	7	49	3	51	1	6	1	0	2	13	.446	.395
Hazewood, Drungo, Balt	.000	6	5	1	0	0	0	0	0	0	0	0	0	4	0	0	0	0	0	0	.000	.000
Heath, Mike, Oak	.243	92	305	27	74	91	10	2	1	33	5	16	2	28	7	1	0	3	3	7	.298	.280
Hebner, Richie, Det.*	.290	104	341	48	99	159	10	7	12	82	8	38	3	45	2	5	2	0	3	7	.466	.365

Henderson, Rickey, Oak	.383	158	591	111	179	236	22	4	9	53	4	117	7	54	6	3	5	100	26	6	.399	.422
Hill, Marc, Sea.	.229	29	70	8	16	26	2	1	2	9	1	3	0	10	1	0	0	0	0	3	.371	.260
Hisle, Larry, Milw.	.283	17	60	16	17	35	0	0	6	16	1	14	2	7	0	1	1	1	1	1	.583	.427
Hobson, Butch, Bos.	.228	93	324	35	74	113	6	0	11	39	5	25	2	69	0	3	0	1	1	10	.349	.284
Hodgson, Paul, Tor	.220	20	41	5	9	14	0	1	1	5	0	3	0	12	2	0	0	0	1	2	.341	.273
Hoffman, Glenn, Bos	.285	114	312	37	89	124	15	4	4	42	7	19	2	41	9	4	2	2	4	8	.397	.330
Holt, Roger, N.Y.†	.167	2	6	0	1	1	0	0	0	1	0	1	0	2	0	0	0	0	0	0	.167	.286
Horton, Willie, Sea	.221	97	335	32	74	110	10	1	8	36	2	39	2	70	2	4	4	0	4	5	.328	.310
Howell, Roy, Tor.*	.269	142	528	51	142	218	28	9	10	57	10	50	8	91	4	5	5	0	0	10	.413	.338
Hoyt, Lamarr, Chgo	—	25	0	0	0	0	0	0	0	0	0	0	0	0	0	0	0	0	0	0	—	—
Hurdle, Clint, K.C.*	.294	130	395	50	116	181	31	2	10	60	5	34	5	61	2	5	2	0	0	11	.458	.353
Iorg, Garth, Tor	.248	80	222	24	55	73	10	1	2	14	3	12	0	39	3	0	0	2	1	5	.329	.286
Jackson, Reggie, N.Y.*	.300	143	514	94	154	307	22	4	41	111	17	83	15	122	0	2	2	1	2	7	.597	.399
Jackson, Darrell, Minn.*	—	33	0	0	0	0	0	0	0	0	0	0	0	0	0	0	0	0	0	0	—	—
Jackson, Ron, Minn.	.265	131	396	48	105	155	29	3	5	42	4	28	5	41	4	3	3	1	8	15	.391	.319
Johnson, Cliff, Clev.	.230	54	174	25	40	63	3	1	6	28	5	25	5	30	0	4	0	0	1	8	.362	.327
Johnson, Lamar, Chgo	.277	147	541	51	150	221	26	3	13	81	10	48	5	53	1	7	0	1	3	15	.409	.336
Johnson, Randy, Chgo.*	.200	12	20	0	4	4	0	0	0	3	1	2	0	4	0	2	1	0	0	0	.200	.304
Johnston, Greg, Minn.*	.185	14	27	3	5	8	3	0	0	1	0	2	0	4	1	1	0	0	0	3	.296	.241
Jones, Lynn, Det	.255	30	55	9	14	20	2	2	0	6	0	10	0	5	0	1	0	1	0	3	.364	.369
Jones, Ruppert, N.Y.*	.223	83	328	38	73	117	11	3	9	42	5	34	3	50	5	3	3	18	8	5	.357	.301
Kelly, Harold Pat, Balt.*	.260	89	280	38	52	73	10	1	3	26	4	34	0	54	0	3	0	16	2	4	.365	.368
Kelly, Dale Pat, Tor.	.286	3	7	0	2	2	0	0	0	0	0	0	0	4	0	0	0	0	0	0	.286	.286
Kemp, Steve, Det.*	.293	135	508	88	149	241	23	3	21	101	10	69	3	64	1	9	4	5	1	24	.474	.382
Kimm, Bruce, Chgo.	.243	100	251	20	61	73	10	1	0	19	0	17	0	26	4	1	0	1	3	10	.291	.291
Klutts, Mickey, Oak	.269	75	197	20	53	79	14	0	4	21	2	13	1	41	1	1	0	1	4	5	.401	.314
Krenchicki, Wayne, Balt.*	.143	9	14	1	2	2	0	0	0	0	0	1	0	3	0	0	0	0	0	0	.143	.200
Kubski, Gil, Calif.*	.254	22	63	11	16	19	3	0	0	6	1	6	0	10	0	0	0	1	1	2	.302	.319
Kuiper, Duane, Clev.*	.282	42	149	10	42	47	5	0	0	9	1	13	3	8	3	1	0	0	1	1	.315	.340
Kuntz, Russell, Chgo	.226	36	62	5	14	18	4	0	0	3	1	5	0	13	0	0	0	1	0	2	.290	.284
LaCock, Pete, K.C.*	.205	114	156	14	32	41	6	0	1	18	3	17	1	10	0	2	1	1	0	7	.263	.287
LaRoche, Dave, Calif.*	—	53	0	0	0	0	0	0	0	0	0	0	0	0	0	0	0	0	0	0	—	—
Landreaux, Ken, Minn.*	.281	129	484	56	136	202	23	11	7	62	9	39	4	42	6	5	2	8	6	13	.417	.337
Lansford, Carney, Calif.	.261	151	602	87	157	235	27	3	15	80	10	50	2	93	7	11	0	14	5	12	.390	.317
Lefebvre, Joe, N.Y.*	.227	74	150	26	34	61	1	1	8	21	2	27	3	30	1	0	0	0	0	5	.407	.345
Lemon, Chet, Chgo	.292	146	514	76	150	227	32	6	11	51	7	71	6	56	4	3	12	6	6	12	.442	.390
Lentine, Jim, Det	.261	67	161	19	42	55	8	1	1	17	1	28	1	30	4	0	2	2	1	3	.342	.377
Lezcano, Sixto, Milw.	.229	112	411	51	94	173	19	3	18	55	4	39	3	76	3	4	3	1	1	6	.421	.300
Lowenstein, John, Balt.*	.311	104	196	38	61	81	8	0	4	27	5	32	1	29	0	3	0	7	3	2	.413	.408
Lynn, Fred, Bos.*	.301	110	415	67	125	199	32	3	12	61	7	58	3	39	0	5	0	12	0	10	.480	.387
Macha, Mike, Tor	.000	5	8	0	0	0	0	0	0	0	0	0	0	1	0	0	0	0	0	0	.000	.000

*Bats Lefthanded †Switch Hitter

Batter and Club	AVG	G	AB	R	H	TB	2B	3B	HR	RBI	GW RBI	IBB	IBB	SO	SH	SF	HB	SB	CS	GI DP	SLG	OBP
Mackanin, Pete, Minn.	.266	108	319	31	85	115	18	0	4	35	5	14	2	33	7	2	0	6	2	7	.361	.297
Manning, Rick, Clev.*	.234	140	471	55	110	144	17	4	3	52	2	63	11	66	10	9	2	12	6	12	.306	.326
Martinez, Buck, Milw.	.224	76	219	16	49	67	9	0	3	17	0	12	0	33	5	1	1	1	0	3	.306	.267
Martinez, Dennis, Balt.	—	26	0	0	0	0	0	0	0	0	0	0	0	0	0	0	0	0	0	0	—	—
Martinez, Tippy, Balt.*	—	53	0	0	0	0	0	0	0	0	0	0	0	0	0	0	0	0	0	0	—	—
May, Lee, Balt.	.243	78	222	20	54	89	10	2	7	31	3	15	1	53	0	2	0	2	0	11	.401	.291
Mayberry, John, Tor.*	.248	149	501	62	124	237	19	2	30	82	7	77	9	81	3	4	3	0	0	9	.473	.351
McGregor, Scott, Balt.†	—	37	0	0	0	0	0	0	0	0	0	0	0	0	0	0	0	0	0	0	—	—
McKay, Dave, Oak.†	.244	123	295	29	72	93	16	1	1	29	4	10	0	57	11	0	6	1	1	4	.315	.283
McRae, Hal, K.C	.297	124	489	73	145	236	39	5	14	83	8	29	4	56	0	6	8	10	2	13	.483	.346
Medich, Doc, Tex	—	35	0	0	0	0	0	0	0	0	0	0	0	0	0	0	0	0	0	0	—	—
Mendoza, Mario, Sea	.245	114	277	27	68	86	6	3	2	14	1	16	0	42	11	1	0	3	4	5	.310	.287
Meyer, Dan, Sea.*	.275	146	531	56	146	216	25	6	11	71	9	31	4	42	4	3	1	8	4	11	.407	.316
Milbourne, Larry, Sea.†	.264	106	258	31	68	86	6	6	0	26	4	19	4	13	15	3	1	7	6	8	.333	.317
Miller, Rick, Calif.*	.274	129	412	52	113	139	14	3	2	38	2	48	4	71	6	3	1	7	3	3	.337	.351
Minoso, Minnie, Chgo	.000	2	2	0	0	0	0	0	0	0	0	0	0	0	0	0	0	0	0	0	.000	.000
Molinaro, Bob, Chgo.*	.291	119	344	48	100	139	16	4	5	36	6	26	7	29	2	5	7	18	7	4	.404	.353
Molitor, Paul, Milw	.304	111	450	81	137	197	29	2	9	37	2	48	4	48	6	5	3	34	7	9	.438	.375
Money, Don, Milw	.256	86	289	39	74	144	17	1	17	46	6	40	0	36	6	0	1	0	0	4	.498	.348
Moore, Alvin, Chgo	.256	45	121	9	31	40	4	1	1	10	1	7	0	11	1	1	0	0	2	5	.331	.297
Moore, Charlie, Milw	.291	111	320	42	93	116	13	2	2	30	3	24	2	28	8	4	0	10	5	7	.363	.340
Mora, Andres, Clev	.111	9	18	0	2	2	0	0	0	0	0	0	0	0	0	0	0	0	0	0	.111	.111
Morales, Jose, Minn.	.303	97	241	36	73	118	17	2	8	36	5	22	4	19	3	2	1	0	0	11	.490	.364
Morris, Jack, Det	—	44	0	0	0	0	0	0	0	0	0	0	0	0	0	0	0	0	0	0	—	—
Morrison, Jim, Chgo	.283	162	604	66	171	256	40	0	15	57	4	36	2	74	12	6	8	8	6	19	.424	.332
Moseby, Lloyd, Tor.*	.229	114	389	44	89	142	24	1	9	46	4	25	4	85	10	2	4	4	6	11	.365	.282
Mulliniks, Rance, K.C.*	.259	36	54	8	14	17	3	0	0	6	1	7	0	10	0	1	0	0	0	2	.315	.344
Mullins, Fran, Chgo.	.194	21	62	9	12	16	4	0	0	3	0	9	0	8	0	1	0	0	1	3	.258	.296
Murcer, Bobby, N.Y.*	.269	100	297	41	80	130	9	1	13	57	10	34	2	28	3	9	2	2	0	9	.438	.348
Murphy, Dwayne, Oak.*	.274	159	573	86	157	218	18	2	13	68	8	102	7	96	22	3	2	26	15	12	.380	.386
Murray, Eddie, Balt.†	.300	158	621	100	186	322	36	2	32	116	16	64	10	71	0	6	2	7	2	18	.519	.367
Narron, Jerry, Sea.*	.196	48	107	7	21	36	3	0	4	18	0	13	2	18	1	2	0	0	0	2	.336	.283
Nettles, Graig, N.Y.*	.244	89	324	52	79	141	14	0	16	45	4	42	5	42	0	2	1	0	0	8	.435	.332
Newman, Jeff, Oak	.233	127	438	37	102	168	19	1	15	56	11	25	8	81	5	5	1	3	4	10	.384	.276
Nichols, Reid, Bos	.222	12	36	5	8	10	0	1	0	3	0	3	0	8	0	0	0	0	1	0	.278	.282
Nordhagen, Wayne, Chgo	.277	123	415	45	115	190	22	4	15	59	10	10	3	45	0	2	1	0	1	13	.468	.296
Norman, Nelson, Tex.†	.219	17	32	4	7	7	0	0	0	1	0	1	0	1	1	0	0	0	1	2	.219	.242
Norris, Jim, Tex.*	.247	119	174	23	43	48	5	0	0	16	2	23	2	16	3	5	0	6	3	11	.276	.335
Norwood, Willie, Minn	.164	34	73	6	12	17	2	0	1	8	0	3	0	13	0	0	0	1	1	3	.233	.197

Oates, Johnny, N.Y.*	.183	39	64	6	12	18	3	0	1	3	1	2	0	3	0	0	1	1	2	1	.281	.224
Oglivie, Ben, Milw.*	.304	156	592	94	180	333	26	2	41	118	12	54	19	71	0	9	5	11	9	5	.563	.367
Oliver, Al, Tex.*	.319	163	656	96	209	315	43	3	19	117	16	39	9	47	1	8	6	5	7	14	.480	.361
Orta, Jorge, Clev.*	.291	129	481	78	140	194	18	3	10	64	9	71	2	44	2	8	2	6	5	8	.403	.384
Otis, Amos, K.C.	.251	107	394	56	99	151	16	3	10	53	7	39	0	70	2	10	3	16	1	9	.383	.323
Paciorek, Tom, Sea	.273	126	418	44	114	180	19	1	15	59	4	17	1	67	3	2	1	3	2	13	.431	.303
Page, Mitchell, Oak.*	.244	110	348	58	85	154	10	4	17	51	5	35	3	87	4	5	1	14	7	9	.443	.315
Palmer, Jim, Balt	—	37	0	0	0	0	0	0	0	0	0	0	0	0	0	0	0	0	0	0	—	—
Papi, Stan, Bos.-Det.	.237	47	114	12	27	47	3	4	3	17	0	5	0	24	2	1	0	0	0	3	.412	.269
Parrish, Lance, Det	.286	144	553	79	158	276	34	6	24	82	2	31	3	109	2	3	3	6	4	24	.499	.327
Patek, Fred, Calif	.264	86	273	41	72	107	10	5	5	34	1	15	1	26	8	2	1	7	6	11	.392	.304
Perez, Tony, Bos	.275	151	585	73	161	273	31	3	25	105	9	41	11	93	0	8	1	1	0	25	.467	.324
Peters, Rick, Det.†	.291	133	477	79	139	178	19	7	2	42	3	54	2	48	7	2	6	13	7	17	.373	.371
Phelps, Ken, K.C.*	.000	3	4	0	0	0	0	0	0	0	0	0	0	2	0	0	0	0	0	0	.000	.000
Picciolo, Rob, Oak	.240	95	271	32	65	93	9	2	5	18	2	2	0	63	8	0	0	1	1	6	.343	.245
Piniella, Lou, N.Y.	.287	116	321	39	92	116	18	0	2	27	2	29	5	20	2	3	0	0	2	17	.361	.346
Poff, John, Milw.*	.250	19	68	7	17	25	1	2	1	7	0	3	2	7	0	0	0	0	0	1	.368	.282
Porter, Darrell, K.C.*	.249	118	418	51	104	143	14	2	7	51	8	69	6	60	0	6	2	1	1	10	.342	.358
Powell, Hosken, Minn.*	.262	137	435	58	127	172	17	5	6	35	1	32	2	46	3	0	3	14	3	14	.355	.312
Pruitt, Ron, Clev.-Chgo.	.302	56	106	9	32	41	3	0	2	15	0	12	1	13	2	1	0	0	0	5	.387	.373
Pryor, Greg, Chgo	.240	122	338	32	81	110	18	4	1	29	6	12	0	35	9	6	2	2	2	10	.325	.270
Putnam, Pat, Tex.*	.263	147	410	42	108	167	16	2	13	55	7	36	6	49	3	5	0	0	2	13	.407	.323
Quirk, Jamie, K.C.*	.276	62	163	13	45	65	5	0	5	21	4	7	2	24	3	3	1	3	2	7	.399	.310
Rader, Dave, Bos.*	.328	50	137	14	45	65	11	0	3	17	0	14	1	12	0	1	0	1	1	4	.474	.381
Ramos, Domingo, Tor	.125	5	16	0	2	2	0	0	0	0	0	2	0	5	0	0	0	0	0	0	.125	.222
Randall, Bobby, Minn	.200	5	15	2	3	4	1	0	0	0	0	1	0	0	0	0	0	0	0	1	.267	.250
Randolph, Willie, N.Y	.294	138	513	99	151	209	23	7	7	46	5	119	4	45	5	3	2	30	5	6	.407	.429
Rayford, Floyd, Balt	.222	8	18	1	4	4	0	0	0	1	0	0	0	5	0	0	0	0	0	1	.222	.222
Remy, Jerry, Bos.*	.313	63	230	24	72	83	7	2	0	9	0	10	0	14	7	2	0	14	6	6	.361	.342
Rettenmund, Merv, Calif.	.250	2	4	0	1	1	0	0	0	0	0	1	0	1	0	0	0	0	0	0	.250	.400
Revering, Dave, Oak.*	.290	106	376	48	109	185	21	5	15	62	11	32	6	37	2	2	0	1	0	6	.492	.346
Rice, Jim, Bos	.294	124	504	81	148	254	22	6	24	86	8	30	5	87	1	3	4	8	3	16	.504	.338
Richardt, Mike, Tex	.225	22	71	2	16	18	2	0	0	8	2	1	0	7	0	0	0	0	0	1	.254	.236
Rivera, Bombo, Minn.	.221	44	113	13	25	41	7	0	3	10	1	4	0	20	0	0	0	0	0	4	.363	.248
Rivers, Mickey, Tex.*	.333	147	630	96	210	275	32	6	7	60	5	20	1	34	6	4	1	18	7	4	.437	.355
Roberts, Dave, Tex	.238	101	235	27	56	90	4	0	10	30	1	13	2	38	1	1	1	0	1	5	.383	.281
Roberts, Leon, Sea	.251	119	374	48	94	148	18	3	10	33	5	43	1	59	3	6	1	8	4	12	.396	.330
Robinson, Bruce, N.Y.*	.000	4	5	0	0	0	0	0	0	0	0	0	0	4	0	0	0	0	0	0	.000	.000
Rodriguez, Aurelio, N.Y.	.220	52	164	14	36	53	6	1	3	14	3	7	1	35	11	0	0	0	0	7	.323	.251
Roenicke, Gary, Balt	.239	118	297	40	71	114	13	0	10	28	4	41	5	49	2	3	6	2	0	10	.384	.343
Romero, Ed, Milw	.260	42	104	20	27	37	7	0	1	10	1	9	0	11	2	0	0	2	0	3	.356	.319

*Bats Lefthanded †Switch Hitter

Batter and Club	AVG	G	AB	R	H	TB	2B	3B	HR	RBI	GW RBI	TBB	IBB	SO	SH	SF	HB	SB	CS	GI DP	SLG	OBP
Rosello, Dave, Clev	.248	71	117	16	29	38	3	0	2	12	0	9	0	19	2	3	0	0	0	2	.325	.302
Rudi, Joe, Calif	.237	104	372	42	88	155	17	1	16	53	6	17	2	84	2	3	5	1	0	10	.417	.279
Sakata, Lenn, Balt	.193	43	83	12	16	26	3	2	1	9	2	6	0	10	0	1	0	2	1	3	.313	.247
Sample, Billy, Tex	.260	99	204	29	53	75	10	0	4	19	3	18	2	15	4	2	6	8	5	4	.368	.338
Schrom, Ken, Tor.	—	18	0	0	0	0	0	0	0	0	0	0	0	0	0	0	0	0	0	0	—	—
Seilheimer, Ricky, Chgo.*	.212	21	52	4	11	19	3	1	1	3	0	4	1	15	1	0	0	1	0	0	.365	.268
Sherrill, Dennis, N.Y	.250	3	4	0	1	1	0	0	0	0	0	0	0	1	0	0	0	0	0	1	.250	.250
Simpson, Joe, Sea.*	.249	129	365	42	91	121	15	3	3	34	3	28	3	43	12	3	1	17	4	6	.332	.305
Singleton, Ken, Balt.†	.304	156	583	85	177	283	28	3	24	104	19	92	1	94	0	4	1	0	2	19	.485	.399
Sizemore, Ted, Bos	.217	9	23	1	5	6	1	0	0	0	0	0	0	0	0	0	0	0	0	1	.261	.217
Skaggs, Dave, Balt.-Calif	.197	26	71	7	14	17	0	0	1	9	1	9	0	14	1	1	0	0	0	1	.239	.288
Smalley, Roy, Minn.†	.278	133	486	64	135	197	24	1	12	63	12	65	4	63	2	9	2	3	3	15	.405	.365
Soderholm, Eric, N.Y.	.287	95	275	38	79	127	13	1	11	35	6	27	2	25	1	0	1	0	0	9	.462	.353
Sofield, Rick, Minn.*	.247	131	417	52	103	156	18	4	9	49	6	24	2	92	9	7	2	4	5	3	.374	.291
Spencer, Jim, N.Y.*	.236	97	259	38	61	109	9	0	13	43	6	30	2	44	1	4	1	1	0	7	.421	.317
Squires, Mike, Chgo.*	.283	131	343	38	97	120	11	3	2	33	3	32	1	24	11	0	1	8	9	6	.350	.346
Stanley, Fred, N.Y	.209	49	86	13	18	21	3	0	0	5	1	5	0	5	1	1	2	0	0	0	.244	.269
Stapleton, Dave, Bos	.321	106	449	61	144	208	33	5	7	45	7	13	1	32	5	4	1	3	2	10	.463	.341
Staub, Rusty, Tex.*	.300	109	340	42	102	156	23	2	9	55	4	39	3	18	1	6	2	1	1	16	.459	.376
Stegman, Dave, Det.	.177	65	130	12	23	34	5	0	2	9	2	14	0	23	2	1	0	1	1	0	.262	.257
Stein, Bill, Sea.	.268	67	198	16	53	75	5	1	5	27	2	16	4	25	7	3	1	1	1	5	.379	.326
Stieb, Dave, Tor.	.000	36	1	0	0	0	0	0	0	0	0	0	0	0	0	0	0	0	0	0	.000	.000
Stinson, Bob, Sea.*	.215	48	107	6	23	28	2	0	1	8	0	9	0	19	2	2	1	0	0	2	.262	.282
Stone, Steve, Balt	—	49	0	0	0	0	0	0	0	0	0	0	0	0	0	0	0	0	0	0	—	—
Summers, Champ, Det.*	.297	120	347	61	103	175	19	1	17	60	4	52	6	52	1	3	5	4	3	10	.504	.396
Sundberg, Jim, Tex	.273	151	505	59	138	194	24	1	10	63	5	64	3	67	6	5	1	2	2	15	.384	.356
Sutherland, Leo, Chgo.*	.258	34	89	9	23	26	3	0	0	5	0	1	1	11	1	1	0	4	1	2	.292	.267
Terrell, Jerry, K.C.	.063	23	16	4	1	1	0	0	0	0	0	0	0	0	0	0	0	0	0	0	.063	.063
Thomas, Gorman, Milw	.239	162	628	78	150	296	26	3	38	105	13	58	4	170	3	6	2	8	5	7	.471	.305
Thompson, Jason, Det.-Calif.*	.288	138	438	69	126	208	19	0	21	90	7	83	10	86	2	5	1	2	1	12	.476	.402
Thon, Dickie, Calif	.255	80	267	32	68	84	12	2	0	15	1	10	0	28	5	2	1	7	5	5	.315	.284
Torres, Rusty, K.C.†	.167	51	72	10	12	12	0	0	0	3	0	8	0	7	0	0	0	1	3	1	.167	.250
Trammell, Alan, Det	.300	146	560	107	168	226	21	5	9	65	9	69	2	63	13	7	3	12	12	10	.404	.380
Upshaw, Willie, Tor.*	.213	34	61	10	13	21	3	1	1	5	0	6	1	14	1	0	0	1	0	0	.344	.284
Valdez, Julio, Bos.	.263	8	19	4	5	9	1	0	1	4	0	0	0	5	1	0	1	2	0	0	.474	.300
Vega, Jesus, Minn	.167	12	30	3	5	5	0	0	0	4	1	3	0	7	1	0	0	1	0	1	.167	.242
Velez, Otto, Tor.	.269	104	357	54	96	174	12	3	20	62	7	54	8	86	0	4	2	0	0	8	.487	.368
Veryzer, Tom, Clev	.271	109	358	28	97	115	12	0	2	28	3	10	1	25	4	3	8	0	5	11	.321	.306
Wagner, Mark, Det	.236	45	72	5	17	18	1	0	0	3	1	7	0	11	2	0	0	0	1	0	.250	.304

Walker Chico, Bos.†	.211	19	57	3	12	15	0	0	1	5	2	6	1	10	1	1	1	3	2	1	.263	.297
Walton, Danny, Tex.†	.200	10	10	2	2	2	0	0	0	1	0	3	0	5	0	0	0	0	0	0	.200	.385
Walton, Reggie, Sea.	.277	31	33	8	23	35	6	0	2	9	1	3	0	10	0	1	1	2	2	1	.422	.310
Ward, Gary, Minn	.463	13	41	11	19	32	6	2	1	10	0	3	1	6	1	1	0	0	0	0	.780	.500
Washington, Claudell, Chgo.*	.289	32	90	15	26	37	4	2	1	12	2	5	0	19	1	0	1	4	2	5	.411	.333
Washington, U.L., K.C.†	.273	153	549	79	150	206	16	11	6	53	7	53	0	78	10	2	0	20	7	13	.375	.337
Wathan, John, K.C	.305	126	453	57	138	184	14	7	6	58	5	50	6	42	3	1	3	17	3	19	.406	.377
Watson, Bob, N.Y.	.307	130	469	62	144	214	25	3	13	68	11	48	5	56	1	6	1	2	1	20	.456	.373
Werth, Dennis, N.Y	.308	39	65	15	20	32	3	0	3	12	1	12	0	19	1	0	0	0	1	3	.492	.416
Whitaker, Lou, Det.*	.233	145	477	68	111	135	19	1	1	45	7	73	0	79	12	6	0	8	4	9	.283	.335
White, Frank, K.C.	.264	154	560	70	148	200	23	4	7	60	11	19	0	69	9	4	2	19	6	11	.357	.291
Whitmer, Dan, Calif.	.241	48	87	8	21	24	3	0	0	7	0	4	0	21	9	2	0	1	0	3	.276	.275
Whitt, Ernie, Tor.*	.237	106	295	23	70	104	12	2	6	34	3	22	0	29	5	3	0	1	3	11	.353	.290
Wilborn, Ted, N.Y.†	.250	8	8	2	2	2	0	0	0	1	0	0	0	1	0	0	0	0	0	0	.250	.250
Wilcox Milt, Det	––	33	0	0	0	0	0	0	0	0	0	0	0	0	0	0	0	0	0	0	––	––
Wilfong, Rob, Minn.*	.248	131	416	55	103	153	16	5	8	45	6	34	3	61	11	2	3	10	6	8	.368	.309
Wills, Bump, Tex.†	.263	146	573	102	152	208	31	5	5	58	3	51	1	71	15	8	3	34	9	8	.360	.326
Wilson, Willie, K.C.†	.326	161	705	133	230	297	28	15	3	49	4	28	3	81	5	1	6	79	10	4	.421	.357
Wockenfuss, John, Det.	.274	126	372	56	102	167	13	2	16	65	8	68	4	64	0	1	3	1	4	7	.449	.391
Wolfe, Larry, Bos	.138	18	23	3	3	7	1	0	1	4	2	0	0	5	0	1	0	0	0	1	.304	.130
Woods, Al, Tor.*	.300	109	373	54	112	179	18	2	15	47	6	37	3	35	5	1	1	4	4	4	.480	.365
Wynegar, Butch, Minn.†	.255	146	486	61	124	163	18	3	5	57	4	63	6	36	7	6	2	3	1	9	.335	.343
Yastrzemski, Carl, Bos.*	.275	105	364	49	100	168	21	1	15	50	8	44	5	38	1	3	0	0	2	9	.462	.353
Yost, Ed, Milw	.161	15	31	0	5	5	0	0	0	0	0	0	0	6	0	0	0	0	0	1	.161	.161
Yount, Robin, Milw	.293	143	611	121	179	317	49	10	23	87	9	26	1	67	6	3	1	20	5	8	.519	.323
Zisk, Richie, Tex	.290	135	443	48	130	206	17	1	19	77	6	39	5	72	1	4	0	0	2	18	.460	.347

DESIGNATED HITTERS

(Individual Statistics – Players Listed Alphabetically)

*Bats Lefthanded †Switch Hitter											GW									GI		
Batter & Club	AVG	G	AB	R	H	TB	2B	3B	HR	RBI	RBI	TBB	1BB	SO	SH	SF	HB	SB	CS	DP	SLG	OBP
Adams, Minn.*	.280	81	214	29	60	88	11	1	5	33	5	14	1	19	6	4	0	1	3	8	.411	.326
Aikens, K.C.*	.302	13	53	6	16	23	1	0	2	12	0	2	1	9	0	0	1	1	0	1	.434	.339
Ainge, Tor	.000	2	6	0	0	0	0	0	0	0	0	0	0	2	0	0	0	0	0	1	.000	.000
Alexander, Clev	.217	40	129	15	28	43	6	0	3	17	0	15	1	39	0	1	0	0	4	8	.333	.299
Allenson, Bos	.313	6	16	3	5	5	0	0	0	1	0	2	0	4	0	0	0	1	0	0	.313	.389
Alston, Clev.*	.000	6	1	1	0	0	0	0	0	0	0	0	0	0	0	0	0	0	1	0	.000	.000
Anderson, Sea.	.200	5	10	1	2	3	1	0	0	0	0	2	0	1	1	0	0	0	0	0	.300	.333
Ault, Tor.	.203	21	64	6	13	18	3	1	0	5	0	5	0	10	0	0	0	0	0	1	.281	.261
Ayala, Balt.	.236	41	110	17	26	57	4	0	9	23	2	12	3	16	0	1	0	0	0	2	.518	.311

*Bats Lefthanded †Switch Hitter Batter & Club	AVG	G	AB	R	H	TB	2B	3B	HR	RBI	GW RBI	TBB	IBB	SO	SH	SF	HB	SB	CS	GI DP	SLG	OBP
Bailor, Tor	.000	1	2	1	0	0	0	0	0	0	0	0	0	1	0	0	0	0	0	0	.000	.000
Baines, Chgo.*	.500	1	2	0	1	1	0	0	0	0	0	0	0	0	0	0	0	0	0	0	.500	.500
Bando, Milw	.154	15	52	3	8	9	1	0	0	5	0	5	1	10	0	0	0	1	1	2	.173	.228
Baylor, Calf	.223	36	130	14	29	37	5	0	1	18	3	13	3	14	0	3	4	1	4	3	.285	.313
Bell, Chgo	.429	3	7	0	3	4	1	0	0	0	0	2	0	1	0	0	0	0	0	0	.571	.556
Beniquez, Sea	.000	1	1	0	0	0	0	0	0	0	0	0	0	1	0	0	0	0	0	0	.000	.000
Bochte, Sea.*	.395	11	43	7	17	32	4	1	3	8	0	5	0	3	0	0	0	0	0	0	.744	.458
Bonnell, Tor	.273	3	11	0	3	3	0	0	0	0	0	0	0	2	0	0	0	0	0	0	.273	.273
Brant, N.Y	.000	1	1	0	0	0	0	0	0	0	0	0	0	1	0	0	0	0	0	0	.000	.000
Braun, 1-K.C. 13-Tor.*	171	14	35	2	6	9	0	0	1	5	1	5	1	3	0	0	0	0	0	2	.257	.276
Brohamer, 3-Bos. 1-Clev.*	.400	4	10	1	4	7	0	0	1	1	0	0	0	1	0	0	0	0	0	0	.700	.400
Brookens, Det	.000	1	1	0	0	0	0	0	0	0	0	0	0	0	0	0	0	0	0	0	.000	.000
Brouhard, Milw	.203	21	69	11	14	26	3	0	3	7	2	4	0	12	0	0	1	0	0	2	.377	.257
Brown, N.Y.†	.000	1	1	1	0	0	0	0	0	0	0	0	0	1	0	0	0	0	0	0	.000	.000
Butera, Minn.	.000	2	2	0	0	0	0	0	0	0	0	0	0	0	0	0	0	0	0	1	.000	.000
Campaneris, Calf	1.000	2	1	1	1	1	0	0	0	0	0	0	0	0	0	0	0	0	1	0	1.000	1.000
Cannon, Tor.*	.000	1	1	0	0	0	0	0	0	0	0	0	0	0	0	0	0	0	0	0	.000	.000
Carew, Calf.*	.362	32	127	20	46	59	8	1	1	16	1	13	0	5	1	2	1	4	2	2	.465	.426
Castillo, K.C.†	.500	2	2	0	1	1	0	0	0	0	0	0	0	0	0	0	0	0	0	0	.500	.500
Chalk, K.C	.273	6	22	3	6	7	1	0	0	3	0	3	0	1	0	0	0	0	0	2	.318	.360
Chappas, Chgo.†	.100	2	10	1	1	1	0	0	0	1	0	1	0	1	1	0	0	0	0	0	.100	.182
Charboneau, Clev	.278	57	209	32	58	105	6	1	13	46	5	21	0	29	0	3	0	1	0	15	.502	.343
Cooper, Milw.*	.317	11	41	4	13	16	0	0	1	6	0	3	2	5	0	1	0	0	0	2	.390	.364
Corcoran, Det.*	.125	5	8	0	1	1	0	0	0	0	0	2	1	2	0	0	0	0	0	0	.125	.300
Cowens, 1-Calf. 1-Det	.500	2	2	1	1	4	0	0	1	3	1	0	0	0	0	0	0	0	0	0	2.000	.500
Crowley, Balt.*	.290	65	207	30	60	99	6	0	11	46	6	25	2	20	1	2	0	0	0	6	.478	.366
Cruz, Sea.†	.429	3	7	2	3	7	1	0	1	1	0	1	0	1	1	0	0	2	0	0	1.000	.500
Cubbage, Minn.*	.000	1	0	0	0	0	0	0	0	0	0	1	1	0	0	0	0	0	0	0	.000	1.000
Davis, Milw	.262	63	233	34	61	89	15	2	3	21	3	5	0	27	0	1	2	2	2	4	.382	.283
Davis, Oak.*	.071	6	14	1	1	1	0	0	0	0	0	2	0	3	0	0	0	1	0	0	.071	.188
Dempsey, Balt.	.000	1	1	0	0	0	0	0	0	0	0	0	0	1	0	0	0	0	0	0	.000	.000
Dilone, Clev.†	.475	11	40	9	19	24	3	1	0	7	1	2	0	1	0	1	1	9	1	0	.600	.512
Downing, Calf	.357	13	42	2	15	21	3	0	1	14	1	5	0	3	0	2	0	0	1	2	.500	.426
Dwyer, Bos.*	.538	12	39	8	21	24	3	0	0	4	1	2	0	1	1	0	2	1	0	1	.615	.581
Dybzinski, Clev	.000	2	0	0	0	0	0	0	0	0	0	0	0	0	0	0	0	0	0	0	.000	.000
Dyer, Det	.160	10	25	2	4	10	0	0	2	4	0	3	1	7	2	0	0	0	0	0	.400	.250
Edwards, Minn	.000	3	0	1	0	0	0	0	0	0	0	0	0	0	0	0	0	0	0	0	.000	.000
Edwards, Oak	.111	5	9	3	1	1	0	0	0	0	0	1	0	0	2	0	0	0	0	1	.111	.200
Elliott, Oak	.139	11	36	4	5	8	3	0	0	1	0	1	0	11	0	0	0	0	0	1	.222	.162

Ellis, Tex.	.242	20	66	6	16	22	4	1	0	8	1	3	0	4	0	1	0	0	0	3	333	.275
Essian, Oak	.237	11	38	2	9	10	1	0	0	1	0	3	0	4	0	0	0	0	0	2	263	.293
Evans, Bos	.333	2	3	0	1	1	0	0	0	0	0	1	0	2	0	0	0	0	0	0	333	.500
Fisk, Bos	.350	5	20	3	7	12	2	0	1	3	0	1	0	3	0	0	0	0	1	0	600	.381
Ford, Calf	.276	15	58	5	16	19	3	0	0	5	0	7	0	11	0	1	1	0	1	4	328	.364
Gamble, N.Y.*	.250	20	52	8	13	21	2	0	2	10	1	4	2	4	0	1	2	0	0	0	404	.328
Garcia, Tor.	.000	1	4	0	0	0	0	0	0	1	0	0	0	0	0	0	0	0	0	0	000	.000
Garr, Calf.*	.241	8	29	4	7	8	1	0	0	2	0	2	2	4	0	0	0	0	0	0	276	.290
Gedman, Bos.*	.231	4	13	2	3	3	0	0	0	0	0	0	0	3	0	0	0	0	0	1	.231	.231
Gibson, Det.*	.000	1	0	0	0	0	0	0	0	0	0	0	0	0	0	0	0	0	0	0	.000	.000
Gonzales, Det.*	.000	1	2	0	0	0	0	0	0	0	0	0	0	1	0	0	0	0	0	0	.000	.000
Gonzales, Oak.*	.233	8	30	3	7	7	0	0	0	0	0	3	0	3	1	0	0	0	0	0	.233	.303
Goodwin, Minn.*	.188	38	80	8	15	18	3	0	0	6	2	14	0	27	1	0	0	0	0	2	.225	.309
Graham, Balt.*	.000	2	4	0	0	0	0	0	0	0	0	0	0	1	0	0	0	0	0	0	.000	.000
Gray, Clev	.129	9	31	3	4	8	1	0	1	1	0	3	1	7	0	0	0	0	0	2	.258	.206
Gross, Oak.*	1.000	1	1	0	1	1	0	0	0	1	0	0	0	0	0	0	0	0	0	0	1.000	1.000
Grubb, Tex.*	.316	8	19	2	6	10	1	0	1	4	0	3	0	2	0	0	0	0	1	0	.526	.409
Hancock, Bos.*	.320	12	25	2	8	12	1	0	1	4	0	0	0	3	0	0	0	0	0	0	.480	.320
Harlow, Calf.*	1.000	1	1	1	1	2	1	0	0	1	1	0	0	0	0	0	0	0	0	0	2.000	1.000
Harrah, Clev	.167	3	6	0	1	1	0	0	0	0	0	1	0	0	0	0	0	0	0	0	.167	.286
Hassey, Clev.*	.400	7	5	1	2	2	0	0	0	2	0	2	0	1	0	0	0	0	0	0	.400	.571
Heath, Oak.	.267	31	105	10	28	34	2	2	0	12	3	6	0	11	3	0	0	1	2	3	.324	.306
Hebner, Det.*	.182	5	11	1	2	5	0	0	1	2	0	3	1	0	0	0	0	0	0	0	.455	.357
Henderson, Oak	.333	1	6	0	2	2	0	0	0	0	0	0	0	1	0	0	0	0	0	0	.333	.333
Hisle, Milw.	.283	17	60	16	17	35	0	0	6	16	1	14	2	7	0	1	1	1	1	1	.583	.427
Hobson, Bos	.177	36	130	9	23	26	0	0	1	10	1	7	1	25	0	2	0	0	0	6	.200	.219
Hodgson, Tor	.000	3	7	1	0	0	0	0	0	0	0	1	0	3	0	0	0	0	0	0	.000	.125
Horton, Sea	.218	92	330	31	72	105	10	1	7	34	2	39	2	63	2	4	4	0	4	5	.318	.308
Howell, Tor.*	.143	2	7	1	1	2	1	0	0	1	1	0	0	1	0	0	0	0	0	0	.286	.143
Iorg, Tor	.500	2	2	0	1	2	1	0	0	0	0	0	0	0	0	0	0	0	0	0	1.000	.500
Jackson, N.Y.*	.331	46	169	25	56	101	8	2	11	29	6	23	7	33	0	0	1	0	0	3	.598	.416
Jackson, R., Minn.	.000	1	1	0	0	0	0	0	0	0	0	0	0	0	0	0	0	0	0	0	.000	.000
Johnson, Clev	.226	45	168	23	38	55	3	1	4	23	4	23	4	30	0	3	0	0	1	7	.327	.319
Johnson, L., Chgo.	.277	66	253	25	70	99	11	3	4	39	7	19	2	24	0	3	0	1	0	8	.391	.327
Johnson, R., Chgo.*	.182	4	11	0	2	2	0	0	0	1	0	0	0	4	0	1	1	0	0	0	.182	.250
Jones, Det	.133	6	15	2	2	2	0	0	0	1	0	5	0	0	0	1	0	0	0	0	.133	.350
Kelly, Balt.*	.205	30	88	8	18	27	4	1	1	14	3	9	0	31	0	1	0	1	1	3	.307	.278
Kemp, Det.*	.325	46	169	31	55	87	6	1	8	27	3	25	2	23	1	1	3	4	1	10	.515	.421
Klutts, Oak	1.000	1	1	0	1	1	0	0	0	0	0	0	0	0	0	0	0	0	0	0	1.000	1.000
Krenchicki, Balt.*	.500	1	2	0	1	1	0	0	0	0	0	0	0	0	0	0	0	0	0	0	.500	.500
Landreaux, Minn.*	.300	6	20	1	6	10	1	0	1	3	0	0	0	2	1	0	0	0	0	0	.500	.300

*Bats Lefthanded †Switch Hitter

Batter & Club	AVG	G	AB	R	H	TB	2B	3B	HR	RBI	GW RBI	TBB	IBB	SO	SH	SF	HB	SB	CS	GI DP	SLG	OBP
Lemon, Chgo	.217	6	23	1	5	10	2	0	1	1	0	1	0	0	0	0	0	0	0	3	.435	.250
Lentine, Det	.438	9	16	1	7	8	1	0	0	2	0	7	0	4	0	0	0	0	0	0	.500	.609
Lezcano, Milw	.250	4	16	2	4	9	0	1	1	1	0	1	0	3	0	0	0	0	0	1	.563	.294
Lowenstein, Balt.*	.125	3	8	0	1	2	1	0	0	1	1	0	0	3	0	0	0	0	0	0	.250	.125
Mackanin, Minn	.500	5	6	3	3	4	1	0	0	1	1	1	0	0	0	0	0	0	0	0	.667	.571
May, Balt.	.228	58	184	16	42	69	8	2	5	23	3	13	1	46	0	1	0	2	0	10	.375	.279
Mayberry, Tor.*	.167	8	30	3	5	9	1	0	1	4	1	2	1	2	0	1	0	0	0	3	.300	.219
McRae, K.C	.293	110	450	63	132	215	35	3	14	75	6	26	3	50	0	6	6	9	2	13	.478	.340
Meyer, Sea.*	.387	7	31	10	12	26	2	0	4	8	1	1	0	0	0	1	0	0	0	0	.839	.406
Milbourne, Sea.†	.190	8	21	1	4	4	0	0	0	2	0	2	0	1	0	0	0	1	0	0	.190	.261
Molinaro, Chgo.*	.319	47	160	27	51	76	9	2	4	16	3	16	5	11	2	1	2	5	4	1	.475	.388
Molitor, Milw	.161	7	31	3	5	5	0	0	0	1	0	2	0	7	1	1	0	4	2	0	.161	.212
Money, Milw.	.313	14	48	6	15	25	4	0	2	8	3	5	0	4	0	0	1	0	0	0	.521	.389
Moore, Chgo.	.200	2	5	0	1	1	0	0	0	0	0	0	0	1	0	0	0	0	0	0	.200	.200
Morales, Minn	.304	86	227	34	69	111	17	2	7	32	5	20	3	19	3	2	1	0	0	11	.489	.363
Morris, Det.	.000	2	0	0	0	0	0	0	0	0	0	0	0	0	0	0	0	0	0	0	.000	.000
Morrison, Chgo	.000	1	4	0	0	0	0	0	0	0	0	0	0	0	0	0	0	0	0	0	.000	.000
Moseby, Tor.*	.300	6	20	2	6	11	2	0	1	4	1	3	0	4	0	0	0	0	0	1	.550	.391
Murcer, N.Y.*	.242	33	120	14	29	41	4	1	2	18	3	11	2	15	0	3	0	1	0	7	.342	.305
Murray, Balt.†	.400	1	5	1	2	5	0	0	1	2	0	1	0	1	0	0	0	0	0	0	1.000	.500
Narron, Sea.*	.000	1	1	0	0	0	0	0	0	0	0	0	0	0	0	0	0	0	0	0	.000	.000
Newman, Oak	.286	9	21	0	6	7	1	0	0	5	3	2	1	4	1	2	0	1	1	1	.333	.348
Nichols, Bos	.000	1	0	0	0	0	0	0	0	0	0	0	0	0	0	0	0	0	0	0	.000	.000
Nordhagen, Chgo	.250	32	120	15	30	53	7	2	4	16	3	3	2	14	0	1	1	0	0	3	.442	.274
Norris, Tex.*	.000	1	1	0	0	0	0	0	0	0	0	0	0	0	0	0	0	0	0	0	.000	.000
Norwood, Minn	.000	9	19	0	0	0	0	0	0	0	0	0	0	4	0	0	0	0	0	0	.000	.000
Oglivie, Milw.*	.294	4	17	1	5	9	1	0	1	4	1	0	0	1	0	1	0	0	0	0	.529	.294
Oliver, Tex.*	.333	4	15	2	5	5	0	0	0	1	1	1	0	1	0	0	0	0	0	0	.333	.375
Orta, Clev.*	.400	7	20	2	8	9	1	0	0	5	1	0	0	2	0	2	0	0	0	0	.450	.400
Paciorek, Sea	.315	23	92	11	29	43	5	0	3	10	0	6	1	13	0	0	0	0	0	2	.467	.357
Page, Oak.*	.247	101	340	56	84	153	10	4	17	49	5	35	3	84	4	5	1	14	7	9	.450	.319
Parrish, Det	.306	16	62	8	19	31	6	0	2	11	0	2	0	15	0	1	0	1	1	5	.500	.328
Perez, Bos	.204	13	54	3	11	16	2	0	1	5	0	1	0	8	0	1	0	0	0	2	.296	.218
Peters, Det.†	.172	11	29	4	5	11	1	1	1	4	0	3	0	4	2	0	0	0	0	0	.379	.250
Piniella, N.Y	.118	7	17	1	2	3	1	0	0	0	0	0	0	2	0	0	0	0	0	0	.176	.118
Poff, Milw.*	.200	7	30	1	6	9	0	0	1	3	0	2	2	3	0	0	0	0	0	1	.300	.250
Porter, K.C.*	.275	34	131	14	36	52	5	1	3	28	5	21	3	11	0	3	0	0	1	2	.397	.375
Pruitt, 2-Clev. 7-Chgo.	.179	9	28	1	5	9	1	0	1	2	0	2	0	4	2	0	0	0	0	0	.321	.233
Pryor, Chgo	.000	1	1	0	0	0	0	0	0	0	0	0	0	0	1	0	0	0	0	0	.000	.000

Putnam, Tex.*	1.000	1	1	1	1	4	0	1	1	0	1	0	0	0	0	0	0	0	0	4.000	1.000
Quirk, K.C.*	.250	1	4	1	1	1	0	0	0	1	0	0	0	0	0	0	0	0	0	.250	.250
Rader, Bos.*	.222	9	27	3	6	14	2	0	2	7	0	3	0	3	0	1	0	0	0	.519	.300
Ramos, Tor	.000	1	4	0	0	0	0	0	0	0	0	0	0	2	0	0	0	0	0	.000	.000
Rayford, Balt	1.000	1	1	1	1	1	0	0	0	0	0	0	0	0	0	0	0	0	0	1.000	1.000
Rettenmund, Calf.	.333	1	3	0	1	1	0	0	0	0	0	1	0	1	0	0	0	0	0	.333	.500
Revering, Oak.*	.176	5	17	2	3	3	0	0	0	1	0	4	1	2	0	0	0	0	0	.176	.333
Rice, Bos.	.397	15	58	13	23	44	4	1	5	6	2	4	2	7	1	0	0	3	0	2	.759	.435
Richardt, Tex	.333	1	3	0	1	1	0	0	0	0	0	0	0	0	0	0	0	0	0	.333	.333
Rivera, Minn.	.000	1	2	0	0	0	0	0	0	0	0	1	0	0	0	0	0	0	0	.000	.333
Rivers, Tex.*	.400	4	15	1	6	6	0	0	0	0	0	0	0	0	0	0	0	0	1	0	.400	.400
Roberts, Sea	.417	4	12	3	5	9	1	0	1	3	1	4	0	3	0	1	1	0	0	0	.750	.588
Rosello, Clev.	.000	1	0	1	0	0	0	0	0	0	0	0	0	0	0	0	0	0	0	0	.000	.000
Rudi, Calf	.182	3	11	0	2	3	1	0	0	1	0	1	0	3	0	0	1	0	0	0	.273	.308
Sakata, Balt	1.000	1	1	0	1	1	0	0	0	1	1	0	0	0	0	0	0	0	0	0	1.000	1.000
Sample, Tex	.143	4	7	0	1	1	0	0	0	0	0	0	0	1	0	0	0	0	0	0	143	.143
Singleton, Balt.†	.450	5	20	2	9	9	0	0	0	4	2	1	0	3	0	0	0	0	0	1	.450	.476
Smalley, Minn.†	.600	3	5	0	3	3	0	0	0	1	0	1	0	1	0	0	0	0	0	0	.600	.667
Soderholm, N.Y	.305	51	151	24	46	78	6	1	8	22	5	18	2	11	1	0	1	0	0	5	.517	.382
Sofield, Minn.*	.400	2	5	1	2	2	0	0	0	1	0	0	0	3	0	0	0	1	0	0	.400	.400
Spencer, N.Y.*	.214	15	28	3	6	9	0	0	1	3	1	6	1	4	0	0	0	0	0	3	.321	.353
Stapleton, Bos.	.375	3	8	2	3	8	0	1	1	5	1	0	0	1	0	1	0	0	0	0	1.000	.375
Staub, Tex.*	.291	57	139	29	58	88	10	1	6	37	2	23	1	9	1	5	1	1	1	9	.442	.368
Stegman, Det	.000	2	4	0	0	0	0	0	0	0	0	1	0	1	0	0	0	0	0	0	.000	.200
Stein, Sea	.167	5	18	0	3	4	1	0	0	1	0	0	0	3	0	0	0	0	0	0	.222	.167
Summers, Det.*	.302	64	139	38	60	104	11	0	11	38	3	36	3	33	0	3	2	3	2	6	.523	.414
Terrell, K.C	.000	1	0	1	0	0	0	0	0	0	0	0	0	0	0	0	0	0	0	0	.000	.000
Thomas, Milw	.125	2	8	1	1	2	1	0	0	0	0	0	0	2	0	0	0	0	0	0	.250	.125
Thompson, Calf	.351	45	148	34	52	89	4	0	11	36	0	31	4	28	0	2	0	2	0	4	.601	.464
Thon, Calf	.310	15	58	6	18	23	3	1	0	5	0	1	0	5	0	1	0	1	2	1	.397	.322
Torres, K.C.†	.000	1	0	1	0	0	0	0	0	0	0	0	0	0	0	0	0	0	0	0	.000	.000
Upshaw, Tor.*	.161	12	31	3	5	6	1	0	0	2	0	4	0	7	0	0	0	1	0	0	.194	.257
Vega, Minn.	.179	9	28	2	5	5	0	0	0	3	0	3	0	7	1	0	0	1	0	1	.179	.258
Velez, Tor	.269	97	342	51	92	167	12	3	19	59	7	51	7	81	0	4	1	0	0	8	.488	.365
Walker, Bos.†	.130	7	23	0	3	3	0	0	0	3	1	2	1	5	0	1	1	1	0	1	.130	.231
Walton, Tex.†	.000	1	3	1	0	0	0	0	0	0	0	1	0	2	0	0	0	0	0	0	.000	.250
Walton, Sea	.256	11	43	4	11	15	4	0	0	4	1	1	0	4	0	1	0	1	1	0	.349	.273
Washington, Chgo.*	.600	2	5	1	3	3	0	0	0	2	0	0	0	1	0	0	0	0	0	0	.600	.600
Watson, N.Y	.313	21	83	15	26	42	4	0	4	8	0	12	0	9	0	0	0	0	1	6	.506	.400
Werth, N.Y.	.133	8	15	3	2	5	0	0	1	1	0	0	0	6	0	0	0	0	0	1	.333	.133
Wockenfuss, Det	.281	28	64	6	18	26	2	0	2	15	2	5	1	11	0	1	0	1	1	1	.406	.333

*Bats Lefthanded †Switch Hitter

Batter & Club	AVG	G	AB	R	H	TB	2B	3B	HR	RBI	GW RBI	TBB	IBB	SO	SH	SF	HB	SB	CS	GI DP	SLG	OBP
Wolfe, Bos	.167	4	6	1	1	4	0	0	1	2	1	0	0	1	0	1	0	0	0	0	.667	.167
Woods, Tor.*	.147	13	34	3	5	5	0	0	0	3	2	4	0	11	1	0	0	0	0	0	.147	.237
Wynegar, Minn.†	.000	1	1	0	0	0	0	0	0	0	0	0	0	1	0	0	0	0	0	0	.000	.000
Yastrzemski, Bos.*	.270	49	174	23	47	81	11	1	7	25	4	24	2	20	0	2	0	0	1	6	.466	.359
Yount, Milw	.343	9	35	7	12	17	2	0	1	1	0	2	0	2	0	0	0	2	2	1	.486	.378
Zisk, Tex	.318	86	302	30	96	147	16	1	11	46	5	30	5	43	1	2	0	0	2	10	.487	.380

PITCHING

TOP FIFTEEN QUALIFIERS FOR EARNED-RUN LEADERSHIP

(162 or more innings)

*Throws Lefthanded

Pitcher and Club	W	L	PCT	ERA	G	GS	CG	GF	SHO	SV	IP	H	BFP	R	ER	HR	SH	SF	TBB	IBB	SO	HB	WP	BK
May, Rudy, N.Y.*	15	5	.750	2.47	41	17	3	13	1	3	175	144	690	56	48	14	6	2	39	2	133	0	9	1
Norris, Mike, Oak	22	9	.710	2.54	33	33	24	0	1	0	284	215	1135	88	80	18	9	7	83	2	180	6	9	4
Burns, Britt, Chgo.*	15	13	.536	2.84	34	32	11	1	1	0	238	213	970	83	75	17	15	5	63	2	133	4	1	4
Keough, Matt, Oak	16	13	.552	2.92	34	32	20	0	2	0	250	218	1041	94	81	24	12	6	94	3	121	5	13	2
Gura, Larry, K.C.*	18	10	.643	2.96	36	36	16	0	4	0	283	272	1175	107	93	20	14	12	76	6	113	5	2	0
Haas, Moose, Milw	16	15	.516	3.11	33	33	14	0	3	0	252	246	1023	96	87	25	3	9	56	6	146	1	5	1
Stone, Steve, Balt	25	7	.781	3.23	37	37	9	0	1	0	251	224	1048	103	90	22	6	3	101	3	149	6	7	0
Erickson, Roger, Minn	7	13	.350	3.25	32	27	7	1	0	0	191	198	811	83	69	13	5	6	56	0	97	4	5	2
Langford, Rick, Oak	19	12	.613	3.26	35	33	28	2	2	0	290	276	1166	119	105	29	5	12	64	6	102	1	7	1
Clancy, Jim, Tor	13	16	.448	3.30	34	34	15	0	2	0	251	217	1075	108	92	19	9	4	128	4	152	2	10	0
McGregor, Scott, Balt.*	20	8	.714	3.32	36	36	12	0	4	0	252	254	1037	101	93	16	10	9	58	3	119	2	3	2
Stanley, Bob, Bos	10	8	.556	3.39	52	17	5	25	1	14	175	186	737	75	66	11	5	5	52	8	71	7	1	0
John, Tommy, N.Y.*	22	9	.710	3.43	36	36	16	0	6	0	265	270	1089	115	101	13	15	5	56	1	78	6	5	0
Bannister, Floyd, Sea.*	9	13	.409	3.47	32	32	8	0	0	0	218	200	918	96	84	24	8	5	66	6	155	2	7	0
Guidry, Ron, N.Y.*	17	10	.630	3.56	37	29	5	4	3	1	220	215	929	97	87	19	9	12	80	1	166	1	5	0

INDIVIDUAL PITCHING

(All Pitchers Listed Alphabetically)

*Throws Lefthanded

Pitcher and Club	W	L	PCT	ERA	G	GS	CG	GF	SHO	SV	IP	H	BFP	R	ER	HR	SH	SF	TBB	IBB	SO	HB	WP	BK
Aase, Don, Calif	8	13	.381	4.06	40	21	5	6	1	2	175	193	761	83	79	13	12	9	66	3	74	1	2	1
Abbott, Glenn, Sea	12	12	.500	4.10	31	31	7	0	2	0	215	228	903	110	98	27	10	4	49	4	78	3	1	1
Allard, Brian, Tex	0	1	.000	5.79	5	2	0	2	0	0	14	13	67	13	9	0	0	1	10	1	10	1	1	0

Anderson, Rick, Sea	0	0	--	3.60	5	2	0	3	0	0	10	8	46	5	4	1	1	0	10	2	7	0	1	0
Aponte, Luis, Bos.	0	0	--	1.29	4	0	0	3	0	0	7	6	28	1	1	0	2	0	2	1	1	0	0	0
Arroyo, Fernando, Minn . .	6	6	.500	4.70	21	11	1	4	1	0	92	97	396	55	48	7	1	6	32	2	27	2	4	3
Augustine, Jerry, Milw.* . .	4	3	.571	4.50	39	1	0	17	0	2	70	83	321	37	35	5	4	3	36	5	22	2	3	0
Babcock, Bob, Tex	1	2	.333	4.70	19	0	0	8	0	0	23	20	98	13	12	3	1	3	8	1	15	2	1	0
Bacsik, Mike, Minn	0	0	—	4.30	10	0	0	9	0	0	23	26	104	12	11	1	1	1	11	0	9	0	0	0
Bailor, Bob, Tor.	0	0	—	9.00	3	0	0	2	0	0	2	4	12	2	2	0	0	0	1	0	0	0	0	0
Bannister, Floyd, Sea.* . . .	9	13	.409	3.47	32	32	8	0	0	0	218	200	918	96	84	24	8	5	66	6	155	2	7	0
Barker, Len, Clev	19	12	.613	4.17	36	36	8	0	1	0	246	237	1052	127	114	17	7	9	92	3	187	3	14	1
Barlow, Mike, Tor.	3	1	.750	4.09	40	1	0	19	0	5	55	57	237	29	25	4	4	1	21	4	19	2	5	0
Barr, Jim, Calif	1	4	.200	5.56	24	7	0	7	0	1	68	90	311	43	42	12	0	6	23	2	22	3	2	0
Barrios, Francisco, Chgo . .	1	1	.500	5.06	3	3	0	0	0	0	16	21	75	9	9	4	0	1	8	0	2	1	0	0
Baumgarten, Ross, Chgo.* .	2	12	.143	3.44	24	23	3	0	1	0	136	127	566	60	52	10	10	6	52	0	66	1	6	2
Beard, Dave, Oak	0	1	.000	3.38	13	0	0	9	0	1	16	12	64	6	6	0	0	1	7	1	12	1	0	0
Beattie, Jim, Sea	5	15	.250	4.86	33	29	3	1	0	0	187	205	831	115	101	19	6	6	98	9	67	4	4	2
Billingham, Jack, Det.-Bos .	1	3	.250	10.13	15	4	0	3	0	0	32	56	166	36	36	7	2	2	18	1	7	4	1	0
Bird, Doug, N.Y.	3	0	1.000	2.65	22	1	0	7	0	1	51	47	205	16	15	3	3	4	14	1	17	1	1	0
Boddicker, Mike, Balt . . .	0	1	.000	6.43	1	1	0	0	0	0	7	6	34	6	5	1	0	0	5	0	4	0	0	0
Boitano, Dan, Milw	0	1	.000	8.00	11	0	0	1	0	0	18	26	85	17	16	7	1	1	6	0	11	1	4	0
Bordi, Rich, Oak	0	0	--	4.50	1	0	0	0	0	0	2	4	10	1	1	0	0	0	0	0	0	0	0	0
Botting, Ralph, Calif.* . . .	0	3	.000	5.88	6	6	0	0	0	0	26	40	130	20	17	1	1	1	13	0	12	0	2	0
Brett, Ken, K.C.*	0	0	—	.00	8	0	0	3	0	1	13	8	54	0	0	0	2	0	5	0	4	1	0	0
Burgmeier, Tom, Bos.* . . .	5	4	.556	2.00	62	0	0	39	0	24	99	87	391	30	22	3	6	2	20	3	54	2	1	0
Burns, Britt, Chgo.*	15	13	.536	2.84	34	32	11	1	1	0	238	213	970	83	75	17	15	5	63	2	133	4	1	4
Busby, Steve, K.C.	1	3	.250	6.21	11	6	0	2	0	0	42	59	199	30	29	3	0	2	19	0	12	2	4	0
Buskey, Tom, Tor.	3	1	.750	4.43	33	0	0	9	0	0	67	68	279	35	33	11	3	5	26	6	34	0	1	0
Butcher, John, Tex	3	3	.500	4.11	6	6	1	0	0	0	35	34	152	19	16	2	2	0	13	0	27	0	1	0
Caldwell, Mike, Milw.* . . .	13	11	.542	4.04	34	33	11	1	2	1	225	248	940	112	101	29	6	7	56	2	74	2	3	2
Camacho, Ernie, Oak	0	0	--	6.75	5	0	0	2	0	0	12	20	61	9	9	2	0	0	5	0	9	1	2	0
Campbell, Bill, Bos	4	0	1.000	4.83	23	0	0	11	0	0	41	44	180	26	22	1	0	3	22	0	17	0	3	0
Castro, Bill, Milw	2	4	.333	2.79	56	0	0	36	0	8	84	89	350	35	26	2	3	3	17	6	32	2	5	0
Chamberlain, Craig, K.C . .	0	1	.000	7.00	5	0	0	2	0	0	9	10	43	8	7	3	0	1	5	2	3	0	1	0
Christenson, Gary, K.C.* . .	3	0	1.000	5.23	24	0	0	8	0	1	31	35	148	23	18	4	0	2	18	1	16	2	1	0
Clancy, Jim, Tor	13	16	.448	3.30	34	34	15	0	2	0	251	217	1075	108	92	19	9	4	128	4	152	2	10	0
Clay, Ken, Tex	2	3	.400	4.60	8	8	0	0	0	0	43	43	202	24	22	4	1	1	29	2	17	3	7	0
Clear, Mark, Calif	11	11	.500	3.31	58	0	0	41	0	9	106	82	461*	51	39	2	8	3	65	9	105	5	4	0
Cleveland, Reggie, Milw . .	11	9	.550	3.74	45	13	5	16	2	4	154	150	657	73	64	9	4	9	49	2	54	5	5	0
Collins, Don, Clev.*	0	0	--	7.50	4	0	0	2	0	0	6	9	33	5	5	0	0	0	7	1	0	0	1	0
Comer, Steve, Tex	2	4	.333	7.93	12	11	0	0	0	0	42	65	205	41	37	6	3	1	22	0	9	2	0	0
Contreras, Nardi, Chgo . . .	0	0	--	5.79	8	0	0	6	0	0	14	18	65	10	9	1	1	1	7	2	8	2	0	0
Corbett, Doug, Minn	8	6	.571	1.99	73	0	0	63	0	23	136	102	531	31	30	7	7	2	42	8	89	1	3	0

*Throws Lefthanded Pitcher and Club	W	L	PCT	ERA	G	GS	CG	GF	SHO	SV	IP	H	BFP	R	ER	HR	SH	SF	TBB	IBB	SO	HB	WP	BK
Crawford, Steve, Bos	2	0	1.000	3.66	6	4	2	1	0	0	32	41	142	14	13	3	0	0	8	2	10	0	0	0
Cruz, Victor, Clev	6	7	.462	3.45	55	0	0	40	0	12	86	71	355	36	33	10	5	10	27	8	88	3	4	0
Darwin, Danny, Tex	13	4	.765	2.62	53	2	0	35	0	8	110	98	468	37	32	4	5	7	50	7	104	2	3	0
Davis, Ron, N.Y	9	3	.750	2.95	53	0	0	29	0	7	131	121	544	50	43	9	10	6	32	3	65	5	5	1
Denny, John, Clev	8	6	.571	4.38	16	16	4	0	1	0	109	116	464	54	53	4	1	3	47	2	59	5	4	1
Devine, Adrian, Tex	1	1	.500	4.82	13	0	0	3	0	0	28	49	142	22	15	4	0	2	9	1	8	1	0	0
Dorsey, Jim, Calif	1	2	.333	9.00	4	4	0	0	0	0	16	25	78	16	16	2	0	1	8	0	8	1	0	0
Dotson, Richard, Chgo	12	10	.545	4.27	33	32	8	1	0	0	198	185	863	105	94	20	15	7	87	2	109	6	6	2
Drago, Dick, Bos	7	7	.500	4.13	43	7	1	18	0	3	133	127	564	67	61	17	7	2	44	7	63	5	0	0
Dressler, Rob, Sea	4	10	.286	3.99	30	14	3	9	0	0	149	161	624	75	66	14	4	8	33	7	50	3	1	1
Eastwick, Rawly, K.C	0	1	.000	5.32	14	0	0	8	0	0	22	37	114	14	13	2	1	1	8	2	5	2	1	0
Eckersley, Dennis, Bos	12	14	.462	4.27	30	30	8	0	0	0	198	188	818	101	94	25	7	8	44	7	121	2	0	0
Erickson, Roger, Minn	7	13	.350	3.25	32	27	7	1	0	0	191	198	811	83	69	13	5	6	56	0	97	4	5	2
Farmer, Ed, Chgo	7	9	.438	3.33	64	0	0	55	0	30	100	92	438	37	37	6	3	1	56	11	54	1	7	0
Felton, Terry, Minn	0	3	.000	7.00	5	4	0	0	0	0	18	20	83	18	14	2	2	1	9	1	14	1	0	0
Ferris, Bob, Calif	0	2	.000	6.00	5	3	0	0	0	0	15	23	74	13	10	2	0	0	9	0	4	0	1	0
Fidrych, Mark, Det	2	3	.400	5.73	9	9	1	0	0	0	44	58	215	35	28	5	5	1	20	2	16	1	3	0
Figueroa, Ed, N.Y.-Tex	3	10	.231	6.52	23	17	0	4	0	1	98	152	462	76	71	12	1	6	36	2	25	1	4	1
Flanagan, Mike, Balt.*	16	13	.552	4.12	37	37	12	0	2	0	251	278	1065	121	115	27	10	12	71	3	128	2	12	1
Flinn, John, Milw	2	1	.667	3.89	20	1	0	8	0	2	37	31	164	20	16	3	1	2	20	2	15	0	2	0
Ford, Dave, Balt	1	3	.250	4.24	25	3	1	9	0	1	70	66	281	34	33	11	3	0	13	2	22	2	4	0
Frost, Dave, Calif	4	8	.333	5.31	15	15	2	0	0	0	78	97	343	53	46	8	2	3	21	1	28	2	3	0
Gale, Rich, K.C	13	9	.591	3.91	32	28	6	1	1	1	191	169	799	90	83	16	8	3	78	2	97	2	6	0
Garland, Wayne, Clev	6	9	.400	4.62	25	20	4	1	1	0	150	163	657	85	77	18	7	6	48	2	55	6	5	0
Garvin, Jerry, Tor.*	4	7	.364	2.28	61	0	0	24	0	8	83	70	336	23	21	6	8	0	27	7	52	0	0	0
Gleaton, Jerry, Tex.*	0	0	——	2.57	5	0	0	2	0	0	7	5	30	2	2	0	0	2	4	0	2	0	0	0
Gossage, Rich, N.Y	6	2	.750	2.27	64	0	0	58	0	33	99	74	401	29	25	5	8	4	37	3	103	1	4	0
Griffin, Mike, N.Y	2	4	.333	4.83	13	9	0	3	0	0	64	64	250	36	29	6	1	2	23	2	25	1	3	0
Grimsley, Ross, Clev.*	4	5	.444	6.72	14	11	2	0	0	0	75	103	342	63	56	11	2	4	24	1	18	1	2	0
Guidry, Ron, N.Y.*	17	10	.630	3.56	37	29	5	4	3	1	220	215	929	97	87	19	9	12	80	1	166	1	5	0
Gura, Larry, K.C.*	18	10	.643	2.96	36	36	16	0	4	0	283	272	1175	107	93	20	14	12	76	6	113	5	2	0
Haas, Moose, Milw	16	15	.516	3.11	33	33	14	0	3	0	252	246	1023	96	87	25	3	9	56	6	146	1	5	1
Halicki, Ed, Calif	3	1	.750	4.89	10	6	0	3	0	0	35	39	153	22	19	5	0	2	11	0	16	0	1	0
Hamilton, Dave, Oak.*	0	3	.000	11.40	21	1	0	3	0	0	30	44	164	39	38	6	3	2	28	2	23	3	0	1
Hartzell, Paul, Balt	0	2	.000	6.50	6	0	0	4	0	0	18	22	80	14	13	3	0	0	9	2	5	0	1	0
Hassler, Andy, Calif.*	5	1	.833	2.49	41	0	0	25	0	10	83	67	354	25	23	8	2	1	37	8	75	1	1	0
Heaverlo, Dave, Sea	6	3	.667	3.87	60	0	0	38	0	4	79	75	341	37	34	9	1	4	35	12	42	5	1	1
Hiller, John, Det.*	1	0	1.000	4.35	11	0	0	2	0	0	31	38	140	15	15	3	1	2	14	1	18	0	1	1
Hoffman, Guy, Chgo.*	1	0	1.000	2.61	23	1	0	8	0	1	38	38	161	12	11	1	1	1	17	2	24	0	1	0

Holdsworth, Fred, Milw . .	0	0	--	4.50	9	0	0	3	0	0	20	24	93	12	10	2	0	0	9	0	12	0	0	0
Honeycutt, Rick, Sea.* . . .	10	17	.370	3.95	30	30	9	0	1	0	203	221	871	99	89	22	11	7	60	7	79	3	4	0
Hough, Charlie, Tex	2	2	.500	3.98	16	2	2	7	1	0	61	54	270	30	27	2	4	1	37	2	47	3	8	0
Hoyt, Lamarr, Chgo	9	3	.750	4.58	24	13	3	5	1	0	112	123	496	66	57	8	8	7	41	3	55	2	3	0
Hurst, Bruce, Bos.*	2	2	.500	9.00	12	7	0	2	0	0	31	39	147	33	31	4	0	2	16	0	16	2	4	2
Jackson, Darrell, Minn.* . .	9	9	.500	3.87	32	25	1	4	0	1	172	161	724	81	74	15	6	4	69	2	90	2	3	0
Jefferson, Jesse, Tor	4	13	.235	5.46	29	18	2	4	2	0	122	130	535	78	74	12	14	5	52	2	53	2	0	2
Jenkins, Ferguson, Tex. . .	12	12	.500	3.77	29	29	12	0	0	0	198	190	827	90	83	22	5	5	52	8	129	4	5	0
John, Tommy, N.Y.*	22	9	.710	3.43	36	36	16	0	6	0	265	270	1089	115	101	13	15	5	56	1	78	6	5	0
Johnson, John Henry, Tex.*.	2	2	.500	2.31	33	0	0	17	0	4	39	27	154	12	10	2	1	1	15	4	44	1	2	0
Jones, Jeff, Oak.	1	3	.250	2.86	35	0	0	13	0	5	44	32	192	21	14	2	5	3	26	2	34	1	3	0
Jones, Mike, K.C.*	0	1	.000	10.80	3	1	0	1	0	0	5	6	24	7	6	0	1	0	5	1	2	0	0	0
Kaat, James, N.Y.*	0	1	.000	7.20	4	0	0	3	0	0	5	8	27	5	4	0	1	1	4	2	1	0	1	0
Kainer, Don, Tex	0	0	--	1.80	4	3	0	0	0	0	20	22	91	7	4	0	3	0	9	1	10	3	0	0
Keeton, Rickey, Milw . . .	2	2	.500	4.82	5	5	0	0	0	0	28	35	127	15	15	4	2	2	9	0	8	0	0	0
Keough, Matt, Oak	16	13	.552	2.92	34	32	20	0	2	0	250	218	1041	94	81	24	12	6	94	3	121	5	13	2
Kern, Jim, Tex	3	11	.214	4.86	38	1	0	15	0	2	63	65	295	38	34	4	9	6	45	10	40	2	3	1
Kerrigan, Joe, Balt	0	0	--	4.50	1	0	0	1	0	0	2	3	11	1	1	0	0	0	0	0	1	0	0	0
Kingman, Brian, Oak	8	20	.286	3.84	32	30	10	0	1	0	211	209	912	105	90	21	5	3	82	5	116	4	6	0
Kinnunen, Mike, Minn.* . .	0	0	--	5.04	21	0	0	10	0	0	25	29	112	18	14	1	0	2	9	1	8	1	2	0
Kison, Bruce, Calif	3	6	.333	4.93	13	13	2	0	1	0	73	73	321	46	40	5	7	2	32	2	28	3	0	2
Knapp, Chris, Calif	2	11	.154	6.15	32	20	1	3	0	1	117	133	535	83	80	18	9	6	51	1	46	8	4	1
Koosman, Jerry, Minn.* . .	16	13	.552	4.04	38	34	8	2	0	2	243	252	1022	119	109	24	17	6	69	5	149	5	2	1
Kravec, Ken, Chgo.*	3	6	.333	6.91	20	15	0	1	0	0	82	100	394	71	63	13	4	5	44	3	37	5	5	1
Kucek, Jack, Tor	3	8	.273	6.75	23	12	0	5	0	1	68	83	325	56	51	9	5	1	41	1	35	1	3	0
LaRoche, Dave, Calif.* . . .	3	5	.375	4.08	52	9	1	17	0	4	128	122	530	62	58	14	7	5	39	3	39	3	0	1
Lacey, Bob, Oak.*	3	2	.600	2.93	47	1	1	31	1	6	80	68	322	29	26	7	5	4	21	5	45	1	5	0
Langford, Rick, Oak	19	12	.613	3.26	35	33	28	2	2	0	290	276	1166	119	105	29	5	12	64	6	102	1	7	1
Lapoint, Dave, Milw.* . . .	1	0	1.000	6.00	5	3	0	1	0	1	15	17	75	14	10	2	2	2	13	1	5	0	0	1
Leal, Luis, Tor.	3	4	.429	4.50	13	10	1	1	0	0	60	72	270	35	30	6	6	3	31	2	26	1	0	0
Lemanczyk, Dave, Tor.-Calif.	4	9	.308	4.79	31	10	0	10	0	0	109	138	498	69	58	12	4	4	42	2	28	2	3	3
Leonard, Dennis, K.C. . . .	20	11	.645	3.79	38	38	9	0	3	0	280	271	1174	127	118	30	13	8	80	5	155	1	12	1
Lewallyn, Dennis, Tex . . .	0	0	--	7.50	4	0	0	1	0	0	6	7	27	5	5	0	0	0	4	1	1	0	0	0
Lockwood, Skip, Bos. . . .	3	1	.750	5.28	24	1	0	16	0	2	46	61	211	31	27	4	1	3	17	3	11	0	0	0
Lollar, Tim, N.Y.*	1	0	1.000	3.38	14	1	0	5	0	2	32	33	144	14	12	3	4	2	20	2	13	0	2	1
Lopez, Aurelio, Det.	13	6	.684	3.77	67	1	0	59	0	21	124	125	534	56	52	15	7	3	45	5	97	3	6	1
Lyle, Sparky, Tex.*	3	2	.600	4.67	49	0	0	32	0	8	81	97	353	47	42	9	5	3	28	6	43	0	1	2
Lysander, Rick, Oak	0	0	--	7.71	5	0	0	3	0	0	14	24	67	13	12	3	0	0	4	0	5	0	0	0
MacWhorter, Keith, Bos . .	0	3	.000	5.57	14	2	0	5	0	0	42	46	189	27	26	3	4	1	18	3	21	2	1	0
Marshall, Mike, Minn	1	3	.250	6.19	18	0	0	12	0	1	32	42	150	23	22	2	3	3	12	1	13	2	4	0
Martin, Renie, K.C	10	10	.500	4.40	32	28	2	8	0	2	137	133	599	84	67	18	3	4	70	2	68	1	4	0

*Throws Lefthanded Pitcher and Club	W	L	PCT	ERA	G	GS	CG	GF	SHO	SV	IP	H	BFP	R	ER	HR	SH	SF	TBB	IBB	SO	HB	WP	BK
Martinez, Alfredo, Calif	7	9	.438	4.53	30	23	4	3	1	0	149	150	649	81	75	14	5	4	58	2	57	1	5	0
Martinez, Dennis, Balt	6	4	.600	3.96	25	12	2	8	0	1	100	103	428	44	44	12	1	3	44	6	42	2	0	1
Martinez, Tippy, Balt.*	4	4	.500	3.00	52	0	0	26	0	10	81	69	329	30	27	5	4	2	34	5	68	1	6	0
Matlack, Jon, Tex.*	10	10	.500	3.68	35	34	8	1	1	1	235	265	985	111	96	17	9	6	48	1	142	0	9	0
May, Rudy, N.Y.*	15	5	.750	2.47	41	17	3	13	1	3	175	144	690	56	48	14	6	2	39	2	133	0	9	1
McCatty, Steve, Oak	14	14	.500	3.85	33	31	11	2	1	0	222	202	960	104	95	27	2	8	99	2	114	8	5	0
McClure, Bob, Milw.*	5	8	.385	3.07	52	5	2	23	1	10	91	83	390	34	31	6	1	5	37	2	47	2	0	2
McGregor, Scott, Balt.*	20	8	.714	3.32	36	36	12	0	4	0	252	254	1037	101	93	16	10	9	58	3	119	2	3	2
McLaughlin, Byron, Sea	3	6	.333	6.82	45	4	0	15	0	2	91	124	439	74	69	15	10	2	50	14	41	2	3	0
McLaughlin, Joey, Tor	6	9	.400	4.50	55	10	0	27	0	4	136	159	600	79	68	16	10	6	53	11	70	4	4	0
Medich, Doc, Tex	14	11	.560	3.93	34	32	6	0	0	0	204	230	877	104	89	13	8	3	56	1	91	3	7	1
Minetto, Craig, Oak.*	0	2	.000	7.88	7	1	0	1	0	1	8	11	38	7	7	2	0	1	3	1	5	0	1	0
Mirabella, Paul, Tor.*	5	12	.294	4.33	33	22	3	2	1	0	131	151	596	73	63	11	9	5	66	3	53	3	4	0
Mitchell, Paul, Milw.	5	5	.500	3.54	17	11	1	4	1	1	89	92	368	40	35	7	5	3	15	3	29	1	0	0
Monge, Sid, Clev.*	3	5	.375	3.64	67	0	0	42	0	14	94	80	401	40	38	12	4	1	40	6	60	3	2	1
Montague, John, Calif	4	2	.667	5.11	37	0	0	18	0	3	74	97	330	47	42	8	4	5	21	1	22	1	2	0
Moore, Balor, Tor.*	1	1	.500	5.26	31	3	0	14	0	1	65	76	290	43	38	6	6	3	31	3	22	4	1	0
Morris, Jack, Det	16	15	.516	4.18	36	36	11	0	2	0	250	252	1074	125	116	20	10	13	87	5	112	4	6	2
Norris, Mike, Oak	22	9	.710	2.54	33	33	24	0	1	0	284	215	1135	88	80	18	9	7	83	2	180	6	9	4
Ojeda, Bob, Bos.*	1	1	.500	6.92	7	7	0	0	0	0	26	39	122	20	20	2	0	0	14	1	12	0	1	0
Owchinko, Bob, Clev.*	2	9	.182	5.29	29	14	1	2	1	0	114	138	516	71	67	13	4	4	47	2	66	2	7	0
Palmer, Jim, Balt	16	10	.615	3.98	34	33	4	0	0	0	224	238	959	108	99	26	11	5	74	0	109	3	2	3
Parrott, Mike, Sea.	1	16	.059	7.28	27	16	1	8	0	3	94	136	442	83	76	16	6	2	42	9	53	1	2	0
Pattin, Marty, K.C	4	0	1.000	3.64	37	0	0	21	0	4	89	97	378	39	36	7	1	3	23	7	40	1	2	0
Paxton, Mike, Clev	0	0	--	12.38	4	0	0	0	0	0	8	13	40	11	11	4	0	1	6	1	6	0	0	0
Perry, Gaylord, Tex.-N.Y	10	13	.435	3.67	34	32	6	2	2	0	206	224	884	107	84	14	9	7	64	3	135	8	9	0
Petry, Dan, Det	10	9	.526	3.93	27	25	4	1	3	0	165	156	716	82	72	9	10	5	83	14	88	1	5	2
Proly, Mike, Chgo.	5	10	.333	3.06	62	3	0	31	0	8	147	136	618	67	50	7	9	11	58	9	56	3	2	1
Quisenberry, Dan, K.C	12	7	.632	3.09	75	0	0	68	0	33	128	129	526	47	44	5	8	6	27	15	37	1	1	0
Rainey, Chuck, Bos.	8	3	.727	4.86	16	13	2	1	1	0	87	92	383	49	47	7	1	2	41	3	43	2	4	0
Rajsich, Dave, Tex.*	2	1	.667	6.00	24	1	0	5	0	2	48	56	221	34	32	7	2	4	22	0	35	3	3	0
Rawley, Shane, Sea.*	7	7	.500	3.32	59	0	0	39	0	13	114	103	484	44	42	3	15	3	63	16	68	3	2	1
Redfern, Pete, Minn	7	7	.500	4.54	23	16	2	3	0	2	105	117	455	58	53	11	5	4	33	3	73	0	2	0
Remmerswaal, Win, Bos	2	1	.667	4.63	14	0	0	5	0	0	35	39	144	18	18	4	2	1	9	1	20	0	0	0
Renko, Steve, Bos.	9	9	.500	4.20	32	23	1	3	0	0	165	180	708	86	77	17	5	5	56	4	90	1	2	1
Robbins, Bruce, Det.*	4	2	.667	6.58	15	6	0	0	0	0	52	60	241	40	38	12	2	2	28	0	23	0	4	0
Roberts, Dave, Sea.*	2	3	.400	4.39	37	4	0	13	0	3	80	86	355	46	39	7	3	6	27	7	47	1	4	0
Robinson, Dewey, Chgo	1	1	.500	3.09	15	0	0	5	0	0	35	26	141	13	12	2	2	2	16	0	28	0	0	0
Rozema, Dave, Det	6	9	.400	3.91	42	13	2	17	1	4	145	152	620	68	63	11	13	4	49	14	49	5	9	0

Sarmiento, Manny, Sea. . .	0	1	.000	3.60	9	0	0	6	0	1	15	14	63	7	6	2	0	2	6	1	15	0	0	0
Scarbery, Randy, Chgo. . .	1	2	.333	4.03	15	0	0	7	0	2	29	24	116	14	13	1	5	1	7	0	18	2	4	0
Schatzeder, Dan, Det.* . . .	11	13	.458	4.01	32	26	9	2	2	0	193	178	794	88	86	23	6	3	58	9	94	3	8	0
Schrom, Ken, Tor.	1	0	1.000	5.23	17	0	0	6	0	1	31	32	140	18	18	2	3	1	19	3	13	0	0	0
Schuler, Dave, Calif.*	0	1	.000	3.46	8	0	0	4	0	0	13	13	53	5	5	3	1	2	2	1	7	0	0	0
Slaton, Jim, Milw	1	1	.500	4.50	3	3	0	0	0	0	16	17	68	10	8	3	0	0	5	0	4	0	1	0
Sorensen, Lary, Milw. . . .	12	10	.545	3.67	35	29	8	3	2	1	196	242	839	91	80	13	7	8	45	6	54	2	3	0
Souza, Mark, Oak.*	0	0	——	7.71	5	0	0	0	0	0	7	9	34	6	6	1	0	0	5	0	2	0	0	0
Spillner, Dan, Clev	16	11	.593	5.29	34	30	7	1	1	0	194	225	865	122	114	23	3	5	74	2	100	3	10	0
Splittorff, Paul, K.C.* . . .	14	11	.560	4.15	34	33	4	0	0	0	204	236	861	101	94	17	11	8	43	1	53	1	1	0
Stanley, Bob, Bos	10	8	.556	3.39	52	17	5	25	1	14	175	186	737	75	66	11	5	5	52	8	71	7	1	0
Stanton, Mike, Clev.	1	3	.250	5.34	51	0	0	27	0	5	86	98	385	67	51	6	5	3	44	1	74	3	3	0
Stewart, Sammy, Balt	7	7	.500	3.55	33	3	2	20	0	3	119	103	507	51	47	8	4	3	60	8	78	2	5	0
Stieb, Dave, Tor.	12	15	.444	3.70	34	32	14	0	4	0	243	232	1004	108	100	12	12	9	83	6	108	6	6	2
Stoddard, Tim, Balt.	5	3	.625	2.51	64	0	0	52	0	26	86	72	352	27	24	2	2	2	38	1	64	1	3	0
Stone, Steve, Balt	25	7	.781	3.23	37	37	9	0	1	0	251	224	1048	103	90	22	6	3	101	3	149	6	7	0
Tanana, Frank, Calif.* . . .	11	12	.478	4.15	32	31	7	1	0	0	204	223	870	107	94	18	8	4	45	0	113	8	3	1
Terrell, Jerry, K.C.	0	0	——	.00	1	0	0	1	0	0	1	1	5	0	0	0	0	0	1	0	0	0	0	0
Tiant, Luis, N.Y.	8	9	.471	4.90	25	25	3	0	0	0	136	139	588	79	74	10	6	7	50	3	84	1	2	0
Tobik, Dave, Det	1	0	1.000	3.98	17	1	0	6	0	0	61	61	253	27	27	7	1	2	21	4	34	0	1	0
Todd, Jackson, Tor	5	2	.714	4.02	12	12	4	0	0	0	85	90	361	40	38	14	2	1	30	1	44	2	4	0
Torrez, Mike, Bos	9	16	.360	5.09	36	32	6	1	1	0	207	256	918	124	117	18	13	11	75	10	97	1	9	3
Travers, Billy, Milw.*	12	6	.667	3.92	29	25	7	1	1	0	154	147	650	76	67	20	2	4	47	2	62	6	2	0
Trout, Steve, Chgo.*	9	16	.360	3.69	32	30	7	1	2	0	200	229	866	102	82	14	14	3	49	5	89	9	5	2
Tudor, John, Bos.*	8	5	.615	3.03	16	13	5	0	0	0	92	81	382	35	31	4	4	3	31	1	45	3	1	0
Twitty, Jeff, K.C.*	2	1	.667	6.14	13	0	0	2	0	0	22	33	103	17	15	4	1	1	7	3	9	0	0	0
Ujdur, Jerry, Det	1	0	1.000	7.71	9	2	0	2	0	0	21	36	107	20	18	5	1	1	10	2	8	1	0	0
Underwood, Pat, Det.* . . .	3	6	.333	3.58	49	7	0	24	0	5	113	121	481	51	45	12	6	1	35	7	60	2	2	0
Underwood, Tom, N.Y.* . .	13	9	.591	3.66	38	27	2	5	2	2	187	163	771	85	76	15	9	4	66	4	116	4	2	0
Verhoeven, John, Minn. . .	3	4	.429	3.96	44	0	0	13	0	0	100	109	425	53	44	10	7	9	29	5	42	3	1	2
Veselic, Bob, Minn	0	0	——	4.50	1	0	0	0	0	0	4	3	15	2	2	1	0	0	1	0	2	0	0	0
Waits, Rick, Clev.*	13	14	.481	4.46	33	33	9	0	2	0	224	231	955	118	111	18	10	7	82	6	109	1	5	0
Weaver, Roger, Det	3	4	.429	4.08	19	6	0	6	0	0	64	56	268	32	29	5	2	4	34	3	42	1	2	0
Wheelock, Gary, Sea	0	0	——	6.00	1	1	0	0	0	0	3	4	13	2	2	0	0	0	1	0	1	0	1	1
Wihtol, Sandy, Clev.	1	0	1.000	3.60	17	0	0	10	0	1	35	35	156	18	14	2	3	1	14	2	20	2	2	1
Wilcox, Milt, Det	13	11	.542	4.48	32	31	13	1	1	0	199	201	854	112	99	24	7	7	68	5	97	6	5	0
Williams, Albert, Minn . . .	6	2	.750	3.51	18	9	3	5	0	1	77	73	321	33	30	9	2	0	30	1	35	0	3	1
Willis, Mike, Tor.*	2	1	.667	1.73	20	0	0	10	0	3	26	25	114	6	5	3	0	1	11	4	14	1	2	0
Wirth, Alan, Oak	0	0	——	4.50	2	0	0	2	0	0	2	3	9	1	1	0	0	0	0	0	1	0	0	0
Wortham, Richard, Chgo.* .	4	7	.364	5.97	41	10	0	9	0	1	92	102	430	73	61	4	4	7	58	5	45	3	8	0
Zahn, Geoff, Minn.*	14	18	.438	4.40	38	35	13	0	5	0	233	273	993	138	114	17	11	11	66	3	96	2	3	1

1980 Official National League Records

(Compiled by Elias Sports Bureau, New York)

STANDINGS AT CLOSE OF SEASON

EASTERN DIVISION

					vs Eastern Division						vs Western Division					
Club	WON	LOST	PCT	GB	PHIL	MTL	PITT	STL	NY	CHI	HOU	LA	CIN	ATL	SF	SD
Philadelphia	91	71	.562	--	--	9	7	9	12	13	9	6	5	7	6	8
Montreal	90	72	.556	1	9	--	6	12	10	12	7	1	9	7	7	10
Pittsburgh	83	79	.512	8	11	12	--	10	8	10	5	6	6	1	8	6
St. Louis	74	88	.457	17	9	6	8	--	9	9	5	5	7	6	5	5
New York	67	95	.414	24	6	8	10	9	--	8	4	5	4	9	3	1
Chicago	64	98	.395	27	5	6	8	9	10	--	1	5	7	4	5	4

WESTERN DIVISION

					vs Western Division						vs Eastern Division					
Club	WON	LOST	PCT	GB	HOU	LA	CIN	ATL	SF	SD	PHIL	MTL	PITT	STL	NY	CHI
Houston	93	70	.571	--	--	9	10	11	11	11	3	5	7	7	8	11
Los Angeles	92	71	.564	1	10	--	9	7	13	9	6	11	6	7	7	7
Cincinnati	89	73	.549	3½	8	9	--	16	7	15	7	3	6	5	8	5
Atlanta	81	80	.503	11	7	11	2	--	11	12	5	5	11	6	3	8
San Francisco	75	86	.466	17	7	5	11	6	--	8	6	5	4	7	9	7
San Diego	73	89	.451	19½	7	9	3	6	10	--	4	2	6	7	11	8

CHAMPIONSHIP SERIES: Philadelphia defeated Houston 3 games to 2

Batting

INDIVIDUAL BATTING LEADERS

Average	:	.324	Buckner, Chi.
Games	:	163	Garvey, L.A.
At Bats	:	676	Moreno, Pitt.
Runs	:	111	Hernandez, St.L.
Hits	:	200	Garvey, L.A.
Total Bases	:	342	Schmidt, Phil.
Singles	:	155	Richards, S.D.
Doubles	:	42	Rose, Phil.
Triples	:	13	Moreno, Pitt. & Scott, Mtl.
Home Runs	:	48	Schmidt, Phil.
Runs Batted In	:	121	Schmidt, Phil.
Game Winning Hits	:	18	Clark, S.F.
Sacrifice Hits	:	23	Smith, S.D.
Sacrifice Flies	:	13	Schmidt, Phil.
Stolen Bases	:	97	LeFlore, Mtl.
Caught Stealing	:	33	Moreno, Pitt.
Longest Batting Streak	:	21	Randle, Chi. August 6 - 29

During the 1980 season 431 players participated in regular season games

TOP FIFTEEN QUALIFIERS FOR BATTING CHAMPIONSHIP

(*Bats Lefthanded #Switch Hitter)

Player & Club	AVG	G	AB	R	H	TB	2B	3B	HR	RBI	GW	SH	SF	SB	CS
Buckner, William, Chi.*	.324	145	578	69	187	264	41	3	10	68	7	0	6	1	2
Hernandez, Keith, St.L.*	.321	159	595	111	191	294	39	8	16	99	13	1	4	14	8
Templeton, Garry, St.L.#	.319	118	504	63	161	210	19	9	4	43	3	1	1	31	15
McBride, Arnold, Phil.*	.309	137	554	68	171	251	33	10	9	87	14	2	6	13	10
Cedeno, Cesar, Hou.	.309	137	499	71	154	232	32	8	10	73	7	1	2	48	15
Dawson, Andre, Mtl.	.308	151	577	96	178	284	41	7	17	87	17	1	10	34	9
Garvey, Steven, L.A.	.304	163	658	78	200	307	27	1	26	106	13	3	4	6	11
Collins, David, Cin.#	.303	144	551	94	167	204	20	4	3	35	6	3	3	79	21
Simmons, Ted, St.L.#	.303	145	495	84	150	250	33	2	21	98	12	0	6	1	0
Hendrick, George, St.L.	.302	150	572	73	173	285	33	2	25	109	11	1	4	6	1
Cruz, Jose, Hou.*	.302	160	612	79	185	261	29	7	11	91	15	0	8	36	11
Richards, Eugene, S.D.*	.301	158	642	91	193	247	26	8	4	41	6	7	0	61	16
Mumphrey, Jerry, S.D.#	.298	160	564	61	168	210	24	3	4	59	7	5	4	52	5
Parker, David, Pitt.*	.295	139	518	71	153	237	31	1	17	79	11	0	5	10	7
Griffey, G. Kenneth, Cin.*	.294	146	544	89	160	247	28	10	13	85	13	3	5	23	1

ALL PLAYERS LISTED ALPHABETICALLY

Player & Club	AVG	G	AB	R	H	TB	2B	3B	HR	RBI	GW	SH	SF	SB	CS
Aguayo, Luis, Phil.	.277	20	47	7	13	21	1	2	1	0	1	0	1	1	1
Alexander, Doyle, Atl.	.181	35	83	7	15	18	3	0	0	3	0	3	0	0	0
Alexander, Matthew, Pitt.#	.333	37	3	13	1	2	1	0	0	0	0	0	0	10	3
Allen, Neil, N.Y.	.143	59	14	0	2	2	0	0	0	0	0	1	0	0	0
Almon, William, Mtl.-N.Y.#	.193	66	150	15	29	39	4	3	0	7	1	0	1	2	0
Andujar, Joaquin, Hou.#	.172	35	29	3	5	10	0	1	1	3	0	5	0	0	0
Armstrong, Michael, S.D.	.000	11	3	0	0	0	0	0	0	0	0	0	0	0	0
Ashby, Alan, Hou.#	.256	116	352	30	90	122	19	2	3	48	4	2	5	0	0
Asselstine, Brian, Atl.*	.284	87	218	18	62	86	13	1	3	25	2	2	3	1	3
Auerbach, Frederick, Cin.	.333	24	33	5	11	17	1	1	1	4	0	1	0	0	3
Aviles, Ramon, Phil.	.277	51	101	12	28	40	6	0	2	9	0	2	2	0	0
Backman, Walter, N.Y.#	.323	27	93	12	30	33	1	1	0	9	0	4	1	2	3
Bahnsen, Stanley, Mtl.	.111	57	9	1	1	2	1	0	0	0	0	0	0	0	0
Bair, C. Douglas, Cin.	.000	61	2	0	0	0	0	0	0	0	0	0	0	0	0
Baker, Charles, S.D.	.136	9	22	0	3	4	1	0	0	0	0	0	0	0	0
Baker, Johnnie, L.A.	.294	153	579	80	170	291	26	4	29	97	17	1	12	12	10
Bass, Randy, S.D.*	.286	19	49	5	14	25	0	1	3	8	2	0	0	0	0
Beall, Robert, Pitt.#	.000	3	3	0	0	0	0	0	0	0	0	0	0	0	0
Beckwith, T. Joseph, L.A.*	.000	38	2	0	0	0	0	0	0	0	0	0	0	0	0
Bench, Johnny, Cin.	.250	114	360	32	90	174	12	0	24	68	6	0	4	4	2
Benedict, Bruce, Atl.	.253	120	359	18	91	113	14	1	2	34	5	13	1	3	3
Benton, Alfred, N.Y.	.048	12	21	0	1	1	0	0	0	0	0	0	0	0	0
Berenguer, Juan, N.Y.	---	6	0	0	0	0	0	0	0	0	0	0	0	0	0
Berenyi, Bruce, Cin.	.000	6	7	1	0	0	0	0	0	0	0	4	0	0	0
Bergman, David, Hou.*	.256	90	78	12	20	28	6	1	0	3	0	3	0	1	0
Bernazard, Antonio, Mtl.#	.224	82	183	26	41	65	7	1	5	18	2	1	1	9	2
Berra, Dale, Pitt.	.220	93	245	21	54	84	8	2	6	31	4	4	2	2	0
Bevacqua, Kurt, S.D.-Pitt.	.228	84	114	5	26	35	7	1	0	16	2	1	1	1	1
Bibby, James, Pitt.	.156	35	77	6	12	18	3	0	1	7	0	10	1	0	0
Biittner, Larry, Chi.*	.249	127	273	21	68	87	12	2	1	34	2	0	6	1	3
Blackwell, Timothy, Chi.#	.272	103	320	24	87	126	16	4	5	30	3	2	3	0	1
Blair, Dennis, S.D.	.200	5	5	0	1	1	0	0	0	0	0	0	0	0	0
Blanks, Larvell, Atl.	.204	[illegible]	221	[illegible]	45	57	6	0	2	12	3	4	2	1	2
Blue, Vida, S.F.*	.074	31	68	3	5	6	1	0	0	1	0	7	1	0	0
Blyleven, R. Aalbert, Pitt.	.082	37	61	0	5	6	1	0	0	2	0	9	0	0	0
Bochy, Bruce, Hou.	.182	22	22	0	4	5	1	0	0	0	0	0	0	0	0
Boggs, Thomas, Atl.	.159	32	63	2	10	10	0	0	0	2	0	6	1	0	0
Bomback, Mark, N.Y.	.233	36	43	5	10	13	3	0	0	5	0	5	0	0	0
Bonds, Bobby, St.L.	.203	86	231	37	47	73	5	3	5	24	2	1	3	15	5
Bonham, William, Cin.	.000	4	6	1	0	0	0	0	0	0	0	0	0	0	0
Boone, Robert, Phil.	.229	141	480	34	110	162	23	1	9	55	6	4	2	3	4
Borbon, Pedro, St.L.	.250	10	4	0	1	1	0	0	0	1	0	0	0	0	0
Bordley, William, S.F.*	.167	8	6	0	1	1	0	0	0	0	0	2	0	0	0
Bourjos, Christopher, S.F.	.227	13	22	4	5	9	1	0	1	2	0	0	0	0	0
Bowa, Lawrence, Phil.#	.267	147	540	57	144	174	16	4	2	39	6	7	3	21	6
Bradford, Larry, Atl.	.000	56	3	0	0	0	0	0	0	0	0	0	0	0	0
Breining, Fred, S.F.	---	5	0	0	0	0	0	0	0	0	0	0	0	0	0
Brooks, Hubert, N.Y.	.309	24	81	8	25	32	2	1	1	10	0	1	0	1	1
Brusstar, Warren, Phil.	.000	26	1	0	0	0	0	0	0	0	0	0	0	0	0
Buckner, William, Chi.*	.324	145	578	69	187	264	41	3	10	68	7	0	6	1	2
Burnside, Sheldon, Cin.	.000	7	1	0	0	0	0	0	0	0	0	0	0	0	0
Burris, B. Ray, N.Y.	.098	29	51	1	5	5	0	0	0	0	0	3	0	0	1
Burroughs, Jeffrey, Atl.	.263	99	278	35	73	126	14	0	13	51	3	1	2	1	1
Bystrom, Martin, Phil.	.071	6	14	1	1	1	0	0	0	1	0	0	0	0	0
Cabell, Enos, Hou.	.276	152	604	69	167	212	23	8	2	55	10	1	5	21	13
Camp, Rick, Atl.	.111	77	9	0	1	2	1	0	0	0	0	0	0	0	0
Candelaria, John, Pitt.*	.195	35	77	5	15	18	3	0	0	7	1	3	1	0	0
Capilla, Douglas, Chi.*	.190	40	21	1	4	6	0	1	0	1	1	1	0	0	0
Carbo, Bernardo, St.L.-Pitt.*	.235	21	17	0	4	4	0	0	0	1	0	1	0	0	0
Cardenal, Jose, N.Y.	.167	26	42	4	7	8	1	0	0	4	1	0	1	0	1
Carlton, Steven, Phil.*	.188	38	101	7	19	20	1	0	0	6	0	6	3	0	0
Carter, Gary, Mtl.	.264	154	549	76	145	267	25	5	29	101	13	1	8	3	2
Cash, David, S.D.	.227	130	397	25	90	111	14	2	1	23	2	2	3	6	5
Castillo, Robert, L.A.	.111	62	9	0	1	1	0	0	0	0	0	1	0	0	0
Caudill, William, Chi.	.222	72	9	0	2	3	1	0	0	1	0	1	0	0	0
Cedeno, Cesar, Hou.	.309	137	499	71	154	232	32	8	10	73	7	1	2	48	15
Cey, Ronald, L.A.	.254	157	551	81	140	249	25	0	28	77	12	4	1	2	2

Player & Club	AVG	G	AB	R	H	TB	2B	3B	HR	RBI	GW	SH	SF	SB	CS
Chambliss, C. Christopher, Atl.*	.282	158	602	83	170	265	37	2	18	72	13	2	4	7	3
Christenson, Larry, Phil.	.368	14	19	6	7	10	0	0	1	4	0	3	0	0	0
Clark, Jack, S.F.	.284	127	437	77	124	226	20	8	22	82	18	1	10	2	5
Collins, David, Cin.#	.303	144	551	94	167	204	20	4	3	35	6	3	3	79	21
Combe, Geoffrey, Cin.	---	4	0	0	0	0	0	0	0	0	0	0	0	0	0
Concepcion, David, Cin.	.260	156	622	72	162	224	31	8	5	77	10	2	6	12	2
Cooper, Gary, Atl.#	.000	21	2	3	0	0	0	0	0	0	0	0	0	2	1
Correll, Victor, Cin.	.421	10	19	1	8	9	1	0	0	3	1	0	0	0	0
Cromartie, Warren, Mtl.*	.288	162	597	74	172	257	33	5	14	70	11	4	3	8	8
Cruz, Hector, Cin.	.213	52	75	5	16	25	4	1	1	5	1	0	0	0	0
Cruz, Jose, Hou.*	.302	160	612	79	185	261	29	7	11	91	15	0	8	36	11
Curtis, John, S.D.*	.194	31	62	2	12	13	1	0	0	2	1	5	0	0	0
D'Acquisto, John, S.D.-Mtl.	.000	50	8	1	0	0	0	0	0	0	0	2	0	0	0
Dade, L. Paul, S.D.	.189	68	53	17	10	10	0	0	0	3	1	0	0	4	5
Davalillo, Victor, L.A.*	.167	7	6	1	1	1	0	0	0	0	0	0	0	0	0
Davis, Mark, Phil.*	.500	2	2	1	1	1	0	0	0	0	0	0	0	0	0
Dawson, Andre, Mtl.	.308	151	577	96	178	284	41	7	17	87	17	1	10	34	9
DeJesus, Ivan, Chi.	.259	157	618	78	160	201	26	3	3	33	4	8	2	44	16
Dernier, Robert, Phil.	.571	10	7	5	4	4	0	0	0	1	0	0	0	3	0
DeSa, Joseph, St.L.*	.273	7	11	0	3	3	0	0	0	0	0	0	0	0	0
Dillard, Stephen, Chi.	.225	100	244	31	55	77	8	1	4	27	4	0	2	2	2
Driessen, Daniel, Cin.*	.265	154	524	81	139	219	36	1	14	74	10	0	9	19	6
Dues, Hal, Mtl.	.000	6	3	0	0	0	0	0	0	0	0	0	0	0	0
Durham, Leon, St.L.*	.271	96	303	42	82	129	15	4	8	42	5	3	5	8	5
Easler, Michael, Pitt.*	.338	132	393	66	133	229	27	3	21	74	9	0	9	5	9
Eichelberger, Juan, S.D.	.111	15	27	1	3	3	0	0	0	0	0	4	0	1	0
Espinosa, Arnulfo, Phil.	.115	13	26	4	3	4	1	0	0	2	0	3	0	0	0
Evans, Barry, S.D.	.232	73	125	11	29	39	3	2	1	14	0	2	3	1	1
Evans, Darrell, S.F.*	.264	154	556	69	147	230	23	0	20	78	14	6	6	17	5
Fahey, William, S.D.*	.257	93	241	18	62	69	4	0	1	22	1	1	2	2	0
Falcone, Peter, N.Y.*	.146	37	41	2	6	6	0	0	0	3	2	6	0	0	0
Ferguson, Joseph, L.A.	.238	77	172	20	41	75	3	2	9	29	7	1	3	2	2
Figueroa, Jesus, Chi.*	.253	115	198	20	50	58	5	0	1	11	1	2	0	2	1
Fingers, Roland, S.D.	.278	66	18	0	5	8	3	0	0	0	0	1	0	0	0
Fischlin, Michael, Hou.	.000	1	1	0	0	0	0	0	0	0	0	0	0	0	0
Flannery, Timothy, S.D.*	.240	95	292	15	70	82	12	0	0	25	3	4	1	2	2
Flynn, R. Douglas, N.Y.	.255	128	443	46	113	138	9	8	0	24	5	6	3	2	2
Foli, Timothy, Pitt.	.265	127	495	61	131	162	22	0	3	38	7	13	7	11	7
Foote, Barry, Chi.	.238	63	202	16	48	81	13	1	6	28	3	0	1	1	1
Forsch, Kenneth, Hou.	.234	32	77	3	18	21	3	0	0	8	0	6	0	1	0
Forsch, Robert, St.L.	.295	32	78	11	23	37	5	0	3	10	0	9	0	1	0
Forster, Terry, L.A.*	---	9	0	0	0	0	0	0	0	0	0	0	0	0	0
Foster, George, Cin.	.273	144	528	79	144	250	21	5	25	93	16	0	4	1	0
Frazier, George, St.L.	---	22	0	0	0	0	0	0	0	0	0	0	0	0	0
Frias, Jesus, L.A.	.222	14	9	1	2	3	1	0	0	0	0	0	0	0	0
Fryman, Woodrow, Mtl.	.167	61	12	0	2	2	0	0	0	2	0	2	0	0	0
Fulgham, John, St.L.	.000	16	27	1	0	0	0	0	0	0	0	3	0	0	0
Garber, H. Eugene, Atl.	.500	68	2	0	1	1	0	0	0	1	0	0	0	0	0
Garner, Philip, Pitt.	.259	151	548	62	142	196	27	6	5	58	3	7	7	32	7
Garvey, Steven, L.A.	.304	163	658	78	200	307	27	1	26	106	13	3	4	6	11
Geronimo, Cesar, Cin.*	.255	103	145	16	37	48	5	0	2	9	0	2	1	2	1
Glynn, Edward, N.Y.	.000	38	6	0	0	0	0	0	0	0	0	2	0	0	0
Goltz, David, L.A.	.128	35	47	1	6	6	0	0	0	4	0	7	0	0	0
Gomez, Luis, Atl.	.191	121	278	18	53	59	6	0	0	24	2	10	1	0	4
Gonzalez, Julio, Hou.	.115	40	52	5	6	7	1	0	0	1	0	1	0	1	0
Griffey, G. Kenneth, Cin.*	.294	146	544	89	160	247	28	10	13	85	13	3	5	23	1
Griffin, Thomas, S.F.	.111	44	18	1	2	5	0	0	1	1	0	2	0	0	0
Grimsley, Ross, Mtl.*	.222	11	9	1	2	3	1	0	0	0	0	0	0	0	0
Gross, Gregory, Phil.*	.240	127	154	19	37	48	7	2	0	12	2	3	0	1	1
Guerrero, Pedro, L.A.	.322	75	183	27	59	91	9	1	7	31	2	1	3	2	1
Gullickson, William, Mtl.	.175	24	40	2	7	8	1	0	0	0	0	10	0	0	0
Halicki, Edward, S.F.	.167	11	6	0	1	1	0	0	0	0	0	0	0	0	0
Hanna, Preston, Atl.	.143	32	14	1	2	4	0	1	0	0	0	0	0	0	0
Hargesheimer, Alan, S.F.	.182	15	22	2	4	5	1	0	0	2	1	1	0	0	0
Harper, Terry, Atl.	.185	21	54	3	10	14	2	1	0	3	1	0	0	2	1
Hassler, Andrew, Pitt.*	.000	6	2	0	0	0	0	0	0	0	0	0	0	0	0
Hatcher, Michael, L.A.	.226	57	84	4	19	24	2	0	1	5	1	4	0	0	2
Hausman, Thomas, N.Y.	.063	55	16	0	1	1	0	0	0	0	0	1	0	0	0
Hayes, William, Chi.	.222	4	9	0	2	3	1	0	0	0	0	0	0	0	0
Heep, Daniel, Hou.*	.276	33	87	6	24	32	8	0	0	6	0	0	1	0	0
Henderson, Kenneth, Chi.#	.195	44	82	7	16	25	3	0	2	9	2	0	0	0	0
Henderson, Stephen, N.Y.	.290	143	513	75	149	206	17	8	8	58	9	3	3	23	12
Hendrick, George, St.L.	.302	150	572	73	173	285	33	2	25	109	11	1	4	6	1
Hernandez, Guillermo, Chi.*	.211	53	19	0	4	5	1	0	0	1	0	1	0	0	0
Hernandez, Keith, St.L.*	.321	159	595	111	191	294	39	8	16	99	13	1	4	14	8
Herndon, Larry, S.F.	.258	139	493	54	127	190	17	11	8	49	2	4	4	8	8
Herr, Thomas, St.L.#	.248	76	222	29	55	77	12	5	0	15	2	1	2	9	2
Hill, Marc, S.F.	.171	17	41	1	7	9	2	0	0	0	0	1	0	0	0
Hodges, Ronald, N.Y.*	.238	36	42	4	10	12	2	0	0	5	2	1	1	1	1
Holland, Alfred, S.F.	.200	54	5	2	1	3	0	1	0	2	0	2	0	0	0
Holman, R. Scott, N.Y.	---	4	0	0	0	0	0	0	0	0	0	0	0	0	0
Hood, Donald, St.L.*	.200	35	20	3	4	4	0	0	0	1	0	2	0	0	0
Hooton, Burt, L.A.	.063	34	64	4	4	7	0	0	1	6	0	14	0	0	0
Horner, J. Robert, Atl.	.268	124	463	81	124	245	14	1	35	89	5	0	4	3	1
Hough, Charles, L.A.	.500	19	2	0	1	1	0	0	0	1	0	0	0	0	0
Householder, Paul, Cin.#	.244	20	45	3	11	14	1	1	0	7	0	0	0	1	0
Howe, Arthur, Hou.	.283	110	321	34	91	143	12	5	10	46	6	4	4	1	0
Howe, Steven, L.A.*	.091	59	11	1	1	1	0	0	0	0	0	0	0	0	0
Howell, Jay, Cin.	---	5	0	0	0	0	0	0	0	0	0	0	0	0	0
Hrabosky, Alan, Atl.	.000	45	1	0	0	0	0	0	0	0	0	0	0	0	0
Hubbard, Glenn, Atl.	.248	117	431	55	107	161	21	3	9	43	6	2	5	7	5
Hume, Thomas, Cin.	.188	78	16	2	3	5	2	0	0	4	0	1	0	0	0
Hutton, Thomas, Mtl.*	.218	62	55	2	12	14	2	0	0	5	1	2	1	0	0
Iorg, Dane, St.L.*	.303	105	251	33	76	110	23	1	3	36	2	0	4	1	1
Isales, Orlando, Phil.	.400	3	5	1	2	4	0	1	0	3	0	0	0	0	0
Ivie, Michael, S.F.	.241	79	286	21	69	99	16	1	4	25	3	0	1	1	2
Jackson, Grant, Pitt.#	.000	61	10	0	0	0	0	0	0	0	0	0	0	0	0

Player & Club	AVG	G	AB	R	H	TB	2B	3B	HR	RBI	GW	SH	SF	SB	CS
Jackson, Roy, N.Y.	.188	26	16	2	3	5	0	1	0	0	0	0	0	0	1
Jefferson, Jesse, Pitt.	.000	1	1	0	0	0	0	0	0	0	0	1	0	0	0
Johnson, Clifford, Chi.	.235	68	196	28	46	84	8	0	10	34	6	0	1	0	0
Johnstone, John, L.A.*	.307	109	251	31	77	102	15	2	2	20	2	2	0	3	2
Jones, Randall, S.D.	.067	25	45	1	3	3	0	0	0	0	0	7	0	0	0
Jorgensen, Michael, N.Y.*	.255	119	321	43	82	114	11	0	7	43	4	1	0	0	3
Joshua, Von, S.D.*	.238	53	63	8	15	25	2	1	2	7	1	0	0	0	1
Kaat, James, St.L.*	.143	49	35	4	5	9	1	0	1	2	0	4	0	1	0
Kelleher, Michael, Chi.	.146	103	96	12	14	17	1	1	0	4	1	1	1	1	3
Kendall, Fred, S.D.	.292	19	24	2	7	7	0	0	0	2	0	0	0	0	0
Kennedy, Junior, Cin.	.261	104	337	31	88	113	16	3	1	34	3	4	8	3	1
Kennedy, Terrence, St.L.*	.254	84	248	28	63	93	12	3	4	34	3	1	4	0	0
Kingman, David, Chi.	.278	81	255	31	71	133	8	0	18	57	4	0	4	2	2
Kinney, Dennis, S.D.*	.083	50	12	0	1	1	0	0	0	0	0	1	0	0	0
Knepper, Robert, S.F.*	.152	35	66	3	10	13	3	0	0	7	0	9	2	1	0
Knicely, Alan, Hou.	.000	1	1	0	0	0	0	0	0	0	0	0	0	0	0
Knight, C. Ray, Cin.	.264	162	618	71	163	258	39	7	14	78	12	5	4	1	2
Knowles, Darold, St.L.*	---	2	0	0	0	0	0	0	0	0	0	0	0	0	0
Kobel, Kevin, N.Y.	.000	14	2	0	0	0	0	0	0	0	0	0	0	0	0
Krukow, Michael, Chi.	.246	34	65	5	16	19	0	0	1	6	1	7	0	0	0
LaCorte, Frank, Hou.	.167	55	6	0	1	1	0	0	0	1	0	2	0	0	0
LaCoss, Michael, Cin.	.091	34	55	2	5	6	1	0	0	1	1	6	0	0	0
Lacy, Leondaus, Pitt.	.335	109	278	45	93	142	20	4	7	33	4	2	4	18	9
LaGrow, Lerrin, Phil.	.250	25	4	0	1	1	0	0	0	0	0	0	0	0	0
Lamp, Dennis, Chi.	.098	41	61	3	6	6	0	0	0	1	0	7	0	0	0
Landestoy, Rafael, Hou.#	.247	149	393	42	97	129	13	8	1	27	3	6	1	23	12
Landrum, Terry, St.L.	.247	35	77	6	19	25	2	2	0	7	0	0	1	3	2
Larson, Daniel, Phil.	.154	12	13	0	2	3	1	0	0	0	0	0	0	0	0
Lavelle, Gary, S.F.#	.000	62	11	0	0	0	0	0	0	0	0	3	0	0	0
Law, Rudy, L.A.*	.260	128	388	55	101	117	5	4	1	23	4	3	1	40	13
Law, Vance, Pitt.	.230	25	74	11	17	23	2	2	0	3	1	1	0	2	0
Lea, Charles, Mtl.	.081	21	37	1	3	5	0	1	0	1	0	0	1	0	0
Lee, Mark, Pitt.	---	4	0	0	0	0	0	0	0	0	0	0	0	0	0
Lee, William, Mtl.*	.220	25	41	2	9	10	1	0	0	0	0	0	0	0	0
LeFlore, Ronald, Mtl.	.257	139	521	95	134	189	21	11	4	39	4	2	1	97	19
Leibrandt, Charles, Cin.	.196	36	56	2	11	13	0	1	0	4	1	4	1	0	0
LeMaster, Johnnie, S.F.	.215	135	405	33	87	124	16	6	3	31	2	7	5	0	1
Lentine, James, St.L.	.100	9	10	1	1	1	0	0	0	1	0	0	0	0	0
Leonard, Jeffrey, Hou.	.213	88	216	29	46	72	7	5	3	20	4	1	2	4	1
Lerch, Randy, Phil.*	.267	34	45	5	12	14	2	0	0	3	0	4	0	0	0
Lezcano, Carlos, Chi.	.205	42	88	15	18	33	4	1	3	12	2	2	2	1	2
Littell, Mark, St.L.*	.000	14	1	0	0	0	0	0	0	0	0	0	0	0	0
Little, D. Jeffery, St.L.	.167	7	6	1	1	1	0	0	0	0	0	0	0	0	0
Littlefield, John, St.L.	.000	52	11	1	0	0	0	0	0	0	0	1	0	0	0
Littlejohn, Dennis, S.F.	.241	13	29	2	7	8	1	0	0	2	0	0	2	0	0
Lopes, David, L.A.	.251	141	553	79	139	190	15	3	10	49	5	9	4	23	7
Loucks, Scott, Hou.	.333	8	3	4	1	1	0	0	0	0	0	0	0	0	0
Loviglio, John, Phil.	.000	16	5	7	0	0	0	0	0	0	0	0	0	1	2
Lucas, Gary, S.D.*	.171	46	35	1	6	6	0	0	0	2	0	7	0	0	0
Lum, Michael, Atl.*	.205	93	83	7	17	20	3	0	0	5	0	1	1	0	0
Luzinski, Gregory, Phil.	.228	106	368	44	84	162	19	1	19	56	8	0	4	3	0
Lyle, Albert, Phil.*	---	10	0	0	0	0	0	0	0	0	0	0	0	0	0
Lynch, Edward, N.Y.	.333	5	6	0	2	2	0	0	0	0	0	0	0	0	0
Macha, Kenneth, Mtl.	.290	49	107	10	31	41	5	1	1	8	1	1	0	0	2
Macko, Steven, Chi.*	.300	6	20	2	6	8	2	0	0	2	0	0	0	0	0
Maddox, Elliott, N.Y.	.246	130	411	35	101	131	16	1	4	34	4	5	4	1	9
Maddox, Garry, Phil.	.259	143	549	59	142	212	31	3	11	73	3	7	9	25	5
Madlock, Bill, Pitt.	.277	137	494	62	137	197	22	4	10	53	8	0	3	16	10
Mahler, Michael, Pitt.#	---	2	0	0	0	0	0	0	0	0	0	0	0	0	0
Mahler, Richard, Atl.	---	2	0	0	0	0	0	0	0	0	0	0	0	0	0
Mankowski, Philip, N.Y.*	.167	8	12	1	2	3	1	0	0	1	0	0	0	0	0
Manuel, Jerry, Mtl.#	.000	7	6	0	0	0	0	0	0	0	0	0	0	0	0
Martin, Jerry, Chi.	.227	141	494	57	112	207	22	2	23	73	9	0	6	8	3
Martin, John, St.L.#	.273	9	11	0	3	3	0	0	0	1	0	0	1	0	0
Martinez, Silvio, St.L.	.086	25	35	3	3	3	0	0	0	1	0	3	0	0	0
Martz, Randy, Chi.*	.111	6	9	0	1	1	0	0	0	0	0	0	0	0	0
Matthews, Gary, Atl.	.278	155	571	79	159	239	17	3	19	75	13	1	3	11	3
Matula, Richard, Atl.	.105	33	57	0	6	6	0	0	0	0	0	5	0	0	0
May, Milton, S.F.*	.260	111	358	27	93	131	16	2	6	50	7	3	6	0	1
Mazzilli, Lee, N.Y.#	.280	152	578	82	162	249	31	4	16	76	9	0	5	41	15
McBride, Arnold, Phil.*	.309	137	554	68	171	251	33	10	9	87	14	2	6	13	10
McCarver, J. Timothy, Phil.*	.200	6	5	2	1	2	1	0	0	2	0	1	0	0	0
McCormack, Donald, Phil.	1.000	2	1	0	1	1	0	0	0	0	0	0	0	0	0
McCovey, Willie, S.F.*	.204	48	113	8	23	34	8	0	1	16	2	0	3	0	0
McGlothen, Lynn, Chi.*	.196	41	51	6	10	14	4	0	0	1	1	8	0	0	0
McGraw, Frank, Phil.	.250	57	8	0	2	2	0	0	0	1	0	3	0	0	0
McWilliams, Larry, Atl.*	.157	30	51	3	8	8	0	0	0	1	0	4	0	0	0
Mejias, Samuel, Cin.	.278	71	108	16	30	40	5	1	1	10	0	2	0	4	2
Metzger, Roger, S.F.#	.074	28	27	5	2	2	0	0	0	0	0	1	0	0	0
Miller, Dyar, N.Y.	.000	31	1	0	0	0	0	0	0	0	0	1	0	0	0
Miller, Edward, Atl.#	.158	11	19	3	3	3	0	0	0	0	0	0	0	1	2
Mills, J. Bradley, Mtl.*	.300	21	60	1	18	19	1	0	0	8	0	0	1	0	1
Milner, Eddie, Cin.*	.000	6	3	1	0	0	0	0	0	0	0	0	0	0	0
Milner, John, Pitt.*	.244	114	238	31	58	88	6	0	8	34	6	1	1	2	2
Minton, Gregory, S.F.#	.125	68	8	0	1	1	0	0	0	1	0	2	0	0	0
Mitchell, Robert, L.A.*	.333	9	3	1	1	1	0	0	0	0	0	0	0	0	0
Moffitt, Randall, S.F.	.000	13	1	0	0	0	0	0	0	0	0	0	0	0	0
Monday, Robert, L.A.*	.268	96	194	35	52	91	7	1	10	25	4	0	0	2	2
Montanez, Guillermo, S.D.-Mtl.*	.272	142	500	40	136	174	12	4	6	64	6	0	6	3	5
Montefusco, John, S.F.	.033	22	30	1	1	1	0	0	0	0	0	3	0	0	0
Moore, Donnie, St.L.*	.750	11	4	1	3	4	1	0	0	2	0	2	0	0	0
Morales, Julio, N.Y.	.254	94	193	19	49	67	7	1	3	30	5	1	8	2	3
Moreland, B. Keith, Phil.	.314	62	159	13	50	70	8	0	4	29	7	1	3	3	1
Moreno, Jose, N.Y.#	.196	37	46	6	9	19	2	1	2	9	2	1	1	1	0
Moreno, Omar, Pitt.*	.249	162	676	87	168	220	20	13	2	36	6	3	7	96	33
Morgan, Joe, Hou.*	.243	141	461	66	112	172	17	5	11	49	11	3	5	24	6
Moskau, Paul, Cin.	.159	33	44	4	7	8	1	0	0	1	0	8	0	0	0

Player & Club	AVG	G	AB	R	H	TB	2B	3B	HR	RBI	GW	SH	SF	SB	CS
Mota, Manuel, L.A.	.429	7	7	0	3	3	0	0	0	2	1	0	0	0	0
Mumphrey, Jerry, S.D.#	.298	160	564	61	168	210	24	3	4	59	7	5	4	52	5
Munninghoff, Scott, Phil.	1.000	4	1	1	1	3	0	1	0	0	0	0	0	0	0
Mura, Stephen, S.D.	.137	39	51	3	7	9	2	0	0	8	0	0	0	0	0
Murphy, Dale, Atl.	.281	156	569	98	160	290	27	2	33	89	13	2	2	9	6
Murray, Dale, Mtl.	.000	16	3	0	0	0	0	0	0	0	0	0	0	0	0
Murray, Richard, S.F.	.216	53	194	19	42	66	8	2	4	24	5	1	0	2	1
Nahorodny, William, Atl.	.242	59	157	14	38	65	12	0	5	18	2	0	0	0	2
Nastu, Philip, S.F.*	---	6	0	0	0	0	0	0	0	0	0	0	0	0	0
Nicosia, Steven, Pitt.	.216	60	176	16	38	49	8	0	1	22	3	2	3	0	1
Niekro, Joseph, Hou.	.275	37	80	7	22	27	5	0	0	10	1	18	0	0	0
Niekro, Philip, Atl.	.133	40	90	2	12	17	5	0	0	5	0	5	0	0	0
Niemann, Randy, Hou.*	.333	22	6	0	2	2	0	0	0	0	0	0	0	0	0
Nolan, Joseph, Atl.-Cin.*	.307	70	176	16	54	71	8	0	3	26	2	3	6	0	0
Noles, Dickie, Phil.	.308	48	13	1	4	4	0	0	0	2	0	2	0	0	0
Norman, Daniel, N.Y.#	.185	69	92	5	17	26	1	1	2	9	2	0	0	5	0
Norman, Fredie, Mtl.#	.050	48	20	1	1	1	0	0	0	0	0	2	0	0	0
North, William, S.F.#	.251	128	415	73	104	121	12	1	1	19	1	2	1	45	19
Oberkfell, Kenneth, St.L.*	.303	116	422	58	128	176	27	6	3	46	6	9	3	4	4
O'Berry, P. Michael, Chi.	.208	19	48	7	10	11	1	0	0	5	1	2	2	0	0
Oester, Ronald, Cin.#	.277	100	303	40	84	110	16	2	2	20	2	5	0	6	2
Office, Rowland, Mtl.*	.267	116	292	36	78	117	13	4	6	30	5	3	4	3	3
Olmsted, Alan, St.L.	.182	5	11	0	2	2	0	0	0	1	0	2	0	0	0
Ontiveros, Steven, Chi.#	.208	31	77	7	16	22	3	0	1	3	0	0	0	0	0
Ott, N. Edward, Pitt.*	.260	120	392	35	102	140	14	0	8	41	7	4	1	1	6
Otten, James, St.L.	.200	31	5	0	1	1	0	0	0	0	0	0	0	0	0
Pacella, John, N.Y.	.100	32	20	0	2	3	1	0	0	1	0	2	0	0	0
Palmer, David, Mtl.	.200	25	45	3	9	11	2	0	0	3	1	2	0	0	0
Parker, David, Pitt.*	.295	139	518	71	153	237	31	1	17	79	11	0	5	10	7
Parrish, Larry, Mtl.	.254	126	452	55	115	193	27	3	15	72	4	1	8	2	6
Pastore, Frank, Cin.	.156	27	64	0	10	10	0	0	0	5	0	6	0	0	0
Pate, Robert, Mtl.	.256	23	39	3	10	12	2	0	0	5	1	1	2	0	1
Pena, Antonio, Pitt.	.429	8	21	1	9	12	1	1	0	1	0	0	0	0	1
Perconte, John, L.A.*	.235	14	17	2	4	4	0	0	0	2	0	2	0	3	0
Perez, Pascual, Pitt.	.250	2	4	1	1	1	0	0	0	0	0	0	0	0	0
Perkins, Broderick, S.D.*	.370	43	100	18	37	52	9	0	2	14	2	0	0	2	1
Pettini, Joseph, S.F.	.232	63	190	19	44	52	3	1	1	9	0	11	0	5	2
Phillips, Michael, St.L.*	.234	63	128	13	30	35	5	0	0	7	1	0	1	0	0
Pladson, Gordon, Hou.	.000	12	10	1	0	0	0	0	0	0	0	0	0	0	0
Pocoroba, Biff, Atl.#	.265	70	83	7	22	32	4	0	2	8	2	1	1	1	0
Price, Joseph, Cin.	.128	24	39	1	5	5	0	0	0	0	0	3	0	0	0
Puhl, Terry, Hou.*	.282	141	535	75	151	224	24	5	13	55	11	6	3	27	11
Pujols, Luis, Hou.	.199	78	221	15	44	52	6	1	0	20	2	1	2	0	0
Raines, Timothy, Mtl.#	.050	15	20	5	1	1	0	0	0	0	0	1	0	5	0
Ramirez, Mario, N.Y.	.208	18	24	2	5	5	0	0	0	0	0	1	0	0	0
Ramirez, Rafael, Atl.	.267	50	165	17	44	58	6	1	2	11	2	3	0	2	1
Ramos, Roberto, Mtl.	.156	13	32	5	5	7	2	0	0	2	1	0	0	0	0
Ramsey, Michael, St.L.#	.262	59	126	11	33	43	8	1	0	8	1	0	0	0	0
Randle, Leonard, Chi.#	.276	130	489	67	135	181	19	6	5	39	3	7	2	19	13
Rasmussen, Eric, S.D.	.095	40	21	0	2	4	2	0	0	0	0	6	0	0	0
Ratzer, Stephen, Mtl.	.000	1	1	0	0	0	0	0	0	0	0	0	0	0	0
Reardon, Jeffrey, N.Y.	.000	61	8	0	0	0	0	0	0	0	0	0	0	0	0
Reed, Ronald, Phil.	.300	55	10	0	3	4	1	0	0	0	0	0	0	0	0
Reitz, Kenneth, St.L.	.270	151	523	39	141	198	33	0	8	58	3	8	5	0	1
Reuschel, Ricky, Chi.	.159	44	82	4	13	18	3	1	0	5	0	10	0	0	0
Reuss, Jerry, L.A.*	.088	37	68	4	6	10	1	0	1	3	0	4	0	0	0
Reynolds, G. Craig, Hou.*	.226	137	381	34	86	116	9	6	3	28	2	13	4	2	1
Rhoden, Richard, Pitt.	.375	20	40	3	15	21	3	0	1	11	0	4	0	0	0
Richard, James, Hou.	.154	17	39	2	6	11	2	0	1	3	0	4	0	0	0
Richards, Eugene, S.D.*	.301	158	642	91	193	247	26	8	4	41	6	7	0	61	16
Riley, George, Chi.*	.000	22	1	0	0	0	0	0	0	0	0	1	0	0	0
Rincon, Andrew, St.L.	.250	4	12	0	3	3	0	0	0	1	0	1	0	0	0
Ripley, Allen, S.F.	.150	23	40	2	6	8	0	1	0	2	0	3	0	0	0
Roberge, Bertrand, Hou.	.000	14	3	0	0	0	0	0	0	0	0	1	0	0	0
Roberts, David, Pitt.*	---	2	0	0	0	0	0	0	0	0	0	0	0	0	0
Robinson, Don, Pitt.	.333	30	57	4	19	26	4	0	1	8	0	0	0	0	1
Robinson, William, Pitt.	.287	100	272	28	78	126	10	1	12	36	7	3	4	1	4
Rodriguez, Aurelio, S.D.	.200	89	175	7	35	52	7	2	2	13	3	2	0	1	1
Rogers, Stephen, Mtl.	.160	38	81	7	13	13	0	0	0	7	0	15	0	0	0
Romo, Enrique, Pitt.	.455	75	11	2	5	8	0	0	1	4	0	2	0	0	0
Rooker, James, Pitt.	.143	4	7	1	1	4	0	0	1	2	0	1	0	0	0
Rosado, Luis, N.Y.	.000	2	4	0	0	0	0	0	0	0	0	0	0	0	0
Rose, Peter, Phil.#	.282	162	655	95	185	232	42	1	1	64	12	4	4	12	8
Rowland, Michael, S.F.	---	19	0	0	0	0	0	0	0	0	0	0	0	0	0
Royster, Jeron, Atl.	.242	123	392	42	95	125	17	5	1	20	4	4	1	22	13
Ruhle, Vernon, Hou.	.245	28	49	7	12	15	3	0	0	2	0	4	0	0	0
Ruiz, Manuel, Atl.	.308	25	26	3	8	12	2	1	0	2	1	0	0	0	1
Russell, William, L.A.	.264	130	466	38	123	159	23	2	3	34	3	12	1	13	2
Ruthven, Richard, Phil.	.235	33	68	7	16	23	5	1	0	8	1	12	0	1	1
Ryan, L. Nolan, Hou.	.086	35	70	5	6	9	0	0	1	6	0	5	1	0	1
Sadek, Michael, S.F.	.252	64	151	14	38	47	4	1	1	16	0	4	1	0	0
Salazar, Luis, S.D.	.337	44	169	28	57	78	4	7	1	25	1	3	1	11	2
Sambito, Joseph, Hou.*	.000	64	9	0	0	0	0	0	0	0	0	0	0	0	0
Sanderson, Scott, Mtl.	.078	33	64	3	5	8	3	0	0	1	0	8	0	0	0
Sanguillen, Manuel, Pitt.	.250	47	48	2	12	15	3	0	0	2	0	2	0	3	2
Saucier, Kevin, Phil.	.000	40	8	0	0	0	0	0	0	0	0	0	0	0	0
Schmidt, Michael, Phil.	.286	150	548	104	157	342	25	8	48	121	17	0	13	12	5
Scioscia, Michael, L.A.*	.254	54	134	8	34	44	5	1	1	8	0	5	1	1	0
Scott, Anthony, St.L.#	.251	143	415	51	104	129	19	3	0	28	5	5	4	22	10
Scott, Michael, N.Y.	.111	6	9	0	1	1	0	0	0	1	0	0	0	0	0
Scott, Rodney, Mtl.#	.224	154	567	84	127	166	13	13	0	46	4	11	6	63	13
Scurry, Rodney, Pitt.*	.250	20	4	0	1	1	0	0	0	0	0	0	0	0	0
Seaman, Kim, St.L.*	.000	26	1	0	0	0	0	0	0	0	0	0	0	0	0
Seaver, G. Thomas, Cin.	.130	26	46	5	6	9	3	0	0	3	0	7	0	0	0
Shirley, Robert, S.D.	.033	59	30	3	1	1	0	0	0	1	1	4	0	0	0
Simmons, Ted, St.L.#	.303	145	495	84	150	250	33	2	21	98	12	0	6	1	0
Smith, C. Reginald, L.A.#	.322	92	311	47	100	158	13	0	15	55	7	0	9	5	6

Player & Club	AVG	G	AB	R	H	TB	2B	3B	HR	RBI	GW	SH	SF	SB	CS
Smith, David, Hou.	.000	57	12	0	0	0	0	0	0	0	0	2	0	0	0
Smith, Keith, St.L.	.129	24	31	3	4	5	1	0	0	2	1	0	0	0	0
Smith, Lee, Chi.	---	18	0	0	0	0	0	0	0	0	0	0	0	0	0
Smith, Lonnie, Phil.	.339	100	298	69	101	132	14	4	3	20	1	1	2	33	13
Smith, Osborne, S.D.#	.230	158	609	67	140	168	18	5	0	35	5	23	4	57	15
Solomon, Eddie, Pitt.	.219	27	32	3	7	9	2	0	0	1	0	3	0	0	0
Sosa, Elias, Mtl.	.091	67	11	0	1	1	0	0	0	1	0	1	0	0	0
Soto, Mario, Cin.	.043	54	46	3	2	2	0	0	0	0	0	8	0	0	0
Speier, Chris, Mtl.	.265	128	388	35	103	128	14	4	1	32	2	6	1	0	3
Spikes, L. Charles, Atl.	.278	41	36	6	10	11	1	0	0	2	0	0	0	0	0
Spilman, W. Harry, Cin.*	.267	65	101	14	27	43	4	0	4	19	1	1	2	0	0
Sprowl, Robert, Hou.*	---	1	0	0	0	0	0	0	0	0	0	0	0	0	0
Stablein, George, S.D.	.000	4	3	0	0	0	0	0	0	0	0	0	0	0	0
Stanhouse, Donald, L.A.	.000	21	2	0	0	0	0	0	0	0	0	0	0	0	0
Stargell, Wilver, Pitt.*	.262	67	202	28	53	98	10	1	11	38	3	0	1	0	0
Stearns, John, N.Y.	.285	91	319	42	91	118	25	1	0	45	4	2	8	7	3
Stember, Jeffrey, S.F.	.000	1	1	0	0	0	0	0	0	0	0	0	0	0	0
Stennett, Renaldo, S.F.	.244	120	397	34	97	120	13	2	2	37	5	2	2	4	4
Stimac, Craig, S.D.	.220	20	50	5	11	13	2	0	0	7	2	2	3	0	0
Strain, Joseph, S.F.	.286	77	189	26	54	60	6	0	0	16	0	7	1	1	2
Sularz, Guy, S.F.	.246	25	65	3	16	19	1	1	0	3	0	2	1	1	0
Sutcliffe, Richard, L.A.*	.148	44	27	1	4	4	0	0	0	3	0	3	0	0	0
Sutter, H. Bruce, Chi.	.111	60	9	0	1	1	0	0	0	1	0	1	0	0	0
Sutton, Donald, L.A.	.078	32	64	3	5	5	0	0	0	1	0	8	0	0	0
Swan, Craig, N.Y.	.219	21	32	1	7	7	0	0	0	5	0	7	0	0	0
Swisher, Steven, St.L.	.250	18	24	2	6	7	1	0	0	2	0	0	0	0	0
Sykes, Robert, St.L.#	.103	27	39	2	4	4	0	0	0	2	0	3	1	0	0
Tamargo, John, Mtl.#	.275	37	51	4	14	20	3	0	1	13	1	0	1	0	0
Taveras, Franklin, N.Y.	.279	141	562	65	157	184	27	0	0	25	1	10	2	32	18
Tekulve, Kenton, Pitt.	.000	78	9	0	0	0	0	0	0	0	0	0	0	0	0
Tellmann, Thomas, S.D.	.125	6	8	0	1	1	0	0	0	1	0	0	0	0	0
Templeton, Garry, St.L.#	.319	118	504	83	161	210	19	9	4	43	3	1	1	31	15
Tenace, F. Gene, S.D.	.222	133	316	46	70	134	11	1	17	50	6	0	4	4	4
Thomas, Derrel, L.A.#	.266	117	297	32	79	106	18	3	1	22	2	7	1	7	9
Thomas, Roy, St.L.	.154	24	13	0	2	2	0	0	0	0	0	0	0	0	0
Thomasson, Gary, L.A.*	.216	80	111	6	24	30	3	0	1	12	1	0	0	0	0
Thompson, V. Scot, Chi.*	.212	102	226	26	48	66	10	1	2	13	1	1	1	6	6
Tidrow, Richard, Chi.	.000	84	4	1	0	0	0	0	0	0	0	0	0	0	0
Tomlin, David, Cin.*	---	27	0	0	0	0	0	0	0	0	0	0	0	0	0
Tracy, James, Chi.*	.254	42	122	12	31	49	3	3	3	9	1	2	0	2	2
Trevino, Alejandro, N.Y.	.256	106	355	26	91	106	11	2	0	37	5	2	5	0	3
Trillo, J. Manuel, Phil.	.292	141	531	68	155	219	25	9	7	43	5	4	3	8	3
Turner, John, S.D.*	.288	85	153	22	44	58	5	0	3	18	0	1	2	8	3
Tyson, Michael, Chi.#	.238	123	341	34	81	115	19	3	3	23	1	4	1	1	2
Unser, Delbert, Phil.*	.264	96	110	15	29	43	6	4	0	10	2	1	2	0	1
Urrea, John, St.L.	.231	30	13	0	3	3	0	0	0	0	0	2	0	0	0
Vail, Michael, Chi.	.298	114	312	30	93	132	17	2	6	47	2	1	0	2	5
Valentine, Ellis, Mtl.	.315	86	311	40	98	163	22	2	13	67	12	0	4	5	5
Valenzuela, Fernando, L.A.*	.000	10	1	0	0	0	0	0	0	0	0	0	0	0	0
Venable, W. McKinley, S.F.*	.268	64	138	13	37	42	5	0	0	10	0	1	3	8	2
Virgil, Osvaldo, Phil.	.200	1	5	1	1	2	1	0	0	0	0	0	0	0	0
Vuckovich, Peter, St.L.	.183	32	71	4	13	19	6	0	0	7	0	9	0	1	0
Vukovich, George, Phil.*	.224	78	58	6	13	16	1	1	0	8	0	0	0	0	0
Vukovich, John, Phil.	.161	49	62	4	10	13	1	1	0	5	0	0	1	0	1
Walk, Robert, Phil.	.140	27	50	5	7	8	1	0	0	2	0	7	0	0	0
Wallach, Timothy, Mtl.	.182	5	11	1	2	5	0	0	1	2	0	0	0	0	0
Waller, E. Tyrone, St.L.	.083	5	12	3	1	1	0	0	0	0	0	0	0	0	0
Walling, Dennis, Hou.*	.299	100	284	30	85	110	6	5	3	29	3	0	2	4	3
Washington, Claudell, N.Y.*	.275	79	284	38	78	132	16	4	10	42	4	0	1	17	5
Weiss, Gary, L.A.*	---	8	0	2	0	0	0	0	0	0	0	0	0	0	0
Welch, Robert, L.A.	.243	34	70	1	17	20	3	0	0	3	1	5	0	0	0
Werner, Donald, Cin.	.172	24	64	2	11	13	2	0	0	5	0	0	1	1	0
White, Jerome, Mtl.#	.262	110	214	22	56	92	9	3	7	22	2	1	3	8	7
Whitfield, Terry, S.F.*	.296	118	321	38	95	127	16	2	4	26	8	4	2	4	2
Whitson, Eddie, S.F.	.091	34	66	2	6	6	0	0	0	4	0	9	0	0	0
Wilson, William, N.Y.#	.248	27	105	16	26	37	5	3	0	4	0	2	0	7	7
Winfield, David, S.D.	.276	162	558	89	154	251	25	6	20	87	10	0	4	23	7
Wise, Richard, S.D.	.138	28	58	1	8	10	2	0	0	4	1	2	0	0	0
Wohlford, James, S.F.	.280	91	193	17	54	71	6	4	1	24	4	0	3	1	4
Woods, Gary, Hou.	.377	19	53	8	20	31	5	0	2	15	2	0	0	1	0
Yeager, Stephen, L.A.	.211	96	227	20	48	62	8	0	2	20	4	0	1	2	3
Youngblood, Joel, N.Y.	.276	146	514	58	142	196	26	2	8	69	3	0	9	14	11
Zachry, Patrick, N.Y.	.043	28	46	0	2	2	0	0	0	1	0	5	1	0	0

CLUB BATTING

Club	PCT	G	AB	R	H	TB	2B	3B	HR	RBI	SH	SF	SB	CS	LOB	SHO
St. Louis	.275	162	5608	738	1541	2242	300	49	101	688	73	49	117	54	1110	8
Philadelphia	.270	162	5625	728	1517	2248	272	54	117	674	77	58	140	62	1131	12
Pittsburgh	.266	162	5517	666	1469	2142	249	38	116	626	75	56	209	102	1087	12
Los Angeles	.263	163	5568	663	1462	2163	209	24	148	638	96	41	123	72	1173	4
Cincinnati	.262	163	5516	707	1445	2130	256	45	113	668	78	54	156	43	1149	9
Houston	.261	163	5566	637	1455	2045	231	67	75	599	89	45	194	74	1200	11
Montreal	.257	162	5465	694	1407	2121	250	61	114	647	76	56	237	82	1116	10
New York	.257	162	5478	611	1407	1890	218	41	61	554	73	53	158	99	1125	13
San Diego	.255	163	5540	591	1410	1892	195	43	67	546	92	38	239	73	1239	9
Chicago	.251	162	5619	614	1411	2053	251	35	107	578	69	40	93	64	1119	17
Atlanta	.250	161	5402	630	1352	2054	226	22	144	597	69	33	73	52	1054	11
San Francisco	.244	161	5368	573	1310	1837	199	44	80	539	100	54	100	58	1116	16
TOTALS	.259	973	66272	7852	17186	24817	2856	523	1243	7354	967	577	1839	835	13619	132

Pitching

INDIVIDUAL PITCHING LEADERS

Earned Run Average	:	2.21	Sutton, L.A.
Won & Lost Percentage	:	.760	Bibby, Pitt. (19-6)
Games Won	:	24	Carlton, Phil.
Games Lost	:	18	Niekro, Atl.
Appearances	:	84	Tidrow, Chi.
Games Started	:	38	Carlton, Phil., Niekro, Atl. & Reuschel, Chi.
Complete Games	:	14	Rogers, Mtl.
Games Finished	:	62	Hume, Cin.
Saves	:	28	Sutter, Chi.
Shutouts	:	6	Reuss, L.A.
Innings	:	304	Carlton, Phil.
Hits	:	281	Reuschel, Chi.
Batsmen Faced	:	1228	Carlton, Phil.
Runs	:	123	Lamp, Chi.
Earned Runs	:	117	Lamp, Chi.
Home Runs	:	30	Niekro, Atl.
Sacrifice Hits	:	19	Reuschel, Chi. & Rogers, Mtl.
Sacrifice Flies	:	14	Reuschel, Chi.
Bases on Balls	:	98	Ryan, Hou.
Intentional Bases on Balls	:	16	Tekulve, Pitt. & Tidrow, Chi.
Hit Batsmen	:	8	Griffin & Knepper, S.F. & Krukow, Chi.
Strikeouts	:	286	Carlton, Phil.
Wild Pitches	:	17	Carlton, Phil.
Balks	:	7	Carlton, Phil.
Games Won, Consecutive	:	8	Carlton, Phil. May 14 - June 22 Bibby, Pitt. June 1 - July 27
Games Lost, Consecutive	:	8	Hernandez, Chi. May 6 - August 7 Capilla, Chi. July 13 - October 5

Phillies' Steve Carlton won the Cy Young Award.

NATIONAL LEAGUE PITCHING AVERAGES
(Top Fifteen Qualifiers for Earned Run Leadership)
* Throws Lefthanded

Pitcher & Club	ERA	W	L	PCT	G	GS	CG	GF	SV	SHO	IP	H	BFP	R	ER	HR	SH	SF	TBB	IBB	HB	SO	WP	BK
Sutton, Donald, L.A.	2.21	13	5	.722	32	31	4	1	1	2	212	163	833	56	52	20	8	3	47	5	2	128	0	1
Carlton, Steven, Phil.* ...	2.34	24	9	.727	38	38	13	0	0	3	304	243	1223	87	79	15	14	8	90	12	2	286	17	7
Reuss, Jerry, L.A.*	2.52	18	6	.750	37	29	10	7	3	6	229	193	907	74	64	12	10	5	40	9	0	111	3	1
Blue, Vida, S.F.*	2.97	14	10	.583	31	31	10	0	0	3	224	202	914	79	74	14	13	6	61	8	0	129	3	2
Rogers, Stephen, Mtl.	2.98	16	11	.593	37	37	14	0	0	4	281	247	1151	101	93	16	19	7	85	7	3	147	7	0
Zachry, Patrick, N.Y.	3.00	6	10	.375	28	26	7	1	0	3	165	145	680	65	55	16	9	4	58	5	5	88	2	2
Soto, Mario, Cin.	3.03	10	8	.556	53	12	3	10	4	1	190	126	777	72	65	11	10	8	84	10	2	182	6	4
Whitson, Eddie, S.F.	3.10	11	13	.458	34	34	6	0	0	2	212	222	898	88	73	7	10	9	56	7	4	90	1	1
Sanderson, Scott, Mtl.	3.11	16	11	.593	33	33	7	0	0	3	211	206	874	76	73	18	11	5	56	3	3	125	6	0
Forsch, Kenneth, Hou.	3.20	12	13	.480	32	32	6	0	0	3	222	230	927	90	79	15	9	4	41	1	7	84	1	3
Pastore, Frank, Cin.	3.26	13	7	.650	27	27	9	0	0	2	185	161	744	72	67	13	6	5	42	3	0	110	0	1
Welch, Robert, L.A.	3.28	14	9	.609	32	32	3	0	0	2	214	190	889	85	78	15	12	10	79	6	3	141	7	5
Bibby, James, Pitt.	3.33	19	6	.760	35	34	6	1	0	1	238	210	985	95	88	20	6	4	88	3	6	144	5	3
Ryan, L. Nolan, Hou.	3.35	11	10	.524	35	35	4	0	0	2	234	205	982	100	87	10	7	7	98	1	3	200	10	1
Reuschel, Ricky, Chi.	3.40	11	13	.458	38	38	6	0	0	0	257	281	1094	111	97	13	19	14	76	10	4	140	3	1

ALL PITCHERS LISTED ALPHABETICALLY
* Throws Lefthanded

Pitcher & Club	ERA	W	L	PCT	G	GS	CG	GF	SV	SHO	IP	H	BFP	R	ER	HR	SH	SF	TBB	IBB	HB	SO	WP	BK
Alexander, Doyle, Atl.	4.19	14	11	.560	35	35	7	0	0	1	232	227	981	120	108	20	12	4	74	5	4	114	3	0
Allen, Neil, N.Y.	3.71	7	10	.412	59	0	0	47	22	0	97	87	407	43	40	7	6	4	40	9	0	79	2	1
Andujar, Joaquin, Hou.	3.91	3	8	.273	35	14	0	5	2	0	122	132	531	59	53	8	7	3	43	2	0	75	2	0
Armstrong, Michael, S.D. ..	5.79	0	0	---	11	0	0	4	0	0	14	16	67	10	9	3	0	0	13	5	0	14	0	0
Bahnsen, Stanley, Mtl.	3.07	7	6	.538	57	0	0	19	4	0	91	80	383	40	31	7	6	3	33	4	0	48	6	0
Bair, C. Douglas, Cin.	4.24	3	6	.333	61	0	0	38	6	0	85	91	377	42	40	7	4	4	39	10	1	62	5	0
Beckwith, T. Joseph, L.A. .	1.95	3	3	.500	38	0	0	16	0	0	60	60	258	17	13	1	4	2	23	4	1	40	4	0
Berenguer, Juan, N.Y.	6.00	0	1	.000	6	0	0	4	0	0	9	9	46	9	6	1	0	0	10	2	0	7	0	0
Berenyi, Bruce, Cin.	7.71	2	2	.500	6	6	0	0	0	0	28	34	132	26	24	1	2	0	23	0	0	19	3	0
Bibby, James, Pitt.	3.33	19	6	.760	35	34	6	1	0	1	238	210	985	95	88	20	6	4	88	3	6	144	5	3
Blair, Dennis, S.D.	6.43	0	1	.000	5	1	0	0	0	0	14	18	61	10	10	3	0	0	3	0	0	11	1	0
Blue, Vida, S.F.*	2.97	14	10	.583	31	31	10	0	0	3	224	202	914	79	74	14	13	6	61	8	0	129	3	2
Blyleven, R. Aalbert, Pitt.	3.82	8	13	.381	34	32	5	1	0	2	217	219	907	102	92	20	10	2	59	5	0	168	2	1
Boggs, Thomas, Atl.	3.42	12	9	.571	32	26	4	1	0	3	192	180	792	80	73	14	13	7	46	0	4	84	4	2

Pitcher & Club	ERA	W	L	PCT	G	GS	CG	GF	SV	SHO	IP	H	BFP	R	ER	HR	SH	SF	TBB	IBB	HB	SO	WP	BK
Bomback, Mark, N.Y.	4.09	10	8	.556	36	25	2	2	0	1	163	191	710	80	74	17	7	6	49	3	4	68	4	0
Bonham, William, Cin.	4.74	2	1	.667	4	4	0	0	0	0	19	21	81	10	10	1	0	0	5	0	0	13	0	0
Borbon, Pedro, St.L.	3.79	1	0	1.000	10	0	0	4	1	0	19	17	84	10	8	3	2	4	10	2	0	4	1	0
Bordley, William, S.F.* ...	4.65	2	3	.400	8	6	0	0	0	0	31	34	141	19	16	3	2	0	21	1	0	11	1	0
Bradford, Larry, Atl.*	2.45	3	4	.429	56	0	0	24	4	0	55	49	232	20	15	3	5	2	22	8	1	32	3	0
Breining, Fred, S.F.	5.14	0	0	----	5	0	0	1	0	0	7	8	30	4	4	0	1	0	4	1	1	3	0	0
Brusstar, Warren, Phil. ...	3.69	2	2	.500	26	0	0	12	0	0	39	42	165	16	16	3	5	0	13	2	0	21	0	0
Burnside, Sheldon, Cin.* ..	1.80	1	0	1.000	7	0	0	3	0	0	5	6	19	1	1	1	0	0	1	0	0	2	0	0
Burris, B. Ray, N.Y.	4.02	7	13	.350	29	29	1	0	0	0	170	181	726	86	76	20	8	7	54	5	4	83	5	2
Bystrom, Martin, Phil.	1.50	5	0	1.000	6	5	1	1	0	1	36	26	142	6	6	1	0	0	9	0	0	21	1	0
Camp, Rick, Atl.	1.92	6	4	.600	77	0	0	44	22	0	108	92	440	26	23	3	10	5	29	8	4	33	2	0
Candelaria, John, Pitt.* ..	4.02	11	14	.440	35	34	7	1	1	0	233	246	969	114	104	14	14	12	50	4	3	97	0	2
Capilla, Douglas, Chi.* ...	4.10	2	8	.200	39	11	0	6	0	0	90	82	388	46	41	7	4	5	51	5	3	51	6	4
Carlton, Steven, Phil.* ...	2.34	24	9	.727	38	38	13	0	0	3	304	243	1228	87	79	15	14	8	90	12	2	286	17	7
Castillo, Robert, L.A.	2.76	8	6	.571	61	0	0	29	5	0	98	70	395	31	30	4	4	5	45	5	1	60	3	0
Caudill, William, Chi.	2.18	4	6	.400	72	2	0	27	1	0	128	100	527	37	31	10	10	9	59	12	1	112	2	4
Christenson, Larry, Phil. .	4.01	5	1	.833	14	14	0	0	0	0	74	62	308	35	33	4	4	1	27	4	3	49	2	4
Combe, Geoffrey, Cin.	10.29	0	0	---	4	0	0	0	0	0	7	9	31	8	8	0	1	0	4	1	0	10	1	0
Curtis, John, S.D.*	3.51	10	8	.556	30	27	6	0	0	0	187	184	787	84	73	9	15	2	67	13	2	71	10	2
D'Acquisto, John, S.D.-Mtl.	3.38	2	5	.286	50	0	0	14	3	0	88	81	373	36	33	2	5	6	45	9	1	59	9	0
Davis, Mark, Phil.*	2.57	0	0	---	2	1	0	0	0	0	7	4	30	2	2	0	0	0	5	0	0	5	0	0
Dues, Hal, Mtl.	6.75	0	1	.000	6	1	0	1	0	0	12	17	57	9	9	1	2	0	4	1	0	2	0	0
Eichelberger, Juan, S.D. ..	3.64	4	2	.667	15	13	0	0	0	0	89	73	377	41	36	8	6	2	55	4	1	43	3	3
Espinosa, Arnulfo, Phil. ..	3.79	3	5	.375	12	12	1	0	0	0	76	73	317	36	32	9	2	2	19	2	2	13	0	0
Falcone, Peter, N.Y.*	4.53	7	10	.412	37	23	1	5	1	0	157	163	684	89	79	16	12	7	58	9	2	109	9	1
Fingers, Roland, S.D.	2.80	11	9	.550	66	0	0	46	23	0	103	101	428	35	32	3	6	6	32	13	0	69	5	1
Forsch, Kenneth, Hou.	3.20	12	13	.480	32	32	6	0	0	3	222	230	927	90	79	15	9	4	41	1	7	84	1	3
Forsch, Robert, St.L.	3.77	11	10	.524	31	31	8	0	0	0	215	225	878	102	90	12	8	9	33	6	4	87	7	0
Forster, Terry, L.A.*	3.00	0	0	---	9	0	0	7	0	0	12	10	49	4	4	0	0	0	4	0	0	2	0	0
Frazier, George, St.L.	2.74	1	4	.200	22	0	0	12	3	0	23	24	96	10	7	2	1	0	7	3	0	11	0	0
Fryman, Woodrow, Mtl.*	2.25	7	4	.636	61	0	0	40	17	0	80	61	332	23	20	1	5	2	30	9	2	59	1	1
Fulgham, John, St.L.	3.39	4	6	.400	15	14	4	0	0	1	85	66	338	33	32	7	2	1	32	1	1	48	1	2
Garber, H. Eugene, Atl. ...	3.84	5	5	.500	68	0	0	31	7	0	82	95	359	42	35	6	4	1	24	5	0	51	0	0
Glynn, Edward, N.Y.*	4.15	3	3	.500	38	0	0	11	1	0	52	49	228	26	24	5	4	2	23	4	0	32	1	0
Goltz, David, L.A.	4.32	7	11	.389	35	27	2	2	1	2	171	198	739	91	82	12	10	8	59	3	0	91	3	1
Griffin, Thomas, S.F.	2.75	5	1	.833	42	4	0	8	0	0	108	80	447	35	33	8	8	4	49	6	8	79	4	3
Grimsley, Ross, Mtl.*	6.37	2	4	.333	11	7	0	2	0	0	41	61	196	31	29	5	4	5	12	1	1	11	1	0
Gullickson, William, Mtl. .	3.00	10	5	.667	24	19	5	1	0	2	141	127	593	53	47	6	3	4	50	2	2	120	5	0

Halicki, Edward, S.F.	5.40	0	0	---	11	2	0	4	0	0	25	29	110	15	15	5	0	1	10	1	0	14	0	0
Hanna, Preston, Atl.	3.19	2	0	1.000	32	2	0	3	0	0	79	63	338	28	28	3	5	4	44	4	3	35	5	0
Hargesheimer, Alan, S.F. ..	4.32	4	6	.400	15	13	0	1	0	0	75	82	325	38	36	3	4	1	32	2	0	40	2	2
Hassler, Andrew, Pitt.* ...	3.75	0	0	---	6	0	0	2	0	0	12	9	45	6	5	2	3	1	4	0	0	4	0	0
Hausman, Thomas, N.Y.	3.98	6	5	.545	55	4	0	14	1	0	122	125	513	63	54	12	11	3	26	8	3	53	2	0
Hernandez, Guillermo, Chi.*	4.42	1	9	.100	53	7	0	13	0	0	108	115	473	58	53	8	6	3	45	4	2	75	6	1
Holland, Alfred, S.F.*	1.76	5	3	.625	54	0	0	31	7	0	82	71	349	21	16	2	5	4	34	8	1	65	1	3
Holman, R. Scott, N.Y.	1.29	0	0	---	4	0	0	1	0	0	7	6	26	2	1	0	0	1	1	1	0	3	1	1
Hood, Donald, St.L.*	3.40	4	6	.400	33	8	1	4	0	0	82	90	359	39	31	2	8	3	34	5	2	35	5	2
Hooton, Burt, L.A.	3.65	14	8	.636	34	33	4	1	1	2	207	194	858	90	84	22	11	5	64	1	0	118	4	1
Hough, Charles, L.A.	5.63	1	3	.250	19	1	0	5	1	0	32	37	156	21	20	4	3	3	21	0	2	25	3	0
Howe, Steven, L.A.*	2.65	7	9	.438	59	0	0	36	17	0	85	83	359	33	25	1	8	3	22	10	2	39	1	0
Howell, Jay, Cin.	15.00	0	0	---	5	0	0	1	0	0	3	8	19	5	5	0	0	1	0	0	1	1	0	0
Hrabosky, Alan, Atl.*	3.60	4	2	.667	45	0	0	25	3	0	60	50	250	27	24	8	2	4	31	5	0	31	2	0
Hume, Thomas, Cin.	2.56	9	10	.474	78	0	0	62	25	0	137	121	554	44	39	6	7	1	38	14	3	68	2	0
Hutton, Thomas, Mtl.*	27.00	0	0	---	1	0	0	1	0	0	1	3	7	3	3	1	0	0	1	0	0	1	0	0
Jackson, Grant, Pitt.*	2.92	8	4	.667	61	0	0	27	9	0	71	71	239	24	23	4	6	5	20	3	0	31	3	0
Jackson, Roy, N.Y.	4.18	1	7	.125	24	8	1	4	1	0	71	78	299	37	33	4	3	4	20	4	0	58	4	1
Jefferson, Jesse, Pitt. ...	1.29	1	0	1.000	1	1	0	0	0	0	7	3	23	1	1	0	0	0	2	0	0	4	1	0
Jones, Randall, S.D.*	3.92	5	13	.278	24	24	4	0	0	3	154	165	638	71	67	14	11	1	29	5	0	53	1	0
Kaat, James, St.L.*	3.81	8	7	.533	49	14	6	22	4	1	130	140	546	61	55	6	8	6	33	11	0	36	3	1
Kinney, Dennis, S.D.*	4.23	4	6	.400	50	0	0	18	1	0	83	79	359	45	39	3	5	3	37	15	1	40	2	0
Knepper, Robert, S.F.*	4.10	9	16	.360	35	33	8	1	0	1	215	242	943	114	98	15	9	5	61	10	8	103	2	1
Knowles, Darold, St.L.* ...	9.00	0	1	.000	2	0	0	0	0	0	2	3	8	2	2	1	0	0	0	0	0	1	0	0
Kobel, Kevin, N.Y.*	7.13	1	4	.200	14	1	0	3	0	0	24	36	114	21	19	5	1	0	11	3	0	8	0	0
Krukow, Michael, Chi.	4.39	10	15	.400	34	34	3	0	0	0	205	200	884	117	100	13	9	13	80	5	8	130	5	2
LaCorte, Frank, Hou.	2.82	8	5	.615	55	0	0	44	11	0	83	61	341	29	26	4	3	5	43	5	0	66	2	0
LaCoss, Michael, Cin.	4.63	10	12	.455	34	29	4	1	0	2	169	207	762	101	87	9	7	3	68	8	1	59	3	2
LaGrow, Lerrin, Phil.	4.15	0	2	.000	25	0	0	8	3	0	39	42	173	22	18	5	1	3	17	2	0	21	3	2
Lamp, Dennis, Chi.	5.19	10	14	.417	41	37	2	3	0	1	203	259	921	123	117	16	17	4	82	7	1	83	10	0
Larson, Daniel, Phil.	3.13	0	5	.000	12	7	0	2	0	0	46	46	201	24	16	4	6	1	24	6	0	17	1	2
Lavelle, Gary, S.F.*	3.42	6	8	.429	62	0	0	28	9	0	100	106	434	43	38	4	8	4	36	11	0	66	1	3
Lea, Charles, Mtl.	3.72	7	5	.583	21	19	0	1	0	0	104	103	458	51	43	5	5	3	55	4	2	56	2	0
Lee, Mark, Pitt.	4.50	0	1	.000	4	0	0	3	0	0	6	5	26	3	3	0	1	0	3	0	0	2	1	0
Lee, William, Mtl.*	4.96	4	6	.400	24	18	2	4	0	0	118	156	522	71	65	13	3	5	22	1	3	34	1	0
Leibrandt, Charles, Cin.* .	4.24	10	9	.526	36	27	5	3	0	2	174	200	754	84	82	15	12	2	54	4	2	62	1	6
Lerch, Randy, Phil.*	5.16	4	14	.222	30	22	2	3	0	0	150	178	664	98	86	15	10	10	55	5	0	57	6	2
Littell, Mark, St.L.	9.00	0	2	.000	14	0	0	12	2	0	11	14	52	11	11	2	1	0	7	2	0	7	2	0
Little, D. Jefferey, St.L.*	3.79	1	1	.500	7	2	0	2	0	0	19	18	81	9	8	0	0	0	9	0	0	17	1	0

Pitcher & Club	ERA	W	L	PCT	G	GS	CG	GF	SV	SHO	IP	H	BFP	R	ER	HR	SH	SF	TBB	IBB	HB	SO	WP	BK
Littlefield, John, St.L. ..	3.14	5	5	.500	52	0	0	31	9	0	66	71	280	31	23	2	1	6	20	9	1	22	1	1
Lucas, Gary, S.D.*	3.24	5	8	.385	46	18	0	14	3	0	150	138	614	59	54	8	12	7	43	14	1	85	6	2
Lyle, Albert, Phil.*	1.93	0	0	---	10	0	0	5	2	0	14	11	59	5	3	0	1	2	6	1	0	6	1	0
Lynch, Edward, N.Y.	5.21	1	1	.500	5	4	0	0	0	0	19	24	86	12	11	0	0	1	5	0	1	9	0	0
Mahler, Michael, Pitt.	63.00	0	0	---	2	0	0	1	0	0	1	4	10	7	7	1	0	0	3	0	0	1	0	0
Mahler, Richard, Atl.	2.25	0	0	---	2	0	0	0	0	0	4	2	13	1	1	0	0	0	0	0	0	1	0	0
Martin, John, St.L.*	4.29	2	3	.400	9	5	1	2	0	0	42	39	169	20	20	1	0	2	9	1	0	23	1	0
Martinez, Silvio, St.L. ...	4.80	5	10	.333	25	20	2	0	0	0	120	127	525	75	64	8	4	5	48	3	2	39	3	3
Martz, Randy, Chi.	2.10	1	2	.333	6	6	0	0	0	0	30	28	130	14	7	1	1	2	11	1	0	5	0	0
Matula, Richard, Atl.	4.58	11	13	.458	33	30	3	2	0	1	177	195	761	100	90	17	8	10	60	9	0	62	3	3
McGlothen, Lynn, Chi.	4.80	12	14	.462	39	27	2	3	0	2	182	211	804	105	97	24	11	9	64	7	1	119	4	0
McGraw, Frank, Phil.*	1.47	5	4	.556	57	0	0	48	20	0	92	62	355	16	15	3	7	4	23	9	2	75	1	0
McWilliams, Larry, Atl.* ..	4.94	9	14	.391	30	30	4	0	0	1	164	188	715	97	90	27	8	2	39	2	7	77	5	1
Miller, Dyar, N.Y.	1.93	1	2	.333	31	0	0	12	1	0	42	37	170	9	9	1	4	2	11	3	0	28	0	1
Minton, Gregory, S.F.	2.47	4	6	.400	68	0	0	38	19	0	91	81	377	28	25	0	8	1	34	6	0	42	7	1
Moffitt, Randall, S.F.	4.76	1	1	.500	13	0	0	5	0	0	17	18	69	10	9	2	0	0	4	2	1	10	1	0
Montefusco, John, S.F.	4.38	4	8	.333	22	17	1	0	0	0	113	120	498	61	55	15	2	3	39	6	2	85	2	1
Moore, Donnie, St.L.	6.14	1	1	.500	11	0	0	3	0	0	22	25	93	15	15	1	2	1	5	1	1	10	0	1
Moskau, Paul, Cin.	4.00	9	7	.563	33	19	2	4	2	1	153	147	630	69	68	13	11	5	41	2	1	94	8	5
Munninghoff, Scott, Phil. .	4.50	0	0	---	4	0	0	0	0	0	6	8	31	3	3	0	0	1	5	0	0	2	1	0
Mura, Stephen, S.D.	3.67	8	7	.533	37	23	3	5	2	1	169	149	719	74	69	9	15	10	86	4	3	109	3	1
Murray, Dale, Mtl.	6.21	0	1	.000	16	0	0	6	0	0	29	39	137	23	20	3	0	1	12	2	0	16	1	1
Nastu, Philip, S.F.*	6.00	0	0	---	6	0	0	1	0	0	6	10	33	9	4	1	0	0	5	1	0	1	1	0
Niekro, Joseph, Hou.	3.55	20	12	.625	37	36	11	1	0	2	256	268	1096	119	101	12	9	11	79	3	4	127	12	0
Niekro, Philip, Atl.	3.63	15	18	.455	40	38	11	2	1	3	275	256	1137	119	111	30	14	5	85	3	3	176	9	1
Niemann, Randy, Hou.*	5.45	0	1	.000	22	1	0	3	1	0	33	40	147	21	20	2	0	1	12	1	0	18	0	1
Noles, Dickie, Phil.	3.89	1	4	.200	48	3	0	20	6	0	81	80	367	42	35	5	7	2	42	11	1	57	2	0
Norman, Fredie, Mtl.*	4.13	4	4	.500	48	8	2	9	4	0	98	96	426	50	45	8	9	4	40	4	3	58	0	1
Olmsted, Alan, St.L.*	2.83	1	1	.500	5	5	0	0	0	0	35	32	147	13	11	2	1	0	14	1	1	14	1	0
Otten, James, St.L.	5.56	0	5	.000	31	4	0	9	0	0	55	71	255	38	34	3	3	4	26	7	2	38	1	1
Pacella, John, N.Y.	5.14	3	4	.429	32	15	0	6	0	0	84	89	388	51	48	5	9	0	59	2	2	68	5	3
Palmer, David, Mtl.	2.98	8	6	.571	24	19	3	0	0	1	130	124	529	53	43	11	8	2	30	1	2	73	1	2
Pastore, Frank, Cin.	3.26	13	7	.650	27	27	9	0	0	2	185	161	744	72	67	13	6	5	42	3	0	110	0	1
Perez, Pascual, Pitt.	3.75	0	1	.000	2	2	0	0	0	0	12	15	51	6	5	0	1	2	2	0	2	7	0	0
Pladson, Gordon, Hou.	4.39	0	4	.000	12	6	0	1	0	0	41	38	175	23	20	3	2	1	16	0	0	13	0	0
Price, Joseph, Cin.*	3.57	7	3	.700	24	13	2	3	0	0	111	95	448	45	44	10	8	0	37	0	1	44	1	1
Rasmussen, Eric, S.D.	4.38	4	11	.267	40	14	0	12	1	0	111	130	488	60	54	9	9	3	33	6	3	50	1	1
Ratzer, Stephen, Mtl.	11.25	0	0	---	1	1	0	0	0	0	4	9	22	5	5	0	0	0	2	0	0	0	0	0

Reardon, Jeffrey, N.Y.	2.62	8	7	.533	61	0	0	35	6	0	110	96	475	36	32	10	8	5	47	15	0	101	2	0
Reed, Ronald, Phil.	4.05	7	5	.583	55	0	0	29	9	0	91	88	387	45	41	4	4	4	30	10	1	54	5	0
Reuschel, Ricky, Chi.	3.40	11	13	.458	38	38	6	0	0	0	257	281	1094	111	97	13	19	14	76	10	4	140	3	1
Reuss, Jerry, L.A.*	2.52	18	6	.750	37	29	10	7	3	6	229	193	907	74	64	12	10	5	40	9	0	111	3	1
Rhoden, Richard, Pitt.	3.83	7	5	.583	20	19	2	0	0	0	127	133	536	58	54	9	3	3	40	4	3	70	6	0
Richard, James, Hou.	1.89	10	4	.714	17	17	4	0	0	4	114	65	438	31	24	2	5	2	40	1	0	119	2	0
Riley, George, Chi.*	5.75	0	4	.000	22	0	0	10	0	0	36	41	166	29	23	2	4	0	20	5	2	18	0	1
Rincon, Andrew, St.L.	2.61	3	1	.750	4	4	1	0	0	0	31	23	116	9	9	1	2	0	7	1	0	22	1	2
Ripley, Allen, S.F.	4.14	9	10	.474	23	20	2	2	0	0	113	119	486	59	52	10	6	5	36	6	4	65	5	3
Roberge, Bertrand, Hou. ...	6.00	2	0	1.000	14	0	0	2	0	0	24	24	106	16	16	2	1	1	10	1	2	9	3	0
Roberts, David, Pitt.*	4.50	0	1	.000	2	0	0	0	0	0	2	2	9	1	1	0	0	0	1	0	0	1	0	0
Robinson, Don, Pitt.	3.99	7	10	.412	29	24	3	1	1	2	160	157	671	74	71	14	8	3	45	5	5	103	7	2
Rogers, Stephen, Mtl.	2.98	16	11	.593	37	37	14	0	0	4	281	247	1151	101	93	16	19	7	85	7	3	147	7	0
Romo, Enrique, Pitt.	3.27	5	5	.500	74	0	0	38	11	0	124	117	507	53	45	10	9	5	28	4	1	82	0	2
Rooker, James, Pitt.*	3.50	2	2	.500	4	4	0	0	0	0	18	16	75	7	7	0	1	1	12	0	0	8	0	0
Rowland, Michael, S.F.	2.33	1	1	.500	19	0	0	14	0	0	27	20	109	8	7	2	2	1	8	2	1	8	0	0
Ruhle, Vernon, Hou.	2.38	12	4	.750	28	22	6	1	0	2	159	148	638	51	42	7	11	5	29	1	3	55	0	2
Ruthven, Richard, Phil. ...	3.55	17	10	.630	33	33	6	0	0	1	223	241	944	99	88	9	8	6	74	9	3	86	4	3
Ryan, L. Nolan, Hou.	3.35	11	10	.524	35	35	4	0	0	2	234	205	982	100	87	10	7	7	98	1	3	200	10	1
Sambito, Joseph, Hou.*	2.20	8	4	.667	64	0	0	40	17	0	90	65	354	26	22	3	4	1	22	3	2	75	3	0
Sanderson, Scott, Mtl.	3.11	16	11	.593	33	33	7	0	0	3	211	206	874	76	73	18	11	5	56	3	3	125	6	0
Saucier, Kevin, Phil.*	3.42	7	3	.700	40	0	0	9	0	0	50	50	207	21	19	2	1	4	20	8	4	25	1	0
Scott, Michael, N.Y.	4.34	1	1	.500	6	6	1	0	0	1	29	40	132	14	14	1	2	1	8	1	0	13	1	0
Scurry, Rodney, Pitt.*	2.13	0	2	.000	20	0	0	4	0	0	38	23	153	12	9	2	3	0	17	3	2	28	2	1
Seaman, Kim, St.L.*	3.38	3	2	.600	26	0	0	10	4	0	24	16	99	9	9	2	1	0	13	1	0	10	0	0
Seaver, G. Thomas, Cin. ...	3.64	10	8	.556	26	26	5	0	0	1	168	140	692	74	68	24	2	8	59	3	1	101	4	0
Shirley, Robert, S.D.*	3.55	11	12	.478	59	12	3	32	7	0	137	143	585	58	54	12	8	4	54	15	0	67	1	2
Smith, David, Hou.	1.92	7	5	.583	57	0	0	35	10	0	103	90	420	24	22	1	6	1	32	7	4	85	3	1
Smith, Lee, Chi.	2.86	2	0	1.000	18	0	0	6	0	0	22	21	97	9	7	0	1	1	14	5	0	17	0	0
Solomon, Eddie, Pitt.	2.70	7	3	.700	26	12	2	1	0	0	100	96	428	44	30	8	3	4	37	5	4	35	1	1
Sosa, Elias, Mtl.	3.05	9	6	.600	67	0	0	43	9	0	94	104	394	33	32	5	7	3	19	3	1	58	1	1
Soto, Mario, Cin.	3.03	10	8	.556	53	12	3	10	4	1	190	126	777	72	65	11	10	8	84	10	2	182	6	4
Sprowl, Robert, Hou.*	0.00	0	0	---	1	0	0	0	0	0	1	1	5	0	0	0	0	0	1	0	0	3	0	0
Stablein, George, S.D.	3.00	0	1	.000	4	2	0	0	0	0	12	16	51	4	4	0	1	0	3	0	0	4	1	0
Stanhouse, Donald, L.A. ...	5.04	2	2	.500	21	0	0	12	7	0	25	30	117	14	14	4	2	1	16	3	0	5	0	0
Stember, Jeffrey, S.F.	3.00	0	0	---	1	1	0	0	0	0	3	2	14	3	1	1	0	0	2	0	0	0	0	1
Sutcliffe, Richard, L.A. ..	5.56	3	9	.250	42	10	1	19	5	1	110	122	491	73	68	10	4	3	55	2	1	59	4	5
Sutter, H. Bruce, Chi.	2.65	5	8	.385	60	0	0	43	28	0	102	90	423	35	30	5	14	2	34	8	1	76	2	4
Sutton, Donald, L.A.	2.21	13	5	.722	32	31	4	1	1	2	212	163	833	56	52	20	8	3	47	5	2	128	0	1

Pitcher & Club	ERA	W	L	PCT	G	GS	CG	GF	SV	SHO	IP	H	BFP	R	ER	HR	SH	SF	TBB	IBB	HB	SO	WP	BK
Swan, Craig, N.Y.	3.59	5	9	.357	21	21	4	0	0	1	128	117	520	59	51	20	12	4	30	3	0	79	0	1
Sykes, Robert, St.L.*	4.64	6	10	.375	27	19	4	0	0	3	126	134	545	67	65	12	5	3	54	3	0	50	3	0
Tekulve, Kenton, Pitt.	3.39	8	12	.400	78	0	0	57	21	0	93	96	407	39	35	6	6	0	40	16	1	47	0	0
Tellmann, Thomas, S.D.	1.64	3	0	1.000	6	2	2	1	1	0	22	23	95	5	4	0	0	0	8	0	0	9	0	0
Thomas, Roy, St.L.	4.75	2	3	.400	24	5	0	8	0	0	55	59	248	32	29	3	1	4	25	5	3	22	0	0
Tidrow, Richard, Chi.	2.79	6	5	.545	84	0	0	38	6	0	116	97	495	44	36	10	9	4	53	16	5	97	1	0
Tomlin, David, Cin.*	5.54	3	0	1.000	27	0	0	8	0	0	26	38	123	17	16	2	4	1	11	5	0	6	1	0
Urrea, John, St.L.	3.46	4	1	.800	30	1	0	8	3	0	65	57	287	28	25	2	3	3	41	9	2	36	3	2
Valenzuela, Fernando, L.A.*	0.00	2	0	1.000	10	0	0	4	1	0	18	8	66	2	0	0	1	1	5	0	0	16	0	1
Vuckovich, Peter, St.L. ...	3.41	12	9	.571	32	30	7	1	1	3	222	203	907	96	84	18	8	6	68	5	2	132	5	2
Walk, Robert, Phil.	4.56	11	7	.611	27	27	2	0	0	0	152	163	673	82	77	8	5	5	71	2	2	94	6	3
Welch, Robert, L.A.	3.28	14	9	.609	32	32	3	0	0	2	214	190	889	85	78	15	12	10	79	6	3	141	7	5
Whitson, Eddie, S.F.	3.10	11	13	.458	34	34	6	0	0	2	212	222	898	88	73	7	10	9	56	7	4	90	1	1
Wise, Richard, S.D.	3.68	6	8	.429	27	27	1	0	0	0	154	172	651	69	63	14	7	3	37	10	0	59	1	2
Zachry, Patrick, N.Y.	3.00	6	10	.375	28	26	7	1	0	3	165	145	680	65	55	16	9	4	58	5	5	88	2	2

CLUB PITCHING

Club	ERA	G	CG	SV	SHO	IP	H	BFP	R	ER	HR	SH	SF	TBB	IBB	HB	SO	WP	BK
Houston	3.10	163	31	41	18	1482.2	1367	6160	589	511	69	64	42	466	26	25	929	38	8
Los Angeles	3.24	163	24	42	19	1472.2	1358	6117	591	531	105	77	49	480	48	12	835	32	15
Philadelphia	3.43	162	25	40	8	1480.	1419	6251	639	564	87	75	53	530	83	20	889	51	23
San Francisco	3.46	161	27	35	10	1448.1	1446	6177	634	556	92	78	44	492	78	30	811	31	21
Montreal	3.48	162	33	36	15	1456.2	1447	6160	629	563	100	83	45	460	42	22	823	37	6
Pittsburgh	3.58	162	25	43	8	1458.1	1422	6091	646	580	110	74	42	451	52	27	832	28	12
San Diego	3.65	163	19	39	9	1466.1	1474	6214	654	595	97	99	46	536	113	12	728	39	14
Atlanta	3.77	161	29	37	9	1428.	1397	6028	660	598	131	81	44	454	49	26	696	36	7
Cincinnati	3.85	163	30	37	12	1459.1	1404	6143	670	624	113	74	38	506	60	13	833	35	19
New York	3.85	162	17	33	9	1451.1	1473	6204	702	621	140	96	51	510	77	21	886	38	13
Chicago	3.89	162	13	35	6	1479.	1525	6402	728	639	109	105	66	589	85	28	923	39	17
St. Louis	3.93	162	34	27	9	1447.	1454	6113	710	632	90	61	57	495	76	21	664	39	17
TOTALS	3.60	973	307	445	132	17529.2	17186	74060	7852	7014	1243	967	577	5969	789	257	9849	443	172

(BFP total includes 18 batsmen awarded first base because of interference or obstruction)

NOTE: Total earned runs for several clubs do not agree with composite total of respective club's pitchers due to provisions of Scoring Rule Section 10:18(i). The following differences are to be noted: Houston pitchers add to 512; Los Angeles 534; New York 626; Philadelphia 569; San Diego 596

TV/RADIO ROUNDUP

NETWORK COVERAGE

ABC-TV: The World Series, several Monday night and late-season Sunday afternoon games will be shown on ABC.

NBC-TV: The American and National League playoffs, the All-Star Game and Saturday Game of the Week are scheduled on NBC.

AMERICAN LEAGUE

BALTIMORE ORIOLES: Chuck Thompson, Bill O'Donnell and Tom Marr call the action over radio station WFBR (1300). Brooks Robinson joins Thompson and O'Donnell on WMAR-TV (Channel 2).

BOSTON RED SOX: Ken Coleman and Jon Miller broadcast over radio station WITS (1510). Ned Martin and Ken Harrelson handle television on WSBK (Channel 38).

CALIFORNIA ANGELS: Bob Starr and Steve Shannon describe the action on KMPC (710). Games will be telecast by KTLA-TV (Channel 5), but announcers were not determined at press time.

CHICAGO WHITE SOX: Joe McConnell and Rich King do the broadcasting on WBBM (780) and WGN-TV (Channel 9).

CLEVELAND INDIANS: Herb Score and Nev Chandler are behind the mike for WWWE (1100) and a three-state radio network. Joe Tait and Bruce Drennan work the telecasts on WUAB-TV (Channel 43).

DETROIT TIGERS: Ernie Harwell and Paul Carey broadcast on a 50-station radio network originating with WJR (760). George Kell and Al Kaline do the honors for WDIV-TV (Channel 4) and a seven-station network.

KANSAS CITY ROYALS: Five-state TV network originates with WDAF-TV (Channel 4), as Al Wisk and Denny Trease call the shots. Fred White and Denny Matthews share radio time on a network headed by KMBZ (980) and WIBW (580).

MILWAUKEE BREWERS: Bob Uecker and Lorn Brown do commentary on WTMJ (620) and are joined by Mike Hegan for the telecasts originating from WTMJ-TV (Channel 4).

MINNESOTA TWINS: Bob Kurtz and Larry Osterman telecast on KMSP-TV (Channel 9) and Frank Quilici and Herb Carneal call the plays on a 32-station radio network headed by WCCO (830).

NEW YORK YANKEES: Frank Messer, Phil Rizzuto and Bill White share duties on a TV network headed by WPIX-TV (Channel 11). Fran Healy joins the same crew on a radio network originating with WABC (770).

OAKLAND A'S: Bill King and Lon Simmons do the broadcasting for KSFO (560). The TV outlet is KPIX-TV (Channel 5), but announcers were not determined at press time.

SEATTLE MARINERS: Dave Niehaus and Ken Wilson describe the action on radio station KVI (570). TV arrangements were still to be finalized.

TEXAS RANGERS: Bill Merrill, Mel Proctor and Eric Nadel broadcast over WBAP (820) and KXAS-TV (Channel 5).

TORONTO BLUE JAYS: Tom Cheek and Early Wynn announce for a network originating with flagship station CKFH (1430). TV arrangements were not set.

NATIONAL LEAGUE

ATLANTA BRAVES: WSB radio (750) and WTBS-TV (Channel 17) are the anchor stations for the Braves' network. Ernie Johnson, Pete Van Wieran, Darrel Chaney and Skip Caray provide the coverage on both TV and radio.

CHICAGO CUBS: Jack Brickhouse, Milo Hamilton, Vince Lloyd and Lou Boudreau are at the mike for WGN (720) and WGN-TV (Channel 9) and a 13-station network.

CINCINNATI REDS: Joe Nuxhall and Marty Brennaman call 'em as they see 'em over WLW (700). The TV voices were not set for WLWT-TV (Channel 5).

HOUSTON ASTROS: KPRC (950) and KRIV-TV (Channel 26) are the flagship stations. Gene Elston, Dewayne Staats and Larry Dierker handle TV and Elston and Staats double up on radio.

LOS ANGELES DODGERS: Vin Scully, Ross Porter and Jerry Doggett broadcast over KABC (790) and KTTV (Channel 11). Spanish coverage is done by Jaime Jarrin and Rudy Hoyos on KTNQ (950).

MONTREAL EXPOS: Dave Van Horne and Duke Snider follow the ball on CFCF (600) and the CBS-TV network. Jacques Doucet and Claude Raymond do French broadcasts on CKAC (730) and 16 provincial stations, and Guy Ferron and Jean-Pierre Roy provide the French play-by-play on CBC-TV's French network.

NEW YORK METS: Ralph Kiner, Bob Murphy and Steve Albert are the talent on WMCA (570) and WOR-TV (Channel 9).

PHILADELPHIA PHILLIES: Harry Kalas, Richie Ashburn, Andy Musser, Chris Wheeler and Tim McCarver describe the action for KYW radio (1060) and WPHL (Channel 17).

PITTSBURGH PIRATES: Lanny Frattare and John Sanders line up for KDKA radio (1020) and KDKA-TV (Channel 2).

ST. LOUIS CARDINALS: Mike Shannon, Dan Kelly and Jack Buck are on KMOX radio (1120) and are joined by Jay Randolph for television on KSD (Channel 5).

SAN DIEGO PADRES: Jerry Coleman and Dave Campbell handle the play-by-play on radio KFMB (760). TV arrangements were not set at press time.

SAN FRANCISCO GIANTS: Action can be heard on radio station KNBR (680) and seen on television station KTVU (Channel 2). Lindsey Nelson and Hank Greenwald team up on radio, and Nelson and Gary Park are the TV announcers.

1981 AMERICAN LEAGUE SCHEDULE

BOLD = **SUNDAY** ( ) = HOLIDAY * = NIGHT GAME TN = TWI-NIGHT DOUBLEHEADER (2) or **(2)** = DOUBLEHEADER

	AT SEATTLE	AT OAKLAND	AT CALIFORNIA	AT TEXAS	AT KANSAS CITY	AT MINNESOTA	AT CHICAGO
SEATTLE		April 17*, 18, **19 (2)** Aug. 4*, 5	April 20*, 21*, 22* June 26*, 27*, **28**	May 29*, 30*, **31*** Sept. 21*, 22*, 23*, 24*	June 1*, 2*, 3* Sept. 25*, 26*, **27**	April 27, 28, 29 Aug. 13*, 14*, 15*, **16**	July 10*, 11, **12 (2)** Sept. (7), 8*, 9*
OAKLAND	April 24*, 25*, **26** July 6*, 7*, 8*, 9		April 13*, 14*, 15*, 16* Aug. 7*, 8*, **9**	July 3*, (4)*, **5*** Sept. 14*, 15*, 16*	June 22*, 23*, 24* Oct. 2*, 3*, **4**	April 9, 10, 11, **12** Aug. 10*, 11*, 12*	June 2*, 3*, 4* Sept. 18*, 19, **20**
CALIFORNIA	April 9*, 10*, 11* **12** Aug. 10*, 11*, 12	April 27*, 28*, 29 Aug. 14*, 15, **16**		June 23*, 24*, 25* Oct. 2*, 3*, **4**	July 9*, 10*, 11, **12** Sept. (7)*, 8*, 9*	April 24, 25, **26 (2)** July 6*, 7*, 8*	May 29*, 30, **31 (2)** Sept. 29*, 30*
TEXAS	May 22*, 23*, **24** Sept. 28*, 29*, 30*	June 26*, 27, **28 (2)** Sept.(7), 8*, 9*	June 29*, 30* July 1*, 2* Sept. 11*, 12*, **13**		May 11*, 12* 13*, 14* July 24*, 25*, **26**	June 2*, 3*, 4 Sept. 25*, 26, **27**	May 15*, 16*, **17** July 27*, 28*, 29*
KANSAS CITY	May (25) TN, 26*, 27* Sept. 18*, 19*, **20**	June 29*, 30* July 1*, 2 Sept. 11*, 12 , **13**	July 3*, (4)*, **5** Sept. 14*, 15*, 16*	April 30* May 1*, 2*, **3** July 16*, 17*		May 29*, 30*, **31** Sept. 28, 29, 30	May 8*, 9*, **10** July 21*, 22 TN, 23*
MINNESOTA	April 14*, 15* Aug. 6*, 7*, 8*, **9**	April 20*, 21*, 22 July 10*, 11, **12**	April 17*, 18*, **19** Aug. 3*, 4*, 5*	May (25)*, 26*, 27*, 28* Sept. 18*, 19*, **20***	May 22*, 23*, **24** Sept. 21*, 22*, 23*, 24*		June 29*, 30* July 1*, 2 Oct. 2*, 3, **4**
CHICAGO	July 3*, (4)*, **5*** Sept. 14*, 15*, 16*	May (25), 26*, 27 Sept. 25*, 26, **27 (2)**	May 22*, 23*, **24** Sept. 21*, 22*, 23*, 24*	May 5*, 6*, 7* July 18 TN, **19***, 20*	June 15*, 16*, 17* July 31* Aug. 1*, **2**	June 23*, 24*, **25** Sept. 11*, 12*, **13**	

MILWAUKEE	May 4*, 5*, 6*, 7* July 18*, 19*	May 8*, 9, 10 July 20*, 21*, 22	April 30* May 1*, 2*, 3 July 16*, 17*	June 19*, 20*, 21* Aug. 17*, 18*, 19*	June 5*, 6*, 7 Aug. 31* Sept. 1*, 2*	June 8*, 9* Sept. 3, 4*, 5, 6	April 14, 15 Aug. 6*, 7*, 8*, 9
DETROIT	April 30* May 1*, 2*, 3 July 16*, 17	May 5*, 6*, 7 July 18, 19 (2)	May 8*, 9*, 10 July 20*, 21*, 22*	June 8*, 9* Sept. 3*, 4*, 5*, 6	April 13*, 15* Aug. 6*, 7*, 8*, 9	June 10*, 11* Aug. 27*, 28*, 29*, 30	June 19*, 20, 21 Aug. 31* Sept. 1*, 2*
CLEVELAND	June 5*, 6*, 7 Aug. 18*, 19*, 20*	June 12*, 13, 14 (2) Aug. 24*, 25	June 8*, 9*, 10* Aug. 21*, 22*, 23	April 14*, 15 Aug. 6*, 7*, 8*, 9*	April 20*, 21*, 22* June 26*, 27*, 28	May 8*, 9, 10 July 21*, 22*, 23	May 11*, 12*, 13* July 24*, 25*, 26
TORONTO	June 22*, 23*, 24* Oct. 2*, 3*, 4	May 22*, 23, 24 (2) Sept. 29, 30	May (25)*, 26*, 27* Sept. 25*, 26, 27	June 5*, 6*, 7* Aug. 31* Sept. 1*, 2*	June 19*, 20*, 21 Aug. 17*, 18*, 19*	July 3*, (4)*, 5 Sept. (7), 8*, 9*	June 8*, 9* Sept. 3*, 4*, 5*, 6
BALTIMORE	June 11*, 12*, 13*, 14* Aug. 24*, 25*	June 9 TN, 10 Aug. 21* 22, 23	June 5*, 6*, 7 Aug. 18*, 19*, 20*	May 8*, 9*, 10 July 21*, 22*, 23*	April 17*, 18, 19 Aug. 3*, 4*, 5*	May 15*, 16, 17 July 27*, 28*, 29*	April 20*, 21*, 22* June 26*, 27*, 28
NEW YORK	May 8*, 9*, 10* July 20*, 21*, 22*	May 1*, 2, 3 (2) July 16*, 17*	May 4*, 5*, 6*, 7* July 18*, 19	April 17*, 18,19 Aug. 3*, 4*, 5*	June 8*, 9* Sept. 3*, 4*, 5, 6	June 12*, 13, 14 Aug. 31* Sept. 1*, 2*	June 10*, 11* Aug. 27*, 28*, 29*, 30
BOSTON	June 8*, 9*, 10* Aug. 21*, 22*, 23*	June 5*, 6, 7 Aug. 18*, 19*, 20*	June 11*, 12*, 13*, 14 Aug. 24*, 25*	April 27*, 28*, 29* Aug. 14*, 15*, 16*	May 4*, 5*, 6* July 18*, 19, 20*	May 12*, 13*, 14 July 24*, 25, 26	April 17, 18, 19 Aug. 3*, 4*, 5*

ALL-STAR GAME AT CLEVELAND, JULY 14
HALL OF FAME GAME, COOPERSTOWN, N.Y., AUGUST 3 — OAKLAND VS. CINCINNATI

1981 AMERICAN LEAGUE SCHEDULE

BOLD = **SUNDAY**   ( ) = HOLIDAY   * = NIGHT GAME   TN = TWI-NIGHT DOUBLEHEADER   (2) or **(2)** = DOUBLEHEADER

	AT MILWAUKEE	AT DETROIT	AT CLEVELAND	AT TORONTO	AT BALTIMORE	AT NEW YORK	AT BOSTON
SEATTLE	June 15*, 16*, 17 July 24*, 25, **26**	May 12*, 13*, 14* July 31* Aug. 1, **2**	May 20*, 21* Aug. 27*, 28*, 29*, **30**	June 30* July 1 TN Sept. 10*, 11*, 12	June 19*, 20*, **21** Aug. 31* Sept. 1*, 2*	May 15*, 16*, **17** July 27*, 28*, 29	May 18*, 19* Sept. 3*, 4*, 5, **6**
OAKLAND	May 15*, 16*, **17** July 27*, 28*, 29*	June 16*, 17*, 18* July 24*, 25, **26**	June 19*, 20*, **21** Aug. 31* Sept. 1*, 2*	May 29*, 30, **31** Sept. 21*, 22*, 23*	May 18*, 19* Sept. 3*, 4*, 5*, **6**	May 12*, 13*, 14* July 31* Aug. 1*, **2**	May 20*, 21* Aug. 27*, 28*, 29, **30**
CALIFORNIA	May 12*, 13*, 14 July 31* Aug. 1*, **2**	May 15*, 16, **17** July 27*, 28*, 29*	May 18*, 19* Sept. 3*, 4*, 5, **6**	June 1*, 2*, 3* Sept. 18*, 19, **20**	May 20*, 21* Aug. 27*, 28*, 29*, **30**	June 16*, 17*, 18* July 24*, 25*, **26**	June 19*, 20, **21** Aug. 31* Sept. 1*, 2*
TEXAS	June 10*, 11* Aug. 27*, 28*, 29, **30**	May 18*, 19*, 20* Aug. 21*, 22, **23**	April 24*, 25, **26** July 7*, 8*, 9*	June 12*, 13, **14**, 15* Aug. 24, 25	June 16*, 17*, 18* July 31* Aug. 1*, **2**	April 9, 11, **12** Aug. 10*, 11*, 12	April 20, 21, 22 July 10*, 11, **12**
KANSAS CITY	April 24*, 25, **26** July 6*, 7*, 8	June 12*, 13, **14** Aug. 24*, 25*, 26*	April 28*, 29* Aug. 14*, 15, **16 (2)**	June 10*, 11* Aug. 27, 28, 29, **30**	April 10, **12** Aug. 10*, 11*, 12*, 13*	May 18*, 19*, 20* Aug. 21*, 22, **23**	May 15*, 16, **17** July 27*, 28*, 29*
MINNESOTA	May 19*, 20*, 21 Aug. 21*, 22*, **23**	June 5*, 6, **7** Aug. 17*, 18*, 19*	June 16*, 17*, 18* July 31* Aug. 1*, **2**	June 26*, 27, **28** Sept. 14*, 15*, 16*	May 4*, 5*, 6* July 18*, **19***, 20*	June 19*, 20*, **21** Aug. 24*, 25*, 26*	April 30* May 1*, 2, **3** July 16*, 17*
CHICAGO	June 12*, 13*, **14** Aug. 24*, 25*, 26*	April 24, 25, **26** July 7*, 8*, 9*	April 30* May 1*, 2, **3** July 16*, 17*	May 18, 19*, 20* Aug. 21, 22, 23	April 27*, 28*, 29* Aug. 14*, 15*, **16**	June 5*, 6*, **7** Aug. 17*, 18*, 19*	April 10, **12** Aug. 10*, 11*, 12*, 13

MILWAUKEE		June 1*, 2*, 3* Sept. 25*, 26, 27	April 11, 12 Aug. 10*, 11 TN, 12*, 13*	April 20, 21*, 22* Aug. 14*, 15, 16 (2)	June 22*, 23*, 24*, 25* Sept. 18*, 19*, 20	July 3*, (4)* 5 Sept. (7), 8*, 9*	May 29*, 30, 31 Sept. 21*, 22*, 23*
DETROIT	May (25), 26*, 27* 28 Oct. 2*, 3, 4		June 29*, 30* July 1* Sept. 18*, 19, 20	April 16*, 17, 18, 19 Aug. 3, 4*, 5*	May 29*, 30*, 31 Sept. 21*, 22*, 23*	April 20*, 21*, 22* July 10*, 11, 12	June 26*, 27, 28 Sept. 14*, 15*, 16*, 17*
CLEVELAND	April 16, 18, 19 Aug. 3*, 4*, 5	June 22*, 23*, 24 TN Sept. 11*, 12, 13		May 5*, 6*, 7* July 18, 19, 20*	July 10*, 11*, 12 Sept (7)*, 8*, 9*, 10*	May 22*, 23* 24 Sept. 21*, 22*, 23*	May (25)*, 26*, 27* Sept. 24*, 25*, 26, 27
TORONTO	April 27, 28, 29 July 10*, 11*, 12	April 9, 11, 12 Aug. 10*, 11*, 12*	May 15*, 16, 17 (2) July 27*, 28*, 29*		April 30* May 1*, 2*, 3 July 16 TN, 17*	April 23*, 24*, 25, 26 July 7*, 8*, 9*	June 16*, 17*, 18* July 31* Aug. 1, 2
BALTIMORE	June 30* July 1*, 2* Sept. 11*, 12*, 13	May 22*, 23, 24 (2) Sept. 28*, 29*, 30*	July 3*, (4), 5 (2) Sept. 15*, 16*	May 12*, 13*, 14* July 24*, 25, 26		June 2*, 3*, 4* Sept. 24*, 25*, 26*, 27	April 13, 14, 15 Aug. 6*, 7*, 8, 9
NEW YORK	June 26*, 27*, 28, 29* Sept. 14*, 15*, 16*	April 27*, 28*, 29 Aug. 13*, 14*, 15*, 16	May 29*, 30, 31 June 1* Sept. 28*, 29*, 30*	April 13, 15* Aug. 6*, 7*, 8, 9	May (25)*, 26*, 27* Oct. 2*, 3*, 4		June 30* July 1*, 2* Sept. 18*, 19, 20
BOSTON	May 22*, 23, 24 (2) Sept. 28*, 29*, 30*	July 3*, (4)*, 5 Sept. (7)*, 8*, 9*	June 2*, 3*, 4* Oct. 2*, 3, 4	May 8*, 9, 10, 11* July 21*, 22*, 23*	April 25, 26 July 6*, 7*, 8*, 9*	June 22*, 23*, 24*, 25* Sept. 11*, 12, 13	

ALL-STAR GAME AT CLEVELAND, JULY 14
HALL OF FAME GAME, COOPERSTOWN, N.Y., AUGUST 3 — OAKLAND VS. CINCINNATI

NATIONAL LEAGUE

EAST

	AT CHICAGO	AT MONTREAL	AT NEW YORK
CHICAGO............		April 14, 15, 16 June 26*, 27*, **28** Sept. 18*, 19, **20**	May 29*, 30, **31** June 29*, 30* July 1*, 2 Sept. 30*, Oct. 1*
MONTREAL..........	May 22, 23, **24** July 7, 8, 9 Sept. 11, 12, **13**		April 18, **19-19** Aug. 4*, 5*, 6 Oct. 2*, 3, **4**
NEW YORK..........	April 9, 11, **12** Aug. 10, 11, 12, 13 Sept. 23, 24	April 24, 25, **26** June 23*, 24*, 25* Sept. 25*, 26, **27**	
PHILADELPHIA...	April 24, 25, **26** June 23, 24, 25 Sept. 25, 26, **27**	April 20, 21, 22 Aug. 7*, 8, **9-9** Sept. 21*, 22*	May 25, 26*, 27* Aug. 14*, 15, **16** Sept. 15*, 16*, 17*
PITTSBURGH.......	May 25, 26, 27, 28 Aug. 14, 15, **16** Sept. 15, 16	May 29*, 30, **31** July 1*, 2* Aug. 10*, 11* Sept. 23*, 24*	April 28*, 29*, 30* Aug. 7*, 8, **9-9** Sept. 21*, 22*
ST. LOUIS...........	April 28, 29 July 3, 4-4, **5**, 6 Sept. 21, 22	May 25*, 26*, 27* Aug. 14*, 15*, **16** Sept. 15*, 16*, 17*	April 14, 15, 16 June 26*, 27*, **28** Sept. 18*, 19, **20**
ATLANTA............	May 1, 2, **3** July 16, 17, 18	June 9*, 10*, 11* Aug. 28*, 29*, **30**	June 15 (Tn), 16* Sept. 4*, 5, **6**
CINCINNATI........	May 19, 20, 21 July 31 Aug. 1, **2**	June 12*, 13, **14** Aug. 25*, 26*, 27*	June 9*, 10*, 11* Aug. 28*, 29*, **30**
HOUSTON............	May 4, 5, 6, 7 July **19**, 20	June 15*, 16* Sept. 3*, 4*, 5, **6**	June 12*, 13*, **14** Aug. 25*, 26*, 27
LOS ANGELES....	June 5, 6, **7** Aug. 17, 18, 19	May 1*, 2, **3**, 4* July 16*, 17*	May 8*, 9, **10** July 21*, 22*, 23
SAN DIEGO.........	June 12, 13, **14** Aug. 24, 25, 26	May 5*, 6*, 7* July 18*, **19**, 20*	May 1*, 2, **3-3** July 16, 17*
SAN FRANCISCO	June 9, 10, 11 Aug. 21, 22, **23**	May 8*, 9, **10-10** July 21*, 22*	May 5*, 6*, 7* July 18*, **19**, 20*

*NIGHT GAME

HEAVY BLACK FIGURES DENOTE SUNDAY
NIGHT GAMES: ANY GAME STARTING AFTER 5:00 p.m.

1981 SCHEDULE

EAST

	AT PHILADELPHIA	AT PITTSBURGH	AT ST. LOUIS
CHICAGO	April 17*, 18*, **19** Aug. 4*, 5*, 6* Oct. 2*, 3*, **4**	June 2*, 3*, 4* July 10*, 11*, **12-12** Sept. 28*, 29*	April 20, 21, 22 Aug. 7*, 8*, **9** Sept. 7, 8*, 9*
MONTREAL	April 27*, 28*, 20* July 3*, 4*, **5** Sept. 7*, 8*, 9*	April 9, 11, **12** June 29*, 30* Aug. 12*, 13* Sept. 30*, Oct. 1*	June 1*, 2*, 3*, 4 July 10*, 11*, **12** Sept. 28*, 29*
NEW YORK	June 1*, 2*, 3* July 10*, 11 (Tn), **12** Sept. 28*, 29*	April 22*, 23 July 3*, 4, **5-5** Sept. 7*, 8*, 9*	May 22*, 23*, **24** July 7*, 8*, 9* Sept. 11*, 12*, **13**
PHILADELPHIA		May 22*, 23*, **24** July 7*, 8*, 9* Sept. 11*, 12*, **13**	April 11, **12** June 29*, 30 (Tn) July 1*, 2 Sept. 23*, 24*
PITTSBURGH	April 13*, 15*, 16* June 26*, 27, **28** Sept. 18*, 19*, **20**		May 8*, 9*, **10** July 16*, 17*, 18 Sept. 25*, 26, **27**
ST. LOUIS	May 29*, 30*, **31** Aug. 10*, 11*, 12*, 13* Sept. 30*, Oct. 1*	April 24*, 25, **26** Aug. 3*, 4*, 5* Oct. 2*, 3, **4**	
ATLANTA	June 12*, 13*, **14** Aug. 24*, 25*, 26*	May 19*, 20* July 31* Aug. 1*, **2-2**	May 4*, 5*, 6*, 7 July **19**, 20*
CINCINNATI	June 15*, 16* Sept. 3*, 4*, 5*, **6**	May 15*, 16, **17** July 27*, 28*, 29*	May 1*, 2, **3** July 21*, 22*, 23*
HOUSTON	June 8*, 9*, 10* Aug. 21*, 22, **23***	May 1*, 2*, **3** June 23*, 24*, 25*	May 19*, 20*, 21 July 31* Aug. 1*, **2**
LOS ANGELES	May 5*, 6*, 7* July 18*, **19**, 20*	June 12*, 13, **14** Aug. 24*, 25*, 26	June 9*, 10*, 11* Aug. 21*, 22*, **23**
SAN DIEGO	May 8*, 9*, **10** July 21*, 22*, 23	June 8*, 9*, 10* Aug. 21*, 22*, **23**	June 5*, 6*, **7** Aug. 17*, 18*, 19*
SAN FRANCISCO	May 1*, 2*, **3**, 4* July 16*, 17*	June 5*, 6*, **7** Aug. 17*, 18*, 19*	June 12*, 13*, **14** Aug. 24*, 25*, 26

JULY 14 – ALL STAR GAME AT CLEVELAND
AUG. 3 – HALL OF FAME GAME AT COOPERSTOWN, N.Y. (Cincinnati vs. Oakland)

NATIONAL LEAGUE

WEST

	AT ATLANTA	AT CINCINNATI	AT HOUSTON
CHICAGO............	May 8*, 9*, **10** July 21*, 22*, 23*	May 12*, 13*, 14* July 24*, 25*, **26**	May 15*, 16*, **17** July 27*, 28*, 29*
MONTREAL..........	June 17*, 18* Aug. 21*, 22 (Tn), **23**	June 5*, 6*, **7** Aug. 31* Sept. 1*, 2*	June 19*, 20*, **21*** Aug. 17*, 18*, 19*
NEW YORK..........	June 19*, 20*, **21** Aug. 18*, 19*, 20*	June 17*, 18* Aug. 21*, 22*, **23**, 24*	June 5*, 6*, **7*** Aug. 31* Sept. 1*, 2*
PHILADELPHIA...	June 5*, 6, **7** Aug. 31* Sept. 1*, 2*	April 8 June 19*, 20*, **21** Aug. 18*, 19*	June 17*, 18* Aug. 28*, 29 (Tn), **30***
PITTSBURGH.......	May 11*, 12*, 13* July 24*, 25*, **26**	May 5*, 6*, 7* July **19-19**, 20*	April 17*, 18, **19** July 21*, 22*, 23*
ST. LOUIS............	May 15*, 16*, **17** July 27*, 28*, 29*	April 17*, 18, **19** June 23*, 24, 25*	May 12*, 13*, 14* July 24*, 25*, **26***
ATLANTA............		April 21*, 22 June 26 (Tn), 27*, **28** Oct. 2*, 3, **4**	April 13*, 14*, 15* July 10*, 11*, **12*** Sept. 22*, 23*, 24*
CINCINNATI........	April 10*, 11*, **12** July 7*, 8*, 9* Sept. 25*, 26*, **27**		April 23*, 24*, 25, **26** June 29*, 30* July 1* Sept. 14*, 15
HOUSTON............	April 28*, 29*, 30* July 3*, 4*, **5** Sept. 7*, 8*, 9*	May 8*, 9, **10**, 11* July 16*, 17*, 18 Sept. 30*, Oct. 1	
LOS ANGELES....	May 25*, 26*, 27*, 28* Aug. 7*, 8*, **9** Sept. 28*, 29*	May 22*, 23, **24-24** Aug. 4*, 5* Sept. 11*, 12*, **13**	April 20*, 21*, 22* June 26*, 27*, **28** Sept. 25*, 26, **27**
SAN DIEGO.........	May 22*, 23*, **24** Aug. 4*, 5*, 6* Sept. 11*, 12*, **13**	April 28*, 29*, 30* July 10*, 11*, **12** Sept. 7*, 8*, 9	May 25*, 26*, 27* Aug. 7*, 8 (Tn), **9** Sept. 28*, 29*
SAN FRANCISCO	April 17*, 18*, **19** June 30 (Tn) July 1*, 2* Sept. 30*, Oct. 1*	May 25*, 26*, 27*, 28 Aug. 14*, 15*, **16** Sept. 28*, 29*	May 22*, 23*, **24*** Aug. 3*, 4*, 5* Sept. 11*, 12*, **13**

***NIGHT GAME** **HEAVY BLACK FIGURES DENOTE SUNDAY**
NIGHT GAMES: ANY GAME STARTING AFTER 5:00 p.m.

1981 SCHEDULE

WEST

	AT LOS ANGELES	AT SAN DIEGO	AT SAN FRANCISCO
CHICAGO	June 15*, 16* Aug. 27*, 28*, 29*, **30**	June 19*, 20*, **21** Aug. 31* Sept. 1*, 2*	June 17, 18 Sept. 3, 4*, 5, **6**
MONTREAL	May 12*, 13*, 14* July 24*, 25*, **26**	May 18*, 19*, 20* July 31* Aug. 1*, **2**	May 15*, 16, **17** July 28*, 29, 30
NEW YORK	May 15*, 16*, **17** July 27*, 28*, 29*	May 12*, 13*, 14 July 24*, 25*, **26**	May 18*, 19*, 20 July 31* Aug. 1, **2**
PHILADELPHIA	May 18*, 19*, 20* July 31* Aug. 1, **2**	May 15*, 16*, **17** July 27*, 28*, 29*	May 12*, 13, 14 July 24*, 25, **26**
PITTSBURGH	June 19*, 20*, **21** Aug. 31* Sept. 1*, 2*	June 17*, 18 Sept. 3, 4*, 5*, **6**	June 15*, 16* Aug. 27*, 28*, 29, **30**
ST. LOUIS	June 17*, 18* Sept. 3*, 4*, 5*, **6**	June 15*, 16* Aug. 27*, 29(Tn), **30**	June 19*, 20, **21-21** Sept. 1*, 2
ATLANTA	June 1*, 2*, 3* Aug. 13*, 14*, 15*, **16** Sept. 16*, 17*	May 29*, 30*, **31** Aug. 10*, 11*, 12* Sept. 18*, 19, **20**	April 23, 24*, 25, **26-26** June 23*, 24 Sept. 14*, 15*
CINCINNATI	May 29*, 30, **31** Aug. 10*, 11*, 12* Sept. 18*, 19*, **20**	April 13*, 14*, 15* July 3*, 4*, **5** Sept. 21*, 22*, 23*	June 1*, 2*, 3* Aug. 7*, 8, **9-9** Sept. 16*, 17*
HOUSTON	April 9, 11*, **12** July 7*, 8*, 9 Oct. 2*, 3, **4**	June 2*, 3*, 4 Aug. 13, 14*, 15*, **16** Sept. 16*, 17*	May 29*, 30, **31** Aug. 10*, 11*, 12 Sept. 18*, 19, **20**
LOS ANGELES		April 17*, 18*, **19** June 29*, 30* July 1*, 2* Sept. 14*, 15*	April 13*, 14*, 15* July 3*, 4, **5** Sept. 22*, 23*, 24*
SAN DIEGO	April 23*, 24*, 25*, **26** June 22*, 23*, 24* Sept. 30*, Oct. 1*		April 9, 10*, 11, **12** July 7*, 8 Oct. 2*, 3, **4**
SAN FRANCISCO	April 27*, 28*, 29* July 10*, 11*, **12** Sept. 7*, 8*, 9*	April 20*, 21*, 22* June 26*, 27*, **28** Sept. 25*, 26*, **27**	

JULY 14 – ALL STAR GAME AT CLEVELAND
AUG. 3 – HALL OF FAME GAME AT COOPERSTOWN, N.Y. (Cincinnati vs. Oakland)